'This timely publication addresses the escalating global demand for health and wellbeing coaching. With each chapter underpinned by rigorous research, the book stands as a beacon of knowledge, insights and inspiration to professionals dedicated to advancing this dynamic field.'

Dr Suzy Green, *CEO, The Positivity Institute*

'Now is the perfect time for the publication of this book on the science and practice of wellbeing coaching. In the wake of a pandemic that brought the world to its knees, it has become increasingly clear that human wellbeing is the province of all coaching, whether in leadership, career, team/organizations or specifically, health. We have all become aware that wellbeing – in every human domain – is critical for success in life, which is why this book is important and well-timed. The editors have compiled a rich set of resources both scholarly and practical to support coaches in navigating the complexities of modern life that plague us all: time management, diet, lifestyle, balance, motivation, technology overload and so on. This book will be a "go-to" resource for coaches committed to coaching with compassion, while grounded in science. A must-read!'

Jeffrey Hull, *Executive Director, Institute of Coaching*

'Since Hippocrates created holistic medicine, scholars have hunted for mind-body-spirit links. This is an amazing compilation of essays on coaching Parasympathetic Nervous System activation (i.e., renewal), somatic techniques and emotional contagion to improve wellbeing. Read it, your future health, happiness and joy, and that of your family, friends and colleagues at work is at stake!'

Richard Boyatzis, *PhD, Distinguished University Professor,*
Case Western Reserve University, Co-author of the international best seller
Primal Leadership *and the new* Helping People Change

T0298824

The Health and Wellbeing Coaches' Handbook

This comprehensive volume offers ideas, examples, and guidance to help coaches develop skills in their coaching practice, specifically in the areas of health and wellbeing as they are experienced by their clients.

The book also explores the growing importance of wellbeing coaching within the wider coaching world and the health sector. Starting with definitions of wellbeing and health coaching, then delving into health and wellbeing issues faced by clients, and tools for coaches, along with their practical applications, this book includes theory, case studies, and reflection exercises so that readers can use it in a personal and practical way.

The Health and Wellbeing Coaches' Handbook is an essential resource for coach practitioners, supervisors, and consultants working with clients, as well as for students in post-graduate programmes, including coaching, health and allied health professional programmes, and human resource professionals focusing on employee wellness.

Jonathan Passmore is an award-winning and internationally respected chartered psychologist. He has written or edited over 40 books including *The Coaches' Handbook, Becoming a Coach: The Essential ICF Guide* and *Coaching Tools Volume 1, 2 and 3* and over 250 book chapters and scientific articles. He holds five degrees and is the Professor of Coaching and Behavioural Change at Henley Business School and Senior Vice President EZRA.

Badri Bajaj is a coaching and wellbeing thought leader and an award-winning coach. He is Associate Professor at Jaypee Institute of Information Technology. He has published widely across various media. He has conducted workshops and provided coaching globally. He has contributed immensely to promoting coaching in India. As the former president of International Coaching Federation (ICF) Delhi Chapter, he orchestrated impactful initiatives and won prestigious awards for the chapter.

Lindsay G. Oades is an internationally acclaimed and award-winning wellbeing science researcher, author, and educator. He is currently Professor of Wellbeing Science and Deputy Dean of the Faculty of Education, at The University of Melbourne. Lindsay has over 150 refereed journal articles and book chapters related to wellbeing, recovery, and coaching, and five books with publishers including Cambridge University Press, Routledge, Wiley-Blackwell and the SAGE text *Coaching and Mentoring Research: A Practical Guide*.

The Coaches' Handbook Series
Series Editor: Jonathan Passmore

This series provides an accessible and comprehensive set of handbooks for all who are new to coaching and those who want to enhance their coaching skills. Edited by a global authority on executive coaching, Jonathan Passmore, it includes books and chapters from leading coach practitioners from across the world.

The Coaches' Handbook
The Complete Practitioner Guide for Professional Coaches
Edited By Jonathan Passmore

The Digital and AI Coaches' Handbook
The Complete Guide to the Use of Online, AI and Technology in Coaching
Edited by Jonathan Passmore, Sandra J. Diller, Sam Isaacson and Maximilian Brantl

The Health and Wellbeing Coaches' Handbook
A Practitioner's Guide for Clinicians, Coaches and Health Professionals
Edited by Jonathan Passmore, Badri Bajaj and Lindsay G. Oades

For more information about this series, please visit: https://www.routledge.com/The-Coaches-Handbook-Series/book-series/Coaches

The Health and Wellbeing Coaches' Handbook

A Practitioner's Guide for Clinicians, Coaches and Health Professionals

Edited by Jonathan Passmore, Badri Bajaj and Lindsay G. Oades

LONDON AND NEW YORK

Designed cover image: © Getty Images / ArtemisDiana

First published 2025
by Routledge
4 Park Square, Milton Park, Abingdon, Oxon OX14 4RN

and by Routledge
605 Third Avenue, New York, NY 10158

Routledge is an imprint of the Taylor & Francis Group, an informa business

British Library Cataloguing-in-Publication Data
A catalogue record for this book is available from the British Library

Library of Congress Cataloging-in-Publication Data
Names: Passmore, Jonathan, editor. | Bajaj, Badri, editor. | Oades, Lindsay G.,
    editor.
Title: The health and wellbeing coaches' handbook : a practitioner's guide for
    clinicians, coaches and health professionals / edited by Jonathan Passmore,
    Badri Bajaj and Lindsay G. Oades.
Description: Abingdon, Oxon ; New York, NY : Routledge, 2025. | Includes
    bibliographical references.
Identifiers: LCCN 2024034150 (print) | LCCN 2024034151 (ebook) |
    ISBN 9781032333007 (hardback) | ISBN 9781032332994 (paperback) |
    ISBN 9781003319016 (ebook)
Subjects: LCSH: Personal coaching—Methodology. | Personal coaching—
    Vocational guidance. | Well-being.
Classification: LCC BF637.P36 H43 2025 (print) | LCC BF637.P36 (ebook) |
    DDC 158.3—dc23/eng/20241114
LC record available at https://lccn.loc.gov/2024034150
LC ebook record available at https://lccn.loc.gov/2024034151

ISBN: 978-1-032-33300-7 (hbk)
ISBN: 978-1-032-33299-4 (pbk)
ISBN: 978-1-003-31901-6 (ebk)

DOI: 10.4324/9781003319016

Contents

Editors and contributors

Editors

Jonathan Passmore, DOccPsyc

Jonathan is professor of coaching at Henley Business School and Senior VP at EZRA-LHH, part of the Adecco Group. He is a chartered psychologist, holds five degrees, is an EMCC master coach, ICF PCC, and holds qualifications in coaching supervision and team coaching. He has published widely with over 250 scientific papers and book chapters, and 40 books on coaching, leadership, mindfulness, and I/O psychology, making him one of the most published researchers in the field of coaching. He is also listed in the top 20 coaching Global Gurus (2023) and Top 8 Coaches for the Thinkers 50 Awards (2023). He coaches leaders in business, politics, and sport. His recent published titles include *The Coaches' Handbook* (2021), The Ethical Coaches' Handbook (2023), *Becoming a Coach: The Essential ICF Guide 2nd edition* (2024), *The Digital & AI Coaches' Handbook* (2024), and three volumes in the *Coaching Tools* series (2021, 2022, 2023).

Badri Bajaj, PhD

Badri is a thought leader and practitioner in coaching and wellbeing. He is Associate Professor at Jaypee Institute of Information Technology, Noida, India. He has published highly cited articles in reputed journals, newspapers, and magazines. He is Associate Editor for the *Frontiers in Psychology* journal. He received 'The 100 Best Global Coaching Leaders Award' in 2017. He has conducted training for senior management and supervisors in information technology (IT) organisations, the retail sector, the Indian Navy, and professional associations He has given presentations in the UK, India, and the United States for different types of organisations. He has contributed immensely to promoting coaching in India. He has served as President on the Board of ICF Delhi-NCR Chapter for two terms: 2019–2021 and 2021–2023. During his stint as president of ICF chapter, he orchestrated impactful initiatives and won prestigious awards for the chapter. He is a Professional Certified Coach (PCC), ICF.

Lindsay G. Oades, PhD

Lindsay is an internationally acclaimed wellbeing science researcher, educator, and author. He is currently Deputy Dean and a Professor of Wellbeing Science at the Faculty of Education at The University of Melbourne. He was a coordinating lead author with a United Nations Educational, Scientific and Cultural Organization (UNESCO) assignment examining the relationship between education and human flourishing. As a sought-after speaker known to provoke thought, he has given keynote or invited presentations in Australia, Canada, China, Hong Kong, India, Ireland, Italy, Japan, Mexico, New Zealand, Singapore, Taiwan, United Arab Emirates, the UK and the United States. He was previously the Director of the Centre for Wellbeing Science/Centre for Positive Psychology, a co-editor for the *International Journal of Wellbeing*, a scientific panel member at the Institute of Coaching (Harvard University), and was visiting researcher at Kings College London. Lindsay's current work involves wellbeing literacy – (how we communicate about and for wellbeing) is part of his new theory, Thriveability Theory. Lindsay believes wellbeing is everyone's business – a shared responsibility. He has published over 165 refereed journal articles and book chapters related to wellbeing, recovery, and coaching, and five books with esteemed publishers including Cambridge University Press, Wiley-Blackwell, Routledge and Sage.

Contributors

Vita Akstinaite, PhD

Vita is a Professor at ISM University of Management and Economics in Vilnius, Lithuania and a business consultant. He is an expert in leadership, hubris and innovative research methodologies (machine learning, computational linguistics).

Tim Anstiss, MD

Tim is a medical doctor specialising in behaviour change, wellbeing improvement, and workforce development. He has trained thousands of healthcare professionals and has written several book chapters on different aspects of coaching.

Jolanta Burke, PhD

Jolanta is a chartered psychologist specialising in positive psychology and a senior lecturer at the Centre for Positive Health Sciences, Royal College of Surgeons in Ireland (RCSI) University of Medicine and Health Sciences.

Mary Collins, EdD

Mary is a chartered coaching psychologist specialising in leadership and talent development at the Centre for Positive Health Sciences, RCSI University of Medicine and Health Sciences.

Jane Daly

Jane is a behavioural scientist and an accredited coach. She has held several executive roles and is the founder of Peoplestar, an evidence-based multidisciplinary agency specialising in complex culture and capability change systems.

Ian Day

Ian is a leadership coach with 20 years' experience working at C-suite level. Ian is course director for the post-graduate coaching courses delivered by the University of Warwick.

Emma Donaldson-Feilder

Emma is a coaching psychologist and occupational psychologist who aims to help create kinder, wiser workplaces. She offers coach development based on relational mindfulness.

Nancy Doyle

Nancy is an occupational psychologist and visiting professor at the Centre for Neurodiversity Research at Birkbeck, and the founder of the non-profit Genius Within.

Rosie Evans-Krimme

Rosie is a coach, psychologist, researcher, and speaker on positive psychology, mental health, wellbeing, and digital coaching.

Zoe Fisher

Zoe is a consultant clinical psychologist and associate professor in Swansea Bay University Health Board and Swansea University.

Eliana Gialain

Eliana is a human resources executive, and is currently responsible for behavioural science at CoachHub. Eliana holds an MSc in HR and is certified in NeuroLeadership, Gallup Strengths, and Systemic Coaching approaches.

Andrea Giraldez-Hayes, PhD

Andrea is a chartered psychologist, positive psychology coach, supervisor, consultant, and researcher on wellbeing arts and creative coaching.

Augusto Gonzalez-Bonorino

Augusto is an Economics PhD candidate at Claremont Graduate University, studying the intersection of behavioural sciences, game theory, and computation.

Alexandra Hamill

Alex is a highly specialist clinical psychologist on the Swansea Bay University Health Board.

Karen Hayns

Karen is an experienced, integrative business lifestyle and health coach with a corporate background. She holds a MSc in coaching and behavioural change and is a certified eating disorders coach practitioner with the National Centre for Eating Disorders (NCFED).

Ray Tak-yin Hui, PhD

Ray is an associate professor at NUCB Business School, Nagoya University whose academic interests include employee development, coaching, and motivation.

Aaron Jarden, PhD

Aaron is an associate professor at the Centre for Wellbeing Science, University of Melbourne, Australia. He is a wellbeing consultant and social entrepreneur; has multiple qualifications in philosophy, computing, education, and psychology; and is a prolific author and presenter.

Rebecca Jarden, PhD

Rebecca is a senior lecturer in nursing at The University of Melbourne, Australia. Rebecca's background focused on psychology and anthropology before nursing, and her research continues a health workforce focus, exploring wellbeing during transition and beyond.

Maggie João

Maggie is a ICF MCC and EMCC senior practitioner. She has published books in English, Portuguese, and Spanish, and teaches at Porto Business School, as well as managing her coaching practice.

Robert Kelly

Robert is professor at RCSI University of Health Sciences, Dublin and Consultant Cardiologist at University College Dublin (UCD) Beacon Hospital, Ireland.

Andrew H. Kemp

Andrew is a personal chair and professor of psychology at Swansea University, and an honorary clinical researcher on the Swansea Bay University Health Board.

Oriane J. B. Kets de Vries

Oriane is the Managing Director at the Kets de Vries Institute. She is responsible for leadership programme design, management, and delivery.

Danny Martin

Daniel s a positive organizational psychology PhD student at Claremont Graduate University, where he studies workplace communication and wellbeing.

Kelly Davis Martin, PhD

Kelly is a coach trainer and healthcare provider in underserved populations, and has a doctorate degree in behavioural health and a Masters degree in public health.

Simon Matthews

Simon is an Australian executive coach, coach trainer, and psychologist with a particular interest in the role of inquiry as a health behaviour change process.

Almuth McDowall, PhD

Almuth is a professor of organizational psychology at Birkbeck, University of London and co-directs the Centre for Neurodiversity Research at Work. She is committed to helping businesses make their people happy.

Trudy Meehan

Trudy is a chartered clinical psychologist and lecturer at the Centre for Positive Health Sciences, RCSI University of Medicine and Health Sciences, Ireland, where she researches creative health, art, and identity.

Margaret Moore

Margaret, a dual U.S. and Canadian citizen, is an executive coach, coach trainer, and leader in the field, having co-founded three coaching organizations since 2000.

Ana Paula Nacif

Ana is an academic, coach, and consultant who works with individuals and organisations in the private, public, and not-for-profit sectors. She specialises in wellbeing, leadership, and inclusion.

Róisín O'Donovan, PhD

Róisín is a post-doctoral researcher at the RCSI Centre for Positive Health Sciences. Her PhD research focused on understanding and improving psychological safety in healthcare teams.

Bergsveinn Olafsson

Bergsveinn is a PhD student in positive organizational psychology at Claremont Graduate University, a leadership coach, and a professional speaker.

Nwachi Gamba Eze Pressley-Tafari, PhD

Nwachi Gamba Eze Pressley-Tafari has been a developmental educator and group coach for over 20 years. He holds an EdD in higher education and a PhD in the human sciences with a specialisation in creativity studies, with a research focus on spirituality and personal mythology.

Sheryl Richard, PhD

Sheryl is a coach trainer and academic educator, with a doctorate in community health and a Masters degree in organizational management.

Annalise Roache

Annalise is a PhD candidate at Auckland University of Technology, and a positive psychology practitioner, coach, mentor, and wellbeing researcher. She works with individuals, teams, and organizations using an evidence-based approach to bring about lasting positive change.

Caroline Rook

Caroline is a researcher at Henley Business School. Her research relates to creating healthy workplaces, with research and practice related to leadership, wellbeing and coaching.

Eugene Sadler-Smith, PhD

Eugene is Professor of Organizational Behaviour at Surrey Business School, University of Surrey, UK. His research interests are intuition in decision-making and hubris in leadership.

Tatiana Schifferle Rowson, PhD

Tatiana is a social gerontologist and psychologist, and an academic and executive coach with expertise in midlife transitions and ageing at work.

Ciara Scott

Ciara is a PhD scholar at the RCSI Centre for Positive Health Sciences on the SPHeRE Programme. She is an experienced specialist orthodontist and an accredited coach.

Julia Vaughan Smith

Julia is an accredited master executive coach and supervisor, and the author of three books, including *Coaching and Trauma* (2019).

Wendy-Ann Smith

Wendy-Ann Smith is a coaching psychologist, co-founder of the Coaching Ethics Forum, researcher, author, and coach supervisor for coach development and wellbeing.

Gill Tanner

Gill is a senior HR professional and coach whose career spans more than 20 years. She has been influential in driving behavioural and cultural change in organisations, and has a strong academic background.

Christian van Nieuwerburgh, PhD

Christian is Professor of Coaching and Positive Psychology at the Centre for Positive Health Sciences at RCSI University of Medicine and Health Sciences.

Lowri Wilkie

Lowri is a mindfulness teacher, assistant psychologist and a PhD student in the School of Psychology at Swansea University.

Section 1

Concepts in health and wellbeing coaching

Chapter 1

Coaching for health and wellbeing

Badri Bajaj and Jonathan Passmore

Introduction

Health and wellbeing are recognised as important goals by people in all cultures. Research findings suggest that health and wellbeing are interrelated. There are some common strategies which may work for improving both health and wellbeing. One of these, coaching for health and wellbeing, is gaining momentum across the globe. There are coach training programmes focussing on health and wellbeing, and there are a growing number of coaches who specialise in providing health and wellbeing coaching. Organisations are also focussing on supporting their employees for health and wellbeing. This chapter will explore how health and wellbeing are interrelated, and what coaching theories and practice can inform our work in this area.

Theory and research

Defining health coaching

Health coaching is a form of coaching applied with a focus on health and wellbeing. But it may help if we start by exploring what we mean in this book when we are referring to as 'coaching', as the use of the term varies widely. While it is fair to say there is no universally agreed definition, there is a broad consensus around the use of the term. Whitmore (2009:11), for example, suggested coaching; involves "unlocking people's potential to maximise their own performance. It is helping them to learn rather than teaching them". This supports Coulter's (2011:2) view about the importance of empowering people to learn, rather than "doing things to people". Passmore and Tee (2023) have offered a process-based definition in an attempt to differentiate coaching from mentoring, counselling and other conversational based approaches to change:

> A voluntary intervention involving a series of future-focused, structured, purposeful conversations characterised by open questions, listening, summaries, reflections and affirmations intended to facilitate the client in generating and acting upon strategies which result in developing greater self-awareness, enhancing personal responsibility and achieving meaningful progress towards a desired change.

Unlike some forms of coaching where there is a strong directive (teaching) aspect, such as in many aspects of sports coaching, health coaching encourages personal responsibility.

DOI: 10.4324/9781003319016-2

Wolever and colleagues (2013:38) suggested health coaching is: "a patient-centered process that is based upon behavior change theory and . . . entails goal setting determined by the patient, encourages self-discovery in addition to content education, and incorporates mechanisms for developing accountability in health behaviors".

This definition dove-tails nicely with the broader coaching definitions but also includes patient-led goal setting and content education and accountability for healthy behaviours. The educational element has been highlighted as a limitation because coaching is difficult to extrapolate in terms of it being standalone in delivering outcomes versus other mechanisms – particularly in relation to educational programmes and other inventions. "The health coach's main role is not to teach, advise or counsel people but rather to support people to plan and reach their own goals" (The Evidence Centre, 2014:12).

However, in a healthcare setting, there is always going to be an element of explanation and education, as clients may lack health knowledge about prognosis or treatment. The question is whether this is invited by the patient (patient-led) or imposed, or the view is that coaching should remain patient-led, which would require the health coach to seek consent before providing a socio-educational input.

In the UK, the National Health Service (NHS) England Health Coaching describes health coaching as helping "people gain and use the knowledge, skills, tools and confidence to become active participants in their care so that they can reach their self-identified health and wellbeing goals" (NHS Lancashire and South Cumbria Integrated Care Board, n.d.). This definition, however, falls short in our view, and risks confusing coaching with other behavioural change interventions.

Palmer, Tubbs, and Whybrow (2003) suggested that for coaching for health, the coach may help to educate the client on specific health-related topics and subsequently support them in achieving their health-related goals. They defined health coaching as "Health coaching is the practice of health education and health promotion within a coaching context, to enhance the wellbeing of individuals and to facilitate the achievement of their health-related goals" (p. 92). In a more recent review of health coaching (Salathiel & Passmore, 2021:4), the authors proposed a new definition of health coaching:

> health coaching is a client-centred process that draws on psychological, evidenced based models of behavioural change to help clients make effective and sustained changes in their thoughts, feelings and behaviours, and thus contributes to enhanced wellbeing and quality of life.

Importance of wellbeing and importance of health

Wellbeing coaching can improve both health and wellbeing outcomes (Anstiss & Passmore, 2017). Good health improves wellbeing, and enhanced wellbeing leads to better health. There is empirical scientific evidence that as an approach coaching may be efficient in enhancing health and wellbeing (Boyatzis et al., 2022; Boyatzis, Smith, & Beveridge, 2013; Jarosz, 2021; Theeboom, Beersma, & van Vianen, 2014).

The field of health psychology is beginning to shift away from a narrow, 'ill-health', sickness model focus, toward a broader view that includes prevention and wellbeing (Hernandez et al., 2018). There is good evidence which shows positive emotions influence variables vital for workplace success such as positive beliefs, creativity, work engagement, positive coping, health, teamwork and collaboration, customer satisfaction, leadership, and performance. Further, optimism and other positive emotions appear to protect individuals from physical illness (Seligman, 2008). Accumulating evidence shows that a higher sense of purpose in life is associated with lower risk of chronic conditions and premature mortality (Kim, Shiba, Boehm, & Kubzansky, 2020). Positive emotional states may promote healthy perceptions, beliefs, and physical wellbeing itself. Optimistic mind and an exhilarated spirit accompany a healthy body. Positive emotional experiences provide people with psychological resources that enable them more effectively to prevent or deal with health problems (Salovey, Rothman, Detweiler, & Steward, 2000). The tendency to experience positive emotions is associated with greater resistance to objectively verifiable colds (Cohen, Doyle, Turner, Alper, & Skoner, 2003). Protective psychological assets that may promote improved physical health and longevity (Hernandez et al., 2018).

Health levels of people may affect their wellbeing levels. A study by Levine and colleagues suggested that interventions to improve psychological health can have a beneficial impact on cardiovascular health (Levine et al., 2021). Evidence has shown that gut-health promoting diets may reduce depressive symptoms through improving physical health (Lai & Boag, 2023). Cho, Martin, Margrett, MacDonald, and Poon (2011), found that health is an essential factor for psychological wellbeing in later life. Other factors such as exercise, sport and healthy diet can also have positive effects on wellbeing.

Practice

Many coaching areas in health and wellbeing may include coaching for sleep, healthy sex life, menopause, stress, mental health, ageing, weight management, heart health, trauma, inner critic, physical recovery, etc. We found that evidence for the effects of health coaching in many areas is increasing. A health coach is not necessarily a medical expert, but in our view, they should be an expert in behaviour change (Normand & Bober, 2020). Health coaching is capable of inducing improvements in health-related quality of life and cardiorespiratory fitness (Huber et al., 2022). Coaching intervention is a suitable method to improve quality of life by reducing weight, waist circumference, body mass index, depression, and menopausal symptoms in postmenopausal and perimenopausal women (Shokri-Ghadikolaei, Bakouei, Delavar, Azizi, & Sepidarkish, 2022). We found evidence that health coaching helped in better sleep (Sedkaoui et al., 2015), managing stress (Junker, Pömmer, & Traut-Mattausch, 2021), and healthy sex (Britton, 2011).

The field of health coaching is just emerging, and much work remains to shape it into an organised and – most importantly – an effective professional practice (Normand & Bober, 2020).

Anstiss and Moore (2018) suggested that coaching for improved health and wellbeing might have one or more of the following three aims.

- Helping leaders to reduce one or more unhealthy behaviours.
- Helping them to adapt or increase one or more healthy or protective behaviours.
- Helping them take steps to be associated with improvements in one or more of Seligman's five pillars of wellbeing, i.e., positive emotions, engagement, relationships, meaning, and achievement.

Coaching may help in improving in one or more wellbeing dimensions, such as psychological wellbeing, social wellbeing, or subjective wellbeing (Diener, Emmons, Larsen, & Griffin, 1985; Keyes, 1998; Ryff, 1989; Watson, Clark, & Tellegen, 1988). Coaching for psychological wellbeing may help clients improve their autonomy, environmental mastery, personal growth, positive relations with others, purpose in life, and self-acceptance. Coaching for social wellbeing can contribute to improving social integration, social acceptance, social contribution, social actualisation, and social coherence. Coaching for subjective wellbeing can contribute to enhancing life satisfaction and more positive affect and less negative affect or improving affect balance, and happiness.

Characteristics of people having higher scores in various dimensions of psychological wellbeing are described in Table 1.1.

Characteristics of people having higher scores in various dimensions of social wellbeing are described in Table 1.2.

Table 1.1 Description of dimensions of psychological wellbeing

Psychological wellbeing dimension	Description
Autonomy	self-determining, independent and regulated internally; resist social pressures to think and act in certain ways; evaluate self by personal standards
Environmental mastery	Feel competent and able to manage complex environments; choose or create personally suitable community
Personal growth	Have feelings of continued development and potential and open to new experience; feel increasingly knowledgeable and effective
Positive relations with others	Have warm, satisfying, trusting relationships; are concerned about other's welfare; capable of strong empathy, affection and intimacy; understand give and take of relationships
Purpose in life	Have goals and a sense of direction in life; past life is meaningful; hold beliefs that give purpose to life
Self-acceptance	Possess positive attitude toward the self; acknowledge and accept multiple aspects of self; feel positive about past life

Table 1.2 Description of dimensions of social wellbeing

Social wellbeing dimension	Description
Social integration	Feel part of community; think they belong, feel supported, and share commonalities with community
Social acceptance	Have positive attitudes towards people; acknowledge others and generally accept people despite others' sometimes complex and perplexing behaviour
Social contribution	Feel they have something valuable to give to the present and society; think their daily activities are valued by their community
Social actualisation	Care about and believe society is evolving positively; think society has potential to grow positively, think self/society is realising potential
Social coherence	Involves appraisals that society is discernible, sensible, and predictable

Table 1.3 Description of dimensions of subjective wellbeing

Subjective wellbeing dimension	Description
Life satisfaction	A sense of contentment, peace, and satisfaction from small discrepancies between wants and needs with accomplishments and attainments
Positive affect	Experience symptoms that suggest enthusiasm, joy, and happiness for life
Negative affect	Experience at times that life is undesirable and unpleasant
Happiness	Having a general feeling and experience of pleasure, contentment, and joy

Characteristics of people having higher scores in various dimensions of subjective wellbeing are described in Table 1.3.

Clifton and Harter (2021) suggested five elements of wellbeing:

- Career wellbeing: You like what you do every day.
- Social wellbeing: You have meaningful friendships in your life.
- Financial wellbeing: You manage your money well.
- Physical wellbeing: You have energy to get things done.
- Community wellbeing: You like where you live.

Coaching complexity

Working with clients is complex. People are different. They have different needs and different presenting issues. Equally coaches and clinicians know different wellbeing models and draw on these frameworks to support their clients.

Coaches also help clients to raise their wellbeing by helping clients work on the factors for enhancing wellbeing. These might include factors such as self-esteem, resilience, mindfulness, emotional intelligence, mindsets, proactive personality, psychological capital, etc., which affect wellbeing levels of individuals.

In addition, the impact of wellbeing on the organisation should also be recognised. These may include factors such as organisational climate, social support, leadership style, policies, opportunities for job crafting, resources, and challenges.

Conclusion

Coaching for health and wellbeing includes a focus on both aspects. Awareness of different health issues and wellbeing models may help coaches in supporting their clients for health and wellbeing goals. Though coaching for health and wellbeing is not well defined, the evidence presented throughout this book suggests greater use should be made across the health system to encourage wellbeing and preventative health coaching, as well as health coaching for recovery. To achieve these outcomes with diverse patients and diverse presenting issues, we believe an integrative approach is likely to best serve the needs of health coaches and health professionals in achieving their goals (Wang, Lai, Xu, & McDowall, 2022).

Reflective questions

1. How can coaches help clients raise their motivation to engage in preventative health and wellbeing programmes?
2. What do coaches need to learn to better support their clients to enhance their health and wellbeing?
3. What systemic changes are needed to achieve enhanced health and wellbeing?

References

Anstiss, T., & Moore, M. (2018). Coaching leaders towards improved health and well-being. In *Mastering Executive Coaching* (pp. 194–211). Routledge.

Anstiss, T., & Passmore, J. (2017). Wellbeing coaching. In *The Routledge companion to wellbeing at work* (pp. 237–248). Routledge.

Boyatzis, R. E., Hullinger, A., Ehasz, S. F., Harvey, J., Tassarotti, S., Gallotti, A., & Penafort, F. (2022). The grand challenge for research on the future of coaching. *The Journal of Applied Behavioral Science*, 58(2), 202–222.

Boyatzis, R. E., Smith, M. L., & Beveridge, A. J. (2013). Coaching with compassion: Inspiring health, well-being, and development in organizations. *The Journal of Applied Behavioral Science*, 49(2), 153–178.

Britton, P. (2011). *The art of sex coaching: Expanding your practice*. WW Norton & Company.

Cho, J., Martin, P., Margrett, J., MacDonald, M., & Poon, L. W. (2011). The relationship between physical health and psychological well-being among oldest-old adults. *Journal of Aging Research*, 2011.

Clifton, J., & Harter, J. (2021). *Wellbeing at work*. Simon and Schuster.

Cohen, S., Doyle, W. J., Turner, R. B., Alper, C. M., & Skoner, D. P. (2003). Emotional style and susceptibility to the common cold. *Psychosomatic Medicine*, 65(4), 652–657.

Coulter, A. (2011). *Engaging patients in healthcare*. Open University Press/McGraw-Hill.

Diener, E. D., Emmons, R. A., Larsen, R. J., & Griffin, S. (1985). The satisfaction with life scale. *Journal of Personality Assessment*, 49(1), 71–75.

The Evidence Centre. (2014). *Does health coaching work? A rapid review of empirical evidence*. Health Education East of England: NHS.

Hernandez, R., Bassett, S. M., Boughton, S. W., Schuette, S. A., Shiu, E. W., & Moskowitz, J. T. (2018). Psychological well-being and physical health: Associations, mechanisms, and future directions. *Emotion Review*, 10(1), 18–29.

Huber, D., Mayr, M., Hartl, A., Sittenthaler, S., Traut-Mattausch, E., Weisböck-Erdheim, R., & Freidl, J. (2022). Sustainability of hiking in combination with coaching in cardiorespiratory fitness and quality of life. *International Journal of Environmental Research and Public Health*, 19(7), 3848.

Jarosz, J. (2021). The impact of coaching on well-being and performance of managers and their teams during pandemic. *International Journal of Evidence Based Coaching and Mentoring*, 19(1), 4–27.

Junker, S., Pömmer, M., & Traut-Mattausch, E. (2021). The impact of cognitive-behavioural stress management coaching on changes in cognitive appraisal and the stress response: A field experiment. *Coaching: An International Journal of Theory, Research and Practice*, 14(2), 184–201.

Keyes, C. L. M. (1998). Social well-being. *Social Psychology Quarterly*, 121–140.

Kim, E. S., Shiba, K., Boehm, J. K., & Kubzansky, L. D. (2020). Sense of purpose in life and five health behaviors in older adults. *Preventive Medicine*, 139, 106172.

Lai, C. C. W., & Boag, S. (2023). The association between gut-health promoting diet and depression: A mediation analysis. *Journal of Affective Disorders*, 324, 136–142.

Levine, G. N., Cohen, B. E., Commodore-Mensah, Y., Fleury, J., Huffman, J. C., Khalid, U.,. . . Spatz, E. S. (2021). Psychological health, well-being, and the mind-heart-body connection: A scientific statement from the American Heart Association. *Circulation*, 143(10), e763–e783.

NHS Lancashire and South Cumbria Integrated Care Board. (n.d.). *Health coaching*. Retrieved on 14 October 2024 from www.lancashireandsouthcumbria.icb.nhs.uk/our-work/

prevention-and-health-inequalities/population-health-academy/personalised-care-training/health-coaching

Normand, M. P., & Bober, J. (2020). Health coaching by behavior analysts in practice: How and why. *Behavior Analysis: Research and Practice*, 20(2), 108.

Palmer, S., Tubbs, I., & Whybrow, A. (2003). Health coaching to facilitate the promotion of healthy behaviour and achievement of health-related goals. *International Journal of Health Promotion and Education*, 41(3), 91–93.

Passmore, J. & Tee, D. (2023). Coaching, Milton Keynes, Open University, *Conference presentation*, 26th January 2023, (Online).

Ryff, C. D. (1989). Happiness is everything, or is it? Explorations on the meaning of psychological well-being. *Journal of Personality and Social Psychology*, 57(6), 1069.

Salathiel, E., & Passmore, J. (2021). *Does health coaching work? A critical review of the evidence for coaching in the health care system*. Henley Business School.

Salovey, P., Rothman, A. J., Detweiler, J. B., & Steward, W. T. (2000). Emotional states and physical health. *American Psychologist*, 55(1), 110.

Sedkaoui, K., Leseux, L., Pontier, S., Rossin, N., Leophonte, P., Fraysse, J.-L., & Didier, A. (2015). Efficiency of a phone coaching program on adherence to continuous positive airway pressure in sleep apnea hypopnea syndrome: A randomized trial. *BMC Pulmonary Medicine*, 15, 1–8.

Seligman, M. E. P. (2008). Positive health. *Applied Psychology*, 57, 3–18.

Shokri-Ghadikolaei, A., Bakouei, F., Delavar, M. A., Azizi, A., & Sepidarkish, M. (2022). Effects of health coaching on menopausal symptoms in postmenopausal and perimenopausal women. *Menopause*, 29(10), 1189–1195.

Theeboom, T., Beersma, B., & van Vianen, A. E. M. (2014). Does coaching work? A meta-analysis on the effects of coaching on individual level outcomes in an organizational context. *The Journal of Positive Psychology*, 9(1), 1–18.

Wang, Q., Lai, Y.-L., Xu, X., & McDowall, A. (2022). The effectiveness of workplace coaching: A meta-analysis of contemporary psychologically informed coaching approaches. *Journal of Work-Applied Management*, 14(1), 77–101.

Watson, D., Clark, L. A., & Tellegen, A. (1988). Development and validation of brief measures of positive and negative affect: The PANAS scales. *Journal of Personality and Social Psychology*, 54(6), 1063.

Whitmore, J. (2009). *Coaching for performance: Growing human potential and purpose: The principles and practice of coaching and leadership*, 4th edn. Nicholas Brealey.

Wolever, R. Q., Simmons, L. A., Sforzo, G. A., Dill, D., Kaye, M., Bechard, E. M., . . . Yang, N. (2013). A systematic review of the literature on health and wellness coaching: Defining a key behavioral intervention in healthcare. *Global Advances in Health and Medicine*, 2(4), 38–57.

Chapter 2

The wellbeing coach

Dimensions, concepts, and language-use of wellbeing

Lindsay G. Oades

Introduction

There is a growing research base for both coaching (Oades, Siokou & Slemp, 2019) and for wellbeing science (van Agteren et al., 2021). For a coach aiming to assist a client with their wellbeing, it may be enticing to believe that learning more and more of the numerous and contested theories and models of wellbeing will be an advantage. Whilst this will likely broaden the coach's breadth of understanding of wellbeing, and the coach's scholarly vocabulary about elements of wellbeing, it is unlikely to expose implicit dimensions of wellbeing, both in theory and for the client. Moreover, the many theories and models of wellbeing – several of which are summarised well in the chapters in this book – may not help the coach understand the lay concepts and theories of wellbeing that the client may bring to the coaching relationship. A lay concept is how a person as a non-expert conceptualises something, in this case wellbeing. A lay theory is how a person as non-expert theorises about how one thing causes another, in this case wellbeing, particularly at a personal level: that is, what improves my own wellbeing?

In addition to understanding lay concepts and broader dimensions of wellbeing, it is imperative to remember that coaching is a relationship, with language-use at its heart. Hence, rather than repeating the well documented existing contemporary – and mainly western – theories of wellbeing, this chapter focuses on understanding dimensions of wellbeing (relevant to most theories); lay concepts of wellbeing and how language is used about and for wellbeing, including the model of wellbeing literacy; and how we communicate *about* and *for* wellbeing. These areas are relevant to coaching for wellbeing and can be considered as a way of understanding the range of theories, but through highlighting the importance of lay concepts and the wellbeing literacy of coach and client, the complex, culturally bound and fluid aspects of coaching communication are honoured.

This chapter first considers dimensions of wellbeing, with reference to the way scholars attempt to categorise and classify wellbeing, and how some understand wellbeing along one or several dimensions. The debate about whether mental health and wellbeing has one or two dimensions is described, highlighting the real-life relevance of this debate. Lay concepts and lay theories in wellbeing are described as an example of understanding wellbeing from the perspective of the client, rather than from the perspective of established theory and models. The understanding of the language of wellbeing, and how it is used, i.e., literacy, the model of wellbeing literacy is then described, highlighting how existing theories and models of wellbeing at the very least add to the wellbeing vocabulary of the coach and client, as toolkits of concepts and language, even if not applied directly. The

DOI: 10.4324/9781003319016-3

chapter concludes with practice implications and recommendations derived from these important ideas, and with key reflective questions.

Theory and research related to wellbeing

Theory can be considered as a concept toolkit (Alexandrova, 2017). This means that we do not simply apply a single theory for a particular issue. Rather, we choose concepts from within theories to make sense of the issue at hand; otherwise, we would need a new theory for an expert problem. Within each theory or model are an array of concepts, which rely on language and language-use to understand and signify them. At the heart of most non-physical and psychological phenomena are root metaphors. For example, Freud's theories were based on root metaphors of hydraulics and steam, whilst cognitive science sees the mind as analogous to a computer.

Wellbeing is a contested and capacious concept (Baumeister et al., 2013; Dodge et al., 2012; Kemp & Edwards, 2022; Salvador-Carulla et al., 2014) and it is closely related to the concept of human flourishing (de Ruyter et al., 2022). This means that there are many debates about the definition of wellbeing, and it is a general or "high order" concept into which we may fit many other concepts. Moreover, it is examined by many disciplines of scholarship, yet is relevant to all our day-to-day experiences. Stated simply, everyone has a view on wellbeing in ways that they may not have views on aspects of the natural sciences, such as the cellular structure of plants. It is beyond the scope of this chapter to review the numerous theories and models of wellbeing, some of which are well documented in other chapters in this handbook. Moreover, a practising coach may have neither the time nor the inclination to become a wellbeing scientist or wellbeing philosopher; however, there are useful meta frameworks to help coaches work with clients, and work beyond a particular model of wellbeing, which is particularly important given the multicultural and multilingual contexts in which coaching happens. Three useful ways for a coach to understand the complexity of wellbeing are: (1) dimensions; (2) concepts, including lay concepts; and (3) language-use. Each of these three issues are now examined before outlining some practice implications for wellbeing coaches.

Dimensions of wellbeing

In mathematics, dimensions refer to the direction of something in space. For example, a three-dimensional space includes height, width, and depth. Whilst this may seem a long way from the average person's thinking about wellbeing, it has some significant consequences, and is all around us in our social world today. For example, gender and gender roles are very key issues of debate in many parts of the world. If we say someone is masculine, do we imply that they are not feminine? If so, we are implying one dimension, in which masculine and feminine are at the opposite ends, a bipolar dimension. However, a single person could have some masculine characteristics and some feminine characteristics (Bem, 2011). If we use two dimensions in our conceptualisation, we can make sense of a person's overall behaviour, using a dimension of low to high feminine characteristics, as well as low to high masculine characteristics. That is, they are not opposites, and a male, for example, can be high on feminine characteristics, as well as high on masculine characteristics, rather than seeing them as opposite ends of one dimension. Hence, we rapidly move from something seemingly abstract to something at the heart of contemporary social debates. The same issues apply to mental health and wellbeing (Linton, Dieppe & Medina-Lara, 2016). Is mental illness the opposite of wellbeing, or are there two dimensions? A further example is extraversion and introversion. Are they opposites on one dimension, or two separate dimensions?

Dimensions are an alternative to classic categories (in which you are either in or out) or prototypical categories (in which there needs to be a certain number of characteristics to be within a category). Given that wellbeing is a complex concept, it is useful to examine issues of dimensionality, beyond simply thinking of it in terms of what are the elements that may cause it and/or constitute it. For example, Seligman's (2018) PERMA model identifies positive emotions, engagement, relationships, meaning, and accomplishment as elements of wellbeing. For a coach, these are useful to know, and as will be described further, represent a useful vocabulary for wellbeing – but does the client think of them each as a dimension from zero to high, or do they think in all-or-none categorical ways?

One well known and most relevant model to understand the importance of dimensions is Keyes' dual continua model of complete mental health, recently summarised as a bivariate approach to mental health and wellbeing (Iasiello et al., 2020; Kessler, 2002; Keyes, 2002, 2007). The dual continua model, stated simply, assumes two dimensions to understand mental health and wellbeing. This means they are not required to be opposites. The absence of psychopathology (mental illness), such as anxiety or depression, does not mean the person is experiencing wellbeing, be it emotional wellbeing, psychological wellbeing, or social wellbeing (Zhao & Tay, 2022).

A person can have high to low mental illness symptoms, and high to low wellbeing. The distinction becomes increasingly important for people who live with chronic illness, including mental illness. For example, a person may live with long-term depression but may still function well and experience levels of emotional, psychological, and social wellbeing. Hence, the two dimensions of mental health and wellbeing become very important to the person's real life and understanding the complexity and changing nature of the experience. This distinction is also relevant in the mental health recovery movement in which people with mental illness seek to experience life recovery as defined by them, not solely in terms of symptom reduction (Andresen, Oades & Caputi, 2011). Hence, the notion of a dimension – or multiple dimensions – is useful to a coach in helping a client understand the complexity and changing nature of wellbeing. Some coaches may use scaling methods with clients, for example, when they ask a client to rate how important something is from 0–10. Dimensional thinking lends itself to quantitative scaling, and finer grained discussions around wellbeing. The rating occurs on a dimension. A key issue is the question of who chooses the dimensions – and understanding lay conceptions of wellbeing and language-use related to wellbeing are very informative in this regard.

Expert concepts and lay concepts of wellbeing

What is wellbeing? For literally thousands of years, philosophers have debated this question. During the twentieth century, scientists also came to the question. However, the public have always had a view, explicitly or implicitly. A rapid overview of expert terms regarding wellbeing are likely to yield a vocabulary of terms related to concepts, such as eudaimonia, hedonia, emotional wellbeing, psychological wellbeing, social wellbeing, happiness, thriving, flourishing, life satisfaction, resilience, stress, coping, meaning, optimism, etc. A different vocabulary and implicit concepts will arise from different non-experts, in different communicates and cultures (Disabato et al., 2016). Following the previous discussion of dimensions, Kelly's (1991/1955) theory of personal constructs is relevant. Kelly proposes that we each have personal psychological constructs which we use to make sense of the world. Kelly's bipolar personal constructs are like the previous discussion of dimensions. For some, a bipolar construct of *happy–sad* may be relevant, whilst for others, it may be *happy–tired* (Winter & Reed, 2016). The opposite end of a construct is often implicit. Hence, a personal construct approach recognises that people make meaning of the world, using their own constructs. The world is understood from the inside looking out, rather than the outside looking in. This is like the idea of lay concepts; we understand wellbeing through the concepts that non-experts use, rather than from the position of expert theory (Zedelius, Müller & Schooler, 2017).

Examining lay concepts and lay theories of wellbeing is relevant to a coach and the coaching process (Bojanowska & Zalewska, 2016). Gazal et al., 2019; Joshanloo, 2019). As mentioned, a lay concept is how a person as a non-expert conceptualises something – in this case, wellbeing (Huang, Kern & Oades, 2020; Oades & Jarden, 2021). A lay theory is how a person as non-expert theorises how something causes wellbeing, particularly at a personal level – in this case, what improves my own wellbeing.

Because wellbeing is a ubiquitous concept, most people have a lay concept, which is often implicit. They will also have a self-theory about what improves their own wellbeing. Hence, in both cases, the coach, in having coaching conversations with a client, will be well served by understanding and exploring the lay concept and lay theory of wellbeing of the client. People will also have their own vocabulary and communication preferences in the way they discuss wellbeing. Hence, not only do coaches have their own lay concepts and lay theories of wellbeing, they have personal vocabularies and language preferences, drawn from their language communities, in the way that they compose and comprehend wellbeing. The important role of language-use in understanding and constructing wellbeing is now described.

Language-use and coaching for wellbeing

The well-known analogy of whether the chicken or the egg came first is like the debate about whether thought came first or language came first. More specifically: if we learn a new word, does that lead us to a new concept – or is it the other way around? A relevant example is words that are not directly translatable across different languages, such as the term mindfulness in English, or eudaimonia/flourishing (Lomas, 2016). The strong version of the Whorfian hypothesis is that language creates thought, whilst a weaker version is that language influences thought. Given that many aspects of wellbeing are non-physical and psychological, the use of analogy and metaphors are central, and the language very much not only describes but constructs the way we think about and experience wellbeing. For this reason, a wellbeing coach not only needs to understand broader dimensions of wellbeing and lay concepts of wellbeing, but be skilled in the language used about and for wellbeing. For many, the language of wellbeing – as opposed to the language of ill-being – may seem like a second language. Wellbeing literacy refers to how we communicate about and for wellbeing (Hou et al., 2021; Oades et al., 2020; Oades et al., 2021). Wellbeing literacy is a capability consisting of five components: (1) vocabulary and knowledge; (2) comprehension of multimodal texts; (3) composition of multimodal texts; (4) context-sensitivity; and (5) intentionality (Table 2.1).

Table 2.1 Five-component capability model of wellbeing literacy

Component	Description
1. Vocabulary and knowledge *about* wellbeing	Words and information about wellbeing – possessing words (vocabulary) and knowledge about wellbeing that is consistent with our values and social context.
2. Comprehension *related to* wellbeing	Clients' comprehension in multiple modes, including viewing, listening, and reading about and for wellbeing.
3. Composition *related to* wellbeing	Clients' expression in multiple modes, including writing, creating, and speaking about and for wellbeing
4. Context awareness and adaptability	Awareness of differences across contexts and adapting language use to fit the relevant context.
5. Intentionality *for* wellbeing	Habit of intentionally using language to maintain or improve wellbeing of self or others.

Vocabulary and knowledge of wellbeing

Wellbeing vocabulary includes language associated with the wellbeing of oneself and others. Wellbeing knowledge includes declarative knowledge about and for wellbeing (refer to Table 2.1 and Table 2.2). One example may be a person who is involved in coaching, who has a limited vocabulary that relates to wellbeing, and uses terms drawn largely from the mental illness lexicon, for example anxiety, depression, or mental breakdown. They may view wellbeing as not having these experiences. That is, the client understands wellbeing as not having illness, thinking along one dimension. Hence, examination of the different language and related concepts may provide new opportunity and insights within the coaching process.

Multimodal comprehension of and for wellbeing: reading, listening, viewing

Communicating about and for wellbeing includes both receiving (comprehension) and producing (composition) aspects of literacy (see Table 2.1). Wellbeing literacy is multimodal (using different modes of communicating), reflecting a real-world, societal view of literacy (Perry, 2012). Similar to previous comments about lay concepts and lay theories, contemporary views of literacy examine how people use language in real life and culturally varied contexts, rather than only reading-writing within educational institutions. Comprehension of wellbeing communication occurs through reading, listening, and viewing (Australian Curriculum, Assessment and Reporting Authority [ACARA], 2020). For example, reading about wellbeing could include recommending to the client specific reading about wellbeing-related issues, whereas reading for wellbeing refers to experiences of the actual reading process. Listening about or for wellbeing could involve intentionally listening to music to boost the mood of the client before work. Viewing about or for wellbeing could involve viewing a portrait, which generates positive feelings such as awe or inspiration.

Multimodal composition of and for wellbeing: writing, speaking, creating

Composition of wellbeing communication is also multimodal and occurs through writing, speaking, and creating (ACARA, 2020) (See Table 2.1). Literacy is understood here as pivotal for relationships and wellbeing, as a sociocultural phenomenon, and as occurring between people (Gee, 1998).

Wellbeing experiences are likely composed in congruence with values and the sociocultural context. Examples of intentionally composing for wellbeing could include a client sending regular text messages to a sibling who lives outside their local area to strengthen their sense of family connection. Speaking for wellbeing could involve deliberately singing personally favourite songs, exercising one's strength of playfulness, and boosting positive emotion. Creating about wellbeing, could involve painting or choreographing a dance, representing the joys and sorrows of life. The multimodal aspect of wellbeing literacy is relevant to the many different modes of communication that may occur within a coaching relationship itself, and for the other relationships of the client.

Context-sensitivity

The meaning of language varies with context. A person who is viewed as wellbeing literate will be able to identify and adapt their language-use for the context, in the service of their own wellbeing and the wellbeing of the person or people to whom they are communicating. For example, words and communication modes differ across a person's life domains, such as home, school, the workplace, and with grandparents, friends, or work colleagues. Sensitivity to context is demonstrated when an individual can select language and communication modes that meet different situations and the contexts' communication needs. clients often raise relationship challenges, either at work or home, that may be hindering their career or life progress. As relationships require language, and emphasis on wellbeing related language-use is a relevant approach for coaches.

Intentionality of language-use

Language does not use itself; it has the user's intentions and awareness of contexts in which they use the language. Malle and Knobe (1997) provide a folk model of intentionality which involves belief, desire, intention, and awareness. Intentionality relates to the *for* component of wellbeing literacy; that is, not just what language is about or signifies, but why it is being used. Does the sender or receiver of communication aim for positive wellbeing of self, others, or the world? Intentionality is more than a single good intention. Rather, it involves the ongoing habit of those intentions – or more specifically, the capability to keep having good intentions regarding language-use for wellbeing. In everyday communication, *mindful* or *skilful* language-use are relevant to intentionality awareness. Intentionality in this context refers to an ongoing mental state, rather than a solitary instance or action. Hence, within a coaching context, a skilful wellbeing communicator will not only understand the role of language in shaping and constructing wellbeing, but also develop the habit of using it with care.

How are dimensions, lay concepts, and language-use of wellbeing relevant to coaching practice?

Dimensions, lay concepts and language-use may all seem abstract and removed from the coaching relationship. However, once one seeks to pay close attention to each of these phenomena, their prevalence and relevance becomes clear. Table 2.2 outlines some key implications to wellbeing coaching of the dimensions of wellbeing, lay concepts of wellbeing, and language-use of wellbeing. Within italics of Table 2.2 are some specific practical recommendations to explore each issue within coaching. There are many other practices and techniques that could be used, contingent on the context and the characteristics of the coach, client, and the relationship (Oades, Siokou & Slemp, 2019; Fisher et al., 2023).

Table 2.2 Implications and recommendations for wellbeing coaching practice

	Implications and recommendations for coaching practice
Dimensions of wellbeing	Coaches and coaches may vary in how they conceptualise wellbeing in terms of categories or dimensions. *Draw dimensions of wellbeing with the client (e.g., a line on a whiteboard) and ask them to label both ends. Ask them whether they need more dimensions (e.g., another line) to understand wellbeing. Ask the client about the opposites of words. This will lead to more dimensional thinking about wellbeing.*
Lay concepts of wellbeing	Coaches and coaches have their own concepts of wellbeing, and what causes their own wellbeing (i.e., lay concepts and lay theories). These may be different from each other and different from well-known theories and models, which may lead to misunderstandings in the coaching relationship. *Leave time within the coaching relationship to explicitly discuss what wellbeing is to the person, and what they believe may cause it in their own life, and compare it when relevant to established models and evidence.*
Language-use of wellbeing	Relationships always involve language. To many, wellbeing language – rather than ill-being language – may seem like a foreign language. Close attention to language and language-use is particularly relevant to wellbeing coaching, because wellbeing is often abstract and psychological, giving language an even greater role. *Pay close attention to the vocabulary of the client in the way they discuss issues related to wellbeing. Examine whether it involves positive words, or solely the low level of negative words. For example, do they say "don't feel sad" or do they say "feeling happy"?* *Introduce new language – and hence concepts – when appropriate, if it opens new avenues beyond stuck points.* *Use a multimodal approach in assisting the client with wellbeing; that is, reading and writing, speaking and listening, creating and viewing. Wellbeing is constructed in different language modes.*
Theories and models of wellbeing as "concept and language toolkits"	Wellbeing and related concepts such as flourishing and happiness and contested and complex areas. It is difficult for the coach to understand them all. It is not possible to have a different theory or model for each issue that arises. *Consider coaching theories and models as concept and language tool kits. A coach can take language and concepts from a particular model or theory as part of the coaching conversation. Whilst it may not be "applying the theory", because language-use itself can assist wellbeing and its conceptualisations, this can assist the coach and client to co-construct relevant aspects of wellbeing, more closely in line with the clients' language and lay concepts, whilst also adding to them.*

Conclusion

Wellbeing is complex and contested, and has many parts to it. For this reason, it is useful to understand its dimensions, how it is viewed by non-experts, and how it is created and recreated through language-use. By viewing theories and models as toolkits of concepts and language, a coach will be able to adapt to resonate more closely with the client's own concepts and language-use about and for wellbeing.

Reflective questions

1. What is your definition of wellbeing compared to the definition of those who you may coach?
2. In your coaching practice, do you tend to rely more on a formal model of wellbeing, or do you work from the lay concept of the client?
3. What language do you use to discuss wellbeing in your own life, compared to the language of those who you may coach?

References

Alexandrova, A. (2017). *A philosophy for the science of wellbeing*. New York: Oxford University Press.

Andresen, R., Oades, L. G, & Caputi, P. (2011). *Psychological recovery: Beyond mental illness*. Chichester: John Wiley & Sons.

Australian Curriculum, Assessment and Reporting Authority. (2020b, June 16). *Literacy*. https://www.australiancurriculum.edu.au/f-10-curriculum/general-capabilities/literacy/

Baumeister, R. F., Vohs, K. D., Aaker, J. L., & Garbinsky, E. N. (2013). Some key differences between a happy life and a meaningful life. *The Journal of Positive Psychology*, 8(6), 505–516. https://doi.org/10.1080/17439760.2013.830764

Bem, S. (2011). Bem sex role inventory. *Bem Sex Role Inventory*. https://doi.org/10.1037/t00748-000

Bojanowska, A., & Zalewska, A. M. (2016). Lay understanding of happiness and the experience of well-being: Are some conceptions of happiness more beneficial than others? *Journal of Happiness Studies*, 17(2), 793–815. https://doi.org/10.1007/s10902-015-9620-1

de Ruyter, D. J., Oades, L. G., Waghid, Y., Ehrenfeld, J., Gilead, T, & Singh, N. C. (2022). Education for flourishing and flourishing in education. In A. K. Duraiappah, N. M. van Atteveldt, G. Borst, S. Bugden, O. Ergas, T. Gilead, L. Gupta, J. Mercier, K. Pugh, N. C. Singh, & E. A. Vickers (Eds.), *Reimagining education: The international science and evidence based assessment* (pp. 72–130). New Delhi: UNESCO MGIEP.

Disabato, D. J., Goodman, F. R., Kashdan, T. B., Short, J. L., & Jarden, A. (2016). Different types of well-being? A cross-cultural examination of hedonic and eudaimonic well-being. *Psychological Assessment*, 28(5), 471–482. https://doi.org/10.1037/pas0000209

Dodge, R., Daly, A. P., Huyton, J., & Sanders, L. D. (2012). The challenge of defining wellbeing. *International Journal of Wellbeing*, 2(3), 222–235.

Fisher, Z., Wilkie, L., Hamill, A., & Kemp, A. H. (2023). Theories of wellbeing, practical applications and implications for coaching. In J. Passmore, B. Badri, & L. Oades (Eds.), *The health & wellbeing coaches handbook*. Abingdon: Routledge.

Gazal, B., Duncan, S., Jarden, A., & Hinckson, E. (2019). A prototype analysis of New Zealand adolescents' conceptualizations of wellbeing. *International Journal of Wellbeing*, 9(4), 1–25. https://doi.org/10.5502/ijw.v9i4.975

Gee, J. P. (1998). What is literacy? In V. Zamel & R. Spack (Eds.), *Negotiating academic literacies: Teaching and learning across languages and cultures* (1st ed., pp. 51–59). New York, NY: Routledge. https://doi.org/10.4324/978020343234

Hou, H., Chin, T. C., Slemp, G. R., & Oades, L. G. (2021). Wellbeing literacy: Conceptualization, measurement, and preliminary empirical findings from students, parents and school staff. *International Journal of Environmental Research and Public Health*, 18(4), 1485. https://doi.org/10.3390/ijerph18041485

Huang L., Kern M. L., & Oades, L. G. (2020). Strengthening university student wellbeing: Language and perceptions of Chinese international students. *International Journal of Environmental Research and Public Health*, 17(15), 5538. https://doi.org/10.3390/ijerph17155538

Iasiello, M., van Agteren, J., & Muir-Cochrane, E. (2020). Mental health and/or mental illness: A scoping review of the evidence and implications of the dual-continua model of mental health. *Evidence Base*, 2020(1), 1–45.

Joshanloo, M. (2019). Lay conceptions of happiness: Associations with reported well-being, personality traits, and materialism.*Frontier in Psychology*, 10, 2377. https://doi.org/10.3389/fpsyg.2019.02377

Kelly, G. (1991) [1955]. *The psychology of personal constructs*. London; New York: Routledge in association with the Centre for Personal Construct Psychology. ISBN 978-0415037990. OCLC 21760190. Originally published as: Kelly, G. (1955). *The psychology of personal constructs*. New York: W. W. Norton & Company. OCLC 217761.

Kemp, A. H., & Edwards, D. J. (Eds.). (2022). *Broadening the scope of wellbeing science: Multidisciplinary and interdisciplinary perspectives on human flourishing and wellbeing*. Switzerland: Springer Nature, Palgrave Macamillan.

Kessler, R. C. (2002). The categorical versus dimensional assessment controversy in the sociology of mental illness. *Journal of Health Social Behavior*, 43(2), 171–188. https://www.ncbi.nlm.nih.gov/pubmed/12096698

Keyes, C. L. (2002). The mental health continuum: From languishing to flourishing in life. *Journal of Health Social Behavior*, 43(2), 207–222. https://www.ncbi.nlm.nih.gov/pubmed/12096700

Keyes C. L. (2007, February–March). Promoting and protecting mental health as flourishing: A complementary strategy for improving national mental health. *American Psychologist*, 62(2), 95–108. https://doi.org/10.1037/0003-066X.62.2.95. PMID: 17324035

Linton, M.-J., Dieppe, P., & Medina-Lara, A. (2016). Review of 99 self-report measures for assessing wellbeing in adults: Exploring dimensions of well-being and developments over time. *BMJ Open*, e010641. https://doi.org/10.1136/bmjopen-2015-010641

Lomas, T. (2016). Towards a positive cross-cultural lexicography: Enriching our emotional landscape through 216 "untranslatable" words pertaining to well-being. *The Journal of Positive Psychology*, 11(5), 546–558. https://doi.org/10.1080/17439760.2015.1127993

Malle, B. F., & Knobe, J. (1997). The folk concept of intentionality. *Journal of Experimental Social Psychology*, 33(2), 101–121. https://doi.org/10.1006/jesp.1996.1314

Oades, L. G., & Jarden, A. (2021). Personalised wellbeing planning. In Allen, K. A., Reupert, A., & Oades, L (Eds.), *Building better schools with evidence-based policy: Adaptable policy for teachers and school leaders*. New York: Taylor and Francis.

Oades, L. G., Jarden, A., Hou, H., Ozturk, C., Williams, P., R Slemp, G., & Huang, L. (2021). Wellbeing literacy: A capability model for wellbeing science and practice. *International Journal of Environmental Research and Public Health*, 18(2), 719. https://www.mdpi.com/1660-4601/18/2/719

Oades, L. G., Ozturk, C., Hou, H., & Slemp, G. R. (2020). Wellbeing literacy: A language-use capability relevant to wellbeing outcomes of positive psychology intervention. *The Journal of Positive Psychology*, 15(5), 696–700. https://doi.org/10.1080/17439760.2020.1789711

Oades, L. G., Siokou, C., & Slemp, G. R. (2019). *Coaching and mentoring research: A practical introduction*. London: Sage.

Perry, K. H. (2012). What is literacy?: A critical overview of sociocultural perspectives. *Journal of Language and Literacy Education*, 8(1), 50–71. https://files.eric.ed.gov/fulltext/EJ1008156.pdf

Salvador-Carulla, L., Lucas, R., Ayuso-Mateos, J. L., & Miret, M. (2014, January–March). Use of the terms "wellbeing" and "quality of life" in health sciences: A conceptual framework. *European Journal of Psychiatry*, 28(1), 50–65. https://doi.org/Doi 10.4321/S0213–61632014000100005

Seligman, M. (2018). PERMA and the building blocks of well-being. *Journal of Positive Psychology*, 13(4), 333–335. https://doi.org/10.1080/17439760.2018.1437466

van Agteren, J., Iasiello, M., Lo, L., Bartholomaeus, J., Kopsaftis, Z., Carey, M., & Kyrios, M. (2021). A systematic review and meta-analysis of psychological interventions to improve mental wellbeing. *Nature Human Behaviour, 5*(5), 631–652. https://doi.org/10.1038/s41562-021-01093-w

Winter, D. A., & Reed, N. (Eds.). (2016). *The wiley handbook of personal construct psychology.* Chichester: Wiley.

Zhao, M. Y., & Tay, L. (2022). From ill-being to well-being: Bipolar or bivariate? *The Journal of Positive Psychology,* 1–11. https://doi.org/10.1080/17439760.2022.2109204

Zedelius, C. M., Müller, B. C., & Schooler, J. W. (2017). *The science of lay theories.* Cham, Switzerland: Springer International Publishing. http://doi. org/10.1007/978-3-319-57306-9

Chapter 3

Theories of wellbeing, practical applications and implications for coaching

Zoe Fisher, Lowri Wilkie, Alexandra Hamill and Andrew H. Kemp

Introduction

Wellbeing science includes numerous – and sometimes competing – theoretical models (see Table 3.1 for summary). These include the tripartite model of subjective wellbeing (Diener, 1984, 2000; Diener et al., 1999), the six-factor model of psychological wellbeing (Ryff, 1989, 2014; Ryff & Keyes, 1995), PERMA model highlighting the core components of wellbeing including positive emotions, engagement, social relationships, meaning and purpose and accomplishment (Butler & Kern, 2016; Seligman, 2012, 2017), self-determination theory (Ryan & Deci, 2000, 2001), salutogenic theory (Antonovsky, 1996; Mittelmark & Bull, 2013), social identity theory (Haslam et al., 2017, 2009, 2021), social wellbeing (Keyes, 1998), social determinants of health (Marmot & Wilkinson, 2005; Wilkinson & Pickett, 2010), the biophilia hypothesis (Wilson, 1984), psycho-evolutionary theory (Ulrich et al., 1991) and different conceptualisations of 'sustainable' happiness and wellbeing (Corral-Verdugo et al., 2015; Corral-Verdugo & Frías-Armenta, 2016; Kjell, 2011; Lyubomirsky et al., 2005; Sheldon & Lyubomirsky, 2021; O'Brien, 2012, 2016; Verdugo, 2012). Recent developments in wellbeing science – including our own work – have been characterised by attempts to integrate various and often competing models, developments that have been described as second-, third- and even fourth-wave positive psychology (Lomas, 2022; Lomas et al., 2020; Wong, 2019) and systems-informed positive psychology (Kern et al., 2020).

Recent developments in the field demonstrate a broadening of positive psychology to encompass communities and the natural environment alongside the individual themselves, a development in which we are actively engaged (Kemp et al., 2022a,b; Kemp & Edwards, 2022; Kemp & Fisher, 2022; Wilkie et al., 2022a). A focus on social identity – defined as "the knowledge that [we] belong to certain social groups together with some emotional and value significance to [us] of this group membership" (Tajfel, 1972, p. 31) – has encouraged reflection on the considerable psychological benefits of social relationships and community. This includes meaning, purpose and belonging with profound implications for health and wellbeing (Haslam et al., 2009). For instance, a recent study (N = 3,700) (Cruwys et al., 2022) reported that neighbourhood identification is a mechanism through which neighbourhood socioeconomic status affects wellbeing. The authors also presented experimental evidence that showed neighbourhood identification could be enhanced through a subtle framing manipulation that required participants to judge the degree to which they were similar – rather than different – to their neighbours. The extent

DOI: 10.4324/9781003319016-4

Table 3.1 Summary of major theories and models of wellbeing

Domain	Theory	Description
Individual	Tripartite model (Diener)	Focused on life satisfaction, positive and negative affect. Typically characterised as tapping into hedonic wellbeing. Diener argued that subjective wellbeing does not involve making value judgements by 'experts' on what a good life entails, such as proponents of 'eudaimonic wellbeing'.
	Psychological flow (Csikszentmihalyi)	Refers to the experience of being completely absorbed in an activity, with the ideal challenge–skill balance. Flow is a highly enjoyable experience linked to creativity, productivity and happiness.
	Six-factor model (Ryff)	Encompasses positive relationships with others, personal mastery, autonomy, a feeling of purpose and meaning in life, and personal growth and development. This model is characterised as tapping into 'eudaimonic wellbeing', as distinct from 'hedonic' wellbeing.
	PERMA model (Seligman)	An integration of hedonic (affect) and eudaimonic (psychological wellbeing) theory. Encompasses positive emotion, engagement, social relationships, meaning and achievement all contribute to wellbeing.
	Self-determination (macro) theory (Deci & Ryan)	Autonomy, competence and relatedness as psychological needs essential for self-motivation, health and wellbeing, regardless of culture or stage of development. Emphasises importance of intrinsic motivation for psychological growth and development.
	'Sustainable' happiness	Focused on sustained positive change and improvements in wellbeing. This definition is distinct from other proposals linking to concepts of 'environmental sustainability', which focus on happiness and wellbeing within an environmental context. See in what follows.
	Salutogenic theory (Antonovsky)	'Salutogenesis' is based on the Latin term 'salus' (meaning health, wellbeing) and the Greek word 'genesis' (meaning emergence or creation). The salutogenic concept emphasises a role for a 'sense of coherence' in managing and overcoming stress.
	Relational frame theory (RFT) (Hayes)	Relations between concepts as the foundations for human language. While not usually thought of as a theory of wellbeing, RFT underpins Acceptance and Commitment Therapy, on which researchers are increasingly drawing – often in combination with principles from positive psychology – to promote values-based behavioural activation and exploration despite suffering.
Community	Social identity theory (Haslam)	Groups provide individuals with a sense of meaning and purpose with positive psychological consequences. This theory has led to 'The New Psychology of Health', which emphasises the importance of positive social ties and social relationships for health and wellbeing.

(Continued)

Table 3.1 (Continued)

Domain	Theory	Description
	Social wellbeing (Keyes)	The sense that society is meaningful and understandable (social coherence), and provides an opportunity for growth (social actualisation), is something that one belongs to and is accepted by (social acceptance and integration) and that one can meaningfully contribute to it (social contribution).
	Social determinants of health (Marmot)	Social determinants include disability, poverty and loneliness, which are major determinants of health (and wellbeing). Role of health equity and social gradients are major concepts.
Environmental	Biophilia hypothesis (Wilson)	Core assumption is that human beings have a strong, innate affiliation with the biological world.
	Psycho-evolutionary theory (Ulrich)	Restorative influences of nature involve a shift toward more positive emotions, parasympathetic dominated responses (heart rate deceleration) and sustained – yet non-taxing – attention.
	'Sustainable' happiness and wellbeing (O'Brien)	Here, 'sustainable happiness' is defined as individual, community and/or global wellbeing that does not involve exploitation of other people, the environment or future generations. Complementary proposals have been made by Kjell and Corral-Verdugo highlighting interdependencies between the individual, others and nature, and explicit links between concepts like character strengths and pro-environmental behaviours.

Note. Table adapted from Mead and colleagues (2019)

to which participants judged themselves as similar or different had subsequent impacts on wellbeing, loneliness and social cohesion. The authors concluded that manipulation of neighbourhood identification has potential for addressing the adverse outcomes associated with living in disadvantaged areas. This focus on social identity has been described as "the new psychology of health" and wellbeing (Haslam et al., 2017), highlighting a recent shift in disciplinary thinking beyond what has been an often-restricted focus on the individual.

Another key component of wellbeing is nature connectedness. Large-scale population-based studies and meta-analyses have demonstrated that time spent in nature and nature connectedness increases wellbeing (Capaldi et al., 2015; McMahan and Estes, 2015) and reduces mental health difficulties (Feng et al., 2022), as well as morbidity and mortality, due to cardiovascular disease and stroke (Liu et al., 2022). Unfortunately, humans have become increasingly disconnected from nature for many reasons which include advances in technology, globalisation and urbanisation (Louv, 2005; Hartig et al., 2014). It has been argued that this disconnection from the natural environment contributes to the degradation of the planet (Nisbet et al., 2009). Critically, as humans derive significant wellbeing from the natural environment, one cannot ignore the inverse relationship between the pernicious impact of climate change and wellbeing.

Interestingly, emerging research shows that connection to nature not only improves wellbeing but also promotes pro-environmental behaviours (e.g., Martin et al., 2020). Thus, connection with natural environment can simultaneously improve individual and planetary wellbeing. These observations have led researchers to call for a new relationship with nature that will transform attitudes and behaviours into positive and meaningful outcomes for the environment while also tackling the crisis in mental health and wellbeing (Pritchard & Richardson, 2022). Such calls are motivated by the sheer challenge and scale of the climate and nature emergency and its implications for health and wellbeing. While research has long demonstrated that wellbeing may be promoted by spending more time in, and engaging with, the natural environment (Kaplan & Kaplan, 1989; Kaplan, 1995; Ulrich, 1981; Ulrich et al., 1991), it has now become impossible to discuss this work without also reflecting on the implications for planetary health and wellbeing (Antó et al., 2021; Isham & Jackson, 2022; Kemp & Fisher, 2022; Martin et al., 2020).

The construct of wellbeing is clearly complex and has even been described as a "wicked problem", given the difficulty in defining the construct and avoidance of straightforward solutions (Bache et al., 2016). To combat this complexity, we have sought to develop our own theoretical framework that we refer to as 'GENIAL' around which we have developed previously unimagined interventions including a five-week undergraduate module on wellbeing science for university students (Kemp & Fisher, 2021a; Kemp et al., 2022a), an eight-week positive psychotherapy intervention (e.g., Fisher et al., 2024) and a five-week surf therapy intervention for people living with an acquired brain injury (e.g., Wilkie et al., 2022b), as three concrete examples among many others. Our framework has allowed us to bring into focus the multifaceted determinants of wellbeing and their interactions across multiple domains and levels of scale. 'GENIAL' is an acronym referring to the relationships among genomics, environment, vagus nerve, social interaction, allostatic regulation and longevity (Fisher et al., 2020; Kemp, 2019; Kemp et al., 2017), reflecting a life-course framework through which wellbeing – versus 'ill-being' – is realised. A key component of the GENIAL model centres around the regulatory function of the vagus nerve, the tenth cranial nerve connecting many different organs including heart, gut, liver and lungs and which is also the major nerve supporting the parasympathetic nervous system. A large body of research now links the vagus nerve to a wide range of constructs associated with wellbeing, including positive emotions, social connectedness, time spent in nature, morbidity and premature mortality (Fang et al., 2020; Jandackova et al., 2016; Kok et al., 2013; Richardson et al., 2016). The English word 'genial' also means 'friendly and cheerful', reflecting important aspects of connection, social relationships and community. More recently, we have characterised wellbeing as 'connection' to ourselves, others and nature, connecting the frequently isolated constructs of individual, collective and planetary wellbeing (Kemp & Fisher, 2022; Wilkie et al., 2022a). We have argued that functioning of the vagus nerve may underpin the experience of wellbeing and provides a target for 'inner development' and transformation of the self (Wilkie et al., 2022a) with potential application in the context of coaching psychology. We further recognise the wider socio-structural factors in our work that either serve to promote or adversely affect the vagus nerve, and are guided by a more ethical approach to promoting wellbeing (Mead et al., 2019) that takes into account many societal challenges, such as the climate and nature emergency.

Practice

In this section, we describe how we have begun to apply our GENIAL model in the education and healthcare sectors, focusing on how we have sought to improve wellbeing in university students and people living with acquired brain injury, in particular. While we acknowledge that this work has been conducted within the context of university teaching and clinical psychology, our work is readily applicable to coaching psychology, and we reflect on opportunities for such application in the discussion below. In particular, our work has led to the development of two new tools, which we make available in Chapters 29 and 35. These tools include the 'GENIAL Roadmap to Wellbeing' and the 'Snakes and Ladders' tool designed to support wellbeing through the promotion of evidence-based techniques and behaviours.

In the education sector, we have developed a five-week module for third-year university students (Kemp et al., 2022a; Kemp & Fisher, 2021a) focused on theory and background (week 1) and connection to self (week 2), others (week 3) and nature (week 4), as well as positive behaviour change (week 5), while reflecting on socio-structural promoters and barriers to wellbeing alongside each week's content. We have adopted an Nof1 study design (Kemp & Fisher, 2021a) to facilitate objective assessment of the impact that the module has on individual student wellbeing, encouraging students to engage in a process of active learning and to focus on how the taught content can be applied to improve their own wellbeing. Findings from a typical student report are presented in Figure 3.1 and Figure 3.2, illustrating the impact the module has had on student-chosen questionnaire and psychophysiological measures of wellbeing. In this example, both questionnaire and psychophysiological measures improved over the course of the module and these improvements were maintained during the two-week follow-up period, indicated by points lying above the upper control line, reflecting three standard deviations above the baseline mean. Measuring objective change in this way has become easier to implement in recent years with increasing interest in the 'quantified self' and associated

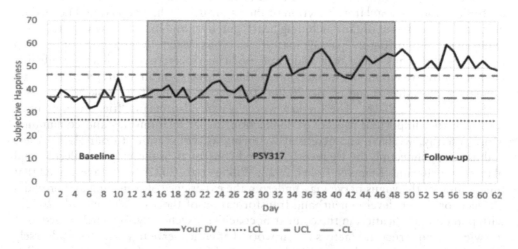

Figure 3.1 Impact of module (PSY317) on subjective happiness as operationalised by the nineitem Global Wellbeing Scale (Diener et al., 2020) on a single third-year student during the 2020–2021 academic year

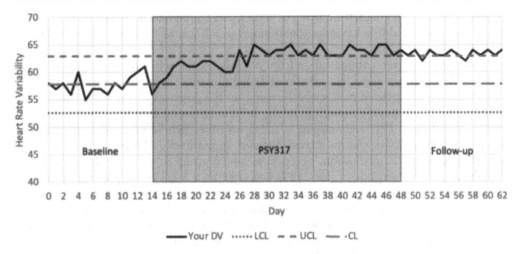

Figure 3.2 Impact of module (PSY317) on heart rate variability (HRV), an index of the functioning of the vagus nerve, using the CooSpo heart rate monitor and the freely available EliteHRV app, on a single third-year student

improvements in technology (e.g., the Oura ring, the Garmin watch or the 'EliteHRV' and 'Welltory' apps), supporting a real world focus on psychophysiological indices of wellbeing such as heart rate variability, an index of the vagus nerve (Wilkie et al., 2022a), that would be readily applicable in coaching psychology contexts.

Our module encourages students to self-select positive psychological interventions, guided by the 'GENIAL Roadmap to Wellbeing' (Chapter 29), a goal-setting exercise that helps individuals to identify the wellbeing domains on which they may wish to focus over the course of the module. The task is to read through each domain of the roadmap and to use the questions as a prompt to reflect on how they feel about each component in their life over the past two weeks. They then mark a number (from 1–6) on each arm to indicate the extent to which these components are being experienced right now. Lower scores indicate components that need attention (with a score of 1 indicating the least optimal score). Then, people are encouraged to use their responses as a guide to set goals and daily habits based on recognised areas for improvement. For example, if they scored 'connection to nature' as low on the roadmap, they might set a goal to walk for 30 minutes a day in nature at least four times a week, given findings that indicate spending at least 120 minutes a week in nature is good for health and wellbeing (White et al., 2019).

This approach is consistent with calls for a more personalised approach to wellbeing promotion (Ciarrochi et al., 2022), aligning with coaching-based practice. Over a period of four weeks, students are introduced to a variety of positive psychology intervention (PPIs) from which they select specific interventions that they are intrinsically motivated to carry out, guided by processes known to be effective in groups of people, including strengths (Schutte & Malouff, 2019), personal values (Bojanowska et al., 2022), positive emotions (Fredrickson, 1998), psychological flow (Tse et al., 2021), equanimity (Eberth et al., 2019), fierce compassion (Kirby et al., 2017), kindness (Hui et al., 2020), active hope (Pleeging et al., 2021), meaning and purpose (Vos & Vitali, 2018), meditation (van

Agteren et al., 2021), goal setting (Klug & Maier, 2015), physical activity (Buecker et al., 2021) and other health behaviours (Stenlund et al., 2022; see also van Agteren et al., 2021; Carr et al., 2020).

Recommended interventions range from a focus on the self, others and planet. For instance, PPIs encouraging a focus on the self might involve the student learning to apply their character strengths in new ways, focusing on the positives through the three good things activity and paying attention to the present moment through mindful breath-focused meditation. PPIs encouraging a focus on other people and community might involve students carrying out an activity focused on gratitude, adopting a Loving Kindness Meditation (LVK meditation) practice, joining a group or volunteering for a cause that aligns with the student's values. PPIs encouraging a focus on nature might involve the student practising a nature-based meditation, journaling or exercising in nature or engaging in fierce compassion through, for example, nonviolent social action. Students are encouraged to focus on activities that they are intrinsically motivated to carry out, focused on individual, collective and planetary wellbeing and supporting sustained positive change. Students might focus their selection around a particular theme. For instance, they might decide on a theme relating to 'meditation' and in order to promote individual wellbeing, they may decide to carry out a simple breath-focused meditation designed to calm the mind and facilitate connection to the self. In the following week, to promote collective wellbeing, they might shift to a meditation involving LVK meditation facilitating connections to others (social connection). In the subsequent week and focusing on planetary wellbeing, they might adapt their practice to nature-based meditation, facilitating connection to nature. In the final week, they might reflect on how to sustain positive changes they have made over the course of the module through a goal-setting activity. Interested readers are directed to specific guidance (developed for students) in regards to how individuals might carry out specific activities (Kemp & Fisher, 2021b).

Our GENIAL framework has also led to the development of an eight-week positive psychotherapy intervention delivered within a community brain injury service (Fisher et al., 2024), including many of the strategies included in the student module, contextualised for a different audience. Recent theoretical developments (described earlier) have guided the development of this intervention, which focuses on connecting people living with brain injury to the self, others and nature. A session-by-session summary of this intervention is provided in Table 3.2, and interested readers are referred to a range of resources in which topics covered in our intervention have been applied in coaching contexts (Green & Palmer, 2018; Palmer & Whybrow, 2019), highlighting the applicability of our work to the practice of coaching psychology. For example, researchers have described an approach that draws heavily on ideas from positive psychology and the mindfulness literature, emphasising a strengths-based approach characterised as 'positive psychology coaching' (Green & Palmer, 2018). More specifically, 'PERMA-powered coaching' provides a framework based on Seligman's PERMA model through which coaches can work with their clients to facilitate the experience of wellbeing through different components of PERMA including positive emotions, engagement (or psychological flow), social relationships, meaning and purpose and accomplishment (Falecki et al., 2018). However, our framework moves beyond PERMA by encouraging reflection on collective wellbeing through for example, volunteering, and even planetary wellbeing through for example, activism. There are opportunities for coaches to encourage collective and planetary

Table 3.2 Current session-by-session summary of eight-week positive psychotherapy course for people living with acquired brain injury

Session no. and name	Summary of session content
Session 1: Living With Difficult Emotions	Before focusing on positive emotions and wellbeing, it is important to acknowledge the role and value of difficult emotions and thoughts. Following a major life event, experiences of difficult thoughts and emotions are both understandable and common. It is important to recognise this and point out that the aim of the course is not to 'get rid' of negative thoughts and emotions but recognise their value where possible and to learn skills to make room for these experiences when they become overwhelming. The techniques outlined in this session are informed by Acceptance and Commitment Therapy, Mindfulness Therapy and Compassion-Focused Therapy, drawing on the work of Harris, Hayes Kabat-Zinn and Gilbert (Harris, 2019; Hayes & Lillis, 2014; Kabat-Zinn, 2003; Gilbert & Simos, 2022).
Session 2: Identifying and Using Character Strengths	Identifying one's character strengths is the foundation to 'building on what is strong, rather than fixing what is wrong'. In this session, group members introduce themselves by their character strengths and provide examples of how they use their strengths. We discuss new ways to use character strengths and making positive statements based on participants strengths, talents and values. Niemiec's (2018) work provides a solid foundation in this regard.
Session 3: Building Positive Emotion	Positive emotions are fundamental to theories of hedonic wellbeing. Barbara Fredrickson's (2004) 'Broaden and Build Model' is a major focus of this section, as well as the work of Seligman and Dieners. A core feature of positive psychology is to promote task engagement by facilitating 'psychological flow', as coined by Csikszentmihalyi (1997). In this session, we explore and practise several evidence-based techniques to build and savour positive emotions and experiences including flow, gratitude and optimism.
Session 4: Connection Between Body and Mind	In this session, we emphasise the importance of building positive health behaviours to facilitate vagal function, which in turn positively affects wellbeing. This session is influenced by our own GENIAL model (Kemp & Fisher, 2022), and the work of Porges, Dana and Thayer (Porges, 2011; Porges & Dana, 2018; Thayer & Lane, 2000). In this session, we teach participants about the mechanisms that underpin the connection between the mind and the body, emphasising the regulatory role of the vagus nerve (as indexed by heart rate variability [HRV]). Participants learn about techniques/lifestyle factors that have been shown to improve HRV including diet, exercise, sleep, meditation, etc. To maximise engagement in the session, participants explore the acute impact of different activities on their own HRV, through engagement in a variety of exercises.
Session 5: Connection to Others and the Natural Environment	In part one of this session, we explore the importance of social connection to health and wellbeing outcomes. We practise techniques shown to facilitate social connection (and social relational emotions) including 'acts of kindness' and 'gratitude' exercises. We talk in more detail about the positive emotion of love in keeping with Fredrickson's (2014) work on positivity resonance. We learn about techniques to elicit feelings of love, including 'Loving Kindness Meditation'. We talk about the importance of connection with our communities and explore

(Continued)

Table 3.2 Continued

Session no. and name	Summary of session content
	how disconnection following brain injury may affect one's sense of identity. This section is influenced by the theoretical work of Tajfel (1979) and Haslam et al. (2017). Finally, we talk about the importance of nature connectedness for health and wellbeing, drawing on key theories such as ecological systems theory, biophilia, stress reduction theory and attention restoration theory, inspired by the work of Wilson (1984), Kaplan (1995), Ulrich et al. (1991) and O'Brien (2016).
Session 6: Meaning and Purpose	Meaning and purpose in life are major components to eudaimonic wellbeing. The theoretical work by Ryff (1989, 2014), Frankl (1985, 2011) and Wong (2019) are particularly influential in this regard. We argue that meaning and purpose in life might be enhanced and facilitated through a combination of interventions that focus on the individual, community and environment. In this session, we explore photos that represent areas of meaning for participants (inspired by the work of Steger et al. (2013, 2014)) and link these areas of meaning to each participant's values using a values clarification exercise. We talk about meaning as providing a sense of direction in life and values as a global positioning system (GPS) to help us move in the right direction.
Session 7: Translating Values Into Action	In this session, we recap on each participant's strengths, values and areas of meaning. We explore the extent to which participants are living a values-based life or are 'acting out their values'. Participants identify and share areas where they are acting out their values and areas where they could better connect with their values. Using a 'goal-setting' framework, participants set goals that support them to reconnect with some of their values in the coming months. We explore some of the challenges and opportunities for growth that participants might encounter while trying to achieve their goals. This session is inspired by Acceptance and Commitment Therapy, and positive psychology as it relates to the human values system, inspired by the work of Bojanowska et al. (2022) and the theoretical work of Schwartz (Schwartz, 2012; Schwartz & Sortheix, 2018) related to values and the basic human needs system.
Session 8: Behaviour Change and Managing the Ups and the Downs	This session explores factors that predict sustainable behaviour change. Participants are given a behaviour change planner based on these factors. This session is based on the work of Kwasnicka and Van Cappellen and colleagues (Kwasnicka et al. 2016; Van Cappellen et al. 2018). The group explores some of the goals identified in session 7 and refines them to work in predictors of behaviour change. In the second half of the session, we revisit many of the challenges typically encountered when moving toward wellbeing. We recap on many of the strategies that we learnt throughout the group to help manage these challenges. We also recap on many techniques and strategies that can be practised anytime to support wellbeing. The ups and downs are conceptualised as snakes and ladders to help make the session as engaging and memorable as possible.

wellbeing (in addition to individual wellbeing) through for example, compassion-focused coaching (e.g., Irons et al., 2019) and outdoor coaching (e.g., Burn & Passmore, 2022).

To facilitate the promotion of wellbeing in the people we work with, we have developed an adaptation of the 'Snakes and Ladders' game (Chapter 35) and use this as a conceptual framework to bring together and simplify ideas that we introduce to students, clients and patients. The 'Snakes and Ladders' board is used to symbolise our individual life journeys at a given time, with each consecutive square representing the passage of time. Since our aim is to improve wellbeing, squares of increasingly higher numbers will represent moving towards greater wellbeing. Throughout the group we refer to 'ladders' which represent things we can do, or strategies we can implement, to move us towards wellbeing. The 'snakes' represent the difficult internal experiences and unhelpful actions that we can take that inadvertently move us away from wellbeing. When confronted with a snake, people face a 'choice point' (Harris, 2017). That is, people may choose to respond in a way that moves them towards or away from their values and goals. For instance, someone may have set a goal of attending a local community group. However, when the time comes to attend the group, the person may experience anxiety. This takes them to a choice point where they may go down the 'avoidance' snake in an attempt to 'get rid' of difficult thoughts, overwhelming emotions and physiological sensations. This ultimately moves them further away from their goal of social connection and maintains anxiety in the future. We show our participants the techniques (ladders) to help them make room for and expect anxiety in these situations so that when faced with this choice point, they may choose to practise, for example, 'expansion techniques' (making room for difficult thoughts and feelings). This framework therefore helps people become more consciously aware of 'snakes', so that they can acknowledge the snake without falling down and continue to move in the direction of their goals. Choices toward wellbeing are represented by ladders, while moves away from wellbeing are represented by snakes. Importantly, falling down snakes is inevitable at times and participants are encouraged to make room for this in a way that facilitates acceptance and growth. We broadly define two types of ladders as 'wooden ladders' and 'rainbow ladders'. Wooden ladders represent a range of different strategies that can be used in response to a variety of different types of snakes that may be encountered when trying to improve wellbeing. 'Rainbow ladders' represent opportunities to use evidence-based strategies that help to improve wellbeing, even in the absence of snakes. The tool includes a 'Snakes and Ladders' board and a series of cards (see Figures 35.1, 35.2 and 35.3 and Chapter 35) featuring different snakes and wooden and rainbow ladders. It should be noted that the tool is not intended to provide an exhaustive range of snakes that may be encountered, or evidence-based techniques to manage downfalls or improve wellbeing. The snakes have been derived from common experiences described by participants in our clinical work and evidence-based techniques that we draw on in our work.

Conclusions

Wellbeing science is a focus of much research interest and significant debate, motivating us to develop a theoretical framework that brings into focus the multifaceted determinants of wellbeing and their interactions across multiple domains and levels of scale. In this chapter, we provided an overview of the different theories in the field on which we have developed this framework, encompassing a focus on the individual, community and the natural environment within which a range of socio-structural opportunities (barriers) arise for promoting (restricting) positive change at multiple levels. We also described a range of interventions in the education and healthcare sectors, including a five-week module to promote wellbeing in undergraduate students and an eight-week positive psychotherapy intervention for people living with acquired brain injury. Finally, we presented two recently developed tools to support reflections around goal setting and the various wellbeing-promoting strategies that we introduce. While our work has been inspired by positive psychology and conducted within the context of clinical psychology and undergraduate teaching (Fisher et al., 2020; Gibbs, Fisher et al., 2022; Kemp et al., 2022a), there is much overlap with coaching psychology, including a focus on building trust and rapport, self-efficacy, motivation to change, collaborative relationships and working alliances (Passmore & Evans-Krimme, 2021; Passmore & Lai, 2021).

Our work with university student populations encourages students to adopt a proactive and independent approach to promote wellbeing, which may have subsequent effects on academic achievement (Cárdenas et al., 2022; Waters et al., 2019). As students engage in self-selected PPIs, they are building emotional, cognitive, psychological and social resources for positive change on which future improvements may be made in an upward spiral model of lifestyle change (Cappellen et al., 2017; Fredrickson, 2004, 2013). Our work in the healthcare sector is more focused around group work to build social connections and reconnect the patients we work with to their local communities and the natural environment. However, this work can be and is adapted for individual therapy across our service. Overall, our approach is based around a social ecological framework for improving individual, collective, and even planetary wellbeing, including a focus on individual people along with the groups and systems in which they are embedded (Haslam et al., 2017; Kemp & Edwards, 2022; Lomas et al., 2020; Morgan et al., 2022).

This multi-dimensional and multi-levelled view of positive psychological interventions demonstrates a person-focused approach that is informed by context-appropriate variation, selection and retention of processes that have helped to align developments in positive psychology, Acceptance and Commitment Therapy, and process-based coaching (Ciarrochi et al., 2022). This work also aligns well with recent discussions on the need to progress the United Nations Sustainable Development Goals (UNSDGs) through a focus on inner development including a focus on self, cognitive skills, caring for others and the world, collaboration and driving change (https://www.innerdevelopment-goals.org/framework; see also Böhme et al., 2022; Mead, Gibbs, Fisher & Kemp, 2023; Wamsler & Bristow, 2022; Woiwode et al., 2021). Together, this work represents a multi-levelled approach to promote individual, collective and planetary wellbeing, providing many opportunities for coaching psychologists and their clients to lead much-needed positive societal change and transformation.

Reflective questions

1. How might coaches harness recent developments in wellbeing science to improve their practice?
2. How should coaches working with clients promote wellbeing (broadly defined)?
3. In what ways could taking a broader approach to wellbeing focused on promoting community integration and engaging with nature add value to coaching practice?

Acknowledgements

We gratefully acknowledge Ms Alina Dray for her assistance in designing the wellbeing cards (Figure 35.3) and referred to in this chapter.

References

Antó, J. M., Martí, J. L., Casals, J., Bou-Habib, P., Casal, P., Fleurbaey, M., Frumkin, H., Jiménez-Morales, M., Jordana, J., Lancelotti, C., Llavador, H., Mélon, L., Solé, R., Subirada, F., & Williams, A. (2021). The planetary wellbeing initiative: Pursuing the sustainable development goals in higher education. *Sustainability, 13*(6), 3372. https://doi.org/10.3390/su13063372

Antonovsky, A. (1996). The salutogenic model as a theory to guide health promotion. *Health Promotion International, 11*(1), 11–18.

Bache, I., Reardon, L., & Anand, P. (2016). Wellbeing as a wicked problem: Navigating the arguments for the role of government. *Journal of Happiness Studies, 17*(3), 893–912. https://doi.org/10.1007/s10902-015-9623-y

Böhme, J., Walsh, Z., & Wamsler, C. (2022). Sustainable lifestyles: Towards a relational approach. *Sustainability Science, 17*(5), 2063–2076. https://doi.org/10.1007/s11625-022-01117-y

Bojanowska, A., Kaczmarek, Ł. D., Urbanska, B., & Puchalska, M. (2022). Acting on values: A novel intervention enhancing hedonic and eudaimonic well-being. *Journal of Happiness Studies, 23*(8), 3889–3908. https://doi.org/10.1007/s10902-022-00585-4

Buecker, S., Simacek, T., Ingwersen, B., Terwiel, S., & Simonsmeier, B. A. (2021). Physical activity and subjective well-being in healthy individuals: A meta-analytic review. *Health Psychology Review, 15*(4), 574–592. https://doi.org/10.1080/17437199.2020.1760728

Burn, A., & Passmore, J. (2022). Outdoor coaching: The role of attention restoration theory as a framework for explaining the experience and benefit of eco-psychology coaching. *International Coaching Psychology Review, 17*(1), 22–36.

Butler, J., & Kern, M. L. (2016). The PERMA-profiler: A brief multidimensional measure of flourishing. *International Journal of Wellbeing, 6*(3), 1–48. https://doi.org/10.5502/ijw.v6i3.526

Capaldi, C. A., Passmore, H.-A., Nisbet, E. K., Zelenski, J. M., & Dopko, R. L. (2015). Flourishing in nature: A review of the benefits of connecting with nature and its application as a wellbeing intervention. *International Journal of Wellbeing, 5*(4), 1–16. https://doi.org/10.5502/ijw.v5i4.1

Cappellen, P. V., Rice, E. L., Catalino, L. I., & Fredrickson, B. L. (2017). Positive affective processes underlie positive health behaviour change. *Psychology & Health, 33*(1), 1–21. https://doi.org/10.1080/08870446.2017.1320798

Cárdenas, D., Lattimore, F., Steinberg, D., & Reynolds, K. J. (2022). Youth well-being predicts later academic success. *Scientific Reports, 12*(1), 2134. https://doi.org/10.1038/s41598-022-05780-0

Carr, A., Cullen, K., Keeney, C., Canning, C., Mooney, O., Chinseallaigh, E., & O'Dowd, A. (2020). Effectiveness of positive psychology interventions: A systematic review and meta-analysis. *The Journal of Positive Psychology*, 1–21. https://doi.org/10.1080/17439760.2020.1818807

Ciarrochi, J., Hayes, S. C., Oades, L. G., & Hofmann, S. G. (2022). Toward a unified framework for positive psychology interventions: Evidence-based processes of change in coaching, prevention, and training. *Frontiers in Psychology, 12*, 809362. https://doi.org/10.3389/fpsyg.2021.809362

Corral-Verdugo, V., & Frías-Armenta, M. (2016). The sustainability of positive environments. *Environment, Development and Sustainability, 18*(4), 965–984. https://doi.org/10.1007/s10668-015-9701-7

Corral-Verdugo, V., Tapia-Fonllem, C., & Ortiz-Valdez, A. (2015). On the relationship between character strengths and sustainable behavior. *Environment and Behavior, 47*(8), 877–901. https://doi.org/10.1177/0013916514530718

Cruwys, T., Fong, P., Evans, O., Batterham, P., & Calear, A. L. (2022). Boosting neighbourhood identification to benefit wellbeing: Evidence from diverse community samples. *Journal of Environmental Psychology, 81*, 101816. https://doi.org/10.1016/j.jenvp.2022.101816

Csikszentmihalyi, M. (1997). *Finding flow: The psychology of engagement with everyday life.* Basic Books.

Diener, E. (1984). Subjective well-being. *Psychological Bulletin*, *95*(3), 542. https://doi.org/10.1037/0033-2909.95.3.542

Diener, E. (2000). Subjective well-being: The science of happiness and a proposal for a national index. *American Psychologist*, *55*(1), 34–43. https://doi.org/10.1037//0003-066x.55.1.34

Diener, E., Miyata, H., Kawakami, T., Chen, D., Kitagawa, T., Lai, A., Ishikawa, Y., Harter, J., Joshanloo, M., Weijer, M. van de, Lambert, L., Passmore, H.-A., & Lomas, T. (2020). Towards a greater global understanding of wellbeing: A proposal for a more inclusive measure. *International Journal of Wellbeing*, *10*(2), 1–18. https://doi.org/10.5502/ijw.v10i2.1037

Diener, E., Suh, E. M., Lucas, R. E., & Smith, H. L. (1999). Subjective well-being: Three decades of progress. *Psychological Bulletin*, *125*(2), 276–302. https://doi.org/10.1037/0033-2909.125.2.276

Eberth, J., Sedlmeier, P., & Schäfer, T. (2019). PROMISE: A model of insight and equanimity as the key effects of mindfulness meditation. *Frontiers in Psychology*, *10*, 2389. https://doi.org/10.3389/fpsyg.2019.02389

Falecki, D., Leach, C., & Green, S. (2018). PERMA-powered coaching: Building foundations for a flourishing life. In S. Green & S. Palmer (Eds.), *Positive psychology coaching in practice* (1st edition). Routledge.

Fang, S.-C., Wu, Y.-L., & Tsai, P.-S. (2020). Heart rate variability and risk of all-cause death and cardiovascular events in patients with cardiovascular disease: A meta-analysis of cohort studies. *Biological Research for Nursing*, *22*(1), 45–56. https://doi.org/10.1177/1099800419877442

Feng, X., Astell-Burt, T., Standl, M., Flexeder, C., Heinrich, J., & Markevych, I. (2022). Green space quality and adolescent mental health: Do personality traits matter? *Environmental Research*, *206*(112591). https://doi.org/10.1016/j.envres.2021.112591.

Fisher, Z., Field, S., Fitzsimmons, D., Hutchings, H., Carter, K., Tod, D., Gracey, F., Knight, A., & Kemp, A. H. (2024). Group-based positive psychotherapy for people living with acquired brain injury: A protocol for a feasibility study. *Pilot and Feasibility Studies*, *10*(1), 38. https://doi.org/10.1186/s40814-024-01459-7

Fisher, Z., Galloghly, E., Boglo, E., Gracey, F., & Kemp, A. (2020). Emotion, wellbeing and the neurological disorders. In *Reference module in neuroscience and biobehavioral psychology*. Elsevier. https://doi.org/10.1016/b978-0-12-819641-0.00013-x

Frankl, V. E. (1985). *Man's search for meaning*. Simon and Schuster.

Frankl, V. E. (2011). *Man's search for ultimate meaning*. Random House.

Fredrickson, B. L. (1998). What good are positive emotions? *Review of General Psychology*, *2*(3), 300–319. https://doi.org/10.1037/1089-2680.2.3.300

Fredrickson, B. L. (2004). The broaden-and-build theory of positive emotions. *Philosophical Transactions of the Royal Society of London: Series B, Biological Sciences*, *359*(1449), 1367–1378. https://doi.org/10.1098/rstb.2004.1512

Fredrickson, B. L. (2013). Updated thinking on positivity ratios. *American Psychologist*, *68*(9), 814. https://doi.org/10.1037/a0033584

Fredrickson, B. L. (2014). *Love 2.0: Creating happiness and health in moments of connection*. Plume.

Gibbs, K., Fisher, Z., & Kemp, A. H. (2022). Towards a culture of care for societal wellbeing: A perspective from the healthcare sector. In *Broadening the scope of wellbeing science, multidisciplinary and interdisciplinary perspectives on human flourishing and wellbeing* (pp. 43–58). https://doi.org/10.1007/978-3-031-18329-4_4

Gibbs, K., Wilkie, L., Jarman, J., Barker-Smith, A., Kemp, A. H., & Fisher, Z. (2022). Riding the wave into wellbeing: A qualitative evaluation of surf therapy for individuals living with acquired brain injury. *PLoS ONE*, *17*(4), e0266388. https://doi.org/10.1371/journal.pone.0266388

Gilbert, P., & Simos, G. (Eds.). (2022). *Compassion focused therapy: Clinical practice and applications* (1st edition). Routledge. https://doi.org/10.4324/9781003035879

Green, S., & Palmer, S. (Eds.). (2018). *Positive psychology coaching in practice* (1st edition). Routledge. https://doi.org/10.4324/9781315716169

Harris, R. (2017). *The choice point 2.0: A brief overview*. ACT Mindfully. https://www.actmindfully.com.au/free-stuff/worksheets-handouts-book-chapters/

Harris, R. (2019). *ACT made simple: An easy-to-read primer on acceptance and commitment therapy* (2nd edition). New Harbinger Publications.

Hartig T, Mitchell R, de Vries S, & Frumkin H. (2014). Nature and health. *Annual Review of Public Health, 35*, 207–228. https://doi.org/10.1146/annurev-publhealth-032013-182443

Haslam, C., Jetten, J., Cruwys, T., Dingle, G., & Haslam, A. (2017). *The new psychology of health: Unlocking the social cure.* Routledge. https://www.routledge.com/The-New-Psychology-of-Health-Unlocking-the-Social-Cure/Haslam-Jetten-Cruwys-Dingle-Haslam/p/book/9781138123885

Haslam, S. A., Haslam, C., Cruwys, T., Jetten, J., Bentley, S. V., Fong, P., & Steffens, N. K. (2021). Social identity makes group-based social connection possible: Implications for loneliness and mental health. *Current Opinion in Psychology, 43*, 161–165. https://doi.org/10.1016/j.copsyc.2021.07.013

Haslam, S. A., Jetten, J., Postmes, T., & Haslam, C. (2009). Social identity, health and well-being: An emerging agenda for applied psychology. *Applied Psychology, 58*(1), 1–23. https://doi.org/10.1111/j.1464-0597.2008.00379.x

Hayes, S. C., & Lillis, J. (2014). Acceptance and commitment therapy. In G. R. VandenBos, E. Meidenbauer, & J. Frank-McNeil (Eds.), *Psychotherapy theories and techniques: A reader* (pp. 3–8). American Psychological Association. https://doi.org/10.1037/14295-001

Hui, B. P. H., Ng, J. C. K., Berzaghi, E., Cunningham-Amos, L. A., & Kogan, A. (2020). Rewards of kindness? A meta-analysis of the link between prosociality and well-being. *Psychological Bulletin, 146*(12), 1084–1116. https://doi.org/10.1037/bul0000298

Irons, C., Palmer, S., & Hall, L. (2019). Compassion focused coaching. In S. Palmer & A. Whybrow (Eds.), *Handbook of coaching psychology: A guide for practitioners* (2nd edition). Routledge.

Isham, A., & Jackson, T. (2022). Finding flow: Exploring the potential for sustainable fulfilment. *The Lancet Planetary Health, 6*(1), e66–e74. https://doi.org/10.1016/s2542-5196(21)00286-2

Jandackova, V. K., Britton, A., Malik, M., & Steptoe, A. (2016). Heart rate variability and depressive symptoms: A cross-lagged analysis over a 10-year period in the Whitehall II study. *Psychological Medicine, 46*(10), 1–11. https://doi.org/10.1017/s003329171600060x

Kabat-Zinn, J. (2003). Mindfulness-based interventions in context: Past, present, and future. *Clinical Psychology: Science and Practice, 10*(2), 144–156. https://doi.org/10.1093/clipsy.bpg016

Kaplan, R., & Kaplan, S. (1989). *The experience of nature: A psychological perspective.* Cambridge University Press.

Kaplan, S. (1995). The restorative benefits of nature: Toward an integrative framework. *Journal of Environmental Psychology, 15*, 169–182. https://doi.org/10.1016/0272-4944(95)90001-2

Kemp, A. H. (2019). *Toward a transdisciplinary science of health and wellbeing spanning psychological science and epidemiology: A focus on vagal function.* University of Melbourne. http://hdl.handle.net/11343/222444

Kemp, A. H., Arias, J. A., & Fisher, Z. (2017). Social ties, health and wellbeing: A literature review and model. In *Neuroscience and social science, the missing link* (Vol. 59, pp. 397–427). Springer International Publishing. https://doi.org/10.1007/978-3-319-68421-5_17

Kemp, A. H., & Edwards, D. J. (Eds.). (2022). *Broadening the scope of wellbeing science: Multidisciplinary and interdisciplinary perspectives on human flourishing and wellbeing.* Springer International Publishing.

Kemp, A. H., & Fisher, Z. (2021a). Application of single-case research designs in undergraduate student reports: An example from wellbeing science. *Teaching of Psychology.* https://doi.org/10.1177/00986283211029929

Kemp, A. H., & Fisher, Z. (2021b). Student guidance on potential interventions. *Open Science Framework.* https://osf.io/6fvd2

Kemp, A. H., & Fisher, Z. (2022). Wellbeing, whole health and societal transformation: Theoretical insights and practical applications. *Global Advances in Health and Medicine, 11*, 21649561211073076. https://doi.org/10.1177/21649561211073077

Kemp, A. H., Mead, J., & Fisher, Z. (2022a). Improving student wellbeing: Evidence from a mixed effects design and comparison to normative data. *Teaching of Psychology, 009862832211124.* https://doi.org/10.1177/00986283221112428

Kemp, A. H., Tree, J., Gracey, F., & Fisher, Z. (2022b). Editorial: Improving wellbeing in patients with chronic conditions: Theory, evidence, and opportunities. *Frontiers in Psychology, 13*, 868810. https://doi.org/10.3389/fpsyg.2022.868810

Kern, M. L., Williams, P., Spong, C., Colla, R., Sharma, K., Downie, A., Taylor, J. A., Sharp, S., Siokou, C., & Oades, L. G. (2020). Systems informed positive psychology. *The Journal of Positive Psychology*, *15*(6), 705–715. https://doi.org/10.1080/17439760.2019.1639799

Keyes, C. L. M. (1998). Social well-being. *Social Psychology Quarterly*, *61*(2), 121. https://doi.org/10.2307/2787065

Kirby, J. N., Tellegen, C. L., & Steindl, S. R. (2017). A meta-analysis of compassion-based interventions: Current state of knowledge and future directions. *Behavior Therapy*, *48*(6), 778–792. https://doi.org/10.1016/j.beth.2017.06.003

Kjell, O. N. E. (2011). Sustainable well-being: A potential synergy between sustainability and well-being research. *Review of General Psychology*, *15*(3), 255. https://doi.org/10.1037/a0024603

Klug, H. J. P., & Maier, G. W. (2015). Linking goal progress and subjective well-being: A meta-analysis. *Journal of Happiness Studies*, *16*(1), 37–65. https://doi.org/10.1007/s10902-013-9493-0

Kok, B., Coffey, K., Cohn, M., Catalino, L., Vacharkulksemsuk, T., Algoe, S., Brantley, M., & Fredrickson, B. (2013). How positive emotions build physical health: Perceived positive social connections account for the upward spiral between positive emotions and vagal tone. *Psychological Science*, *24*(7), 1123–1132. https://doi.org/10.1177/0956797612470827

Kwasnicka, D., Dombrowski, S. U., White, M., & Sniehotta, F. (2016). Theoretical explanations for maintenance of behaviour change: A systematic review of behaviour theories. *Health Psychology Review*, *10*(3), 277–296. https://doi.org/10.1080/17437199.2016.1151372

Liu, X. X., Ma, X. L., Huang, W. Z., Luo, Y. N., He, C. J., Zhong, X. M., Dadvand, P., Browning, M. H. E. M., Li, L., Zou, X. G., Dong, G. H., & Yang, B. Y. (2022). Green space and cardiovascular disease: A systematic review with meta-analysis. *Environmental Pollution*, *301*, 118990. https://doi.org/10.1016/j.envpol.2022.118990.

Lomas, T. (2022). Making waves in the great ocean: A historical perspective on the emergence and evolution of wellbeing scholarship. *The Journal of Positive Psychology*, *17*(2), 257–270. https://doi.org/10.1080/17439760.2021.2016900

Lomas, T., Waters, L., Williams, P., Oades, L. G., & Kern, M. L. (2020). Third wave positive psychology: Broadening towards complexity. *The Journal of Positive Psychology*, 1–15. https://doi.org/10.1080/17439760.2020.1805501

Louv, R. (2005). *Last child in the woods: Saving our children from nature-deficit disorder* (Paperback edition). Algonquin Books.

Lyubomirsky, S., Sheldon, K. M., & Schkade, D. (2005). Pursuing happiness: The architecture of sustainable change. *Review of General Psychology*, *9*(2), 111–131. https://doi.org/10.1037/1089-2680.9.2.111

Marmot, M., & Wilkinson, R. G. (2005). *Social determinants of health*. 54–77. https://doi.org/10.1093/acprof:oso/9780198565895.003.04

Martin, L., White, M. P., Hunt, A., Richardson, M., Pahl, S., & Burt, J. (2020). Nature contact, nature connectedness and associations with health, wellbeing and pro-environmental behaviours. *Journal of Environmental Psychology*, *68*, 101389. https://doi.org/10.1016/j.jenvp.2020.101389

McMahan, E. A., & Estes, D. (2015). The effect of contact with natural environments on positive and negative affect: A meta-analysis. *The Journal of Positive Psychology*, *10*(6), 507–519. https://doi.org/10.1080/17439760.2014.994224

Mead, J., Fisher, Z., & Kemp, A. H. (2021). Moving beyond disciplinary silos towards a transdisciplinary model of wellbeing: An invited review. *Frontiers in Psychology*, *12*, 642093. https://doi.org/10.3389/fpsyg.2021.642093

Mead, J., Fisher, Z., Wilkie, L., Gibbs, K., Pridmore, J., Tree, J., & Kemp, A. (2019). Toward a more ethical science of wellbeing that considers current and future generations. *Authorea*. https://doi.org/10.22541/au.156649190.08734276

Mead, J., Gibbs, K., Fisher, Z., & Kemp, A. H. (2023). What's next for wellbeing science? Moving from the anthropocene to the symbiocene. *Frontiers in Psychology*, *14*. https://doi.org/10.3389/fpsyg.2023.1087078

Mittelmark, M. B., & Bull, T. (2013). The salutogenic model of health in health promotion research. *Global Health Promotion*, *20*(2), 30–38. https://doi.org/10.1177/1757975913486684

Morgan, G., Barnwell, G., Johnstone, L., Shukla, K., & Mitchell, A. (2022). The power threat meaning framework and the climate and ecological crises. *Psychology in Society*, *63*, 83–109.

Niemiec R. M. (2018). *Character strengths interventions: A field guide for practitioners*. Hogrefe.

Nisbet, E. K., Zelenski, J. M., & Murphy, S. A. (2009). The nature relatedness scale: Linking individuals' connection with nature to environmental concern and behavior. *Environment and Behavior, 41*(5), 715–740. https://doi.org/10.1177/0013916508318748

O'Brien, C. (2012). Sustainable happiness and well-being: Future directions for positive psychology. *Psychology, 03*(12), 1196–1201. https://doi.org/10.4236/psych.2012.312a177

O'Brien, C. (2016). *Education for sustainable happiness and well-being.* https://doi.org/10.4324/9781315630946

Palmer, S., & Whybrow, A. (Eds.). (2019). *Handbook of coaching psychology: A guide for practitioners* (2nd edition). Routledge.

Passmore, J., & Evans-Krimme, R. (2021). The future of coaching: A conceptual framework for the coaching sector from personal craft to scientific process and the implications for practice and research. *Frontiers in Psychology, 12*, 715228. https://doi.org/10.3389/fpsyg.2021.715228

Passmore, J., & Lai, Y. (2021). *Coaching researched* (pp. 3–22). Wiley. https://doi.org/10.1002/9781119656913.ch1

Pleeging, E., Burger, M., & van Exel, J. (2021). The relations between hope and subjective wellbeing: A literature overview and empirical analysis. *Applied Research in Quality of Life, 16*(3), 1019–1041. https://doi.org/10.1007/s11482-019-09802-4

Porges, S. W. (2011). *The polyvagal theory: Neurophysiological foundations of emotions, attachment, communication, and self-regulation.* W W Norton & Co.

Porges, S. W., & Dana, D. (Eds.). (2018). *Clinical applications of the polyvagal theory: The emergence of polyvagal-informed therapies.* W. W. Norton & Company.

Pritchard, A., & Richardson, M. (2022). The relationship between nature connectedness and human and planetary wellbeing: Implications for promoting wellbeing, tackling anthropogenic climate change and overcoming biodiversity loss. In A. H. Kemp & D. J. Edwards (Eds.), *Broadening the scope of wellbeing science.* Palgrave Macmillan, Cham. https://doi.org/10.1007/978-3-031-18329-4_6

Richardson, M., McEwan, K., Maratos, F., & Sheffield, D. (2016). Joy and calm: How an evolutionary functional model of affect regulation informs positive emotions in nature. *Evolutionary Psychological Science, 2*(4), 308–320. https://doi.org/10.1007/s40806-016-0065-5

Ryan, R. M., & Deci, E. L. (2000). Self-determination theory and the facilitation of intrinsic motivation, social development, and well-being. *American Psychologist, 55*(1), 68–78. https://doi.org/10.1037/0003-066x.55.1.68

Ryan, R. M., & Deci, E. L. (2001). On happiness and human potentials: A review of research on hedonic and eudaimonic well-being. *Annual Review of Psychology, 52*(1), 141–166. https://doi.org/10.1146/annurev.psych.52.1.141

Ryff, C. D. (1989). Happiness is everything, or is it? Explorations on the meaning of psychological well-being. *Journal of Personality and Social Psychology, 57*, 1069–1081. https://doi.org/10.1037//0022-3514.57.6.1069

Ryff, C. D. (2014). Psychological well-being revisited: Advances in the science and practice of eudaimonia. *Psychotherapy and Psychosomatics, 83*(1), 10–28. https://doi.org/10.1159/000353263

Ryff, C. D., & Keyes, C. L. M. (1995). The structure of psychological well-being revisited. *Journal of Personality and Social Psychology, 69*(4), 719–727.

Schutte, N. S., & Malouff, J. M. (2019). The impact of signature character strengths interventions: A meta-analysis. *Journal of Happiness Studies, 20*(4), 1179–1196. https://doi.org/10.1007/s10902-018-9990-2

Schwartz, S. H. (2012). An overview of the schwartz theory of basic values. *Online Readings in Psychology and Culture, 2*(1). https://doi.org/10.9707/2307-0919.1116

Schwartz, S. H., & Sortheix, F. M. (2018). Values and subjective well-being. In E. Diener, S. Oishi, & L. Tay (Eds.), *Handbook of well-being.* Noba Scholar Handbook series: Subjective well-being, DEF Publishers.

Seligman, M. (2012). *Flourish: A visionary new understanding of happiness and well-being.*

Seligman, M. (2017). PERMA and the building blocks of well-being. *The Journal of Positive Psychology, 13*(4), 1–3. https://doi.org/10.1080/17439760.2018.1437466

Sheldon, K. M., & Lyubomirsky, S. (2021). Revisiting the sustainable happiness model and pie chart: Can happiness be successfully pursued? *The Journal of Positive Psychology, 16*, 145–154. https://doi.org/10.1080/17439760.2019.1689421

Steger, M. F., Shim, Y., Barenz, J., & Shin, J. Y. (2014). Through the windows of the soul: A pilot study using photography to enhance meaning in life. *Journal of Contextual Behavioral Science*, *3*(1), 27–30. https://doi.org/10.1016/j.jcbs.2013.11.002

Steger, M. F., Shim, Y., Rush, B. R., Brueske, L. A., Shin, J. Y., & Merriman, L. A. (2013). The mind's eye: A photographic method for understanding meaning in people's lives. *The Journal of Positive Psychology*, *8*(6), 530–542. https://doi.org/10.1080/17439760.2013.830760

Stenlund, S., Koivumaa-Honkanen, H., Sillanmäki, L., Lagström, H., Rautava, P., & Suominen, S. (2022). Changed health behavior improves subjective well-being and vice versa in a follow-up of 9 years. *Health and quality of life outcomes*, *20*(1), 66. https://doi.org/10.1186/s12955-022-01972-4

Tajfel, H. (1972). Experiments in a vacuum. In J. Israel & H. Tajfel (Eds.), *The context of social psychology: A critical assessment*. Academic Press.

Tajfel, H. (1979). Individuals and groups in social psychology. *British Journal of Social and Clinical Psychology*, *18*(2), 183–190. https://doi.org/10.1111/j.2044-8260.1979.tb00324.x

Thayer, J. F., & Lane, R. D. (2000). A model of neurovisceral integration in emotion regulation and dysregulation. *Journal of Affective Disorders*, *61*(3), 201–216. https://doi.org/10.1016/s0165-0327(00)00338-4

Tse, D. C. K., Nakamura, J., & Csikszentmihalyi, M. (2021). Living well by "flowing' well: The indirect effect of autotelic personality on well-being through flow experience. *The Journal of Positive Psychology*, *16*(3), 310–321. https://doi.org/10.1080/17439760.2020.1716055

Tulip, C., Fisher, Z., Bankhead, H., Wilkie, L., Pridmore, J., Gracey, F., Tree, J., & Kemp, A. H. (2020). Building wellbeing in people with chronic conditions: A qualitative evaluation of an 8-week positive psychotherapy intervention for people living with an acquired brain injury. *Frontiers in Psychology*, *11*. https://www.frontiersin.org/article/10.3389/fpsyg.2020.00066

Ulrich, R. S. (1981). Natural versus urban scenes. *Environment and Behavior*, *13*(5), 523–556. https://doi.org/10.1177/0013916581135001

Ulrich, R. S., Simons, R. F., Losito, B. D., Fiorito, E., Miles, M. A., & Zelson, M. (1991). Stress recovery during exposure to natural and urban environments. *Journal of Environmental Psychology*, *11*(3), 201–230. https://doi.org/10.1016/s0272-4944(05)80184-7

van Agteren, J., Iasiello, M., Lo, L., Bartholomaeus, J., Kopsaftis, Z., Carey, M., & Kyrios, M. (2021). A systematic review and meta-analysis of psychological interventions to improve mental wellbeing. *Nature Human Behaviour*, *5*(5), 631–652. https://doi.org/10.1038/s41562-021-01093-w

Van Cappellen, P., Rice, E. L., Catalino, L. I., & Fredrickson, B. L. (2018). Positive affective processes underlie positive health behaviour change. *Psychology & Health*, *33*(1), 77–97. https://doi.org/10.1080/08870446.2017.1320798

Verdugo, V. C. (2012). The positive psychology of sustainability. *Environment, development and sustainability*, *14*(5), 651–666. https://doi.org/10.1007/s10668-012-9346-8

Vos, J., & Vitali, D. (2018). The effects of psychological meaning-centered therapies on quality of life and psychological stress: A metaanalysis. *Palliative and Supportive Care*, *16*(5), 608–632. https://doi.org/10.1017/s1478951517000931

Wamsler, C., & Bristow, J. (2022). At the intersection of mind and climate change: Integrating inner dimensions of climate change into policymaking and practice. *Climatic Change*, *173*(1–2), 7. https://doi.org/10.1007/s10584-022-03398-9

Waters, L. E., Loton, D., & Jach, H. K. (2019). Does strength-based parenting predict academic achievement? The mediating effects of perseverance and engagement. *Journal of Happiness Studies*, *20*(4), 1121–1140. https://doi.org/10.1007/s10902-018-9983-1

White, M. P., Alcock, I., Grellier, J., Wheeler, B. W., Hartig, T., Warber, S. L., Bone, A., Depledge, M. H., & Fleming, L. E. (2019). Spending at least 120 minutes a week in nature is associated with good health and wellbeing. *Scientific Reports*, *9*(1), 7730. https://doi.org/10.1038/s41598-019-44097-3

Wilkie, L., Fisher, Z., & Kemp, A. H. (2022a). The complex construct of wellbeing and the role of vagal function. *Frontiers in Integrative Neuroscience*, *16*, 925664. https://doi.org/10.3389/fnint.2022.925664

Wilkie, L., Fisher, Z., & Kemp, A. H. (2022b). The 'rippling' waves of wellbeing: A mixed methods evaluation of a surf-therapy intervention on patients with acquired brain injury. *Sustainability*, 14(15), 9605. https://doi.org/10.3390/su14159605

Wilkinson, R. G., & Pickett, K. (2010). *The spirit level: Why greater equality makes societies stronger*. Bloomsbury Press.

Wilson, E. O. (1984). *Biophilia*. Harvard University Press.

Woiwode, C., Schäpke, N., Bina, O., Veciana, S., Kunze, I., Parodi, O., Schweizer-Ries, P., & Wamsler, C. (2021). Inner transformation to sustainability as a deep leverage point: Fostering new avenues for change through dialogue and reflection. *Sustainability Science*, 16(3), 841–858. https://doi.org/10.1007/s11625-020-00882-y

Wong, P. T. P. (2019). Second wave positive psychology's (PP 2.0) contribution to counselling psychology. *Counselling Psychology Quarterly*, 1–10. https://doi.org/10.1080/09515070.2019 .1671320

Chapter 4

The essentials of 'The Good Life'

*Wendy-Ann Smith, Andrea Giraldez-Hayes and
Rosie Evans-Krimme*

Introduction

Humanity intrinsically seeks to experience 'The Good Life'. Yet, what are the essential components and processes to facilitate such an experience? There is evidence for the importance of psychologically informed coaching that is both a process of influencing wellbeing and the striving for The Good Life, and an important component of The Good Life itself. This chapter will focus on psychological wellbeing and explore various theories and frameworks that constitute The Good Life. Psychology theories fundamental to subjective wellbeing are explored such as: the emotional life, the importance of relationships, the emotional life, creativity and play to support emotional health, the identification and use of strengths, and the rich life for perspective taking and fostering wisdom, to fulfil the basic psychological needs: autonomy, relatedness and mastery – the cornerstone of self-determination theory. The second half of this chapter is practice focused for enhancing The Good Life. Examples of coaching questions within the six dimensions of psychological wellbeing: self-acceptance, positive relations, autonomy, environmental mastery, purpose in life and growth. The questions are crafted to link the explored wellbeing theories to each domain to facilitate the development and sustainment for and of psychological wellbeing within the coaching context to bring The Good Life to life. Finally, we present various physical activities examples that have a reciprocal effect on wellbeing helping to construct the experience of living The Good Life and be a point of exploration within the coaching context.

Wellbeing Theories and Frameworks

The Good Life

Philosophers throughout the ages have tried to answer the undying question 'What is The Good Life?'. In more contemporary times, happiness and wellbeing have been used interchangeably. Wellbeing, generally a more readily accepted term, has several working definitions that speak to the need of both happiness and meaning for The Good Life. For example, Diener (1984) identified three subjective components to wellbeing: (1) *life satisfaction*; (2) *experience of pleasant/positive emotions*; and (3) *relative absence of negative/unpleasant emotions*. How people evaluate their lives (in areas such as marriage and work, for example) influences their perception of life satisfaction and wellbeing (Diener et al., 2003) and a striving for self-growth (Rogers, 1961). Juster and colleagues (1981)

DOI: 10.4324/9781003319016-5

refer to wellbeing as "a consequence of the intrinsic benefits from all activities engaged in by individuals" (p. 1).

Frisch and colleagues (2005) define life satisfaction as a cognitive–experiential 'function', in which a general sense of satisfaction/happiness/contentment is experienced. This functionality provides three important elements for wellbeing: (1) *a pleasant conscious inner experience* that (2) *motivates goal pursuit*; and (3) *makes one attractive to friends and loved ones who then may share resources and social support*. Wellbeing is a vital human experience as well as the ability to love, work and care for oneself (Frisch et al., 1992) and can occur in the presence of ill-being (see Yue Zhao & Tay, 2022 for discussion).

Living The Good Life is a process, not a destination.

The What of The Good Life

Wellbeing and happiness are multidimensional in nature, with over 180 domains/subconstructs of wellbeing found; but just a few are: satisfaction with self, education, relationships (family, friends, colleagues, and intimates), academic abilities, recreation, work, health and money (Diener et al., 2000; Oishi & Diener, 2001). Several authors have proposed different frameworks to define wellbeing, including Ryff (1989), Seligman (2011), and Deci and Ryan (2012).

Carol Ryff (1989) offered a perspective on psychological wellbeing that was mostly based on two conceptions of positive functioning, one that considers happiness is the result of a balance between positive and negative affect and the other focused on life satisfaction. Ryff's and Keyes' subsequent model (1995), the psychological wellbeing theory (PWBT), identified six dimensions of wellbeing: (1) *self-acceptance*; (2) *personal growth*; (3) *purpose in life*; (4) *positive relations with others*; (5) *environmental mastery*; and (6) *autonomy*. These dimensions form the basis of facilitating The Good Life in action as described later in this chapter.

Martin Seligman's PERMA model (Seligman, 2011), more recently extended to PERMA-H and PERMA-V, hypotheses that positive emotions, engagement, positive relationships, meaning and accomplishment are the five components of wellbeing. In the extended models, H stands for health, and recognises the importance of physical and psychological health on wellbeing (Lai et al., 2018), and V stands for vitality, adding a body-related dimension (Petersen et al., 2021).

A third categorisation has been offered by Deci and Ryan. Edward Deci and Richard Ryan's (2012) self-determination theory (SDT) differs from the aforementioned frameworks because of the consideration of social and cultural conditions that can affect wellbeing. The theory suggests that individuals have three innate and universal psychological needs: *competence*, *autonomy* and *relatedness*. The fulfilment of these core needs motivates people to grow and change, and be self-determined. We, the authors, suggest that the three psychological needs map to the aforementioned PWBT dimensions; examples of coaching questions with the model in mind are shown later in the chapter.

The How of The Good Life

It would be easy to have a one-size-fits-all approach to The Good Life, but humans are much more complex. The best route is to understand the individual needs and apply strategies to meet those needs (Diener et al., 1999). Psychological active constructs such as hope, optimism, motivation and emotional intelligence have given humanity "a better understanding of the basic human traits and competencies associated with life satisfaction", wellbeing and happiness (Adler & Fagley, 2005, p. 80). Additionally, strengths-based approaches (see Miglianico et al., 2020), engagement in creative pursuits (see Peterson & Seligman, 2004) and a regular dose of playfulness for connection and restorative purposes (see Biswas-Diener, 2022; O'Brien & Seydel, 2022) support enhanced wellbeing, as well as being moderating and protective mechanisms (Kafka & Kozma, 2002). Finally, expanding on the two foundations to wellbeing noted earlier (happiness and meaning), a third pillar – 'The Psychologically Rich Life' characterised by actively engaging in life experiences that stretch an individual's capacities and expand understanding of often complex circumstances that support personal growth and wisdom (Oishi & Westgate, 2021) – can also be said to contribute to The Good Life.

Connection for Protection

Stronger together or alone? Social connections arrive and grow into various forms but some are friendship, romantic, family, social media channels and colleagues. Relatedness, a sense of belonging, is one of three core psychological needs (Ryan & Deci, 2000), and as such is the foundation of both nurturing and predicting wellbeing (Biswas-Diener & Diener, 2001; Diener & Seligman, 2002), and is what gives meaning to life (Baumeister & Leary, 1995).

Social connections and the belief that social support is available significantly influences physical health perceptions and symptoms (Harandi et al., 2017), are a protective mechanism against ageing and the impairment of cognitive and physiological functioning (Blieszner et al., 2019). People who experience quality, energising, reciprocal relationships can tolerate a greater range of negative and positive emotions within the relationship, with the capacity to bend and flex to relationship strains and challenges (Dutton & Ragins, 2017). Relationships are the foundational nutrients for experiencing The Good Life.

Nutrients for connection

Relationships motivation theory (for summary, see Spence & Deci, 2016) and high-quality connections (HQCs: Dutton, 2003) stipulates certain mutually experienced conditions, such as positive mutual regard, interest, warmth, support, autonomy and a trusting connection whereby safety to express vulnerability exists. Importantly, having a sense of control significantly influences the quality of social relationships and has a reciprocal effect on wellbeing (Vella-Brodrick et al., 2022).

Mattering and belonging in connection

Somewhat different to connection, is a feeling of belonging (Biswas-Diener & Diener, 2001; Diener & Seligman, 2002), the kind of knowing and sense of belonging when, for example, you are part of a choir or swimming club, etc. One could argue the elements of mattering discussed in what follows are vital for a sense of belonging.

People need to perceive and feel that they matter; that is, they feel as though they are valued and add value to themselves, others and the broader world they engage in (Prilleltensky & Prilleltensky, 2021).

Schlossberg (1989) identified five psychological dimensions of mattering: (1) attention, the feeling that others notice them; (2) importance, to believe that others care about and support them; (3) pride, that others will be proud of their efforts; (4) dependence, the feeling or knowing that others can be depended on; and (5) appreciation, knowing that others show appreciation for efforts. While mattering has more recently been refined to the following three components (Prilleltensky & Prilleltensky, 2021).

1. Awareness, meaning that others notice their presence and are interested.
2. Importance, meaning that they care about others and others care about them.
3. Reliance, meaning that they can rely on and be relied on to contribute in a meaningful way.

Both frameworks of mattering add important dimensions to how people initiate, build and maintain emotionally sustaining valued relationships.

The emotional Good Life

Happiness is understood by some to occur only in the absence of experiencing unpleasant emotions such as sadness, anger or fear. However, the experience of a full emotional life that embraces emotions both positive (joy, hope, gratitude) and negative (sadness, anger, fear) is important for wellbeing (Kashdan & Biswas-Diener, 2015; Ivtzan et al., 2016). Quoidbach and colleagues (2014) define this emphasis on the whole emotional self as 'emodiversity'.

Unpleasant emotions and The Good Life

An excess of unpleasant emotional experiences is detrimental to long-term physical and psychological wellbeing (Diener & Tov, 2012). Baumeister and colleagues (2007) argue that unpleasant emotions hold adaptive significance because they enable humans to be more attuned to potential threats. Further to this, Kashdan and Biswas-Diener (2015) describe negative or unpleasant emotions as an important part of our emotional architecture that increases wisdom, stating that without them, humans simply would not function.

An example being a modern-day epidemic of 'loneliness' (Murthy, 2017) often experienced as pain provides important guidance that action is required to feel connection and a sense of belonging (Smith et al., 2021).

Pleasant emotions and The Good Life

Fredrickson's 'broaden-and-build' theory of positive emotion (pleasant emotions: Fredrickson, 1998, 2001, 2013) asserts that the more awareness and attention is given to pleasant emotional experiences, the more you are protected from spiralling to 'ill-being' during challenging life experiences. In order to develop this rich emotional life, or 'emodiversity', it is essential to enhance emotional literacy (see Oades, 2020), recognise emotions within ourselves and others, and manage our emotions.

Awareness of pleasant emotional experiences has various functional outcomes, such as temporarily expanding awareness so that more contextual information is brought to consciousness; having an increased tendency to grow and play, explore and expand the self; and facilitating new creative and flexible thinking (Fredrickson & Branigan, 2005). Further benefits are increased health and longevity; people thus become more likely to contribute to community and societies, and engage in virtuous actions (Diener & Tov, 2012). Finally, longer-lasting pleasant emotions are experienced by those who pursue valued goals (Diener & Tov, 2012) and tend to approach goals more often (Cacioppo & Berntson, 1999), suggesting that levels of hope is a moderating factor.

Hope for The Good Life

Hope, more than a future thought of wishful thinking, is a dynamic reciprocating goal-oriented way of being. Snyder and colleagues define hope as "a cognitive set that is based on a reciprocally derived sense of successful (a) agency (goal directed determination), and (b) pathways (planning of ways to meet goals)" (1991, p. 571). Hope helps people to define and stay committed to their goals despite adversity and obstacles, to connect to their 'why', or meaning (Feldman et al., 2018), and self-concordant goals whereby goals reflect their values, beliefs, interests, passions and autonomy (Sheldon et al., 2004), and they are more likely to have better life outcomes and experience wellbeing (Snyder et al., 1991).

Snyder (2002) asserted that by studying hope, he was able to observe the spectrum of human strength and that reminded him of the rainbow that is usually used as a symbol of hope: "a rainbow is a prism that sends shards of multi-coloured light in various directions. It lifts our spirits and makes us think about what is possible. Hope is the same – a personal rainbow in the mind" (p. 269).

If The Good Life is a process, a direction, not a destination (Rogers, 1961), we can conclude that hope is an essential component of people's pursuit of The Good Life.

Strengths Mastery for The Good Life

What is right with people? Do they know and use their strengths? Can strengths be developed? If so, how do we create strengths to experience mastery and autonomy?

Among other topics, positive psychology is interested in people's positive traits, including character strengths; that is, "positive traits reflected in thoughts, feelings and behaviours" (Park et al., 2004, p. 603), such as bravery, curiosity, love of learning, kindness or perspective. A significant number of studies have considered how strengths can help to enhance and maintain a 'Good Life' for oneself and others (Peterson & Seligman, 2004). Among others, Biswas-Diener and colleagues (2011) draw attention to the optimal use of character strengths, and the risk of both overusing and underusing them.

Young and colleagues (2015) suggest that using signature strengths and improving less-developing strengths is an important factor to promote wellbeing, and Biswas-Diener et al. (2011), Proyer et al. (2015). With this in mind, we suggest that a balanced and appropriate use of character strengths, that is finding the golden mean or "the expression of the right combination of strengths" (Niemiec, 2013, p. 453) can increase our sense of self-efficacy (Bandura et al., 1999), and in turn, our sense of competency or mastery as defined by SDT (Deci & Ryan, 2012) and psychological wellbeing (Ryff & Keyes, 1995).

Creativity and play for The Good Life

Many people are inclined to view creativity as a gift or to think of creativity solely in the domains of arts and science. However, creativity is a much broader concept. In fact, research on creativity refers to both eminent-level creativity – sometimes referred to as the "Big-C" and primarily focused on the lives of renowned and exceptional scientists, thinkers, creators, and artists such as Albert Einstein, Walt Disney, Maire Curie, Frida Kahlo, Michael Jackson and Rukmini Devi Arundale; and everyday creativity – usually called the "little-c" (Richards, 2010).

Everyday creativity alludes to the everyday informal creativity characteristic of all human beings, an essential ingredient of The Good Life (Dolan & Metcalfe, 2012; Richards, 2018; Wright & Pascoe, 2013). Examples of everyday creativity include activities related to the arts, such as drawing, dancing or singing, but also to everyday activities such as "mundane creative experiences, such as having small moments of insight or working on a creative hobby" (Conner et al., 2018, p. 187); creative writing, knitting or crochet (Conner & Silvia, 2015); decorating a room or combining pieces of clothes to have a new outfit (Helfand et al., 2016); creating flower arrangements (Morelock & Feldman, 1999); and cooking (Richards, 2010). Furthermore, creativity is one of the 24 character strengths belonging to the subcategory of wisdom (Peterson & Seligman, 2004), and as such, although to different degrees, it is a strength we all possess.

Benefits of a range of arts and humanities interventions for flourishing in healthy adults has been found to be related to a range of psychological flourishing outcomes (Shim et al., 2021). Studies have examined the relationship between positive emotions and creativity (Conner & Silvia, 2015; Karwowski et al., 2017), suggesting that creativity relates to successful ageing and longevity (Smith & van der Meer, 1997), improves the function of our immune system (Lowe, 2006), reduces depression (Nan & Ho, 2017), helps focus the mind (Csikszentmihalyi, 1997) and reduces anxiety and stress (Martin et al., 2018). However, the number of studies looking at creativity specifically for wellbeing enhancement is limited (Forgeard & Eichner, 2014).

Creativity – rather more specifically, everyday creativity – is one of the critical factors that "contributes to various fulfilments that comprise the good life, for oneself and for others" (Peterson & Seligman, 2004, p. 17). It is the process of everyday creativity, more than the product, that can improve health and wellbeing. As Richards (2018) suggests, creativity can be a happy path of "growth and further development that feels good, open us to inspiration, brings us deeper self-knowledge, adds more meaningful contributions to the world, . . . , [enhances] self-awareness in a greater system, and more mature knowledge tempered by childlike fun and joy" (p. 47).

Purposeful Meaning Making for the Good Life

What do you mean? The challenge with defining the words 'meaning' and 'purpose' is highlighted by this question, as the answer depends on the context. While topics such as meaning in life have their religious, spiritual and philosophical roots, modern theories and empirical research on meaning and purpose have demonstrated the importance of these constructs within secular societies (for example, Wong, 2012; Martela & Steger, 2016). Simply put, meaning is when an individual perceives something to be meaningful, purposeful or significant, makes sense and matters. To clarify the core components of meaning that are interconnected yet independent, models of meaning tend to include senses of coherence (they can make sense of their experiences), significance (the event has importance and value to the person), and purpose (what and how they action their intent) (Steger, 2017).

Steger and colleagues (2012) propose a multidimensional three-level model of meaning, or work but can also apply to life generally.

The meaningful work model involves three levels of meaning an individual can potentially perceive from their work and other areas of life. The first-level (inner-level) activities of work are *perceived* to be meaningful; second-level (middle-level) activities are *perceived* to be in harmony with one's personal life and transcend into an opportunity to have a positive impact on others, societies or even the wider ecosystem (the outer level). The key to the pursuit of purposeful meaning is the type of action an individual takes and the intent behind it (Steger, 2017). Perceiving and actioning for purposeful meaning supports psychological wellbeing and experiencing The Good Life.

The rich life for wise action increasing access to The Good Life

The Good Life as explored earlier in this chapter has been determined to require meaning and purpose in life pursuits, which when deconstructed supports the fulfilment of the basic psychological needs: autonomy, connectedness and mastery (Ryan & Deci, 2000), yet what might a moderating factor be for the best use of the psychological and external resources available and fulfilment of basic psychological needs? – wisdom! Oishi and Westgate (2021) argue that wisdom is the third wheel to The Good Life.

Wisdom

Wisdom is challenging to attain for some, while others develop it over time with life experience, available sometimes and not at other times; hence, it is dynamic in its development and expression (Smith & Bretherton, 2021). It is described as multidimensional, requiring integration and balance of cognitive, affective and reflective domains of the psyche born of experience (Bangen et al., 2013); requiring prudence and ability to make complex decisions between competing goals; and having access to many resources available as needed (Schwartz & Sharpe, 2006).

Psychologically Rich Life – Wise Action

Oishi and Westgate (2021) explain the conditions of life that are *novel, complex* and *perspective-changing* (that do not require happiness or be meaningful) as *a 'Psychologically Rich Life'*. Some examples are living interstate or abroad, learning through higher education or languages, or from romantic or platonic relationships gone wrong, taking time out for a day to sit upon a mountain. These life experiences provide the conditions to feed the psychological nutrients for enhancing character (e.g., empathy, prosociality, awareness, reflectivity, openness, and emodiversity: Smith & Bretherton, 2021) needed for developing wisdom for efficient use of resources to be experiencing The Good Life.

Practice **Coaching for The Good Life**

Coaching is a fun and challenging future-oriented endeavour defined as a co-created relationship that is a "thought-provoking and creative process that inspires them [client] to maximise their personal and professional potential" (ICF, 2022), with psychology being the foundations of development, change and wellbeing. Atad and colleagues (2021, pp. 43–44) argue that " 'Coaching Psychology' is simply the science of human emotion, cognition and behaviour (i.e., psychology) that underpins coaching practice" and that "Evidence-based Coaching as the applied arm of Coaching Psychology, which draws on the best current knowledge of theory, research and practice from scientific domains of psychology, education and business management to coaching practice" (Atad et al., 2021, p. 44).

While research is very limited to the effectiveness of coaching for The Good Life essentials, there are a number of evidenced-based examples of coaching with various components of wellbeing at the heart of the coaching; for example: coaching strengths (Boniwell & Smith, 2018, 2021; Smith et al., 2021; MacKie, 2021), acceptance and commitment coaching (Skews et al., 2021), coaching for HQCs and emotions (Smith et al., 2021), coaching for compassion (Dhar et al., 2021), coaching for meaning (Jacob & Steger, 2021) and coaching for wisdom (Smith & Bretherton, 2021) and job crafting (Silapurem et al., 2021).

There is acknowledgement that coaching is a process, and as Atad and colleagues (2021) argue, a wellbeing and development intervention in and of itself. A meta-analysis by Wang and colleagues (2021) supports this argument, highlighting the importance of the coach and coaching being psychologically informed for coaching to be an evidenced-based practice and have a stronger influence on coaching outcomes. Scholz and colleagues (2022) argue wellbeing interventions that are taught have limited longevity efficacy and require a process whereby the individual is more active in their knowledge acquisition for greater wellbeing effects. Furthermore, the work of Dixit and Sinha (2022) investigating the transfer of training in the workplace found coaching to be a worthy process to facilitate learning and development. Hence, we the authors suggest that coaching informed positive psychology or psychology more broadly is an important and fundamental activity, and that those are the ingredients that both support and facilitate nourishing conditions for the experience of The Good Life, as depicted in Figure 4.1.

Coaching for The Good Life

The following coaching questions are to illustrate the types of questions a coach might ask in relation to each domain of 'psychological wellbeing' to help facilitate the experience of The Good Life. It is not a prescription for a step-by-step process of coaching. Rather, it is suggested that the coach gets to know the model and the previously explored theories intimately and allow this to inform the coaching. Table 4.1 showcases coaching for the 'Good Life' framed by the psychological wellbeing dimensions of Ryff and Keyes (1995) and intertwining the aforementioned theories and the following discussed activities.

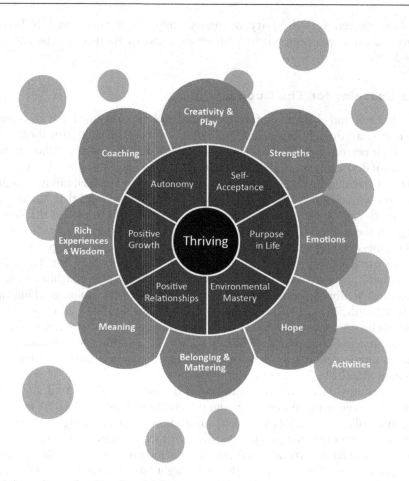

Figure 4.1 Ingredients for The Good Life

Physical activities for The Good Life

Psychological wellbeing requires working with cognitions and emotions directly and indirectly through physical activities (for discussion and activities, see: Spence, 2022; Spence & Spence, 2022). There is an unimaginable number of activities that could be created but would require research to understand their impact. Those readily available have been reviewed by Sakuraya and colleagues (2020), who conducted a meta-analysis of activities and their effect on wellbeing generally, and found interventions/activities psychological in nature to be the most impactful wellbeing, such as the following.

- Physical activity interventions (walking, yoga, resistance training, muscle relaxation, physical exercise).
- Psychological interventions (mindfulness, CBT, resilience, meaning-centred training, etc).
- Others (emotion-oriented, music making and eating fresh fruit).

Table 4.1 Coaching for The Good Life

Ryff and Keyes' (1995) psychological wellbeing dimensions	Coaching questions
1. **Self-acceptance** The degree to which one accepts and is satisfied or not with their whole self both good and negative qualities and their evaluation of their life up to the present	• *What do you believe you do best? How has that shown up in your life previously?* • *Describe a time when you felt most at ease with yourself. What does that time tell you about yourself now?* • *Describe a time when you felt as if you could have shown up better than you did. What did you learn about yourself from that experience? What has come from that event in how you feel about yourself?* • *Today, how would you rate your life on a scale from 0 (poor)–10 (very satisfied)? What area of life do you feel has room to increase your life satisfaction?*
2. **Positive relations** Having valued, warm, trusting quality relationships grounded on the capacity to experience empathy, affection and intimacy and the reciprocity of human relationships	• *With whom do you feel most energised and connected?* • *How do you engage others with play at home or work? Who are you most playful with?* • *What emotions do you experience when you are playful?* • *Who do you trust? What does that trust look like?* • *How do you let others know they matter to you?* • *Who do you feel/think values you? How do you know this?* • *Who do you have to rely on if you have a strained relationship?*
3. **Autonomy** The degree one is living in accordance with their values, both personally and socially; how independent, self-determining, and self-regulated their behaviours are	• *What and how can you tweak your activities to include something out of the ordinary?* • *What do you understand creativity to be? How does creativity show up in your life?* • *How can you incorporate creativity and playfulness in your relationships?* • *How can you ensure your decision making is in accordance with your known values?* • *How can you regularly take time away from the usual to gain perspective on life's events, big and small?* • *What have you planned today/this week/this month that is not of your own making, or desire or that you are not obliged to do? How can you change who owns it?*
4. **Environmental mastery** Having a sense of control and competency in complex circumstances and activities; identifying, choosing and making effective use of arising opportunities in contexts congruent to personal needs and values	• *What would help you make best use of events to better meet your needs? Under what circumstances do you feel or believe you make the best decisions?* • *How can you widen the lens with which you see the world?* • *When have you felt as if you were able to see all opportunities available to you? What was happening for you at the time?* • *When life is most challenging or complex, how can you remain steadfast in your value aligned decision making? What strengths do you rely on too much or too little?* • *When faced with many opportunities, how can you best work with them to decide which ones are best for you to engage with?*

(Continued)

Table 4.1 (Continued)

Ryff and Keyes' (1995) psychological wellbeing dimensions	Coaching questions
5. Purpose in life Having a sense that their life both present and past has purpose and a sense of direction, with significant objectives and goals	• *What activities have you engaged with previously that have significance for you?* • *What did you do recently that resonated strongly with you?* • *When you mentioned that [insert comment or scenario], you appeared to be joyful/uncomfortable/[coach inserts their perception]. Would you like to tell me more about that? –* Note: this question is to help the client explore their story to help them make sense of it. This is a component of meaning making/coherence. • *How do you make sense of your life experiences? What activities or resources do you have available to help make sense of life experiences?* • *What are your driving ambitions? How often do you review your short-term and long-term goals?*
6. Growth Valuing and actualising continued self-development, reflecting on life experiences to promote self-growth through self-knowledge and effective behaviour	• *How have you contributed to your (personal and professional) successes to date?* • *When thinking about unfavourable circumstances or less successful projects/events, what have you learned about yourself and others?* • *What actions will support your commitment to understanding yourself as you strive for your valued goals and objectives?* • *What experiences have you had in the back of your mind to try but have eluded you until now? What would it take for you to plan for them and see them through?* • *If you had the choice to stay home after an extraordinarily stressful week at work or go for a drive or visit somewhere new or some other activity that would be unusual for you, what would that be? Who would you like to share this experience with? When will you do this?*

The question would be: What are the activities that contribute to a client's psychological wellbeing? Besides the meta-analysis of Sakuraya and colleagues (2020), several studies have considered a wide variety of intentional activities, including creating craft hobbies such as quilting (Burt & Atkinson, 2012), savouring positive experiences (Smith & Hollinger-Smith, 2015), tourist and travelling activities (Steyn et al., 2004), choral singing (Clift et al., 2010), play and playfulness (Biswas-Diener, 2022; Proyer, 2013), humour and humorous experiences (Mannell & McMahon, 1982) volunteering (Gil-Lacruz et al., 2019); and social prescribing activities such as visiting museums (Thomson et al., 2018), engaging in nature-based community services (Leavell et al., 2019), and walking in nature (Sudimac et al., 2022).

It is not possible to say that one activity is better than others. The best activities are ones that contribute to the individual's psychological wellbeing and provide meaning, enjoyment, challenge, the opportunity to engage in strengths or connect with others, or time alone; preferences will vary. However, to have an impact, these activities should be engaged in regularly and for an extended period. When working with individuals and groups, it would be a good idea for the coach to start by asking what activities their client enjoys most and what are the ones they would like to try but, for different reasons, have not.

Conclusion

The Good Life – wellbeing – is one full of promise, with a sense of satisfaction with life, even if all is not rosy. However, it does not appear without effort. There are many factors that influence one's appraisal of their wellbeing and happiness. Some we have addressed in this chapter, such as connection, emotions, hope, meaning and purpose; strengths, creativity and play; making sense of novel life experiences to build wisdom; and engagement and coaching as both a wellbeing facilitator but also a process to support striving and experience of The Good Life. A coach is obliged to understand the vital nutrients/dimensions of psychological wellbeing and engagement of well-chosen activities to best support and facilitate a client's psychological and physical wellbeing to build the resources needed to experience The Good Life.

Reflective questions

1. Reflecting on the six psychological wellbeing domains of Ryff and Keyes (1995), what is your score on each on a scale from 0 (not good)–10 (the best it could be)? Which would you choose to begin work on?
2. How could you add creativity to your daily life?
3. What physical activities are you drawn to that you could implement more regularly into your life?

References

Atad, O., Smith, W. A., & Green, S. (2021). Coaching as the missing ingredient in the application and training of positive psychological science. In W. A. Smith, I. Boniwell, & S. Green (Eds.), *Positive psychology coaching in the workplace*. Springer. https://doi.org/10.1007/978-3-030-79952-6_3

Baard, P. P., Deci, E. L., & Ryan, R. M. (2004). Intrinsic need satisfaction: A motivational basis of performance and well-being in two work settings. *Journal of Applied Social Psychology, 34*, 2045–2068.

Bandura, A., Freeman, W. H., & Lightsey, R. (1999). Self-efficacy: The exercise of control. *Journal of Cognitive Psychotherapy, 13*(2), 158–166.

Bangen, K. J., Meeks, T. W., & Jeste, D. V. (2013). Defining and assessing wisdom: A review of the literature. *The American Journal of Geriatric Psychiatry, 21*(12), 1254–1266.

Baumeister, R. F., & Leary, M. R. (1995). The need to belong: Desire for interpersonal attachments as a fundamental human motivation. *Psychological Bulletin, 117*(3), 497–529.

Baumeister, R. F., Vohs, K. D., DeWall, C. N., & Zhang, L. (2007). How emotion shapes behavior: Feedback, anticipation, and reflection, rather than direct causation. *Personality and Social Psychology Review, 11*(2), 167–203. https://doi.org/10.1177/1088868307301033

Birren, J. E., & Renner, V. J. (1980). Concepts and issues of mental health and aging. In J. E. Birren & R. B. Sloane (Eds.), *Handbook of mental health and aging* (pp. 3–33). Prentice Hall.

Biswas-Diener, R. (2022). Be playful. In C. van Nieuwerburgh & P. Williams (Eds.), *From surviving to thriving: A student's guide to feeling and doing well at university*. Sage.

Biswas-Diener, R., & Diener, E. (2001). Making the best of a bad situation: Satisfaction in the slums of Calcutta. *Social Indicators Research, 55*, 329–352.

Biswas-Diener, R., Kashdan, T. B., & Minhas, G. (2011). A dynamic approach to psychological strength development and intervention. *The Journal of Positive Psychology*, 6(2), 106–118.

Blieszner, R., Ogletree, A. M., & Adams, R. G. (2019). Friendship in later life: A research agenda. *Innovation in Aging*, 3(1), igz005. https://doi-org.elib.tcd.ie/10.1093/geroni/igz005

Boniwell, I., & Smith, W.-A. (2018). Positive psychology coaching for positive leadership. In S. Green & S. Palmer (Eds.), *Positive psychology coaching in practice*. Routledge.

Boniwell, I., & Smith, W.-A. (2021). Positive psychology: Coaching leadership tensions. In A. Kostić & D. Chadee (Eds.), *Positive psychology: An international perspective* (pp. 69–84). Wiley.

Buhler, C. (1935). The curve of life as studied in biographies. *Journal of Applied Psychology*, 19, 405–409.

Burt, E. L., & Atkinson, J. (2012). The relationship between quilting and wellbeing. *Journal of Public Health*, 34(1), 54–59.

Cacioppo, J. T., & Berntson, G. G. (1999). The affect system: Architecture and operating characteristics. *Current directions in psychological science*, 8(5), 133–137.

Cacioppo, J. T., Gardner, W. L., & Berntson, G. G. (1999). The affect system has parallel and integrative processing components: Form follows function. *Journal of Personality and Social Psychology*, 76(5), 839.

Clift, S., Hancox, G., Morrison, I., Hess, B., Kreutz, G., & Stewart, D. (2010). Choral singing and psychological wellbeing: Quantitative and qualitative findings from English choirs in a cross-national survey. *Journal of Applied Arts & Health*, 1(1), 19–34.

Conner, T. S., DeYoung, C. G., & Silvia, P. J. (2018). Everyday creative activity as a path to flourishing. *The Journal of Positive Psychology*, 13(2), 181–189.

Conner, T. S., & Silvia, P. J. (2015). Creative days: A daily diary study of emotion, personality, and everyday creativity. *Psychology of Aesthetics, Creativity, and the Arts*, 9(4), 463.

Csikszentmihalyi, M. (1997). Flow and creativity. *Namta Journal*, 22(2), 60–97.

Deci, E. L., & Ryan, R. M. (2012). Self-determination theory. In P. A. M. Van Lange, A. W. Kruglanski, & E. T. Higgins (Eds.), *Handbook of theories of social psychology* (pp. 416–436). Sage Publications Ltd. https://doi.org/10.4135/9781446249215.n21

Deci, E. L., & Ryan, R. M. (2014). Autonomy and need satisfaction in close relationships: Relationships motivation theory. *In Human motivation and interpersonal relationships* (pp. 53–73). Springer.

Dhar, U., Schaffner, J. J., & Smith, W. A. (2021). Coaching with compassion. In W. A. Smith, I. Boniwell, & S. Green (Eds.), *Positive psychology coaching in the workplace*. Springer. https://doi.org/10.1007/978-3-030-79952-6_25

Diener, E. (1984). Subjective wellbeing. *Psychological Bulletin*, 95(3), 542–575.

Diener, E., Napa Scollon, C., Oishi, S., Dzokoto, V., & Suh, E. (2000). Positivity and the construction of life satisfaction judgements: Global happiness is not the sum of its parts. *Journal of Happiness Studies*, 1, 15–176.

Diener, E., Oishi, S., & Lucas, R. (2003). Personality, culture, and subjective wellbeing: Emotional and cognitive evaluations of life. *Annual Review Psychology*, 54, 403–425.

Diener, E., & Seligman, M. E. P. (2002). Very happy people. *Psychological Science*, 13, 81–84.

Diener, E., & Suh, E. (1997). Measuring quality of life: Economic, social, and subjective indicators, *Social Indicators Research*, 40, 189–216.

Diener, E., Suh, E., Lucas, R., & Smith, H. (1999). Subjective wellbeing: Three decades of progress. *Psychological Bulletin*, 125(2), 276–302.

Diener, E., & Tov, W. (2012). National accounts of well-being. In *Handbook of social indicators and quality of life research* (pp. 137–157). Springer.

Dixit, R., & Sinha, V. (2022). Leveraging coaching as an instrument for training transfer: A case of learners in a Fintech firm. *Development and Learning in Organizations*, Vol. ahead-of-print No. ahead-of-print. https://doi.org/10.1108/DLO-07-2022-0129

Dolan, P., & Metcalfe, R. (2012). The relationship between innovation and subjective wellbeing. *Research Policy*, 41(8), 1489–1498.

Dutton, J. E. (2003). *Energize your workplace: How to create and sustain high-quality connections at work* (Vol. 50). John Wiley & Sons.

Dutton, J. E., & Ragins, B. R. (Eds.). (2017). *Exploring positive relationships at work: Building a theoretical and research foundation*. Psychology Press.

Erikson, E. (1959). Identity and the life cycle. *Psychological Issues, 1*, 18–164.

Feldman, D. B., Balaraman, M., & Anderson, C. (2018). Hope and meaning-in-life: Points of contact between hope theory and existentialism. In M. W. Gallagher & S. J. Lopez (Eds.), *The Oxford handbook of hope* (pp. 353–362). Oxford University Press.

Forgeard, M. J., & Eichner, K. V. (2014). Creativity as a target and tool for positive interventions. *The Wiley Blackwell handbook of positive psychological interventions* (pp. 135–154). Wiley Blackwell.

Fredrickson, B. L. (1998). What good are positive emotions?. *Review of general psychology, 2*(3), 300–319.

Fredrickson, B. L. (2001). The role of positive emotions in positive psychology: The broaden-and-build theory of positive emotions. *American psychologist, 56*(3), 218.

Fredrickson, B. L., & Branigan, C. (2005). Positive emotions broaden the scope of attention and thought-action repertoires. *Cognition & Emotion, 19*(3), 313–332.

Fredrickson, B. L. (2013). Positive emotions broaden and build. In *Advances in experimental social psychology* (Vol. 47, pp. 1–53). Academic Press.

Frisch, M. B., Clark, M. P., Rouse, S. V., Rudd, M. D., Paweleck, J. K., Greenstone, A., & Kopplin, D. A. (2005). Predictive and treatment validity of life satisfaction and the quality of life inventory. *Assessment, 12*(1), 66–78.

Frisch, M. B., Cornell, J., Villanueva, M., & Retzlaff, P. (1992). Clinical validation of the quality of life inventory: A measure of life satisfaction for use in treatment planning and outcome assessment. *Psychological Assessment, 4*(1), 92–101.

Gilbert, D. (2004). Affective forecasting. . . or. . . the big wombassa-a talk with Daniel Gilbert. *The Edge.* http://www.edge.org/3rd_culture/gilbert03/gilbert_index.html

Gil-Lacruz, M., Saz-Gil, M. I., & Gil-Lacruz, A. I. (2019). Benefits of older volunteering on wellbeing: An international comparison. *Frontiers in Psychology, 10*, 2647.

Hackman, J. R., & Oldham, G. R. (1976). Motivation through the design of work: Test of a theory. *Organization Behavior and Human Decision Processes, 16*, 250–279.

Harandi, T. F., Taghinasab, M. M., & Nayeri, T. D. (2017). The correlation of social support with mental health: A meta-analysis. *Electronic Physician, 9*(9).

Headey, B. W., & Wearing, A. J. (1992). *Understanding happiness: A theory of subjective wellbeing.* Longman Cheshire.

Heintzelman, S. J., & King, L. A. (2014). Life is pretty meaningful. *American Psychologist, 69*, 561–574.

Helfand, M., Kaufman, J. C., & Beghetto, R. A. (2016). The four-C model of creativity: Culture and context. In *The Palgrave handbook of creativity and culture research* (pp. 15–36). Palgrave Macmillan.

International Coach Federation (ICF). (2022). *ICF core competencies.* https://coachingfederation.org/credentials-and-standards/core-competencies

Ivtzan, I., Young, T., Martman, J., Jeffrey, A., Lomas, T., Hart, R., & Eiroa-Orosa, F. J. (2016). Integrating mindfulness into positive psychology: A randomised controlled trial of an online positive mindfulness program. *Mindfulness, 7*, 1396–1407.

Jacob, Y., & Steger, M. F. (2021). Meaning-centred coaching in the workplace. In W. A. Smith, I. Boniwell, & S. Green (Eds.), *Positive psychology coaching in the workplace.* Springer. https://doi.org/10.1007/978-3-030-79952-6_29

Jahoda, M. (1958). *Current concepts of positive mental health.* Basic Books.

Juster, F., Courant, P., & Dow, G. (1981). A theoretical framework for the measurement of wellbeing. *Review of Income and Wealth, 27*(1), 1–31.

Kafka, G., & Kozma, A. (2002). The construct validity of Ryff's scales of psychological well-being (SPWB) and their relationship to measures of subjective well-being. *Social Indicators Research, 57*, 171–190.

Karwowski, M., Lebuda, I., Szumski, G., & Firkowska-Mankiewicz, A. (2017). From moment-to-moment to day-to-day: Experience sampling and diary investigations in adults' everyday creativity. *Psychology of Aesthetics, Creativity, and the Arts, 11*(3), 309.

Kashdan, T. B., & Biswas-Diener, R. (2015). *The upside of your dark side: Why being your whole self-not just your "good" self-drives success and fulfillment.* Penguin.

Kiernan, F., Davidson, J., & Oades, L. (2020). Researching creativity and wellbeing: Interdisciplinary perspectives. *International Journal of Wellbeing, 10*(5).

Lai, M. K., Leung, C., Kwok, S. Y., Hui, A. N., Lo, H. H., Leung, J. T., & Tam, C. H. (2018). A multidimensional PERMA-H positive education model, general satisfaction of school life, and character strengths use in Hong Kong senior primary school students: Confirmatory factor analysis and path analysis using the APASO-II. *Frontiers in Psychology, 9*, 1090. https://doi.org/10.3389/fpsyg.2018.01639

Leavell, M. A., Leiferman, J. A., Gascon, M., Braddick, F., Gonzalez, J. C., & Litt, J. S. (2019). Nature-based social prescribing in urban settings to improve social connectedness and mental well-being: A review. *Current Environmental Health Reports, 6*(4), 297–308.

Leontiev, D. (2013). Personal meaning: A challenge for psychology. *The Journal of Positive Psychology, 8*(6), 459–470.

Lowe, G. (2006). Health-related effects of creative and expressive writing. *Health Education, 106.*

MacKie, D. (2021). Strength-based coaching and sustainability leadership. In W. A. Smith, I. Boniwell, & S. Green (Eds.), *Positive psychology coaching in the workplace.* Springer. https://doi.org/10.1007/978-3-030-79952-6_20

Mannell, R. C., & McMahon, L. (1982). Humor as play: Its relationship to psychological well-being during the course of a day. *Leisure Sciences, 5*(2), 143–155.

Martela, F., & Steger, M. F. (2016). The three meanings of meaning in life: Distinguishing coherence, purpose, and significance. *The Journal of Positive Psychology, 11*(5), 531–545.

Martin, L., Oepen, R., Bauer, K., Nottensteiner, A., Mergheim, K., Gruber, H., & Koch, S. C. (2018). Creative arts interventions for stress management and prevention—a systematic review. *Behavioral Sciences, 8*(2), 28.

Maslow, A. H. (1968). *Toward a psychology of being* (2nd ed.). Van Nostrand.

Miglianico, M., Dubreuil, P., Miquelon, P., Bakker, A. B., & Martin-Krumm, C. (2020). Strength use in the workplace: A literature review. *Journal of Happiness Studies, 21*(2), 737–764.

Morelock, M. J., & Feldman, D. H. (1999). Prodigies. *Encyclopedia of Creativity, 2*, 449–456.

Murthy, V. (2017). Work and the loneliness epidemic: reducing isolation at work is good business. *Harvard Business Review.* Retrieved from https://hbr.org/cover-story/2017/09/work-and-the-loneliness-epidemic

Nan, J. K., & Ho, R. T. (2017). Effects of clay art therapy on adults outpatients with major depressive disorder: A randomized controlled trial. *Journal of Affective Disorders, 217*, 237–245.

Neugarten, B. L., Havighurst, R., & Tobin, S. (1961). The measurement of life satisfaction. *Journal of Gerontology, 16*, 134–143.

Niemiec, R. M. (2013). VIA character strengths: Research and practice (The first 10 years). In *Well-being and cultures* (pp. 11–29). Springer.

Oades, L. (2020). Towards a wellbeing literate society. *Innovations in a Changing World*, 14–18.

O'Brien, E., & Seydel, A. (2022). *The power of play: Optimize your joy potential.* Live Life happy Publishing.

Oishi, S., & Diener, E. (2001). Re-examining the general positivity model of subjective well-being: The discrepancy between specific and global domain satisfaction. *Journal of Personality, 69*(4), 641–666.

Oishi, S., & Westgate, E. C. (2021). A psychologically rich life: Beyond happiness and meaning. *Psychological Review, 129.*

Park, N., Peterson, C., & Seligman, M. E.(2004). Strengths of character and well-being. *Journal of Social and Clinical Psychology, 23*, 603–619. https://doi.org/10.1521/jscp.23.5.603.50748

Petersen, E., Bischoff, A., Liedtke, G., & Martin, A. J. (2021). How does being solo in nature affect well-being? Evidence from Norway, Germany and New Zealand. *International Journal of Environmental Research and Public Health, 18*(15), 7897.

Peterson, C., & Seligman, M. E. (2004). *Character strengths and virtues: A handbook and classification* (Vol. 1). Oxford University Press.

Prilleltensky, I., & Prilleltensky, O. (2021). *How people matter: Why it affects health, happiness, love, work, and society.* Cambridge University Press.

Proyer, R. T. (2013). The well-being of playful adults: Adult playfulness, subjective well-being, physical well-being, and the pursuit of enjoyable activities. *The European Journal of Humour Research, 1*(1), 84–98.

Proyer, R. T., Gander, F., Wellenzohn, S., & Ruch, W. (2015). Strengths-based positive psychology interventions: A randomized placebo-controlled online trial on long-term effects for a signature strengths-vs. a lesser strengths-intervention. *Frontiers in Psychology, 6*, 456.

Quoidbach, J., Taquet, M., Desseilles, M., de Montjoye, Y. A., & Gross, J. J. (2019). Happiness and social behavior. *Psychological science*, *30*(8), 1111–1122.

Richards, R. (2007). Everyday creativity: Our hidden potential. In R. Richards (Ed.), *Everyday creativity and new views of human nature: Psychological, social, and spiritual perspectives* (pp. 25–53). American Psychological Association. https://doi.org/10.1037/11595-001

Richards, R. (2010). Everyday creativity: Process and way of life—four key issues. In J. C. Kaufman & R. J. Sternberg (Eds.), *The Cambridge handbook of creativity* (pp. 189–215). Cambridge University Press. https://doi.org/10.1017/CBO9780511763205.013

Richards, R. (2018). *Everyday creativity and the healthy mind: Dynamic new paths for self and society*. Springer.

Rogers, C. (1961). *On becoming a person*. Houghton Mifflin.

Ryan, R. M. (2009). Self determination theory and well being. *Social Psychology*, *84*(822), 848.

Ryan, R. M., & Deci, E. L. (2000). Self-determination theory and the facilitation of intrinsic motivation, social development, and well-being. *American Psychologist*, *55*, 68–78.

Ryan, R. M., & Deci, E. L. (2001). On happiness and human potentials: A review of research on hedonic and eudaimonic well-being. *Annual Review of Psychology*, *52*(1), 141–166.

Ryan, R. M., & Deci, E. L. (2018). *Self-determination theory: Basic psychological needs in motivation, development, and wellness*. Guilford Press.

Ryff, C. D. (1989). Happiness is everything, or is it? Explorations on the meaning of psychological well-being. *Journal of Personality and Social Psychology*, *57*(6), 1069–1081.

Ryff, C. D. (1995). Psychological well-being in adult life. *Current Directions in Psychological Science*, *4*(4), 99–104.

Ryff, C. D., & Keyes, C. L. M. (1995). The structure of psychological well-being revisited. *Journal of Personality and Social Psychology*, *69*(4), 719.

Sakuraya, A., Imamura, K., Watanabe, K., Asai, Y., Ando, E., Eguchi, H., Nishida, N., Kobayashi, Y., Arima, H., Iwanaga, M., Otsuka, Y., Sasaki, N., Inoue, A., Inoue, R., Tsuno, K., Hino, A., Shimazu, A., Tsutsumi, A., & Kawakami, N. (2020). What kind of intervention is effective for improving subjective well-being among workers? A systematic review and meta-analysis of randomized controlled trials. *Frontiers in Psychology*, *11*, 528656.

Schlossberg, N. K. (1989). Marginality and mattering: Key issues in building community. *New Directions for Student Services*, 1–7.

Scholz, D., Taylor, A., & Strelan, P. (2022). Factors contributing to the efficacy of universal mental health and wellbeing programs in secondary schools: A systematic review. *Adolescent Research Review*, 1–20.

Schwartz, B., & Sharpe, K. E. (2006). Practical wisdom: Aristotle meets positive psychology. *Journal of Happiness Studies*, *7*(3), 377–395.

Seligman, M. E. (2002). Positive psychology, positive prevention, and positive therapy. In *Handbook of positive psychology* (Vol. 2, pp. 3–12). Oxford University Press.

Seligman, M. E. (2011). *Flourish*. Free Press.

Sheldon, K., Elliot, A., Ryan, R., Chirkov, V., Kim, Y., Wu, C., Demir, M., & Sun, Z. (2004). Self-concordance and subjective well-being in four cultures. *Journal of Cross-Cultural Psychology*, *35*(2), 209–223.

Shim, Y., Jebb, A. T., Tay, L., & Pawelski, J. O. (2021). Arts and humanities interventions for flourishing in healthy adults: A mixed studies systematic review. *Review of General Psychology*, *25*(3), 258–282.

Silapurem, L., Slemp, G. R., & Jarden, A. (2021). Encouraging Job Crafting through a Coaching Partnership. *Positive Psychology Coaching in the Workplace*, 417–435.

Skews, R., West, A., & Archer, R. (2021). Acceptance and commitment coaching in the workplace. In W. A. Smith, I. Boniwell, & S. Green (Eds.), *Positive psychology coaching in the workplace*. Springer. https://doi.org/10.1007/978-3-030-79952-6_26

Smith, G. J., & van der Meer, G. (1997). Creativity in old age. *Eminent Creativity, Everyday Creativity, and Health*, 333–353.

Smith, J. L., & Hollinger-Smith, L. (2015). Savoring, resilience, and psychological well-being in older adults. *Aging & Mental Health*, *19*(3), 192–200.

Smith, S., & Bretherton, R. (2021). Coaching wisdom in the workplace: Coaching from an integrative model of wisdom. In W. A. Smith, I. Boniwell, & S. Green (Eds.), *Positive psychology coaching in the workplace*. Springer. https://doi.org/10.1007/978-3-030-79952-6_28

Smith, W. A., King, S., & Lai, Y. L. (2021). Coaching with emotions and creating high quality connections in the workplace. In W. A. Smith, I. Boniwell, & S. Green (Eds.), *Positive psychology coaching in the workplace*. Springer. https://doi.org/10.1007/978-3-030-79952-6_10

Snyder, C. R. (1995). Conceptualizing, measuring, and nurturing hope. *Journal of Counseling & Development, 73*(3), 355–360.

Snyder, C. R. (2002). Hope theory: Rainbows in the mind. *Psychological Inquiry, 13*(4), 249–275.

Snyder, C. R., Harris, C., Anderson, J. R., Holleran, S. A., Irving, L. M., Sigmon, S. T., Yoshinobu, L., Gibb, J., Langelle, C., & Harney, P. (1991). The will and the ways: Development and validation of an individual-differences measure of hope. *Journal of Personality and Social Psychology, 60*, 570–585.

Snyder, C. R., Irving, L., & Anderson, J. R. (1991). Hope and health: Measuring the will and the ways. In C. R. Snyder & D. R. Forsyth (Eds.), *Handbook of social and clinical psychology: The health perspective* (pp. 285–305). Pergamon Press.

Spence, G. B., & Deci, E. L. (2016). Self-determination theory within coaching contexts: Supporting motives and goals that promote optimal functioning and well-being. In *Beyond goals* (pp. 85–108). Routledge.

Spence, G. B. (2022). *Get moving. Keep moving: Healthy ageing and how physical activity loves you back*. Longueville Media.

Spence, G. B., & Spence, R. J. (2022). *26 ways to keep moving: The joyful connections people make with their physical selves*. Longueville Media.

Steger, M. F. (2017). Creating meaning and purpose at work. In L. G. Oades, M. Steger, A. Delle Fave, & J. Passmore (Eds.), *The Wiley Blackwell handbook of the psychology of positivity and strengths-based approaches at work* (pp. 60–81). John Wiley & Sons.

Steger, M. F., & Dik, B. J. (2010). Work as meaning. In P. A. Linley, S. Harrington, & N. Page (Eds.), *Oxford handbook of positive psychology and work* (pp. 131–142). Oxford University Press.

Steger, M. F., Dik, B. J., & Duffy, R. D. (2012). Measuring meaningful work: The work and meaning inventory (WAMI). *Journal of Career Assessment, 20*, 322–337.

Steyn, S., Saayman, M., & Nienaber, A. (2004). The impact of tourist and travel activities on facets of psychological well-being. *South African Journal for Research in Sport, Physical Education and Recreation, 26*(1), 97–106.

Sudimac, S., Sale, V., & Kühn, S. (2022). How nature nurtures: Amygdala activity decreases as the result of a one-hour walk in nature. *Molecular Psychiatry, 27*.

Thomson, L. J., Lockyer, B., Camic, P. M., & Chatterjee, H. J. (2018). Effects of a museum-based social prescription intervention on quantitative measures of psychological wellbeing in older adults. *Perspectives in Public Health, 138*(1), 28–38.

Vella-Brodrick, D., Joshanloo, M., & Slemp, G. R. (2022). Longitudinal relationships between social connection, agency, and emotional well-being: A 13-year study. *The Journal of Positive Psychology*, 1–11.

Wang, Q., Lai, Y. L., Xu, X., & McDowall, A. (2021). The effectiveness of workplace coaching: A meta-analysis of contemporary psychologically informed coaching approaches. *Journal of Work-Applied Management, 14*.

Wong, P. T. P. (Ed.). (2012). From logotherapy to meaning-centered counseling and therapy. In *The human quest for meaning* (2nd ed., pp. 619–647). Taylor and Francis.

Wood, A. M., Linley, P. A., Maltby, J., Kashdan, T. B., & Hurling, R. (2011). Using personal and psychological strengths leads to increases in well-being over time: A longitudinal study and the development of the strengths use questionnaire. *Personality and Individual Differences, 50*(1), 15–19.

Wright, P. R., & Pascoe, R. (2015). Eudaimonia and creativity: The art of human flourishing. *Cambridge Journal of Education, 45*(3), 295–306.

Young, K. C., Kashdan, T. B., & Macatee, R. (2015). Strength balance and implicit strength measurement: New considerations for research on strengths of character. *The Journal of Positive Psychology, 10*(1), 17–24.

Zhao, M. Y., & Tay, L. (2022). From ill-being to well-being: Bipolar or bivariate? *The Journal of Positive Psychology*. https://doi.org/10.1080/17439760.2022.2109204

Section 2

Coaching in health and wellbeing practice

Chapter 5

Weight management coaching

Jane Daly and Karen Hayns

Introduction

Weight management coaching is a vital component of empowering clients to better manage and sustain healthy weight behaviours. Issues associated with poor weight management are well-documented, complex and multi-faceted challenges that affect a significant portion of the global population (WHO, 2022a, 2022b). Left untreated, the consequences of poor weight management are likely to escalate and cause an increased risk of other non-communicable diseases (NCDs) such as diabetes, heart disease and some cancers (Institute for Health Metrics and Evaluation, 2020a, b). Practicing sustainable healthy weight behaviours is more complex than meets the eye, with most people – including healthcare professionals, policymakers and others – being guilty of seeing it as a simple lack of personal responsibility, when fragmented health systems, stigma and misunderstanding are at the root of a problem that is both chronic and relapsing in nature (WHO, 2018, 2022c).

In this chapter, we will consider the fields of research associated with weight management and the critical role coaching needs to play in reversing a global health crisis that is preventable. We will explore some practical client-centred approaches that support clients to systemically investigate their own health behaviours in the context of a confusing landscape of expert advice and within the lived experience of bias often associated with being over- or under-weight. We will conclude this chapter by noting that there is no one best model that suits all clients. Instead, each coach should – through practice, reflection and training, and by connecting with relevant evidence-based communities of practice – seek to formulate their own integrated approach that allows clients to better understand why they may have formed unhealthy weight behaviours and how this new insight can empower clients to make life changes that lead to better health outcomes and to sustainable weight behaviours.

Theoretical approaches

Scale of the problem

The World Obesity Federation predicts that by 2030, 1 billion people globally, including 1 in 5 women and 1 in 7 men, will be living with obesity (World Obesity Federation, 2021). Childhood obesity is expected to double between 2020 and 2035. In the UK, the NHS costs attributable to overweight and obesity-related conditions stands at £6 billion per annum and are projected to reach almost £10 billion by 2050, together with a wider economic and social burden estimated at £50 billion.

DOI: 10.4324/9781003319016-7

At the other end of the spectrum, a rise in eating distress is noted in the *British Medical Journal*, which reported an 84% increase in hospital admissions for eating disorders over the last five years, together with new guidance for general practitioners (GPs) to spot the danger signs for illnesses such as anorexia nervosa (Wise, 2022).

During the COVID19 pandemic, imposed restrictions on our social freedoms had a profound effect on lifestyles as the business world moved online – and, for many, hybrid working became the norm with longer periods of sedentary behaviour and higher levels of physical inactivity. Furthermore, push factors in our environment like the proliferation of food apps and 24/7 doorstep deliveries resulted in changes to dietary habits as the food industry and food tech cashed in on enforced periods of lockdown.

A closely related and perhaps less well understood aspect of weight management is body image, a dynamic and life-long construct which is largely determined by social experience. As human beings, our very existence is embodied, and so it is quite natural to be wrapped up in a whole range of private thoughts and feelings about the degree to which we feel comfortable in our bodies.

Deep concerns about size and shape can cause high levels of body dissatisfaction in some people; a consequence of internalisation – a cognitive process that influences and disrupts our body image in unhelpful ways caused by a perceived discrepancy between their body and the 'ideal' body. This phenomenon increasingly affects men, women and children.

Nutrition and nutritional psychiatry

This approach focuses on the role of diet and nutrition in weight management. Researchers in this field investigate the effects on weight of diet, dietary information and/or dietary supplements.

Nutrition advice is constantly changing, and this volatility in education has been one source of confusion amongst consumers who are unsure what nutritional advice and sources are trustworthy.

Professor Tim Spector, a founder of the ZOE Health study and largest nutrition science study in the world, has argued (Spector, 2022) that nutrition advice has been part of the problem. He argues that while diabetes, heart disease and other chronic health problems associated with poor nutrition are not improving, the current approaches which have focused on weight gain are unhelpful. He proposes that instead, a better approach is to focus on poor metabolic health.

Key to research in this field is the role of data, with many studies drawing on digital technologies and global university collaboration projects to better understand food behaviours and changing attitudes towards nutrition.

A parallel field of research is nutritional psychiatry. Studies here have tended to focus on the role of nutrition and its impacts on the body as an integrated complex structure (Felice Jacka et al., 2015). One example is the work of Professor Felice Jacka (2015, 2019) in uncovering the links between diet, brain function and depressive behaviour. Jacka has highlighted the lack of evidence-based nutrition advice and education, provided by the global food industry, and the lack of political will to reduce their collective influence on consumers.

Epidemiology

Epidemiology is the study of distribution and determinants of health and disease in populations. Researchers in this field focus on the environmental and social factors that contribute to obesity, such as socioeconomic status, access to food and cultural norms.

Many epidemiologists believe that obesity fits the model of a disease process, except that the toxic or pathological agent is food rather than a microbe. Bray and colleagues (2017) argue that obesity is a chronic relapsing disease process which operates in a systemic context.

World Obesity Federation (2022a) believes that the magnitude of obesity and its adverse effects in individuals may relate to the virulence or toxicity of the environment and its interaction with the host. The WOF are calling for obesity to be seen as a twenty-first century pandemic, one potentially which can cause more death than the COVID19 pandemic.

Spector (2015) has argued that society needs to change the way it thinks about food before change is possible in addressing the obesity pandemic facing the developed world. Spector argues that personalised nutrition, supported by data, is the key to weight management and reversing illnesses associated with obesity, with the main focus being on the microbes in our guts, which need a varied diet themselves in order to process the food that makes us healthy.

Exercise physiology

Exercise physiology explores the role of physical activity in weight management and body image. Researchers in this field study the impact and side effects of different types of exercise, as well as the optimal duration and frequency of exercise for healthy weight maintenance (Kent, 2021). Exercise physiologists require a solid foundation in biochemistry, physics, molecular biology and computer sciences.

The term 'metabolic flexibility' was introduced to describe the interplay between fat and carbohydrate as substrates for energy metabolism in response to fasting or feeding (Goodpaster & Kelley, 2002; Hood et al., 2006). Exercise physiologists have used exercise as a probe for understanding the aetiology and reversibility of metabolic inflexibility, which is a problem most evident in the context of obesity and insulin resistance. The associations between metabolic inflexibility – generally measured as insulin resistance or impaired fatty acid metabolism – and mitochondrial function have been established in several studies (Dubé et al., 2014; Stephenson & Hawley, 2014). Notably, Meex et al. (2010) showed that exercise training can reverse this problem in part through an improvement in mitochondrial capacity.

Exercise physiologists continue to push the boundaries of this field, with the rapid adoption of advanced technologies and artificial intelligence expected to revolutionise the self-regulation and personalised aspects of exercise and weight management.

Endocrinology

Endocrinology is the study of the hormones that regulate appetite, metabolism and energy expenditure. Researchers in this field focus on the role of hormones like insulin, leptin and ghrelin in weight management.

Bray & Ryan (2021) suggest that despite continued attempts to identify superior dietary approaches, most studies have found there is not a significant difference between low-carbohydrate and low-fat diets; however, studies that explore the role of diet across the human lifespan – including during childhood, the menopause and ageing – suggest that it is our unique combination of gut microbes that may hold the key to weight management success, rather than our DNA. Spector (2015) suggests our gut health may change over our lifetime and therefore it needs monitoring and nurturing through a rich, colourful, diverse, fermented, less processed diet but also through allowing space between eating so that our gut bugs have time to rest and recover so they can support a healthy gut and immune system.

Many endocrinologists believe that obesity may be impacted by 'set point theory'. Kennedy (1953) and Speakman et al. (2011) suggested that body fat storage might be a regulated phenomenon involving a set point. He suggested that fat might produce a signal that was sensed by the brain, where it was compared with a target level of body fatness. Leibel et al. (1984, 1995) has built on this theory, observing that when the system is perturbed, for example by a period of dieting or overfeeding, people lose or gain weight, respectively. However, once dieting or overfeeding ceases, they tend to regain any lost fat, or lose the accumulated fat, and return to a level approximating their original fatness (Bouchard et al., 1996; Anderson et al., 2001).

Genetics

This field explores the genetic factors that influence body weight and the risk of obesity. Researchers in this field typically investigate the role of specific genes in regulating metabolism and appetite.

There has been much research into the relationship between DNA and weight management. The first large-scale genome-wide analysis of the association between adult body mass index (BMI) and deoxyribonucleic acid (DNA) methylation has shown that BMI is associated with methylation of the protein HIF3A in blood and adipose tissue. These findings provide a strong foundation for further exploration of the part played by the epigenome in regulation of BMI and the downstream detrimental effects of increased bodyweight (Dick et al., 2014).

In addition to obesity, eating disorders now affect a growing proportion of the population, including anorexia nervosa, bulimia nervosa and binge-eating disorder. Eating disorders have the highest mortality rate amongst all psychiatric disorders. Currently, less than half of individuals reach full recovery; as a result, there is a need to make research into eating disorders faster, cheaper and more effective to identify more effective treatments.

Behavioural psychology

This field investigates the psychological factors that influence eating behaviour in weight management and body image. Researchers in this field typically study extrinsic and intrinsic motivation, self-regulation, self-control, body image and social support in maintaining a healthy weight and body image.

Few people are successful in long-term weight maintenance. Those that are more successful demonstrate more frequent practice of dietary choices, physical activity, self-monitoring, and psychological coping strategies (Phelan et al., 2020). Phelan and colleagues state that specific psychological coping strategies included "thinking about past successes" and "remaining positive in the face of weight regain."

Behavioural psychologists study the relationships and interrelationships people have with food and their subsequent impact on weight management success or failure. The importance of consistency, goal regulation and self-control for healthy-weight behaviour was found in the study by McKee et al. (2013). Within these overarching themes, successful weight management was related to long-term, realistic goal setting, consistent use of routines and self-monitoring, avoiding deprivation and effective coping skills. Unsuccessful maintenance was related to short-term unrealistic goal setting, inconsistent routines and self-monitoring, experiencing deprivation and poor coping skills.

The abstinence violation effect (AVE) Collins (2013) is a theory of weight management whereby obsessive behaviour and behaviours related to obsession can be found. AVE refers to the negative cognitive (i.e., internal, stable, uncontrollable attributions; cognitive dissonance) and affective responses (i.e., guilt, shame) experienced by an individual after a return to the use of a substance following a period of self-imposed abstinence from substances (Curry et al., 1987) an affect that is more commonly referred to as lapsing or relapsing.

Public health and digital health

This field focuses on developing policies and interventions to prevent and manage obesity at the population level. Researchers in this field typically investigate the effectiveness of policies designed to improve food environments, public education campaigns that promote healthy eating and weight management behaviours, and the impact of community-based programmes. In the Institute for Government report "Tackling Obesity", Metcalf and Sasse (2023) recommend significant and urgent changes as well as systemic approaches by policy makers if we are to improve health behaviours as well as food and health policies (Madigan et al., 2022).

Digital healthcare offers new opportunities to support weight management. Areas of most interest are those that support people with their self-efficacy so they can integrate successful health behaviours into their lifespan. Research by Hinchliffe et al. (2022), suggested that:

> Existing technologies, such as telehealth and mobile health apps and wearable devices, offer emerging opportunities to improve access to obesity care and enhance the quality, efficiency and cost-effectiveness of weight management interventions and long-term patient support. Future application of machine learning and artificial intelligence to obesity care could see interventions become increasingly automated and personalised.

A substantial and rising percentage of healthcare costs are associated with weight management, obesity, childhood obesity, eating disorders and illnesses associated with weight management. Lower middle income is seen as a barrier to healthy behaviour education. Food education is also confusing and more needs to be done to change how food is produced, sold and marketed, and how cultures pass on the right health behaviours. The socioeconomic and health costs of weight management are now unmanageable, and a call for new and systemic thinking is required (WHO, 2022a, 2022b, 2022c).

Coaching research

Weight management is a complex and multi-faceted global challenge. For a significant and growing proportion of the population, the inability to self-regulate weight is a chronic relapsing condition that is preventable, but practicing and sustaining healthy weight behaviours requires a holistic approach whereby both the system and the client work well together, and the client is supported to maintain healthy weight behaviours.

Opportunity for coaching

The rise in obesity rates and an obesogenic environment has brought increased attention to the importance of weight management and the need for effective interventions. On the face of it, there is a mountain to climb; however, this challenge also presents the professional coaching community with the opportunity to bring their skills, experience and compassion to help clients find a balance between weight and shape satisfaction.

Weight management coaching offers a lifeline to empower clients so they can make long-term changes that revolutionise their relationship with food and uncover the root causes of these relationships. Motivational interviewing (MI), a client-centred approach focused on enhancing intrinsic motivation and behaviour change, is a powerful medium within weight management coaching. Clients who are able to maintain healthy weight behaviours for 12 months beyond the initial coaching mentioned the coach/client relationship as a key contributor to their personal success. MI techniques were used by the coaches to build dynamic and trusted relationships with their clients, with clients feeling empowered to integrate weight management behaviours into their daily living, resulting in life changing experiences (Newnham-Kanas et al., 2011).

Newnham-Kanas et al. (2011) credited increased self-confidence, learning to cope with life in a healthy manner, putting self first, increased emotional healing, the importance of social networks in weight loss and learning to step outside comfort zones to the coaching intervention that combined MI with co-active life coaching skills. The Newnham-Kanas et al. (2011) study revealed systemic themes: weight was a symptom, increased self-care, life coaching and weight loss as a journey, support required as a motivator and importance of the coach/client relationship; however, more studies are required to increase fidelity including groups across gender, age, class and ethnicity.

A meta-analysis by Barnes & Ivezaj (2015) also supports the effectiveness for MI in weight management. Barnes & Ivezaj (2015) conducted a comprehensive review and highlight significant barriers within primary care when clients may face treatment challenges due to the quality of actions by clinicians. Barnes & Ivezaj (2015) suggest there is potential for MI to help clients lose weight, but they also call for more MI treatment fidelity. MI was also credited in a systemic review by Patel et al. (2019), the study concluded that MI was easily translated to use as part of eHealth interventions and resulted in more effective weight management but more research is required to increase fidelity.

Acceptance and commitment therapy (ACT) is a behaviourally based person-centred approach that has been identified as effective in healthy weight coaching. A Finnish web-based clinical care study credited healthy weight coaching incorporating ACT as a potential addition to the repertoire of obesity management in a clinical setting Kupila et al. (2022). Kupila et al. (2022), conducted a comprehensive 12-month cohort study focused on lifestyle, general health and psychological factors. Results concluded that ACT coaching supported clients with success of long-term weight management, but the study highlights the need for a systemic approach whereby coaching is part of a systemic approach.

Budden et al. (2017) credited the concepts of ontological approaches to weight management coaching of men. Budden et al. (2017) integrated weight management coaching as part of a lived experience approach that included a team sport. All participants in the study agreed to weekly team coaching and one-to-one coaching, both focused on weight management. The study aimed to provide men with an environment where sport provided the activity programme and the coaching provided a trusted platform for men to express their lived experiences and behavioural and psychological challenges because they have built dynamic relationships.

A systemic review and meta-analysis conducted by Sieczkowska et al. (2021) suggests that although health coaching has emerged as a potential supporting tool for health professionals to overcome behavioural barriers, its efficacy in weight management remains unclear. The study concluded that health professionals marginally favour coaching compared to the usual care routes; however, due to a high risk of bias, Sieczkowska and colleagues suggest that quality improvements are necessary to effectively conclude that coaching leads to more effective client outcomes. Exploring this study further reveals that a lack of consistency in the application of best practice when using high-quality behavioural approaches made it difficult to analyse the results conclusively. The study highlights that to increase the impact of health coaching for weight management, there is an urgent need to raise the quality of the coaching, as well as to introduce more rigour, regulation and particularly focus on: (1) defining what health coaching actually is; (2) better defining and describing the most effective coaching interventions; (3) properly training coaches who can successfully apply interventions consistently; and (4) conducting more pragmatic randomised controlled trails following the Consolidated Standards of Reporting Trials (CONSORT) guidelines to test clinically significant outcomes. In contrast to this study, Madigan et al. (2022) conducted randomised controlled trials to examine the effectiveness of behavioural weight management interventions for adults with obesity delivered in primary care. The Madigan and colleagues systematic review and meta-analysis of randomised controlled trials concluded that behavioural weight management interventions are effective for weight management.

The elements of weight management coaching – discussed in more detail earlier in this chapter – combines nutrition (food quality and quantity), behavioural, mindset and self-esteem interventions. These elements should also guide learning and discovery and the appropriate challenge of pseudo-science and mis information, so that clients feel better equipped to take responsibility for their health behaviour within the system as it is. Coaches should look to increase their ability in practice to apply high quality behavioural approaches consistently and as they were intended to be used. Cutting corners is likely to reduce the desired health outcomes for clients.

Practice

Coaches who align their work with client-centred approaches will enable clients to investigate their health behaviour amidst a confusing landscape of pseudo-science and expert advice, and through the lens of their lived experience.

No one model suits all; rather, an integrated approach that empowers the client to look beyond diet to support and sustain healthy weight behaviours. A systemic model of weight management coaching (Figure 5.1) combines personal, lifestyle and environmental elements to offer clients a holistic way to manage their weight sustainably and over the long term, no matter where their starting point might be in terms of mindset and health

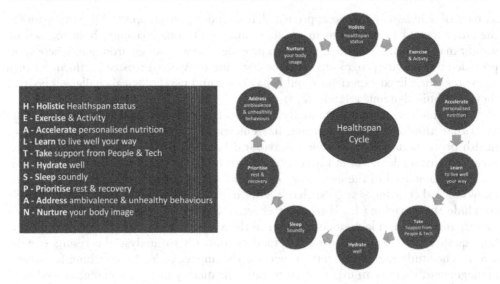

H - **Holistic** Healthspan status
E - **Exercise** & Activity
A - **Accelerate** personalised nutrition
L - **Learn** to live well your way
T - **Take** support from People & Tech
H - **Hydrate** well
S - **Sleep** soundly
P - **Prioritise** rest & recovery
A - **Address** ambivalence & unhealthy behaviours
N - **Nurture** your body image

Figure 5.1 Healthspan approach – client-centred weight management coaching to increase adherence and reduce ambivalence

behaviour. This is particularly important if there is a history of failed attempts to lose weight, and given the very high failure rates of dieting where weight regain is a certainty.

In this way, coaching enables the client to establish the root causes, focussing on specific behavioural, cognitive or physical areas, for example. Passmore (2020) explains that for cognitive issues, an integrated approach would seek to combine different approaches such as visualisation, disputation and self-compassion. Increasing change-talk by practicing MI in this context would further increase a client's ability to succeed and cope when they may relapse.

As weight management coaching is complex and multi-faceted, coaches should be prepared to experience a variety of emotions and resistance from clients. Coaches will need to deploy high standards in their practice and set up relevant support systems for themselves and their clients before they start to help clients to look beyond the surface and focus on the long term beyond diet alone. Coaches should take the time to contract carefully, making sure it is clear what successful health coaching for weight management looks like so that clients know what to expect. This also provides both parties with the opportunity to outline any specific requirements or steps that may need to be taken as the coaching relationship develops.

Coaches who are well practiced in cognitive and behavioural approaches, and apply these interventions as they are intended, will achieve more impact because approaches like MI build self-efficacy and self-regulation. Leading with empathy and practicing unconditional positive regard is not only imperative but will also support coaches to build trust swiftly and provide clients with the quality led, valuable and safe space they deserve and a place that allows them to find a more peaceful relationship with their health behaviours.

Coaches should seek to stay ahead through practice, reflection and training, and by connecting with relevant evidence-based communities of practice. Coaches should formulate their own integrated client-centred approaches that optimise successful techniques such as MI, The Trans-Theoretical Model (TTM) of health behaviour change (Prochaska, 1997), ACT and ontological coaching. These approaches will not only build the trusted and dynamic client relationships required but also enable the coach to create the unique blend needed for each client.

Healthspan – the benefits of a systemic weight management approach

By exploring the ten lenses in this model, clients will be able to identify the aspects that require the most attention to restore a more peaceful relationship with food, weight and shape, the benefits of which will have a positive impact on their sense of wellness by reducing stress, improving body image and self-esteem, and reducing the risk of developing an eating disorder. In a relatively short period of time, improved nutritional status may improve sleep, raise energy levels and stabilise mood.

Introducing the concept of a healthspan not only encourages long-term thinking; it also brings into focus the degree of satisfaction and fulfilment a person may be experiencing in key health areas where weight management is causing distress. It is likely to be welcomed and come as something of a relief to know that losing weight and keeping it off has less to do with genetics and more to do with building self-esteem and self-efficacy, and by embedding and then maintaining healthy behaviour in an obesogenic environment.

A guided conversation of this nature will begin to deepen a client's understanding of what is important as they begin to realise that the aim is not only the weight they lose; it is the life they gain in return. Coaching could be conducted with the client on a one-to-one basis, in a group setting or as part as a wider client support system.

Setting goals

Setting a specific weight loss target is not recommended in weight management coaching because this can lead to disappointment when less weight is lost than had been hoped for. Instead, it is recommended that a partnership of equals is created where the coaching relationship guides learning and discovery and provides the prioritisation of the client's healthspan focus.

If appropriate, weighing in at intervals is recommended providing that weighing scales do not present an issue. For some this can be problematic where persistent weighing and weight sabotage behaviours may adversely interfere with the client's weight management journey.

Coaches should be sensitive to the limiting belief that weight loss is not rapid enough and progress is slow or perhaps there is a sense of not feeling slimmer despite losing weight or feel overwhelmed by the process. It is recommended that contracting sets realistic expectations that incorporates lifestyle, environmental and behavioural elements, together with any barriers which may disrupt or impede the client's progress.

Nutrition and health status

Coaches should begin by establishing how motivated the client is to improve the quality of their diet and health. Techniques proven to increase intrinsic motivation include MI,

ACT and ontological approaches. In parallel, it is vital that coaches encourage their clients to understand why it is important to improve their gut health and mood by using a variety of methods that challenge their attitude and beliefs. Open-mindedness, a willingness to learn and experiment with a wider variety of foods will help the client to become more confident in increasing their nutritional profile and health status.

It is important for coaches to know that eating a better balance of healthy fats, protein, carbohydrate and fibre is a crucial part and long-term aim of a client's weight management programme. It is important to highlight the critical role that healthy fats play in helping the body to protect vital organs, transport nutrients and in the control of blood pressure, blood sugar and cholesterol.

Simple meal planning should be encouraged and food label understanding highlighted when shopping because this will help clients to improve the quality of food bought into the home. Calorie counting should be discouraged because not all calories are equal, notably energy-dense nutrient-poor foods, i.e., those foods high in fat, salt and sugar (HFSS). An improved diet is likely to improve mood – the effects of increased levels of serotonin and endorphins – reduce lethargy and cravings which are both associated with poor blood sugar control and a potential contributory factor in mood swings.

Obesogenic values require exploration and appropriate challenge. For example becoming wise to food industry marketing ploys and 'healthy eating' claims. Education plays a vital role in this from the outset. Stimulus control measures will be easier to manage if clients are able to switch to healthier snack alternatives, particularly if there are children in the home. This will not only help clients, but it may also have a positive effect on their family's health at the same time.

Hunger and satiety ratings can be used to raise appetite sensitivity awareness and hunger cues. This will help clients distinguish between real hunger and other hungers (i.e., worry, boredom, stress). Self-care and gratitude work will help to self-soothe in ways other than through food.

Other eating strategies include adopting healthy mealtime rituals by eating together as a family and at a table, without distraction and strengthening assertion skills when others (usually a spouse or close family and friends) may try to hamper efforts.

Learning the skills of portion control can be accomplished by downsizing plates and bowls, being mindful of up-sizing tactics in supermarkets, using back of pack labelling for portion guidance as well as taking time to present meals, clearing away and eating slowly to savour food and feel nourished.

Behavioural (self-regulation and skills acquisition)

Clients that build the vital skills of self-awareness, problem-solving, planning and flexibility are more likely to manage eating setbacks effectively. The National Weight loss Control Registry (NWCR), a longstanding study in the US whose 10,000 members have successfully lost and maintained at least a 30lb loss for more than a year, finds that food tracking and weight monitoring, eating breakfast, meal frequency, diet quality, daily exercise are important weight management and maintenance skills.

The completion of a food diary for at least a consecutive seven-day period, eating with regularity throughout the day, starting with breakfast is a proven behavioural strategy for weight loss and weight maintenance. This may help clients to overcome nibbling, grazing where eating events have no beginning or end and where restraint behaviours earlier in the day may lead to food immoderation later on. Lunch and dinner are recommended with a smaller snack in between each meal. In addition to monitoring dietary patterns, it can be useful to capture notes about eating guilt, distress, food triggers as well as binge or craving episode and explored in session.

Rating hunger levels using a simple 0–10 scale should be recorded on the food diary so that clients do not allow themselves to become too hungry whilst offering a useful method to recognise appetitive cues and the urge to eat when not hungry. The food diary is a useful monitoring and feedback tool which will include learning about lapse management a common feature in weight management work. Lapses (or eating setbacks) should be re-framed as learning events and marked on the diary and viewed as opportunities to problem-solve and learn new skills.

Lapse management is a critical part of weight loss, weight management and maintenance. AVE is well referenced in the literature and describes the process of lapse, relapse and collapse in addiction therapies, including weight loss and eating disorder (ED) work. It is important that clients understand AVE – and the degrees of escalation – although coaches may prefer to use term eating setback. A lapse can be described as a one-off event where something unplanned happens, like eating a trigger food, or breaching a dietary rule, which then may trigger the dichotomous mindset of "I've blown it', I may as well eat the lot" or an undesired amount of food. In turn this response may diminish feelings of worthiness and increase feelings of guilt or disappointment (Marlatt, 1985).

Environment and lifestyle

The key elements that guide client understanding of this topic is the creation of a unique system of support and a renewed awareness of their wider environment including, their relationships, their home, place, or places of work and environments that challenge health behaviour (supermarkets, coffee shops, garages, restaurants and so on). This is important because an abundance of food in developed countries like the UK means that those who find it difficult to control their weight are also likely to struggle with poor dietary habits and weight gain. Epidemiologists argue in their research that food is the primary agent, particularly through the increased consumption of energy-dense, nutrient-poor (high fat, sugar, salt) foods.

Encouraging your client to use a diverse variety of tools and techniques to support them is key, if applicable, suggesting the introduction of digital health monitoring tools such as wearables may increase a client's awareness of the impact of diet, rest and exercise on their health. Digital tools will also help to educate clients on their ability to cope and their energy levels. As clients start to increase their self-efficacy, digital health tools will support them to notice their successes, limitations and triggers, e.g., their critical strategies needed to embed long-term behaviours for managing weight successfully even in the face of ambivalence.

Biology, mood and mindset

Creating a health manifesto will help to build assertion and communication skills so that clients protect their weight management efforts and feel more equipped to not bow to the pressure or persuasion of others.

For most people, losing weight is not easy and so those who appear 'normal' in terms of body size are almost certainly adopting a number of personal weight management strategies to achieve this. Part of the reason for this difficulty is the hedonic brain which releases dopamine, a neurotransmitter associated with pleasure and reward which then makes it difficult 'to stick' to a healthy diet because the brain's drive to seek out the foods that activate the reward system will overcome authentic food needs which can lead to overeating and weight gain.

Strategies that address the pleasure and reward response, include stimulus control measures to limit the amount of ultra processed foods kept at home by switching to healthier options. This will improve the client's sensitivity to sugar and their food palette as they begin to strike a better balance between authentic food needs and hedonic wants.

Dieting has a short-term effect on metabolism and is now known to be responsible for eating disordered behaviour, food cravings with binge eating, eating disinhibition (eating in response to non-appetitive cues) and dysregulation (losing touch with hunger and satiation). Few people realise that by the end of a weight loss programme, fewer calories are needed to maintain body weight.

Dichotomous thinking is often a feature of diet mentality, accompanied by throwaway remarks like having 'good and bad days', and by eliminating or demonising certain foods. This should be actively discouraged because it may lead to restraint-binge patterns of eating which can be hard to break. Stereotype beliefs like 'healthy food is boring' fat phobia and stigma may contribute to an unhelpful food script.

Clients also need to learn to eat mindfully. This is a gradual process of change which involves dealing with judgemental thoughts about food. Building emotional literacy skills will foster understanding about food meanings and incorporating treat foods as part of a main meal so that they gradually lose power and their association with reward. Cravings can be managed by reducing anxiety through breath work and calming techniques like cognitive defusion. Emotional eating is a common side effect of dieting because it changes the neurochemical profile associated with mood and wellbeing.

Food script and lifeline

Many coaches will be familiar with lifeline work; here it is used to understand the client's personal journey with food. Working with 5-year intervals to illicit earliest memories, schooling and forming social bonds, mealtimes growing up, parental influences and attitudes about diet, cooking and eating. What do they notice about their weight and dietary pattern over time? What have been the weight management strategies that have succeeded, and failed? Who or what are their stressors? Timeline and food script work is a valuable tool to help to overcome an obese mindset by setting some non-food goals to help improve other elements in the healthspan.

Energy balance and physical activity

MI may be a useful approach to establish what your client would be able to do if they were to become more active. This may be a case of taking ownership with small increases to activity levels on a daily basis. Activities related to hobbies can work well like gardening, walking, running and swimming. Increased activity also confers other health benefits such as improved mood, increased aerobic capacity, reduced resting heart rate, blood pressure, and insulin sensitivity.

Related to this idea is set point theory which argues that when someone attempts to diet the body's natural response is to slow down metabolism to conserve energy, reduce fullness signals, and increase the drive to eat in order to resist weight loss and return to the set point range (thought to be between 5–20 lbs). The hypothalamus is the primary brain region responsible for regulating appetite, satiety, and metabolism, crucial components of this theory. A variety of hormones, including leptin (fullness and satiety), ghrelin (the hunger hormone), insulin, and others, provide feedback to the hypothalamus about the body's energy needs. This response is quite primitive and with each attempt at weight loss the set point may actually increase as a way to protect the body in case the threat occurs again.

Increased levels of physical activity is associated with personal growth and a sense of mastery and self-worth – although most studies argue that significant weight loss cannot be achieved by exercise alone because it is not possible to exercise our way out of a poor diet.

There is no one size fits all activity programme which can predict weight loss and some clients may compensate for activity by rewarding or restricting food. Simply being aware of this can help to change this relationship.

Body image

The aim of this work may simply be to make body image matter less by diverting positive attention into other areas of the client's healthspan. This is because body image may or may not improve with weight loss efforts. Internalisation (Jung et al., 2022) of the 'slim ideal', social comparison and size estimation amongst female clients in particular may be an issue because of the tendency for women to think they are bigger than they are.

If a client complains about feeling fat it is most likely due to the mislabelling of feelings in the body that cannot be recognised or expressed. Plutchik's emotion wheel (Karimova, 2017) is a useful tool to share with clients to help clients learn to identify and welcome any and all feelings, including 'dangerous' ones like anger and disgust; gentle exploration will help to diminish their power. An increase in emotional vocabulary will enable a client to connect with their body in a more positive way.

Questions that support clients to recognise unhelpful thinking styles about their appearance by challenging core beliefs and assumptions – e.g., Where in the body do you feel fat? Is this all the time? Is it certain clothing? Is it a certain body part you dislike? Or, who makes you feel fat? What might calm you when you feel upset about your weight? Compassion focussed approaches including daily gratitude work and acknowledging what our bodies do for us can to build confidence and self-esteem.

Mirror work may also help. A positive daily self-care routine, a little personal grooming, wearing clothes that someone feels good in clothes, a little makeup, perfume or aftershave can all make the world of difference. Research (Alleva & Martijn, 2019) suggests that encouraging clients to think about what their body does for them rather than how it looks may open up a conversation to foster kinder thoughts.

Coaches should aim to keep up to date by aligning themselves with reputable organisations and evidence-based and relevant communities of practice. Coaching supervision and peer support is highly recommended. Four leading organisations that can support coaches and clients with EDs are: The National Centre for Eating Disorders (UK), Beat Eating Disorders UK, ARFID Awareness UK and NHS Eating Disorders.

ARFID Awareness UK
National Centre for Eating Disorder Help | Treatment and Training (eating-disorders. org.uk)
Overview – Eating disorders – NHS (www.nhs.uk)
The UK's Eating Disorder Charity – Beat (beateatingdisorders.org.uk)

Weight loss drugs and surgery

Unless qualified it will be inappropriate to make recommendations about drugs or surgery. However, it is appropriate to advise that as it stands there is no one drug that is totally effective for weight loss. Side effects may cause raised blood pressure, nausea, restlessness, lethargy, insomnia, and weight plateau/gain when treatment stops.

Some drugs may suppress appetite, reducing hunger and increasing feelings of fullness and prevent the absorption of dietary fat, where undigested fat passes through faeces. SSRIs (selective serotonin reuptake inhibitors) are a class of antidepressant medication that works by increasing the amount of serotonin, a neurotransmitter in the brain that is associated with mood regulation and feelings of wellbeing like Prozac and Fluoxetine. They are sometimes prescribed for providing short-term relief from bingeing, cravings and appetite suppression.

Semaglutides, Ozempic and Wegovy, available on the NHS from September 2023 may also be prescribed alongside lifestyle advice to treat type 2 diabetes and managing overweight and obesity respectively. Treatment eligibility is assessed as part of a specialist weight management service.

Weight loss surgery, also known as bariatric surgery, is usually considered a last resort for people who have tried and failed to lose weight through diet and exercise. Gastric bypass surgery is considered the gold standard in bariatric surgery. It has been performed for over 50 years with a long track record of success in helping patients achieve significant and sustainable weight loss, as well as improvements in obesity-related health conditions such as type 2 diabetes, high blood pressure, and sleep apnoea.

It is typically performed as a keyhole surgery and considered advantageous with fewer complications and faster recovery time than open surgeries. Appetite is also curbed because of the changed gut hormone profile post-surgery. Patients can also lose up to 75% of their excess weight in the first 5 years. The downsides are the procedure is irreversible and that stomach stretch and excess drinking can lead to weight gain. Leakage from sleeve stapling can also be serious and loose skin may also cause body image distress.

These surgeries are typically reserved for individuals who have a BMI of 40 or higher, or a BMI of 35 or higher with obesity-related health problems such as diabetes or high blood pressure.

Conclusion

Weight management is a growing strand of coaching that offers coaches an opportunity to support clients to increase their health and contribute to a global and societal issue that urgently needs addressing. Coaches who build a client-centred and integrated coaching practice will not only reap the rewards of being able to optimise the medium of coaching to change lives, but also play a valuable role in joining the dots of fragmented systems and by empowering clients to embed healthier weight management behaviours.

Reflective questions

1. What does a healthy, balanced lifestyle mean to you (or your client)?
2. How do you (or your client) see yourself in relation to your body and weight?
3. What kind of relationship do you (or your client) have with your health behaviour?

References

Alleva, J. M., Martijn, C. (2019). Body functionality. In T. L. Tylka & N. Piran (Eds.), Handbook of positive body image and embodiment: Constructs, protective factors, and interventions (pp. 33–41). Oxford University Press.

Anderson J. W., Konz E. C., Frederich R. C., Wood C. L. (2001). Long-term weight-loss maintenance: A meta-analysis of US studies. The American Journal of Clinical Nutrition, 74, 579–584.

Barnes, R. D., Ivezaj, V. (2015). Motivational interviewing, weight loss and primary care. Obesity Reviews, 16, 304–318.

Bouchard, C., Tremblay, A., Després, J. P., Nadeau, A., Lupien, P. J., Moorjani, S., et al. (1996, August). Overfeeding in identical twins: 5-year post overfeeding results. Metabolism, 45(8), 1042–1050.

Bray, G. A., Kim, K. K., Wilding, J. P. H., World Obesity Federation. (2017, July). Obesity: A chronic relapsing progressive disease process: A position statement of the world obesity federation. Obesity Reviews, 18(7), 715–723.

Bray, G. A., Ryan, D. H. (2021). Evidence-based weight management interventions: Individualized treatment options to maximize patient outcomes'. Diabetes, Obesity & Metabolism, 23(1), 50–62.

Budden, K. F., Gellatly, S. L., Wood, D. L., Cooper, M. A., Morrison, M., Hugenholtz, P., Hansbro, P. M. (2017 Jan). Emerging pathogenic links between microbiota and the gut-lung axis. Nat Rev Microbiol, 15(1), 55–63. doi: 10.1038/nrmicro.2016.142. Epub 2016 Oct 3. PMID: 27694885.

Collins, S., Witkiewitz, K. (2013). Abstinence violation effect. Encyclopaedia of Behavioral Medicine, 8–9.

Curry, S., Marlatt, G. A., & Gordon, J. R. (1987). Abstinence violation effect: Validation of an attributional construct with smoking cessation. Journal of Consulting and Clinical Psychology, 55, 145–149.

Dick, K. J., Nelson, C. P., Tsaprouni, L, Sandling, J. K., Aïssi, D, Wahl, S., et al. (2014). DNA methylation and body-mass index: A genome-wide analysis. The Lancet, 383(9933), 1990–1998.

Dubé J. J., Coen, P. M., DiStefano, G, Chacon, A. C., Helbling, N. L., Desimone M. E., et al. (2014). Effects of acute lipid overload on skeletal muscle insulin resistance, metabolic flexibility, and mitochondrial performance. American Journal of Physiology – Endocrinology and Metabolism, 307(12), E1117–E1124.

Goodpaster, B. H., Kelley, D. E. (2002). Skeletal muscle triglyceride: Marker or mediator of obesity-induced insulin resistance in type 2 diabetes mellitus? Current Diabetes Reports, 2(3), 216–222, 10.

Hinchliffe, N., Capehorn, M. S., Bewick, M., Feenie, J. (2022, October). The potential role of digital health in obesity care. Advances in Therapy, 39(10), 4397–4412.

Hood, D. A., Irrcher, I., Ljubicic, V., & Joseph, A.-M. (2006). Coordination of metabolic plasticity in skeletal muscle. Journal of Experimental Biology, 209(12), 2265–2275.

Institute for Health Metrics and Evaluation. (2020a). Global burden of 87 risk factors in 204 countries and territories, 1990–2019: A systematic analysis for the global burden of disease study 2019. Lancet, 396(10258), 1129–1306.

72 The Health and Wellbeing Coaches' Handbook

Institute for Health Metrics and Evaluation. (2020b). Measuring universal health coverage based on an index of effective coverage of health services in 204 countries and territories, 1990–2019: A systematic analysis for the global burden of disease study 2019. Lancet, 396(10258), 1250–1284.

Jacka, F. (2019). Brain changer: How diet can save your mental health – cutting-edge science from an expert (pp. 3–19). Macmillan by Pan Macmillan Austria Pty Ltd.

Jacka, F. N. (2015). Lifestyle factors in preventing mental health disorders: An interview with Felice Jacka. BMC Medicine, 13, 264.

Jacka, F. N., O'Neil, A., Opie, R., et al. (2015). A randomised controlled trial of dietary improvement for adults with major depression (the 'SMILES' trial). BMC Medicine, 15, 23(2017).

Jung, J., Barron, D., Lee Y. A., Swami, V. (2022). Social media usage and body image: Examining the mediating roles of internalization of appearance ideals and social comparisons in young women. Computers in Human Behavior, 135, 2022.

Karimova, H. (2017, December 24). The emotion wheel: What it is and how to use it (Plutchik's emotion wheel). Positive Psychology.

Kent, J. A., Hayes, K. L. (2021, August). Exercise physiology from 1980 to 2020: Application of the natural sciences. Kinesiology Review (Champaign), 10(3), 238–247.

Kennedy G. C. (1953). The role of depot fat in the hypothalamic control of food intake in the rat. Proc. R. Soc. B 140, 578–592 [DOI] [PubMed] [Google Scholar].

Kupila, S. K. E., Venäläinen, M. S., Suojanen, L., Rosengård-Bärlund, M., Ahola, A. J., Elo, L. L., Pietiläinen, K. H. (2022). Weight loss trajectories in healthy weight coaching: Cohort study. The Journal of Medical Internet Research: Formative Research, 6(3), e26374.

Leibel, R. L., Hirsch, J. (1984). Diminished energy requirements in reduced obese patients. Metabolism, 33, 164–170.

Leibel, R. L., Rosenbaum, M., Hirsch, J. (1995). Changes in energy expenditure resulting from altered body weight. New England Journal of Medicine,332, 621–628.

Madigan, C. D., Graham, H. E., Sturgiss, E., Kettle, V. E., Gokal, K., Biddle, G., et al. (2022). Effectiveness of weight management interventions for adults delivered in primary care: Systematic review and meta-analysis of randomised controlled trials. British Medical Journal.

Marlatt, G. A., Gordon, J. R. (1985). Relapse prevention: Maintenance strategies in the treatment of addictive behaviors. New York: The Guilford Press.

McKee, H., Ntoumanis, N., Smith, B. (2013). Weight maintenance: Self-regulatory factors underpinning success and failure. Psychological Health, 28, 1207–1223.

Meex, R. C. R., Schrauwen-Hinderling, V. B., Moonen-Kornips, E., Schaart, G., Mensink, M., Phielix, E, Hesselink, M. K. C. (2010). Restoration of muscle mitochondrial function and metabolic flexibility in type 2 diabetes by exercise training is paralleled by increased myocellular fat storage and improved insulin sensitivity. Diabetes, 59(3), 572–579.

Merrill, R. M., Aldana, S. G., Bowden, D. E. (2010). Employee weight management through health coaching. Eating and Weight Disorders, 15(1–2), e52–e59.

Metcalfe, S., Sasse, T. (2023). Tackling obesity: Improving policy making on food and health. Institute for Government.

Newnham-Kanas, C., Morrow, D., Irwin, J. D. (2011). Participants' perceived utility of motivational interviewing using co-active life coaching skills on their struggle with obesity. Coaching: An International Journal of Theory, Research and Practice, 4(2), 104–122.

Passmore, J. (2020). The coaches' handbook: The complete practitioner guide for professional coaches. Routledge.

Patel, M. L., Wakayama, L. N., Bass, M. B., Breland, J. Y. (2019). Motivational interviewing in eHealth and telehealth interventions for weight loss: A systematic review. Preventative Medicine, 126, 105738.

Phelan, S., Halfman, T., Pinto, A. M., Foster, G. D. (2020). Behavioral and psychological strategies of long-term weight management maintainers in a widely available weight management program. Obesity, 28, 421–428.

Prochaska, J. O., Velicer, W. F. (1997, September–October). The transtheoretical model of health behavior change. American Journal of Health Promotion, 12(1), 38–48.

Sieczkowska, S. M., de Lima, A. P., Swinton, P. A., Dolan, E., Roschel, H., Gualano, B. (2021). Health coaching strategies for weight loss: A systematic review and meta-analysis. Advances in Nutrition, 12(4), 1449–1460.

Speakman, J. R., Levitsky, D. A., Allison, D. B., Bray, M. S., de Castro, J. M., Clegg, D. J., et al. (2011, November). Set points, settling points and some alternative models: Theoretical options to understand how genes and environments combine to regulate body adiposity. Disease Models & Mechanisms, 4(6), 733–745.

Spector, T. (2015). The Diet Myth | W&N – Ground-breaking, award-winning, thought-provoking books since 1949.

Spector, T. (2022). Food for life. Penguin Random House.

Stephenson, E. J., Hawley, J. A. (2014). Mitochondrial function in metabolic health: A genetic and environmental tug of war. Biochimica et Biophysica Acta (BBA) – General Subjects, 1840(4), 1285–1294. https://doi.org/10.1016/j.bbagen.2013.12.004

Wise, J. (2022). Eating disorders: Guidance is issued to doctors after 84% rise in past five years. British Medical Journal, 2022, 377.

World Health Organization: World Obesity Federation. (2018). Taking action on childhood obesity. DOI:9789289057738-eng.pdf

World Health Organization (WHO). (2022a). Global health observatory. Premature NCD deaths (under age 70), data by country.

World Health Organization (WHO). (2022b). Global health observatory. NCD-related tests and procedures in primary health care, response by country.

World Health Organization (WHO). (2022c). Global health observatory. Policies, strategies and action plans, data by country.

World Obesity Federation. (2021). Obesity is a disease. One billion people globally estimated to be living with obesity by 2030 | World Obesity Federation.

Useful organisations

https://eating-disorders.org.uk/
https://slam.nhs.uk/eating-disorders-condition, https://www.arfidawarenessuk.org/
https://www.beateatingdisorders.org.uk/

Chapter 6

The importance of meaning and purpose in coaching for health and wellbeing

Christian van Nieuwerburgh and Trudy Meehan

Introduction

Human beings have been asking and answering questions about meaning and purpose throughout their history. The field of positive psychology has highlighted that these questions are central to our concept of wellbeing. In this chapter, we will consider specific approaches to coaching that may be particularly suited to the context of health and wellbeing. We start with a review of narrative approaches and then present practical ideas about integrating these into coaching conversations about health and wellbeing. We then propose a conversational framework that draws attention to questions about meaning and purpose. It is our contention that raising awareness of meaning and purpose can lead to more empowering and helpful conversations about health and wellbeing.

When considering meaning and purpose, it is helpful to divide the concept of 'meaning in life' into three dimensions: coherence, purpose and significance (Martela & Steger, 2016). Steger explains them in this way: coherence "is about how people make sense of their lives and come to understand the degree to which life is consistent and predictable"; purpose "is about the kinds of aspirations and dreams people want to achieve in their lives"; and significance "is about the strength of our beliefs that our own life has inherent value" (Steger, 2022, p. 119). Each dimension has an important part to play in our assessment of the meaningfulness of our lives.

Meaning- and purpose-based interventions

Increasingly, meaning- and purpose-based interventions are being deployed in health settings. For example, Meaning-Centred Group Psychotherapy (MCGP) has been used with patients to support them to find a sense of meaning as they live with cancer (Breitbart et al., 2004). In another case, an individualised therapeutic approach called a Meaning-Making Intervention (MMI) (Henry et al., 2010) supported people with the search for meaning following cancer diagnosis. Such interventions are designed to support people with the search for meaning and purpose. At the same time, it is suggested that people with higher purpose in life are more likely to have better health behaviours, such as engaging with preventive healthcare services (Kim et al., 2014). The studies presented here highlight the potential of positive conversations about meaning and purpose in the context of health and wellbeing.

Coaching has become a preferred methodology for supporting desired behavioural change over the last few decades (Passmore, 2021; Wang et al., 2022). According to one

DOI: 10.4324/9781003319016-8

of the field's leading pioneers, Sir John Whitmore, coaching is an intervention that is designed to "maximise a person's performance" by adopting a facilitative approach that raises awareness and a sense of personal responsibility (1992, p. 5). It is essentially a conversational intervention that supports people to set objectives and then make incremental behavioural changes towards those goals (Grant, 2012). While definitions of coaching abound, there is broad agreement that it "is a managed conversation that takes place between two people"; "aims to support sustainable change to behaviours or ways of thinking"; and "focuses on learning and development" (van Nieuwerburgh, 2020, p. 6). The academic literature indicates that coaching is 'working' in the sense that it has been shown to support people to implement desired changes (Theeboom et al., 2014). Coaching is used in a broad range of contexts, including financial services, professional services, governmental institutions, education and healthcare (van Nieuwerburgh, 2016).

Theory and research

Seligman (2011) defines "meaning" in positive psychology as "belonging to and serving something that you believe is bigger than the self" (p. 17). It is one of the core features of Seligman's PERMA model of wellbeing. However, unlike positive emotion, engagement, relationships, and accomplishment, it is often pursued for its own sake, not just to feel good or happy. Seligman emphasises that meaning often comes at a cost to personal hedonic wellbeing. Importantly, meaning is defined and measured independently of the other factors in the PERMA model. It is subjectively defined by oneself and others depending on the culture and the prevailing values and what counts as impactful in each situation or society. Wong (2014) has criticised Seligman's incorporation of meaning into the PERMA model of wellbeing, arguing that the pursuit of happiness directly conflicts with self-transcendence. However, it is evident in Seligman's work that he sees personal hedonic happiness as just one piece of the wellbeing puzzle. Seligman is clear that one needs both hedonic and eudemonic happiness for us individually but, most importantly, if we are to thrive as a society and culture (Seligman, 2011).

   Whilst the exact biological and neurological mechanisms of meaning are not yet fully understood, research has shown the importance of meaning for physical and psychological wellbeing. Research has shown meaning to be important in the following areas.

- Life satisfaction and positive affect (Chamberlain & Zika, 1988; King et al., 2006; Ryff, 1989; Zika & Chamberlain, 1992).
- Wellbeing and mental health (Debats, 1998; Mascaro & Rosen, 2006, 2008; Steger, 2012; Steger et al., 2006).
- Stress reduction, through functional attributions (Seligman, 1990; Weiner, 1985; Wong & Weiner, 1981).
- Post-traumatic growth (Janoff-Bulman, 2004; Steger et al., 2008).
- Better cognitive health, through reduced risk of cognitive impairment (Boyle et al., 2010; Boyle et al., 2012).
- Better physical health, through reduced risk of cardiovascular disease and stroke (Cohen et al., 2016; Kim et al., 2013).
- Improved resilience, through mediating reactions to negative stimuli, allowing for faster emotional recovery (Schaefer et al., 2013).

Carol Ryff's work on wellbeing (2014) has demonstrated the absolute necessity and value of meaning for achieving eudemonic wellbeing. According to her, purpose, meaning and intention are required for physical and psychological wellbeing. Ryff's work highlights the connection between developing a rich sense of personal meaning and engaging in health-promoting behaviours. Essentially, talking about meaning and purpose seems to strengthen intentions around health and wellbeing. From a narrative therapeutic point of view, this means that we are scaffolding agency for our clients. Agency is a key factor in determining to what extent we can be optimistic in our imaginations of the future and progress (Seligman, 2021). From a health coaching perspective, it is interesting to note that Kim and colleagues (2014) have shown that people with a higher purpose in life are more likely to have better health behaviours, such as engaging with preventive healthcare services. Their work highlights the importance of having conversations about meaning, purpose and intention before inviting clients to consider specific health and wellbeing-promoting behaviours.

The concept of meaning remains contested across different schools of psychology, philosophy and theology. The positive psychology view articulated previously is predominantly a cognitive behavioural understanding of meaning. Meaning is conceptualised as originating within an individual, evidenced in their actions and thoughts. However, this is just one perspective. We can also examine meaning from an existential standpoint (Frankl, 1985), a constructivist approach (Raskin et al., 2010) and also a social constructionist perspective (Gergen, 2010; White & Epston, 1990). In what follows, we will consider meaning from a social constructionist perspective, specifically the work of narrative therapists Michael White and David Epston. We bring the more individualistic focus of positive psychology together with the social constructionist narrative view of meaning, not to be contrary, but because we believe that together, they are more informative and helpful in health coaching. This integration of competing approaches to meaning is called for by Wong (2014), one of the leading experts in meaning. He reflects on the failure of global summits on meaning, stating, "we have not had much success in integrating different schools of thought, but that does not mean we should not continue the effort" (p. 20). Similarly, in health psychology, Cornish and Gillespie (2009) call for a pragmatic approach to help us avoid unnecessary theoretical silos and endless debate, with few practical recommendations for action.

Within the framework of narrative therapy, there is a preference for models of understanding human experience – what White and Epston (1990) call "analogies" (p. 6) that are socially constructionist, not based on an external objective reality. This approach argues that our experiences are a combination of the analogies we use to make sense of the world, our lived experience and the cultural context that we are living. They draw on the work of Gregory Bateson (systems theorist), Clifford Geertz (anthropologist) and Edward Bruner (educational psychologist), pulling these ideas together through the writing of post-structural philosopher Michel Foucault. The essence of this approach is the understanding that people need to 'story their experiences' to make meaning of them. These stories are shaped across time and include a sense of the past and the future self. Significantly, stories are limited in that they can be multiple and fragmented and do not totally capture our experience. Hence, in narrative therapy, there are always at least two possible stories, the problem-saturated/dominant story and the preferred/alternative story. Human beings are constituted by stories and use stories to construct themselves socially in relation to others. Stories support agency and develop meaning and coherence (Meehan & Guilfoyle, 2015). Within narrative therapy, this assumption is built on complex theoretical approaches that are outside the scope of this chapter. White and Epston's (1990) first chapter on story, knowledge and power is still one of the most comprehensive introductions to these theories and is worth reading for anyone who would like to engage with the conceptual base for narrative therapeutic work. The view of agency in narrative therapy is linked to intentional states and actions driven by socially constituted meaning and values rather than an internal cognitive state or personality trait (White, 2007). Meaning is viewed as actively storied and negotiated within a person's socio-relational context. Meaning is an active and hence agentive event. When we practise agency, we live "according to intentions that they embrace in the pursuit of what they give value to in life" (White, 2007, p. 101).

Etchison and Kleist (2000) set out to review studies using narrative therapy but struggled to find sufficient research studies. Neimeyer (1993) argues that constructionism and narrative therapy are relatively recent, and the paradigms they use often conflict with mainstream positivist research paradigms, further complicating the availability of outcome studies. Perhaps the best body of research we have available currently is the work of Miguel Gonçalves, who has designed a standardised coding manual to analyse narrative therapeutic conversations. Gonçalves' work has demonstrated a directional causal relationship between more moments he describes as 'innovative moments' in the therapeutic dialogue and better client outcomes. He describes five types of innovative moments. The two most relevant to the concept of meaning are "re-conceptualisation innovative moments" and "new experience innovative moments" (Matos et al., 2009, p. 69). Both moments in the therapeutic conversation provide space for the client to reflect on and generate new meanings or, as Gonçalves and colleagues (2016) describe them, "narrative markers of meaning transformation" (p. 425). For Gonçalves and colleagues, these shifts in meaning facilitate "the emergence of a meta-level perspective about the change process itself and, in turn, enables the active positioning of the person as an author of the new narrative" (Gonçalves et al., 2009, p. 1).

Narrative approaches to meaning have moved beyond the psychotherapeutic space and have started to be incorporated into medical training and practice. Narrative medicine draws on the social constructionist and relational theories of meaning. Launer and Wohlmann (2023) give a good overview of these theories in narrative medicine. They conclude their review with the hope that narrative approaches can help us explore possibilities for co-creating meaning in medicine. Like evidence for narrative therapeutic approaches, the consensus is that we need more rigorous studies before conclusions can be drawn about the value of narrative medicine (Laskow et al., 2019). However, there are promising studies in niche areas such as genetics where the value of narrative and supporting the client/patient in co-constructing meaning are shown to be valuable. Nowaczyk (2012) reports on Frank's (2010) description of a narrative type he calls the "illness as normality narrative". The plot for this story

> involves minimising the effects of illness, living in spite of the illness. As geneticists we are most familiar with this narrative where our patients become experts at living with illness, either their own, or their child's. We witness stories of life around the illness and not of illness defining the life of patients.
>
> (Nowaczyk, 2012, p. 1946)

In summary, meaning is theorised to be essential to achieving eudemonic happiness, a sense of happiness that transcends our immediate hedonic sense of what feels good in the moment in favour of what is good in the long run. Research in the positive health field has started to link meaning to positive outcomes for wellbeing, resilience, heart, and cognitive health. In narrative approaches to meaning, people are documented using it to develop and support agency, such as situations when one experiences a life-defining illness or significant mental health issue such as depression.

Practice

As described in this chapter, meaning is helpful in supporting agency and allowing one to develop preferred stories and trajectories for one's life. It is helpful in scaffolding a view of what is good in the long run over the hedonic pull of what feels good right now. Supporting agency, committing to preferred stories and focusing on living well can be used in coaching conversations about engaging in health promoting behaviours. Coaches can add value by finding opportunities to talk about meaning and purpose in conversations about health and wellbeing. Essentially, increasing a sense of meaning and purpose is likely to strengthen agency around health and wellbeing.

Focusing on intention

In addition to supporting clients to re-author their own stories, coaches can also support health and wellbeing by focusing on "intention" rather than specific goals. The simple act of exploring a client's intention can lead to conversations about meaning and purpose. An approach called Coaching for Alignment, which is based on the Ershad Coaching Framework (van Nieuwerburgh & Allaho, 2018) sets out a framework that is designed to support clients to clarify their intentions and then align these with their values, behaviours and practices. This coaching framework is a useful way of supporting meaningful conversations about health and wellbeing.

In Coaching for Alignment, it is the role of the coach to facilitate the conversation in a way that encourages agency and self-belief. As with most facilitative forms of coaching, coaches should adopt a "way of being" that is characterised by patience, humility and humanity. In other words, the coach allows their clients ample space and time for quiet reflection, creating a safe environment for them to do their best thinking. The humility aspect relates to the coach adopting the stance of curiosity about what will work best for their clients. It is a non-directive, non-prescriptive stance that prioritises agency by supporting clients to find their own reasons for changing. Once these reasons are clear, clients are supported to develop their own strategies for bringing about the desired change. The 'humanity' of coaches refers to the need for them to bring a high level of compassion to coaching conversations. Conversations about health and wellbeing can sometimes be difficult; people's circumstances can be incredibly challenging; clients can blame themselves for being unable to make progress. In all these situations, a compassionate and kind response from the coach is needed.

As a coaching framework, the Coaching for Alignment model is slightly unusual for a number of reasons. First, it starts by acknowledging where the client is at the moment rather than moving straight into discussions about a desired future. This opportunity for acknowledgement is an important starting point and foundation for meaningful conversations. Second, rather than ignoring the past, the framework invites exploration and celebration of the client's history and heritage. Third, uniquely for a coaching framework, it does not involve explicit goal-setting. Fourth, the framework considers discussions about the alignment of the client as integral to the conversation.

The conversational process starts with the discovery phase. The term 'discovery' is borrowed from the field of Appreciative Inquiry (Cooperrider & Srivastva, 1987). This phase provides an opportunity for the client to tell the coach about who they are. Clients are invited to talk about their history to date, focusing on strengths, achievements and successes. The coach may also share a little bit about their own background. This is so as to build the foundation for a strong coaching relationship. It is also helpful for the coach to understand the self-image or the 'story' of the client to date. As with all forms of facilitative coaching, the primary role of the coach in this phase is to listen and appreciate, occasionally summarising or paraphrasing. When used in health and wellbeing contexts, this phase should include a review of the client's health and wellbeing history. The coach should also ask about their client's attitude to health and wellbeing.

Once there is greater clarity about the client's story and what is happening at the moment, the next phase is the intention phase. This *is* an opportunity to talk about the future, but the focus of the conversation is to determine the positive intention of the client – not particular goals or outcomes. Instead of talking about achieving a certain health-related goal, the client is asked to identify a positive intention they have in relation to the future. For example, a positive intention could be to "be a better parent"; "make a bigger impact in the world" or "be an inspiration to others". Sometimes the coach will have to persist in asking the question "What is the positive intention behind that?" numerous times if clients continue to identify specific outcomes. The reason that it is helpful to identify positive intentions is that these are usually closely connected to people's values. There is often great synergy between a person's positive intentions and their sense of what is meaningful. By identifying this at this point in the coaching framework, the coach and the client are able to harness a source of energy and motivation that will support clients to move forwards positively.

With a good understanding of the client and clarity about a broad-ranging positive intention, the next phase supports the client to identify a number of pathways that would allow them to move closer to their positive intention. The concept of pathways is derived from Hope Theory. Snyder's Cognitive Model of Hope incorporates three core concepts: goals, pathways and agency (Snyder, 1995). Pathways are understood as the different ways that a person can move towards desired outcomes. Agency relates more to the perceived ability (on the part of a client) to be able to make progress towards desired outcomes. This coaching framework supports both of these aspects by supporting the client to generate pathways and encouraging agency in the client through the non-directive, non-prescriptive and facilitative stance of the coach. In this phase, the coach works with the client to come up with various ideas that would move the client towards what they would like to be doing or thinking. To encourage creativity and lateral thinking, the coach would remind the client that the next phase of the conversation will allow them to assess and evaluate the pathways. It is helpful for the client to generate between four and six possible pathways. These should be captured, preferably by the client, so that they can be reviewed in the next phase.

At this point, the coach and client move into the Alignment Wheel, which is at the centre of the conversational framework. This wheel is an integral part of the coaching framework because it ensures that clients have an opportunity to ensure that their chosen pathways are aligned to their own principles and values (self), important relationships and alliances in their lives (relationships) and their personal, social and professional context (environment). Once clients select some pathways that they think they would like to pursue, they would be guided through the following three questions: "How aligned is your chosen pathway with your own personal values and beliefs?"; "When you think about the important personal and professional relationships in your life, how would they be affected if you followed this pathway?"; "What is the context in which you will be pursuing this pathway?" The purpose of asking clients to address these questions is to ensure that the pathways do not go against their own principles or damage important relationships. Clients are then asked to think about how their pursuit of this pathway will be received in their social contexts and also how it will affect their environment.

Once clients have explored these questions for their preferred pathways, they should make a decision whether to proceed or not. If not, other pathways that were identified earlier in the conversation should now be considered. When a pathway has been selected, the conversation moves into the final phase: effort. In discussing effort, two aspects are addressed – what the client needs to *do* differently and how the client may need to *think* differently. The coach supports the client to identify practical, tangible ways in which they will start to make progress on their pathway. It is important to check that the proposed steps are aligned with the positive intention which was highlighted earlier in the conversation. This is the phase in which the client should make specific, tangible commitments to undertake. These will be reviewed in the next coaching conversation.

In this section, we have outlined the Coaching for Alignment process, covering the key stages in the conversational process. In what follows, we will consider how to implement the narrative approach discussed earlier and present some practical ideas for having conversations about alignment.

Using the Coaching for Alignment framework

In Table 6.1, we have provided some sample questions for each phase of the Coaching for Alignment model. They should not be taken as a guide or list of questions to ask in each stage. Coaching conversations are most effective when they are organic and the questions asked respond directly to what the client is saying.

Implementing narrative strategies

Narrative therapeutic approaches are scaffolded around developing agency through fostering and/or excavating meaning and intentions in conversations with clients. Agency can be generated through a sense of meaning and purpose. In turn, this can lead to people adopting intentional positions in relation to the problems and challenges that they face. This intentional position-taking deliberately separates the person from the problem. This is described in narrative therapy as 'externalising the problem'. For example, one would describe a client as "someone who experiences anxiety" instead of as "anxious". Externalising the problem and taking a position on the problem both increase agency. This is helpful when working with changing health behaviours or exploring a client's relationship to health and wellbeing. The conversations start by building agency and focusing on the potential of bringing about change, rather than assuming that clients are completely

Table 6.1 Questions for each stage of the Coaching for Alignment framework

Phase	
Discovery	• "Tell me a bit about yourself". • "What is important to you?" • "What is your purpose in life?" • "What is meaningful about what you do?" • "In relation to your health/wellbeing, what are you most proud of?" • "How would you describe your life so far, from a health/wellbeing perspective?" • "What is your attitude to health/wellbeing in general?" • "What is your attitude to your *own* health/wellbeing?"
Intention	• "What is your positive intention for the future?" • "What motivates you to spend time talking about your health/wellbeing?" • "What would you like in the future for yourself?" • "What would you like in the future for loved ones?" • "What would you like in the future for colleagues?"
Pathways	• "How many pathways can you see towards your intention?" • "What are the possibilities for moving towards your intention?" • "What else can you do?" • "What is calling you forward?" • "Which of these most energises you?"
Alignment wheel	• "How will your chosen pathway affect important relationships in your life?" • "How does your chosen pathway sit alongside your values and beliefs?" • "How will pursuing this pathway affect your context/environment?"
Effort	• "What will you need to do to make progress?" • "How might you need to think differently if you are to make progress?" • "How will you manifest your positive intention in your context?" • "When you consider the original positive intention, will these ideas support you to bring that intention into fruition?"

at the mercy of circumstances that affect their health and wellbeing. By taking a position on the problem, clients are forced to describe alternative positions. These new positions become starting points for authorship/agency in alternative, more empowering stories (Nowaczyk, 2012).

Coaches can harness their clients' story-telling abilities to support them to 're-author' the stories that they tell about their lives. The most empowering stories reveal agency and present narratives that may not be predicted by the circumstances that clients may be facing. People are always capable of resisting particular discourses and associated personal stories. Through the process of 're-authoring', it is possible for people to surpass the limitations that their own stories impose on them, ultimately relocating themselves with respect to existing power/knowledge formations. "These resistances, and displays of being 'more than' a prescribed position, are the 'unique outcomes' of which narrative practitioners speak" (e.g., White & Epston, 1990, p. 15). The fact that both an alternative story and unique outcomes exist allow openings for inserting agency into a client's experience of their lives.

Assumptions from narrative therapy are that people naturally 'story' their experiences. Within those stories are subject positions. A subject position is a stance given to someone by the power/knowledge framework that they are living in. It is the dominant way of knowing, doing and saying/thinking in a given culture. These dominant ways offer people positions for ways to be in the world that are somewhat limited. Essentially, narrative coaches encourage people to observe who they are as a character in the story of their life. Because narrative therapy takes a social constructionist/post-structural perspective on the person, the stories available to clients are given by their cultures and are therefore not limitless. People are bound by discourse and practices in their cultures.

In coaching conversations about health and wellbeing, we can be interested in the subject positions related to these areas of life. The initial task is to question subject positions that have become entrenched and that might be hiding positions that support agency and a healthy life. This involves having an 'externalising conversation' whereby the client is separated discursively from the problem. The client is then asked to take a position on the problem. The following questions can be useful when supporting clients to externalise.

- "What would you call this thing that is affecting your health and wellbeing?"
- "What is your position on this thing that is affecting your health and wellbeing?"; "Do you want more or less of it in your life?"; "What would be the impact of having less of it?"; "What would be the impact of having more of it?"
- "Are there any thoughts or behaviours or intentions in your life now that would not be predicted by this problem thing that is affecting your health and wellbeing?"
- "What would you call these alternative thoughts/behaviours/intentions, and what is your position on them?"; "Do you want more of fewer of these in your life?"

Having taken a position, usually *against* the problem, the client is invited to re-author (rewrite/reimagine) an alternative story that is not dominated by the problem. The aim of the first part of the conversation is to get a position on the problem, to establish an agentive perspective. The aim of the second part of the conversation is to develop agency and to 'thicken' the story of agency in the landscape of action and the landscape of identity and across time (distant past, past, present, near future, future, distant future). This means that the client's story of themselves as agentive is woven across two areas of their life and across multiple time points. Weaving a new story and grounding it in a temporal reality gives it more support and grounding.

The landscape of action is the practical realm, the land of acts and behaviours. In this world, the client tells stories about things they did or did not do, events that happened and people they did those things with. Questions in this part of the conversation plot sequences of events through time: "What happened?"; "In what sequence?"; "Involving which characters?"; "When, where and how?" These questions highlight agency: "How did you do that?"; "What did you do that led you to feeling this new feeling?"; "How did you notice the different ways others were treating you?"

The landscape of identity is the realm of values, meaning and purpose. In this realm, the client explains how their actions in the landscape of action connect to their beliefs, values, meaning and/or purpose in life. The first part of the conversation asks "What happened?". The second part of the conversation asks "Why did you make that happen?". Questions in the landscape of identity plot meanings, desires, intentions, beliefs, commitments, motivations and values that the client relates to their actions.

The coach's questions are designed to help clients reflect on the implications of actions taken. Coaches ask things like "What do these actions mean?"; "Why did you do that rather than this?"; "What do you hope will or will not happen by doing that action?"; "What does that action say about your character?" By linking action to intention, coaches strengthen agency. By weaving these links across time, coaches make them multiple events of agency, not rare unique outcomes. By highlighting the presence of agency across clients' lives, coaches thicken the story of agency. These conversations are conducted through the process of asking questions, generating curiosity, paying attention to openings (absent but implicit), telling and retelling (outsider witnessing), creating the loop between what a client does (landscape of action) and how they make meaning about it (landscape of identity). The following questions can be helpful in highlighting agency during coaching conversations.

- "How might you name this alternative thought/behaviour/intention?" (e.g., being healthy/choosing life).
- "How does this fit/resonate with some of your values, intentions, purpose, hopes, explanations, motives and desires for your life?"
- "What would you name this new thought/behaviour/intention?" (The name needs to be given by the client, not an expert label).
- "Can you tell me a story of that behaviour/thought/intention in your life now in the present?"; "Is this something you want more or less of in your life?"
- "If more, what impact will bringing this thought/behaviour/intention into your life have on your future (both near and distant future)?"; "Can you describe these future selves and your life with this intention in it?"

Importantly, when using narrative approaches, these unique outcomes and preferred stories are maintained and thickened in community. Part of the practice of narrative conversations is to bring members of the community into the conversation. This is because of the power of social norms to reduce our agency. Foucault and White have used the term "normalising judgement" to describe these social norms and the ways of talking and doing, with which they are connected (Foucault, 1977, p. 177; see also White, 2007). This means that clients constantly assess themselves and others based on these norms in terms of what is expected, what is valued, what is normal or what makes sense. For Kendall and Wickham (1999), discourse achieves such normalisation by making some things sayable, doable and visible (e.g., valued stories, activities, and institutions).

As White (2007) has put it, we govern ourselves and each other "through the construction of norms about life and identity and by inciting people to engage in operations on their own and each other's lives to bring their actions and thoughts into harmony with these norms" (p. 268). This means that any particular individual will face both their own internal struggles to make change but will be challenged also by the norms of their community or culture. Agency can best be built up and maintained by identifying enabling communities who will support the client and resist normalising judgements. The coaching conversation then must expand outside of the room by asking the client questions that track the history of their healthy intentions and actions in their history as a person embedded within a community. The questions must also embed any new intentions or behaviours back within the community so that there is a supportive space in which to enact and support the agency and meaning developed. The following questions can support clients to think about how their topic may relate to others.

- "Do you have a story of this value/intention making an appearance in your life in the past?"; "Did you witness someone else performing that intention?"; "How did you first come to know about this value?"
- "Who would not be surprised by your commitment to this new health behaviour?"; "Is there someone in your life now that you would like to tell about this intention/ value and your hope to bring it more into your life?"; "Who? Why do you want to tell them?"; "How do you think they will hear it?"
- "What action do you need to take today to help you carry that intention forward?; "Who will join you to do that?"

Conclusion

The stance suggested for a narrative coach is to be either slightly behind or just beside the client, never in front. If we find ourselves going too far in front of where our client is, there's a danger of the client feeling like a failure or that they are not measuring up to the coach's expectations. It is important to acknowledge that there will be times when coaches get too far ahead and there will be moments of failure in the work. Those moments are the failure of the coach, not of the client. They are simply indications that the coach may have gone too far forward. It is worth acknowledging these moments with our clients and saying something like "Wow, I think I went way too far ahead in our last session! The suggestion I made was way off. I will do my best to not jump ahead again".

The idea of "walking alongside" the client is critically important in sensitive conversations about health and wellbeing. The power of coaching is that it is non-prescriptive and non-judgemental. It is a supportive conversation that should feel empowering, allowing our clients to experience agency and become their own storytellers. By bringing meaning and purpose into the coaching conversations, we encourage our clients to take a step back from the topic so that they can see it from a broader perspective. By reflecting on one's purpose, it becomes possible to connect with a source of sustained and sustainable motivation. Change requires energy, and one's purpose can provide that. The coach brings a non-judgemental, appreciative approach that provides the client with a sense of being valued and respected as they determine the best way forward. The coach's belief that the client can and will make progress will boost a sense of agency in the client, while the conversational frameworks of coaching provide an opportunity to consider pathways towards a more desirable future.

Reflective questions

1. In what ways might our clients be locked into normalising judgements about health and wellbeing?
2. How can we authentically and respectfully integrate conversations about meaning and purpose into our coaching conversations?
3. How do our own attitudes and understanding of the concepts of "health" and "wellbeing" affect our clients?

References

Boyle, P. A., Buchman, A. S., Barnes, L. L., & Bennett, D. A. (2010). Effect of a purpose in life on risk of incident Alzheimer disease and mild cognitive impairment in community-dwelling older persons. *Archives of General Psychiatry*, 67(3), 304–310. DOI:10.1001/archgenpsychiatry.2009.208

Boyle, P. A., Buchman, A. S., Wilson, R. S., Yu, L., Schneider, J. A., & Bennett, D. A. (2012). Effect of purpose in life on the relation between Alzheimer disease pathologic changes on cognitive function in advanced age. *Archives of General Psychiatry*, 69(5), 499–504. DOI:10.1001/archgenpsychiatry.2011.1487

Breitbart, W, Gibson, C, Poppito, S. R., & Berg, A. (2004). Psychotherapeutic interventions at the end of life: A focus on meaning and spirituality. *Canadian Journal of Psychiatry. Revue canadienne de psychiatrie*, 49(6), 366–372. DOI:10.1177/070674370404900605

Chamberlain, K., & Zika, S. (1988). Religiosity, life meaning and wellbeing: Some relationships in a sample of women. *Journal for the Scientific Study of Religion*, 411–420.

Cohen, R., Bavishi, C., & Rozanski, A. (2016). Purpose in life and its relationship to all-cause mortality and cardiovascular events: A meta-analysis. *Psychosomatic Medicine*, 78(2), 122–133. DOI:10.1097/PSY.0000000000000274

Cooperrider, D. L., & Srivastva, S. (1987). Appreciative inquiry in organizational life. In W. Pasmore & R. Woodman (Eds.), *Research in organization change and development*. Vol. 1 (pp. 129–169). JAI Press.

Cornish, F., & Gillespie, A. (2009). A pragmatist approach to the problem of knowledge in health psychology. *Journal of Health Psychology*, 14(6), 800–809. DOI:10.1177/1359105309338974

Debats, D. L. (1998). *Measurement of personal meaning: The psychometric properties of the life regard index*. Lawrence Erlbaum Associates Publishers.

Etchison, M., & Kleist, D. M. (2000). Review of narrative therapy: Research and utility. *The Family Journal*, 8(1), 61–66.

Foucault, M. (1977). *Discipline and punish: The birth of the prison*. Penguin Books.

Frank, A. W. (2010). *Letting stories breathe: A socio-narratology*. University of Chicago Press.

Frankl, V. E. (1985). *Man's search for meaning*. Simon and Schuster.

Gergen, K. J. (2010). Meaning in relationship. In J. D. Raskin, S. K. Bridges, & R. A. Neimeyer (Eds.), *Studies in meaning 4: Constructivist perspectives on theory, practice, and social justice* (pp. 9–25). Pace University Press.

Gonçalves, M. M., Matos, M., & Santos, A. (2009). Narrative therapy and the nature of "innovative moments" in the construction of change. *Journal of Constructivist Psychology*, 22(1), 1–23.

Gonçalves, M. M., Ribeiro, A. P., Silva, J. R., Mendes, I., & Sousa, I. (2016). Narrative innovations predict symptom improvement: Studying innovative moments in narrative therapy of depression. *Psychotherapy Research*, 26(4), 425–435.

Grant, A. (2012). An integrative goal-focused approach to executive coaching. *International Coaching Psychology Review*, 7(2), 146–165.

Henry, M., Cohen, S. R., Lee, V., Sauthier, P., Provencher, D., Drouin, P., Gauthier, P., Gotlieb, W., Lau, S., Drummond, N., Gilbert, L., Stanimir, G., Sturgeon, J., Chasen, M., Mitchell, J., Huang, L. N., Ferland, M. K., & Mayo, N. (2010). The Meaning-Making intervention (MMi) appears to increase meaning in life in advanced ovarian cancer: A randomized controlled pilot study. *Psychooncology*, 19(12), 1340–1347. DOI:10.1002/pon.1764

Janoff-Bulman, R. (2004). Posttraumatic growth: Three explanatory models. *Psychological Inquiry*, 15(1), 30–34.

Kendall, G., & Wickham, G. (1999). *Using Foucault's methods*. Sage.

Kim, E. S., Strecher, V. J., & Ryff, C. D. (2014). Purpose in life and use of preventive health care services. *Proceedings of the National Academy of Sciences*, 111(46), 16331–16336.

Kim, E. S., Sun, J. K., Park, N., Kubzansky, L. D., & Peterson, C. (2013). Purpose in life and reduced risk of myocardial infarction among older U.S. adults with coronary heart disease: A two-year follow-up. *Journal of Behavioral Medicine*, 36, 124–133. DOI:10.1007/sl0865.012.2906.4

King, L. A., Hicks, J. A., Krull, J. L., & Del Gaiso, A. K. (2006). Positive affect and the experience of meaning in life. *Journal of Personality and Social Psychology*, 90(1), 179.

Laskow, T., Small, L., & Wu, D. S. (2019). Narrative interventions in the palliative care setting: A scoping review. *Journal of Pain and Symptom Management*, 58(4), 696–706.

Launer, J., & Wohlmann, A. (2023). The art of medicine: Narrative medicine, narrative practice and the creation of meaning. *The Lancet, 401,* 98–99.

Martela, F., & Steger, M. F. (2016). The three meanings of meaning in life: Distinguishing coherence, purpose, and significance. *The Journal of Positive Psychology, 11*(5), 531–545.

Mascaro, N., & Rosen, D. H. (2006). The role of existential meaning as a buffer against stress. *Journal of Humanistic Psychology, 46*(2), 168–190.

Mascaro, N., & Rosen, D. H. (2008). Assessment of existential meaning and its longitudinal relations with depressive symptoms. *Journal of Social and Clinical Psychology, 27*(6), 576–599.

Matos, M., Santos, A., Gonçalves, M., & Martins, C. (2009). Innovative moments and change in narrative therapy. *Psychotherapy Research, 19*(1), 68–80.

Meehan, T., & Guilfoyle, M. (2015). Case formulation in poststructural narrative therapy. *Journal of Constructivist Psychology, 28*(1), 24–39. DOI:10.1080/10720537.2014.938848

Neimeyer, R. A. (1993). An appraisal of constructivist psychotherapies. *Journal of Consulting & Clinical Psychology, 61*(2), 221–234.

Nowaczyk, M. J. (2012). Narrative medicine in clinical genetics practice. *American Journal of Medical Genetics Part A, 158*(8), 1941–1947.

Passmore, J. (2021). *Excellence in coaching: Theory, tools and techniques to achieve outstanding coaching performance.* 4th Ed. Kogan Page.

Raskin, J. D., Bridges, S. K., & Neimeyer, R. A. (2010). *Studies in meaning 4: Constructivist perspectives on theory, practice, and social justice.* Pace University Press.

Ryff, C. D. (1989). Happiness is everything, or is it? Explorations on the meaning of psychological well-being. *Journal of Personality and Social Psychology, 57*(6), 1069.

Ryff, C. D. (2014). Psychological well-being revisited: Advances in the science and practice of eudaimonia. *Psychotherapy and Psychosomatics, 83*(1), 10–28. DOI:10.1159/000353263

Schaefer, S. M., Morozink Boylan, J., Van Reekum, C. M., Lapate, R. C., Norris, C. J., Ryff, C. D., & Davidson, R. J. (2013). Purpose in life predicts better emotional recovery from negative stimuli. *PloS One, 8*(11), e80329. DOI:10.1371/journal.pone.0080329

Seligman, M. E. P. (1990). Why is there so much depression today? The waxing of the individual and the waning of the commons. In R. E. Ingram (Ed.), *Contemporary psychological approaches to depression: Theory, research, and treatment* (pp. 1–9). Plenum Press. DOI:10.1007/978-1-4613-0649-8_1

Seligman, M. E. P. (2011). *Flourish: A visionary new understanding of happiness and well-being.* Free Press.

Seligman, M. E. P. (2021). Agency in Greco-Roman philosophy. *The Journal of Positive Psychology, 16*(1), 1–10. DOI:10.1080/17439760.2020.1832250

Snyder, C. R. (1995). Conceptualizing, measuring, and nurturing hope. *Journal of Counselling and Development, 73,* 355–360.

Steger, M. F. (2012). Making meaning in life. *Psychological Inquiry, 23*(4), 381–385.

Steger, M. F. (2022). Find meaning. In C. van Nieuwerburgh & P. Williams (Eds.), *From surviving to thriving: A student's guide to feeling and doing well at university* (pp. 117–125). Sage.

Steger, M. F., Frazier, P. A., Oishi, S., & Kaler, M. (2006). The meaning in life questionnaire: Assessing the presence of and search for meaning in life. *Journal of Counseling Psychology, 53*(1), 80.

Steger, M. F., Frazier, P. A., & Zacchanini, J. L. (2008). Terrorism in two cultures: Stress and growth following September 11 and the Madrid train bombings. *Journal of Loss and Trauma, 13*(6), 511–527.

Theeboom, T., Beersma, B., & van Vianen, A. E. M. (2014). Does coaching work? A meta-analysis on the effects of coaching on individual level outcomes in an organizational context. *The Journal of Positive Psychology, 9*(1), 118. DOI:10.1080/17439760.2013.837499

van Nieuwerburgh, C. (2016). *Coaching in professional contexts.* Sage.

van Nieuwerburgh, C. (2020). *An introduction to coaching skills: A practical guide.* Sage.

van Nieuwerburgh, C., & Allaho, R. (2018). *Coaching in Islamic culture: The principles and practice of Ershad.* Routledge.

Wang, Q., Lai, Y.-L., Xu, X., & McDowall, A. (2022). The effectiveness of workplace coaching: A meta-analysis of contemporary psychologically informed coaching approaches. *Journal of Work-Applied Management, 14*(1), 77–101.

Weiner, B. (1985). An attributional theory of achievement motivation and emotion. *Psychological Review*, 92(4), 548.

White, M. (2007). *Maps of narrative practice*. W. W. Norton.

White, M., & Epston, D. (1990). *Narrative means to therapeutic ends*. W. W. Norton.

Whitmore, J. (1992). *Coaching for performance: A practical guide for growing your own skills*. Nicholas Brealey.

Wong, P. T. P. (2014). Viktor Frankl's meaning-seeking model and positive psychology. In A. Batthyany & P. Russo Netzer (Eds.), *Meaning in existential and positive psychology*. Springer.

Wong, P. T. P., & Weiner, B. (1981). When people ask "why" questions, and the heuristics of attributional search. *Journal of Personality and Social Psychology*, 40(4), 650.

Zika, S., & Chamberlain, K. (1992). On the relation between meaning in life and psychological well-being. *British Journal of Psychology*, 83(1), 133–145.

Chapter 7

Coaching for stress

Tim Anstiss

Introduction

Our ability to respond rapidly and effectively to threat and danger is essential to our survival. Much of this response is hardwired into our nervous system and bodies, and the stress response is commonly triggered automatically when the conditions are right. We tend to notice the accompanying motivational, feeling, behavioural and physiological changes which accompany it. However, the innate stress reactions suited to our environment of evolutionary adaptation may now be causing us to experience poor health, wellbeing, quality of life and performance (Taborsky et al., 2022). In this chapter, I will review the evidence that coaching can favourably affect client levels of stress, distress and resilience. I will then explore how an integrated and process-based approach to stress coaching can help the coach collaboratively develop a tailored stress management and reduction plan with the client.

Research

Over the last two decades, research into the effectiveness of coaching on stress and related variables has grown in quantity and quantity. In one of the earliest studies, Gyllensten and Palmer (2005) explored whether or not workplace coaching can reduce stress. The study involved 31 participants from a UK finance organisation and used a quasi-experimental study design measuring depression, anxiety and stress before and after coaching in the coaching and control groups. They found levels of anxiety and stress decreased more in the coaching group than the control group, and that levels of depression decreased more in the control group than the coaching group.

Ruotsalainen and colleagues (2014) examined randomised controlled trials (RCTs) of interventions aimed at preventing psychological stress in healthcare workers. They categorised interventions as cognitive-behavioural training (CBT) (n = 14), mental and physical relaxation (n = 21), combined CBT and relaxation (n = 6), and organisational interventions (n = 20), and categorised outcomes as stress, anxiety or general health. They found that at 1–6 months follow-up (in seven studies) and at more than six months follow-up (in two studies), CBT with or without relaxation reduced stress more than no intervention. They concluded that there is low-quality evidence that CBT and mental and physical relaxation reduce stress more than no intervention and recommended that more RCTs are needed with at least 120 participants that compare the intervention to a placebo-like intervention.

DOI: 10.4324/9781003319016-9

Gardiner and colleagues (2013) explored the relationship between cognitive behavioural coaching, the wellbeing of rural general practitioners (GPs), their intentions to leave and actual leaving of rural general practice. The intervention was a nine-hour cognitive behavioural coaching programme. They found that GPs who underwent cognitive behavioural coaching had lower rural doctor distress scores, that before coaching 81% of rural GPs in the intervention group had considered leaving general practice, which reduced to 40% after coaching, and that over a three-year period 94% of the coaching group remained in general practice compared with 80% of the control group. They concluded that cognitive behavioural coaching reduced the stress levels of rural GPs who self-identified the need for managing stress and reduced their intention to leave rural general practice, and that despite initially being more stressed compared with the general population of rural GPs, more GPs from the coaching group remained in rural general practice.

Vanhove and colleagues (2016) performed a meta-analytic review of resilience-building programmes in organisational settings to explore their effectiveness. Conducting 42 independent samples across 37 studies implemented in organisational contexts, they found that the overall effect of such programmes was small (d = 0.21) and that programme effects tended to diminish over time, although moderator analyses revealed that programmes targeting individuals thought to be at greater risk of experiencing stress and lacking core protective factors may show improved effect over time. Programmes employing a one-on-one delivery format (e.g., coaching) were most effective, followed by the classroom-based group delivery format.

David and colleagues (2016) conducted a study to test the effectiveness of an executive cognitive behavioural coaching programme in enhancing managerial stress resilience and performance during the financial recession. Their sample consisted of 59 middle and top-managers from an Italian multinational banking group. Results suggest that the programme was effective in helping managers to improve their performance and manage their distress and depressed mood. The authors found that changes in beliefs after the programme can function as mechanisms for both managing depressed mood and boosting managers' performance levels.

Dyrbye and colleagues (2019) explored the effect of individualised coaching on the wellbeing of physicians. Using a pilot randomised clinical trial design involving 88 physicians, they found that participants who received professional coaching (six sessions with a professional coach) experienced a significant reduction in emotional exhaustion and overall symptoms of burnout, as well as improvements in overall quality of life and resilience. The authors concluded that coaching may be an effective way to reduce emotional exhaustion and overall burnout, as well as improve quality of life and resilience for some physicians.

Spinelli and colleagues (2019) performed a meta-analysis on data from RCTs examining the effect of mindfulness-based interventions on healthcare professionals, including healthcare professionals in training. They found interventions had a significant moderate effect on anxiety (Hedge's g = 0.47), depression (Hedge's g = 0.41), psychological distress (Hedge's g = 0.46), and stress (Hedge's g = 0.52), with small to moderate effects observed for burnout (Hedge's g = 0.26) and wellbeing (Hedge's g = 0.32). They concluded that mindfulness-based interventions are effective in reducing distress and improving wellbeing in health care professionals (HCPs) and HCPs in training.

Aboalshamat and colleagues (2020) assessed the effect of a life coaching program on dental students' psychological status, using a quasi-experiment design with two arms involving 88 female dental students. Psychological status was assessed with the Depression and Anxiety Stress Scale (DASS-21), Resilience Scale (RS-14) and the Psychological Wellbeing Scale – Short (PWB-S). The intervention group received a coaching program comprising a one-hour lecture and five phone coaching sessions over five weeks, while the control group received no intervention. They found that the study group showed significant reductions in depression, anxiety, stress, resilience and self-acceptance compared to the control group.

Okeke and colleagues (2021) investigated the efficacy of a 12-week, blended Rational Emotive Occupational Health Coaching course in reducing occupational stress among teachers of children with special needs, using a group-randomised waitlist control trial design. Participants (N = 83) included teachers of children with special education needs in inclusive and specialised schools. Outcome measures included the Single Item Stress Questionnaire (SISQ), Teachers' Stress Inventory and Participants' Satisfaction Questionnaire (PSQ). Results showed significant reduction in perceived stress, stress symptoms and the total teachers' stress score in the intervention group compared to the waitlisted group. The authors concluded that that blended Rational Emotive Occupational Health Coaching is effective in occupational stress management among teachers of children with special education needs.

Auer and colleagues (2022) examined the buffering effects of virtual coaching during the COVID19 pandemic, using a pre-post quasi-experimental design. They compared changes in wellbeing, social behaviour, and work outcomes for coached and non-coached samples (n = 1,005) and found that post–COVID19 outcomes were generally more positive for those who received coaching: they experienced positive gains in optimism, life satisfaction, authenticity, and productivity, while those who did not receive coaching experienced a decline in those outcomes. They also found that those who received coaching experienced larger growth in resilience and social connection and concluded that external, virtual coaching can be an effective solution in supporting employees through times of crisis and change.

Tamminga and colleagues (2023) conducted a systematic review of the effectiveness of stress-reduction interventions targeting individual healthcare workers. Interventions were compared to no intervention, wait list, placebo or another type of stress-reduction intervention. Included were 117 studies involving a total of 11,119 participants. They categorised interventions into ones that: (1) focus one's attention on the (modification of the) experience of stress (thoughts, feelings, behaviour); (2) focus one's attention away from the experience of stress by various means of psychological disengagement (e.g., relaxing, exercise); (3) alter work-related risk factors on an individual level; and (4) combine two or more of these three. The main outcome measure was stress symptoms measured with various self-reported questionnaires such as the Maslach Burnout Inventory (MBI). They found that overall, such interventions may result in a reduction in stress symptoms in the short term (standardised mean difference (SMD) -0.37, 95% confidence interval (CI) -0.52–-0.23) and medium term (SMD -0.43, 95% CI -0.71–-0.14), and concluded that: (1) there may be an effect on stress reduction in healthcare workers from individual-level stress interventions; (2) this effect may last up to a year after the end of the intervention; (3) a combination of interventions may be beneficial; and (4) the long-term effects of individual-level stress management interventions remain unknown. They recommended methodologically better designed and executed studies with larger sample sizes to increase the certainty of the evidence.

This brief overview of the research shows us that coaching can and does help some people experience less stress and more resilience, but better studies are needed so that the field can get a better understanding of what types of coaching work best for who, with what stress-related issues, etc.

Practice

Integrative model

Due to the wide variation in coaching approaches, tools and strategies offered to people to help them better cope with stress (e.g., cognitive behavioural, mindfulness-based, compassion-based, positive psychology–based, acceptance and commitment–based, solution-focussed, etc.), it may be helpful to view the field through the lens of the classic and influential Stress, Appraisal and Coping model of Lazarus and Folkman (1984) (Figure 7.1).

This model outlines a transactional model of stress involving the interaction between stressors (things which cause stress) and the stress response, with the stress response being influence by appraisal (primary and secondary) and ways of coping (including emotion-focussed and problem-focussed coping). We can also include various 'buffers' which moderate the impact of stress on outcomes. The model includes feedback loops and reciprocal determinism, in which variable A influences variable B which can in turn lead back to variable A. For instance, work stress may lead to excessive drinking, which can in turn lead to more work stress, which can drive a vicious circle and downward spiral in a person's life. The model is dynamic in that the nature of the stressor, a person's appraisal of it, their ways of coping and the effects of this interaction change over time.

Adopting this more granular view of the dynamics of stress and reactions to stress can help the coach better understand how stress may be negatively affecting the health,

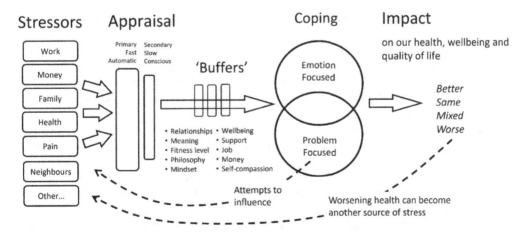

Figure 7.1 The Stress, Appraisal and Coping Model (adapted)

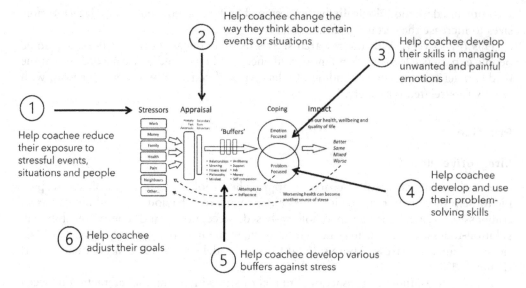

Figure 7.2 Six main areas to intervene in the Stressor-Stress Response Dynamic Process

wellbeing, quality of life and performance of the client, as well as guide the co-design of a personalised plan.

The model suggests six main ways for a coach to guide a client towards experiencing less stress over time (Figure 7.2), and adapt well to what remains.

The first way a coach can help a client can be to help them explore how to reduce their exposure to threat and stress. This could include such options as changing jobs, reducing their contact with certain people, becoming more assertive or taking a break from certain situations or environments. It can also involve exploring ways in which the client might reduce their exposure to 'internal' threats such as a harsh, attacking inner critic (Chapter 25).

> Men are disturbed not by things, but by the views which they take of them.
>
> Epictetus

Another way a coach can help is to help the client to re-appraise or reframe the way they think about their situation. This can best be done via such cognitive behavioural strategies such as identifying cognitive errors and thinking traps, inference chaining, disputing and debating unhelpful beliefs, cognitive restructuring, and behavioural experimentation (Palmer and Szymanska, 2018). Helping clients shift their explanatory (or attributional) style for unwanted events away from the three P's can also be helpful – from seeing the cause as Permanent, Pervasive and/or Personal to seeing the cause as temporary, specific and not entirely due to them (Seligman, 2006). It can also be helpful to share various messages from compassionate mind approaches including 'It's not your fault'; 'we all have tricky brains'; 'our brains are made for us, not by us'; and the common humanity message that we all tend to suffer in similar ways. Of course, these messages need to be shared in a caring and empathic way, not dismissively or in any way suggesting that you are not taking their struggle and issues seriously.

A third way the coach may help the client is to help them develop and make better use of various emotion-focussed coping strategies. This might include some of the previously mentioned cognitive behavioural approaches, as well as practising relaxation, using mindfulness-based techniques such as defusion; acceptance; present moment awareness and self-as-context (Anstiss, 2020); exercising; yoga; various positive psychology methods such as cultivating positive emotions, increasing contact with nature, etc. (Anstiss and Passmore, 2017); and/or techniques and strategies from Compassionate Mind Coaching such as soothing breathing rhythm, cultivating feelings of safeness, cultivating and experience self-compassion, etc. (Anstiss and Gilbert, 2014). It can also be helpful to help the client understand and reduce secondary emotional disturbance – for example, getting anxious about the possibility of getting anxious, or getting angry with oneself for getting anxious, or becoming depressed as a result of getting angry and anxious, and then feeling guilty or shame about ones inability to cope, etc.

The coach might also guide and support the client in taking effective action on the sources of stress using various problem-focussed coping strategies. This might include developing their general problem-solving skills, becoming more assertive, seeking professional help, generating solutions via solution-focussed coaching methods (Passmore, 2020; Cavanagh & Grant, 2010), making better use of lists, etc. It might also be helpful to have the client discover, learn more about and use/apply their strengths of character (Burke and Passmore, 2019). And since approaching and dealing with problems can be uncomfortable it might be necessary to use some emotional focussed coping strategies (e.g., cultivating experiential acceptance) to help increase the likelihood that problems are approached and acted upon rather than avoided.

The coach might also help their client develop and strengthen various non-specific 'buffers' against stress. This might include positive psychology interventions to help them experience more psychological wellbeing (van Agteren et al., 2021), more positive emotions, better social connections and social support, improved fitness levels, more meaning and purpose, better sleep, better diet, etc. Guided by self-determination theory (Deci and Ryan, 2012), the coach might also help the client explore ways to have their three core psychological needs met more fully, e.g., their need for autonomy, for competence and for relatedness (or belonging).

Since research shows that failure to disengage from unachievable goals can be a cause of stress, poor physical health and poor mental health (Wrosch et al., 2013), another thing a coach can do for some clients is to help them adjust or even let go of certain goals, while reassuring them that they can still make progress towards a value-based life, even if that goal is not achievable – e.g., a professional athlete's need to retire before they wished to.

Additional considerations

Leverage evidence-based relationship factors

While the evidence suggests that helping clients use various techniques (e.g., cognitive behavioural, mindfulness, positive psychology, etc.) can be helpful in reducing their experience of stress, very good evidence supports the importance of practitioners paying as much attention to relational factors as technical factors for instance to empathy, alliance, warmth and goal congruence (Anstiss, 2021; Sommers-Flanagan, 2015).

Hope

Hope theory suggests that hope is related to both goals and pathways (Rand and Cheavens, 2009). To be as helpful as possible to a client experiencing stress, the coach may wish to help their client have realistic and believable goals about a future with less stress, as well as to see one or more pathways to their desired future.

A process-based approach to coaching for stress

Informed by the discussed research and suggestions, as well as the four processes of Motivational Interviewing (Rollnick et al., 2022), the following is a six-step process for guiding and supporting a client towards becoming less stressed over time.

1. Engage.
2. Focus.
3. Evoke and Strengthen.
4. Decide.
5. Plan.
6. Support.

Engage: It is important that the coach gets and keeps engagement throughout the coaching session, using active listening and other core coaching skills.

Focus: In this step, the coach and client agree on the focus of the coaching session. In this case, the focus would be stress, how to have less of it over time and how to cope better with what remains.

Evoke and Strengthen: In this step, the coach and client might explore what the client is experiencing, and where they feel the stress is coming from, as well as the steps the client may already have taken to cope with their stress. They then might explore the stress, appraisal and coping model, and explore options in each of the six main areas highlighted in this chapter. Things the coach might seek to strengthen during the coaching session might include understanding, insight, readiness to change and self-efficacy for (or confidence about) changing, as well as hope, alliance, empathy, rapport, goal congruence, connection with values and feelings of autonomy and achievement.

Decide: At some stage in session, the client will need to come to a decision about what to do about their stress and their reaction to it. Of course, this decision might be to not do anything just yet. But coming to a decision about what to do is an important step in the coaching process.

Plan: Once the previous steps have been engaged in, then it might be time to transition to working collaboratively and develop a person-centred plan, with some details including the desired outcome, the changes that are going to be made, the reasons why they changes are to be made, some specifics around when the changes will be made, how and how often they will be made, and with what kind of support. The plan might also cover anticipated obstacles and how the client might find a way around them if they arise, as well as a date to review the plan and update it according to progress made and what has been learned.

Support: Once a person-centred plan has been generated and the client has started to implement their plan, then the coach will need to support them in their efforts, which may include additional coaching sessions, as well as text messaging and other virtual methods.

Conclusion

Excessive worry, stress, anxiety and distress are common presentations for coaching. To get better at coaching clients towards experiencing less stress over time, coaches may wish to view the client's situation through the less of the dynamic stress, appraisal and coping model; help the client to explore which combination of six main approaches they may wish to take action on; and then guide and support them towards helpful action, possibly using the six-step coaching process model outlined in the chapter. Other coaching models are available.

Reflective questions

1. What percentage of your clients do you believe experience adverse effects of stress – e.g., poor health, sleep, relationships, performance at work, quality of life, etc.?
2. What do you feel might be the advantages of sharing the Stress, Appraisal and Coping model of Folkman and Lazarus with some clients, and using is to agree the focus of any stress management/reduction approach?
3. What are your main sources of stress, and how well do you feel you are coping with them?

References

Aboalshamat, K., Al-Zaidi, D., Jawa, D., Al-Harbi, H., Alharbi, R., & Al-Otaibi, S. (2020). The effect of life coaching on psychological distress among dental students: Interventional study. *BMC Psychol.* 14;8(1):106.

Anstiss, T. (2020). Acceptance and commitment coaching. In J. Passmore (Ed.), *The coaches handbook*. Routledge.

Anstiss, T. (2021). Affirmations, reflections and summaries in coaching. In J. Passmore (Ed.), *The coaches handbook* (pp. 114–124). Routledge.

Anstiss, T., & Gilbert, P. (2014). Compassionate mind coaching. In J. Passmore (Ed.), *Mastery in coaching: A complete psychological toolkit for advanced coaching*. Routledge.

Anstiss, T., & Passmore, J. (2017). Wellbeing coaching. In C. Cooper & M. Leiter (Eds.), *The Routledge companion to wellbeing at work* (pp. 237–248). Routledge.

Auer, E. M., Hutchinson, D., Eatough, E., Carr, E. W., Sinar, E. F., & Kellerman, G. (2022). The buffering effects of virtual coaching during crisis: A quasi-experimental study of changes in well-being, work, and social outcomes before and during the COVID-19 pandemic. *Int J Evid Based Coach Mentor.* 20(2):3–19.

Burke, J., & Passmore, J. (2019). Strengths based coaching—a positive psychology intervention. In L. Van Zyl & S. Rothmann Sr. (Eds.), *Theoretical approaches to multi-cultural positive psychological interventions* (pp. 463–475). Springer.

Cavanagh, M., & Grant, A. M. (2010). The solution-focused approach to coaching. In E. Cox, T. Bachkirova, & D. Clutterbuck (Eds.), *The complete handbook of coaching*. Sage.

David, O. A., Ionicioiu, I., Imbăruş, A. C., & Sava, F. A. (2016). Coaching banking managers through the financial crisis: Effects on stress, resilience, and performance. *J Ration-Emot Cogn-Behav Ther*. 34(4):267–281.

Deci, E. L., & Ryan, R. M. (2012). Motivation, personality, and development within embedded social contexts: An overview of self-determination theory. In R. M. Ryan (Ed.), *Oxford handbook of human motivation* (pp. 85–107). Oxford University Press.

Dyrbye, L. N., Shanafelt, T. D., Gill, P. R., Satele, D. V., & West, C. P. (2019). Effect of a professional coaching intervention on the well-being and distress of physicians: A pilot randomized clinical trial. *JAMA Intern Med*. 1;179(10):1406–1414.

Epictetus: the discourses as reported by Arrian, the manual, and fragments. Chapter 5. page 29. Volume 1. By Epictetus; Oldfather, William Abbott. Loeb Classical Library No. 218. Publication date: 1926. Publisher: Heinemann, London.

Gardiner, M., Kearns, H., & Tiggemann, M. (2013). Effectiveness of cognitive behavioural coaching in improving the well-being and retention of rural general practitioners. *Aust J Rural Health*. Jun;21(3):183–189.

Gyllensten, K., & Palmer, S. (2005). Can coaching reduce workplace stress? A quasi-experimental study. *Int J Evid Based Coach Ment*. 3(2): 75–85.

Lazarus, R. S., & Folkman, S. (1984). *Stress, appraisal, and coping*. Springer Publishing Company.

Okeke, F. C., Onyishi, C. N., Nwankwor, P. P., & Ekwueme, S. C. (2021). A blended rational emotive occupational health coaching for job-stress among teachers of children with special education needs. *Internet Interv*. 11;26:100482.

Palmer, S., & Szymanska, K. (2018). Cognitive behavioural coaching: An integrative approach. In S. Palmer & A. Whybrow (Eds.), *Handbook of coaching psychology* (2nd ed.). Routledge.

Passmore, J. (2020). Solution-focused coaching. In J. Passmore (Ed.), *The coaches handbook*. Routledge.

Rand, K. L., & Cheavens, J. S. (2009). Hope theory. In S. J. Lopez & C. R. Snyder (Eds.), *Oxford handbook of positive psychology* (pp. 323–333). Oxford University Press.

Rollnick, S., Miller, R., & Butler, C. (2022). *Motivational interviewing in health care* (2nd ed.: Helping Patients Change Behavior). Guilford Press.

Ruotsalainen, J. H., Verbeek, J. H., Mariné, A., & Serra, C. (2014). Preventing occupational stress in healthcare workers. *Cochrane Database Syst Rev*. 8;(12):CD002892.

Seligman, M. E. P. (2006). *Learned optimism: How to change your mind and your life*. Vintage.

Sommers-Flanagan, J. (2015). Evidence-based relationship practice: Enhancing counselor competence. *J Ment Health Couns*. 37:95–108.

Spinelli, C., Wisener, M., & Khoury, B. (2019). Mindfulness training for healthcare professionals and trainees: A meta-analysis of randomized controlled trials. *J Psychosom Res*. May;120:29–38.

Taborsky, B., Kuijper, B., Fawcett, T. W., English, S., Leimar, O., McNamara, J. M., & Ruuskanen, S. (2022). An evolutionary perspective on stress responses, damage and repair. *Horm Behav*. 142:105180.

Tamminga, S. J., Emal, L. M., Boschman, J. S., Levasseur, A., Thota, A., Ruotsalainen, J. H., Schelvis, R. M., Nieuwenhuijsen, K., & van der Molen, H. F. (2023). Individual-level interventions for reducing occupational stress in healthcare workers. *Cochrane Database Syst Rev*. May 12;5(5):CD002892.

van Agteren, J., Iasiello, M., Lo, L., et al. (2021). A systematic review and meta-analysis of psychological interventions to improve mental wellbeing. *Nat Hum Behav*. 5:631–652.

Vanhove A. J., Herian M., Perez A. L. U., Harms P. D., & Lester P. B. (2016). Can resilience be developed at work? A meta-analytic review of resilience-building programme effectiveness. *J Occup Organ Psycho*. 89(2):278–307.

Wrosch, C., Scheier, M. F., & Miller, G. E. (2013). Goal adjustment capacities, subjective well-being, and physical health. *Soc Personal Psychol Compass*. Dec 1;7(12):847–860.

Chapter 8

Coaching for the menopause

Gill Tanner and Eliana Gialain

Introduction

This chapter addresses a relatively new phenomenon: coaching for the menopause. The term 'menopause coach' appeared in the late 2010s and has been growing in popularity during the 2020s. However, while there are a number of short courses available, little formal health coach training has emerged in this space. This chapter aims to clarify what is meant by the term menopause coaching and why it is an important topic for the 2020s; outline the context for menopause coaching, including the philosophical, cultural, societal and economic considerations; review the emerging research for menopause coaching and health coaching in general; suggest ways in which coaching can help with the menopause; and finally, look at next steps and draw conclusions.

What is coaching for the menopause?

In order to outline what is meant by coaching for the menopause, let's start by looking at definitions for both.

Coaching is an activity involving an equal relationship between coach and client and one that believes the client is the expert on themselves and that they have the resources within them to resolve issues and move forward; the coach helps to facilitate that movement.

Menopause is a period of life experienced by women when there is a hormonal change in the body leading to the end of menstruation. This change is experienced differently by different women, but can include physical symptoms such as hot flashes, disrupted sleep, fatigue, weight gain and low energy; and psychological indications such as stress, anxiety, low confidence, poor concentration levels, memory lapses and mood swings. It can also be seen as a turning point in life when many women are wondering about their purpose and how useful they now are.

For this chapter, we will consider menopause as a biological stage in a woman's life when menstruation stops permanently due to loss of ovarian follicular activity, accordingly to the World Health Organization (n.d.).

Coaching for the menopause is about helping women gain insight into how they wish to manage this transition period and what it means for them, and defining tangible outcomes to help them take control of this key moment in their lives.

DOI: 10.4324/9781003319016-10

Table 8.1 Menopause coaching areas

- Identifying needs.
- Resilience.
- Relationships.
- Nutrition and exercise.
- Career.
- Self care.
- Communication skills.
- Mindset.
- Sleep.
- Boundaries.
- Confidence.
- Managing symptoms and making choices.
- Managing stress.
- Identity and acceptance.
- Finding a meaning/purpose.
- Dealing with a sense of loss.
- Gaining new perspectives.

Why is coaching for the menopause important?

Usher (2022), a menopause coach, noted that due to lengthening life expectancy, the current generation is only the third to experience menopause as part of an average life. Before that, women often died not long after the menopause and therefore it was considered by many cultures an end-of-life experience. Many would argue that menopause and obsolescence are still very closely associated when women today can have more than 20 years of their career left, and three, four or five decades of life after this change.

Unfortunately, menopause is still a taboo subject in many societies, yet it can have a significant impact on many women physically, emotionally and psychologically. Not only is it often reduced to medicalisation, meaning only the physical symptoms are treated, but often there is a lack of information and women can struggle to access appropriate treatment. Organisations historically have not been good at supporting women through their menopause; however, there has been a growing interest in the potential impact of the menopause on women's careers. Women in the 50+ age bracket are, after all, the most economically active population (Brewis et al., 2020).

Often when the menopause is discussed, it is from a negative standpoint. According to Hickey and colleagues (2022), women could feel more empowered and confident to manage menopause by changing the narrative around it and emphasising positive or neutral aspects such as freedom from menstruation, pregnancy and contraception.

Table 8.2 Key statistics: The menopause

- Nearly 50% of the population experience or will experience the menopause.
- One in ten women who worked during the menopause have left a job due to their symptoms.
- Eight out of ten women say their employer has not shared information, trained staff or put in place a menopause absence policy.
- It can take over four years for women to access effective support to manage their symptoms.
- Doctors are not routinely trained in menopause.

Menopause does not happen in isolation. It occurs at the same time as changing body conditions, changing lifestyle, changing role (particularly if children have grown up) and potentially different relationships (Deeks, 2003). It is therefore a key moment in a woman's life and yet, to date, it is little spoken about.

What are the philosophical, economic, cultural and social considerations?

Martin (1997) argues that women's bodies have been regarded as machines that produce products. Menstruation is a sign of the breakdown of continuous functioning, as it has failed to produce a baby, and the menopause can be seen as a breakdown of the body's reproductive capacity, thereby falling into disrepair and uselessness. She challenges this negative perspective of menopause and asks the question: shouldn't the transition to menopause be seen more as a move from one kind of order to another, rather than from order to disorder?

Gullette (1997) argued that menopause is something that divides women both from other women and from men. She believes that the public narrative is very much around menopausal women being infirm, contaminated and ageing, and that marketing favours youth, health, fitness and sexuality. Menopause can be seen by many women as a time of loss: loss of womanliness, childbearing, youth, usefulness of the womb, ovaries, menstruation, and sexuality. She advocates for women managing the change with competence and making their own sense of the end of fertility and the meaning of ageing, illness and death.

Cross cultural studies of the menopause demonstrate that it is experienced differently across the world, and caution needs to be exercised in a single western-centric experience and 'solution' (Kelly, 2011). For example, Singh and Arora (2005) note that women in India view menopause as a rite of passage into a newfound stage of womanhood which frees them from the restrictions of menstruation. In Latin America, many women also look forward to their newfound freedom and status. While in Japan, women tend not to report hot flushes or negative bodily effects reported in other cultures. It is thought it could be due to the respect women receive when they become menopausal such that they feel a greater sense of importance and move to a place of honour, making the transition less traumatic (Kelly, 2011).

Women everywhere experience menopause – but in which way is influenced by cultural and societal norms. In a culture where ageing is viewed as a loss or a journey towards death, and where menopause is medicalised, it can be very stressful. In societies where it is seen as something to aspire or look forward to, it can be much more life-affirming (Kelly, 2011). It is not just cultural norms which determine a woman's experience of menopause, but also socioeconomic status, education level and social attitudes to menopause, along with hormonal changes, diet, smoking, and body mass index (Hickey et al., 2022).

In terms of economic impact, there are some key reasons as to why women experiencing the menopause can be financially worse off, in some cases needing to work reduced hours, lacking time off or losing employment as a result of menopause-related absence.

Whilst some organisations are addressing these issues, in part driven by a desire to retain skilled and experienced workers, much work still needs to be done in most organisations to normalise menopause.

The positive benefits of health coaching

Whilst coaching has developed over the past three decades largely within sport and business environments, the past decade has seen the emergence of coaching being used to support improvements in health outcomes (Salathiel & Passmore, 2021).

A study of 779 healthcare professionals trained in health coaching skills showed significant increases in patient self-efficacy and satisfaction, increased patient confidence and motivation, change in health-related behaviours, reduction in dependency and improvements in medical compliance (Newman & McDowell, 2016).

In a 2016 study of health coaches, the researchers found that key factors in successful outcomes included the equal relationship between health coach, a relationship based on trust and the availability of the health coach mutual trust; the provision of practical support, as well as talking; and the role of the health coach to act as a bridge between the patient and the clinician (Thom et al., 2016).

Rodger (2021) noted that health coaching engages patients in managing their own health, encourages behaviour change and has proved beneficial in caring for people with long-term conditions. She considers that a mindset shift is needed amongst patients and healthcare professionals in order for it to become an integral part of patient care.

Rogers and Maini (2016) developed this thinking, arguing that in a health setting, coaching can improve patient outcomes, as well as reduce the stress levels of the healthcare professional: patients gain confidence in managing their own health, thereby reducing the number of medical appointments and emergency admissions, and patients are more likely to take their medication. They outline how a coaching approach acknowledges that people do not like to be told what to do, no matter how much they respect the person telling them. They outlined the following six fundamentals of health coaching, which are taken from coaching in business.

- Patients are resourceful.
- The practitioner's role is to move from expert to enabler.
- It is best to take a whole-life approach.
- The patient brings the agenda for the consultation.
- Practitioner and patient are equals in the consultation.
- Coaching is about change and action.

Given the research, there is no doubt that coaching can be a powerful force for change in improving health outcomes.

Coaching for menopause research

Very little research has been done specifically on coaching for the menopause to date. One phenomenological study was conducted by Dunn (2022) on coaching in the workplace for menopausal women. It found that coaching provided an opportunity for women to address issues arising from the menopause such as confidence, identity and transitions, but they did not speak directly about the menopause in the coaching sessions.

In a Japanese randomised control trial (Fujimoto, 2017) on cognitive (GROW model) behavioural coaching intervention for women with menopause symptoms to encourage engagement in health behaviours, results indicated that the coach was effective in enhancing the health of these menopausal Japanese women. The intervention group received information and three monthly coaching sessions.

Path analysis on the results for the intervention group showed that self-efficacy negatively affected menopause symptoms; menopause symptoms negatively affected mental symptoms; and goal achievement positively affected mental health directly, rather than through menopause symptoms. In the control group, both self-efficacy and goal achievement negatively affected menopause symptoms. Particularly the coaching process itself (goal-oriented actions) enhanced self-efficacy, reduced menopausal symptoms and improved quality of life. The study found that three months of coaching aimed at promoting health among women with menopausal symptoms increases self-efficacy.

In 2020, Verburgh and colleagues undertook a study of female workers in low-paid jobs who were experiencing menopause and midlife issues (Verburgh et al., 2020). They reviewed the effects of a workplace health promotion programme which included menopause consultations, work–life coaching sessions and training. The results indicated a positive impact of the workplace health promotion programme, including a significant improvement in menopausal symptoms. It also demonstrated that the workplace health promotion programme initiated a process of empowerment which had a positive impact on the participants' behaviour, physical health and mental wellbeing, and in the workplace itself. This was brought about, to some extent, by giving the women the opportunity to speak openly about their issues and the fact that they felt recognised for what they were going through. Integrated programmes such as this drawing together coaching with education and wider organisational changes point a possible way forward. More generally, health coaching has also shown positive impacts on workplace populations.

How can coaching help with the menopause?

Harrison (undated) has outlined how coaching can help with the menopause. She highlights that the client can use the coach as a sounding board, someone who will allow space for the client to talk, while the coach can help the client normalise their experiences. It is also a safe space for the client to discuss concerns and make action plans. While coaching has tended to focus exclusively on the importance of reflective space and the view that all the resources exist within the client, in health coaching, there is a recognition that psycho-social education should also form part of the intervention. This does not mean the coach tells the client what to do. Instead, the coach can help the client to assess their existing knowledge, identify gaps, share information and invite the client to reflect on what the information may mean for them. A third aspect is resilience. Change brings challenges and emotions. The coach can help the client recognise these aspects and to prepare mentally for the ups and downs which are arising. Harrison suggests that the coach can also facilitate discussions around career and career flexibility. For some people, discussions with line managers about absence, emotions, or job performance can enable others inside the organisation to better understand what may be happening. Finally, Harrison suggests, the coach can help the client find a renewed interest in the future by reflecting on their new identity and setting new goals and ambitions for the future. Whether it is coaching for the menopause, or some other kind of coaching, there are some fundamental principles that govern how coaching works. Following are some of the key ones and an illustration of how they may help within a menopause conversation.

Setting goals: SMART (specific, measurable, achievable, relevant and time-bound) goals are used in the work environment, but they are also essential for coaching and could be key for menopause coaching. The coach can partner with the woman to break down the goal into achievable chunks, be it to learn more about the menopause or to be clear about what areas are important for her, how she would like to address them and, where appropriate, work out potential solutions. The client is held accountable each time she meets the coach. Then, when a goal has been accomplished, it helps to reinforce the sense of achievement and wellbeing.

Personalised: one-to-one coaching is a personal and confidential experience which lends itself well to the subject of menopause – which is also a very personal experience. Each woman experiences it differently and so she can ensure that the support she needs is individual to her. She needs to be sure she can open up to the coach and therefore the coaching relationship is crucial. We know from research that the coaching relationship is one of the key determinants of coaching success (Pandolfi, 2020), so before embarking on any coaching, the client needs to be sure she can work with the coach.

Increasing self-awareness: even though most people believe they are self-aware, only 10–15% of people in a study actually fitted the criteria (Eurich, 2018). Research suggests that self-awareness leads to confidence, creativity, sound decision-making, strong relationships and effective communication (Eurich, 2018) – the outcomes we have been discussing in this chapter. Lee Lai Keen (2018) states that self-awareness is about understanding one's own needs, desires, habits and everything that makes the person being who they are, to a point that the more one's know about themselves, the better the adaptation to life changes. Coaching is a very effective medium for helping someone develop their self-awareness and act on the insights gained. In a study looking at self-awareness during the menopause, Bloch (2002) found that those women who had a negative attitude towards the menopause suffered much more from symptoms than women who had a positive one. Additionally, women who were satisfied with their appearance suffered from fewer symptoms. There was a significant association between high self-esteem and fewer menopausal symptoms.

Developing personal resources: the person's psychological capital or also known as the individual's positive psychological state of development accordingly to Luthans et al. (2007) and is a set of resources an individual can develop through coaching and then use to help them resolve their issues. It is made up of four different elements: self-efficacy, hope, optimism and resilience, which are central to a number of life challenges – not least the menopause.

Developing accountability: all too often in western cultures where menopause is medicalised, the woman looks up to the healthcare professional as the expert and implements whatever she is advised to do. The truth is that menopause is a very individual experience and the woman is the expert on herself. Coaching can help her to take control of her own mind and body, and to develop accountability rather than relying solely on medical professionals.

Improving interpersonal skills: Burleson and colleagues write that "Interpersonal skills are vital to the development of human relationships. Interpersonal communication is the means through which relationships are initiated, negotiated, maintained and ended" (Burleson, Metts & Kirch, 2000). Interpersonal skills are fundamental for women to be able to communicate effectively with those around them and get what they need, be it support from male partners, family members, friends, colleagues or healthcare professionals. Coaching can support women in developing these skills to have the confidence to not only speak up but also negotiate for themselves and maintain relationships which may otherwise be damaged.

Managing emotions: this is a problematic one when it comes to the menopause because, due to hormonal changes, emotions can easily be triggered and they can be hard to control. Nevertheless, turbulent emotions can be quite damaging whether or not a woman is experiencing the menopause, so it is important that she finds tools that can help her. A coach can work with her to understand what is happening in the moment and to find ways to recognise the signs and implement coping strategies.

Learning strategies for life: Accordingly to Grant (2013), success is not about who you are but what you do. Whilst the quote relates to success in business, it also translates well into other areas of life. Menopause should not define a woman; it is a life transition and therefore dealing with it is very much about what you do. As has already been mentioned, coaching can help a client define the issues and how to approach and solve them. It can also help the client develop strategies, not only for dealing with this transition but for other big changes – and therefore effectively for life.

As we have seen, it is essential to look beyond just the menopausal symptoms, important though they are, and look at how coaching can provide support to the whole person.

Men and menopause

Menopause does not only affect women, of course. It has an impact on the men in their lives, predominantly partners or men who are close to them, including direct reports, team members and colleagues at work. It is a significant change for them, too, when the woman starts to experience the physical, emotional and psychological changes that the menopause brings.

The most obvious answer is for men to educate themselves on the menopause so that they know what to expect and can begin to understand why the woman is behaving as she is. Men are also advised to not put any pressure on their partner, ask her for what she needs, accept the silence, resist the urge to snap back, encourage the woman to seek medical help; be prepared to change their plans and – most of all – communicate. This is a tall order and could be intimidating, so how can men respond?

First, they can encourage the woman concerned to participate in coaching for the menopause. As we have already seen, it can help her in so many ways, including how she deals with the physical, emotional and psychological aspects. Second, the man could consider coaching himself. But crucially, organisations have a role to play in education, both by normalising menopause through open discussion, inclusion of the issue within organisational policies and generic training, but fundamentally by offering specific psycho-social education on the topic for all employees. An easy way to achieve this is through online courses in a similar way to information technology (IT) security training, ensuring that all employees have a basic understanding of an issue which will affect 50% of the population – and possibly 10% of their current workforce at this moment in time.

Who should do coaching for the menopause?

When it comes to general health coaching, there are a number of programmes designed to train healthcare professionals, and there has been some success as a result. Newman and McDowell (2016) identified a number of barriers in their study on health coaching in the East of England: clinicians identify strongly with the expert role and many do not feel they are psychologically minded, the workforce is not sufficiently trained or skilled in this level of patient-centred care because the system is designed around a biomedical model, concern about length of consultations and losing control of the clinical risk, and the patient expects to go to the doctor to be fixed and to be told by the expert what to do. Bearing all of this in mind, the responsibility of coaching for menopause is probably not one that is best carried out by medical professionals.

Can menopause coaching be carried out by someone who is not medically qualified? We have seen that many of the health/menopause coaching principles align with those from business and other types of coaching. To what extent does a coach need to have a sound knowledge of the menopause to have credibility and build the all important working alliance? To what extent does a menopause coach need to be a female who has experienced, or is experiencing, menopause? To date, there are a number of coaches who specialise in the menopause and they seem to be older females, some of whom do not have any medical background, but what is their rate of success? These are questions which are yet to be answered.

Where do we go from here?

In some cultures, menopause is beginning to be discussed more openly. Organisations are realising the importance of keeping their older female workforce and so are developing policies and support; high-profile celebrities are also talking about it and creating awareness and interest. Nevertheless, there is still a way to go before it becomes less of a taboo.

There is a need for more education for everyone on the topic such that people are well informed about what it is, how to identify it and how to support individuals going through it. People need to feel that they can talk openly and without embarrassment about it and it needs to be a much more culturally acceptable topic.

Further research around the effectiveness of coaching for the menopause would be helpful looking at areas such as the following.

- In which areas related to the menopause does coaching have the most impact?
- What is the impact of male partners receiving coaching?
- What is the difference between a healthcare professional and someone not medically qualified doing the menopause coaching?
- How much does a non-medically trained menopause coach need to know about the menopause?
- What level of credibility does a coach have if they are not a female who is experiencing or has experienced the menopause?
- Which wider contextual issues affect coaching for menopause, e.g., cultural, societal, financial, educational?

Finally, in spite of the lack of research on coaching for the menopause, there is a body of evidence demonstrating how effective coaching is as a practice.

Conclusion

Menopause has been a taboo subject for many years and is only now emerging as an important topic to be discussed openly. That being said, it is different in different cultures. While there is limited evidence about how coaching can support women and men at this transition phase in life, there is a substantial body of research demonstrating both the general value of coaching and more specifically the benefits from health coaching. Menopause is an individualised experience and, as coaching is generally a personalised, confidential, forward-looking and solution-oriented approach, we believe it can offer a significant element of the solution for organisations and individuals.

Reflective questions

1. Should health service providers offer menopause coaching for women, and why?
2. What role can men play in managing menopause?
3. How might culture affect the responses of men and women to menopausal changes in women?

References

Bloch, A. (2002). Self-awareness during the menopause. *National Library of Medicine*, 30;41(1), 61–68. DOI: 10.1016/s0378-5122(01)00252-3

Brewis, J., Atkinson, C., Beck, V., Davies, A., & Duberley, J. (2020). Menopause and the workplace: New directions in HRM research and HR. *Human Resource Management Journal*, 31(1), 49–64.

Burleson, B. R., Metts, S., & Kirch, M. W. (2000). *Close Relationships*. Sage Books Chapter. DOI: 10.4135/9781452220437.n18

Deeks, A. (2003). Psychological aspects of menopause management. *Best Practice & Research Clinical Endocrinology & Metabolism*, 17(1), 17–31.

Dunn, S. (2022). The experience of workplace coaching for menopausal women. A descriptive phenomenological study. *International Journal of Evidence Based Coaching & Mentoring*, (Supplement), 97–108.

Eurich, T. (2018). What self-awareness really is (and how to cultivate it). *Harvard Business Review*, January.

Fujimoto, K. (2017). Effectiveness of coaching for enhancing the health of menopausal Japanese women. *Journal of Women & Aging*, 29(3), 216–229. DOI: 10.1080/08952841.2015.1137434

Grant, H. (2013). The most effective strategies for success. *Harvard Business Review*, March 25.

Gullette, M. (1997). Menopause as a magic marker: Discursive consolidation in the United States, and strategies for cultural combat (pp. 179–199). In P. A. Komesaroff, P. Rothfield, & J. Daly (eds.), *Reinterpreting Menopause, Cultural and Philosophical Issues*. London: Routledge.

Harrison, J. (undated). *How Coaching Can Help Your Career During Menopause*. Retrieved on 5 September 2022 from https://henpicked.net/how-coaching-can-help-your-career-during-menopause/

Hickey, M., Hunter, M. S., Santoro, N., & Ussher, J. (2022). Normalising menopause. *British Medical Journal*, 377. DOI: 10.1136/bmj-2021-069369

Kelly, B. (2011). Menopause as a social and cultural construction, *XULAneXUS*, 8(2), Article 4. Retrieved on 5 September 2022 from https://digitalcommons.xula.edu/xulanexus/vol8/iss2/4

Lee Lai Keen, I. (2018). *Why Is Self-Awareness Important in Coaching? International Coach Academy*. Retrieved on 5 September 2022 from https://coachcampus.com/coach-portfolios/research-papers/irene-lee-lai-kean-why-is-self-awareness-important-in-coaching/

Luthans, F., Avolio, B. J., Avey, J., & Norman, S. M. (2007). Positive psychological capital: Measurement and relationship with performance and satisfaction. *Personnel Psychology*, 60, 541–572.

Martin, E. (1997). The woman in the menopausal body (pp. 239–254). In P. A. Komesaroff, P. Rothfield, & J. Daly (eds.), *Reinterpreting Menopause, Cultural and Philosophical Issues*. London: Routledge.

Newman, P. & McDowell, A. (2016). Health changing conversations: Clinicians' experience of health coaching in the East of England. *Future Hospital Journal*, 3(2), 147–151.

Pandolfi, C. (2020). Active ingredients in executive coaching: A systematic literature review. *International Coaching Psychology Review*, 15(2), 6–30.

Rodger, S. (2021). How health coaching can help patients manage their own health. *Nursing Times [Online]*, 117(1).

Rogers, J. & Maini, A. (2016). *Coaching for Health: Why It Works and How to Do It.* Maidenhead: Open University Press.

Salathiel, E. & Passmore, J. (2021). *Does Health Coaching Work: A Critical Review of Coaching in the Health system.* Henley on Thames: Henley Business School, UK. Retrieved on 6 September from https://assets.henley.ac.uk/v3/fileUploads/Does-Health-Coaching-Work_-Salathiel-and-Passmore-April2021.pdf?

Singh, A. & Arora, A. K. (2005). Profile of menopausal women in rural North India. *Climacteric*, 8(2), 177–184.

Thom, D. A., Wolf, J., Gardner, H., DeVore, D., Lin, M., Ma, A., Ibarra-Castro, A., & Saba, G. (2016). A qual study of how health coaches support patients in making health-related decisions and behavioural changes. *Annals of Family Medicine*, 14(6), 509–516. DOI: 10.1370/afm.1988

Usher, K. (2022, June 8). *It's Time to Change the Narrative Around Menopause.* Retrieved on 5 September 2022 from https://menopauseinbusiness.com/2022/06/08/its-time-to-change-the-narrative-around-menopause/

Verburgh, M., Verdonk, P., Appelman, Y., Brood-van Zanten, M., & Nieuwenhuijsen, K. (2020). "I get that spirit in me" – Mentally empowering workplace health promotion for female workers in low paid jobs during menopause and mid-life. *International Journal of Environmental Research and Public Health*, 17, 6462.

World Health Organization (n.d.). *Menopause.* Retrieved on 30 September 2024 from www.who.int/news-room/fact-sheets/detail/menopause

Chapter 9

Coaching for heart health and recovery

Robert Kelly and Jolanta Burke

Introduction

Non-communicable diseases, such as heart disease, are responsible for 74% of deaths worldwide. They account for almost 80% of recurring hospital visits. Most can be prevented, managed, and potentially reversed by engaging in simple activities such as stopping smoking, regular exercise, good nutrition and managing stress and sleep (i.e., lifestyle medicine). Yet, many patients either do not follow their doctor's advice or do not sustain their health behaviour over the long term. In this chapter, we will review how coaching can assist patients in changing their behaviour and thereby prolonging their lives. We will start by reviewing the latest literature on the current approaches to behavioural change used by practitioners. We will then delve into the past research on how coaching has been used with cardiac patients to date and reflect on what future potential it has for saving people's lives. Finally, we will provide practical examples of the coaching application in heart failure, coronary artery disease, cardiac rehabilitation and lifestyle medicine cardiology programmes.

Theory and research

Heart disease is the leading cause of death worldwide, leading to almost 17 million deaths annually (Roth, 2020). Four out of five deaths occur from heart attacks and strokes, with 32% of premature deaths from heart disease. Chronic non-communicable diseases such as high blood pressure, diabetes, obesity, smoking-related illnesses, and metabolic syndromes cause 70% of these deaths each year. Risk factors for heart disease include smoking, drug misuse, obesity, diet, diabetes, high cholesterol, high blood pressure, poor sleep, stress, loneliness and isolation. Ideal heart health is present in less than 1% of the U.S. population, regardless of age (Lloyd-Jones et al., 2022). Furthermore, these chronic diseases are reversible in 80% of cases (Frates et al., 2019).

The World Health Organization (WHO) defines chronic conditions as those encompassing disability and disease that people 'live with' for extended periods (WHO, 2002). The Chronic Care Model (Wagner et al., 1996) is an internationally accepted model for managing non-communicable diseases and specifies self-management support as a critical component. In addition, the concept of patient empowerment for self-management was introduced into the WONCA Europe (2011) definition of general practice. Thus, self-management and patient empowerment support are crucial components in managing chronic conditions.

DOI: 10.4324/9781003319016-11

Heart failure (HF) is a chronic disease which often leads to premature deaths (7) and significantly lowers the quality of life (McDonagh et al., 2021). Standard treatment, as declared in national and international guidelines on HF (Heidenreich et al., 2022), includes self-care as a crucial part of maintenance. Examples of self-care behaviours comprise daily weighing, medication adherence, regular physical activity and monitoring of fluid intake and symptoms to prevent exacerbations (Jaarsma et al., 2021). Adherence to these behaviours has been found effective for alleviating illness symptoms, increasing the quality of life and reducing hospital readmissions and mortality better than drug therapy alone (Jaarsma et al., 2021), while non-adherence results in the opposite (Heidenreich et al., 2022; McDonagh et al., 2021). Still, many patients fail to implement ongoing self-care into their daily lives (Jaarsma et al., 2021). Therefore, it is crucial to change the behaviour of patients towards better self-care adherence and to close the gap between guideline-advised care and what patients do.

Changing health-related behaviour is a complex goal, as many factors determine behaviours. Informing patients about desirable behaviours is not enough; neither is applying common sense models, as they rarely result in the desired outcome (Lachman et al., 2018). Hence, it is necessary to base behaviour change interventions on evaluated scientific models. A review of interventions promoting HF self-care found that few studies used direct theory-based interventions; thus, it is unsurprising that the evidence on the efficacy of such interventions remains inconsistent (Alageel et al., 2017). There is increasing recognition of the importance of using strong theory to support intervention design (Frates et al., 2019; Kushner, 2015; Lloyd-Jones et al., 2022). One such theory is the lifestyle medicine six-pillar model.

Lifestyle medicine is an evidence-based therapeutic approach delivered by doctors to prevent, treat and potentially reverse lifestyle-related chronic diseases (Frates et al., 2019; Kushner, 2015). It is the application of medical, behavioural, motivational and environmental principles in a clinical setting. It teaches self-care and self-management, and it comprises pillars similar to heart risk factors: addiction behaviours, physical activity, healthy eating, sleep, stress and social connection. These factors have been shown to increase the risk for heart disease and premature death: smoking increases mortality by 25%, poor sleep by 30%, social isolation by 30%, inactivity by 12% and poor diet by over 40% (Visseren et al., 2021). Therefore, applying changes associated with lifestyle medicine pillars can support patients with cardiovascular disease.

The Diabetes Remission Clinical Trial (DiRECT) in the UK in 2017 showed that a 12week low-calorie diet with dietician lead coaching reverses type 2 diabetes and reduces weight in 60% of cases. This has a long-lasting effect of five years (Lean et al., 2018). Lifestyle Health Study in the United States shows that stress management supplemented with diet and activity as part of an intensive lifestyle program can reverse coronary atherosclerosis (Ornish et al., 1998). Mediterranean and plant-based diets lower heart disease risk by over 30% (Danesh et al., 2007). A 150-minute exercise, physical activity and one-hour resistance training weekly regimen lowers risk by 20–30%. The EPIC trial showed that multiple lifestyle interventions reduced heart attack risk by 80% (EPIC, 2007). Thus, lifestyle medicine offers a solution to prevent and treat heart disease. The challenge is empowering patients to take medicine and make lifestyle changes.

Despite mounting evidence, many patients respond less well to lifestyle interventions (Alonso et al., 2021). For example, a European study of patients with established cardiovascular disease showed that most have failed to modify their behaviour and continued to enjoy a sedentary lifestyle, used unhealthy substances and practised unhealthy eating despite increased mortality risks (DeBacquer et al., 2022). This puts additional pressure on primary care, which becomes vital in supporting patient autonomy and enabling them to develop expertise in managing their health and wellness (Mola et al., 2008). This support has been identified as a potentially impactful avenue, with education and training noted as potential ways of engaging primary care clinicians in patient self-management support (Wagner et al., 2001). However, it is also recognised that visits in primary care may be brief and that low readiness to change may exist among patients. As such, alternative ways to support patients in lifestyle interventions are required.

Focusing on person-centred care, where the care delivered is aligned with patients' needs and expectations and is interlinked to chronic disease management, increases the effectiveness of intervention programmes (Lloyd-Jones et al., 2022). However, low uptake of some patient interventions – such as goal-setting, action-planning, and patient motivation – were noted as factors that may have reduced the impact of lifestyle interventions (Winter et al., 2016). The reason may be due to the complexity of interventions not being delivered as planned or their effectiveness being difficult to assess (British Heart Foundation, 2018). In these situations, drawing on the assistance of health coaches may prove particularly beneficial for patients and healthcare staff.

Behavioural changes

Regardless of the approach used to help patients modify their behaviour, behavioural change techniques (BCT) are essential to consider to ensure the success of an intervention (Davis et al., 2015; Dombrowski et al., 2016). Some of the most prevalent BCTs used with patients with cardiovascular disease to improve physical activity were habit-reversal and self-monitoring of behaviour (Patterson et al., 2022; Rahman et al., 2015). A meta-analysis of studies of patients with post-myocardial infarction (MI; heart attack) and HF showed that the only cardiac rehabilitation programme ineffective in reducing cardiovascular disease risk factors was the one that did not include instructions on how participants can change their behaviours (Heron et al., 2016). Thus, the conscious application of BCT is fundamental when working with cardiac patients.

In the context of preventing and reducing the risk of cardiovascular disease, the most effective techniques for weight management including the provision of explicit instruction, self-monitoring, relapse and prompt practice (Dombrowski et al., 2012; Patnode et al., 2017); whereas the BCTs for engaging with physical activity and/or weight management included self-monitoring supplemented with one of the following techniques: prompting intention formation, specific goal-setting, review of behavioural goals or providing feedback on performance (Michie et al., 2009; Wolever et al., 2013). Thus, an effective method for behavioural change is required when working with individuals, and coaching practice may offer a solution to this challenge.

Coaching as a solution

Growing evidence suggests coaching improves behaviour change in heart disease/risk factor interventions in primary and secondary care settings (Gordon, 2016). The impact of studies has a significant variation between the UK and the United States, as well as between groups and individual samples. However, findings to date are inconclusive.

Moreover, studies are designed with a follow-up of usually 3–6 months, and little is known about how the coaching intervention affects cardiac patients long-term. Furthermore, of the published studies, many show little power and inconsistency of benefits for coaching in CCF and CAD/risk management, especially that related to weight, diabetes, stopping smoking and physical activity. Thus, better-powered quality research is required.

A meta-analysis of coaching interventions in patients with cardiovascular risk factors showed that motivational interviewing was the most common approach to coaching and had a negligible impact on participants' healthy behaviours (An & Song, 2020; Li et al., 2020; Masterson-Creber et al., 2016). It is currently considered a standard coaching model by AHA and ESC for lifestyle interventions based on more than 1,000 studies (e.g., Blumenhthal et al., 2019; Visseren et al., 2021). However, these studies vary in size and have long-term effects. Moreover, cultural differences were noted with several UK angina studies showing no effect of MI compared with U.S. studies (Ismail et al., 2020; Michie et al., 2009). At the same time, compared with other BCTs, motivational interviewing was one of the least effective techniques (Li et al., 2020). Thus, alternative coaching approaches should be explored when working with individuals to prevent or reduce the risk of cardiovascular disease.

The Trans-Theoretical Model (TTM) of behaviour change (Prochaska & Velicer, 1997) matches the benefits of MI in heart health and risk factor prevention and is a vital tool to address patients who may not be ready to change. The cardiac benefits of both methods relate to risk factor reduction, but the sustained benefit data is non-existent, so the impact on heart mortality is difficult to define. Nevertheless, a clear lifestyle benefit exists in using TMC in smoking cessation, alcohol reduction, diet, exercise, and weight management (Li et al., 2020). Similarly, the self-determination theory informs rehab exercise and weight programmes with 12 monthly benefits (Boehm et al., 2020).

Fogg Behaviour Model (Fogg, 2020) has been used for mobile health tools and has been shown to improve weight, diet and diabetes management when its principles are applied (see Anchora Health Holland) (Forte et al., 2022). It is based on the principle of behaviour design: making behaviour changes easy to do and reducing the motivation needed for behaviour to happen. Once prompted, the behaviour will happen. If easy and likely to be successful in helping to reach the desired health goal, e.g., eating one piece of fruit with breakfast and dinner each day to drive healthy eating. Changing the patient's ability to do behaviour and finding suitable prompts are critical to making behaviour happen. Adding emotion to the action whereby patients feel rewarded for doing the behaviour will encourage them to repeat the same behaviour, ultimately creating new habits. Prompting can be achieved by nudging patients with technology or patient reminders. Further research is required to test this method in helping cardiology patients to achieve long-lasting health behaviour change and thereby improve their cardiac outcomes.

An emerging approach comes from positive psychology coaching (PPC), which incorporates research and techniques that aim to facilitate wellbeing, optimise the use of personal strengths and utilise other evidence-based interventions to assist people in reaching an optimal level of functioning (van Zyl et al., 2020). Several models of PPC exist (e.g., Burke, 2018; Passmore & Oades, 2014). While evidence for individual positive psychology assets – such as the use of character strengths, optimism or gratitude activities – exists (Huffman et al., 2011; Nikrahan et al., 2016), further research is required to establish the effect of using positive psychology tools as part of a PPC programme in helping cardiac patients engage more effectively with healthy behaviours, not only wellbeing.

Applying positive psychology concepts in cardio coaching is associated with lower all-cause mortality in type 2 diabetes (Massey et al., 2019) and improved heart disease health outcomes (Dubois et al., 2015). The Gratitude Research in Acute Coronary Events (GRACE) study (Huffman et al., 2015) showed that optimism predicted exercise habits at six-month follow-ups in angina patients and was associated with less frequent hospital readmission than low optimism patients. Gratitude improved future exercise habits and medication adherence but did not affect rehospitalisation. Furthermore, the Prevention of Events with Angiotensin Converting Enzyme (PEACE) trial in acute coronary syndrome (ACS) and heart attack patients included positive psychology and motivational interviewing either daily or weekly for six weeks. Physical activity, medication adherence and mood significantly improved compared to usual care. Finally, the REACH study of positive psychology in heart failure patients also showed improvement in medication adherence, less salt intake, and fewer HF symptoms compared with usual care. Mobile health studies (Planning Advance Care Together, or PACT) providing text messages to heart attack patients to promote physical activity and wellbeing show minor improvements. Of interest, patient feedback emphasised the need to tailor service to individuals to improve engagement in behaviour change.

These studies provided preliminary evidence of the effectiveness of using positive health interventions with cardiac patients. Furthermore, Trom and Burke (2022) showed that when coaching is applied alongside a positive psychology intervention, such as gratitude, it affects eudemonic wellbeing, helping individuals develop life meaning instead of more fleeting hedonic wellbeing associated with higher levels of positive affect, lower levels of negative affect and life satisfaction. This is particularly important for cardiac patients who experience death anxiety and depression (Yildirim et al., 2022) associated with traumatic health-related experiences. Thus, coaching using positive interventions can support patients' health and wellbeing.

Furthermore, a correlation was found between behaviours associated with lifestyle medicine pillars (physical activity, good sleep, nutrition, relationships, stress management and moderate substance use) and psychological flourishing, the highest level of wellbeing (Burke & Dunne, 2022). This means that wellbeing may be essential in motivating individuals to engage in healthy behaviours. For example, evidence shows that positive emotions, such as those experienced by practising wellbeing interventions, can sustain goal pursuit, e.g., weight loss (Carver & Scheier, 1999; Plemmons & Weiss, 2013). Thus, PPC, which is focused on wellbeing as part of the coaching process or its outcome, can play a crucial role in the link between body and mind, although the context within which they are applied may alter the outcome (e.g., Orehek et al., 2011). This allows practitioners and researchers to create a range of coaching interventions that can help improve wellbeing and health behaviours. However, further research is required to identify the impact of the interaction between body and mind interventions and various positive outcomes relating to changes in health behaviours.

Practice

Most doctors are too busy and do not make time to coach their patients. They may refer patients to chronic disease programs (cardiac rehabilitation, heart failure clinic programmes and chronic disease management services), a community-based exercise programme, smoking cessation, stress management and sleep clinics. However, the availability of these services is varied, and they need to be better aligned with patient health problems. A more focused and issue-directed approach is required.

Cardiology programmes like cardiac rehab and HF clinics effectively reduce cardiovascular events and hospital admission rates, but the effect is short-term. For example, many rehab programmes for coronary artery disease, stent, bypass surgery and heart attack patients last no more than 6–8 weeks, and it is estimated that half of the patients who suffer heart attacks stop taking medications after rehabilitation. An opportunity for more significant benefit by coaching exists, as many of these patients return to the hospital with future heart issues. Therefore, a more combined approach to healthcare support is required, with cardiologists/physicians and primary care doctors employing coaching to understand their patients' needs and to offer them immediate support by helping them realise that lifestyle changes are required. At the same time, the existing programmes for cardiac rehabilitation can serve the patients by offering them medium-term support that assists them in providing education and developing some habits.

Finally, an ongoing coaching-led service is needed to offer patients long-term support that allows them to assimilate knowledge from their medical doctor and lifestyle programmes, filter all this through their values and embed a new behaviour into their lives. In this section, we will discuss the role of cardiologists and heart cardio coaching programmes in helping patients assimilate new health behaviours.

Cardiologist support

Whilst cardiologists do not have enough time to coach their patients, the coaching approach is helpful in several situations. Traditional healthcare is delivered in most parts by giving patients information, telling them what to do and leaving it up to the patient to make their changes. The coaching-based approach aims to develop an ongoing relationship between patient and doctor to support patient empowerment, sustained health behaviour change and better patient engagement. This has a whole-patient and lifestyle-practice focus. Patients are active partners in their care, and long-term significant lifestyle changes are expected. It is a collaborative, coordinated, team-based approach shared with allied health professionals. Good communication is, therefore, essential and the coaching approach allows for this to happen.

Primary care is actively trying to bring coaching into clinical practice. However, most heart patients follow up with their GP and then join a chronic disease management programme at that clinic to check blood pressure and cholesterol, and check their medication. Community-based programmes for rehabilitation (essentially physical-exercise driven) provide ongoing community-based rehabilitation for patients, but attendance is traditionally poor. Attempts at using technology to keep contact with patients for longer cardiac rehab follow-up exist with improved behaviour, yet after six months, most patients lose interest. What is missing is ongoing patient support and close communication, which cardio coaches can deliver.

Empathy-based coaching (Frates et al., 2011) highlights the need to better understand patients, align motivation with goals, build confidence, set accountability, and continue the same process. Empathy-based coaching helps patients to help themselves. It builds motivation, confidence, engagement and active listening. It relies on patients increasing their self-awareness and insights, and it strives to help them find their own answers. They have a solution. The focus is on what is working well. It is a collaboration between patient and doctor, and the overall goal is sustained action, self-efficacy and better health. In this approach, the doctor has a crucial coaching role in the patient care path to support behaviour change and health improvement instead of telling the patient what to do.

In cardiology rehabilitation programmes, patients will access exercise, healthy eating, d lifestyle post–heart attack education advice, usually from a physiotherapist/nurse. Some may access stress management services. These programmes are standardised by Heart Association's guidelines around the world (Corrà et al., 2010; Dalal et al., 2015). The objectives for the patient are primarily education, risk factor management and exercise. Most programmes try to put patients on a path to better heart health to reduce another heart attack. Once six weeks pass, the patient is discharged and advised to continue positive behaviours and follow up with their cardiologist or primary care doctor. The more motivated patient may seek out exercise programmes in the community, but for half of the patients, it is the end of their health-change journey, as they find it difficult to keep going. In these circumstances, the help of a coach is essential.

After rehabilitation, the patient may follow up with GP and/or the hospital cardiology clinic. After that, they are discharged from hospital clinic care. Patients often follow up directly with their GP and may enter a chronic disease management programme at the practice. The opportunities are there to coach patients in lifestyle medicine, to facilitate stopping smoking, more exercise, better eating and stress management. Still, it requires a joined-up structure that is patient-centred, doctor-led and multidisciplinary, like ongoing cardiac rehabilitation or a lifestyle health programme (Ornish, 2023). Most programmes are six weeks; a few run for six months. They have multiple allied health professionals like physiotherapists, dieticians and stress management staff. Few have dedicated health coaches. Fewer have a dedicated care pathway from the cardiologist to personalise individual patient health goals and align patient behaviour change with patient risk factors such as eating behaviours or the need to exercise/do more resistance work. Instead, patients are often given everything together at the same time.

The COACH Program in Australia is perceived among cardiologists as the world's best coaching-based practice for chronic disease prevention (British Heart Foundation, 2018; Jelinek et al., 2009). Hospitalised patients with heart disease risk factors and/or chronic diseases are enrolled in a six-month coaching programme (telephone-based, with five in-person one-to-one sessions). The coaches are often nurses trained to guide patients to improve health behaviours and achieve heart health guideline targets such as walking 150 minutes per week. The instructions for each patient come from the doctor's office, and patients can continue the programme beyond six months. The care pathways are standardised by the Australian Heart Association heart disease treatment guidelines (in most other countries with similar guidelines, there is a significant gap between what treatment is advised and what happens for patients).

The COACH Program has five years of follow-up data that shows sustained improvement in all risk factors, reductions in cholesterol, blood pressure control and increases in physical activity and medication adherence, which can be modified during the time frame to better achieve target levels – nurses direct the patient to call the doctor for this (Dalal et al., 2015). At the same time, these interventions have been reported to reduce cardiac mortality in the Australian population. Patients achieve 52% reduction in total cholesterol and 92% increase in physical activity, and 95% stop smoking at 18-month follow up. This translates to 16% reduction in hospital admissions and 15% reduction in cardiac admissions (British Heart Foundation, 2018). The programme is also provided by BUPA Insurance in Australia for all patients. In addition, coaches are trained in cardiology and motivational interviewing skills.

The data relates to The COACH Program vs standard of care. The same programme is also used in type 2 diabetes with similar lifestyle gains enabled by the coaching support of patients (Corrà et al., 2010; Jelinek et al., 2009). The Finnish Diabetes/One Life Programme combines medical clinic visits, group coaching and motivational interviewing, and leads to 3.5% reduction in ten-year heart disease risk, with 15% increase in healthy eating. Of interest, 48% of participants achieved no change in lifestyle (Jelinek et al., 2009). Coaches phone patients, are accessible outside these calls and provide written information to clients. However, somewhat surprisingly, this programme is not practised universally outside Australia. However, it is available in Holland, which has a reimbursed preventative health payment for all citizens.

A web-supported programme in Holland (Vascular Risk Programme) which is nurse led, provides education, messaging and monitoring of patients. This programme results in 7 times greater reduction in smoking rates and 19 times more low-density lipoprotein (LDL) reduction among patients who take part. Canada's Cardio Health Awareness Program (CHAP) identifies heart disease risk awareness in the community and encourages self-management skills. Nurses call, teach, educate and refer patients to doctors if needed to optimise medication or self-testing of blood pressure (BP) at home, and then provide coaching in the community. This programme is associated with significant sustained reductions in blood pressure from 142/78 to 123/69. This in turn affected stroke and heart attack event risk. The Heart of New Ulm (HONU) study based on 19,000 people living in New Ulm, Minnesota, USA was established with individual, community and medical care involvement. Patients were coached in behaviour change and these programmes extended into work, whole family and community. This led to significant uptake of positive lifestyle behaviours in 50–80% of people, reduction in blood pressure and LDL cholesterol control. There was an impressive 200% increase in consumption of five vegetables and two pieces of fruit daily, 50% reduction in smoking, 30% increase in physical activity of at least 150 minutes per week, 70% reduction in cholesterol and 94% increase adherence to medications. This programme included dedicated once-monthly 20-minute coaching sessions for six months, dedicated weight programmes (coaching supported and with community activities, as well). The doctors directed medications and provided additional education. Members of the community supported each other's efforts to be and stay healthy.

HF programmes are usually nurse-led. These closely monitor patients and manage acute HF episodes in the community so that patients do not have to go to the hospital. This support works exceptionally well to empower these patients and keep them as well as possible. The HF nurse role is dedicated to patient coaching and behaviour management. Some primary care practices work with these groups. Unfortunately, like in most areas of healthcare, resources are limited, so patients are expected to take care of themselves. In the absence of accountability, half of the people do not stick with behaviour change (Oscarsson et al., 2020), so they inevitably get more heart problems.

The individuals at risk for heart attacks/HF are those who are overweight, have high blood pressure, smokers, inactive, and chronically stressed. Socially isolated groups have access to selective risk factor coaching-led services (like smoking cessation). Still, most of these are in isolation from their cardiologist and are not managed in a way to support additional behaviour improvements simultaneously. This means an opportunity is lost for helping patients who make progress in stopping a bad habit of adding more good health habits around the same time, especially when motivation is likely to be strong.

Therefore, what should the cardiologist be doing when it comes to longer-term management of the patient or beyond the acute hospital admission and finding ways to prevent or retard the onset of heart disease? The healthcare model needs to better engage patients with greater doctor empathy, coaching leadership and more coordinated extended-lasting lifestyle behaviour change programmes.

The COACH Program is validated as one approach whereby nurses/coaches and primary cardiologists/physicians/doctors can collectively improve heart outcomes and sustain medication compliance – behaviour changes leading to mortality benefits (British Heart Foundation, 2018; Jelinek et al., 2009). In addition, a more empathic model of positive psychology and lifestyle interventions (in stress, sleep and social connection) may improve outcomes and reach a more significant number of at-risk patients.

Either way, the patient's journey from heart risk or after a cardiac event to recovery, rehabilitation and possible disease reversal requires a heart coach/buddy to support and keep the patient accountable. The challenge exists regarding the best coaching method(s) to apply and whether an in-person or technology self-directed coaching approach would work better. The COACH, Effect of Strict Blood Pressure Control and ACE Inhibition on Progression of Chronic Renal Failure in Pediatric Patients (ESCAPE) and HONU programmes might benefit from combining their strengths in coaching, involving all stakeholders, teamwork, evidence-based treatment targets and promoting self-efficacy, aligning behaviours with clear goals and going to where the patients are in the community. Success for coaches happens when they contact clients and provide regular support and accountability.

What can the cardiologist do?

First, the cardiologist must lead health improvement and sustained behaviour change. When doctors practise what they preach, 80% of patients follow (Frates et al., 2019). The doctor can learn/train to be a behaviour change coach. This might be best learned at medical school. The empathetic doctor/healthcare professional is a much more understanding person for a patient to engage with. As a result, patients are more likely to trust and respond. The doctor is ultimately (with the patient) responsible for directing patients' heart care and prescribing medications, rehabilitation and follow-up. Doctors need to self-educate in lifestyle medicine and keep up to date with the short life-changing benefits of exercise, diet, sleep, stress reduction and social connection in heart patients and the entire community. Several doctors prescribe nutrition, exercise and stress tools as part of their patient care instructions. The ESCAPE programme showed good improvement in BP control through doctor engagement and medication adjustment, whereas COACH and HONU achieved greater improvements by adding coaching, community and home support (Jelinek et al., 2009).

Doctors need more time to see multiple patients. However, there are great opportunities for mini-coaching to initiate conversations with patients about their behaviour and help them move through the TTM process to a point where they are ready to change. Bringing additional lifestyle coaches on board at that point can then give patients more time and support, but the doctor must oversee and support the patient's progress or act as the patient's accountability partner. The doctor needs to acquire the empathetic health and lifestyle coaching skillset.

Simplifying the coaching process may also help manage time and patient understanding. Again, that comes from clear and effective coaching tools. For example, in the Fogg Behaviour Model (Fogg, 2020), change happens when people choose simple, easy-to-do behaviours that will make them feel successful so that they will feel great and want to repeat the behaviour, ultimately leading to new healthy habits. Doctors can teach this approach in a relatively simple way, and when patients succeed with this, they will often shift their mindset to making more changes.

It is also possible that the doctor may hold a personal interest like running or yoga that they can teach the patient as a way to become healthier. This still requires a coaching/accountability approach that closely supports patient compliance and links to the cardiology patient record to see how patients' health is improving from these behaviours or if other steps are also needed.

Doctors must help patients stay well and prevent disease because the health system and society cannot be sustained if everyone gets sick. Doctors must also practise what they preach to keep themselves healthy and well, especially during burnout. Doctors, patients and society need to choose health over inaction and do something active about it instead of ignoring it or making excuses for not looking after themselves. Collaboration and coaching are ideally suited to address these problems.

Finally, we see the role of a cardiologist as a quarterback in American football. A patient is the ball, and to get the patient to the goal of health, the quarterback passes the ball to crucial people but will still ultimately keep control of the ball. For the patient, the cardiologist will oversee their heart attack patient care. They will follow up on progress, complete rehabilitation, and liaise with exercise, diet and coaches. They will keep patients accountable via technology or in person. They will use a coaching approach to support the patient's goal to stay and be healthy and deliver in a positive, empathetic manner that genuinely cares for the patient. All this engagement can only be done successfully with a coaching mindset that allows one to get the best out of patients and other professionals involved in patient care – the team that can help them survive and thrive.

Conclusion

Cardiovascular disease is the leading cause of death worldwide, yet most cardiovascular disease is reversible by stopping smoking, eating healthy, taking regular exercise, sleeping for seven hours each night, lowering stress, socialising and looking after blood pressure, blood sugar, and cholesterol medications. Still, physical and mental behaviour change is required to effect lifestyle medicine interventions and reduce the risks of heart disease.

Lifestyle medicine emphasises doctor self-care, and patients will follow the advice of doctors who practice what they preach. However, current cardiology studies highlight a growing prevalence of heart disease and risk factors across all age groups. For example, 98% of the population in the United States is unhealthy regarding physical activity and diet. These risk factors cause chronic diseases, responsible for 80% of hospital admissions and recurrent healthcare costs.

An enormous gap exists between treatment recommendations and how people and patients live. Closing that gap requires a coordinated approach of education, medication, lifestyle interventions and close monitoring, follow-up and accountability delivered by an empathetic physician-guided approach. No doctor alone could succeed. A multidisciplinary team of lifestyle medicine/heart coaches is needed to support the patient's health needs and achieve effective, long-lasting behaviour change.

Coaching is very effective in achieving patient health change. In Australia, It has long-lasting prognostic benefits when used in conjunction with doctor-led care of chronic disease and heart patients. Many patients are at risk for chronic diseases and need to kickstart health and lifestyle behaviour changes before a heart attack or a stroke. The data support finding a way to bring COACH-like programmes into the community. M-technology, virtual coaches and phone coaching services are all known to help once tailored to individual patients. Success also requires a model that connects the patient, a primary doctor looking after patients' chronic disease and the lifestyle/health coach. It also needs to link with family, community and support.

The optimal coaching method needs to be clarified: motivational interviewing, TTM, Fogg, and positive psychology have all been reported in smaller patient populations despite some poorly powered meta-analyses promoting each method for health behaviour improvement but not for measurable cardiac mortality reduction. At the same time, extensive studies have used a blend of coaching methods to manage patients. In fairness, some weakness in the coaching theory definition does limit the quality of available data.

Healthcare is overwhelmed, poorly run and largely dysfunctional worldwide. The best solution is to avoid getting sick in the first place. That is only possible by living a healthier life, avoiding chronic illnesses by not smoking or drinking too much; having a healthy mind, body and diet; exercising and sleeping well; and socialising with friends and family. Coaching programmes are needed to keep everyone healthy, reach out to at-risk people, and help them reduce their risk by effecting meaningful behaviour change in conjunction with a supervising medical doctor. A healthier culture is also needed in society, at home and in the workplace to support this better approach to healthier hearts and longer life.

Reflective questions

1. What are the differences between a health coaching and a specific cardio coaching?
2. What other coaching models can be used in coaching cardiac patients?
3. How much cardiological knowledge is necessary to conduct cardio coaching?

References

Alageel, S., Gulliford, M. C., McDermott, L., & Wright, A. J. (2017). Multiple health behaviour change interventions for primary prevention of cardiovascular disease in primary care: Systematic review and meta-analysis. *BMJ Open, 7*(6), e015375. https://doi.org/10.1136/bmjopen-2016-01537

Alonso, W. W., Kupzyk, K., Norman, J., Bills, S. E., Bosak, K., Dunn, S. L., Deka, P., & Pozehl, B. (2021). Negative attitudes, self-efficacy, and relapse management mediate long-term adherence to exercise in patients with heart failure. *Annals of Behavioral Medicine, 55*(10), 1031–1041. https://doi-org.elib.tcd.ie/10.1093/abm/kaab002

An, S., & Song, R. (2020). Effects of health coaching on behavioral modification among adults with cardiovascular risk factors: Systematic review and meta-analysis. *Patient Education & Counseling, 103*(10), 2029–2038. https://doi-org.elib.tcd.ie/10.1016/j.pec.2020.04.029

Boehm, J. K., Qureshi, F., Chen, Y., Soo, J., Umukoro, P., Hernandez, R., Lloyd-Jones, D., & Kubzansky, L. D. (2020). Optimism and cardiovascular health: Longitudinal findings from the coronary artery risk development in young adults study. *Psychosomatic Medicine*, 82(8), 774–781. https://doi.org/10.1097/PSY.0000000000000855

British Heart Foundation (2018). *International cardiovascular disease prevention case studies.* Retrieved from: https://www.bhf.org.uk/for-professionals/healthcare-professionals/data-and-statistics/international-cardiovascular-disease-case-studies

Burke, J. (2018). Conceptual framework for a positive psychology coaching practice. *Coaching Psychologist*, 14(1), 16–25. https://doi-org.elib.tcd.ie/10.53841/bpstcp.2018.14.1.16

Burke, J., & Dunne, P. J. (2022). Lifestyle medicine pillars as predictors of psychological flourishing. *Frontiers in Psychology*, 13, 963806. https://doi-org.elib.tcd.ie/10.3389/fpsyg.2022.963806

Carver, C. S., & Scheier, M. F. (1999). Stress, coping, and self-regulatory processes. In L. A. Pervin & O. P. John (Eds.), *Handbook of personality: Theory and research* (pp. 553–575). New York: Guilford Press.

Corrà, U., European Association of Cardiovascular Prevention and Rehabilitation Committee for Science Guidelines, EACPR, Piepoli, M. F., Carré, F., Heuschmann, P., Hoffmann, U., Verschuren, M., Halcox, J., Document Reviewers, Giannuzzi, P., Saner, H., Wood, D., Piepoli, M. F., Corrà, U., Benzer, W., Bjarnason-Wehrens, B., Dendale, P., Gaita, D., McGee, H., . . . Schmid, J. P. (2010). Secondary prevention through cardiac rehabilitation: Physical activity counselling and exercise training: Key components of the position paper from the cardiac rehabilitation section of the european association of cardiovascular prevention and rehabilitation. *European Heart Journal*, 31(16), 1967–1974. https://doi.org/10.1093/eurheartj/ehq236

Dalal, H. M., Doherty, P., & Taylor, R. S. (2015). Cardiac rehabilitation. *BMJ (Clinical Research Ed.)*, 351, h5000. https://doi.org/10.1136/bmj.h5000

Danesh, J., Saracci, R., Berglund, G., Feskens, E., Overvad, K., Panico, S., Thompson, S., Fournier, A., Clavel-Chapelon, F., Canonico, M., Kaaks, R., Linseisen, J., Boeing, H., Pischon, T., Weikert, C., Olsen, A., Tjønneland, A., Johnsen, S. P., Jensen, M. K., Quirós, J. R., . . . EPIC-Heart (2007). EPIC-Heart: The cardiovascular component of a prospective study of nutritional, lifestyle and biological factors in 520,000 middle-aged participants from 10 European countries. *European Journal of Epidemiology*, 22(2), 129–141. https://doi.org/10.1007/s10654-006-9096-8

Davis, R., Campbell, R., Hildon, Z., Hobbs, L., & Michie, S. (2015). Theories of behaviour and behaviour change across the social and behavioural sciences: A scoping review. *Health Psychology Review*, 9(3), 323–344. https://doi.org/10.1080/17437199.2014.941722

De Bacquer, D., Astin, F., Kotseva, K., Pogosova, N., De Smedt, D., De Backer, G., Rydén, L., Wood, D., Jennings, C., & EUROASPIRE IV and V surveys of the European Observational Research Programme of the European Society of Cardiology (2022). Poor adherence to lifestyle recommendations in patients with coronary heart disease: Results from the EUROASPIRE surveys. *European Journal of Preventive Cardiology*, 29(2), 383–395. https://doi.org/10.1093/eurjpc/zwab115

Dombrowski, S. U., O'Carroll, R. E., & Williams, B. (2016). Form of delivery as a key 'active ingredient' in behaviour change interventions. *British Journal of Health Psychology*, 21(4), 733–740. https://doi.org/10.1111/bjhp.12203

Dombrowski, S. U., Sniehotta, F. F., Avenell, A., Johnston, M., MacLennan, G., & Araújo-Soares, V. (2012). Identifying active ingredients in complex behavioural interventions for obese adults with obesity-related co-morbidities or additional risk factors for co-morbidities: A systematic review. *Health Psychology Review*, 6(1), 7–32. https://doi.org/10.1080/17437199.2010.513298

DuBois, C. M., Lopez, O. V., Beale, E. E., Healy, B. C., Boehm, J. K., & Huffman, J. C. (2015). Relationships between positive psychological constructs and health outcomes in patients with cardiovascular disease: A systematic review. *International Journal of Cardiology*, 195, 265–280. https://doi.org/10.1016/j.ijcard.2015.05.121

Fogg B. J. (2020). *Tiny habits: Small changes that change everything.* Penguin Press.

Frates, B., Bonnet, J. P., Joseph, R., & Petersen, J. A. (2019). *Lifestyle medicine handbook.* Healthy Learning.

Frates, E. P., Moore, M. A., Lopez, C. N., & McMahon, G. T. (2011). Coaching for behavior change in physiatry. *American Journal of Physical Medicine & Rehabilitation*, 90(12), 1074–1082. https://doi.org/10.1097/PHM.0b013e31822dea9a

Gordon, N. F., Salmon, R. D., Wright, B. S., Faircloth, G. C., Reid, K. S., & Gordon, T. L. (2016). Clinical effectiveness of lifestyle health coaching: Case study of an evidence-based program. *American Journal of Lifestyle Medicine, 11*(2), 153–166. https://doi.org/10.1177/1559827615592351

Heidenreich, P. A., Bozkurt, B., Aguilar, D., Allen, L. A., Byun, J. J., Colvin, M. M., Deswal, A., Drazner, M. H., Dunlay, S. M., Evers, L. R., Fang, J. C., Fedson, S. E., Fonarow, G. C., Hayek, S. S., Hernandez, A. F., Khazanie, P., Kittleson, M. M., Lee, C. S., Link, M. S., & Milano, C. A. (2022). 2022 AHA/ACC/HFSA fuideline for the management of heart failure: Executive summary: A report of the american college of cardiology/american heart association joint committee on clinical practice guidelines. *Journal of The American College of Cardiology (JACC), 79*(17), 1757–1780. https://doi-org.elib.tcd.ie/10.1016/j.jacc.2021.12.011

Heron, N., Kee, F., Donnelly, M., Cardwell, C., Tully, M. A., & Cupples, M. E. (2016). Behaviour change techniques in home-based cardiac rehabilitation: A systematic review. *The British Journal of General Practice: The Journal of the Royal College of General Practitioners, 66*(651), e747–e757. https://doi.org/10.3399/bjgp16X686617

Huffman, J. C., Beale, E. E., Beach, S. R., Celano, C. M., Belcher, A. M., Moore, S. V., Suarez, L., Gandhi, P. U., Motiwala, S. R., Gaggin, H., & Januzzi, J. L. (2015). Design and baseline data from the Gratitude Research in Acute Coronary Events (GRACE) study. *Contemporary Clinical Trials, 44*, 11–19. https://doi.org/10.1016/j.cct.2015.07.002

Huffman, J. C., Mastromauro, C. A., Boehm, J. K., Seabrook, R., Fricchione, G. L., Denninger, J. W., & Lyubomirsky, S. (2011). Development of a positive psychology intervention for patients with acute cardiovascular disease. *Heart International, 6*(2), e14. https://doi.org/10.4081/hi.2011.e14

Jaarsma, T., Hill, L., Bayes-Genis, A., La Rocca, H. B., Castiello, T., Čelutkienė, J., Marques-Sule, E., Plymen, C. M., Piper, S. E., Riegel, B., Rutten, F. H., Ben Gal, T., Bauersachs, J., Coats, A. J. S., Chioncel, O., Lopatin, Y., Lund, L. H., Lainscak, M., Moura, B., Mullens, W., . . . Strömberg, A. (2021). Self-care of heart failure patients: Practical management recommendations from the Heart Failure Association of the European Society of Cardiology. *European Journal of Heart Failure, 23*(1), 157–174. https://doi.org/10.1002/ejhf.2008

Jelinek, M., Vale, M. J., Liew, D., Grigg, L., Dart, A., Hare, D. L., & Best, J. D. (2009). The COACH program produces sustained improvements in cardiovascular risk factors and adherence to recommended medications-two years follow-up. *Heart, Lung & Circulation, 18*(6), 388–392. https://doi.org/10.1016/j.hlc.2009.06.001

Lachman, M. E., Lipsitz, L., Lubben, J., Castaneda-Sceppa, C., & Jette, A. M. (2018). When adults don't exercise: Behavioral strategies to increase physical activity in sedentary middle-aged and older adults. *Innovation in Aging, 2*(1), igy007. https://doi.org/10.1093/geroni/igy007

Lean, M. E. J., Leslie, W. S., Brosnahan, N., Thom, G., McCombie, L., Welsh, P., Sattar, N., Kean, S., Ford, I., McConnachie, A., Barnes, A. C., Adamson, A. J., Mathers, J. C., Peters, C., Zhyzhneuskaya, S., Al-Mrabeh, A., Hollingsworth, K. G., Taylor, R., Rodrigues, A. M., & Rehackova, L. (2018). Primary care-led weight management for remission of type 2 diabetes (DiRECT): An open-label, cluster-randomised trial. *Lancet, 391*(10120), 541–551. https://doi-org.elib.tcd.ie/10.1016/S0140-6736(17)33102

Li, X., Yang, S., Wang, Y., Yang, B., & Zhang, J. (2020). Effects of a transtheoretical model – based intervention and motivational interviewing on the management of depression in hospitalized patients with coronary heart disease: A randomized controlled trial. *BMC Public Health, 20*(1), 420. https://doi.org/10.1186/s12889-020-08568-x

Lloyd-Jones, D. M., Allen, N. B., Anderson, C. A. M., Black, T., Brewer, L. C., Foraker, R. E., Grandner, M. A., Lavretsky, H., Perak, A. M., Sharma, G., Rosamond, W., & American Heart Association (2022). Life's essential 8: Updating and enhancing the american heart association's construct of cardiovascular health: A presidential advisory from the american heart association. *Circulation, 146*(5), e18–e43. https://doi.org/10.1161/CIR.0000000000001078

Massey, C. N., Feig, E. H., Duque-Serrano, L., Wexler, D., Moskowitz, J. T., & Huffman, J. C. (2019). Well-being interventions for individuals with diabetes: A systematic review. *Diabetes Research and Clinical Practice, 147*, 118–133. https://doi.org/10.1016/j.diabres.2018.11.014

Masterson Creber, R., Patey, M., Lee, C. S., Kuan, A., Jurgens, C., & Riegel, B. (2016). Motivational interviewing to improve self-care for patients with chronic heart failure: MITI-HF randomized controlled trial. *Patient Education and Counseling*, 99(2), 256–264. https://doi.org/10.1016/j.pec.2015.08.031

McDonagh, T. A., Metra, M., Adamo, M., Gardner, R. S., Baumbach, A., Böhm, M., Burri, H., Butler, J., Čelutkienė, J., Chioncel, O., Cleland, J. G. F., Coats, A. J. S., Crespo-Leiro, M. G., Farmakis, D., Gilard, M., Heymans, S., Hoes, A. W., Jaarsma, T., Jankowska, E. A., Lainscak, M., . . . ESC Scientific Document Group (2021). 2021 ESC guidelines for the diagnosis and treatment of acute and chronic heart failure. *European Heart Journal*, 42(36), 3599–3726. https://doi.org/10.1093/eurheartj/ehab368

Michie, S., Abraham, C., Whittington, C., McAteer, J., & Gupta, S. (2009). Effective techniques in healthy eating and physical activity interventions: A meta-regression. *Health Psychology*, 28(6), 690–701. https://doi.org/10.1037/a0016136

Mola, E., De Bonis, J. A., & Giancane, R. (2008). Integrating patient empowerment as an essential characteristic of the discipline of general practice/family medicine. *The European Journal of General Practice*, 14(2), 89–94. https://doi.org/10.1080/13814780802423463

Nikrahan, G. R., Suarez, L., Asgari, K., Beach, S. R., Celano, C. M., Kalantari, M., Abedi, M. R., Etesampour, A., Abbas, R., & Huffman, J. C. (2016). Positive psychology interventions for patients with heart disease: A preliminary randomized trial. *Psychosomatics*, 57(4), 348–358. https://doi.org/10.1016/j.psym.2016.03.003

Orehek, E., Bessarabova, E., Chen, X., & Kruglanski, A. W. (2011). Positive affect as informational feedback in goal pursuit. *Motivation and Emotion*, 35, 44–51. https://doi.org/10.1007/s11031-010-9197-2

Ornish (2023). *Lifestyle healht programme*. Retrieved from: www.ornish.com

Ornish, D., Scherwitz, L. W., Billings, J. H., Brown, S. E., Gould, K. L., Merritt, T. A., Sparler, S., Armstrong, W. T., Ports, T. A., Kirkeeide, R. L., Hogeboom, C., & Brand, R. J. (1998). Intensive lifestyle changes for reversal of coronary heart disease. *JAMA*, 280(23), 2001–2007. https://doi.org/10.1001/jama.280.23.2001

Oscarsson, M., Carlbring, P., Andersson, G., & Rozental, A. (2020). A large-scale experiment on new year's resolutions: Approach-oriented goals are more successful than avoidance-oriented goals. *PloS One*, 15(12), e0234097. https://doi.org/10.1371/journal.pone.0234097

Passmore, J., & Oades, L. G. (2014). Positive psychology coaching: A model for coaching practice. *Coaching Psychologist*, 10, 68–70.

Patnode, C. D., Evans, C. V., Senger, C. A., Redmond, N., & Lin, J. S. (2017). Behavioral counseling to promote a healthful diet and physical activity for cardiovascular disease prevention in adults without known cardiovascular disease risk factors: Updated evidence report and systematic review for the US preventive services task force. *JAMA*, 318(2), 175–193. https://doi.org/10.1001/jama.2017.3303

Patterson, K., Davey, R., Keegan, R., Kinstler, B., Woodward, A., & Freene, N. (2022). Behaviour change techniques in cardiovascular disease smartphone apps to improve physical activity and sedentary behaviour: Systematic review and meta-regression. *International Journal of Behavioral Nutrition and Physical Activity*, 19, 81. https://doi.org/10.1186/s12966-022-01319-8

Plemmons, S. A., & Weiss, H. M. (2013). Goals and affect. In E. A. Locke & G. P. Latham (Eds.), *New developments in goal setting and task performance* (pp. 117–132). New York: Routledge.

Prochaska, J. O., & Velicer, W. F. (1997). The transtheoretical model of health behavior change. *American Journal of Health Promotion: AJHP*, 12(1), 38–48. https://doi.org/10.4278/0890-1171-12.1.38

Rahman, R. J., Hudson, J., Thøgersen-Ntoumani, C., & Doust, J. H. (2015). Motivational processes and well-being in cardiac rehabilitation: A self-determination theory perspective. *Psychology, Health & Medicine*, 20(5), 518–529. https://doi.org/10.1080/13548506.2015.1017509

Roth, G. A., Mensah, G. A., Johnson, C. O., Addolorato, G., Ammirati, E., Baddour, L. M., Barengo, N. C., Beaton, A. Z., Benjamin, E. J., Benziger, C. P., Bonny, A., Brauer, M., Brodmann, M., Cahill, T. J., Carapetis, J., Catapano, A. L., Chugh, S. S., Cooper, L. T., Coresh, J., Criqui, M., . . . GBD-NHLBI-JACC Global Burden of Cardiovascular Diseases Writing Group (2020). Global burden of cardiovascular diseases and risk factors, 1990–2019: Update from the GBD 2019 study. *Journal of The American College of Cardiology*, 76(25), 2982–3021. https://doi.org/10.1016/j.jacc.2020.11.010

Trom, P., & Burke, J. (2022) 'Positive psychology intervention (PPI) coaching: An experimental application of coaching to improve the effectiveness of a gratitude intervention', *Coaching: An International Journal of Theory, Research & Practice, 15*(1), 131–142. https://doi.org/10.1080/17521882.2021.1936585

van Zyl, L. E., Roll, L. C., Stander, M. W., & Richter, S. (2020). Positive psychological coaching definitions and models: A systematic literature review. *Frontiers in Psychology, 11*. https://doi-org.elib.tcd.ie/10.3389/fpsyg.2020.00793

Visseren, F. L. J., Mach, F., Smulders, Y. M., Carballo, D., Koskinas, K. C., Bäck, M., Benetos, A., Biffi, A., Boavida, J. M., Capodanno, D., Cosyns, B., Crawford, C., Davos, C. H., Desormais, I., Di Angelantonio, E., Franco, O. H., Halvorsen, S., Hobbs, F. D. R., Hollander, M., Jankowska, E. A., . . . ESC Scientific Document Group (2021). 2021 ESC guidelines on cardiovascular disease prevention in clinical practice. *European Heart Journal, 42*(34), 3227–3337. https://doi.org/10.1093/eurheartj/ehab484

Wagner, E. H., Austin, B. T., Davis, C., Hindmarsh, M., Schaefer, J., & Bonomi, A. (2001). Improving chronic illness care: Translating evidence into action. *Health Affairs, 20*(6), 64. https://doi-org.elib.tcd.ie/10.1377/hlthaff.20.6.64

Wagner, E. H., Austin, B. T., & Von Korff, M. (1996). Organizing care for patients with chronic illness. *The Milbank Quarterly, 74*(4), 511–544.

WANCA (2011). *The European definition of general practice/family medicine.* Retrieved from: https://www.woncaeurope.org/page/definition-of-general-practice-family-medicine

Winter, S. J., Sheats, J. L., & King, A. C. (2016). The use of behavior change techniques and theory in technologies for cardiovascular disease prevention and treatment in adults: A comprehensive review. *Progress in Cardiovascular Diseases, 58*(6), 605–612. https://doi.org/10.1016/j.pcad.2016.02.005

Wolever, R. Q., Simmons, L. A., Sforzo, G. A., Dill, D., Kaye, M., Bechard, E. M., Southard, M. E., Kennedy, M., Vosloo, J., & Yang, N. (2013). A systematic review of the literature on health and wellness coaching: Defining a key behavioral intervention in healthcare. *Global Advances in Health and Medicine, 2*(4), 38–57. https://doi.org/10.7453/gahmj.2013.042

World Health Organisation (WHO) (2002). *Innovative care for chronic diseases: building blocks for action: Global report.* Retrieved from: https://apps.who.int/iris/handle/10665/42500

Yildirim, D., Vives, J., & Ballespí, S. (2022). Anxiety and depression: The moderating effects of attention to emotion and emotional clarity. *Psychological Reports*, 332941211070764. Advance online publication. https://doi.org/10.1177/00332941211070764

Chapter 10

Coaching for oral health

Ciara Scott, Jolanta Burke and Mary Collins

Introduction

Oral health is intricately linked to four primary non-communicable diseases, i.e., cardiovascular disease, cancer, diabetes and chronic respiratory disease (Wolf et al., 2021), which are responsible for 73% of deaths worldwide each year (WHO, 2022b). In addition, tooth decay affects 3.5 billion people (WHO, 2022a), and oral health is associated with lifestyle choices such as increased sugar consumption and insufficient oral hygiene. Furthermore, the current oral health model, which is based on treatment and education for prevention, is not effective, which is why researchers and practitioners highlight the urgency for action and need for change (Watt et al., 2018). One such change relates to oral health coaching, which is emerging as a potential solution to improving oral health. This chapter first explores the research showing why oral health challenges occur and how coaching can support patients to prevent oral disease, reduce the stress associated with dental treatment and assist them in maintaining oral health following treatment. Second, it considers the potential models of coaching that can be applied to maximise its impact on patients.

Theory

In the nineteenth century, miners used to bring a canary into the coal shaft. The canary was sensitive to noxious gases and carbon monoxide levels, so it served as an indicator of the workplace's health. Similarly, our mouths are a window to our bodies, and oral health is an indicator of the overall health status and can represent how well we care for ourselves and our future health risk. Oral health is, therefore, "a canary in the coalmine" (Watt et al., 2018, p. 965), yet many people underestimate it.

Oral health is firmly embedded in overall health (Dörfer et al., 2017). It affects mental and physical wellbeing, especially when oral disease ensues (Glick et al., 2016); and is one of the World Health Organisation's priorities that help reduce the global burden of chronic disease (WHO, 2021). It is associated with an ability to "speak, smile, smell, taste, touch, chew, swallow" (Glick et al., 2016, p. 793), thus affecting basic human needs. When individuals experience pain, discomfort or disease relating to their oral health, it can have a detrimental effect on their daily lives, preventing them from living their lives to the fullest.

Oral diseases are the most common chronic diseases worldwide, affecting up to half the population, i.e., 3.5 billion people (WHO, 2022a). They are linked with non-communicable diseases, such as cardiovascular, cancer, diabetes, and chronic respiratory disease

DOI: 10.4324/9781003319016-12

(Peres et al., 2019), which are responsible for 73% of deaths worldwide (WHO, 2022b). Tooth decay remains the most common chronic disease in children in the UK and Ireland (75% of children), and the most common reason a child is admitted to a hospital in the UK (Levine, 2021). In addition, approximately 30% of adults in the UK and Ireland have untreated tooth decay (WHO, 2022a), which may significantly affect their overall health, raising their inflammatory markers and increasing their risk of other chronic diseases, such as heart disease.

Like other chronic diseases, lifestyle factors such as dietary habits, sugar consumption, insufficient physical activity, overuse of substances and poor oral hygiene increase the risk of oral disease. Public health measures to address this are described as the common risk factors approach (Watt & Sheiham, 2012). Whilst the exact pathogenic pathways are still being researched, the role of chronic inflammatory markers and changes to the oral microbiome can also explain the increased risk and co-existence of chronic diseases such as diabetes and coronary artery disease in patients with oral diseases (Cinar & Schou, 2014a; Cinar et al., 2018; Dörfer et al., 2017). Thus, education and coaching are recommended to help individuals connect their oral health issues with lifestyle choices (Antoniadou & Varzakas, 2020; Vernon & Howard, 2015; Volk et al., 2020).

Tooth decay can be prevented, meaning much of the burden of disease and treatment need could be eliminated by changes in health behaviour. For example, parents supervising their children's toothbrushing until the age of 7 can result in a 15% reduction in tooth decay later in life (Kabiri et al., 2022). Furthermore, longitudinal research that mapped the oral health life course in adults showed that while the pathways to poor oral health in adult life are complex, they can be linked to socioeconomic status, oral health beliefs and behaviours from childhood throughout our life course (Broadbent et al., 2016). Beliefs and behaviours can determine our oral health and oral health–related quality of life (OHRQoL) since childhood. Given that coaching helps individuals to become aware of unhelpful or self-limiting beliefs, oral health coaching can support individuals in overcoming limiting beliefs towards their oral health, thus taking action that may result in saving a lot of money on dental treatments.

Furthermore, the COVID19 pandemic increased oral health issues due to both changes in diet, routine and lifestyle, and the lack of access to the routine non-emergency dental care due to the risk of transmission (de Silva et al., 2022; Watt, 2020). Moreover, the stress associated with the pandemic resulted in an increase of tooth-grinding and teeth clenching (Kardeş & Kardeş, 2022), not to mention that many participants diagnosed with long COVID19 suffer from a range of oral health conditions such as dry mouth, oral lesions and increased orofacial pain (Qi et al., 2022). The resulting surge in demand for dental care and capacity issues (BDA, 2022) highlights the opportunity for new approaches such as coaching and remote patient monitoring complementing surgery visits (Dickson-Swift et al., 2022; Thurzo et al., 2022).

From the positive perspective, the pandemic also brought a paradigm shift in the individual and collective motivation to change lifestyles and health behaviours in response to the emerging threat and an understanding that behavioural interventions focused on individual responsibility also needed broader system support and public health messaging to be effective (Thomas & Daube, 2023). Similarly, systems thinking outlines the active participatory roles of the public, health professionals and policy makers to collectively reduce the burden or chronic oral diseases (Brocklehurst et al., 2021). Coaching has a place in enabling both patients and professionals.

Nature provides its own solution to oral health. Teeth survive in human remains for thousands of years, even in hostile environments. Healthy saliva and oral microbiome are natural defence systems helping protect gums and teeth. Rather than optimise this, many advances in dental care have merely served to diagnose and treat dental problems. Furthermore, the demand for aesthetic treatments has never been greater with a rapid increase in procedures, such as teeth whitening, Hollywood smile, dental veneers, and at-home aligners (Abbasi et al., 2022). These developments have reoriented professionals towards treatment instead of improving health or reducing disease burden. The voices advocating radical change continue to soar (Asimakopoulou et al., 2023; Brocklehurst et al., 2021; Peres et al., 2019; Watt et al., 2019). In the meantime, patients can benefit from oral health coaching that can help them manage pain and improve quality of life during their ongoing, long-term treatment.

The media promotes quick fixes and instant makeovers to achieve oral beauty, but their endeavours are often inconsistent with oral health objectives. Maintaining dental restorations is more demanding than maintaining natural teeth. Treatment inevitably fails. It fails more quickly if the underlying risk factors and habits, such as poor tooth-brushing, have led to treatment needs stay the same (Broadbent et al., 2016). This can create a Sisyphus effect – Sisyphus was doomed to push a boulder uphill continually. As soon as he reached the summit, the boulder would roll off, and he started his uphill struggle again. Successful dental treatment works with patients rather than being done to them. However, this powerful alliance can be lost in important busy clinical settings. Models of care have become increasingly transactional, and this relational element can be devalued. Dentists can perceive that lack of time, lack of understanding and a fear of being perceived to be blaming or judging patients can all be barriers to engaging with patients to address health risks and broader health issues (Arora et al., 2022). Equally, patients may want to defer responsibility and may need more time to contemplate change (Rollnick et al., 2008). In those situations, having an oral health coach in a dental clinic may support patients and improve clinical outcomes.

Coaching for oral health

Positive psychology coaching has been defined as "a conversation intervention that supports people to achieve meaningful goals and improve the quality in their lives by paying particular attention to existing strengths, available resources and psychological wellbeing" (van Nieuwerburgh & Biswas-Diener, 2021, p. 315). In the oral health context, it is "building awareness and empowerment" (Cinar et al., 2018, p. 54) to develop the patient's own agency, competence and confidence to make small steps to achieve their oral health goals outside of the clinical setting. It is worthwhile to consider some foundational coaching theories and their relationship to oral health coaching.

Applying theory to oral health coaching

Newton and Asimakopoulou (2015) identified that there was little evidence that psychological constructs were being applied to understanding the enablers or barriers to change in studies designed to improve oral health behaviour. Historically, patient behaviour related to their own oral care was commonly referred to as "compliance" or "adherence" in the scientific literature, but this has shifted towards an understanding that effective long-term maintenance of behaviour change requires patients' motivation for change to be autonomous, as opposed to controlled (Halvari & Halvari, 2006). Self-Determination Theory (SDT) (Deci & Ryan, 1985) provides a clear framework and evidence-based approach for understanding individual motivation and the importance of enhancing autonomy-supportive relationships with patients in a dental setting (Halvari et al., 2012). Moreover, patients perceive higher subjective dental wellbeing, satisfaction and motivation in environments that maximize support of their need for competence in particular, as well as their need for social relatedness and autonomy (Halvari et al., 2013). Conversely, a negative correlation is found for a perceived controlling clinic style (Halvari et al., 2013, 2019b). Dental satisfaction is linked to autonomous motivation and perceived dental competence. Interventions designed to promote competence in dental home care in an autonomy-supportive way, relative to standard care, have been shown to increase autonomous motivation, improve perceived dental competence and positively affect dental health behaviours, with a significant reduction in dental plaque and gingivitis (Halvari et al., 2012). Coaching provides evidenced-based frameworks and tools to bring awareness and positive actions that build autonomy-supportive practices.

The Trans-Theoretical Model (TTM) of behaviour change (Prochaska & Velicer, 1997) has also been applied to oral health behaviour change (Tillis et al., 2003). The framework can be used to understand what stage of change the dental patient or client is at. Once this is established, the coach or clinician can apply techniques for facilitating change that are specific and effective for that stage, and this has been effectively applied to improving oral hygiene (Wade et al., 2013).

Motivational interviewing (MI) was developed as a technique for exploring ambivalence, identifying limited beliefs and readiness for change and to facilitate movement through the five stages of TTM (Rollnick et al., 2008). Like SDT, it promotes an autonomy-supportive relationship for the client to establish their goals, plan action and build competence and sustainable change, and it has been applied as a patient-centred, therapeutic approach to supporting oral health behaviour change (Kay et al., 2016). A patient with a difficult dental history may feel a level of guilt or shame about their oral health or anger or regret about poor self-care or poor treatment decisions in the past. MI provides a framework for "change talk" that supports people to focus on the future – what they can change and why it matters to them – and this is important for goal-setting and positive actions for a healthier future (Brennan & O'Driscoll, 2021).

The acronym DARN (desire, ability, reasons, need) provides the following MI framework for using open questions that encourage "change talk" (Rollnick et al., 2008, p. 37).

Desire: "What dental future are you hoping for?"
Ability: "What are you able to do?"
Reasons: "Why does this matter to you?"
Need: "Why is it important?"

The COM-B model (Michie et al., 2011) consists of the following three interrelated components that are conceptualised as essential components of behaviour and describe an individual capacity for behaviour change.

C (capability): physical or psychological
O (opportunity): physical access or social environment
M (motivation): conscious decision-making or automatic habits

This has recently been applied to dental health behaviour change (Buchanan et al., 2021). The COM-B Behaviour Change Wheel was developed through a synthesis of 19 behaviour change frameworks, identified by systematic review (Michie et al., 2011). When using the wheel, a client identifies their current behaviour and the factors influencing it, their goals and the broader social, physical, psychological and support elements that they will benefit from in planning and actioning positive health changes.

Stage 1: Understand the behaviour. This stage encourages the client to identify what needs to change and select a target behaviour.
Stage 2: Identify intervention options. This stage encourages the client to design and evaluate interventions using the APEASE (acceptability, practicality, effectiveness, affordability, safety and equity) criteria for the goals they have set.
Stage 3: Identify context and implementation to identify specific behaviour change techniques (again, consideration of APEASE criteria relevant to inform this).

This is not a "magic bullet" but can provide a systematic way of identifying opportunities and support to enable behaviour change and setting goals similar to other coaching models such as GROW. Like SDT and the TTM, when COM-B has been adopted for oral health behaviour change, it emphasises an individual's perception of their own competence and motivation and to identify the supportive relationships that will enable them to achieve their oral health goal (Buchanan et al., 2021). An understanding of the theoretical frameworks for health behaviour can support both clinicians and coaches to bring awareness to an individual's barriers or enablers to change, their existing support dyads and what support they may need to move towards their health goals (Asimakopoulou et al., 2023; Gov.UK, 2014; Kitsaras et al., 2023).

Health services in both the UK and Ireland (Meade et al., 2022; NHS England, 2016) have adopted Making Every Contact Count policies to engage staff and patients in a holistic approach to using interactions and appointments, build awareness and adopt health behaviours that promote whole person health. Old parental models of care have evolved towards patient-centred care. There is an increasing role for health coaches to support health behaviour change, and equally, many healthcare professionals are bringing coaching and motivational interviewing techniques to their role.

Lay person coaching has been successful for the management of chronic diseases such as adult onset diabetes. A number of studies have investigated the effects of coaching interventions to support oral health behaviour change in children (Hurling et al., 2013) and the elderly (Dejonghe et al., 2017) and those with comorbidities such as diabetes (Cinar & Schou, 2014b; Cinar et al., 2018). Coaching has been delivered at both individual (de Silva et al., 2016) and group (Hill et al., 2015) settings, and via mHealth applications (Sharif et al., 2019). Thus, many approaches to oral health coaching already show evidence of effectiveness.

Need for more evidenced-based coaching practice

When delivering coaching methodologies that are effective for clients, such as those who engage in oral health coaching, it is of utmost importance to engage in evidence-based coaching (Grant & O'Connor, 2019). This involves being up to date on coaching literature and the body of research that informs effective coaching practice. Taking an evidence-based approach allows us to work in an ethical and professional way avoiding the "fads and foibles" that permeate the coaching and wellbeing space.

Furthermore, coaches must stay current on emerging coaching research (Grant & O'Connor, 2019). To do that, they must become familiar with the critical foundational evidence for coaching effectiveness, for example, by reading peer-reviewed coaching-specific studies that show what works and what does not work in coaching. They need to become familiar with the coaching-related research that shows *how* coaching works and gives ideas on improving their coaching practice. They should learn to distinguish between high-quality and low-quality research. Also, they need to remember that each journal, book, or published report on coaching will have some implicit bias that needs to be considered when reviewing findings. This is of utmost importance, especially in the emerging field of oral health coaching research.

Practice

Coaching can be used by dental professionals or health coaches in a variety of situations relating to oral health, such as the following.

1. Helping individuals prevent oral health issues.
2. During oral health treatment.
3. Improving their quality of life when experiencing long-term illness associated with adverse oral health outcomes or chronic diseases.
4. Helping them cope with dental anxiety.

Oral health prevention

When coaching for prevention, a coach supports the clients by helping them draw on their existing strengths and resources to set goals, overcome obstacles and work towards a mutually agreed goal. This style is maintained throughout the sessions and the relationship in structured coaching interactions. By contrast, a clinician brings their expertise to a problem and offers solutions, advice and treatment during the patient's visit. A patient often expects the clinician to provide the solution in that dyad. This does not stop clinicians from bringing a coaching style to their practice or coaching with "a small c" in patient interactions, but they should remain aware of when they are coaching and when they are a clinician. Oral health professionals should be mindful of patients' needs for autonomy and competence (Buchanan et al., 2021; Halvari et al., 2019a) and how these affect motivation and sustainable health behaviours and avoid language and behaviours that can be perceived as controlling.

Singh et al. (2019) reviewed the shared competencies of healthcare professionals and coaching professionals, concluding that both groups could communicate effectively the ability to communicate with empathy and the ability to bring evidenced-based, life-long learning into professional practice. Thus, many dental surgeons have their skills somewhat developed but require a coaching model to assist them in using them more effectively.

Fogg (2019) provides a framework for building a sequence of "tiny" habits that build competence, highlighting that small successes positively affect the motivation, competence and confidence that support sustainable change. One of the examples of a "tiny habit" he uses is "brush just one tooth." Practitioners often instruct patients to brush for two minutes twice a day, but big goals and a demand for drastic changes can set up patients for failure and this can be disabling. Whitmore (2010) highlights the role for coaches in supporting clients to break down their high-end goal into smaller manageable chunks to build opportunities to celebrate success and recognise the development of competence. Accomplishment can be associated with an upward spiral of positive emotions and behaviours that broaden and build motivation for further behaviour change (Fredrickson, 2001). As such, sustainable behaviour change can be influenced by recognising, rewarding and celebrating small steps in the direction of the goal to build motivation for further progress.

Coaches understand the relevance of values and beliefs on health behaviour, and the relationship between values and motivation. Oral health values (OHVs) may impact oral health-relevant behaviours, such as toothbrushing, flossing, smoking and nicotine use, and maintenance of a healthy diet (Edwards et al., 2021, p. 455). Edwards and her colleagues defined OHVs as "the extent to which one views dental status as important, or one's prioritization of or dedication to improving or maintaining one's teeth, gingiva, and aspects of orofacial functioning," and developed and validated an oral health values scale to support patients to identify their oral health beliefs and values and set goals for dental treatment and self-care that were connected with their own values and motivation. Coaches can play a pivotal role in applying this tool in practice.

Oral health treatment

Professional training builds expertise in a field, and professionals often feel responsible for others' health and wellbeing and their treatment outcome. Like teachers and parents, much of the advice dentists give patients is well-intentioned, but may not be received positively by the listener (Schein, 2010). Patients may not understand the information they are given or want to take an active role in decisions about their own care (Bennett et al., 2010). Given that dental patients may already feel vulnerable, in pain and sleep deprived, not to mention an existence of a power imbalance in a clinical setting and personal protective equipment (PPE), can all contribute to difficult communication. This is when coaching can assist with improving communication between patients and clinicians.

Dental treatment can involve a series of visits and coaching can be applied by clinicians during treatment, be it via remote technology or in surgery. Such an approach is based on the principle of involving patients in a dialogue, rather than advising patients what is going to be done to them (van der Wouden et al., 2022). As such, personal agency is created that supports a change and creates more trust and respect between all parties involved. After all, dental care is a shared responsibility between the clinicians and their patients, as "it's their mouth at the end of the day" (Barnes et al., 2022, p. 1).

Coaching can be a powerful tool in challenging the misnomer that it is the dentist who makes all the difference and controls the outcome. People who join slimming clubs can benefit from peer support and the accountability to the group, but they understand they do not achieve their goals just by turning up every week to get weighed; it's what they do during the week that matters. Similarly, daily habits improve oral health, whereas visiting a hygienist can provide broader accountability, support, guidance and treatment, as well as the acknowledgement of progress that supports sustained behaviour change. Dental treatment manages disease, whereas dental behaviour helps to reduce the future disease risk. In one study, dental hygienists were trained to provide health counselling to patients with periodontal disease through remote patient monitoring during the course of their treatment. This has shown some promise in improving patient outcomes (Shen et al., 2022), and there are both potential opportunities and ethical considerations to mainstreaming this type of intervention.

Quality of life

Updated definitions of health promote agency and the patient's role in their care. The transition to patient-centred care and shared decision-making promotes an equal partnership. A coaching relationship is an equal partnership, creating a safe space for meaningful engagement for the client to set their own goals. In a clinical setting, dentists adopting a coaching style should know their positionality and tendency to offer guidance or instruction.

Patients with chronic diseases and comorbidities may have multiple appointments, as well as changes to income and additional expenses and may perceive oral health as a low priority. The Making Every Contact Count Policy (NHS England, 2016) identifies the opportunity for all healthcare professionals to support patients in positive behaviour changes and self-care by adopting a broader, whole-patient approach to care. For instance, someone who is admitted to hospital as an emergency is unlikely to bring a toothbrush, but prolonged periods of not brushing will negatively affect long-term dental health, so providing a brush or brushing teeth for a patient who does not have the capacity is a simple way this policy can be applied. Coaching has a valuable place in building awareness of behaviours and beliefs and setting goals for positive habits. Broadbent and colleagues (2006) identified that patients with favourable beliefs about their oral health had a significantly lower prevalence of poor self-rated oral health, better oral hygiene and fewer teeth extracted due to caries, but that this can change during the life course.

Self-management support interventions have been recognised as a promising approach to enhance health outcomes in patients with chronic disease and recognise that health coaching is a valuable patient orientated approach, but there has been little evaluation of the long-term costs and benefits (Oksman et al., 2017). Autonomy-supportive interventions have not only provided some evidence that they can reduce dental anxiety and improve oral health but also led to moderate improvements in eudemonic wellbeing, which can support other health behaviour changes (Halvari et al., 2019b).

Variations in normal oral and facial development and treatment for diseases such as oral and pharyngeal cancers can have a significant effect on facial aesthetics and function, negatively affecting the ability to speak, swallow, eat and socialise, and OHRQoL (Yuwanati et al., 2021). Measures of treatment success can often be orientated towards survival rather than supporting patients to adjust to a life changing "new normal" and coaching and positive psychology interventions can support patients with building acceptance and identifying factors within their control to regain a level of autonomy, competence and connectedness.

Dental anxiety

A dental surgery is a familiar and comfortable place to work for a dentist. They do not associate it with treatment but instead with work-related issues. However, it can be daunting for many patients as they dread, fear or feel vulnerable when visiting the surgery. Stress can activate their sympathetic nervous system or "fight or flight", which has severe consequences. For some patients, walking into a dental surgery can be as reactive for their nervous system as walking into the jungle and being confronted by a tiger. This experience deactivates their frontal cortex and ability to reason and learn. Giving patients advice in this altered state might not be helpful. Clinicians may perceive that patients understand their advice, but their patients' minds focus only on that tiger. Subsequently, a knowledge gap can develop between what is said and knowledge that is transferred to the patient, as well as between patients' intentions and health behaviours. This paves a place for coaching outside the clinical setting and for dental team members or coaches to play a pivotal role in oral health coaching (Watt, 2005; Watt et al., 2015).

Dental phobia is defined as persistent fear, often unnecessary or unreasonable (*DSM-5*) (APA 2015). Anxiety or phobia related to dental care or dental attendance can affect about 20% of the population (Wide Boman et al., 2013) and be a barrier to care, impairing OHRQoL (Mehrstedt et al., 2007). A dental anxiety inventory scale uses three facets to understand the anxiety; time (i.e., is it related to anticipating the appointment at home or being in the dental chair?), situation (the interaction or the procedure) and the reaction (physical, cognitive or subjective) (Stouthard et al., 1993). Understanding this supports more effective coaching.

To date, there is no established approach to use coaching in helping patients overcome their anxiety. Coaching has demonstrated effectiveness when helping individuals overcome their music performance anxiety or retirement anxiety (Jang et al., 2022; Mahony et al., 2022); thus, there is no reason why it should not be used to help individuals with dental anxiety. Halvari and colleagues (2019a) used a SDT framework to analyse dental anxiety. Although the majority of patients perceived their oral healthcare professionals as being non-controlling (51%), others were perceived as moderately (38%) or highly controlling (11%). Patients who perceived a controlling approach had higher dental anxiety and a high dysregulation of dental anxiety also increased perception of a controlled approach through a feedback loop. Perception of control rather than autonomy was associated with low attendance and poorer oral health. Patients perceived that controlling treatment styles were shaped at three levels: the external operational pressures related to appointment timings, the dentist's personality and the pressure from the patient's anxiety. SDT provides a framework to understand why developing a style that supports patient autonomy and builds patient competence and positive relationships can reduce anxiety and improve attendance.

Some practices will have a treatment coordinator or "non-clinical" room for an initial consultation. Even if this is not the case, making time to listen, using language the patients perceive as empathetic and non-controlling, while maintaining eye contact and positive body language, can build psychological safety and rapport and desensitise patients to their environment. Conversely, feeling threatened can impact on patients' cognition, attention and attendance and this negatively affects practitioners' perception of them as a patient (Halvari et al., 2013). When clients describe a perception of feeling "controlled" and anxious, powerful coaching questions such as "Was the intention good?" can break down threatening feelings and help to build trust and perspective.

Conclusion

This chapter highlighted the need for change in how oral health is managed. Currently, half of the world's population suffers from oral health issues. Urgent action is required to remedy this situation. In this chapter, we argued that coaching allows clinicians and health coaches to reduce the burden of oral disease and help individuals manage their emotions, thoughts, and actions while in treatment and preventatively. However, agreed-upon coaching approaches to accomplishing this are required to maximise this opportunity.

To date, a dearth of research exists about the applications of oral health coaching in clinical practice. It is used mainly in the context of other conditions that affect oral health, such as long COVID19, diabetes and cardiovascular disease. However, specific coaching approaches for preventing oral disease and helping patients who need treatment cope with their dental care are needed. This relates to clinicians learning how to use mini-coaching sessions in their daily practice. It also concerns health coaches who can support patients undergoing painful, long-term treatments or those experiencing dental anxiety that prevents them from caring for their mouth. This offers an opportunity for surgeries to employ such coaches to take better care of their patients and individuals living in their community and, as such, contribute to reducing non-communicable diseases related to oral health.

Finally, while there is no precedent for it, we hope that in the future, oral health coaching will become a standard dental approach when educating young people to help them look after their teeth. Many patients experiencing dental anxiety draw on negative experiences they have had from childhood. When using a non-directive coaching approach with young people, they can become more engaged in caring for their teeth. Coaching can help them overcome some of the obstacles they have that prevent them from effective oral health. Finally, it can also help them believe that a life without invasive dental treatment is possible if they find the motivation to look after their oral health effectively. All this can become possible through coaching.

Reflective questions

1. Reflecting on the concept of "Who you are is how you coach," how do your own attitudes, behaviours and beliefs around oral health influence how you would coach your clients about their oral health?
2. Is there a broader role for dental team members to bring coaching to how they would support patients through their dental journey?
3. How do you incorporate questions about oral health into coaching conversations for general health and wellbeing?

References

Abbasi, M. S., Lal, A., Das, G., Salman, F., Akram, A., Ahmed, A. R., Maqsood, A., & Ahmed, N. (2022). Impact of social media on aesthetic dentistry: General Practitioners' perspectives. *Healthcare*, *10*(10), 2055. MDPI AG. https://doi.org/10.3390/healthcare10102055

American Psychiatric Association (APA) (2015). *Anxiety disorders: DSM-5® selections*. American Psychiatric Pub.

Antoniadou, M., & Varzakas, T. (2020). Diet and oral health coaching methods and models for the independent elderly. *Applied Sciences*, *10*(11), 4021. MDPI AG. https://doi.org/10.3390/app10114021

Arora, A., Rana, K., Manohar, N., Li, L., Bhole, S., & Chimoriya, R. (2022). Perceptions and practices of oral health care professionals in preventing and managing childhood obesity. *Nutrients*, *14*(9), 1809.

Asimakopoulou, K., Kitsaras, G., & Newton, J. T. (2023). Using behaviour change science to deliver oral health practice: A commentary. *Community Dentistry and Oral Epidemiology, 51*(5), 697–704.

Barnes, E., Bullock, A., & Chestnutt, I. (2022). 'It's their mouth at the end of the day': Dental professionals' reactions to oral health education outcomes. *British Dental Journal.* https://doi.org/10.1038/s41415-022-4978-z

Bennett, H. D., Coleman, E. A., Parry, C., Bodenheimer, T., & Chen, E. H. (2010). Health coaching for patients with chronic illness. *Family Practice Management, 17*(5), 24.

Brennan, R., & O'Driscoll, R. (2021). A scoping review of motivational interviewing in oral health settings. *Journal of the Irish Dental Association, 67*(5).

British Dental Association [BDA] (2022, August, 8). NHS Dentistry at a Tipping Point. British Dental Association. https://bda.org/news-centre/press-releases/Pages/nhs-dentistry-at-a-tipping-point.aspx

Broadbent, J. M., Thomson, W. M., & Poulton, R. (2006). Oral health beliefs in adolescence and oral health in young adulthood. *Journal of Dental Research, 85*(4), 339–343.

Broadbent, J. M., Zeng, J., Foster, P. L. A., Baker, S. R., Ramrakha, S., & Thomson, W. M. (2016). Oral health-related beliefs, behaviours, and outcomes through the life course. *Journal of Dental Research, 95*(7), 808–813.

Brocklehurst, P. R., Baker, S. R., & Langley, J. (2021). Context and the evidence-based paradigm: The potential for participatory research and systems thinking in oral health. *Community Dentistry and Oral Epidemiology, 49*(1), 1–9.

Buchanan, H., Newton, J. T., Baker, S. R., & Asimakopoulou, K. (2021). Adopting the COM-B model and TDF framework in oral and dental research: A narrative review. *Community Dentistry and Oral Epidemiology, 49*(5), 385–393.

Cinar, A. B., Freeman, R., & Schou, L. (2018). A new complementary approach for oral health and diabetes management: Health coaching. *International Dental Journal, 68*(1), 54–64. https://doi.org/10.1111/idj.12334

Cinar, A. B., & Schou, L. (2014a). Health promotion for patients with diabetes: Health coaching or formal health education? *International Dental Journal, 64*(1), 20–28. https://doi.org/10.1111/idj.12058

Cinar, A. B., & Schou, L. (2014b). The role of self-efficacy in health coaching and health education for patients with type 2 diabetes. *International Dental Journal, 64*(3), 155–163.

Deci, E. L., & Ryan, R. M. (1985). Conceptualizations of intrinsic motivation and self-determination. In: E. L. Deci, & R. M. Ryan (1st ed.), *Intrinsic motivation and self-determination in human behavior* (pp. 11–40). Springer.

Dejonghe, L. A. L., Becker, J., Froboese, I., & Schaller, A. (2017). Long-term effectiveness of health coaching in rehabilitation and prevention: A systematic review. *Patient Education and Counseling, 100*(9), 1643–1653.

de Silva, A. M., Hegde, S., Akudo, N. B., Calache, H., Gussy, M. G., Nasser, M., Morrice, H. R., Dickson-Swift, V., Kangutkar, T., Knevel, R., & Down, S. (2022). The impact of COVID-19 on individual oral health: A scoping review. *BMC Oral Health, 22*(1), 422. https://doi.org/10.1186/s12903-022-02463-0

de Silva, A. M., Hegde, S., Akudo, N. B., Calache, H., Gussy, M. G., Nasser, M., Morrice, H. R., Riggs, E., Leong, P. M., Meyenn, L. K., & Yousefi-Nooraie, R. (2016). Community-based population-level interventions for promoting child oral health. *Cochrane Database of Systematic Reviews, 9.* CD009837. https://doi.org/10.1002/14651858.CD009837.pub2

Dickson-Swift, V., Kangutkar, T., Knevel, R., & Down, S. (2022). The impact of COVID-19 on individual oral health: A scoping review. *BMC Oral Health, 22*(1), 422.

Dörfer, C., Benz, C., Aida, J., & Campard, G. (2017). The relationship of oral health with general health and NCDs: A brief review. *International Dental Journal, 67*, 14–18.

Edwards, C. B., Randall, C. L., & McNeil, D. W. (2021). Development and validation of the oral health values scale. *Community Dentistry and Oral Epidemiology, 49*(5), 454–463.

Fogg, B. J. (2019). *Tiny habits: The small changes that change everything.* Eamon Dolan Books.

Fredrickson, B. L. (2001). The role of positive emotions in positive psychology: The broaden-and-build theory of positive emotions. *American Psychologist, 56*(3), 218.

Glick, M., Williams, D. M., Kleinman, D. V., Vujicic, M., Watt, R. G., & Weyant, R. J. (2016). A new definition for oral health developed by the FDI World Dental Federation opens the door to a universal definition of oral health. *British Dental Journal, 221*(12), 792–793.

Gov.UK (2014, June, 12). Delivering Better Oral Health: An Evidence-Based Toolkit for Prevention. Gov.UK. https://www.gov.uk/government/publications/delivering-better-oral-health-an-evidence-based-toolkit-for-prevention

Grant, A., & O'Connor, S. (2019). A brief primer for those new to coaching research and evidence-based practice. *The Coaching Psychologist, 15*(1), 3–10.

Halvari, A. E. M., & Halvari, H. (2006). Motivational predictors of change in oral health: An experimental test of self-determination theory. *Motivation and Emotion, 30,* 294–305.

Halvari, A. E. M., Halvari, H., Bjørnebekk, G., & Deci, E. L. (2012). Motivation for dental home care: Testing a self-determination theory model 1. *Journal of Applied Social Psychology, 42*(1), 1–39.

Halvari, A. E. M., Halvari, H., Bjørnebekk, G., & Deci, E. L. (2013). Oral health and dental well-being: Testing a self-determination theory model. *Journal of Applied Social Psychology, 43*(2), 275–292.

Halvari, A. E. M., Halvari, H., & Deci, E. L. (2019a). Dental anxiety, oral health-related quality of life, and general well-being: A self-determination theory perspective. *Journal of Applied Social Psychology, 49*(5), 295–306.

Halvari, A. E. M., Halvari, H., Deci, E. L., & Williams, G. C. (2019b). Autonomy-supportive dental treatment, oral health-related eudaimonic well-being and oral health: A randomized clinical trial. *Psychology & Health, 34*(12), 1421–1436.

Hill, B., Richardson, B., & Skouteris, H. (2015). Do we know how to design effective health coaching interventions: A systematic review of the state of the literature. *American Journal of Health Promotion, 29*(5), e158–e168.

Hurling, R., Claessen, J. P., Nicholson, J., Schafer, F., Tomlin, C. C., & Lowe, C. F. (2013). Automated coaching to help parents increase their children's brushing frequency: An exploratory trial. *Community Dental Health, 30*(2), 88–93.

Jang, Y., Cho, H., Kim, M., Lee, J., & Suh, W. (2022). Contextual analysis of retirement anxiety among Koreans: Benefits of retirement coaching. *Educational Gerontology,* 1–10. https://doi-org.elib.tcd.ie/10.1080/03601277.2022.2160567

Kabiri, B., Heidarnia, A., Alavijeh, M. M., & Motlagh, M. E. (2022). Primary tooth decay prevention program in children: Application of intervention mapping approach. *BioMed Research International,* 8901102. https://doi.org/10.1155/2022/8901102

Kardeş, E., & Kardeş, S. (2022). Google searches for bruxism, teeth grinding, and teeth clenching during the COVID-19 pandemic. Google-Suchanfragen zu Bruxismus, Zähneknirschen und Zähnepressen während der COVID-19-Pandemie. *Journal of Orofacial Orthopedics = Fortschritte der Kieferorthopadie: Organ/official journal Deutsche Gesellschaft fur Kieferorthopadie, 83*(6), 1–6.

Kay, E. J., Vascott, D., Hocking, A., & Nield, H. (2016). Motivational interviewing in general dental practice: A review of the evidence. *British Dental Journal, 221*(12), 785–791. https://doi.org/10.1007/s00056-021-00315-0

Kitsaras, G., Asimakopoulou, K., Henshaw, M., & Borrelli, B. (2023). Theoretical and methodological approaches in designing, developing, and delivering interventions for oral health behaviour change. *Community Dentistry and Oral Epidemiology, 51*(1), 91–102. https://doi.org/10.1111/cdoe.12817

Levine, R. S. (2021). Childhood caries and hospital admissions in England: A reflection on preventive strategies. *British Dental Journal, 230*(9), 611–616.

Mahony, S. E., Juncos, D. G., & Winter, D. (2022). Acceptance and commitment coaching for music performance anxiety: Piloting a 6-week group course with undergraduate dance and musical theatre students. *Frontiers in Psychology, 13,* 830230. https://doi.org/10.3389/fpsyg.2022.830230

Meade, O., O'Brien, M., Mc Sharry, J., Lawless, A., Coughlan, S., Hart, J., . . . & Byrne, M. (2022). Enhancing the implementation of the Making Every Contact Count brief behavioural intervention programme in Ireland: Protocol for the Making MECC Work research programme. *HRB Open Research, 5.*

Mehrstedt, M., John, M. T., Tönnies, S., & Micheelis, W. (2007). Oral health-related quality of life in patients with dental anxiety. *Community Dentistry and Oral Epidemiology*, 35(5), 357–363.

Michie, S., Van Stralen, M. M., & West, R. (2011). The behaviour change wheel: A new method for characterising and designing behaviour change interventions. *Implementation Science*, 6, 1–12.

Newton, J. T., & Asimakopoulou, K. (2015). Managing oral hygiene as a risk factor for periodontal disease: A systematic review of psychological approaches to behaviour change for improved plaque control in periodontal management. *Journal of Clinical Periodontology*, 42, S36–S46.

NHS England (2016, April). Making Every Contact Count. NHS. https://www.england.nhs.uk/wp-content/uploads/2016/04/making-every-contact-count.pdf

Oksman, E., Linna, M., Hörhammer, I., Lammintakanen, J., & Talja, M. (2017). Cost-effectiveness analysis for a tele-based health coaching program for chronic disease in primary care. *BMC Health Services Research*, 17(1), 1–7.

Peres, M. A., Macpherson, L. M., Weyant, R. J., Daly, B., Venturelli, R., Mathur, M. R., . . . & Benzian, H. (2019). Oral diseases: A global public health challenge. *The Lancet*, 394(10194), 249–260.

Prochaska, J. O., & Velicer, W. F. (1997). The transtheoretical model of health behavior change. *American Journal of Health Promotion*, 12(1), 38–48.

Qi, X., Northridge, M. E., Hu, M., & Wu, B. (2022). Oral health conditions and COVID-19: A systematic review and meta-analysis of the current evidence. *Aging and Health Research*, 2(1), 100064. https://doi.org/10.1016/j.ahr.2022.100064

Rollnick, S., Miller, W. R., Butler, C. C., & Aloia, M. S. (2008). *Motivational interviewing in health care: Helping patients change behavior*. Guilford Publications.

Schein, E. H. (2010). *Helping: How to offer, give, and receive help*. ReadHowYouWant.com.

Sharif, M. O., Newton, T., & Cunningham, S. J. (2019). A systematic review to assess interventions delivered by mobile phones in improving adherence to oral hygiene advice for children and adolescents. *British Dental Journal*, 227(5), 375–382.

Shen, K. L., Huang, C. L., Lin, Y. C., Du, J. K., Chen, F. L., Kabasawa, Y., . . . & Huang, H. L. (2022). Effects of artificial intelligence-assisted dental monitoring intervention in patients with periodontitis: A randomized controlled trial. *Journal of Clinical Periodontology*, 49(10), 988–998.

Singh, H. K., Kennedy, G. A., & Stupans, I. (2019). A systematic review of pharmacy health coaching and an evaluation of patient outcomes. *Research in Social and Administrative Pharmacy*, 15(3), 244–251.

Stouthard, M. E., Mellenbergh, G. J., & Hoogstraten, J. (1993). Assessment of dental anxiety: A facet approach. *Anxiety, Stress and Coping*, 6(2), 89–105.

Thomas, S., & Daube, M. (2023). New times, new challenges for health promotion. *Health Promotion International*, 38(1), daad012.

Thurzo, A., Urbanová, W., Novák, B., Czako, L., Siebert, T., Stano, P., . . . & Varga, I. (2022). Where is the artificial intelligence applied in dentistry? Systematic review and literature analysis. *Healthcare*, 10(7), 269.

Tillis, T. S., Stach, D. J., Cross-Poline, G. N., Annan, S. D., Astroth, D. B., & Wolfe, P. (2003). The transtheoretical model applied to an oral self-care behavioral change: Development and testing of instruments for stages of change and decisional balance. *Journal of Dental Hygiene: JDH*, 77(1), 16–25.

van der Wouden, P., Hilverda, F., van der Heijden, G., Shemesh, H., & Pittens, C. (2022). Establishing the research agenda for oral healthcare using the Dialogue Model-patient involvement in a joint research agenda with practitioners. *European Journal of Oral Sciences*, 130(1), e12842. https://doi.org/10.1111/eos.12842

van Nieuwerburgh, C. & Biswas-Diener, R. (2021). Positive psychology approach. In J. Passmore (Ed.), *The coaches' handbook: The complete practitioner guide for professional coaches*. Routledge, pp. 314–321.

Vernazza, C. R., Birch, S., & Pitts, N. B. (2021). Reorienting oral health services to prevention: Economic perspectives. *Journal of Dental Research*, 100(6), 576–582. https://doi.org/10.1177/0022034520986794

Vernon, L. T., & Howard, A. R. (2015). Advancing health promotion in dentistry: Articulating an integrative approach to coaching oral health behavior change in the dental setting. *Current Oral Health Reports 2*, 111–122. https://doi.org/10.1007/s40496-015-0056-9

Volk, L., Spock, M., Sloane, P. D., & Zimmerman, S. (2020). Improving evidence-based oral health of nursing home residents through coaching by dental hygienists. *Journal of the American Medical Directors Association, 21*(2), 281–283. https://doi.org/10.1016/j.jamda.2019.09.022

Wade, K. J., Coates, D. E., Gauld, R. D., Livingstone, V., & Cullinan, M. P. (2013). Oral hygiene behaviours and readiness to change using the TransTheoretical Model (TTM). *New Zealand Dental Journal, 109*(2).

Watt, R. G. (2005). Strategies and approaches in oral disease prevention and health promotion. *Bulletin of the World Health Organization, 83*, 711–718.

Watt, R. G. (2020). COVID-19 is an opportunity for reform in dentistry. *The Lancet, 396*(10249), 462.

Watt, R. G., Daly, B., Allison, P., Macpherson, L. M., Venturelli, R., Listl, S., . . . & Benzian, H. (2019). Ending the neglect of global oral health: Time for radical action. *The Lancet, 394*(10194), 261–272.

Watt, R. G., D'cruz, L., Rai, A., & Jones, E. (2015). Reflections on a training course reorienting dental teams towards prevention. *British Dental Journal, 218*(1), 25–28.

Watt, R. G., Mathur, M. R., Aida, J., Bönecker, M., Venturelli, R., & Gansky, S. A. (2018). Oral health disparities in children: A canary in the coalmine? *Pediatric Clinics, 65*(5), 965–979.

Watt, R. G., & Sheiham, A. (2012). Integrating the common risk factor approach into a social determinants framework. *Community Dentistry and Oral Epidemiology, 40*(4), 289–296.

Whitmore, J. (2010). *Coaching for performance: The principles and practice of coaching and leadership*. Hachette.

Wide Boman, U., Carlsson, V., Westin, M., & Hakeberg, M. (2013). Psychological treatment of dental anxiety among adults: A systematic review. *European Journal of Oral Sciences, 121*(3), 225–234.

Wolf, T. G., Cagetti, M. G., Fisher, J., Seeberger, G. K., & Campus, G. (2021). Non-communicable diseases and oral health: An overview. *Frontiers in Oral Health*, 2. https://doi.org/10.3389/froh.2021.725460

World Health Organisation (2021) Resolution 74.1 Oral Health. WHO. https://apps.who.int/gb/ebwha/pdf_files/WHA74/B148_REC1_EXT-en.pdf

World Health Organisation (2022a). Global Status Report on Oral Health. WHO. https://www.who.int/team/noncommunicable-diseases/global-status-report-on-oral-health-2022

World Health Organisation (2022b, September, 16). Non-Communicable Diseases. WHO. https://www.who.int/news-room/fact-sheets/detail/noncommunicable-diseases

Yuwanati, M., Gondivkar, S., Sarode, S. C., Gadbail, A., Desai, A., Mhaske, S., . . . & Khatib, M. N. (2021). Oral health-related quality of life in oral cancer patients: Systematic review and meta-analysis. *Future Oncology, 17*(8), 979–990.

Chapter 11

Trauma-informed and sensitive coaching

Julia Vaughan Smith

Introduction

Understanding how trauma disrupts our health and wellbeing, and being trauma-sensitive, is part of effective coaching. The prevalence and impact of trauma means that coaches cannot ignore its obvious or hidden presence in the coaching. This may challenge ideas that trauma belongs in therapy and is not suitable for coaching. While most trauma integration work needs appropriately trained therapists, clients can benefit from coaches who understand trauma.

Within the expanding field of coaching, how we work with clients depends on our training, competence and orientation. Being trauma-informed and sensitive does not change these boundaries; rather, it offers another lens to work through. Being trauma-informed means understanding what trauma is and how it presents; being trauma-sensitive is responding to symptoms of trauma in ways that enhance a sense of safety and offer appropriate coaching interventions.

Most coaches will have encountered clients affected by trauma – some with overt symptoms, others less obvious – hidden behind behaviour and thought patterns that are hard to shift. This can be the case in coaching that feels stuck or unproductive, or in clients who feel hard to connect to. Coaches also carry their own trauma dynamics, which can get in the way of effective coaching.

This chapter describes what trauma is and how we survive it, and addresses some of the practical implications for coaches and coaching.

What is trauma?

Trauma is a widely misused term. On the one hand, it can bring images of abuse or violence which are disturbing; on the other hand, the term can be used for inconsequential things, for example, "I couldn't find a parking place. It was so traumatic". The language therefore can be a problem. We do not need to feel afraid of what we imagine it will bring into coaching, but we do need to be prepared.

A definition

For this chapter, trauma is defined as "the lasting impact on our neuro-physiology and psyche of being overwhelmed by a sense of danger". It is within us; it is not the event, it is the effect our experience has on our nervous and other body systems. Most of this

DOI: 10.4324/9781003319016-13

experience arises from our early lives as infants and children or being perpetrated upon by another or others at any time.

Theory

What causes the trauma response within us?

To appreciate the lasting impact, we need an awareness of the nervous and hormonal system responses to threat. These arise in response to danger, as sensed by our nervous system; it is not a cognitive process but a body-based response that involves the autonomic nervous and endocrine systems.

What follows is a much simplified description of the autonomic nervous system response.

There are the following four broad stages.

- Calm or social engagement

    In this phase, our breathing is even, our pulse at resting pace and we are grounded without agitation. We feel safe.

- Active awareness

    Something might make us 'sit up', becoming alert, as we see meerkats do. If there is no danger, we revert to the calm phase.

- Fight or flight

    If there is danger, we move into fight or flight. Our pulse rate and breathing rate increase, adrenaline circulates, we feel anxiety and fear, and our body prepares to flee or flight back. We may experience rage or anger, which fuels our desire to act. However, often we can neither flee nor fight, and the arousal level increases to the next phase.

- Freeze, fragment, submission (sometimes referred to as 'fawn')

    In this phase, we become immobilised by fear, we produce endorphins that help numb us to pain, raising the pain threshold; our heart rate and blood pressure decrease, possibly to collapse. This brings dissociation, helplessness, shame, a shut-down in our systems and a preparation for death. We become submissive in our collapse.

(Porges, 2009; Walker, 2020)

This is an intelligent system, designed to help us survive a threat. When the danger is passed, the body may readjust to the changed reality, but the danger pathway has been laid down and can be easily reactivated. This is what happens when we are 'triggered' by situations in the 'here and now'. Porges's Polyvagal Theory (https://integratedlistening. com/polyvagal-theory/), identified the crucial part played by different branches of the vagal nerve, which connects our brains with our gut and all organs within the body.

Stress hormones, including cortisol, are produced to support the stress and trauma response, the impact of which is seen in changes to the immune system, the thymus and lymph glands, and in the lining of the digestive system (Maté, 2003). Maté and Maté (2022) shows how a prolonged stress response has a lasting impact on our physical health in many ways.

Impact on the memory

Memory is fragmented by the trauma response, which means we may not have a coherent cognitive recollection of the experience. In addition, emotional and body experience is stored as intrinsic memory, which is not available to cognitive recall. Before we have language, around the age of 2, all our memories are intrinsic. For example, we have no cognitive memory of being born, but our intrinsic memory does. Just because we cannot recall traumatising experiences does not mean that the memory is not there (Levine, 1997, 2008; Rothschild, 2000; Schore, 2003, 2001), it continues to influence us in the present.

Impact on the body

Maté (2003, Maté and Maté, 2022) has written about the lasting impact of heightened stress and the trauma response on the physical body, especially on the immune system. Multiple writers (Levine, 1997, 2010; Rothschild, 2000; Ogden and Fisher, 2015) have explored how traumatic memory is held in the body and subsequently affects the development of our neural pathways.

Symptoms of trauma include fight-or-flight responses being permanently switched on, with hypervigilance, agitation, hyperactivity, sleep problems and sensitivity to loud noises. We are continually on our guard. We may have forgotten what feeling calm and safe is like, so are unaware that our stress responses are high. It is exhausting, and rest is difficult to achieve.

Previous trauma pathways with fight-or-flight responses can be activated in the 'here and now' by a present circumstance or relationship that in some way mirrors the 'there and then'. We become anxious, feel unsafe, may have panic attacks and experience mood swings. The present may not contain any danger, but the response has been activated. This may happen occasionally or often, and we may be able to experience calm some of the time, to a greater or lesser extent.

We try to numb such feelings and to manage the symptoms through a range of behaviour, which are detailed in the next section. With unresolved trauma, the past is always pushing through into the present. Through regaining self-regulation, we can use the 'executive function' in our higher brain to access the actual danger now; often, though, we can be caught up in the undertow of a past response.

A further symptom of trauma is that the connections between the mind and the felt-experience in the body are disrupted. This happened at the time to help numb us to pain. This means we are unable to 'feel into' our body and can lead us to disregard the body as being a full part of us.

We can all learn to enhance our self-regulation and meditation, mindfulness, yoga, Tai Chi and other practices help facilitate it. If we are not self-regulated, we cannot be in the calm or social engagement phase described by Porges (2009). We need to be self-regulated to have a connection with our body, so that we have a flow of information from body, emotions and mind to do the best thinking and decision-making we can and which is in our best interests.

Post-traumatic stress

This is commonly what people think of when describing the symptoms of trauma. Everyone who is traumatised and stuck in the fight/flight/freeze response is carrying post-traumatic stress. Post-traumatic stress disorder (PTSD) is a diagnostic category for those more seriously affected and who may act out the unprocessed anger or harm themselves because of the emotional pain they experience; and who, at the same time, have 'flashbacks'; that is, sensory memories of the traumatising time, experienced as if they are happening right now – there is no differentiation of the past and present. Working with PTSD requires specially trained practitioners.

Impact on the psyche

Another way of working with and understanding trauma is through the impact on the psyche. I use the term 'psyche' to refer to the process by which we integrate our experience and sense of ourselves as a whole person. The fragmentation phase of trauma disrupts this so that we will not cognitively remember the pain and terror of experience. Ruppert (2014) refers to this as a split in the psyche; it is a way to de-link our experience (Kalsched, 1996).

We develop a range of defensive thoughts and behaviour patterns to block out the pain of deep trauma feelings and high levels of agitation, detailed in the previous section (Schwartz, 2021; Ruppert, 2014; Maté and Maté, 2022). These are our attempts to recreate a sense of protection and safety within us.

These defences are our saviours. However, they can become resisters to change that would release joy and vitality. We meet these in coaching when change becomes stuck or sabotaged by the client. To be always defending our self is exhausting.

The list of defences is long, and includes the following.

- Dissociation.
- Addictions (including overwork).
- Distraction (keeping busy/talking about anything other than the real issue).
- Denial of our experience or how our behaviour is harming us in the 'here and now'.
- Control of ourselves and a need to control others.
- Rescuing.
- Avoidance of experiences and situation.
- Fantasy thinking.
- Collapse and constriction of our life.
- Entangling others in relationships that are inevitably unhealthy and unsatisfying.

The beliefs we generate from trauma experience include having low self-esteem, not feeling lovable, that we have to work hard to be of value, that we have to please people, feeling an imposter, or that no one cares for or about us.

In his Split in the Psyche Model, Ruppert (2014) describes the Trauma Self (containing cut off trauma emotional memories frozen in time at the age they occurred) the Survival Self (containing the survival defence patterns) and the Healthy Self. He states that we all have a Healthy Self, outside of the trauma dynamics, containing our resources for healing and for wholeness.

Schwartz's (2021) Internal Family Systems (IFS) work, calls this entity the Self. The Self and the Healthy Self have similar characteristics, being the part of the psyche where we can be curious, creative, compassionate to ourselves and others; calm, grounded and self-regulated; we do not need to entangle others in our relationships with them; and where we have a good connection through body, emotions and thoughts.

In coaching, our aim is to support connection within this Healthy Self/Self from where the other internal dynamics can be seen clearly and the reality of the present can be engaged with. It is where resilience is possible; that is, the capacity to face reality without collapse or acting out via survival defences (adapted from Halifax, 2018).

The survival defences are part of a self-caring system, and they should be seen as our trying to find safety until we can find a better way. We should not see them as blockages to change or want to 'get rid of them'; they have to become part of the change. We need to see them compassionately and welcome them for what they are trying to do for us. Schwartz (2021) makes this point in talking about 'all parts are welcome'. In his work, he talks about the individual having many different parts within the psyche. I have previously referred to his idea of the Self, alongside that he describes three other groups of parts: 'Managers', 'Firefighters' and 'Exiles'. Managers act to keep the person feeling secure by controlling self, others and events, Firefighters react when trauma pain is felt; this may involve substance abuse, numbing activity, dissociation, distracting and other addictions. Both Managers and Firefighters have similarities with the Survival Self of Ruppert. A third group in Swartz's IFS is the Exiles, the parts affected by the trauma, holding the deep unprocessed emotions of shame, terror, anger and intense vulnerability. These Exiles are similar in concept to the Trauma Self of Ruppert.

It is not clear yet whether these ways of describing the impact on the psyche fully accommodate those who are neurodiverse. In the emerging understanding of neurodiversity, there is the opportunity to enquire into the interplay between neurodiversity and trauma. It might be hard to differentiate what is part of the individual's neurodiversity and what is a trauma symptom. Fortunately, the attention now being given to neurodiversity will add greatly to our understanding (see Chapter 15 on neurodiversity). No coach should try to force a theoretical model onto a client's symptoms, and this is no different. However, we can work with what clients make of it, how they understand it and what is resourcing for them.

With the increasing understanding of trauma, and associated therapeutic approaches, the field continues to develop. Simply understanding these approaches can be helpful for coaches in their work, providing a great appreciation of what clients may be experiencing.

Examples of traumatising experience

Attachment neuroscience makes it clear that we can be traumatised from conception onwards. Understanding that life events, the environment in which we are raised and how we are parented has opened up the field of inquiry while continuing to recognise the major trauma impact of sexual or domestic abuse, and of witnessing violence. Those in the field talk of attachment trauma, or developmental or emotional trauma, being ways to bring together these observations of the impact of adverse experiences as infants and children. Ruppert (2014) talks of trauma biography, a way of understanding the cumulative effect of traumatising experience on our body and psyche.

Table 11.1 Potentially traumatic experiences

- High stress arousal in the mother during pregnancy.
- Difficult birth and separation from mother after birth (for example, if the infant or the mother needs specialised care).
- Death and loss of a close caregiver at a young age.
- Separation due to illness.
- Caregivers who are consistently unable to be attuned to the needs of the infant and child, who offer little reassurance or physical holding, or who are emotionally cool.
- Critical, judgemental and controlling parenting.
- Boarding school.
- Sexual abuse/rape.
- Physical abuse/anger in the household.
- Caregivers who have addiction problems, or who are absent often or who have high levels of narcissism (also a survival defence).
- Racism.
- War – being a refugee.
- Severe shocks, such as a bad accident.

Mary Ainsworth's contribution in 1969 and afterwards further developed the theory of attachment and attachment styles. Attachment has remained a central concept in understanding how early experiences can have a long-lasting effect on us as humans. Maté (2003) talks of authenticity and attachment and that we often given up our authenticity to remain attached to our caregiver(s). We compromise, we seek to please or we rebel through anger. In the past, little recognition was given to the lasting impact of our earlier experience; children were assumed to be resilient or unable to recall early events. However, this understanding has changed, and these early experiences are now widely accepted as being foundational.

Table 11.1 highlights experiences which can increase the likelihood of being traumatised from childhood and as an adult. How an individual responds to different life experiences is unique to them. Factors such as having someone to turn to and who offers caring safety, as well as individual resilience, can influence how an individual is affected by events in both the short and the long term. It can depend on what happens next; for example, there is a big difference between having been sexually abused, feeling able to tell a caregiver or other adult, being believed and supported, and not being believed or feeling unable to tell anyone and keep it a secret. Too often, society and family responses are to blame the victim (Taylor, 2020, 2022).

Why are infants so vulnerable?

Human infants are incapable of independent living, their brains are not fully developed and they are entirely dependent on those around them for their needs for love, warmth, food, safety and touch/physical holding. Whatever happens to them, they cannot flee or fight – they have nowhere to go. In addition, parenting is usually challenging and difficult, and parents are often struggling with many demands.

Our brains and minds start to develop from the fifth week of pregnancy and progress rapidly from the third trimester of pregnancy until the age of around 2 or 3, and then continue to develop until our 20s. The human brain is vulnerable to the relational environment in which it is being raised. There is no protection from what goes in; it is like an open system without filters. The first to develop according to McGilchrist (2009) and Schore (2003, 2001) is the right hemisphere and intrinsic memory.

The human brain also develops in the interaction with our caregivers. Gerhardt (2004) highlights the importance of love, alongside the variety of stimulation infants receive. She argues this is essential for the development of the frontal lobe, and development of an individual's sense of right and wrong, as well as the development of curiosity, creativity, language, learning and habit formation.

Ruppert talks of human needs being to be wanted, loved and protected. When these are not met, our warning responses are activated. Hübl (2020) talks of the human needs as to be, to become and to belong – and similarly, if these are not facilitated, it has a lasting impact on our sense of ourselves, our capacity to love and care for ourselves, our sense of our place in the world, how lovable we feel and how we manage or fail to manage our boundaries.

Some parents will pass on their trauma to their children in how they relate and respond to them. Trauma is inter-generational in that regard. We also live in a traumatised and traumatising society, as is seen in racism and how society and institutions respond to certain groups of people.

Practice

When coaching is flowing freely and the client is self-reflective, able to recognise and change any self-limiting patterns and the working alliance feels good, both client and coach are more likely to be operating from healthy self or parts. However, trauma is likely to be present when clients are clearly in an emotionally disturbed or agitated state or when the coaching feels stuck, as if it is going nowhere, we doubt ourselves, the clients' coaching intentions seem further and further away, or there are things about how the client relates to us – or us to them.

A significant element of being trauma-sensitive is developing the qualities that support that intention and becoming more skilful in particular situations.

Safety

Being trauma-sensitive means recognising issues around safety. Most coach training talks about creating a safe confidential environment through contracting, listening, checking in with the client and not directing the agenda but respecting that of the client. For some clients and coaches, however, being in close contact with some people does not feel safe.

For the coach, it might be that there is a lot of reputation riding on the outcome of the coaching, or perhaps the client triggers trauma memories in us which causes us to pull back or become over concerned about being a 'good coach' or our anxiety is raised, which takes them into fight-or-flight territory.

For the client, it might be the context of the coaching. If it is internal coaching or the coach has been invited in by a company, the client may be concerned about whose 'side' the coach is on and have concerns about confidentiality. The attachment patterns of either coach or client may mean that they are avoidant or anxious in the relationship. A lack of a sense of safety affects the ability to draw on the resources of curiosity, compassion, creativity and connecting with what is healthy for us.

Coaches can inadvertently prompt safety issues within a client by acting unexpectedly or arbitrarily, by not observing the client's boundaries or by not listening properly to the client. This may trigger memories of interactions with caregivers or teachers in the past. We must always remember that our clients are resourceful and respect their autonomy. Our own anxiety might get in the way of doing that.

Whatever the reason for a lack of safety, our first task is to check that we are self-regulated, grounded and attuned to the client – and if not, adjust that in the session and explore afterwards what was being activated within us. We cannot make clients feel safe; we can, however, fully respect the fact that they may not. With a good connection from the coach, the client's sense of safety may shift over a series of sessions.

Social engagement connection/healthy self

The key to our part of providing a safe environment is to ensure, as much as we can, that we are in our healthy self (Ruppert, 2014) and the social engagement phase (Walker, 2020). This means we are self-regulated, grounded, attuned with the client, respectful of how they are and able to bring curiosity and compassion into the relationship, along with a sense of calm acceptance.

This is easier said than done. When the coaching is flowing, we are likely to be in this place. But when it is not, we often move away from it, as our anxiety is activated. When this happens, we lose that connection with our body, our thoughts are swirling about and we may notice familiar survival patterns emerge. These may include giving advice or telling the client what to do, using another tool or technique, talking a lot more than the client, feeling bored, thinking we are the wrong coach for this client, talking about referral, stepping into rescue mode as we find the helplessness of the client almost unbearable or becoming controlling and directive. We will have our own patterns – those to which we return at such times. With supervision and personal reflection, we can become aware of these – and the more we can be in contact with our body, we can sense more quickly when we are not, taking ourselves back to a grounded self-regulated place in the session. We can always say "Let's just pause a moment and see where we are"; this gives us an opportunity to breathe and regroup.

The benefit of autobiography without going into the past

The mantra of some coach training is that coaching does not deal with the past or talk about it. And yet, we know that so much of the present – the 'here and now' – is affected by the past, the 'there and then'. We are not diagnosticians and there is no value in pretending that we can pinpoint the past experience within the client that might be at play. Much of trauma memory is not available to cognitive recall, and it is not our place to try to 'find the cause' of the trauma. What some clients do find helpful, however, is the idea that events and experiences in our childhood have an impact on how we are responding to challenges in the present. It can bring insights that can be helpful.

We have the option of asking clients in the first session about their past in ways that give them space to share as much or as little as they want. For example, we could ask them about what it was like growing up, how safe home life felt, who was a positive figure for them or about significant life events. We can introduce this by referring in the contract to the link between past experience and issues in the present. If, during the coaching, we have a thought that there might be a link between something in the client's past and the issue in the present, we can offer a suggestion such as "I'm wondering if . . . ?", which leaves space for the client to reject it if they do not sense a connection.

Some coaches may be anxious that the client might share something they are unprepared for. Sometimes clients tell us things they have never told anyone else. Our coaching response is the same as for distressed clients – we stay grounded and self-regulated, attentive to the client. How we respond is important to whether the client feels more shame by telling us. It is understandable that coaches may feel anxious about 'getting it right'. We need to be an attuned witness to what clients are sharing and then facilitate clients to access their resourcefulness.

Working with a client who is distressed, agitated or anxious

This may be a new client, or a client who arrives in this state or becomes distressed during the session. Many coaches find this difficult as it does not happen very often, so a skilled response has not had a chance to develop. The first thing to realise is that we do not have to solve it or rescue the client from it. What we do need to do is stay calm and in the healthy self, witnessing the client and showing that we can see how distressed or agitated they are. We can voice this – for example, "I can see that part of you is very distressed here today" or "I can see that you appear to be quite anxious, today" – and ask, for example, "What would be most helpful for you right now?"

We can suggest doing a breathing exercise together, if the client is open to that, and spend 5–10 mins practising self-regulation together. Dr Karen Treisman (Treisman, 2023) presents a range of soothing resources if you have clients for whom this may be useful.

Coaches unfamiliar with clients being like this may feel as if they need to rescue the client from their distress, or become frightened and withdraw from the client. It may remind us of people in our past who became distressed or were agitated and our response is to feel responsible for it, and for making it 'go away'. If we have been disturbed by a client's presentation, supervision is a good place to talk about it, to explore our responses and to learn from the experience.

Becoming aware of potential defensive strategies, thoughts and behaviour patterns

These defensive parts or thoughts and behaviours will appear often in coaching. An individual can challenge them if there is sufficient curiosity and capacity for self-reflection. However, often the defences are rigid and have a driven energy and are not coachable as the client does not feel internally safe enough to let them go. For example, if the issue is about reducing workload, whatever is decided may be sabotaged by a survival part that uses overwork for safety reasons. Our task is to aim our interventions at the healthy parts of the client – the parts that can be curious, creative and compassionate. Coaching has many ways of doing this, including using powerful questions – those that start with how, where or who – and feedback in the 'here and now'; that is, from our own responses to the client in the moment.

We may also hear beliefs clients hold about themselves and narratives they use to hold the survival patterns in place. We can invite clients to question how such stories help them, or ask them where they came from. The answers can sometimes be revealing and helpful to the client.

The challenge for the coach is to stay in their grounded, attuned state so that their survival defences aren't doing the coaching; for example, by being driven to 'get a result' or 'achieve the goals'. It is a delicate balance between having in mind what the client wishes to achieve in coaching and feeling anxious about whether those will be achieved or not.

Using the idea of parts

I have mentioned the IFS model of Richard Schwartz (2021), and his training offers a way of working therapeutically with parts. His U.S.-based organisation is developing training for coaches, and over the next few years, I expect to see such training available outside of North America.

In the meantime, we can use a very simplified way of using the parts idea which can help bring in the healthy self-voice. For example, a client may say "I feel totally overwhelmed" and we might respond "I hear part of you feels totally overwhelmed"; this disconnects the overwhelm from defining me. If the client connects with this, we might then ask "What does this part need?" or "How do you feel about this part?" or "What is this part's positive intention for you?" We can use parts in our exchanges within the coaching, and clients may come to say "Part of me feels really anxious today" or "Part of me really wants to keep doing X and another part really does not". Schwartz reminds us that all the parts think they are acting in our best interest, and should be welcomed, especially the parts that we may want to reject. The more we can welcome in the parts we want to push away, the more we are able to get to know them and understand the function they are fulfilling in the attempt to keep ourselves safe. It is the connection with the Self that brings curiosity to the exploration.

Saying yes when we mean no – rescuing and pleasing others

In 2021, during an online workshop, Dr Gabor Maté highlighted that many people who are traumatised want to please others, be a 'good' child, gain recognition and rescue others in the hope that they will love us, see us, want us and/or need us so that we can get approval and feel as if we finally belong. These are all trauma responses from childhood experience of our relationship with our caregivers. The more we do this, the more stressed and overworked we become, until burnout or being overwhelmed ensures that we have to stop.

One pattern he identified was the habit of saying "yes" to something when we really want to say "no". These means that we are repeatedly putting our needs and wants on hold to service the demands or requests from others. At the same time, we lose the ability to say "yes" to ourselves and so do not resource ourselves sufficiently, getting more and more exhausted and operating in a survival mode; we no longer thrive.

Rescuing is common in all those in the 'people business', as it comes from our anxiety about the apparent helplessness or pain of another and a desire to control the outcome. We are saying, in effect, "Let me solve this for you, as you can't" and undermining the potential resourcefulness of the person. It comes from a place of wanting to be needed, loved and seen. Unfortunately, rescuing rarely gives us that; instead, we get entangled in the dynamics and may feel resentment – we may find we are denying our own needs for rest and space. Readers may be familiar with the Drama Triangle developed by Dr Steven Karpman, and how rescuers or those being rescued can turn into persecutors of each other. As coaches, we may step into rescuing if we accommodate a client's need; for example, for meeting times or dates, or when we do lots of work for the client out of the sessions that the client could have done for themselves, or when we put ourselves forward to too much work or too many clients.

Emotions and the body

Not all coaches feel comfortable talking about emotions or bringing the body into coaching. Being trauma-informed and sensitive means that we need to feel comfortable doing so, not to become counsellors or body therapists but to be the best coach we can be. We need to be able to sit with distress or other emotions we may find difficult, and have ways of responding that enable the client to soften the intensity of the feeling and maybe make sense of it.

Involving the body is part of somatic coaching but may not be something other coaches do. Such questions as "What do you feel in your body right now, if anything?" or "You talk about feeling angry. I wonder if you feel that anywhere in your body?" link an emotion to where it is felt in the body. These types of explorations bring different data into the coaching. Not all clients, or coaches, have good access to their felt-experience in their bodies, so it is important not to push it with such clients and to give the opt out of 'if anything'. If this is an area a coach feels unsure about, it may be useful to get some somatic coaching for themselves, to experience it first-hand and from that place take it into their coaching as an offering to clients.

Mental health first aid

Many in the trauma field, including Maté and Maté (2022) and Ruppert (2014), consider mental ill health to be a symptom of trauma. Taylor (2020, 2022) is vocal in her challenges to psychiatry and to the use of psychiatric diagnoses and what happens next, particularly to women. Many coaches find it helpful to do a mental health first aid course to prepare them for responding to mental ill health. We can coach clients with a diagnosis of mental ill health, if the client has sufficient sense of agency, that is, the capacity to take charge of their life from the healthy self. We can ask them how they think their depression or bipolar symptoms may affect the coaching and allow them to tell us if they are experiencing a problem in any given session. It is not the place of coaching to get involved in trying to shift the diagnosis. We can, though, support a client wanting coaching to live as full and satisfying life as they can given their mental health challenges.

It is very rare that coaching clients talk of ending their life – and again, this is something that if it happens, we may be unprepared for it unless we have undergone some continuing professional development (CPD) to help us know best practice in such a situation. We do have a duty of care, and we need to extend our competence to be able to respond appropriately with the client's safety in mind. Getting training in this will help reduce any anxiety we may feel about it, which ironically may prevent us going to get the training. Supervision is the place to take such fears and to get the support needed.

Such training and supervision helps us be clear about when it may be in the best interests of the client to suggest that a therapeutic route may be valuable. Sometimes, coaches' anxiety drives them to want to refer clients on when coaching could offer a valuable process. Learning how to negotiate this within ourselves and the client is an important skill to develop. The key is to involve the client – what are their thoughts? If they think therapy might be helpful, what might be the next steps?

Resourcing ourselves

This is crucial, as being in survival means we find rest difficult. We all need to be resourced by contact with close friends and beloved family, by doing what we enjoy most with those whom we like being with. We need rest and to be refreshed. The same is true for our clients, and part of coaching is to help clients resource themselves – particularly those who are too busy attending to others to do that. This is very important when working with trauma dynamics, as the healthy self needs good sleep and to be resourced; we are then better able to think clearly and to bring curiosity and creativity into being.

Conclusion

Coaches need not be afraid of trauma in the coaching room. Understanding it better can help reduce any anxiety, as can developing skills in using appropriate interventions. Our coaching can be enhanced by understanding trauma, as we can better recognise survival patterns in us and our clients; we can invite clients to be curious about theirs and assess how well they are serving them right now. We can be with distress or strong emotions and have ways of responding to clients who are agitated and highly anxious. We are less often pulled out of shape by our own trauma responses, so remain coaching and respecting the client's resourcefulness.

As I hope I have demonstrated, being trauma-informed and sensitive is about us as coaches and our own trauma dynamics. We need to look to ourselves and this will be helped if we also engage with therapeutic work on any trauma that we carry within us.

Supervision is the best process for exploring boundaries between coaching and therapy as the question arises with particular clients, and for other concerns we may have about the coaching, including how we are with some clients. It is important we stay within our area of competence for the safety of the client and ourselves.

It is not the place of coaching to diagnose trauma, to tell clients they are traumatised, to work with the cut-off trauma memories or to process trauma history. This is the realm of therapy. We can use psycho-education if we feel it appropriate with particular clients, talk about the trauma response and invite the client to be curious about particular patterns of behaviour and thought.

We all need to recognise the amount of trauma in the world and that it will come into our coaching. Wanting to be the best coaches we can for our clients means using our continuing professional development to deepen our awareness, our skilled interventions and the qualities needed to be trauma-sensitive.

Reflective questions

1. What connections, if any, have you made between the contents of this chapter and aspects of your coaching practice and work with clients?
2. What survival defensive patterns have you recognised in yourself?
3. What next steps will you take towards enhancing your trauma sensitivity?

References

Bowlby, J. (1953) *Child Care and the Growth of Love*. London: Penguin Books

Bowlby, J. (1969) *Attachment and Loss Vols 1 and 2*. London: Penguin Books

Gerhardt, S. (2004) *Why Love Matters: How Affection Shapes a Baby's Brain*. East Sussex: Brunner–Routledge

Halifax, J. (2018) *Standing at the Edge*. New York, NY: Flatiron Books

Hübl, T. (2020) *Healing Collective Trauma: A Process for Integrating Our Intergenerational and Cultural Wounds*. London: Sounds True

Kalsched, D. (1996) *The Inner World of Trauma: Archetypal Defenses of the Personal Spirit: Archetypal Defences of the Personal Spirit*. Abingdon: Routledge

Karpman, S. (unavailable) *A Game Free Life: The Definitive Book on the Drama Triangle and Compassion Triangle by the Originator and Author*. San Fransisco, CA: Drama Triangled Publications

Levine, P. (1997) *Waking the Tiger: Healing Trauma*. Berkely, CA: North Atlantic Books

Levine, P. (2008) *Healing Trauma: A Pioneering Programme for Restoring the Wisdom of your Body*. Colorado: Sounds True

Levine, P. (2010) *In an Unspoken Voice: How the Body Releases Trauma and Restores Goodness*. Berkely, CA: North Atlantic Books

Maté, G. (2003) *When the Body Says No*. New York: Wiley

Maté, G. & Maté, D. (2022) *The Myth of Normal: Trauma, Illness and Healing in a Toxic Culture*. London: Vermillion

McGilchrist, I. (2009) *The Master and His Emissary*. Yale: Yale University Press

Ogden, P. & Fisher, J. (2015) *Sensori-Motor Psychotherapy: Interventions for Trauma and Attachment*. New York: Norton

Porges, S. W. (2009) The polyvagal theory: New insights into adaptive reactions of the autonomous system. *Cleveland Clinic Journal of Medicine*, 76(supplement 2), S86–S90

Rothschild, B. (2000) *The Body Remembers*. New York: Norton

Ruppert, F. (2014) *Trauma, Fear and Love*. Steyning, UK: Green Balloon Publishing

Schore, A. N. (2001) The effects of early relational trauma on right brain development, affect regulation and infant mental health. *Infant Mental Health Journal*, 22(1), 201–269, Michigan Association for Infant Mental Health

Schore, A. N. (2003) The human consciousness: The development of the right brain and its role in early emotional life. In Green, V. (ed), *Emotional Development in Psychoanalysis, Attachment Theory and Neuroscience*. Abingdon: Routledge

Schwartz, R. (2021) *No Bad Parts*. Colorado, USA: Sounds True

Taylor, J. (2020) *Why Women Are Blamed for Everything: Exposing the Culture of Victim Blaming*. London: Constable

Taylor, J. (2022) *Sexy But Psycho*. London: Constable

Treisman (2023) Mindfulness. Retrieved on 20 April 2023 from http://www.safehandsthinkingminds.co.uk/covid-anxiety-stress-resources-links/

Walker, R. J. (2020) www.swtraumatraining.com/polyvagaltheory (diagram describing Stephen Porges's polyvagal theory)

Chapter 12

Coaching and mental health

Ana Paula Nacif

Introduction

Mental health is a universal concern. Positive mental health, or wellbeing, affects all areas of our lives and it is "fundamental to our collective and individual ability as humans to think, emote, interact with each other, earn a living and enjoy life" (WHO, 2013). Yet, mental ill health is highly prevalent in all countries, with 1 in 8 people in the world living with a mental disorder, according to the World Health Organization (2022b). Figures can be even higher among people living with socio-economic deprivation, those who experience social exclusion and stigma, people who live with long-term physical health conditions, carers and those with a history of substance abuse.

Mental disorders remain among the top ten leading causes of disease burden worldwide, with no evidence of global reduction since 1990 (WHO, 2022d). In England, 1 in 4 people will experience a mental health problem of some kind each year (McManus et al., 2009), and 1 in 6 experience a common mental health problem, like anxiety or depression, in any given week in England (McManus et al., 2016).

Given the pervasiveness of mental health issues among the general population, coaches are likely to work with clients who are experiencing some sort of mental distress. What is the role of coaching in supporting clients' mental health and/or as an intervention to help them cope with mental distress or ill health? This chapter will explore theories of mental health and mental illness, the debate about coaching and mental health, professional boundaries and the implications for coaching practitioners.

Theory and research

It is reasonable to expect statistics around mental illness to be reflected in the coaching client population. Past studies revealed that a proportion of coaching clients experience mental health issues (Cavanagh, 2005; Oades et al., 2005). Therefore, the debate about coaching and mental health – including questions about the purpose of coaching in relation to mental health and mental illness, training, professional development and ethical practice – remain important for the coaching field and its clients.

Mental health and mental illness

Mental health diagnosis is a controversial and complex field of research and practice. Categorical classification of mental illnesses – as proposed by the American Psychiatric

DOI: 10.4324/9781003319016-14

Association's *Diagnostic and Statistical Manual of Mental Disorders* (*DSM-5* for its current fifth edition) (American Psychiatric Association 2013) and the World Health Organization's International Classification of Diseases (ICD) (WHO, 2022a) – provides a list of symptoms and descriptors that are used by healthcare professionals to establish if someone meets the criteria for a particular mental health condition. According to categorical classifications, a person either has a mental illness or does not.

Critics of this approach claim that the boundaries between categories are "fuzzy" and that "categorical distinctions among personality disorder diagnoses are difficult to justify" (Livesley et al., 1994, p. 15). These critics tend to favour a dimension approach which conceptualises mental health as a continuum. American sociologist and psychologist Corey Keyes is one such scholar. Keyes, who coined the term 'flourishing', argued that mental health is more than the absence of mental illness; it encompasses positive emotions and positive functioning (2002, p. 208).

Despite the criticisms, categorical classifications are commonly used to diagnose people. What follows are some of the more common conditions that coaches may encounter in their work with clients.

1. Anxiety disorders are usually manifested in excessive and/or disproportionate worry and fear, which affect a person's feelings and behaviours. There are many types of anxiety disorders, including generalised anxiety disorder (excessive worry), panic disorder (panic attacks) and social anxiety disorder (fear and worry in social situations), among others.
2. Mood disorders are those which affect a person's feelings of happiness and sadness, such as depression and bipolar disorders. During a depressive episode, the person experiences a depressed mood and a loss of interest in any activities. They can also experience hopelessness, low energy and lack of appetite, and/or disrupted sleep. Those who experience bipolar disorder will go through a period of depressed mood, followed by manic symptoms, which may include euphoria or irritability, and increased activity or energy. Other symptoms include increased self-esteem and impulsive behaviour.
3. Post-traumatic stress disorder (PTSD) develops after a person is exposed to an extreme event or series of events. It usually involves flashbacks and intrusive memories. People experiencing PTSD may live in a constant perception of heightened alert for threats.
4. Psychotic disorders can cause impairments in perception and changes in behaviour. These can include delusions, hallucinations, disorganised thinking, highly disorganised behaviour, or extreme agitation. There may be difficulties with cognitive functions.
5. Obsessive-compulsive disorder is characterised by the experience of recurring, unwanted thoughts, ideas or sensations (obsessions) and the drive to do something repetitively (compulsions) to deal with those thoughts.

About 15% of working-age adults live with a mental disorder. Depression and anxiety alone cost the world economy some US$1 trillion per year, according to the World Health Organization (2022c). Contributory factors to employees' poor mental health include difficult working conditions such as excessive workloads, uncertainty and poor management practices (WHO, 2022c). Evidence gathered during the COVID19 pandemic has shown that coaching can help mitigate some of the mental health risks posed by an uncertain and stressful working environment (Rosen et al., 2022; Søvold et al., 2021). These findings are aligned with existing literature which suggests that coaching can be used effectively to support wellbeing in organisations (Davis, 2015; Grant et al., 2009; Hultgren et al., 2013; Ladegård, 2011; O'Connor & Cavanagh, 2013). Coaching practitioners working with organisational wellbeing are likely to have clients with personal experience of mental health conditions such as depression and anxiety, which may have been triggered or compounded by poor place practices.

Coaches are also likely to encounter another type of coaching client: those whose dysfunctional behaviour, possibly associated with personality disorders, has a negative impact on others. These employees may be perceived as difficult or challenging. "They may be pushed in the direction of coaching because of strong interpersonal problems highlighted in their relationships with work colleagues" (Szymanska, 2018, p. 542), or they may interpret events and interact with others in a way that poses "significant practical and emotional problems" for themselves and others (Cavanagh, 2005, p. 25).

Personality disorders and challenging behaviour

There are no specific studies about the occurrence of personality disorders among coaching clients. In the general population, the prevalence of any personality disorder is 7.8%, with a higher rate of 9.6% seen in high-income countries (Winsper et al., 2020). The diagnosis and treatment of personality disorders are strictly the domain of psychiatrists and clinicians, but it is helpful for coaches to understand these personality traits and disorders. Clients may display difficult personality traits to various degrees, which may not necessarily indicate they have a personality disorder. When working with challenging clients, Szymanska (2018) suggests coaches to focus on two areas: "the interpersonal process within the coaching relationship and, if required, skills acquisition and practise" (p. 543).

The personality disorders listed in the *DSM-V* (APA 2013), organised into the following three clusters.

CLUSTER A

These personality disorders manifest in what is perceived as odd or eccentric behaviour. These include paranoid personality disorder, characterised by an intense mistrust of others; and schizoid personality disorder, which is manifested in emotional and social detachment and limited emotional expression.

CLUSTER B

This cluster is characterised by larger-than-life, dramatic, emotional and erratic behaviour. It includes the following.

Histrionic personality disorder: tends to be 'overdramatic' and attention seeking, and display patterns of excessive emotionality.
Narcissistic personality disorder: displays a grandiose sense of self-importance, a need for admiration and a lack of empathy.

Antisocial personality disorder: deceitfulness and lack of respect for social norms.
Borderline personality disorder: pattern of unstable and intense interpersonal relationships characterised by alternating between extreme idealisation and devaluation.

CLUSTER C

These disorders are characterised by anxiety and fear. These include the following.

Avoidant personality disorder: pattern of social inhibition, feelings of inadequacy and hypersensitivity to negative evaluation.
Dependent personality disorder: excessive need to be taken care of, clinging behaviour and fears of separation.
Obsessive-compulsive personality disorder (not to be confused with obsessive-compulsive disorder): excessive preoccupation with orderliness, perfectionism and mental and interpersonal control at the expense of flexibility, openness and efficiency.

It may be difficult for coaches to ascertain the best course of action for clients displaying dysfunctional behaviour, and "the coach needs to assess whether their skills match the client's need or whether the client should be referred to a qualified mental health practitioner" (Cavanagh, 2005, p. 25).

Keyes' research (2002) showed that flourishing individuals function markedly better than languishing ones, reporting higher levels of functional goals, resilience and intimacy, along with lower levels of helplessness. Flourishing individuals tend to have high emotional, psychological and social wellbeing. Languishing individuals experience low subjective wellbeing. Individuals who are not languishing or flourishing are said to experience moderate mental health. These states are normally distributed among the population, which means that the majority of the population experience moderate mental health, whilst a minority would be placed on both sides as flourishing on the positive end of the continuum and as languishing on the negative. Keyes' data (2005) showed that only 16.8% of Americans aged between 25 and 74 experience flourishing. On the other end of the spectrum, he found that 9.5% of people were languishing, even though they did not experience mental illness, whilst some 14.5% of people with a moderate level of mental health had a diagnosed mental illness.

Keyes' mental health continuum can help coaches explore the complexities surrounding the mental health and wellbeing of their clients, whilst reflecting on factors that can support and/or hinder clients' readiness for coaching. According to Keyes' mental health continuum, positive mental wellbeing and mental illness are not necessarily mutually exclusive. People can have high levels of wellbeing, whether or not they have a diagnosed mental illness. Equally, they can have low levels of wellbeing with or without a mental illness. Those who are not mentally ill but experience low levels of wellbeing are said to be 'languishing', whereas those with optimal mental wellbeing and minimal mental illness are said to be 'flourishing'. Coaching practitioners are likely to work with clients in all these different categories.

Over the past decade, there has been increasing interest in exploring the role coaching can play in providing mental health support (Bishop et al., 2018; Corrie & Parsons, 2021). Coaching, which is "fundamentally concerned with the enhancement of human functioning, achieved through the improvement of cognitive, emotional and/or behavioural self-regulation" (Spence & Oades, 2011, p. 37), is well placed to support the psychological wellbeing of clients, and there is growing evidence to suggest that coaching can have a positive impact on the wellbeing of clients (Davis, 2015; Grant, 2003; Green et al., 2006; Nacif, 2021).

However, when it comes to working with people who live with a mental illness, views become more polarised, with some raising concerns about the potential risk and harm coaches without psychological training and awareness of mental health issues could inflict on their clients (Cavanagh, 2005). This polarisation is intensified by debates about the boundaries between coaching and psychotherapy, for example, and the challenges in defining clinical and non-clinical populations (Bachkirova & Baker, 2018). These boundaries are elusive, and some argue that there is a grey area where coaching and psychotherapeutic practices become undifferentiated (Bishop et al., 2018). Others emphasise that clients may not "belong either a coaching or counselling population, but rather they moved between the two" (Griffiths & Campbell, 2008, p. 173), as they experienced fluctuation in their psychological wellbeing in their daily lives. Research (Giraldez Hayes, 2021) shows that psychotherapists and coaches see themselves playing distinct roles, but they also recognise the grey area where both practices meet and where they work with clients tackling and exploring similar topics.

In their scoping review, Bishop and colleagues (2018) highlighted the lack of consensus "as to whether coaching is an appropriate mental health intervention", adding that whilst some organisations, such as the Foundation for Recovery Coaching UK and Rethink Mental Illness, endorse this approach, others fiercely criticise it (p. 30). Authors conceded that there is a lack of empirical evidence for either side of the argument but the review points out that, in some cases, there is

> little difference between those considered experts and non-experts in mental health: in several included studies, cognitive-behavioural techniques were used by coaches; this closely reflects the role of a "low-intensity" therapist, who uses coaching techniques to support clients in applying cognitive-behavioural strategies (IAPT, 2015).
>
> (Bishop et al., 2018, p. 38)

It is suggested that coaching could be particularly useful in the context of mental health recovery, a concept which, according to Burhouse and colleagues (2015), is gaining traction and "is commonly used to describe an individual's way of living a meaningful life beyond mental illness and how they conceptualise their own experience of mental illness" (p. 15). Bishop and colleagues (2018) suggest that coaching has multiple purposes and can be used in combination with other interventions or as an alternative: "All of these possibilities require further exploration, perhaps through a cost–benefit analysis to understand the comparative risks and value of mental health coaching" (p. 39).

This could signal a paradigm change which can be supported by existing evidence such as studies in which coaching demonstrated enhanced mental health and quality of life (Grant, 2003), coaching programmes specifically designed to foster an individual's subjective and psychological wellbeing (Nacif, 2021), and theoretical discussions encouraging coaching approaches aligned to wellbeing (Passmore & Oades, 2014).

Professional boundaries

As previously mentioned, the idea of coaching as an intervention to support people living with mental health conditions is contentious and there remain unresolved issues, including the professional boundaries in terms of practice, training and professional development of coaching practitioners, and a better understanding of clients' needs. Crowe (2017, p. 97) has called for more research into needs assessments, case conceptualisation practices, coaching competencies, the prevalence of mental health issues in coaching contexts and interdisciplinary support coaches and psychotherapists faced with client needs complexity.

Whereas discussions about the boundaries of coaching and psychotherapy have sought to find that elusive line between clinical and non-clinical work, "the majority of the literature and research indicates the boundaries are not clear and practitioners deal with them in a pragmatic way" (Bachkirova & Baker, 2018, p. 489). In addition, mental health is not necessarily part of the curriculum of coaching training programmes and studies have raised "concerns relating to coaches' abilities to recognise mental health problems and manage them effectively (Hart et al., 2001; Grant & Zackon, 2004; Turner, 2010; Jinks, 2010)" (Bachkirova & Baker, 2018, p. 488).

It has been argued that this lack of understanding hinders case conceptualisation and could "contribute to a misattribution of slow or minimal coaching progress to client resistance or attitudinal problems, or worse contribute to the exacerbation of underlying client issues" (Crowe, 2017, p. 89).

To mitigate such risks, some advocate basic mental health training to help coaches "recognise the presence of mental disorder, and an understanding of the appropriate evidence-based treatment options for these problems" (Cavanagh, 2005, p. 23). This understanding of mental health can be crucial to ensure clients are supported appropriately or signposted to the most appropriate professional support (Campone, 2014; Cavanagh, 2005).

In addition to more targeted mental health training, supervision can be a helpful resource for coaches who need guidance dealing with difficult issues and/or want to discuss the boundaries of their practice and questions about mental health. Interestingly, some of the questions raised about coaching practitioners' readiness to work with clients experiencing mental health issues are equally valid for supervisors. If supervisors are to fully support this work, should they also have specialist training? Moreover, other professionals formally working with people with mental health issues – such as psychotherapists, social workers and psychologists – are required to take part in supervision as a mandatory component of their professional practice. This is not the case for coaching practitioners. Issues related to training, supervision and professional and ethical practices need to be resolved to ensure clients' needs are fully met.

Practice

Mental health issues are, by their very nature, complex. Cavanagh and Buckley (2014) suggest that coaches should consider their "personal point of referral" when they "have reached the limits of their skills and abilities" (p. 408). They proposed a list of indicators to help coaching practitioners reflect on whether the client may be presenting some signs of mental distress which would require specialist help. These include the following (adapted from Cavanagh and Buckley, 2014, p. 410).

- Appearance: significant and noticeable changes in the client's personal care and body language.
- Behaviour: client displays signs of being agitated and nervous, or incoherent.
- Mood: experience of extreme mood, either positive or negative.
- Thoughts: fixation, appearing irrational or deluded.
- Perception: signs of experiencing reality in an unusual way.
- Intellect: significant changes in intellect over time.

It is important to note that, in isolation, these factors may not be sufficient to give coaches a full picture of the mental state of their clients. Therefore, in addition, Cavanagh (2005) suggests paying attention to the following: how long the client has experienced the issues, the intensity of behaviour and/or experience, whether the issue affects one or more aspects of the client's life and the pervasiveness of the perceived dysfunctional behaviours.

Coaches are not trained to diagnose or assess mental health conditions; hence, they need to be cognisant of the limitations of their skill set and ability to work with specific client groups. A survey among coaching practitioners (Corrie, 2017) revealed that 98% of a sample of 96 respondents agreed with the importance of their ability to identify a client who has poor mental health, with 95% of the sample reported being confident that they could accurately detect when a coaching client has a mental health problem. Another small-scale survey among 148 coaches revealed that 10% of them regularly coached clients "in relation to issues commonly associated with serious psychological distress (e.g., fears about a personal loss, life crises, social isolation and self-esteem)", including those without a background in psychology or counselling (Spence et al., 2006, p. 71).

Coaching practitioners have moral, ethical and professional obligations to be honest about the limitations of their professional training and experience, and to contract with their clients accordingly. If the client is experiencing mental health issues, the options for the client and coach are to delay, continue or stop the coaching programme. Although coaching can be used in parallel to other interventions, the client and coach must give full consideration to the implications of this option, especially as to whether it could interfere with other treatments or put the client under undue stress or pressure. Failing to fully comprehend the client's position can be harmful. For example, Cavanagh (2005) describes how pushing through with stretch goals when working with depressed clients "can further entrench a sense of despair and hopelessness, and these clients can leave coaching significantly worse off" (p. 22). Each case will be different. In England, the guidelines by the National Institute of Health and Care Excellence state that some mental health illnesses, such as depression and anxiety, can be experienced on a scale from mild to moderate to severe (NICE, 2011). This affects people's experiences of symptoms – such as feeling stressed, low, anxious or worried, for example – which can affect their ability to engage with the coaching process.

An example of coaching working simultaneously with psychotherapy was illustrated by a case study (Campone, 2014) that examined the coaching engagement of a client with dissociative identity disorder. The case study made extensive references to the coach's counselling knowledge and skills and how they were instrumental in developing the coaching relationship and a supportive environment for the client. In particular, "his professional education helped him to research and understand the specific mental disorder and to work within the parameters indicated by the particular condition" (p. 11). This is an example of a proactive client who was able to engage with both coaching and psychotherapy. The client also demonstrated a good understanding of their diagnosis and self-awareness about it meant for her to live with that mental health condition. This is not always the case. Some clients will not be fully aware of their mental state, while others may intentionally or unintentionally minimise or mask their symptoms.

Conclusion

The high prevalence of mental health issues among the general population means that coaching practitioners are likely to encounter clients experiencing these issues, regardless of the sector or specialty in which they work.

In working with these clients, coaches will face various dilemmas, including awareness about their knowledge, skills and experience; understanding of how to navigate professional boundaries; professional development and supervision; and, crucially, clarity on their own views and attitudes about where coaching sits within the complex and ambiguous world of mental health-mental illness.

Current literature refers to the need for psychological training for coaching practitioners, but whereas coaching is undoubtedly a useful intervention to foster positive mental health and wellbeing, its role in supporting people living with mental health issues is more contentious. Nevertheless, the literature points to a potential shift in the perception that the remit of coaching is within clearly defined boundaries within non-clinical populations.

As paradigms shift or are challenged, coaching practitioners, educators, academics and professional bodies may have to engage in deeper reflection on how coaching can be responsive to client needs whilst upholding high standards of professional and ethical practice.

Reflective questions

1. How can coaching support clients who are languishing?
2. What are your thoughts about the idea personal 'point of referral'? What are the advantages/risks involved in this concept?
3. What would it be helpful for you to learn, as a coach, to better support a client's positive mental health?

References

American Psychiatric Association. (2013). *Diagnostic and statistical manual of mental disorders* (5th ed.). https://doi.org/10.1176/appi.books.9780890425596
Bachkirova, T., & Baker, S. (2018). Revisiting the issue of boundaries between coaching and counselling. In *Handbook of coaching psychology* (pp. 487–499). Routledge.
Bishop, L., Hemingway, A., & Crabtree, S. A. (2018). Lifestyle coaching for mental health difficulties: Scoping review. *Journal of Public Mental Health*, 17(1), 29–44.
Burhouse, A., Rowland, M., Niman, H. M., Abraham, D., Collins, E., Matthews, H., . . . Ryland, H. (2015). Coaching for recovery: A quality improvement project in mental healthcare. *BMJ Open Quality*, 4(1), u206576. w202641.

Campone, F. (2014). At the border: Coaching a client with dissociative identity disorder. *International Journal of Evidence Based Coaching and Mentoring, 12*(1), 1–13.

Cavanagh, M. (2005). Mental health issues and challenging clients in executive coaching. In *Evidence-based coaching* (Vol. 1, pp. 21–36). Australian Academic Press.

Cavanagh, M., & Buckley, A. (2014). Coaching and mental health. In *The complete handbook of coaching* (Vol. 2, pp. 405–417). Sage.

Corrie, S. (2017). SGCP research network: What role do coaching practitioners have in working with mental health issues? Results of a survey. *The Coaching Psychologist, 13*(1), 41–48.

Corrie, S., & Parsons, A. A. (2021). The contribution of coaching to mental health care: An emerging specialism for complex times. In *Emerging conversations in coaching and coaching psychology* (pp. 60–77). Routledge.

Crowe, T. (2017). Coaching and psychotherapy. *The SAGE handbook of coaching*, (pp. 85–101). Sage.

Davis, S. (2015). *Coaching, well-being and organisational culture: A case study of the Executive Leadership Development Programme (ELDP) in royal mail (UK)* (Doctoral dissertation). Oxford Brookes University.

Giraldez Hayes, A. (2021). Different domains or grey areas? Setting boundaries between coaching and therapy: A thematic analysis. *The Coaching Psychologist, 17*(2), 18–29.

Grant, A. M. (2003). The impact of life coaching on goal attainment, metacognition and mental health. *Social Behavior and Personality: An International Journal, 31*(3), 253–263.

Grant, A. M., Curtayne, L., & Burton, G. (2009). Executive coaching enhances goal attainment, resilience and workplace well-being: A randomised controlled study. *The Journal of Positive Psychology, 4*(5), 396–407. https://doi.org/10.1080/17439760902992456

Green, L., Oades, L., & Grant, A. (2006). Cognitive-behavioral, solution-focused life coaching: Enhancing goal striving, well-being, and hope. *The Journal of Positive Psychology, 1*(3), 142–149.

Griffiths, K., & Campbell, M. A. (2008). Semantics or substance? Preliminary evidence in the debate between life coaching and counselling. *Coaching: An International Journal of Theory, Research and Practice, 1*(2), 164–175.

Hultgren, U., Palmer, S., & O'Riordan, S. (2013). Can cognitive behavioural team coaching increase well-being. *The Coaching Psychologist, 9*(2), 100–110.

Keyes, C. (2002). The mental health continuum: From languishing to flourishing in life. *Journal of Health and Social Behavior, 43*(2), 207–222.

Keyes, C. L. (2005). Mental illness and/or mental health? Investigating axioms of the complete state model of health. *Journal of Consulting and Clinical Psychology, 73*(3), 539.

Ladegård, G. (2011). Stress management through workplace coaching: The impact of learning experiences. *International Journal of Evidence Based Coaching & Mentoring, 9*(1).

Livesley, W. J., Schroeder, M. L., Jackson, D. N., & Jang, K. L. (1994). Categorical distinctions in the study of personality disorder: Implications for classification. *Journal of Abnormal Psychology, 103*(1), 6.

McManus, S., Bebbington, P. E., Jenkins, R., & Brugha, T. (2016). *Mental health and wellbeing in England: The adult psychiatric morbidity survey 2014.* NHS Digital.

McManus, S., Meltzer, H., Brugha, T., Bebbington, P. E., & Jenkins, R. (2009). *Adult psychiatric morbidity in England: Results of a household survey.* Health and Social Care Information Centre.

Nacif, A. (2021). BeWell: A group coaching model to foster the wellbeing of individuals. *International Journal of Evidence Based Coaching and Mentoring, 15*, 171–186.

National Institute for Health and Care Excellence [NICE]. (2011). Common mental health problems: Identification and pathways to care. *Clinical guideline 123.* https://www.nice.org.uk/guidance/cg123

Oades, L. G., Green, S., & Grant, A. (2005). An evaluation of a life coaching group program: Initial findings from a waitlist control study. In M. Cavanagh, A. Grant & T. Kemp (Eds.), *Evidence-based coaching* (pp. 127–142). Australian Academic Press.

O'Connor, S., & Cavanagh, M. (2013). The coaching ripple effect: The effects of developmental coaching on wellbeing across organisational networks. *Psychology of Well-Being: Theory, Research and Practice, 3*(1), 2.

Passmore, J., & Oades, L. G. (2014). Positive psychology coaching: A model for coaching practice. *The Coaching Psychologist, 10*(2), 68–70.

Rosen, B., Preisman, M., Read, H., Chaukos, D., Greenberg, R. A., Jeffs, L., . . . Wiesenfeld, L. (2022). Resilience coaching for healthcare workers: Experiences of receiving collegial support during the COVID-19 pandemic. *General Hospital Psychiatry, 75,* 83–87.

Søvold, L. E., Naslund, J. A., Kousoulis, A. A., Saxena, S., Qoronfleh, M. W., Grobler, C., & Münter, L. (2021). Prioritizing the mental health and well-being of healthcare workers: An urgent global public health priority [Perspective]. *Frontiers in Public Health, 9.* https://doi.org/10.3389/fpubh.2021.679397

Spence, G. B., Cavanagh, M. J., & Grant, A. M. (2006). Duty of care in an unregulated industry: Initial findings on the diversity and practices of Australian coaches. *International Coaching Psychology Review, 1*(1), 71–85.

Spence, G. B., & Oades, L. G. (2011). Coaching with self-determination theory in mind: Using theory to advance evidence-based coaching practice. *International Journal of Evidence-Based Coaching and Mentoring, 9*(2), 37–55.

Szymanska, K. (2018). Coachee mental health: Practice implications for coaching psychologists. In *Handbook of coaching psychology* (pp. 537–547). Routledge.

Winsper, C., Bilgin, A., Thompson, A., Marwaha, S., Chanen, A. M., Singh, S. P., . . . Furtado, V. (2020). The prevalence of personality disorders in the community: A global systematic review and meta-analysis. *The British Journal of Psychiatry, 216*(2), 69–78.

World Health Organization. [WHO] (2013). *Investing in mental health: Evidence for action.* WHO.

World Health Organization. [WHO] (2022a). *ICD-11: International classification of diseases* (11th revision). https://icd.who.int/

World Health Organization. [WHO] (2022b). *Mental health disorders.* Retrieved 12/02/2023 from https://www.who.int/news-room/fact-sheets/detail/mental-disorders

World Health Organization. [WHO] (2022c). *WHO guidelines on mental health at work.* World Health Organization.

World Health Organization. [WHO] (2022d). World mental health report: Transforming mental health for all: Executive summary. In *World mental health report: Transforming mental health for all: Executive summary.*World Health Organization.

Chapter 13

Coaching for a healthy sex life

Nwachi Gamba Eze Pressley-Tafari

Introduction

While sex coaching is not a new paradigm of professional coaching, it is one of the least researched forms of professional coaching when compared to other forms of coaching in the growing literature of evidenced-informed coaching. Perhaps sex coaching's relative absence from evidence-informed literature has less to do with the nature of modern coaching literature and more to do with the nature of human sexuality.

What it means to have a healthy sex life is complicated by how one's body interacts, not only with lovers, but also with the cultural, social, and ecological worlds in which sex acts occur and sexual identity is expressed (Barker, 2013; National Coalition for Sexual Health, 2022; Siegel, 2010). Moreover, what it means to have a healthy sex life is also confounded by the embodied, subjective, creative, and imaginative nature of human sexuality, one's phenomenological experience of being sexual in one's own body (Denman, 2004; Gagnon & Parker, 1995; Morin, 1995; Walker, 2021).

This chapter is organised into two parts. The first part introduces sex coaching and sex therapy research that support positive and respectful approaches to diverse sexual identities, relationship configurations, and sexual expressions; that support safe sexual experiences, free of coercion, discrimination, and violence; and that support the sexual rights of all persons (World Health Organization, 2022). The second part focuses on how to apply the research to the practice of professional sex coaching, particularly through Erotic Mythology Inquiry Approach (Pressley-Tafari, 2020, 2023).

Healthy human sexuality

Sexology was formally established in the late 1800s and early 1900s, but humanity has studied sex and sexual expression since recorded time (Djajic-Horváth, 2022). Much has changed since sexology's inception.

Until the mid-1900s, evidence-informed literature that supported sexology and sex therapy practices did not focus on how individuals defined healthy sexuality for themselves. Particularly in Western civilisation, the definition of a healthy sex life was often

DOI: 10.4324/9781003319016-15

aligned with the perspectives of Christian ideals (Gagnon & Parker, 1995; Seidman, 2015). Gagnon and Parker (1995) summarised this perspective:

> Both Christianity and medicine viewed sex as a basic drive that needed to be thwarted through self-control and environmental purity – a drive that differed between women and men – and that in its socially correct manifestation resulted in sex between men and women in marriage for the purpose of reproduction.
>
> (p. 5)

Thus, in part, the purpose of early sexologists' research was to identify sexual expressions and acts that should be considered "psychologically deviant and morally troubling, and this encompassed almost everything except procreational sex between a wife and husband" (Sharage & Stewert, 2015, p. 232). Therefore, BDSM (bondage, discipline, sadism and masochism) practices, homosexuality, masturbation, and oral sex – among other acts and expressions – were all labelled deviant or morally troubling because they do not bring children into the world nor forward heterosexual marriage.

Constantinides and colleagues (2019) categorised the sexual identities that historically and currently have been deemed perverse, in society and therapy, as erotically marginalised sexualities:

> The term erotically marginalised describes people who are at risk of being pathologized and oppressed both outside and inside the clinical setting due to their sexual identities, orientations and practices. Erotically marginalised people can include those who identify as lesbian, gay, bisexual, pansexual, asexual, demisexual, queer, trans and gender nonconforming, nonbinary, intersex, polyamorous, consensually non-monogamous, kinky, BDSM practitioners, or who have alternative relational and sexual structures in general.
>
> (p. 1)

By way of illustration, BDSM practitioners are an interesting example of a marginalised community's complicated path to healthy sex lives, in part because of sexuality researchers' perspectives about BDSM identities (Goerlich, 2021, 2023; Weinberg, 2006). Sex therapist Goerlich (2023) might best summarise the confusing path of marginalised sexual communities such as BDSM practitioners in some evidence-informed literature:

> Our clinical understanding of the BDSM community is evolving. Over the last century, we have seen our perception of kinksters shift from seeing them as mentally ill, to socially deviant, to stigmatised subculture, to object of cultural fascination. In the same way that our body of research has yet to catch up to these changes, so too do our kinky clients struggle with the various boxes and categories they have been placed in. Inclusion is imperfect.
>
> (p. 234)

Coaching others to happy sex lives is remembering that coaching clients are intersectional beings, connected to many fluid systems that affect them and which they reciprocally affect. Interestingly enough, Iasenza (2020) emphasises that fantasy or imagination is a part of human sexuality: Some researchers of sexuality and human understanding have asserted that creativity and human imagination is the foundation all human understanding, including those focused on healthy sexuality (Denman, 2004; Dilts & Gilligan, 2021; Johnson, 2007; Schulkin, 2011).

Kyriarchal and intersectional sexuality as theoretical starting point

How the World Health Organization (2022) defined sexual health is symbolic of healthy sexuality evolving and complex nature:

> a state of physical, emotional, mental and social well-being in relation to sexuality; it is not merely the absence of disease, dysfunction or infirmity. Sexual health requires a positive and respectful approach to sexuality and sexual relationships, as well as the possibility of having pleasurable and safe sexual experiences, free of coercion, discrimination and violence. For sexual health to be attained and maintained, the sexual rights of all persons must be respected, protected and fulfilled.

Through the lens of this definition, sexual health not only includes biological, psychological, emotional, and social characteristics, but also includes such things as sexual rights, respect, and freedom from coercion, discrimination, and violence, making the path towards a healthy sex life very different for different people.

Kyriarchy is a term that means "axes of difference" causing individuals' relationships with power and oppression to vary from individual to individual "according to social/spatial/temporal location" as well as "race, ethnicity, religion, class, sexuality, gender, gender identity/expression/conformity, relationship status, ability, body type/size, age, colonial status, national identity and more" (Osborne, 2015, pp. 136–137). The term was coined to "conceptually grapple with multiple, intersecting and co-constitutive structures of power and oppression" (Osborne, 2015, p. 137).

As this term pertains to coaching, the concept of kyriarchy is useful in helping sex coaches evaluate evidence-informed practices that best represent the subjective realities of their clients' experiences. Additionally, the term kyriarchy does not limit oppression and intersectionality to narrow categories of gender or racial difference, thus including individuals who identify as nonbinary or multiracial in coaching reflections and discussions about sexual diversity (Osborne, 2015).

Closely related to the term kyriarchy is the term intersectionality (Hill Collins, 2019; Malone et al., 2022; Osborne, 2015). As intersectionality pertains to sex coaching and sex therapy theories, Malone and colleagues (2022) wrote the following:

> Centering human sexuality with an intersectional lens acknowledges and illuminates the relationship of social oppressions and discrimination on sexual health and wellness . . . those who straddle the boundaries of what is perceived as acceptable or those who altogether transcend or reject cultural normatives of sexuality are often in a position of negotiating authentic identity versus discrimination and stigmatisation.
>
> (p. 28)

Evidence-informed, kyriarchal, and intersectional sex therapies are more aligned with the World Health Organization (WHO) definition of what it means to have a healthy sex life than other versions of sex coaching and therapy practices; in that, kyriarchal and intersectional sex coaching and sex therapy practices consider that humans have embodied – and thus subjective – understandings of their sexual lives (Plummer, 2005; Weeks, 2010).

Cultural construction sex coaching theories

One category of evidence-informed sex therapies that have the concepts of kyriarchal and intersectional sexuality woven into it is cultural construction. Sex coaches and therapists who speak from a cultural construction context forward the perspective that sexuality "is a learned way of thinking and acting" (Seidman, 2015, p. 27). While social construction sex theorists do not ignore the body in defining what sexual health is, they do define healthy sexuality and view sexual expression mainly in terms of sexual beings in society and culture contexts:

> Whether it is a mental health issue, a human right, or a private matter, people around the world experience sexual difficulties that greatly impact the quality of their lives. We believe that efforts to help individuals and couples increase their sexual satisfaction will only be effective if informed by an understanding of their social and cultural background, and of the meaning of sexual problems in specific cultural contexts.
>
> (Hall & Graham, 2013, p. 15)

Hall and Graham (2013) asserted that human sexuality cannot be understood outside of a cultural context, and any effort to assist clients in obtaining healthy sex lives must include understanding their social and cultural backgrounds.

Moreover, cultural construction sex theorists and researchers assert that because sexuality is dynamic, it is therefore particularly sensitive to social influences and social learning. In this regard, Weeks (2010) wrote:

> We experience the erotic very subjectively, and in a host of often contradictory ways. At the same time, the very mobility of sexuality, its chameleon-like ability to take many guises and forms, so that what for one might be a source of warmth and attraction, for another might be a cauldron of fear and hate, makes it a peculiarly sensitive conductor of cultural influences, and hence of social, cultural and political divisions.
>
> (p. 27)

Sex coaching within a cultural context means understanding that members of the LGBTQUIA+ (lesbian, gay, bisexual, transgender, queer, unisex, intersex, and asexual, plus other non-heterosexual sexualities) community's paths to healthy sexuality might be vastly different for members born in the 1950s as opposed to the path for members born in the 2000s. Whether these same members live in London or South Africa, are female or gender fluid, are rich or poor, and are persons of colour or not, affects how members of the LGBTQUIA+ individually experience and define healthy sexuality. Axes of difference such as age, time, location, gender, and class alter the cultural context in which all humans experience their erotic ways of being (Osborne, 2015).

Generally, social construction sex theorists state that sexuality is constructed in at least four intersecting manners:

1. Structure: sexuality institutionalised as a particular form or relationship, family structure and practice traditionally based on heterosexual, monogamous marriage.

2. Social and cultural meaning: how sexuality encodes and structures the socially and culturally available "scripts" available to us that inform shared understandings and knowledge about sexuality.
3. Everyday interactions and practices: how we socially interact with each other, live and experience sexualities.
4. Subjectivities: our sense or ourselves, which includes our sexual and gendered identities.

(Richardson, 2018, pp. 21–22)

Through a social construction lens, healthy sexuality can be specifically viewed as "analysis of the relationship between rights of citizenship and the state" (Richardson, 2018, p. 47). Therefore, sex coaches – especially if they coach clients through online means – might be faced with the hurdle that certain clients are not sexual citizens in their own states, providences, or countries (Richardson, 2018; Weeks, 2010).

Though the World Health Organization (2022) asserted that for "sexual health to be attained and maintained, the sexual rights of all persons must be respected, protected and fulfilled", respect, protection, and fulfilment is not a given:

Rights and responsibilities are not 'natural' or 'inalienable' but have to be invented through human activities, and built into the notions of communities, citizenship and identities. Rights and responsibilities depend upon a community of stories which make those same rights plausible and possible. They accrue to people whose identities flow out of the self-same communities.

(Plummer, 2002, p. 176)

Therefore, sex coaches informed by social construction theories use practices that address the premise that they themselves might enjoy certain social and cultural rights that their clients do not recognise for themselves or that their clients presently fight to have. The path to healthy sexuality might include a political fight or social change.

For instance, in some countries in Asia, individuals can be put in prison for being a part of the LGBTQUIA+ community; moreover, in some countries in Africa and the Middle East, members of the LGBTQUIA+ community can legally be put to death (Nunez, 2016). In these countries, these individuals are not sexual citizens, nor can they attain healthy sexual lives according to how the World Health Organization presently defines healthy sexuality (Richardson, 2018; World Health Organization, 2022).

Some sex coaches informed by a social construction context might view themselves as activists; moreover, at the historic foundation of sex coaching, the notion of a healthy sex life is connected to freedom as asserted by the WHO (Britton, 2005; World Health Organization, 2022). Britton (2005) noted: "Sexuality is constructed through the interaction between the individual and social structures" (p. 61).

Those sex coaches informed by a social construction context pay attention to – and in some cases, fight – how a given society constructs sexual rights, for these constructions affect how individuals experience sexual freedom and health.

Finally, sex coaches and therapists informed by social construction sexuality research not only see healthy sexuality through kyriarchal and intersectional lenses, but also see perversion and sexual challenges through the same lenses.

Body-centred sex coaching theories

Body-centred sex coaching and sex therapy evidence-informed research and practices are another body of research that addresses the complex nature of human sexuality, as well as its kyriarchal, intersectional, and creative nature.

In body-centred coaching research literature, terms such as body-centred, embodiment, embodied, somatic, and whole-body might be used; in this section, these terms are used interchangeably (Bloom, 2006; Claxton, 2015; Cornell, 2015; Haines, 2007; Walker, 2021). Sex coaches directed by somatic evidence-informed research view the individual body as the recipient of all human intersections and as the container of individual sexual histories. Body-centred theorists contend that all knowledge – including sexual knowledge – starts with the body, and they also contend that the body is pliable, making sexual identity, sexual expression, and sexual understandings pliable.

Some somatic theorists such as Johnson (2007) asserted that each individual has at least five different somatic bodies: the biological body, the ecological body, the phenomenological body, the social body, and the cultural body.

Johnson's conceptualisation of the body is that the body is never isolated from its surroundings and history. Moreover, the body cannot turn off the effects that culture, society, and ecology have on the biological and phenomenological bodies (Johnson, 2007).

Walker (2021) addressed the interplay of the biological, ecological, phenomenological, social, and cultural bodies as it pertains to human sexuality and called the dynamic interplay among these bodies *sexual ecology of whole-body sexuality*.

From a body-centred context, healthy sexuality can never be defined from an objective perspective (Cornell, 2015; Ellison & Papps, 2020; Haines, 2007; Marlock, 2015; Pressley-Tafari, 2023). In its extreme, an embodiment context has, at its foundations, the notion that only the self can be truly known, and who humans are can only be imperfectly reflected outward and then interpreted publicly by others, never fully known, as asserted by Weinberg (2012):

> only I have my sensations. Nobody else has my perceptions . . . . In that respect there is a partial truth to solipsism . . . . Our subjective lives . . . are embodied . . . . Our intentions, thoughts, feelings, etc., are something that occurs deep within us, being only reflected through our embodied conduct. Rather exist in and through our conduct.
>
> (p. 147)

Practising of sex coaching from a mythic perspective

Sex coaches, therapists, and sexologists, now more than ever, call for and search for new practices to best support clients in acquiring and maintaining healthy sex lives (Barker, 2013; Brown, 2022; Ogden, 2018). The rest of this chapter focuses on such a practice. Erotic Mythology Inquiry Approach (EMIA) is an evidence-informed practice sex coaches use to help clients navigate and normalise an ever-changing, complex sexual landscape (Pressley-Tafari, 2023).

Erotic mythology inquiry approach: EMIA

Pressley-Tafari (2023) described EMIA in the following manner:

> Erotic Mythic Inquiry is intersectional, embodied reflection, which centres the erotic body as the intersection of mind, emotions, and energy as well as recognizes the erotic body as a cultural symbol, a keeper of time, and a tether to geography/environment.
>
> (p. 190)

EMIA's body-centred underpinnings come directly from mythological psychology theory (Feinstein & Krippner, 2006; Keen & Valley-Fox, 1989; Keleman, 1999; Larsen, 1996). This body of literature maintains that human understanding, personal mythology, is created from the body's interactions with the world:

> Mythology is . . . poetics of the body singing about our cellular truth . . . . It is the song of creation.
>
> (Keleman, 1999, p. xiii)

> [M]yths arise in and from the body, as if all our history and our stories were recorded in our muscles, connective tissue, and viscera. Simply to partake of the physical condition . . . is the precondition for a personal mythology.
>
> (Larsen, 1996, p. 19)

Another foundational concept of EMIA is that the embodied mythic imagination is part of every human thought and action: "embodied cognition grounds everything from dance to ethics" (Asma, 2017, p. 127). Most relevant to sex coaches is that aspects of the mythic imagination are dedicated to how humans define, express, and experience sex:

> Humans have an enormous range of sexual tastes, desires, and habits, many of which veer very, very far from anything having to do with reproduction. Humans have . . . created a whole new way to have, think about, represent, regulate, and embody sex.
>
> (Fuentes, 2017, p. 170)

Pressley-Tafari (2023) called these creations *erotic personal mythology*, while Fous (2015) defined erotic mythos as "a story generated and played out deep within your Erotic psyche when you have sex" (p. 47). Though Fous did not directly discuss embodiment in his definition of erotic mythos, he connected erotic mythos to embodiment and Fetishsexuality.

EMIA sex coaches help find misalignments in Johnson's (2007) somatic bodies. Misalignments among the biological, phenomenological, cultural, social, and ecological bodies are erotic mythic conflicts – impediments to healthy sex lives.

Transforming mythic sexual conflict

> A myth creates the plotline that organises the diverse experiences of a person . . . into a single story . . . . But when crisis comes . . . , the mythic mind is at a loss to deal with novelty.
>
> (Keen & Valley-Fox, 1989, p. xiii)

Researchers such as Johnson (2007) and Clark (2023) used the terms 'homeostasis' and 'allostasis' to symbolise states of embodied stability and instability.

> whatever else a living organism does, it must at all costs continually monitor its own internal bodily states. If it fails to do so, it can risk losing the homeostasis necessary for life or, less dramatically, for smooth functioning.
>
> (Johnson, 2007, p. 57)

On the other hand, "allostasis highlights the need to alter the fixed points themselves so as to adapt to changing needs and environments" (Clark, 2023, p. 91).

The terms homeostasis and allostasis fit neatly into the EMIA paradigm: erotic personal mythology organises diverse sexual experience into a stable storyline, *erotic homeostasis* (Johnson, 2007; Schulkin, 2011). *Erotic allostasis* is the embodied cognitive process of reacting to erotic mythic crisis to realign the biological, phenomenological, cultural, social, and ecological bodies (Clark, 2023).

EMIA sex coaches use the following seven-step process to assist clients to become conscious of their erotic mythic conflicts and to create new erotic personal mythologies better suited to bring about temporary erotic homeostasis, which is erotic allostasis (Pressley-Tafari, 2023).

1. Becoming a coaching instrument.
2. Reflecting simultaneously on self and sex coaching clients.
3. Helping clients identify underlying erotic mythic conflict.
4. Assisting clients understand both sides of the erotic mythic conflict.
5. Co-creating and envisioning a new erotic personal mythology.
6. Supporting clients as they move from a vision of new personal erotic mythology to commitment to a new personal erotic mythology.
7. Aiding clients in embodying their new personal erotic mythology.

Sex coaching practice

In this section, we will review one approach to sex coaching using the seven-stage framework. It should be noted this is just one approach of many used by sex coaches with clients.

Step 1: Becoming a coaching instrument

Coaching others toward healthy sex lives is a reflective way of being, not a profession: "Coaching is not just about using skills in specific situations. As coaching gets in your bones, it's a way of being with others. The mental habits of being present, receiving instead of listening, and releasing judgement" (Reynolds, 2020, p. 190).

The first step of an EMIA sex coach might be the most difficult. Looking deeply into self can be very challenging, because what is found there might not be easy to see nor comprehend. Conversely, during those difficult moments in self-reflection, EMIA gains greater empathy for their clients.

Step 2: Reflecting on the self

Next, EMIA sex coaches simultaneously reflect on self and sex coaching clients, helping them become more creative and present. During this stage, EMIA sex coaches use their bodies to be present and to alert them about subtle changes in their clients and themselves. As Bachkirova (2021) notes, a practitioner who develops this ability to reflect deeply can notice their own emotions, hunches and subtle messages from their body as they occur, and utilise them in the session.

During erotic homeostasis, an erotic personal mythology goes unnoticed, inconspicuously providing stability. However, the nature of erotic homeostasis is that it cannot be maintained into perpetuity (Feinstein et al., 1998). Each somatic body evolves (Johnson, 2007). Thus, reflection of self and clients is continuous. Practices such as centring can be regularly used for practitioner reflection and client grounding. Centring is an internal process of bringing attention into our bodies, connecting with ourselves, and becoming aware and present.

EMIA sex coaches do not want to simply respond to triggers and react inappropriately to how our clients differ from us in values, beliefs, sexual orientation, appearance, or sexual understandings and expressions. Equally as important, EMIA sex coaches look to shift clients from simply reacting to the loss of erotic homeostasis and start exploring where the somatic bodies are misaligned (Clark, 2023; Feinstein & Krippner, 2006; Strozzi-Heckler, 2014).

Step 3: Helping clients identify underlying erotic mythic conflict

Helping clients identify underlying erotic mythic conflict is identifying what is at odds with each other, what fights to go backwards to outdated erotic personal mythologies, and what fights for novel behaviours to establish a new erotic homeostasis.

The EMIA sex coach will journey with clients through erotic allostasis, helping clients explore their biological, phenomenological, social, cultural, and ecological bodies to find what has made their existing erotic personal mythologies falter. Perhaps, one of the most challenging aspects of this stage is helping clients explore their erotic shadows.

Often, the erotic imagination is a window into the shadow aspect of self. Also, the shadow self is often the disruptor of erotic homeostasis, as well as the creator of an emerging erotic personal mythology.

Strozzi-Heckler (2014) proposed that three entry points to the body can provide coaches with access to many aspects of clients, including their erotic shadows: "working on the body, working with the body, and working through the body" (p. 32–34). Working on the body

> is the situation where the individual's presenting symptoms are so strong that they need to be attended to before any other issues can be addressed . . . . In this category the Somatic Coach is very clear that if there is an organic cause she will refer this person to a qualified health professional.
>
> (p. 34)

Working with the body is "the situation where the emotional, social life of the individual is addressed" (Strozzi-Heckler, 2014, p. 35). Finally, when working through the body: "the body becomes the shape of our experience . . . the body will reveal our predispositions. . . . . The body will relentlessly disclose our embodied strategies for belonging, for love, safety, and acceptance" (Strozzi-Heckler, 2014, pp. 36–37).

In identifying the mythic conflict, EMIA sex coaches deeply investigate the needs of the biological body and for the patterns of the phenomenological body in relation to the cultural, social, and ecological bodies. How do clients' bodies reflect lived experience? What do their bodies suggest what comes next?

Step 4: Understanding both sides of the erotic mythic conflict

Understanding both sides of the erotic mythic conflict is "bringing . . . opposing internal forces into consciousness, honouring each, and tracing their roots in the individual's culture, personal history, and psychic depths" (Feinstein, 1997, p. 515). For instance, Pressley-Tafari (2023) wrote the following when exploring his mythic conflict after embodying new sexual expressions as BDSM practitioner, an identity that did not align with who he had been culturally and socially:

> To move through this stage of mythic development, who you were and who you are becoming must be met with love and forgiveness . . . . I was ashamed of and angry with the Good Black Man in me. Additionally, I feared the Fetishsexual, for he embraced the shadows, the depths, and dark emotions in me.
>
> (p. 171)

EMIA sex coaches help clients love who they were, representing the faltering erotic personal mythology, and help clients love who they might become, representing the emerging erotic mythology. Even the shadow parts of the faltering erotic personal mythology have purpose. As Limmer notes: "Our shadows are not evil; they merely hold our negativity until we are strong enough to face it and let it go" (Limmer, 2014, p. 37).

The faltering erotic personal mythology was supporting who your clients have been for quite some time. Take the opportunity to help clients praise what has been. Also, help clients forgive and let go. Help them create initiation rituals that mark endings and beginnings simultaneously. As Branscombe (2022) asserted, "Observing the rhythms and rituals with consciousness in your daily life allows you to balance the polarities of work and play, joy and grief, beginnings and endings" (p. 271).

EMIA sex coaches understand that they assist their clients enter unknown and unshaped worlds to find erotic homeostasis. The emergence of an erotic mythic conflict is a death and a birth (Pressley-Tafari, 2023).

Step 5: Co-creating a new personal erotic mythology

Co-creating a new personal erotic mythology is working on, with, and through the body to create new ways of being in the world. Assisting clients in forming new erotic personal mythology is akin to moving from a historical embodiment to new postures by engaging their "sensate imaginations".

During this stage, use of the imagination and creativity is critical. It is the time to co-create embodied images and narratives for our clients to become, leaving behind some of who they had been (Pressley-Tafari, 2020, 2023; Strozzi-Heckler, 2014).

Clients create who they are to become, a sexual being aligned with the diverse somatic bodies we inhabit. EMIA sex help clients embody this new sexual being and explore all that it can do.

Step 6: Moving to commitment

Moving from vision of new personal erotic mythology to commitment to a new personal erotic mythology is moving from the sensate imagination to behaviours, when clients' nervous systems create the neural structures that support change. Clients start to move differently and make decisions that support their new erotic mythologies. They find new erotic homeostasis.

Feinstein and Krippner (1997) wrote that there are six markers that EMIA sex coaches can help their clients obtain. These markers are coherence, openness, credibility, differentiation, reconciliation, and generative integration.

As asserted, the new erotic personal mythology brings novel erotic homeostasis. The biological, phenomenological, social, cultural, and ecological bodies all align. Stability is achieved; ironically, the new erotic personal mythology is immediately moving towards erotic allostasis. Life is dynamic; thus, personal erotic mythology is also dynamic.

Step 7: Embodying from your new personal erotic mythology

Embodying from your new personal erotic mythology is being in a constant state of reflection and awareness about what outward new behaviours, postures, interactions, environments, and novel responses to triggers must be maintained to keep the inner self (biological and phenomenological) aligned with an evolving social, cultural, and ecological world.

Coaching others to healthy sex lives, given a healthy sex life's temporal nature, is assisting clients become more conscious of the conflict between their inner selves and outer selves, assisting in the process of mythic transformation or erotic allostasis (Clark, 2023; Feinstein & Krippner, 1997; Schulkin, 2011).

Conclusion

Coaching for healthy sex life is assisting clients to recognise that they are intersectional, fluid sexual beings, and assisting them to normalise erotic personal mythological transformations, alternating periods of erotic homeostasis and erotic allostasis.

Additionally, coaching for a healthy sex life is aligning the biological, phenomenological, cultural, social, and ecological bodies in order to enjoy sexual expression safely, free of "coercion, discrimination and violence" (World Health Organization, 2022).

On the other hand, sex coaches' biggest challenge in coaching others to healthy sex lives might very well be examining self and being honest with themselves about who they themselves are as sexual beings and coaching instruments.

Reflective questions

1. How might your axis of difference affect who you are as a sex coach?
2. What might you have to heal or forgive for you to be the best sex coach you can be?
3. What is the best way for you to remain present with your clients as they reveal intimately and deeply about their erotic lives?

References

Asma, S. T. (2017). *The evolution of imagination*. Chicago, IL: University of Chicago Press.

Bachkirova, T. (2021). Understanding yourself as a coach. In J. Passmore (Ed.), *The coaches' handbook: The complete practitioner guide for professional coaches* (pp. 38–46). New York, NY: Routledge.

Barker, M.-J. (2013). *Rewriting the rules: An integrative guide to love, sex and relationships*. New York, NY: Routledge.

Bloom, K. (2006). *The embodied self: Movement and psychoanalysis*. New York, NY: Routledge.

Branscombe, M. (2022). *Ritual as remedy: Embodied practices for soul care*. Rochester, VT: Findhorn Press.

Britton, P. (2005). *The art of sex coaching: Expanding your practice*. New York, NY: W. W. Norton & Company.

Brown, S. J. (2022). *Refusing compulsory sexuality: A black asexual lens on our sex-obsessed culture*. Berkeley, CA: North Atlantic Books.

Clark, A. (2023). *The experience machine: How our minds predict and shape reality*. New York, NY: Pantheon Books.

Claxton, G. (2015). *Intelligence in the flesh: Why your mind needs your body much more than it thinks*. New Haven, CT: Yale University Press.

Constantinides, D. M., Sennott, S. L., & Chandler, D. (2019). *Sex therapy with erotically marginalized clients: Nine principles of clinical support*. New York, NY: Routledge.

Cornell, W. F. (2015). Entering the erotic field: Sexuality in body-centered psychotherapy. In G. Marlock, H. Weiss, C. Young, & M. Soth (Eds.), *The handbook of body psychotherapy and somatic psychology* (pp. 692–700). Berkeley, CA: North Atlantic Books.

Denman, C. (2004). *Sexuality, a biopsychosocial approach*. New York, NY: Palgrave MacMillan.

Dilts, R., & Gilligan, S. (2021). *Generative coaching volume 1: The journey of creative and sustainable change*. Santa Cruz, CA: International Association for Generative Change.

Djajic-Horváth, A. (2022, February 27). *Sexology: Interdisciplinary science*. Retrieved from Britannica: https://www.britannica.com/science/sexology/additional-info#history

Ellison, T., & Papps, F. A. (2020, May 30). 'Sexuality, without that mirror': The role of embodied practice in the development of sexual potential. *Complementary Therapies in Clinical Practice*, 40, 1–9. doi:10.1016/j.ctcp.2020.101205

Feinstein, D. (1997). Personal mythology and psychotherapy: Myth-making in psychological and spiritual development. *American Journal of Orthopsychiatry*, 67(4), 508–521. https://doi.org/10.1037/h0080251

Feinstein, D., & Krippner, S. (1997). *The mythic path: Discovering the guiding stories of your past-creating a vision of your future*. New York: G.P. Putnam's Sons.

Feinstein, D., & Krippner, S. (2006). *The mythic path*. Santa Rose, CA: Elite Books.

Feinstein, D., Mortifee, A., & Krippner, S. (1998). Walking to the rhythm of a new myth: Mythic perspectives for a world in distress. *World Futures*, 52, 187–238.

Fous, G. M. (2015). *Decoding your kink: Guide to explore share an enjoy your wildest sexual desire* (digital ed.). Galen Fous.

Fuentes, A. (2017). *The creative spark: How imagination made humans exceptional*. New York, NY: Penguin Random House.

Gagnon, J. H., & Parker, R. G. (1995). Conceiving sexuality. In J. H. Gagnon, & R. G. Parker (Eds.), *Conceiving sexuality: Approaches to sex research in the postmodern world* (pp. 1–16). New York, NY: Routledge.

Goerlich, S. E. (2021). *The leather couch: Clinical practice with kinky clients*. New York, NY: Routledge.

Goerlich, S. E. (2023). *Kink-affirming practice: Culturally competent therapy from the leather chair*. New York, NY: Routledge.

Haines, S. (2007). *Healing sex: A mind-body approach to healing sexual trauma* (2nd ed.). San Francisco, CA: Cleis Press.

Hall, K. S., & Graham, C. A. (2013). Introduction. In C. A. Grahman, & K. S. Hall (Eds.), *The cultural context of sexual pleasure and problems: Psychotherapy with diverse clients* (pp. 15–34). New York, NY: Taylor and Francis.

Hill Collins, P. (2019). *Intersectionality as critical social theory*. Durham, NC: Duke University Press.

Iasenza, S. (2020). *Transforming sexual narratives: A relational approach to sex therapy*. New York, NY: Routledge.

Johnson, M. (2007). *The meaning of the body: Aesthetics of human understanding*. Chicago, IL: The University of Chicago Press.

Keen, S., & Valley-Fox, A. (1989). *Your mythic journey: Finding meaning in your life through writing and storytelling*. New York, NY: Penguin Group.

Keleman, S. (1999). *Myth & the body: A colloquy with Joseph Campbell*. Berkley, CA: Center Press.

Larsen, S. (1996). *The mythic imagination: The quest for meaning through personal mythology*. Rochester, VT: Inner Traditions International.

Limmer, E. (2014). *The body as shadow*. Bloomington, IN: Balboa Press.

Malone, R., Stewart, M. R., Gary-Smith, M., & Wadley, J. C. (2022). Introduction. In R. Malone, M. R. Stewart, M. Gary-Smith, & J. C. Wadley (Eds.), *An intersectional approach to sex therapy: Centering the lives of black, indigenous, racialized, and people of color* (pp. 23–32). New York, NY: Routledge.

Marlock, G. (2015). Body psychotherapy as a revitalization of the self: A depth-psychological and phenomenological-existential perspective. In G. Marlock, H. Weiss, C. Young, & M. Soth (Eds.), *The handbook of body psychotherapy and somatic psychology* (pp. 148–162). Berkeley, CA: North Atlantic Books.

Morin, J. (1995). *The erotic mind*. New York, NY: HarperCollins.

National Coalition for Sexual Health. (2022). *What is sexual health?* Retrieved from National Coalition for Sexual Health: https://www.nationalcoalitionforsexualhealth.org/sexual-health/what-is-sexual-health

Nunez, C. (2016). Map shows where being LGBT can be punishable by law. Retrieved from https://www.nationalgeographic.com/history/article/lgbt-laws-gay-rights-world-map

Ogden, G. (2018). *Expanding the practice of sex therapy (the neuro update edition): An integrative approach for exploring desire and intimacy* (2nd ed.). New York, NY: Routledge.

Osborne, N. (2015). Intersectionality and kyriarchy: A framework for approaching power and social justice in planning and climate. *Planning Theory, 14*(2), 130–151. doi:10.1177/1473095213516443

Plummer, K. (2004). *Telling sexual stories: Power, change, and Social Worlds*. New York , NY: Routledge.

Plummer, K. (2005). Symbols of change. In W. Simon, *Postmodern sexualities* (pp. ix-xvi). New York, NY: Routledge.

Pressley-Tafari, N. (2020). Art and erotic exploration as critical pedagogy with youth. In S. R. Steinberg, & B. Down (Eds.), *The Sage handbook of critical pedagogies* (pp. 1400–1410). Thousand Oaks, CA: Sage. doi:10.4135/9781526486455.n125

Pressley-Tafari, N. (2023). Beyond my own comprehension: Death of a good Black man, BDSM transcendence, and other mythic stories. In *Eros & Psyche: Existential Perspectives on Sexuality* (pp. 125–148). Colorado Springs, CO: University Professors Press.

Reynolds, M. (2020). *Coach the person, not the problem*. Oakland, CA: Berrett-Koehler Publishers.

Richardson, D. (2018). *Sexuality and citizenship*. Medford, MA: Polity Press.

Schulkin, J. (2011). *Adaption and well-being: Social allostasis*. New York, NY: Cambridge University Press.

Seidman, S. (2015). *The social construction of sexuality* (3rd ed.). New York, NY: W. W. Norton.

Sharage, L. J., & Stewert, R. S. (2015). *Philosophising about sex*. Petersborough, ON, Canada: Broadview Press.

Siegel, D. J. (2010). *Mind your brain*. New York, NY: Bantam Books.

Strozzi-Heckler, R. (2014). *The art of somatic coaching: Embodying skillful action, wisdom, and compassion*. Berkeley, CA: North Atlantic Books.

Walker, M. (2021). *Whole-body sex: Somatic sex therapy and the lost language of the erotic body.* New York, NY: Routledge.

Weeks, J. (2010). *Sexuality: Key ideas* (3rd ed.). New York, NY: Routledge.

Weinberg, D. (2012). Social constructionism and the body. In B. S. Turner (Ed.), *Routledge handbook of body studies* (pp. 144–156). New York, NY: Routledge.

World Health Organization. (2022). *Sexual health.* Retrieved from World Health Organization: https://www.who.int/health-topics/sexual-health#tab=tab_2

Chapter 14

Coaching for ageing well

Tatiana Schifferle Rowson

Introduction

Coaching for ageing well is an important and underdeveloped area of activity. Globally, we are living longer and healthier than ever before (Schurman, 2022; WHO, 2002), and this brings opportunities and challenges. This increased longevity, combined with lower birth rates, created a social trend called *superage* (Schurman, 2022). This is not a trend only in countries that are traditionally perceived as old, but a global phenomenon (Schurman, 2022; WHO, 2002, 2020). Therefore, societies will become noticeably more age-diverse. In fact, it is not uncommon today to find multigenerational workplaces where this trend towards age diversity is already a reality. In 2021, the United Nations (UN) and the World Health Organization (WHO) launched a global collaboration to promote healthy ageing named 'Decade of Healthy Ageing' (WHO, 2020). This initiative reflects the urgency and importance of understanding how to better harness the opportunities that come with longevity, not only as societies but also as individuals and workplaces. This is particularly important, given the concerns about the sustainability of an older population (OECD, 2011), more specifically in relation to the funding of retirement and the healthcare costs associated with older people's ill health. Nevertheless, if individuals manage to keep relatively healthy and are in an environment that welcomes their participation, they become a valuable resource to society. In all circumstances, coaching can be a highly effective intervention in helping people to be prepared for age-related adjustments and to make the necessary changes to thrive in old age. This chapter is organised in two main parts. The first part introduces the research background and important conceptual frameworks applied to ageing studies. These are useful to contextualise and inform evidence-based coaching practice. The second part focuses on how to apply this knowledge to coaching for ageing well, with a particular attention to midlife review coaching.

Gerontology and ageing research

Ageing is a process that starts when we are born; however, when we talk about ageing, the focus is generally on mid- to late adulthood. The study of ageing is called gerontology, and as a multidisciplinary field, it covers several aspects of ageing (e.g., social, psychological, biological, economical). For gerontologists, it is accepted that these various aspects contribute to understanding how we age and how we can age better as societies and individuals.

DOI: 10.4324/9781003319016-16

Earlier gerontological studies proposed contrasting – and relatively extreme – perspectives on how people adjust to life as they get older. The disengagement theory (Cumming & Henry, 1961) suggested that the normal way to adjust to ageing, and its 'inevitable' decline, was to slowly relinquish social roles and participation in activities. Hence, it implied that ageing well involved getting ready for old age decline, and eventually death. Contemporary to this theory, an opposing view was also argued. The activity theory (Havighurst, 1961) suggested that ageing well required being actively engaged, and when certain roles and activities are no longer relevant (an example is when the role of worker would cease to exist once one retires), people would replace them with new roles or activities (e.g., volunteering, hobbies). Interestingly, both theories emerged from the same Kansas City study dataset and equally implied a level of discontinuity, either because people would be replacing certain roles and activities with new ones or would be letting go of them altogether. These theories have been challenged in their original form, yet they have been highly influential to our current understanding of ageing (Phillipson & Baars, 2007). Anecdotally, it can be observed that individuals often disengage from certain roles or activities, as well as engaging in new activities or roles, as they enter their late years.

The next generation of studies took a different perspective as a response to these early gerontological theories. They emphasised that old age is a continuation of adulthood. One of the key authors to write about this is Robert Atchley (1972, 1989, 1999), who developed the continuity theory following the Ohio Longitudinal Study. According to the Continuity Theory, people adjust better to ageing when they maintain a sense of continuity. The premise is that by midlife, most people have worked out the defining aspects of their identity and lifestyle. Thus, what aspects are important to continue in later life and what is acceptable or reasonable to let go. Responding to early critics, Atchley (1989) explains that continuity does not mean that life remains unchanged. Instead, adjustments and changes would happen over time and incrementally without posing a threat to individuals' identity and self-concept. He also makes a distinction between internal and external continuity. Internal continuity refers to a sense of self, identity, personality, personal values, etc., and external continuity concerns routines, habits, membership in certain groups, etc. (Atchley, 1989, 1999). Further criticisms to the continuity theory point out that a lot can change in middle and old age, and these changes may be due to circumstances out of individuals' control (Earl & Taylor, 2017; Katz, 2020). Moreover, not all continuity is positive; some things people would prefer to change. Despite its weaknesses, continuity theory has not been completely discredited (Rowson & Phillipson, 2020).

A more accepted approach to understanding the ageing experience is the Life Course Theory. This perspective emphasises that experiences are influenced by what happens during a person's life course: their biographies, historical context (Elder, 1985; Elder et al., 2003) and the accumulation of advantages or disadvantages, such as poor or good health, and availability or lack of financial resources (Crystal et al., 2017; Dannefer, 2003; Ferraro & Shippee, 2009). Therefore, different factors, circumstances or life events incrementally contribute to shaping older adulthood outcomes (Rowson & Phillipson, 2020). The life course perspective has helped researchers to understand what factors contribute to ageing well and how people can change their lifestyle patterns to improve ageing outcomes. While many studies indicate that trends in health and financial circumstances can be traced back to childhood circumstances and events (Crystal et al., 2017;

Ferraro & Shippee, 2009), it is what happens in midlife that exerts the greatest influence on ageing outcomes (Earl & Taylor, 2017; Katz, 2020; Rowson & Phillipson, 2020).

There is no agreed definition of when midlife begins or ends. While some argue this phase to be between the ages of 40 and 60 (Freund & Ritter, 2009; Lachman et al., 2015), this age range may be a bit more malleable and individualised. This is because chronologic age is an incomplete indicator of life stage. Individual circumstances such as the age of children, general health and fitness, and work arrangements may influence whether someone sees themselves as middle-aged or not (Demakakos et al., 2006; Freund & Ritter, 2009). Organisations such as International Labour Office (ILO), Organisation for Economic Co-operation and Development (OECD) or WHO conventionally use the age of 50 or 55 as an indicative of midlife and to mark a period adults may experience significant changes in the work and non-work life domains. With the increased longevity, this phase of life became extremely important as a period when there is still enough time to reverse negative patterns of behaviours and lifestyles (Crystal, 2006; Gilleard & Higgs, 2005). A good example is health, as the impact of bad lifestyle choices can only be felt many years later. Still, lifestyle changes in midlife can significantly revert the effect of bad habits in time to prevent severe ill health and chronic disease in late life. Midlife is also a time of high demand in different life domains (e.g., stressful jobs, caring responsibilities for teenagers, parents) and when many middle-aged adults experience significant changes, such as career transitions, launching their children, divorce, etc. (Gilleard & Higgs, 2005). These changes may also interact or indirectly influence another life domain in a process called cross-domain transitions (Rowson et al., 2022), hence adding another layer of complexity. An example is no longer having caring responsibilities may free some time for volunteering or up taking a hobby, or experiencing ill health may trigger adjustments to career aspirations. Therefore, midlife is a period of transitions, risks, and opportunities, making it a pivotal moment to introduce coaching for ageing well.

Conceptualising ageing well

Several different terminologies have been used to describe positive ageing experiences and outcomes in the grey and academic literature. Two common terms are active ageing (WHO, 2002) and successful ageing (Rowe & Kahn, 1987, 1998). Active ageing 'is the process of optimising opportunities for health, participation and security in order to enhance quality of life as people age' (WHO, 2002, p. 12). This WHO definition, adopted in a 2002 report, still informs their age-friendly policy framework and indicates the importance of social inclusion, participation and supporting a growing older population across the world. Therefore, active ageing is not only about individuals' actions to improve their prospects in later life but also about fostering age-inclusive social environments where older people can thrive.

Another common term used to reflect positive ageing outcomes is successful ageing. This notion gained greater visibility in 1987 when Rowe and Kahn conceptualised 'successful ageing' as distinct from 'normal ageing'. Their definition emphasised not only increased longevity but also an absence of disease and disability. Although widely used in ageing research and praised for its positive outlook (Katz & Calasanti, 2015), this concept has been criticised for its biomedical focus of health and functionality (Katz & Calasanti, 2015; Urtamo et al., 2019), i.e., successful avoidance of disease and disability. While at the same time, this conceptualisation excludes psychosocial aspects of ageing, such as individuals' subjective evaluations of their own health and wellbeing and other social contextual factors (Martinson & Berridge, 2015; Urtamo et al., 2019). Baltes and Baltes (1990) and subsequent authors (see Nosraty et al., 2015; Pruchno & Wilson-Genderson, 2015; Young et al., 2009) suggest that individuals may experience ill health, chronic conditions and disability but still successfully age, hence evaluating their lives positively.

According to Baltes and Baltes (1990), how individuals manage and deploy their personal resources influences their adjustment to ageing. This is reflected in their Selection, Optimisation and Compensation (SOC) model (Baltes & Baltes, 1990). SOC is situated within lifespan developmental psychology theories and builds on the assumption that at any given time, individuals have a limited level of resources (Hobfoll, 2002); for example, money, health, time and social connections. Therefore, managing those resources well is important for individuals to thrive. Life management strategies (Baltes & Baltes, 1990) and conservation of resources (Hobfoll, 2002) are not exclusively applicable to ageing or older adults, and we see many examples of how it has been applied to stress management and occupational health research. Nevertheless, it is particularly important in old age because these resources tend to diminish as life progresses. SOC is a particularly well tested life management approach. It includes three key strategies: (1) elective or loss-based selection or the prioritisation of goals; (2) the optimisation of current resources necessary to achieve a set goal; and (3) a compensation mechanism to make up for resource shortages – for example, if a coaching client is someone who always enjoyed being active, so being active through to old age is one of their goals. This prioritisation is an example of selection. However, if a coaching client has experienced an injury and no longer can engage in high-impact physical activities like football or running, they may decide to continue with more moderate activities like walking. This new scenario is an example of loss-based selection. As the individual is committed to continue with their goal to remain active, they join a local walking club to maintain – or improve – their levels of fitness. This is an example of optimisation, as the client is prepared to invest their efforts and resources to maintain or improve their performance. A couple of years later, imagine the individual has a fall and feels as if it is no longer safe to continue to walk outdoors. Although they could continue exercising, it has to be in a controlled environment, such as on treadmills. This is an example of compensation, as the individual has replaced their activity of choice with a different activity. Compensation strategies can be much more drastic if there is a significant loss of resources.

The SOC model received some criticism (Burnett-Wolle & Godbey, 2007) and the use of its strategies was found to be positively related to job performance, job satisfaction, work engagement (Moghimi et al., 2017) and improved levels of wellbeing (Wiese et al., 2002), among other positive outcomes. Moreover, there is evidence that these SOC behaviours are trainable and their effects for individuals can be maximised by setting clear and individualised goals and an action plan (Müller et al., 2018). This makes SOC a promising model to be incorporated to coaching interventions targeted at bettering the experience of ageing. Hence, it is important to include psychosocial factors and processes when operationalising the idea of successful ageing – especially when it comes to informing coaching practice.

For the purpose of this chapter, I am using the term *ageing well* to talk about positive ageing experiences and outcomes. This terminology implies a broader perspective on the ageing process beyond the original definition of successful ageing by Rowe and

Kahn (1987), while keeping the focus at an individual level. It allows for objective and subjective evaluations of both biomedical and psychosocial factors to be considered as part of positive ageing, including the ideas proposed within the SOC model (see also Fernandez-Ballesteros, 2019). This means that *ageing well* will vary from person to person according to their own personal circumstances, expectations, and social context. This individualised approach to ageing is very appropriate to coaching conversations.

Midlife transitions

In the previous sections of this chapter, it was established that midlife is a critical period in determining late adulthood outcomes. Not only is there still time to make significant lifestyle adjustments, but it is also a period when many external life changes may happen that can disrupt the stability of this life (Gilleard & Higgs, 2005), e.g., children leaving home, or work-related or marital status changes. Moreover, this is a time when internal changes at a psychological level also tend to occur. Some authors differentiate these internal changes (from external changes) by referring to them as transitions (Bridges & Bridges, 2019).

Despite the popular idea of 'midlife crisis', most middle-aged people will not necessarily experience anything as dramatic as a crisis (Freund & Ritter, 2009; Lachman et al., 2015). Still, at this stage, most people will experience a shift in their life priorities, goals and aspirations. Several authors wrote about psychosocial and existential changes middle-aged individuals experience; some notable examples are Erik Erikson (1980, 1985), Carl Jung (1960), Daniel Levinson (1978, 1986, 1996) and Gail Sheehy (1995).

These authors' theories are not incongruent to the ideas from the life course approach as they consider how the various life stages connect. In different ways, they propose that midlife is a time when there is a shift in perspective towards life, and hence it is quite distinct from early adulthood. Sheehy (1995) refers to first and second adulthood. The transition between these key stages involves a certain level of uncertainty and confusion, which in turn can trigger a sense of threat or vulnerability (see Sheehy, 1995; Levinson, 1978, 1986, 1996). However, it was Jung (1960) who popularised the idea of the two halves of life when writing about the structure and dynamics of the psyche. The first half of life is when individuals form their ego selves, hence their sense of self and identity. Therefore, at this stage, individuals will be looking into fitting in with others and securing their place in the world through acquiring material things and group affiliations. The second half of life is when these things are no longer sufficient, and individuals seek greater meaning in life, a sense of purpose. Coming from a slightly different theoretical perspective, Erikson (1980, 1985) suggests a similar shift at this stage. In Erikson's works, each life stage involves a particular developmental task. In the case of midlife, adults strive to establish their legacy and make an active contribution to a better world beyond themselves. This process is called generativity. Failing to engage in this process is called stagnation, whereby adults get stuck in an earlier stage of development that is not compatible with the kind of development they should be pursuing.

While there is a consensus that midlife is a gateway to a new life stage, an in-depth review of the various theories will reveal that these are grounded in different assumptions, with its limitations and criticism. A detailed discussion on the matter is out of the scope of this chapter. However, for the purpose of coaching for ageing well, awareness of this midlife psychosocial shift is essential. Social scientists, academic researchers and policymakers echo the importance of midlife as a period for reflection, re-evaluation and purposeful change (see NIACE, 2015; Illmarinen, 2005; Schurman, 2022). This re-evaluation, sometimes referred to as midlife review, allows middle-aged individuals to take greater control over their ageing process and outcomes.

Research: coaching for ageing well

There is very little research on coaching or even counselling interventions for ageing well. This is particularly the case when it comes to the new realities of increased longevity, e.g., extending working life rather than preparing for a cliff-edge retirement (see Schurman, 2022). However, there is emerging evidence on the potential of coaching conversations to support ageing well. One example is a randomised controlled trial study conducted by Müller and colleagues (2018) to examine the effectiveness of a SOC-based intervention (Baltes & Baltes, 1990) to help workers improve their ability to work for longer. They found that the success of the intervention was enhanced when the participants had the opportunity to reflect and formulate clear goals before designing an action plan, thus engaging these participants in a conversation akin to coaching. Research on health promotion for older workers (see Poscia et al., 2016) also alludes to the role of providing a talking space (e.g., counselling) to help older adults to implement their wellness and wellbeing goals.

Grounded in the same ageing and life course research in the earlier part of this chapter, midlife reviews are the closest evidence-based intervention to ageing well coaching. Midlife reviews refer to a facilitated group-based or one-to-one conversation to help individuals aged 50 and older to reflect and consider work, health, family and finances in light of a longer life (NIACE, 2015). The study conducted in the UK by NIACE (2015) in partnership with trade unions, employers and career services supported the effectiveness of midlife reviews conversations as a way to help older adults to identify and implement ageing well goals. This is further confirmed by similar intervention studies conducted in Finland. These studies demonstrated the value of occupational health conversations at midlife for extending working life (see Illmarinen, 2005).

The success of these midlife conversations can be explained by the extant coaching literature. Several meta-analysis studies evidence the value of coaching, whether it is workplace or life coaching, to help clients to achieve positive changes (Graßmann et al., 2020; Jones et al., 2016; Theeboom et al., 2014; Wang et al., 2022). O'Connor and Lages (2007) highlight that coaching can help the client to gain awareness of possible goals and issues, consider different thinking perspectives, and take action. Therefore, it creates the conditions for individuals to make 'more conscious, intentional decisions about what goals they commit to (or not) in the context of their life or, in situations where there is little perceived choice, by choosing what these goals will mean to them' (Spence & Grant, 2012, p. 1020). Hence, coaching provides the space for those midlife conversations whereby the client can make sense of their goals considering their current situation and potential longevity.

Coaching for ageing can be eclectic and varied to reflect the individualised nature of ageing experiences, as discussed in the earlier part of this chapter. Moreover, it should not be constrained to a single life domain (e.g., career or health). Evidence from similar interventions shows it should instead be holistic and focused on the whole person, therefore allowing older adults to evaluate how life domains affect one another and avoiding the setting of competing or unrealistic goals (see Locke & Latham, 2002).

Coaching for ageing well: a framework

This section outlines an effective framework to start a coaching for ageing well intervention. This is a flexible approach that can be adapted, expanded, and integrated to other coaching strategies.

Identifying life domains for ageing well

While the purpose of coaching for ageing well is self-explanatory, the specific areas a client will work on will most likely vary from person to person, as hinted in the ageing literature. Therefore, it is important to begin the process by mapping the areas of priority within the various life domains. Moreover, the process of mapping areas of priorities also allows the client to identify the ripple effect of issues from one life domain to the other, e.g., a change in health-related behaviours may impact a work routine; or that taking on a hobby may lead to a renegotiation of domestic tasks. Middle-aged adults usually have several roles and are involved in a variety of activities; this increases the complexity of coaching, as cross-domain transitions and changes are likely to occur and would need to be considered in a coaching conversation (Rowson et al., 2022).

One way to start coaching for ageing well is by adapting the 'wheel of life' exercise (Byrne, 2005). The wheel of life, also known as wheel of balance or life wheel, is a very well-known coaching tool and provides a compelling visual representation of different life domains to be explored in coaching. This tool is usually represented by a circle that is sectioned into 6–8 segments (Figure 14.1). It does not matter if the client has done a wheel of life before or is familiar with the process, as the purpose of the wheel of life as

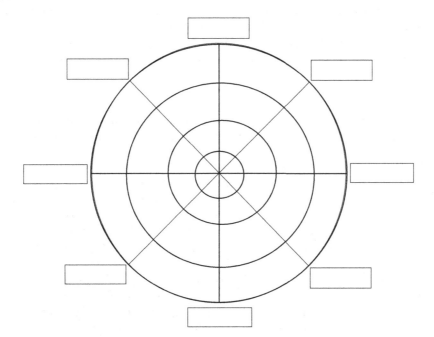

Figure 14.1 The wheel of life

a coaching tool is not simply completing it but to support the coaching conversation. Moreover, the wheel of life is a snapshot of the current situation and will change as life goes on.

The first step is for the client to define what areas of life are important to be represented on the wheel. These may be roles they play (e.g., parent, spouse or partner, professional, friend), life domains or aspirational aspects (e.g., work, leisure, health and wellbeing, fitness and wellness, home, financial freedom, artistic expression, spirituality, volunteering), or a combination of both. There is no set guidance for what dimensions should be represented on the wheel; however, ageing research indicates that it may be important to consider health and wellbeing, learning and skills, finance, social participation and work (see Schurman, 2022). Once these dimensions have been defined, the client should write these down on their wheel of life.

Establishing areas for coaching for ageing well

The second step is divided into three important conversations to explore: how satisfied the client is with different aspects of their lives at the time of the session, how much attention and resources the client devotes to each segment of their wheel and how sustainable this is. The result of this conversation is an assessment of possible areas which the client may like to work on with the coach.

Levels of satisfaction conversation

The first conversation is an evaluation of life satisfaction for each segment of the wheel. For that, the client is asked to score each aspect on a scale of 0–10 (low to full satisfaction) by placing two small 'x's on the appropriate points on the wheel. In addition to exploring areas that the client may like to change based on levels of satisfaction, this step gives an opportunity for a deeper exploration of what is important for the client and is worth investing their time and resources.

Use of resources conversation

The second conversation is an assessment of how much attention and effort the client is currently devoting to each segment. In other words, how much of their resources are being directed to each segment. Given that resources are limited (see Hobfoll, 2002), it is important to explore whether their resources are optimised (Baltes & Baltes, 1990) or used inefficiently. In other words, are their efforts generating the expected results, e.g., satisfaction. To evaluate this, the client is asked to score each aspect again on a scale of 0–10 (low to full effort/resources usage) by placing the desired number for each aspect of the wheel. The results of this conversation, when combined with a set of scores on 'satisfaction', can be revealing. When there is a clear relationship between input and outcomes, e.g., low effort (resources usage) resulting in low satisfaction or high effort (resources usage) generating high satisfaction, it is easy to understand why and think about possible actions. Mismatches, however, offer the possibility of more interesting conversations. At a minimum, the coach should explore with the client how a certain area brings satisfaction and yet requires little effort or 'How can this area be taking so much of their resources and efforts and still not be bringing satisfaction?'. For instance, the client may be putting a lot of effort, hence deploying a sizeable proportion of their resources (a score of 8–9), to their work and career, and still not feeling satisfied enough (score of 3–4). An exploration of possible reasons allows the client to gain insights on why. Maybe the goals they are not pursuing are not aligned with their values, or they are focused on something that no longer brings them a sense of fulfilment or meaning (see Erikson, 1980, 1985; Jung, 1960).

The opposite mismatch is also a fertile ground for exploration. For instance, the client may indicate they are fairly satisfied with their health (a score of 7–8), while putting little effort towards it (score 2–3). While this may be good news, or luck, it may be an area which the coach would like to explore a bit more to learn about why this is working well, and if there are any strategies that may be useful or transferable to other areas.

Sustainable future conversation

At this stage of coaching conversation, the client will have a good idea of what areas could benefit from a change and what areas are not a concern. This may not be enough to trigger them to take action, especially if they are still managing to function in their daily lives (e.g., not satisfied but not overstressed or burnt out). Moreover, when it comes to coaching for ageing well, it is also important to have a future focus to evaluate how sustainable certain choices are in terms of personal resources availability and readiness to deal with unexpected or unwanted changes that may come along. Thus, the client will be encouraged to adopt a life management strategy mindset, such as SOC (Baltes & Baltes, 1990). The coach should help the client to take a long-term perspective and ask them to rate how sustainable each segment of the wheel is with a particular attention to personal resources usage, on a scale from 0–10. If we take the same examples used previously, the coach can explore with the client how sustainable it is to continue focusing so much of their resources on work, or if it is worth considering what could change or what could improve the input–outcome equation to avoid depleting personal resources.

If we use the second example, it may be that the client perceives that their health domain as low effort, because positive lifestyle choices and activities come naturally to them. Hence, it may be a lot of action, but not the associated cognitive strain, which would make this domain quite sustainable as life progresses towards old age; or instead, they are just lucky with their health and never had to pay much attention to it. In this case, it is not unlikely that their health status could deteriorate over time as they age – so it may be more sustainable to make changes to prevent future illness and disability.

Finally, the coach closes the wheel of life activity by supporting the client to set the agenda for the remainder of the coaching engagement, thus asking the client to indicate what domains they think change is needed; how important it is for them to make the changes they identified; and what area they would like to start with.

Committing to the coaching agenda

Like any other kind of coaching, identifying a change agenda is an essential step towards achieving successful results. However, it is important to highlight that despite the client's awareness of the issues they want to address, they may still find it difficult to start the process. This is because current behaviours and lifestyles, however negative or unsatisfying, also bring rewards, despite any longer-term adverse consequences. These gains may be objective or subjective, at a symbolic level. For instance, working unreasonable long hours can resonate with a personal value of being hardworking; or eating a whole tub of ice cream may bring some comfort after a long and hard day. Therefore, these 'hidden gains', if not explored, may impede the client's progress towards their change goals (Kegan & Lahey, 2009; Prochaska & DiClemente, 1984).

The client might not be aware of any opposing attitudes or ambivalence towards the change. The behaviours and lifestyles they may be intending to change are often crystallised by midlife (Atchley, 1999), and the rewards may not be in their mind. Therefore, it is crucial that the client is invited to reflect on what 'rewards' or 'gains' will be forfeited as part of the changes they intend to make; and if there are any better or healthier ways, they can experience similar rewards. There are established, evidence-based, approaches and tools to strengthen readiness for change by addressing underlying resistance (see Kegan & Lahey, 2009; Miller & Rollnick, 2013; Prochaska & DiClemente, 1984). For instance, Kegan and Lahey's Immunity to Change model (2009) and Motivational Interviewing coaching techniques (Anstiss & Passmore, 2011; Anstiss & Passmore, 2013; Passmore, 2014) are useful approaches to deal with ambivalence to change. These can be successfully incorporated into coaching for ageing well conversations.

A simple and powerful technique is the decisional balance sheet (for detailed guidance, see Passmore, 2011). Using a piece of paper, flip chart or open notes document (if the coaching is over a video call), the coach invites the client to explore four questions in the following order for each item of the change agenda.

1. What are the pros (or gains) of not making this change; thus, the advantages of maintaining the status quo?
2. What are the cons (or losses) of not making this change; thus, the downsides of maintaining the status quo?
3. What are the cons (or losses) of making this change; thus, the downsides of changing?
4. What are the pros (or benefits) of making this change; thus, the advantages of changing?

This sophisticated 'pros and cons' list may be better displayed as a 4 x 4 matrix. This can be repeated to explore each aspect the client identified in their change agenda before the coaching process can continue with more specific goals or action plans.

Conclusions

Coaching for ageing well is an important area of coaching with an incredible growing potential considering the demographic shift and the emergence of the *superagers* (Schurman, 2022). Ageing well means to have the opportunity to live a fulfilling life, with relatively good health, social connections, and purpose. Ageing outcomes, however, are highly influenced by lifestyle decisions, choices and behaviours adopted in midlife, making this an optimum time to start making positive changes. Coaching for ageing well, or midlife review coaching, can be an effective intervention to empower individuals to manage their resources and goals so they can thrive in their later years.

There is no set framework for coaching for ageing well, but it is important to take a holistic approach and evaluate how all significant life domains of the client may affect their ageing outcomes. Midlife is a complex stage of life when adults are faced with several competing demands and changing circumstances. Consequently, taking the time to review and reflect on different aspects of life is an essential part of successfully helping the client to define the coaching agenda. Among the challenges of coaching for ageing well is the fact that certain lifestyles can be still manageable in midlife, although unsustainable over the long term – so helping the client to assess future outcomes through reflection or envisioning can be an effective way to help them to define and commit with their goals for ageing well.

Finally, it is important to acknowledge that changes of lifestyle and behaviours adopted in midlife can be challenging and can be met with a certain level of ambivalence. Being equipped to discuss emerging issues that may lead to resistance to change is essential to ensure the success of coaching for ageing well.

Reflective questions

1. If you could describe your ideal future ten years from now, after you made positive changes and adjustments in midlife, what would this be like?
2. Now, if you could imagine ten years has passed, what would your future look like if you have made no changes and life took its natural course?
3. Considering the satisfaction, effort and sustainability of the different domains of your life today, what do you think you need to do to achieve your ideal future?

References

Anstiss, T., & Passmore, J. (2011). Motivational interview. In M. Neenan & S. Palmer (eds.), *Cognitive Behavioural Coaching in Practice: An Evidenced Based Approach* (pp. 33–52). London: Routledge.
Anstiss, T., & Passmore, J. (2013). Motivational interviewing. In J. Passmore, D. Peterson, & T. Freire (eds.), *The Wiley Blackwell Handbook of the Psychology of Coaching & Mentoring* (pp. 339–364). Chichester: Wiley.
Atchley, R. C. (1972). Retirement and leisure participation: Continuity or crisis? *The Gerontologist*, 11, 13–17. DOI: 10.1093/geront/11.1_part_1.13
Atchley, R. C. (1989). A continuity theory of normal aging. *The Gerontologist*, 29(2), 183–190. DOI: 10.1093/geront/29.2.183
Atchley, R. C. (1999). *Continuity and Adaptation in Aging: Creating Positive Experiences*. Baltimore, MD: The Johns Hopkins University Press.
Baltes, P. B., & Baltes, M. M. (1990). Psychological perspectives on successful ageing: The model of selective optimization with compensation. In P. B. Baltes & M. M. Baltes (Eds.), *Successful Aging: Perspectives from the Behavioural Sciences* (pp. 1–34). New York, NY: Cambridge University Press. Chapter 1.
Bridges, W., & Bridges, S. (2019). *Transitions: Making Sense of Life's Changes* (Revised 40th Anniversary Edition). Cambridge: Da Capo Press. Print.
Burnett-Wolle, S., & Godbey, G. (2007). Refining research on older adults' leisure: Implications of selection, optimization, and compensation and socioemotional selectivity theories. *Journal of Leisure Research*, 39(3), 498–513. DOI: 10.1080/00222216.2007.11950119
Byrne, U. (2005). Wheel of life. *Business Information Review*, 22(2), 123–130. DOI: 10.1177/0266382105054770
Crystal, C. (2006). Dynamics of later life inequality: Modelling the interplay of health disparities, economic resources. In J. Baars et al. (ed.), *Globalization and Inequality* (pp. 205–213). Amityville, NY: Baywood Publishing.
Crystal, S., Shea, D. G., & Reyes, A. M. (2017). Cumulative advantage, cumulative disadvantage, and evolving patterns of late-life inequality. *The Gerontologist*, 57, 910–920. DOI: 10.1093/geront/gnw056

Cumming, E., & Henry, W. (1961). *Growing Old*. New York: Basic.

Dannefer, D. (2003). Cumulative advantage and the life course: Cross-fertilizing age and social science knowledge. *Journal of Gerontology*, 58b, 327–S337. DOI: 10.1093/geronb/58.6.S327

Demakakos, P., Hacker, E., & Gjonca, E. (2006). Perceptions of ageing. In J. Banks, E. Breeze, C. Lessof, & J. Nazroo (eds.), *Retirement, Health and Relationships of the Older Population in England: The 2004 English Longitudinal Study of Ageing* (Chapter 11, pp. 339–351). London: The Institute for Fiscal Studies. https://discovery.ucl.ac.uk/id/eprint/15351/1/15351.pdf

Earl, C., & Taylor, P. (2017). Reconceptualising work-retirement transitions: Critiques of the new retirement and bridge employment. In I. Aaltio, A. Mills, & J. H. Mills (eds.), *Ageing, Organizations and Management: Constructive Discourses and Critical Perspectives*. London: Palgrave MacMillan.

Elder, G. H. (1985). Perspectives on the life course. In G. H. Elder (ed.), *Life Course Dynamics* (pp. 23–49). Ithaca, NY: Cornell University Press.

Elder, G. H., Johnson, M. K., & Crosnoe, R. (2003). The emergence and development of life course theory. In J. T. Mortimer & M. J. Shanahan (eds.), *Handbook of the Life Course* (pp. 3–19). New York, NY: Springer.

Erikson, E. H. (1980). *Identity and the Life Cycle*. W. W. Norton & Co.

Erikson, E. H. (1985). *The Life Cycle Completed: A Review*. W. W. Norton & Co.

Fernandez-Ballesteros, R. (2019). The concept of successful aging and related terms. In R. Fernandez-Ballesteros, A. Benetos, & J.-M. Robine (eds.), *The Cambridge Handbook of Successful Aging* (pp. 6–22). Cambridge University Press.

Ferraro, K. F., & Shippee, T. P. (2009). Aging and Cumulative Inequality: How Does Inequality Get under the Skin? *The Gerontologist*, 49, 333–343. DOI: 10.1093/geront/gnp034

Freund, A. M., & Ritter, J. O. (2009). Midlife crisis: A debate. *Gerontology (Basel)*, 55(5), 582–591. DOI: 10.1159/000227322

Gilleard, C. J., & Higgs, P. (2005). *Contexts of Ageing Class, Cohort, and Community*. Cambridge, UK: Polity Press.

Graßmann, C., Schölmerich, F., & Schermuly, C. (2020). The relationship between working alliance and client outcomes in coaching: A meta-analysis. *Human Relations*, 73(1), 35–58. DOI: 10.1177/00187267188197

Havighurst, R. J. (1961). Successful aging. *The Gerontologist*. DOI: 10.1093/geront/1.1.8

Hobfoll, S. E. (2002). Social and psychological resources and adaptation. *Review of General Psychology*, 6(4), 307–324. DOI: 10.1037/1089-2680.6.4.307

Illmarinen, J. (2005) *Towards a Longer Worklife – Ageing and the Quality of Worklife in the European Union*. Helsinki: Finnish Institute of the Occupational Health, Ministry of Social Affairs and Health. DOI: 10.1026/0932-4089.52.1.47

Jones, R., Woods, S., & Guillaume, Y. (2016). The effectiveness of workplace coaching: A meta-analysis of learning and performance outcomes from coaching. *Journal of Occupational and Organizational Psychology*, 89(2), 249–277. DOI: 10.1111/joop.12119

Jung, C. G. (1960). *The Structure and Dynamics of the Psyche*. Hove and New York, NY: Routledge and Kegan Paul.

Katz, S. (2020). Precarious life, human development and the life course: Critical intersections. In A. Grenier, C. Phillipson, & R. Settersten (eds.), *Precarity and Ageing: Understanding Insecurity and Risk in Later Life* (pp. 41–68). Bristol: Policy Press.

Katz, S., & Calasanti, T. (2015;2014). Critical perspectives on successful aging: Does it "appeal more than it illuminates"? *The Gerontologist*, 55(1), 26–33. DOI: 10.1093/geront/gnu027

Kegan, R., & Lahey, L. L. (2009). *Immunity to Change*. Boston, MA: Harvard Business Review Press.

Lachman, M. E., Teshale, S., & Agrigoroaei, S. (2015;2014). Midlife as a pivotal period in the life course: Balancing growth and decline at the crossroads of youth and old age. *International Journal of Behavioral Development*, 39(1), 20–31. DOI: 10.1177/0165025414533223

Levinson, D. J. (1978). *The Seasons of a Man's Life*. New York, NY: Knopf Publishers.

Levinson, D. J. (1986). A conception of adult development. *American Psychologist*, 41(1), 3–13. DOI: 10.1037/0003-066X.41.1.3

Levinson, D. J. (1996). *The Seasons of a Woman's Life*. New York, NY: Knopf Publishers.

Locke, E. A., & Latham, G. P. (2002). Building a practically useful theory of goal setting and task motivation: A 35-year odyssey. *American Psychologist*, 57(9), 705–717. DOI: 10.1037/0003-066X.57.9.705

Martinson, M., & Berridge, C. (2015;2014). Successful aging and its discontents: A systematic review of the social gerontology literature. *The Gerontologist*, 55(1), 58–69. DOI: 10.1093/geront/gnu037

Miller, W. R., & Rollnick, S. (2013). *Motivational Interviewing, Third Edition: Helping People Change: Third Edition: Applications of Motivational Interviewing*. New York: Guildford Press.

Moghimi, D., Zacher, H., Scheibe, S., & Van Yperen, N. W. (2017). The selection, optimization, and compensation model in the work context: A systematic review and meta-analysis of two decades of research. *Journal of Organizational Behavior*, 38, 247–275. DOI: 10.1002/job.2108

Müller, A., Angerer, P., Becker, A., Gantner, M., Gündel, H., Heiden, B., Herbig, B., Herbst, K., Poppe, F., Schmook, R., & Maatouk, I. (2018). Bringing successful aging theories to occupational practice: Is selective optimization with compensation trainable? *Work, Aging and Retirement*, 4(2), 161–174. DOI: 10.1093/workar/wax033

National Institute of Adult Continuing Education [NIACE]. (2015). *Midlife Career Review: Technical Report: Background, Evidence and Methodology*. Leicester: Published by the NIACE. https://www.agediversity.org/wp-content/uploads/2019/04/midlife-career-review.pdf

Nosraty, L., Jylhä, M., Raittila, T., & Lumme-Sandt, K. (2014;2015). Perceptions by the oldest old of successful aging, vitality 90 + study. *Journal of Aging Studies*, 32, 50–58. DOI: 10.1016/j.jaging.2015.01.002

O'Connor, J., & Lages, A. (2007). *How Coaching Works*. London: A & C Black.

Organisation for Economic Co-Operation and Development [OECD]. (2011). *Pensions at a Glance 2011: Retirement-Income Systems in OECD and G20 Countries*. OECD Publishing. https://www.oecd-ilibrary.org/finance-and-investment/pensions-at-a-glance-2011_pension_glance-2011-en

Passmore, J. (2011). MI techniques – Balance sheet. *The Coaching Psychologist*, 7(2), 151–153. http://jonathanpassmore.com/wp-content/uploads/resources/Passmore%20(2011)%20Motivational%20Interviewing%20Techniques%20-%20Balance%20sheet.pdf

Passmore, J. (2014). Motivational interviewing. In J. Passmore (ed.), *Mastery in Coaching*. London: Kogan Page eBook. ISBN: 9781003027164.

Phillipson, C., & Baars, J. (2007). Social theory and social ageing. In J. Bond, et al. (eds.), *Ageing in Society: European Perspectives on Gerontology* (pp. 68–84). Sage Publications.

Poscia, A., Moscato, U., La Milia, D. I., Milovanovic, S., Stojanovic, J., Borghini, A., Collamati, A., Ricciardi, W., & Magnavita, N. (2016). Workplace health promotion for older workers: A systematic literature review. *BMC Health Services Research*, 16(Suppl 5), 329–329. DOI: 10.1186/s12913-016-1518-z

Prochaska, J. O., & DiClemente, C. C. (1984). *The Transtheoretical Approach: Towards a Systematic Eclectic Framework*. Homewood, IL, USA: Dow Jones Irwin.

Pruchno, R. A., & Wilson-Genderson, M. (2015). A Longitudinal Examination of the Effects of Early Influences and Midlife Characteristics on Successful Aging. *The Journals of Gerontology. Series B, Psychological Sciences and Social Sciences*, 70(6), 850–859. DOI: 10.1093/geronb/gbu046

Rowe, J. W., & Kahn, R. L. (1987). Human aging: Usual and successful. *Science*, 237, 143–149. DOI: 10.1126/science.3299702

Rowe, J. W., & Kahn, R. L. (1998). *Successful Aging*. New York: Random House.

Rowson, T. S., Meyer, A., & Houldsworth, E. (2022). Work identity pause and reactivation: A study of cross-domain identity transitions of trailing wives in Dubai. *Work, Employment and Society*, 36(2), 235–252. DOI: 10.1177/0950017021993736

Rowson, T. S., & Phillipson, C. (2020). 'I never really left the university:' Continuity amongst male academics in the transition from work to retirement. *Journal of Aging Studies*, 53. DOI: 10.1016/j.jaging.2020.100853

Schurman, B. (2022). *The Super Age: Decoding Our Demographic Destiny*. New York, NY: HarperCollins Publishers.

Sheehy, G. (1995). *New Passages: Mapping Your Life Across Time*. New York: Random House.

Spence, G. B., & Grant, A. M. (2012). Coaching and well-being: A brief review of existing evidence, relevant theory and implications for practitioners. In S. David & I. Boniwell (eds.), *Oxford Handbook of Happiness* (pp. 1009–1025). London: Oxford University Press.

Theeboom, T., Beersma, B., & van Vianen, A. E. M. (2014). Does coaching work? A meta-analysis on the effects of coaching on individual level outcomes in an organizational context. *The Journal of Positive Psychology*, 9(1), 1–18. DOI: 10.1080/17439760.2013.837499

Urtamo, A., Jyväkorpi, S. K., & Strandberg, T. E. (2019). Definitions of successful ageing: A brief review of a multidimensional concept. *Acta Bio-Medica De l'Ateneo Parmense*, 90(2), 359–363. DOI: 10.23750/abm.v90i2.8376

Wang, Q., Lai, Y.-L., Xu, X., & McDowall, A. (2022). The effectiveness of workplace coaching: A meta-analysis of contemporary psychologically informed coaching approaches. *Journal of Work-Applied Management*, 14(1), 77–101. DOI: 10.1108/JWAM-04-2021-0030

Wiese, B. S., Freund, A. M., & Baltes, P. B. (2002). Subjective career success and emotional well-being: Longitudinal predictive power of selection, optimization and compensation. *Journal of Vocational Behavior*, 60, 321–335. DOI: 10.1006/jvbe.2001.1835

World Health Organization [WHO]. (2002). Active ageing: A policy framework. *World Health Organization.* Apr 1. https://apps.who.int/iris/handle/10665/67215

World Health Organization [WHO]. (2020). Decade of healthy ageing plan of action. *World Health Organization.* Dec 14. https://www.who.int/publications/m/item/decade-of-healthy-ageing-plan-of-action

Young, Y., Frick, K., & Phelan, E. (2009). Can successful aging and chronic illness coexist in the same individual? A multidimensional concept of successful aging. *Journal of the American Medical Directors Association*, 10(2), 87–97. DOI: 10.1016/j.jamda.2008.11.003

Chapter 15

Coaching for neurodiversity

Nancy Doyle and Almuth McDowall

Introduction

With a notable exception, few writers have explicitly acknowledged coaching as a social process including its role as an ideological and instrumental device (Shoukry & Cox, 2018). We situate our chapter on coaching neurodiverse individuals in this new and exciting strand of research. We start by outlining the premises of the advocacy movement, relevant theories and legal considerations, safeguarding risks and contracting considerations. Together, these position the need for particularly considered approaches when working with marginalised populations. We hope that on reading this chapter, coaches will be able to adapt their coaching practice to neurodivergent clients and recognise areas for continuing professional development. Our chapter outlines the key tenets of the neurodiversity paradigm which acknowledges and seeks to harness rather than pathologise differences in functioning. The consideration of theoretical, conceptual and historical underpinnings leads us to outline how coaching in neurodiversity has to acknowledge socio-legal context and the distinct knowledge and skills needed to underpin coaching in this context.

Theory and research

Terminology

The term neurodiversity was conceptualised by Australian sociologist Judy Singer (1998) in the context of online disability self-advocacy of the late 1990s. We have summarised relevant terms in Table 15.1 to orientate our readers, as we believe applying the correct terminology is crucial in this field, as it is in many others.

Understanding the concept

Neurodiversity holds that neurodevelopmental differences such as autism, attention deficit and hyperactivity disorder (ADHD), dyslexia, dyspraxia, dyscalculia and tic disorders are natural variations in the human species – not pathological impairments. The neurodiversity movement has advanced the social model of disability (Charlton, 1998) to assert the right of minority neurotypes to thrive in education, work and community through accommodation of difference, not treatment for deficits. Coaching in this context can empower clients to move on from any internalised limiting beliefs acquired through struggling with mainstream education and social interaction, towards focusing instead on understanding their strengths and talents.

DOI: 10.4324/9781003319016-17

Table 15.1 Key chapter terminology

Term	Our operational definition
Medical model of disability	Holds that disability is an individual-level impairment that causes dysfunction in life
Neurocognition/ neurocognitive	The thinking that we experience, originating from our neurology
Neurodifference	How human neurocognitive functions differ from each other
Neurodivergence/ neurodivergent	Terminology indicating that some neurotypes deviate from a neurotypical norm. This term is seen by some as 'othering', with 'neurodistinct' or 'neurodiverse' preferred
Neurodiversity	Human experience and functioning as a spectrum of difference, akin to biodiversity
Neurominority	Population with a 'spiky profile' which indicates distinct strengths and weaknesses
Neurotypical/ neurotypicality	People who have not been diagnosed with a neurodevelopmental condition and who do not have a spiky profile
Neurotype	More neutral term which references that there are different typologies of behaving and human experience
Neurodevelopmental differences	This term describes a range of conditions which develop over the lifespan. There is ongoing debate as to whether all of these are present from birth or – for example, in the case of attention deficit and hyperactivity disorder (ADHD) – if there is evidence for late onset
Social model of disability	Holds that people are prevented from functioning at their best because of barriers in their environment, not because of how they differ from the norm. Barriers can be physical or due to social norms and beliefs

Yet, conditions vary in intensity and marginalisation. Autism frequently co-occurs with intellectual disability and epilepsy (Zeidan et al., 2022), both of which lead to complex medical and social needs. Autistic people are more likely to be unemployed than any other category of disability (ONS, 2019); dyslexic people represent a third of unemployed people, but only 10% of the population (Jensen et al., 2000). Dyslexia and ADHD are known to be more prevalent in offender groups than in the general population (Snowling et al., 2000; Young et al., 2018), suggesting that any difficulties severely affect life chances and social inclusion. That said, there are considerable potential benefits to neurodifference, depending on how individuals navigate the neuro-normative world (Huijg, 2020), which can be supported by high-quality coaching. ADHD graduates are twice as likely to start a business compared to neurotypical graduates (Lerner et al., 2019); dyslexia is associated with creativity in adulthood (Majeed et al. 2021), and autism is associated with innovation and detailed observational skills (Meilleur et al., 2015).

Relevant history

The majority of neurodevelopmental conditions were documented in the nineteenth and early twentieth centuries (Berlin, 1884; Ssucharewa, 1927), yet genetic and archaeological evidence suggests that minority neurotypes have always been part of the human species. This is proposed as a theory of 'Complementary Cognition' (Taylor et al., 2021), in which there are specialist thinkers (good at some things but not others) and generalist thinkers (jacks of all trades) operating in balance to maximise potential for a tribe. Pejorative and medicalised views of neurodifferences arguably emerged due to the failure of the industrialised education paradigm when attendance at school became mandatory and replaced informal mentoring and apprenticeship learning. In standardised education, success depends on the ability to sit still to concentrate in crowded environments, to be literate and numerate, and to communicate with fine motor control (handwriting/typing). Those who have difficulties with such tasks are deemed 'unusual' or 'impaired', and the terminology accentuates assumptions about negative deviance including *dys*lexia (difficulty with words), *dys*praxia (difficult with movement), and so on.

Yet, such 'disorders' continue to be prevalent at around 15–20% of the human population (Doyle, 2020), with remarkably consistent global prevalence (Elsabbagh et al., 2012). Advocates and researchers have begun to highlight potential evolutionary advantages which are identified with a 'spiky profile' in psychology allowing us to plot cognitive abilities on a graph showing that some people have large disparities between individual strengths and weaknesses (Armstrong, 2010; Grant, 2009). Abilities such as spatial and mechanical reasoning are not examined in schools until the teenage years (design and technology and verbal skills involving language are only examined through literacy), yet both abilities are valued in specific jobs – construction, hairdressing, warehousing logistics, engineering, surgery – all dependent on spatial and mechanical ability. Verbal skills are essential for customer service, teaching, sales, public relations and many other roles. A spiky profile analysis can be cathartic for individuals, creating a road map for coaching activity such that the focus is on understanding and maximising opportunities, harnessing strengths over weaknesses.

The evolutionary critique is essential to understanding why many neurodivergent people prefer neutral terminology. In this chapter, you read words such as 'neurodivergent' or 'neurominority' juxtaposed with 'neurotypical' (Chapman, 2020; Singer, 1999) to indicate a group of people within a minority neurotype. People also identify as having an 'SpLD', or 'specific learning disability', as neurodiverse (indicating the spiky profile) or 'neurodifferent' (Doyle, 2020). It can be challenging to keep up with the changes, and some people are nervous that they might use the wrong word. We recommend checking which terminology people prefer, coupled with a swift apology where unwelcome words have been used in order to build trust and take a position of curiosity and respect. Similar to language describing race, ethnicity, gender identity and sexual orientation, words can be interpreted as pejorative and discriminatory, and they can give rise to strong feelings.

Stigma and fitting in

Research into the psychological experience of neurominorities draws heavily on stigma theory (Goffman, 1963), which can become internalised (Johnson & Joshi, 2016; Masuch et al., 2019) and lead to 'masking'. 'Masking' is the behavioural and psychological process of trying to appear neurotyical, for example by supressing urges to stim, which is cognitively demanding and a risk factor for burnout (Pearson & Rose, 2021; Wissell et al., 2022). In coaching, this requires unpicking of self-limiting beliefs and internalised narratives of shame for uncontrollable differences. Table 15.2 outlines typical issues that lead to social anxiety and self-scolding, which remain prevalent.

Table 15.2 Uncontrollable differences and potential internalised narratives by condition

Condition	Uncontrollable difference	Potential internalised narrative
ADHD	• Higher levels of energy • Tendency to 'hyperfocus' on one topic • Inability to concentrate unless tasks are novel or particularly interesting • Forgetful of day-to-day events, appointments, timing	• I am chaotic, uncontrollable, domineering • I am rude and ignore people because I am intense • I am lacking in motivation or care • I am uncaring and unkind, and disrespectful of others; I don't listen and I am disorganised
Autism	• Higher levels of social overwhelm and need to withdraw • Misunderstanding metaphors and inability to make 'best guess' sense of ambiguous phrases • Detail conscious, sometimes to the exclusion of shortcuts	• I am antisocial and don't like people, I don't have empathy • I ask too many questions, I don't listen properly, I interrogate people • I take too long, I 'go' round the houses', I bore other people
Dyscalculia	• Difficulty making mental representation of numerosity, which includes size, speed, relative comparisons • Mistakes in everyday mental maths	• I didn't try hard enough to think it through • I'm thick; I'm rubbish with numbers
Dyslexia	• Spelling mistakes • Taking a long time to read or write in everyday communication • Difficulty planning and prioritising • Forgetting names and how to spell or pronounce them	• I'm careless, unprofessional • I don't get back to people on time, I am rude and don't take time to consider • I am thoughtless and unreliable • I am uncaring, disinterested, rude or even discriminatory
Dyspraxia	• Dropping things and breaking them • Bumping into things, including when driving • Difficulty planning and prioritising • Difficulty verbalising (can include stammering)	• I am careless and clumsy • I am clumsy and accident-prone • I am thoughtless and unreliable • I am non-communicative and hard to talk to
Tic disorder	• Minor physical tics • Minor verbal tics • Major physical tics • Major verbal tics	• I am fidgety and distracting to others • I interrupt people and throw them off course • I am intentionally disruptive and rude • I am only saying what I actually think or observe; people think I mean it

Autistic sociologist Damian Milton proposed the 'double empathy problem' to explain how neurodivergents and neurotypicals often misinterpret each other's behaviour (Milton et al., 2022), noting that society assumes that inclusion will happen through assimilation to neurotypical norms rather than neurotypical people empathising with marginalisation and making accommodations. There are many therapeutic approaches aimed at this goal, with significant scientific research to support their effectiveness (Kirby et al., 2008), including medication (Engert & Pruessner, 2009). This proposal has some support in the literature as autistic students are more likely to interact with autistic peers than non-autistic peers (Chen, et al., 2021) and more relational than across neurotypes. Chapple and colleagues (2021) found that non-autistic people paired with autistic people for short periods of time were able to shift their understanding, becoming less judgemental and more accepting of difference.

Double empathy shows us that social acceptance needs to go both ways to inform coaching in this context. A coach might be asked to help a client learn how to fit in by the client, their manager or other stakeholders. We advise caution in taking up such coaching goals, due to the high level of cognitive effort required to suppress one's natural thought processes and/or to circumvent a cognitive deficit, with either leading to increased risk of burnout. An ADHD client will undoubtedly seek support for being more organised and consistent in their workflow; a dyspraxic client may approach for support with communication anxiety or staying calm; an autistic client may wish to develop empathy skills. When faced with such challenges, there are limits to what 'trying harder' will achieve; instead, the coach may skilfully challenge internalised beliefs. What evidence do clients have that they lack empathy? Is their self-belief based solely on the critiques that they have received from neurotypical people in times of stress? In what ways are they empathetic, and how could clients communicate this more openly? A robust strategy for working *with* is less likely to reinforce a sense of inadequacy and provides a basis for self-acceptance, preservation and harnessing of individual resources.

Reasonable accommodations and adjustments at work

Work challenges, including performance deficits, are common ground for neurodiversity coaching referrals. Established person–environment–fit theories hold that performance and success are more likely with congruence of individual ability and the resources/demands present in the environment (Lewin, 1936). Neurodivergent individuals may be struggling because their neurotype is not catered for in a standard work environment, which may need to be adapted to maximise conditions for success, although evidence is somewhat sparse and disjointed. The sensory environment is a starting point where we can reduce triggering discomfort and pain through changes to the visual, tactile, auditory, olfactory and gustatory stimuli (Weber et al., 2022). Yet different minority neurotypes have varied needs, and relevant primary research lacks evaluative high-quality evidence to support policy and effective implementation.

Often, the actual environment does not change but people make work structure and flow accommodations (e.g., remote/hybrid work policies and flexible/reduced hours), although we lack evidence that such accommodations will translate directly into success (Doyle & McDowall, 2021). We frequently witness the provision of assistive technology (e.g., text to speech or vice versa), dual screens (to reduce burden on retaining details whilst transferring between tasks) and mind-mapping software (to help retain focus on overview and details simultaneously). Assistive technology effectiveness is better researched, showing improvements that are moderated by familiarity with technology (age) and effective training on implementation (Doyle, 2019; Draffan et al., 2013; Kulow & Thomas, 2019). These sorts of changes are legislative requirements in most developed economies, in line with the United Nations Convention on the Rights of

Persons with Disabilities (United Nations, 2006), and coaches must be aware that stakeholders – including educators, employers and healthcare providers – are legally obliged to exercise accommodations. Yet, psychosocial accommodations have not kept pace with physical accommodations for wheelchair users (Santuzzi & Waltz, 2016); with that said, coaching is an effective mechanism for supporting the client to ask for solutions. From this perspective, coaching is not the reasonable adjustment but the pathway to understanding which adjustments will enable person–environment fit at the individual level.

There is no doubt that neurodivergence is stigmatising and significantly compromises mental wellbeing, leading to anxiety and depression (Hollocks et al., 2019; Snowling, 2010), eating disorders (Levin & Rawana, 2016) and other conditions. Coaching that is focused on the development of self-efficacy – that is, people's belief in their capabilities – reduces stress and the impact of compromised short-term memory, and increases proactive behaviour in adapting one's environment (Doyle et al., 2022b; Doyle & McDowall, 2015). This supports confidence to self-advocate for the changes to the environment, as it may not be the individual who needs to change, but rather the resources available to them and the demands they experience. We discuss practical methods in the next section.

Coaching practice

Contracting

In considering contracting, we draw on the frameworks of the coaching triad and the coaching alliance (O'Broin & Palmer, 2010; Palmer & McDowall, 2010) to highlight the role of third parties, which could be an employer, an educator, a healthcare professional or a statutory service such as probation officer. Many neurominorities qualify as disabled, which is a protected characteristic in many countries, because of the long-term and chronic nature of their daily struggles with communication and learning (Equality Act, 2010). The legal profession in the UK reports a 31% rise in discrimination claims on the basis of autism and dyslexia (Deol, 2022) and the UK Ministry of Justice has recently published guidance on the barriers for neurodivergent people in the criminal justice system (CJJI, 2021). The UK's Department of Work and Pensions offers support for neurodivergent people under the 'Access to Work' scheme aimed at disabled people (Melvill et al., 2015), who are the third-largest group to receive support (Gifford, 2011). Thus, it is wise to assume that a neurodivergent client could qualify as disabled, placing the burden for making change with the organisation and not the individual.

Who changes?

Contracting must consider the environment, including any adjustments the coach needs to make. These will likely include adapting the real or virtual coaching environment regarding minimising social overwhelm, as well as providing opportunity to move and fidget. It is important to double-check and, if necessary, revise reasonable expectations and goals bearing in mind that communication difficulties and managing emotions can be part of a disabling condition. For example, coaches might need to ensure that coaching records/reports use software which is compliant with assistive technology and/or commit to descriptions of visual or diagrammatic handouts which should summarise action points and takeaway practice tasks in a short, written message. Coaches must take time to check mutual understanding of what was heard and carefully consider next steps.

Informed consent and data control

A second issue in coaching contracting is informed consent. If an individual has come to coaching because they are at risk of losing their job, healthcare provision or their freedom, this puts pressure on the coaching relationship. The coach should explore in more detail than usual how to raise concerns with the client and how to ask for a replacement coach if it is not working. Coaches need to be explicit about confidentiality and reporting to the commissioning client depending on the context. Discussing the details of someone's neurominority diagnosis is considered medical grade data by most national and international data protection laws. All coaches need to therefore ensure that consent, data handling and access to data are formalised into a robust process and negotiated with each client.

Safeguarding

Neurodivergent people are vulnerable to mental health distress and abuse (Weiss & Fardella, 2018), so coaches need to plan how they will handle significant indicators of anxiety, depression, suicidal ideation and disclosure. It is wise to have a next of kin contact for neurodivergent clients and to discuss a referral plan for mental health support during contracting. Coaches also need to know how to handle any suspicions of bullying, harassment and/or discrimination by ensuring that they have a contact from the commissioning client (acting transparently if they refer such concerns). Another issue is knowing where to signpost for legal advice. Coaches should undertake training in safeguarding and ensure supervision arrangements for potential escalation of safeguarding concerns.

Managing bias

Neurominority diagnosis is intersectionally biased towards white people and men (Doyle, 2022; Roman-Urrestarazu et al., 2021) and is bound by cultural assumptions regarding diagnosis seeking (Miyasaka et al., 2018), and 'masking' is encouraged in females from a young age (Lai et al., 2017; Young et al., 2020). Sexuality and gender status further complicate diagnosis (Pecora et al., 2020; Warrier et al., 2020), meaning that many of us carry open or hidden assumptions about minority neurotypes. We remember being asked in a meeting, "Oh, but people with ADHD [sic], aren't they all really aggressive?". There are biases in our societal narratives concerning neurominorities and other characteristics. For example, do coaches expect women to be calmer, more nurturing (empathetic) and more diligent, and do they judge them differently when they are not? We invite readers to reflect on Table 15.3, which lists common prejudicial narratives about neurominorities, paired with counter-arguments. We ask coaches to consider whether they recognise narratives and how these might influence their approach to coaching. The first author, Nancy, once had a dyslexic client seek support because their counselling supervisor interpreted their requests for bullet point reminders instead of wordy reports as an unacceptable expression of narcissism.

Table 15.3 Prejudicial narratives and counter statements, per condition

Condition	Example prejudicial narrative	Counter-argument
ADHD	ADHD isn't a real disorder, it's just bad behaviour. It is caused by poor diet and too many video games.	ADHD has been recorded in medical notes since the 1700s with genetic markers and measurable differences in neurological activity.
Autism	There are too many people with autism diagnoses these days who are just jumping on the bandwagon.	Autism diagnosis has increased in recent years because we have reduced cultural and gender biases. As our world becomes noisier and more complex, more autistic people seek support.
Dyscalculia	Some people just don't like maths; that's not a disability.	Dyscalculia affects the ability to perceive and respond to speed, shape and size, which is disabling in many contexts.
Dyslexia	It doesn't matter anymore because there is so much technology.	Feeling dependent on technology is destabilising; it is also expensive and not available to all. Many essential services (for example, hospital information) still depend on paper.
Dyspraxia	Much more of a problem for men than women.	Dyspraxic people are more likely to fall and injure themselves, to break and lose expensive equipment and to struggle to drive, which affects both genders.
Tic disorder	They could control it if they tried.	It is physically effortful/painful to control, which should not be encouraged as a coping mechanism.
All neurominorities	They can do it when they really want to.	Enormous effort required for fitting in is hard. Many wheelchair users with multiple sclerosis can climb stairs on occasion; it doesn't mean they have the resources to do it every day.

Typical topics in neurodiversity coaching

The transdiagnostic mapping project at Cambridge University has found a remarkable level of consistency across neurocognitive differences of neurominorities (Astle et al., 2019; Siugzdaite et al., 2020). Regardless of diagnosis, the same topics reoccur documented in practitioner and coaching literature (Doyle, 2021; Doyle & Bradley, 2022; Pollack, 2009). These include difficulties in executive functions such as short-term and working memory and planning, challenges with understanding one's own emotional responses, communicating needs and communicating in conflict. Coaching is sometimes also used for developing skills such as literacy, numeracy or equipment use. We do not address these areas since this is more akin to tutoring than the scope of this book. We do, however, note that neurodiversity-trained coaches are sometimes asked to problem-solve such activity.

Spoon Theory

A useful metaphor for coaching neurominorities is 'Spoon Theory' (Miserando, 2018), borrowed from the wider disability literature, which holds that we have a limited number of 'spoons' including attention, effort and emotional resilience. Certain activities deplete our spoons, and others refill them. Once we are out of spoons, we cannot go on. For example, working memory capacities are limited to a number of items for our attention, or our social 'batteries' differ in the range of social interactions we can have before we need time alone. All humans differ, but neurominorities start with a lower number of spoons and differ in their experience of everyday life, including noise, social interaction, literacy/numeracy requirements or navigating transport. During coaching, we can be supported to identify when we are out of spoons, which activities/environments reduce our spoons and which activities/environments replenish them. We can also learn to accept that we might have fewer spoons than our peers for social interaction or concentrating in one place.

Executive functions coaching

Coaching needs to be very careful about signposting tools and activities designed for neurotypical brains. A timer to get up and move might help concentration, but it might also disrupt a perfectly productive bout of hyperfocus. Lists could be helpful, but need to be stored, and so mind mapping may be more effective. It is important to flexibly co-produce any effectiveness strategies for neurominorities, taking into account sensory modality, linear versus spatial presentation and emotional state. An effective approach is to work with what they have already tried, or to consider what works in other contexts. One of Nancy's clients was sure that they had no organisational skills, but they were an amazing cook for friends and family in large groups. How did they organise when they cook? They explained, "I get everything out onto the kitchen table and look at it all once. I can then see what will go with what, when it needs to be put on to cook and what I don't need". This strategy translated into one for prioritisation which utilised a twice-weekly flip chart board covered with Post-it notes referencing tasks, which they moved around until they could see the right order and flow. Starting with strengths helps counter the narrative that one is 'useless' and 'needs help', and it affords ownership for positive self-support.

Emotions and behaviour

Many neurominorites struggle to self-regulate emotions, as demands on neurodivergent people to fit in can be draining. This makes tipping into fight, flight, freeze and faun responses (overwhelm) more likely. The key to managing this with clients is to expect, prevent and plan. Coaching can identify common triggers and how to address these one at a time; for example, tackling them at a time of day when the individual has the most resources, and/or learning from instances of successfully handling overwhelm. Understanding successful recovery to discuss them with a manager, partner or service professional could be transformational. One of Nancy's clients identified their feet beginning to tap when they started feeling overwhelmed as a signal for them to retreat to a quiet space. They came to an agreement with their floor manager to pop outside for five minutes to look at the sky. Jointly with their manager, they then agreed that since they were not a smoker and that other colleagues went out more frequently, this was achievable and fair. This made a significant difference to their health and absence record, with fewer 'duvet days'.

Wellbeing and balance

Emotional resilience and executive functions depend on our wellbeing, which is a frequent and important starting point for coaching assignments with neurodiverse clients, but not the end game. Many clients will voice need for support to cope with pressures, but as the causes are unpicked in the coaching process, it may transpire that concentration or organisational difficulties are a root cause. Wellbeing and work/life balance may be different for neurominorities who often prefer to work in bursts of intensity followed by prolonged rest. This can be incompatible with rigid work set-ups necessitating focus on ensuring down time and negotiating boundaries with others.

Nancy worked with a client who had never held onto a job for more than 18 months because of repeated burnout cycles. They found a job that they loved and desperately wanted to avoid burnout. Empowered through coaching, they negotiated a four-day week, with 10-hour days, working weekends when in flow and taking time off in lieu to compensate. They have been in that job for seven years, have been promoted twice and are now head of department.

Wellbeing activities involving diet and exercise depend on good executive functioning, whereby clients need options for when they are well-spooned or otherwise and support to avoid self-reproach. Insomnia is endemic for people with ADHD, autism and tic disorders, and it may require medical treatment if basic advice about sleep hygiene has proved ineffective. In general, an effective approach to wellbeing is to say, "Let's revisit the basics and look at what's been working (or not) to identify what suits your needs". Such joint review of experience does not assume that they have not tried the obvious but acknowledges experience. Of course, there may be further ideas you might be able to suggest at this point.

Useful coaching tools

We recommend person-centred models with explicit positive regard, including clean language, appreciative enquiry, acceptance and commitment coaching.

Clean language

Clean language avoids limiting thought patterns by asking clean questions. For example, a client might say that they "always found it hard to speak up" in meetings. In an unclean approach, you might follow with the question "Are there other situations where you feel self-conscious?", placing ideas of 'self-consciousness' in their minds. Using clean language coaching (e.g., Linder-Pelz & Lawley, 2015), you could ask, "Is there anything else about it being hard to speak up?" or "When you find it hard to speak up, what would you like to have happen?". Your client is then free to articulate their own 'clean' experience; for example, not knowing how to break into a conversation, or not seeing the point in meetings because they would rather be working on their own projects. Clean language coaching enables you to avoid pre-judging their intention which is helpful for neurodiversity coaching because of divergent models of experience and interpretation (Doyle & Waseem, 2022). The clean coaching model uses a template of 10–20 'clean questions' and no other words or observations that did not come from the client.

Client-focused models

Acceptance and Commitment coaching (Hayes et al., 2004) and Appreciative Inquiry (Cooperrider & Whitney, 2000) are also useful approaches for this client group, as they support the development of self-awareness or drawing one's attention to 'loops' (Oliver, 2004) which replay internal scripts that limit our thinking and behaviour. Both approaches focus on 'grounding' in the present, which helps to promote calm and draw our focus as coaches to asking open questions about values and goals. Thus, they promote a social cognitive learning theory perspective on personal learning (Bandura, 1986), developing self-efficacy, which we have referenced as important framing for coaching in our earlier section. Self-efficacy is developed by identifying an ambition or outcome and working towards it with support from positive role modelling, vicarious learning, feedback and noticing success. Previous loops of failure chip away at the self-efficacy of neurominorities (Nalavany et al., 2017), and in coaching, we can redress this balance by setting realistic, short-term and achievable goals to promote positive self-regard.

Conclusion

Neurodiversity coaching requires an understanding of the history and developmental trajectories of the field, an appreciation of working with potentially vulnerable populations and careful attention to contracting. Relevant conditions are medical grade data which require distinct training, professional development and adequate supervision, given likely case histories of exclusion and lack of success. We encourage engagement with literature on theory and historical trajectories as well as the concepts of stigma and bias to underpin professional development. Given prevalence rates, all coaches are likely to encounter neurodivergent clients and therefore recognising boundaries and competence limits is essential for coaches to protect themselves and their clients. Questioning our own biases and assumptions is a good starting point, as is a focus on client-centred techniques with positive regard. Neurodiversity coaching can be incredibly rewarding, and we encourage all coaches working in this field to evaluate and report successes to grow practice literature.

Reflective questions

1. What is your own experience of neurodiversity in coaching?
2. Where have you come across prejudicial narratives about neurodiversity? How would you address these in coaching?
3. Which typical neurodiversity coaching topics are you curious about, and what are your next steps to learn more?

References

Armstrong, T. (2010). *The Power of Neurodiversity*. De Capo Press.
Astle, D. E., Bathelt, J., & Holmes, J. (2019). Remapping the cognitive and neural profiles of children who struggle at school. *Developmental Science*, 22(1), 1–17. https://doi.org/10.1111/desc.12747
Bandura, A. (1986). *Social Foundations of Social Foundations of Thought and Action*. Prentice Hall.

Berlin, R. (1884). Über Dyslexie [About dyslexia]. *Archiv Für Psychiatrie*, 15, 276–278.

Chapman, R. (2020). Defining neurodiversity for research and practice. In H. B. Rosqvist, N. Chown, & A. Stenning (Eds.), *Neurodiversity Studies: A New Critical Paradigm* (pp. 218–220). Routledge, Taylor & Francis. https://doi.org/10.4324/9780429322297-21

Chapple, M., Davis, P., Billington, J., Myrick, J. A., Ruddock, C., & Corcoran, R. (2021). Overcoming the double empathy problem within Pairs of autistic and non-autistic adults through the contemplation of serious literature. *Frontiers in Psychology*, 12, 708375. https://doi.org/10.3389/fpsyg.2021.708375

Charlton, J. (1998). Nothing about us without us: Disability oppression and empowerment. *University of California Press*. http://www.jstor.org/stable/10.1525/j.ctt1pnqn9

Chen, Y. L., Senande, L. L., Thorsen, M., & Patten, K. (2021). Peer preferences and characteristics of same-group and cross-group social interactions among autistic and non-autistic adolescents. *Autism*, 25(7), 1885–1900.

Cooperrider, D. L., & Whitney, D. (2000). A positive revolution in change: Appreciative inquiry. In *Handbook of Organizational Behavior*, pp. 633–652. Routledge.

Criminal Justice Joint Inspection [CJJI]. (2021). Neurodiversity in the criminal justice system: A review of evidence. *Criminal Justice Joint Inspection*, pp. 1–77. HM Inspectorate of Prisons.

Deol, M. (2022, June 16). Employment tribunal discrimination claims. *IBB Law*. https://www.ibblaw.co.uk/insights/employment-tribunal-discrimination-claims

Doyle, N. (2019). Reasonable adjustments for dyslexia. *Occupational Health at Work*, 16(2), 28–31.

Doyle, N. (2020). Neurodiversity at work: A biopsychosocial model and the impact on working adults. *British Medical Bulletin*, 135, 1–18. https://doi.org/10.1093/bmb/ldaa021

Doyle, N. (2021). Neurodiversity in higher education: Support for neurodiverse individuals and professionals. In L. K. Fung (Ed.), *Neurodiversity: From Phenomenology to Neurobiology and Enhancing Technologies*. American Psychiatric Publishing.

Doyle, N., & Bradley, E. (2022). Disability coaching during a pandemic. *Journal of Work-Applied Management*. https://doi.org/10.1108/JWAM-07-2022-0042

Doyle, N., & McDowall, A. (2015). Is coaching an effective adjustment for dyslexic adults? *Coaching: An International Journal of Theory and Practice Coaching*, 8(2), 154–168. https://doi.org/10.1080/17521882.2015.1065894

Doyle, N., & McDowall, A. (2021). Diamond in the rough? An 'empty review' of research into 'neurodiversity' and a road map for developing the inclusion agenda. *Equality, Diversity and Inclusion: An International Journal*. https://doi.org/10.1108/EDI-06-2020-0172

Doyle, N., McDowall, A., & Waseem, U. (2022b). Intersectional stigma for autistic people at work: A compound adverse impact effect on labor force participation and experiences of belonging. *Autism in Adulthood*. https://doi.org/10.1089/aut.2021.0082

Doyle, N., & Waseem, U. (2022). Using clean language interviewing to explore the lived experience of neurodifferent job applicants. In H. Cairns-Lee, J. Lawley, & P. Tosey (Eds.), *Clean Language Interviewing*. Emerald Publishing Ltd.

Draffan, E. A., James, A., Wilkinson, S., & Viney, D. (2013). Assistive technology and associated training: A survey of students who have received the disabled students' allowances. *Journal of Inclusive Practice in Further and Higher Education*, 5(June 2018), 5–10.

Elsabbagh, M., Divan, G., Koh, Y., Kim, Y., Kauchali, S., Marcín, C., Montiel-Nava, C., Patel, V., Paula, C., Wang, C., Yasamy, M., & Fombonne, E. (2012). Global prevalence of autism and other pervasive developmental disorders. *Autism Research*, 5(3), 160–179. https://doi.org/10.1002/aur.239

Engert, V., & Pruessner, J. (2009). Dopaminergic and noradrenergic contributions to functionality in ADHD: The role of methylphenidate. *Current Neuropharmacology*, 6(4), 322–328. https://doi.org/10.2174/157015908787386069

Equality Act. (2010). http://www.legislation.gov.uk/ukpga/2010/15/introduction

Gifford, G. (2011). *Access to Work: Official Statistics*. DWP.

Goffman, E. (1963). *Stigma: Notes on the Management of Spoiled Identity*. Simon & Schuster.

Grant, D. (2009). The psychological assessment of neurodiversity. In D. Pollak (Ed.), *Neurodiversity in Higher Education* (pp. 33–62). Wiley-Blackwell.

Hayes, S. C., Strosahl, K. D., Bunting, K., Twohig, M., & Wilson, K. G. (2004). What is acceptance and commitment therapy? In *A Practical Guide to Acceptance and Commitment Therapy* (pp. 3–29). Springer.

Hollocks, M. J., Lerh, J. W., Magiati, I., Meiser-Stedman, R., & Brugha, T. S. (2019). Anxiety and depression in adults with autism spectrum disorder: A systematic review and meta-analysis. *Psychological Medicine*, 49(4), 559–572.

Huijg, D. D. (2020). Neuronormativity in theorising agency. In H. B. Rosqvist, N. Chown, & A. Stenning (Eds.), *Neurodiversity Studies: A New Critical Paradigm* (pp. 213–217). Routledge. https://doi.org/10.4324/9780429322297-20

Jensen, J., Lindgren, M., Andersson, K., Ingvar, D. H., & Levander, S. (2000). Cognitive intervention in unemployed individuals with reading and writing disabilities. *Applied Neuropsychology*, 7(4), 223–236. https://doi.org/10.1207/S15324826AN0704_4

Johnson, T. D., & Joshi, A. (2016). Dark clouds or silver linings? A stigma threat perspective on the implications of an autism diagnosis for workplace well-being. *Journal of Applied Psychology*, 101(3), 430–449. https://doi.org/10.1037/apl0000058

Kirby, J. R., Silvestri, R., Allingham, B. H., Parrila, R., & La Fave, C. B. (2008). Learning strategies and study approaches of postsecondary students with dyslexia. *Journal of Learning Disabilities*, 41(1), 85–96.

Kulow, M. D., & Thomas, S. (2019). Assistive technology and the Americans with disabilities act: Endearing employers to these reasonable accommodations. *Berkeley Journal of Employment & Labor Law*, 40(2), 257. https://doi.org/10.15779/Z38CZ32542

Lai, M. C., Lombardo, M. V., Ruigrok, A. N. V., Chakrabarti, B., Auyeung, B., Szatmari, P., Happé, F., & Baron-Cohen, S. (2017). Quantifying and exploring camouflaging in men and women with autism. *Autism*, 21(6), 690–702. https://doi.org/10.1177/1362361316671012

Lerner, D. A., Verheul, I., & Thurik, R. (2019). Entrepreneurship and attention deficit/hyperactivity disorder: A large-scale study involving the clinical condition of ADHD. *Small Business Economics*, 53(2), 381–392. https://doi.org/10.1007/s11187-018-0061-1

Levin, R. L., & Rawana, J. S. (2016). Attention-deficit/hyperactivity disorder and eating disorders across the lifespan: A systematic review of the literature. *Clinical Psychology Review*, 50, 22–36. https://doi.org/10.1016/j.cpr.2016.09.010

Lewin, K. (1936). *Principles of Topographical Psychology*. McGraw-Hill.

Linder-Pelz, S., & Lawley, J. (2015). Using clean language to explore the subjectivity of clients' experience and outcomes. *International Coaching Psychology Review*, 10(2), 161–174.

Majeed, N. M., Hartanto, A., & Tan, J. J. (2021). Developmental dyslexia and creativity: A meta-analysis. *Dyslexia*, 27(2), 187–203.

Masuch, T., Bea, M., Alm, B., Deibler, P., & Sobanski, E. (2019). Internalized stigma, anticipated discrimination and perceived public stigma in adults with ADHD. *Attention Deficit and Hyperactivity Disorders*, 11(211–220). https://doi.org/10.1007/s12402-018-0274-9

Meilleur, A. A. S., Jelenic, P., & Mottron, L. (2015). Prevalence of clinically and empirically defined talents and strengths in autism. *Journal of Autism and Developmental Disorders*, 45(5), 1354–1367. https://doi.org/10.1007/s10803-014-2296-2

Melville, D. & Stevens, C. (2015). Access to Work – Cost benefit analysis. *Royal National Institute of Blind People (RNIB)*. Research Report. https://www.rnib.org.uk/professionals/health-social-care-education-professionals/knowledge-and-research-hub/reports-and-insight/access-to-work-cost-benefit-analysis/

Milton, D., Gurbuz, E., & Lopez, B. (2022). The 'double empathy problem': Ten years on. *Autism*. https://doi.org/13623613221129123

Miserando, C. (2018). The spoon theory. In L. Davis (Ed.), *Beginning with Disability* (1st ed., p. 5). Routledge. https://doi.org/10.4324/9781315453217

Miyasaka, M., Kajimura, S., & Nomura, M. (2018). Biases in understanding attention deficit hyperactivity disorder and autism spectrum disorder in Japan. *Frontiers in Psychology*, 9(Feb), 1–13. https://doi.org/10.3389/fpsyg.2018.00244

Nalavany, B. A., Logan, J. M., & Carawan, L. W. (2017). The relationship between emotional experience with dyslexia and work self-efficacy among adults with dyslexia. *Dyslexia*, 24(1), 1–16. https://doi.org/10.1002/dys.1575

O'Broin, A., & Palmer, S. (2010). Introducing an interpersonal perspective on the coaching relationship. In S. Palmer & A. McDowall (Eds.), *The Coaching Relationship* (pp. 9–33). Routledge, Taylor & Francis.

Oliver, C. (2004). Reflexive inquiry and the strange loop tool. *Human Systems: The Journal of Systemic Consultation and Management*, 15(2), 127–140.

Office of National Statistics [ONS]. (2019). Disability and employment, UK. *Office of National Statistics* (pp. 1–19). https://www.ons.gov.uk/peoplepopulationandcommunity/healthandsocialcare/disability/bulletins/disabilityandemploymentuk/2019

Palmer, S., & McDowall, A. (2010). The coaching relationship: Putting people first: An introduction. In S. Palmer & A. McDowall (Eds.), *The Coaching Relationship* (pp. 1–8). Routledge, Taylor & Francis.

Pearson, A., & Rose, K. (2021). A conceptual analysis of autistic masking: Understanding the narrative of stigma and the illusion of choice. *Autism in Adulthood*, 3(1), 52–60. https://doi.org/10.1089/aut.2020.0043

Pecora, L., Hooley, M., Sperry, L., Mesibov, G., & Stokes, M. (2020). Sexuality and gender issues in individuals with autism spectrum disorder. *Child and Adolescent Psychiatric Clinics*, 29(3), 111–124.

Pollack, D. (Ed.). (2009). *Neurodiversity in Higher Education*. Wiley-Blackwell.

Roman-Urrestarazu, A., Van Kessel, R., Allison, C., Matthews, F. E., Brayne, C., & Baron-Cohen, S. (2021). Association of race/ethnicity and social disadvantage with autism prevalence in 7 million school children in England. *JAMA Pediatrics*, 175(6), 1–11. https://doi.org/10.1001/jamapediatrics.2021.0054

Santuzzi, A. M., & Waltz, P. R. (2016). Disability in the workplace: A unique and variable identity. *Journal of Management*, 42(5), 1111–1135.

Shoukry, H., & Cox, E. (2018). Coaching as a social process. *Management Learning*, 49(4), 413–428.

Singer, J. (1998). *Odd People In: The Birth of Community Amongst People on the 'Autistic Spectrum': A Personal Exploration of a New Social Movement based on Neurological Diversity.* University of Technology.

Singer, J. (1999). 'Why can't you be normal for once in your life?' From a problem with no name to the emergence of a new category of difference. In M. Corker & S. French (Eds.), *Disability Discourse* (pp. 59–67). Open University Press.

Siugzdaite, R., Bathelt, J., Holmes, J., & Astle, D. E. (2020). Transdiagnostic brain mapping in developmental disorders. *Current Biology*, 30(7), 1245–1257.e4. https://doi.org/10.1016/j.cub.2020.01.078

Snowling, M. J. (2010). Dyslexia. In C. L. Cooper, J. Field, U. Goswami, R. Jenkins, & B. J. Sahakian (Eds.), *Mental Capital and Mental Wellbeing* (pp. 775–783). Blackwell.

Snowling, M. J., Adams, J. W., Bowyer-Crane, C., & Tobin, V. A. (2000). Levels of literacy among juvenile offenders: The incidence of specific reading difficulties. *Criminal Behaviour and Mental Health*, 10(4), 229–241. https://doi.org/10.1002/cbm.362

Ssucharewa, D. G. E. (1927). Die schizoiden Psychopathien im Kindesalter. *Monatsschrift für Psychiatrie und Neurologie*, 62(3), 171–200.

Sun, J., Zhuang, K., Li, H., Wei, D., Zhang, Q., & Qiu, J. (2018). Perceiving rejection by others: Relationship between rejection sensitivity and the spontaneous neuronal activity of the brain. *Social Neuroscience*, 13(4), 429–438.

Taylor, H., Fernandes, B., & Wraight, S. (2021). The evolution of complementary cognition: Humans cooperatively adapt and evolve through a system of collective cognitive search. *Cambridge Archaeological Journal*, 1–17. https://doi.org/10.1017/s0959774321000329

United Nations (2006). Convention on the Rights of Persons with Disabilities. ixty-first session of the General Assembly by resolution A/RES/61/106. https://www.ohchr.org/en/instruments-mechanisms/instruments/convention-rights-persons-disabilities

Warrier, V., Greenberg, D. M., Weir, E., Buckingham, C., Smith, P., Lai, M.-C., Allison, C., & Baron-Cohen, S. (2020). Elevated rates of autism, other neurodevelopmental and psychiatric diagnoses, and autistic traits in transgender and gender-diverse individuals. *Nature Communications*, 11(1), 3959. https://doi.org/10.1038/s41467-020-17794-1

Weber, C., Krieger, B., Häne, E., Yarker, J., & McDowall, A. (2022). Physical workplace adjustments to support neurodivergent workers: A systematic review. *Applied Psychology*, apps.12431. https://doi.org/10.1111/apps.12431

Weiss, J. A., & Fardella, M. A. (2018). Victimization and perpetration experiences of adults with autism. *Frontiers in Psychiatry*, 9, 203. https://doi.org/10.3389/fpsyt.2018.00203

Wissell, S., Karimi, L., Serry, T., Furlong, L., & Hudson, J. (2022). "You don't look dyslexic": Using the job demands – Resource model of burnout to explore employment experiences of Australian adults with dyslexia. *International Journal of Environmental Research and Public Health*, 19(17), 10719. https://doi.org/10.3390/ijerph191710719

Young, S., Adamo, N., Ásgeirsdóttir, B. B., Branney, P., Beckett, M., Colley, W., Cubbin, S., Deeley, Q., Farrag, E., Gudjonsson, G., Hill, P., Hollingdale, J., Kilic, O., Lloyd, T., Mason, P., Paliokosta, E., Perecherla, S., Sedgwick, J., Skirrow, C.,. . . Woodhouse, E. (2020). Females with ADHD: An expert consensus statement taking a lifespan approach providing guidance for the identification and treatment of attention-deficit/hyperactivity disorder in girls and women. *BMC Psychiatry*, 20(1), 404. https://doi.org/10.1186/s12888-020-02707-9

Young, S., González, R. A., Fridman, M., Hodgkins, P., Kim, K., & Gudjonsson, G. H. (2018). The economic consequences of attention-deficit hyperactivity disorder in the Scottish prison system. *BMC Psychiatry*, 18, 1–11. https://doi.org/10.1186/s12888-018-1792-x

Zeidan, J., Fombonne, E., Scorah, J., Ibrahim, A., Durkin, M. S., Saxena, S., Yusuf, A., Shih, A., & Elsabbagh, M. (2022). Global prevalence of autism: A systematic review update search strategy. *Autism Research*, February, 1–13. https://doi.org/10.1002/aur.2696

Chapter 16

Coaching for health equity

Margaret Moore, Simon Matthews, Kelly Davis Martin, and Sheryl Richard

Introduction

The construct of health equity reminds coaches that the societal variance in levels of health and wellbeing are not simply the result of genetics and behaviours. Health and wellbeing are also affected, if not determined, by social and economic processes that generate uneven distribution of access to health-generating resources. In this chapter, we review the research confirming health inequity, particularly the global disparities in health outcomes. We name the social and economic resources that support health, spanning individual, group, and societal dimensions. We explore the value demonstrated by coaching for under-resourced populations emerging from the coaching outcomes literature. The chapter's coaching framework proposes additional development for individual coaches, enhanced coaching skills and processes, and at the big picture level calls coaches to the societal opportunity of coaching stewardship. Coaches and coaching are well-positioned to step up, lean in, and support health equity for all.

Defining health equity

Since 1946, the World Health Organization (WHO) has defined health as being greater than simply the absence of illness, disease, or infirmity. Instead, health is defined as an individual's state of complete physical, mental, and social wellbeing (WHO, 2024). Implicit in the WHO construct of wellbeing is that all individuals have the right, through good health, to function productively in their societies by producing goods and services, contributing to local economies, seeking opportunities for education, and interacting socially with friends and family members. The tenet that health is a fundamental human right – inalienable from such rights as those of assembly, participation in government, work, leisure, and education – has been upheld to the present time (Hunt, 2016).

Building on the WHO foundation, Braveman and colleagues (2018) offer a useful two-part definition of health equity. The first element confirms that all human beings have the same opportunity to live as healthy and fulfilling a life as possible – the "level playing field" idea. The second element acknowledges that steps to address disparities in healthcare systems and structures are necessary. Access to resources and removal of barriers are not sufficient to ensure that marginalised groups have opportunities for robust health. In many cases, positive societal steps in favour of minority groups are essential.

Most countries fall short of health equity; just as with socioeconomic status, health and wellbeing are not equitably distributed within and across nations. The U.S. federal

DOI: 10.4324/9781003319016-18

health prevention agenda "Healthy People 2020" includes health equity among its four goals: (1) attain high-quality, longer lives free of preventable disease, disability, injury, and premature death; (2) achieve health equity, eliminate disparities, and improve the health of all groups; (3) create social and physical environments that promote good health for all; and (4) promote quality of life, healthy development, and healthy behaviours across all life stages (Koh et al., 2014).

The U.S. "Quintuple Aim of health care" adds health equity to the existing Quadruple Aim of improving the individual experience of care for patients, improving the health of populations, reducing the per capita cost of care, and improving the experience of health care professionals. Elevating health equity to the status of a distinct aim is necessary to address persistent health inequities that disproportionately affect under-represented and minoritised groups (Farrell et al., 2022)

The following findings support consistent themes of health inequity globally related to race, social class, social status, sex, and their impact on access to health resources. By 2022, the New Zealand government reported that equity gains had been made for Māori children in comparison to non-Māori, with respect to vaccination rates, while simultaneously acknowledging that Māori health status generally remains unequal with non-Māori while morbidity and mortality rates remain higher for Māori (Wehipeihana et al., 2022). The Australian government document "Australia's Health: Data insights 2022" (AIHW, 2022) devotes two of its ten chapters to the health gaps of culturally and linguistically diverse populations and the Indigenous Aboriginal Australians, while a 2020 population study in Canada revealed that the Indigenous Métis have a life expectancy 5–6 years lower than other Canadians (Cooper et al., 2020).

Research on health equity and health outcomes

Current research on health equity also highlights major race and social disparities in health outcomes. Importantly, there are also indications that overlapping disadvantages associated with social categorisations increase or compound these disparities.

Several large studies support this position. For example, in a sample of nearly 26,000 participants, researchers identified a lower gender-based rate of ischaemic stroke in white and Black women between the ages of 45 and 64, compared to men in each racial grouping (Albright et al., 2018).

Zimmerman and Anderson (2019) surveyed 25 years of data (1993–2017) to investigate variations and trends in health equity across that time for more than 5.5 million U.S. respondents aged 18–64 years. They used two outcome measures: self-rated general health and the number of healthy days in the previous month. In relation to Black vs white equity, the authors concluded that there was clear evidence of "stagnation" in health equity progress for Blacks by some measures and unambiguous evidence of decline in other measures.

In Australia, Landers and colleagues (2019) reported that despite Australia's world position as an income- and resource-rich country, the prevalence of diabetic retinopathy (as an end-stage complication of type 2 diabetes mellitus) has almost doubled over the previous two decades and is consistently higher in Indigenous compared to non-Indigenous groups.

Lane and colleagues (2018) reported that both immigrant and refugee children arriving in Canada are at risk of disparities in health when compared with Canadian-born

Table 16.1 What are social resources?

Environment	Personal	Societal equity
Neighbourhood conditions	Early childhood experiences	Race
Clean, water, air, environment	Social support	Gender
No crime and violence	Income	Age
Workplace safety	Education	Socio-economic
Transportation	Employment	Healthcare access
Healthy food access	Food security	Mental health
Physical activity	Coaching	

Adapted from Berkowitz (2023).

children due to the impacts of marginalisation and their parents' reduced access to social, health and educational resources and systems.

Data from the UK highlighted similar inequalities during COVID19. There was significant racial disparity in COVID19 mortality among people of Black African descent compared to white British people (Otu et al., 2020).

Responding to this growing body of evidence, in the United States, the descriptor social determinants of health (SDOH) has emerged. These "determinants" may be better described as social resources, summarised in Table 16.1 including environmental, personal, and societal equity factors. To this framework we have added the idea that coaching is a social resource, with the potential to improve social capital in disadvantaged populations.

The U.S. National Academies of Sciences in 2019 published a report titled: "Integrating Social Care into the Delivery of Healthcare: Moving Upstream to Improve the Nation's Health" (NASEM, 2019). The opening paragraph speaks to the broadening of healthcare to improve SDOH:

> The consistent and compelling evidence concerning how social determinants shape health has led to a growing recognition throughout the health care sector that improvements in overall health metrics are likely to depend – at least in part – on attention being paid to these social determinants.

Can coaching improve health equity?

A key question is whether coaching as a modality has the capacity to address issues of inequity. Braveman and colleagues (2018) revises the question to ask: Can coaching provide fair opportunities for all human beings to live as healthily as possible, and can coaching lead to autonomy and empowerment in health-seeking behaviours and remove barriers and obstacles, together generating better health and wellbeing? In summary, can coaches be a positive force in improving health equity?

Though at its core coaching supports autonomy, healthcare systems are not inherently empowering systems; there is a power differential between clinicians and patients. In a review addressing the power imbalance, Strickler (2009) concludes that a lack of patient autonomy is a structural component of healthcare systems, noting that the "mental health care system at times expects that people will be submissive and follow all treatment, but this is at times unhealthy" (p. 316). For patients who are already marginalised in some way – by virtue of income, educational level, gender, and/or social or citizenship status – such differences in power relationships can deepen their experience of disenfranchisement.

A coaching approach can be empowering, since it is natively intended as humble and collaborative (Moore et al., 2016), meeting people where they are as equals and without judgement. Coaching may enable marginalised patients to feel more respected and supported, and to become more engaged and confident.

Evidence for coaching in socially disadvantaged populations

A growing body of empirical evidence, primarily in the United States, demonstrates clinically significant health outcomes of healthcare-based coaching interventions in patients lacking health equity. In 2015, the Camden Coalition of Healthcare Providers published its COACH Manual (COACH framework, n.d.) as a basis for what it calls "hotspotting," bringing intensive resources to low-income patients with the most complex needs. This group emphasises the "authentic healing relationship" as a stabilising force and the core driver of behaviour change. The Coalition also works at the systems-level to improve collaboration and integration of healthcare systems and social services agencies in New Jersey, USA. A randomised study of the hotspotting programme showed reduced hospital readmission rates of 800 hospitalised patients with medically and socially complex conditions from 62% to 23% (Finkelstein et al., 2020). This model provides coaches with inspiration to focus on a trusting one-on-one partnership, while having a systems-based mindset.

Two large, high profile randomised controlled studies are worthy of note. Katzmarzyk and colleagues (2020) conducted a cluster-randomised trial to assess the efficacy of a high-intensity, lifestyle-based programme for primary care-based obesity treatment delivered by health coaches in low-income and rural populations. Approximately two-thirds of the study participants were Black. At the conclusion of the 24-month intervention, those in the coaching group had experienced a clinically significant weight loss, which was also significantly greater than those in the usual care group.

The second study, conducted by Nguyen-Huynh and colleagues (2022), was a four-year randomised controlled study of a 12-month telephone coaching intervention for Black adults, who have higher rates of hypertension, cardiovascular disease, and stroke than do white adults. The authors described telephone delivery as part of a culturally appropriate modality for coaching sessions. Health coaching – but not enhanced pharmacotherapy – effectively helped Black adults control their hypertension (BP < 140/90), with this effect continuing for three years after the intervention. Adherence to the intervention was important, as those in the coaching group who had completed at least six telephone coaching sessions were significantly more likely to achieve blood pressure control than those in usual care.

Beyond these two strong studies, Ruffin (2016) and Dennis and colleagues (2013) demonstrated the efficacy of a coaching approach (including telephone-based coaching) for underserved groups managing chronic disease. Other research has medical assistants (MAs) providing administrative support to physicians in patient care as health coaches. Willard-Grace and colleagues (2015) reported that MA health coaches successfully supported a group of low-income patients to reduce HbA1C (haemoglobin A1C) and LDL-C (low-density lipoprotein cholesterol) levels, thereby improving control over diabetes and hypertension. Ruggiero and colleagues (2014) and Ivey and colleagues (2012) demonstrated the use of coaching approaches by MAs to improve self-care and HbA1c levels for non-English speakers of ethnic/racial minorities.

Thom and colleagues (2014) reported that the coaching approach used by MAs led to an increase in trust in the patients' physicians. This supports the "common factor" ideas of Duncan and colleagues (2010) that the practitioner/patient relationship is key in starting and sustaining behavioural change.

Coaching for health equity in practice

Given that there is strong evidence of the positive effects of coaching in the following subsections, we set out a "coaching for health equity framework" (Table 16.2). It starts by addressing the individual coach level – what coaches need to do to be prepared for this work, including self and system awareness, readiness for growth, and cultural competence. The second level is the coaching work itself, including stabilising and collaborating. The third societal level we call coaching stewardship – the field of coaching as a collective works together to bring equity and social resources into the practice of coaching. This framework builds upon the Astin & Astin Social Change Model of Leadership Development (Astin & Astin, 1996) and starts with the individual, moving to the professional group, and then to society.

Level 1: Individual-level coach

Striving for health equity in coaching requires a shift for coaches. The first priority is not the typical support of an individual's self-determination and self-actualisation. It starts with oneself – recognising one's well-intentioned and unconscious, although collectively harmful, participation in the societal system that creates health inequity. A second shift is feeling a part of societal initiatives that improve individual and systemic health inequity. Coaches have the opportunity to rise to a higher purpose, beyond a healthy patient or client, to embracing the goal of a healthy society. The upward shift of consciousness for coaches includes the following.

1. Finding new meaning and purpose in improving health equity.
2. Seeing individuals within a systemic context – both influencing and being influenced by their place in a community and society.

Table 16.2 Coaching for health equity framework

Individual-level coach	Group-level coaching competencies	Society-level coaching stewardship
Conscious of self: examine bias	Stabilise: esteem, belonging, safety	Stewardship: leverage social resources
Commitment: embrace growth	Collaborate: autonomy, efficacy	Change: build equity into practice
Congruence: broaden cultural competency		

3. Committing to overcoming one's own perceptions and biases toward people lacking social resources.
4. Expanding one's zone of compassion to include everyone, particularly people who are disadvantaged and of different races and backgrounds.
5. Accepting that coaching for health equity is challenging and requires a commitment to personal growth.

Conscious of self: examine bias

The universality of human bias is well-explored by UK psychologist Pragya Agarwal. In the context of improving healthy equity, a coach will notice and greet their own biases toward people who are disadvantaged at every turn. The work of a coach is to constantly examine and re-examine their own biases, tempered by genuine compassion toward themselves as they continuously improve their objectivity. Agarwal describes the common tendency to over-focus on the negative features of a particular category of people (e.g., race, education, income, social status), and then generalise those negative features to everyone in that category. She also observes that in this process, the unique and complex characteristics of everyone are diminished, along with a capacity for empathy and patience. Under stress, all these automatic reactions get worse (Agarwal, 2020).

Biases trigger real harm for those receiving bias. The foundational psychological needs of self-esteem, belonging, and safety are not met. The stress and anxiety of discrimination harms performance and health. The reduced access to resources and opportunities from childhood onward puts brakes on the realisation of potential.

While not immune from the automatic human tendency toward bias, coaches come trained to cultivate a deeper presence to greet others with accepting, trust-generating compassion, as well as a genuine, open interest, without judgement, in the other's experience. A sincere curiosity and exploration of "what it is like to live a day in the other's life" is important to deepen understanding and compassion.

The coach's primary tool for expressing curiosity and approaching the experience of another with a genuinely open mind is the skill of inquiry (Matthews, 2023). Cultivating a capacity for genuine interest in, curiosity about and desire to partner with others is a foundational feature of accomplished coaching which might dismantle the effects of bias.

In summary, when coaching those with limited social resources:

- Accept responsibility, with grace, of one's higher levels of social resources, education, and opportunities.
- Continually examine and challenge one's own biases, attitudes, assumptions, stereotypes, and prejudices.

Commitment: embrace growth

Coaching the underserved is a challenging force of growth for the coach. It is personally uncomfortable to continually examine one's biases, judgements, and preconceived notions about others with social disadvantages. It is not easy to win the trust of someone who has endured major adversity, as well as minor and major aggressions that are the daily experiences of inequity. It is painful to watch the struggles of those dealing with complex and chronic adversity.

In response to these challenges, the *growth mindset* (Dweck, 2012) inherent in the coach approach creates a platform of openness to learning and integration of new perspectives for both client and coach. This mindset can be directed towards learning about oneself, the client, and the intersections each has with the social context in which they find themselves. By adopting a "ground zero" mindset (Moore, 2023, p. 634), the coach "holds space" for the client to feel safe. Importantly, this mindset also creates space for the coach to grow new insights about their own practice and what gets in the way of their coaching – including biases, judgements, and preconceptions about others. Over time, through this growth process, coaches expand their awareness of the social forces that create and sustain identity and begin to see themselves and others as shaped by their social conditions. Thankfully, the higher purpose of improving health equity provides high quality motivation on the steep growth journey.

Coaches must take great care in not fostering a power differential and well-intentioned dependency. Self-care is also vital in order to continually refresh compassion and commitment to help others who are struggling. It takes inner strength to maintain confidence, hope, and optimism in self, coaching, and the other, in the face of low levels of social resources and chronic instability.

Congruence: broaden cultural competency

According to Jones (2000), demonstrating cultural competence is the ability to effectively interact with people from cultures different from one's own. Such competence involves possessing and enacting the knowledge, skills, and abilities necessary for providing equitable, person-centred care despite cultural differences. In coaching, cultural competence starts with being well-informed on cultural norms, perspectives, and practices, and maintaining a deep interest in a client's experiences and social resources. Coaches need to appreciate the depth of cultural factors that affect self-expression (such as clothing, hair, cuisine, family rituals, friendship rituals, and ceremonies) and use culturally appropriate language (such as a person's preferred pronouns, and being sure to learn about and then pronounce names properly). At the same time, it is important to avoid the phenomenon of generalising cultural dimensions to an individual. Being present to the uniqueness of each client is vital.

The notion of "cultural humility" emerged more recently and can be defined as: "a lifelong commitment to self-evaluation and critique, to redressing power imbalances . . . and to developing mutually beneficial and non-paternalistic partnerships with communities on behalf of individuals and defined populations" (Greene-Morton & Minkler, 2020, p. 1). Coaching starts with deep humility and curiosity about a client's perspectives, and this mindset is deepened in coaching those with disadvantaged lives.

Among cultural competence scholars, there is a recent shift from using cultural competence to cultural safety as necessary for achieving health equity (Curtis et al., 2019). Cultural safety requires cultivating a safe environment where there is listening with no challenge, assault, or denial of an individual's identity and needs. It entails stable respect while stretching to attune to the meaning, knowledge, and experiences of people of different cultures and backgrounds (Kickett, 2020).

It is important to call out the importance of race as a social dimension and construct, and recognise the understanding of racism as a system of oppression that harms individual health and wellbeing. Another cultural competency, a way forward to help change the system, is to actively be anti-racist (Kendi, 2019), which means going beyond typical action to provide extra support to people who are experiencing or who have experienced racism. A good example of anti-racist coaching could be to seek out and deliver pro bono coaching exclusively to an underserved population.

Level 2: Group-level coaching competencies

Now we outline two domains of coaching competencies for clients who have low levels of social resources. We start with the focus on helping a client become more stable, and from there collaborate on the way forward.

Stabilise – esteem, belonging, safety

Typically, in health and wellbeing coaching, as encoded in the National Board for Health and Wellness Coaching competencies, the coach supports a client in developing a vision for their health and wellbeing (NBHWC, n.d.). However, clients with low social resources may be experiencing significant instability in their family, home, and work lives, which derails their envisioning of a path to growth. Scott Barry Kaufman recently rebuilt Maslow's hierarchy into a sailboat – whereby the hull represents stabilising forces including psychological safety, social belonging, and self-esteem (Kaufman, 2021). The bottom half of the boat keeps us afloat as the secure base we need to feel physically, intrapersonally, and interpersonally safe. Kaufman distinguishes deficit needs as "what we lack" and growth needs as those that "pull us toward what we value or desire (intrinsic fulfilment) without worrying about mere survival." (Martela, 2020).

The starting place in coaching for health equity is to support a client in becoming more stable. Stability is the prerequisite for cultivating autonomy, efficacy, and a sense of personal achievement, key principles of behaviour change that are essential to effective coaching (Deci & Ryan, 2008). The coach must be aware of both the supports and restraints which may be acting on individual clients in the pursuit of their autonomy.

In considering the supports and restraints, there are several dimensions to which a coach must attend in helping a client create more safety and stability. First, coaches internalise the understanding that reduced access to social resources affects resilience, wellbeing, and health outcomes. Notwithstanding this understanding, a key coaching task is to take an appreciative perspective of any sources of stability which may be present, and then support the client to identify strategies to increase these stabilising resources. In managing this exploration, the coach demonstrates flexibility and agile responsiveness to clients, and competence in appropriately referring clients when the circumstances may be beyond the scope of coaching. For example, many clients with low social resources may have mental health deficits, and it is important for coaches to know where to find mental health resources for their clients.

Coaching for esteem and belonging rests on important coaching principles of curiosity, compassion, and appreciation. Curiosity is the skill which supports understanding each client's unique experience of social resources. Compassion supports coaches to maintain an abiding interest in the circumstances the client faces, in addition to supporting the client to cultivate effective responses to challenging situations. Approaching client interactions with an appreciative mindset allows the coach to draw from, acknowledge, explore, and affirm client strengths, values, and autonomous motivation. Together, these can improve self-esteem.

Collaborate: autonomy and efficacy

Collaboration in coaching for health equity has two dimensions: the "coach–client" collaboration and the "coach–system" collaboration. These will be addressed in turn. Collaboration starts with cultivating autonomy: meeting the client where they are, empowering the client to be in the driver's seat, and honouring a client's choice of focus, goals, and specific behaviours. Another area to cultivate autonomy is to draw out a client's wishes for their wellbeing. A client with low social resources may well have a different perspective on the meaning of wellbeing than the models that are applied in coaching – such as the WHO thriving model (WHO, 2024), self-determination theory (Deci & Ryan, 2008) and concepts from positive psychology, including positive emotion, engagement, relationships, meaning and accomplishments (PERMA) and flourishing (Seligman, 2018), the Virtues in Action character strengths inventory (VIA Institute on Character, n.d.) and Positivity Ratio (Fredrickson, 2013).

It is vital that coaches support clients in identifying or crafting their own model of wellbeing, based on what wellbeing means for the client.

Arao and Clemens (2013) have provided a helpful framework for the development of collaboration in their work on "brave spaces," which is a shift from the notion of "safe spaces" and relevant here. *Safe spaces* are supportive environments of psychological safety where individual expression is encouraged, acknowledged, and affirmed without pressure to educate, fear of judgement or repercussion, or subjection to biases, microaggressions, or any other harm. *Brave spaces* encourage inclusive dialogue and interaction in which learning, sharing, and growing are supported, although they involve some level of vulnerability, discomfort, and accountability.

The five elements of brave spaces in a coaching context which can be drawn from this framework are the embracing of different perspectives and avoidance of binary "right/ wrong" thinking, attuning oneself to the impact of the process of coaching on the client (including owning coaching intentions, and their intended or unintended effects), honouring autonomy by co-creating the space for clients to choose what is important to them and what they wish to focus on, maintaining respect for implicit and explicit capacities of the client, and upholding the principle of *"primum non nocere"* ("first, do no harm) in the coach–client relationship.

The second element of collaboration is that the coach works with other members of the healthcare system to ensure that the client has access to necessary and desirable treatment, support, and encouragement towards the attainment of their own personal vision. This dimension of collaboration is largely operationalised in the International Coaching Federation's Core Competency model (ICF, n.d.). The skills required of the coach in this area include seeking client agreement about contact with other parties (if required), clarifying the specific parties with whom information may be shared, engaging in clear reasoning and justification for sharing information, and involving the client directly in conversations with other healthcare team members (rather than having conversations "about the client").

The process of collaboration enhances the client's role in decision-making about their own health and wellbeing, the goals they wish to set, and the actions which are important to them. Coaches are then enfranchising the disenfranchised in their care of their own health and wellbeing.

Level 3: Society-level coaching stewardship

Perhaps more so in coaching for health equity than other coaching specialties, coaches have the opportunity to be more connected, aligned, and active in improving societal equity at a higher level. There is a unique opportunity for coaching stewardship; the coach or coaches together can engage directly in promoting with societal-level social resources and integration of equity into all aspects of collective coaching practice.

Leverage social resources

At the level of *stewardship* in the Social Change Model (Komives et al., 2017), a coach has a responsibility to support the client to fully harness the social resources available to them, in addition to a responsibility to become an "activist for change." An analogy might be considering whether it is sufficient to support drivers to avoid potholes on a road and to navigate that particular stretch safely and efficiently, or whether that person – now aware of the limitations – also has a responsibility to alert and lobby the relevant authority for change that will make the road inherently more navigable and safe.

These social resources are numerous and may include friendship networks, extended family support networks, educational support, healthcare support, employment relationships, and many others. The skilled coach recognises the social resources available to the client and also discerns, through the coaching relationship, the degree to which the client is connected to and able to make use of those resources. Furthermore, the systemic link between social and personal resources is understood by the coach. Personal resources such as resilience, determination, "stickability" or "grit," and many others, are influenced by and influence the social resources available to a client.

Change: build equity into daily practice

Creating a coaching practice that embodies social and health equity requires an intentional and mindful approach. In drawing together the described competencies, there are three broad tasks in coaching for health equity which summarised in the following list as Dream, Design and Demand, followed by Table 16.2 listing potential strategies for coaching stewardship.

1. Create a coaching practice that is active in increasing health equity (such as by providing pro bono coaching) ("Dream").
2. Experiment and refine competencies, skills, and processes in coaching that can effectively address inequity ("Design").
3. Advocate at community and societal levels for structural change to address inequity ("Demand").

For many coaches and coach communities, among the most meaningful learning and coaching work will focus on improving societal and health equity. Empathic coaching

Table 16.3 Coaching Strategies for Coaching Stewardship

1. Be goal-directed in seeking to address inequity.
2. Increase fair access to coaching services – such as through telehealth – for people who may not be able to meet face-to-face or access video conferencing.
3. Consider equity-based pricing in coaching such as sliding scale fees for service, pro bono work, or being paid per hour what your client is paid per hour.
4. Make a social impact with coaching services. Work for community organisations (or collaborate/volunteer) for populations currently under-represented in coaching.
5. Coach community leaders around health diversity, equity, and inclusion.
6. Receive mentorship and/or supervision for continued professional and personal growth.
7. Be a social change agent. Champion culturally competent organisations. Stand up for social justice causes.
8. Share your financial resources to support diverse populations.
9. Travel, read, ask, and learn.

seeks to be mindful and awake to health inequities and how one can contribute at the individual, community, and societal levels. The journey of attending to and outgrowing one's biases, becoming culturally competent, helping to stabilise, creating safe and brave spaces that empower autonomy and lift up self-efficacy, and engaging in coaching stewardship together enrich the work of coaches and the thriving of coaches and the communities of which they are a part.

Conclusion

Inequity of social and economic resources is pervasive and getting worse in many contexts. Without dedicated attention to improving the factors which generate health inequity, good health outcomes will favour the socially resourced and economically advantaged. The challenge for all coaches in health and wellbeing is to not only deliver high quality, evidence-based services, but to help distribute positive outcomes to all members of a community. It is time for coaches to play a life-giving role as social resources for those dealing with some or many challenges related to childhood experience, social inclusion, education, income, employment, and access to health and social services.

Reflective questions

1. What health inequities have you directly observed (rather than simply being aware of) in your own life?
2. What is an example in your own life in which you have been able to positively affect an inequity (in health or another social dimension)?
3. What next steps do you wish to take on your own coaching journey to improve health equity?

References

Agarwal, P. (2020). *Sway: Unravelling Unconscious Bias*. Bloomsbury.
Albright, K. C., Huang, L., Blackburn, J., Howard, G., Mullen, M., Bittner, V., Muntner, P., & Howard, V. (2018). Racial differences in recurrent ischemic stroke risk and recurrent stroke case fatality. *Neurology*, 91(19), e1741–e1750. https://doi.org/10.1212/WNL.0000000000006467

Arao, B. & Clemens, K. (2013). From safe spaces to brave spaces. In L. Landerman (Ed.), *The Art of Effective Facilitation* (pp. 135–150). Stylus Publishing.

Astin, H. S. & Astin, A. W. (1996). *A Social Change Model of Leadership Guidebook, Version III*. https://www.dickinson.edu/info/20380/student_leadership/3795/social_change_model_of_leadership_development

Australian Institute of Health and Welfare (2022). Australia's Health 2022: Data Insights (2022). https://www.aihw.gov.au/reports/australias-health/australias-health-2022-data-insights/about

Berkowitz, S. A. (2023). Health care's new emphasis on social determinants of health. *NEJM Catalyst Innovations in Care Delivery*. https;//doi.org/10.1056/CAT.23.0070

Braveman, P., Arkin, E., Orleans, T., Proctor, D., Acker, J., & Plough, A. (2018). What is health equity? *Behavioral Science & Policy*, 4(1), 1–14. https://doi.org/10.1177/003335491412915S2

COACH Framework. (n.d.). *Camden Coalition*. Retrieved May 10, 2023, from http://camden-health.org/care-interventions/the-coach-model

Cooper, E. J., Sanguins, J., Menec, V., Chartrand, A. F., Carter, S., & Driedger, S. M. (2020). Culturally responsive supports for Metis Elders and Metis family caregivers. *Canadian Journal on Aging/La Revue Canadienne du vieillissement*, 39(2), 206–219. https://doi.org/10.1017/S0714980819000321

Curtis, E., Jones, R., Tipene-Leach, D., Walker, C., Loring, B., Paine, S., & Reid, P. (2019). Why cultural safety rather than cultural competency is required to achieve health equity: A literature review and recommended definition. *International Journal for Equity in Health* 18, 174. https://doi.org/10.1186/s12939-019-1082-3

Deci, E. L. & Ryan, R. M. (2008). Self-determination theory: A macrotheory of human motivation, development, and health. *Canadian Psychology/Psychologie Canadienne*, 49(3), 182. https://doi.org/10.1037/a0012801

Dennis, S. M., Harris, M., Lloyd, J., Davies, G. P., Faruqi, N., & Zwar, N. (2013). Do people with existing chronic conditions benefit from telephone coaching? A rapid review. *Australian Health Review*, 37(3), 381–388. https://doi.org/10.1071/AH13005

Duncan, B. L., Miller, S. D., Wampold, B. E., & Hubble, M. A. (2010). The heart and soul of change: Delivering what works in therapy. *American Psychological Association*. https://psycnet.apa.org/doi/10.1037/12075-000

Dweck, C. S. (2012). Mindsets and human nature: Promoting change in the Middle East, the schoolyard, the racial divide, and willpower. *American Psychologist*, 67(8), 614. https://doi.org/10.1037/a0029783

Farrell, T. W., Greer, A. G., Bennie, S., Hageman, H., & Pfeifle, A. (2022). Academic health centers and the quintuple aim of health care. *Academic Medicine*, 10–1097. https://doi.org/10.1097/ACM.0000000000005031

Finkelstein, A., Zhou, A., Taubman, S., & Doyle, J. (2020). Health care hotspotting – A randomized, controlled trial. *New England Journal of Medicine*, 382(2), 152–162. https://doi.org/10.1056/NEJMsa1906848

Fredrickson, B. L. (2013). Updated thinking on positivity ratios. *The American Psychologist*, 68(9), 814–822. https://psycnet.apa.org/doi/10.1037/a0033584

Greene-Morton, E., & Minkler, M. (2020). Cultural competence or cultural humility? Moving beyond the debate. *Health Promotion Practice*, 21(1), 142–145. https://doi.org/10.1177/1524839919884912

Hunt, P. (2016). Interpreting the international right to health in a human rights-based approach to health. *Health and Human Rights*, 18(2), 109.

ICF. (n.d.). The gold standard in coaching | ICF – Core competencies. *International Coaching Federation*. https://coachingfederation.org/credentials-and-standards/core-competencies

Jones, C. (2000). Levels of racism: A theoretic framework and a gardener's tale. *American Journal of Public Health*, 90(8), 1212–1215. https://ajph.aphapublications.org/doi/pdfplus/10.2105/AJPH.90.8.1212

Ivey, S. L., Tseng, W., Kurtovich, E., Weir, R. C., Liu, J., Song, H.,. . .& Hubbard, A. (2012). Evaluating a culturally and linguistically competent health coach intervention for Chinese-American patients with diabetes. *Diabetes Spectrum*, 25(2), 93–102. https://doi.org/10.2337/diaspect.25.2.93

Katzmarzyk, P. T., Martin, C. K., Newton, R. L., Jr, Apolzan, J. W., Arnold, C. L., Davis, T. C., Price-Haywood, E. G., Denstel, K. D., Mire, E. F., Thethi, T. K., Brantley, P. J., Johnson, W. D.,

Fonseca, V., Gugel, J., Kennedy, K. B., Lavie, C. J., Sarpong, D. F., & Springgate, B. (2020). Weight loss in underserved patients – A cluster-randomized trial. *The New England Journal of Medicine, 383*(10), 909–918.

Kaufman, S. B. (2021). *Transcend: The New Science of Self-Actualization*. Penguin.

Kendi, I. X. (2019). *How to be an anti-racist*. Penguin Random House.

Kickett, G. (2020). What is cultural safety? *CECTC*. https://www.cetc.org.au/what-is-cultural-safety/

Koh, H. K., Blakey, C. R., & Roper, A. Y. (2014). Healthy People 2020: A report card on the health of the nation. *Jama, 311*(24), 2475–2476.

Komives, S., Wagner, W., & Associates. (2017). *Leadership for a Better World: Understanding the Social Change Model of Leadership Development* (2nd ed.). Jossey-Bass.

Landers, J., Liu, E., Estevez, J., Henderson, T., & Craig, J. E. (2019). Presence of diabetic retinopathy is associated with worse 10-year mortality among Indigenous Australians in Central Australia: The Central Australian ocular health study. *Clinical & Experimental Ophthalmology, 47*(2), 226–232. https://doi.org/10.1111/ceo.13375

Lane, G., Farag, M., White, J., Nisbet, C., & Vatanparast, H. (2018). Chronic health disparities among refugee and immigrant children in Canada. *Applied Physiology, Nutrition, and Metabolism, 43*(10), 1043–1058. https://doi.org/10.1139/apnm-2017-0407

Martela, F. (2020). Replacing the pyramid of needs with a sailboat of needs. *Psychology Today*. https://www.psychologytoday.com/us/blog/insights-more-meaningful-existence/202012/replacing-the-pyramid-needs-sailboat-needs

Matthews, S. M. (2023). The question cube re-imagined – A 5-dimensional model for cultivating coaches' capacity for curious inquiry in health behaviour change. *American Journal of Lifestyle Medicine*. https://doi.org/10.1177/15598276231172910

Moore, M. (2023). Ground zero in lifestyle medicine: Changing mindsets to change behavior. *American Journal of Lifestyle Medicine, 17*(5), 632–638.

Moore, M., Jackson, E., Moran, B. (2016). *Coaching Psychology Manual*. Williams & Wilkins.

National Academies of Sciences, Engineering, and Medicine [NASEM]. (2019). *Integrating Social Care into the Delivery of Health Care: Moving Upstream to Improve the Nation's Health*. The National Academies Press. https://doi.org/10.17226/25467

NBHWC. (n.d.). *NBHWC*. Retrieved May 10, 2023, from https://nbhwc.org/program-approval-standards/

Nguyen-Huynh, M. N., Young, J. D., Ovbiagele, B., Alexander, J. G., Alexeeff, S., Lee, C., Blick, N., Caan, B. J., Go, A. S., & Sidney, S. (2022). Effect of lifestyle coaching or enhanced pharmacotherapy on blood pressure control among black adults with persistent uncontrolled hypertension: A cluster randomized clinical trial. *JAMA Network Open, 5*(5), e2212397. https://doi.org/10.1001/jamanetworkopen.2022.12397

Otu, A., Ahinkorah, B. O., Ameyaw, E. K., Seidu, A. A., & Yaya, S. (2020). One country, two crises: What Covid-19 reveals about health inequalities among BAME communities in the United Kingdom and the sustainability of its health system? *International Journal for Equity in Health, 19*(1), 1–6. https://doi.org/10.1186/s12939-020-01307-z

Ruffin, L. (2016). Health coaching strategy to Improve glycemic control in African American adults with type 2 diabetes: An integrative review. *JNBNA, 28*(1), 54–59. https://doi.org/10.34297/AJBSR.2020.09.001456

Ruggiero, L., Riley, B. B., Hernandez, R., Quinn, L. T., Gerber, B. S., Castillo, A., Day, J., Ingram, D., Wang, Y., & Butler, P. (2014, February 25). Medical assistant coaching to support diabetes self-care among low-income racial/ethnic minority populations. *Western Journal of Nursing Research, 36*(9), 1052–1073. https://doi.org/10.1177/0193945914522862

Seligman, M. (2018). PERMA and the building blocks of well-being. *The Journal of Positive Psychology, 13*(4), 333–335. https://doi.org/10.1080/17439760.2018.1437466

Strickler, D. C. (2009). Addressing the imbalance of power in a traditional doctor-patient relationship. *Psychiatric Rehabilitation Journal, 32*(4), 316. https://doi.org/10.2975/32.4.2009.316.318

Thom, D. H., Hessler, D., Willard-Grace, R., Bodenheimer, T., Najmabadi, A., Araujo, C., & Chen, E. H. (2014). Does health coaching change patients' trust in their primary care provider? *Patient Education and Counseling, 96*(1), 135–138. https://doi.org/10.1016/j.pec.2014.03.018

VIA Institute on Character. (n.d.). The 24 Character strengths. *Viacharacter.org*. https://www.viacharacter.org/character-strengths

Wehipeihana, N., Sebire, K., Spee, K., & Oakden, J. (2022). In pursuit of māori health equity. In *Evaluation of the Māori Influenza and Measles Vaccination Programme*. Ministry of Health.

WHO (2024). Retrieved October 1, 2024, from https://www.who.int/about/frequently-asked-questions

Willard-Grace, R., Chen, E. H., Hessler, D., DeVore, D., Prado, C., Bodenheimer, T., & Thom, D. H. (2015). Health coaching by medical assistants to improve control of diabetes, hypertension, and hyperlipidemia in low-income patients: A randomized controlled trial. *The Annals of Family Medicine, 13*(2), 130–138.

Zimmerman, F. J., & Anderson, N. W. (2019). Trends in health equity in the United States by race/ethnicity, sex, and income, 1993–2017. *JAMA Network Open, 2*(6), e196386–e196386.

Chapter 17

Coaching for bereavement and ill health

Maggie João

Introduction

This chapter focuses on those situations when health and wellbeing are absent, both from the coach's and the client's perspective. Loss is certain to appear in the coaching room, and in some cases shows up in the form of bereavement and in others as loss of function as a result of ill health. In each case, bereavement is unique to the person who is navigating it. We start by exploring theoretical models that might affect the coaching relationship when there is an absence of health and wellbeing, or when there is bereavement, and move on to consider how coaches can manage these issues for themselves or with clients.

Theory

We all know that the whole is made of parts, and when it is not yet whole, it is because something is missing. This missing part – the absence of – very often comes into the coaching room; sometimes clients are truly unaware of it, and other times it is hidden behind objectives or masked by other issues. Clients come to coaching in the pursuit of something that they still do not have or that they have lost. Exploring it and bringing it to the surface is part of the coaching process and in itself is a transformational journey.

Coaching through this loss is extremely relevant. Based on the work of James and Friedman (2009), and as noted by Menaul and João (2022), there are at least 20 different types of loss. As we live our lives, the likelihood of encountering loss is certain. One of these types of losses is health changes; this can lead to people feeling vulnerable or confused, as for some this also involves a change to their own identity. Someone who was once very physically active, suddenly gets diagnosed with a disease that will impair their movement, and thus may have to redefine themselves. This is just an example of how medical coaching, for instance, can help in providing a new sense of identity, navigating through a new self and creating new helpful routines to reach acceptance and wellbeing.

Loss presupposes bereavement. João and Menaul (2019) define bereavement as a deprivation or loss by force and a unique process. The way we deal with loss when bereaved is personal, but will also be culturally situated, with different cultures – both within a society and in a family – responding differently.

Some of the losses that happened in our lives are consciously planned, like choosing to change houses, countries, or jobs. In fact, the bereavement or grief associated with it is much more manageable compared to when we lose the same things unexpectedly or when this loss is outside of our control. The anticipation factor is important in helping

DOI: 10.4324/9781003319016-19

manage our expectations and affecting the intensity of the bereavement. If I can anticipate that I am going to lose something or someone, I can prepare for that moment and work on coping strategies to deal with its impact in advance.

In truth, there is space in the coaching room to deal with, and explore, both expected and unexpected losses. In fact, part of coaching is centred around planning to move forward, to choose one option over another, to prepare for the next stage we need to engage in when letting go or losing something: a new job means leaving the old one; a new relationship may mean letting go of the old one, or of our independence.

However, part of coaching is also holding the space and working on the being, instead of solely of the doing, nurturing, inviting new perspectives, and accepting what is.

Change curve

Bereavement is an experience which works at a different pace, and in different ways, with different people. However, some writers have argued there are common themes or patterns which many people experience, even if they do so at different rates. Kubler-Ross first developed the grief curve (Kubler-Ross, 1969), which was later brought to the organisational world by David Kessler (2019), who relabelled it as the change curve. It proposed that most people move through a cycle of emotions when facing change.

Each individual navigates this curve in a different rhythm or speed. The movement is not always linear or one-directional. An individual might be starting to move into the integration phase when something triggers them, and they move back into the low-energy or depressed phase.

For some, bereavement or loss is a cycle which leads to resolution of healing. For others, it remains a loop, where a new bereavement or loss can trigger a return of feelings of sadness, for example when we hear about a friend's loss or see a news report of a tragedy.

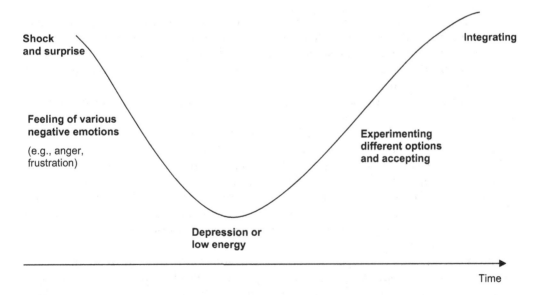

Figure 17.1 Change curve (Adapted from the Kubler-Ross grief curve)

It is exactly in this situation that it is essential the coach becomes fully present and aware of what might be triggering the client. One thing to pay attention to is the coach's presence, reflected in the empathy they display towards the client. The coach needs to remain mindful of staying in a space of empathy and try to avoid moving to sympathy, where rescuer response becomes a feature of the coach's actions. While the rescuer may come from a place of good intention, its effect can be less helpful for the client.

What is at stake here is the coach's impact by holding the space, by respecting that moment for the client, and to be empathetic and supportive while providing a container for the emotions and encouraging authenticity. In these moments, the Arabic proverb may be apt: "Words are silver; silence is gold". Mastering silence management with an empathic presence. Holding the space, respecting the moment for the client, regardless of taking five seconds or five minutes, listening to them externalising their emotions. Respecting the client's speed in navigating through this invisible curve is really important.

In this world, where coaching has become global, it is crucial to recognise and respect differences. Different cultures grieve differently. Health is seen differently from culture to culture, it is lived differently from person to person, and it is shown differently from country to country. Respecting these differences and cohabiting with them in the coaching room is key for the partnership created with the client.

Drama Triangle

Most coaches believe negative or critical judgement do not have a place in the coaching room. As a result, there might be a tendency to move towards positive judgement. These generally come in three forms: a compliment, an encouragement, and an acknowledgement.

A compliment is basically any intervention such as "Well done" or "Good job". This can pass on short-term motivation. It has a place in life, though it might not be the only thing we do in the coaching room.

The encouragement comes in the form of "I know you've got this", "You have everything to succeed with your action plan", or "With these skills you worked on, you will shine in that presentation". It presupposes more involvement from our side as it conveys our trust in them and in their abilities, which might equate to the clients as feelings of security and self-confidence.

The acknowledgement is something in the lines of "I see how determined you were in conducting that task until the end" or "I noticed a sparkle of passion in your eyes for what you've accomplished". Here coaches highlight the qualities seen in the client and is more powerful and transformational than the simple "Well done" statement.

In using such interventions, we need to be conscious of the role they play in the coach–client relationship. One perspective which is worthwhile exploring here are triggers. Coaches might be triggered by their clients, and this might take the partnership dynamics off balance. Even the subtle judgements previously mentioned might lead to it. One can easily accept the invitation and move into rescuer or persecutor or even victim role alluding here to the Drama Triangle.

The Drama Triangle developed by Karpman in 1968 explores the difference in dynamics and social interactions. We can accept (or even resign ourselves) to this power dynamic in our social lives with our peers, managers, team members, or even family and friends. However, we need to pay attention when it enters the coaching room.

When it comes to health and wellbeing, it is easy to be triggered and get stuck in the Drama Triangle. For instance, the young, attractive, and slim client who talks about their approach to counting calories in the session, to their overweight, middle-aged coach, may trigger the coach into thoughts about their own lifestyle, looks, and eating habits, triggering emotions of irritation, shame, guilt in the coach or even to allow the coach to momentarily check out of the coaching conversation and start thinking in what actions they want to put in place to improve their own lifestyle.

Or when the client is sharing how they drink one too many glasses of wine to deal with the loss they are encountering. It is so easy for the voice inside the coach's mind to start judging and counting: "How many glasses did you drink?" or "What other (healthier) ways can you choose to take to cope with this loss?". Here, the coach's judge becomes a controlling parent talking in a very polite way to the client, placing the client in the role of the child. Is this what the client wants to explore, or is the rescuer in the coach showing up to rescue this person from (what the coach considers to be) more turmoil and deception in their lives due to their drinking habits?

Like this there are many other examples where the Drama Triangle comes into play in the coaching room (Cochrane & Newton, 2011).

Covey (2004) describes the '5 Cs' of toxic behaviours: competing, complaining, condemning, comparing, criticising – and what the triggers do is to tap into several of these behaviours, which should not have (any) space in the coaching room.

Another point about the triggers is that they make the story about the coach who suddenly is focusing on their own narrative and emotions leading to reflecting on their actions. In fact, much of this can place the coach in the position of the child, seeking to prove that they are good, too, which again unbalances the coaching partnership.

Hence, it is crucial for the coaches' own wellbeing to have the time to simply do nothing and learn from their own reflections about their self-care, health, somatics. So, when they have a coaching session and the client arrives on screen or physically, the coach is prepared to focus on an adult-to-adult relationship, exclusively on the client's topic.

An alternative to the Karpman's Drama Triangle was offered by David Emerald (2015), who coined TED (The Empowerment Dynamic®). In Emerald's (2015) reframing, the victim's position is now the "Creator". It is the place where the individual takes the matter in their own hands and starts creating initial steps forward – albeit 'baby steps' –out of the victim's role. The rescuer turns into the Coach, who is there to support, to notice and to reflect back the qualities they see in the client, and the persecutor turns

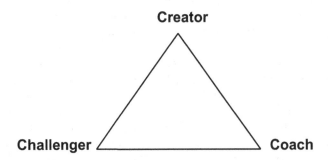

Figure 17.2 The Empowerment Dynamic

into the Challenger, who helps explore different perspectives and see the same situation with a different light.

In essence, it highlights the personal responsibility, accountability, self-awareness, and empowerment of the client, which is a much healthier approach to interpersonal interactions.

Such models can help coaches to conceptualise the experiences they have in the coaching room, but the question remains what the coach can do to manage these challenges of loss and bereavement when it occurs for their clients – or happens to them. In the next section, we explore a series of tools which coaches can apply to help themselves and their clients navigate these challenges.

Practice

In this section, we explore working with coaching clients, and coaches, who are experiencing loss or bereavement. We offer four practical tools which coaches can draw on and apply in their work.

Coaches' 'Self-Care Wheel'

Ross and Wonfor (2019) introduced two very interesting tools, later adapted for coaches by Menaul and João (2022): 'Coaching Excellence' (Figure 17.3) and the 'Self-Care Wheel' (Figure 17.4). These tools can be used in supervision to unveil what can be triggering the coach. Notwithstanding, these tools can also be used by any coach in their own reflection time as a way to think how to build resilience through wellbeing.

The Coaching Excellence tool shows how the combination of two important topics creates an interesting perspective to explore. For instance, when we are dealing with ethical maturity and personal sustainability, it would be valuable for the coach to reflect on what to say yes or no to. When the coach is exploring resourcing self and fitness for practise, a closed question such as "Am I well enough for the work?" might be provocative enough to shake things up.

On the other hand, the Self-Care Wheel includes various perspectives the coach can take when evaluating one's wellbeing. Most probably based on the 'Wheel of Life', the most popular exercise in coaching, the Self-Care Wheel also includes a self-evaluation of the current level of satisfaction the individual has on each of the topics. It works almost as a photograph of the individual's life at that specific moment in time.

Recommendations include using a scale of 1–10 (10 being the strongest) on each topic, and shading the chosen level, so it is much easier to understand whether this wheel would spin or not and if not, on which topic would it get stuck.

The wheel is a simple tool that helps increase our awareness of our current patterns. Because it is so visual, one can easily identify the topics with lower satisfaction. Coaching through the absence of this satisfaction will help the client make connections between topics, understand how to break those habitual patterns, and choose to create a course of action to tackle that dissatisfaction. As we know, tackling that dissatisfaction does not necessarily mean that the individual will choose the topic with the lowest level of satisfaction to work on. Working on the leverage topic might be wiser as it will improve not only that specific topic but will also simultaneously raise the level of satisfaction.

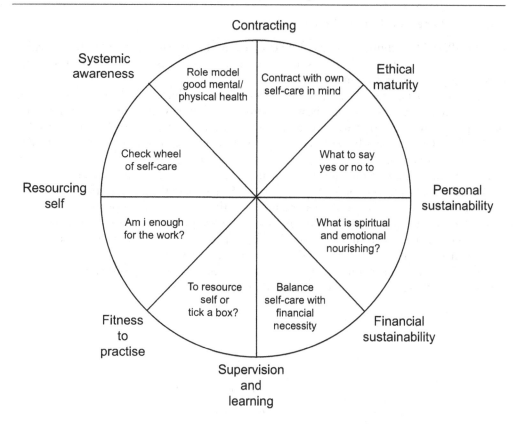

Figure 17.3 Coaching Excellence tool

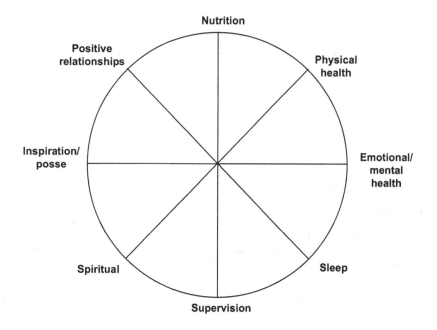

Figure 17.4 Self-Care Wheel for coaches

Presence-Based and embodied coaching

Presence-Based Coaching (Silsbee, 2008) can be a useful approach to use in the coaching room when the absence of health is at stake. Many people rush from task to task, with little regard for the present moment.

According to Hansen (2023), presence resides in the body and it is through being present, attentive to the here and now, and through what is happening in the immediacy of the present moment that we can create awareness of what lies outside of us as well as inside of us. This includes being aware of our bodies and the information they hold. With a heightened awareness comes the power of choice. Hansen notes the present moment is always available and the only moment when change happens is in the present.

A third tool, 'The Awareness Map' (Figure 17.5), can help the coach explore and guide the client's attention. This tool was created with the purpose of supporting the client's increased awareness of the five different channels of experience in the present moment. The coach through curiosity and questioning can help the client explore these dimensions, which may be out of the client's conscious awareness.

Table 17.1 contains examples of questions coaches can use to explore awareness. It is best to adapt these to the individual client and their circumstances.

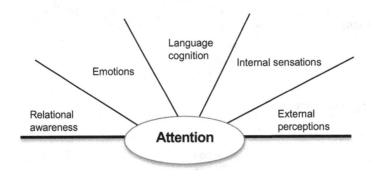

Figure 17.5 The Awareness Map

Table 17.1 Self-awareness questions

- What is going on in my relationship with the thing (the thing being health or its absence, a disease, a pain, a feeling, a project, a topic, an issue, even a person or a part of the body)?
- How are my emotions showing up? How do they affect my relationship with the thing? The outside world? The inside world?
- What narratives have I been telling that have been supportive or have been hindering?
- What are the mental maps that are at service in the here and now?
- What are internal physical sensations (such as urges, breath, heartbeat, numbness, tightness, tingling, etc.) telling me? What do they want to tell me?
- How are my five senses informing me?
- What choices am I making based on my internal perceptions?

The aim here is to offer the client the opportunity to move their attention towards what is going on inside their body, to be present with the body, and through this gain greater understanding of their health and wellbeing.

The 'Coach's Will'

The 'Coach's Will' might be something new to the coaching world, but it has been widely used in therapy. It evolves from the point of what happens to the coaching practice when something happens to the coach. If the coach gets ill, or not fit for practice, how are the other players in the coach's system – meaning clients, sponsors, peers, or members – informed of what is going on with the coach?

For the cases when the coach is sick, but functional and operational, it makes sense that the coach directly informs others about not being able to practise for the time they believe is required. Unfortunately, there are other situations when it is not possible for the coach to inform using their own voice, maybe because they are lying in a hospital bed or simply because they have suddenly passed away. In these cases, the Coach's Will comes into play. This is simply a series of arrangements made by the coach in the event of their unexpected death or serious illness. Making prior arrangements by leaving detailed notes, from passwords for computers, to current client files, financial accounts and bank information, can all reduce the burden on family members (Lane, 2023).

The Coach's Will can be managed by a specific company specialised in these services (you can search online) or by a family member, a peer, or a friend – someone who is responsible to get in touch with the clients and bring them the news of what has happened to the coach (illness, death). Some may argue that it is a breach of confidentiality. However, we suggest it should form part of all coaches' written contracts.

Coaches David Lane and Eve Turner have also suggested another good practice, which includes preparing an email to your clients or wider network and some instructions as to when and who to send to, so all can be informed. We suggest the coach makes specific arrangements and leaves instructions in a "known place" with the list of contact details for clients, peers, professional memberships/accreditation bodies.

Research by Menaul and João (2022) revealed that few coaches have made such arrangements. In their survey conducted in 2022, less than 1 in 5 coaches have a Coach's Will or have made provisions with next of kin or close colleague/business partner. This suggests that more awareness needs to happen so all coaches have these arrangements in place, in the near future.

Conclusion

This chapter focused on exploring important aspects when one is coaching or supervising someone whose health is slowly deteriorating or has shown signs of incapacity or even has received a terminal diagnosis. There are aspects we need to be aware of when it comes to coaching clients who are ill, and there are dimensions the professional coach needs to consider when becoming ill.

We briefly consider theoretical perspectives before exploring four tools. The first two explore self-care for the coach (to be aware of what can impact being fit for practice). The third helps the coach focus their attention, as well as guide the clients to work with their attention to tap into other type of answers. The fourth tool brings to the surface the situation when the coach is the one who is ill or somehow incapacitated. The aim is to help coaches to be better prepared for when these situations arise in their own practice.

Reflective questions

1. What would be the most powerful question to ask you, the coach, about your own self-care habits?
2. In which form your triggers related to loss and bereavement show up in the coaching room?
3. What are you doing to appease them?
4. How do you envision the end of your working days?
5. What new perspectives has this chapter provided you with?

References

Cochrane, H. & Newton, T., (2011). *Supervision for Coaches: A Guide to Thoughtful Work*, Abingdon: Routledge.

Covey, S., (2004). *The 7 Habits of Highly Effective People*, London: Simon & Schuster.

Emerald, D., (2015). *The Power of TED* (*The Empowerment Dynamic)*. London: Polaris Publishing. Available at: https://theempowermentdynamic.com/

Hansen, B. (2023). *The Power of Embodied Transformation Course Materials*.

James, J. & Friedman, R., (2009). *The Grief Recovery Handbook: The Action Program for Moving Beyond Death, Divorce, and Other Losses Including Health*, New York: William Morrow & Company.

João, M. & Menaul, J., (2019, October 23). Coaching and Supervising Through Bereavement. *Coaching Perspectives*.

Kessler, D., (2019). *Finding Meaning: The Sixth Stage of Grief*, London: Penguin Random House.

Kubler-Ross, E., (1969). *On Death and Dying*, New York: MacMillian.

Lane, D. & Turner, E., (2023, April 14). The supervisor's role in developing an ethical exit strategy for unexpected incapacitation and death. *Global Supervisors Network Webinar*.

Menaul, J & João, M., (2022). *Coaching and Supervising through Bereavement: A Practical Guide to Working with Grief and Loss*, Abingdon: Routledge.

Ross, M. & Wonfor D., (2019). Self-Care in Coaching Supervision (webinar). *Association of Coaching Supervisors*. Available at: https://www.associationofcoachingsupervisors.com/community/aocs-april-2019-webinar-self-care-in-coaching-supervision

Silsbee, D., (2008). *Presence-Based Coaching*, San Francisco: Jossey-Bass.

Chapter 18

Digital-enabled coaching for individual wellbeing

Ray Tak-yin Hui and Jonathan Passmore

Introduction

In the post-pandemic era, a growing number of companies have expanded their use of remote-work initiatives (Barrero et al., 2022; Draca et al., 2022). The implementation of remote work, i.e., work virtually from a remote distance, has been proposed as the 'new normal' for organisations (CNBC, 2020; Fujitsu, 2020). As many organisational processes have turned to online or hybrid modes, employee development has also switched to digitally enabled modes of delivery, including employee coaching (Passmore, Qi, & Tewald, 2021).

To support the introduction of remote work, organisations have adopted advanced information and communication technologies (ICT) to provide digital coaching which seeks to both support wellbeing and enhance performance (Hui & Sue-Chan, 2023; Hui, Law, & Lau, 2021; Hui, Wu, & Luo, 2022, 2024). Although there was evidence from other spheres that provide digital solutions, such as counselling and telemedicine, the introduction of digital coaching has created new challenges for both coaches and managers in these new environments (Glass, 2022). One of the most common concerns is how coaches and managers build rapport and demonstrate empathy without personal contact (Straus et al., 2022). When poorly managed, this can lead to feelings of disconnection, with negative feelings in employees (Prasad et al., 2020; Shockley et al., 2021).

Although scholars and practitioners have suggested more widespread use of digital coaching as part of mental health and wellbeing strategy in post-pandemic workplaces (Hagemann & Klug, 2022; Straus et al., 2022), limited studies have focused specifically on how managers coach subordinates' wellbeing online. To address this unfilled gap, this chapter will explore the science of digital coaching and how digital coaching interventions can assist individuals in their wellbeing.

Theory and research of digital coaching

Past studies have shown that effective coaching can significantly increase clients' satisfaction, self-efficacy, adaptation, and performance (Athanasopoulou & Dopson, 2018; Grover & Furnham, 2016; Hui & Sue-Chan, 2018; Hui, Sue-Chan, & Wood, 2019; Jones, Woods, & Guillaume, 2016; Theeboom, Beersma, & van Vianen, 2014). Nevertheless, the COVID19 pandemic of the early 2020s brought significant change to the coaching field as it did to many other sectors, increasing the speed of transition to digital delivery.

DOI: 10.4324/9781003319016-20

Digital-enabled coaching is variously described as 'e-coaching', 'remote coaching', 'online coaching', or 'virtual coaching' (Diller & Passmore, 2023). Digital-enabled coaching can be defined as a one-on-one, ongoing development practice in which coaches use digital technologies – such as chat program, instant messaging program, or video conferencing tools – to facilitate the personal development and wellbeing of clients (Hui, Law, & Lau, 2021). Similar to traditional face-to-face coaching, the focal purpose of digital-enabled coaching is to provide effective personal facilitation to induce the desired behavioural and attitude change, resulting in individual goal achievement (Ribbers & Waringa, 2015). In 2015, Ribbers and Waringa (2015) summarised that digital-enabled coaching had four basic types: email coaching, telephone coaching, video/webcam coaching (e.g., Skype, Zoom, Google Chat), and chat coaching (e.g., Facebook Messenger, WhatsApp, Line). While the most popular form is human-to-human synchronous coaching, other digitally enabled approaches have emerged including 'coachbots' (computer to human). What is also likely as technology develops is that new forms of digital-enabled coaching will emerge through the coming decade as new technologies develop.

To help moving forward, we have sought to summarise the digital-enabled coaching market as it stands now. However, we recognise that the fluid nature of the industry is likely to see continuing change. In our view, the markets have coalesced around two modes of delivery (as per 2024). The first is digital platforms (e.g., BetterUp, CoachHub, Ezra). Digital platforms, which a format popularly called 'digital coaching', involves the delivery of synchronous human-to-human coaching using audio and video channels via a digital connection (Passmore & Woodward, 2023). The second is chatbots, commonly known as coachbots. This involves the use of computer-delivered responses to a human through synchronous delivery (e.g., PocketConfidant and other AI coaching applications). Other forms of digitally enabled coaching persist, such as 'phone coaching', but this is declining. Additionally, asynchronous coaching via coachbots (e.g., Wave) and coaching software that enables independent coaches and in-house coaching pools to offer similar services to platform providers are also prevalent in the market (e.g., coaching.com). We recognise what may be popular in 2024 in a dynamic market may be quite different in 2034 as new technologies become available (see Table 18.1).

Table 18.1 Digital-enabled providers in the field of coaching

Market segments	Digital platforms	Coaching management software	AI chatbots	Asynchronous coaching (using a combination of AI and humans)
Commonly used title or term	Providing 'digital coaching'	Enabling the delivery of 'digital coaching'	'Coachbots'	No commonly used title
Providers	BetterUp CoachHub Ezra-LHH Sounding Board Torch Pluma Bravely AceUp Sharpist UExcelerate	coaching.com Optify Delenta simply.coach Paperbell Profi Honeybook	PocketConfidant Evoach Rocky.ai AI coaching Coach Vici IXCoach	Wave

Source: Adapted from Passmore and Tee (2023, p. 9) (Data as of 31 December 2022)

While digital-enabled coaching has been gaining increasing attention from practitioners in recent years, it has faced challenges with other forms of online developmental practices such as online mentoring, training, and therapy. At the first glance, these development practices share a common objective of promoting behavioural change or improvement, so these suspicions are not without reason. However, as with face-to-face delivery, each of these interventions has a distinct focus which is different and separate from coaching. In mentoring, the focus is towards career development (Iqbal, 2020), in counselling managing psychological distress (Ribbers & Waringa, 2015) and in training and skills acquisition focused on a predetermined syllabus or learning outcomes (Ramayah, Ahmad, & Hong, 2012). Compared with these developmental practices, digital coaching is more goal-focused and aims to improve employees' performance at work (Hui, Law, & Lau, 2021; Hui, Wu, & Luo, 2022; Hui, Wu, & Luo, 2024).

Digital-enabled coaching

Unlike face-to-face coaching, digital-enabled coaching is delivered via an ICT-mediated channel (a platform), with unique characteristics which give rise to new challenges and opportunities in the communication between coaches and clients. As a starting point, it may be helpful to review the foundational theories surrounding ICT-mediated communication.

Mostly based on the *cues-filtered-out (CFO) perspective* (Culnan & Markus, 1987), early studies usually suggested that the absence of non-verbal cues affects information processing and interpretation of the communicators and leads to poorer quality communication in a digital environment (Geissler et al., 2014; Lewandowski et al., 2011). Culnan and Markus (1987) argued that the systematic reduction of non-verbal cues results in more impersonal and de-individuated interactions due to the minimisation of social presence (Short, Williams, & Christie, 1976), media richness (Daft & Lengel, 1986), and media naturalness (Kock, 2004). *Social presence theory* (Short, Williams, & Christie, 1976) suggested that because the digital environment supports fewer social cues, such as emotion and relationship, digital communication is inferior to face-to-face communication for personal and emotional exchanges. Similar to social presence theory, *media richness theory* (Daft & Lengel, 1986) focused on the bandwidth of information cues supported by a medium. It posits that digital communication has fewer media richness than face-to-face communication because digital communication facilitates less support for information cues in the communication process. Later, *media naturalness theory* (Kock, 2004) argued that the inferior naturalness of digital communication creates more cognitive burden on communicators during the information transfer, leading to poorer communication quality than face-to-face communication.

Generally speaking, when non-verbal cues such as facial expression, gesture, tone, and loudness of voice are insufficient to supplement the verbal cues, the amount of meaning delivered (i.e., media richness) will be reduced. Communicators will be less likely to perceive the sense of being with another (i.e., social presence; Short, Williams, & Christie, 1976) and to feel as natural as communicating face to face (i.e., media naturalness) when communicating in digital environment, especially for emotional support and clarification (Hui, Law, & Lau, 2021; Santucci, 2021). Furthermore, previous studies have also shown that a lack of non-verbal cues increases the communicator's cognitive burden in interpreting messages (Fahy, 2003), increases emotional ambiguity (Lee & Wagner,

2002), induces hostility and delayed feedback (Wright, 2002; Wright & Bell, 2003), and creates more disruption in the communication process over time (Walther, 2011). Taken together, these studies manifest the wellbeing problems of remote workers and imply the challenges of coaching in digital environments (Filsinger, 2014; Ghods & Boyce, 2013; Hui, Law, & Lau, 2021; Irving, 2021).

Nevertheless, Walther's (1996) *hyperpersonal communication theory*, which is an extension of social information processing theory (Walther, 1992), challenged the CFO approach (Culnan & Markus, 1987) and proposed that non-verbal cues are only valuable to the extent that they fulfil the purpose of communication and convey subtle meaning (Sumner & Ramirez, 2017). It further explained that minimisation of non-verbal cues in digital communication benefits more effective personal communication because users possess increased abilities to control and to select the information and channel that uphold their desired interpersonal image and fulfil unique communicative needs (Walther, 1996). For example, Hancock (2004) suggested that individuals are more explicit when delivering messages online because digital communication carries fewer information cues. Unlike CFO theories, this theory emphasises the active role which coaches can adopt when coaching in digital spaces if they are aware of these challenges. For example, Cox and Dannahy (2005) and Mortensen (2015) claimed that coach-led transparency and self-disclosure are key to enhancing successful outcomes in the digital coaching process.

For example, integrating Walther's (1996) hyperpersonal communication theory and Hui, Sue-Chan, and Wood's (2013, 2019) model of coaching style, Hui, Wu, and Luo (2022) proposed a new model for management coaching with four distinct communication styles used by the manager: verbal guidance, non-verbal guidance, verbal facilitation, and non-verbal facilitation. In a large-scale study involving managers and their direct reports, the researchers found that both verbal and non-verbal guidance are positively related to employees' proficiency, adaptivity, and proactivity, while verbal and non-verbal facilitation was negatively associated with the same (Hui, Wu, & Luo, 2022). The results from this study suggest that a more directive style (what the researchers termed "verbal guidance") provided more benefits than the non-directive communication style ("verbal facilitation").

Despite the benefit of information control, some studies determined that ICT allows individuals to communicate with a wider audience despite geographical distance and time, and despite looser social ties (Anthony, Gimbert, & Fultz, 2013; Wright, 2002; Wright & Bell, 2003). It has been noted that in theory, a record of the communication can be stored and retrieved for subsequent review, thus enhancing communication quality and learning opportunities (Rossett & Marino, 2005). However, we would urge caution on such an approach, as recording conversations requires both explicit agreement within the organisation, as well as with the individual coach, to ensure compliance with privacy laws in the respective territories where the coach and client are based, as well as where the data may be stored.

Existing studies of digital-enabled coaching on wellbeing

While coaching has traditionally focused on enhancing performance, with the emergence of positive psychology, the focus on outcomes has broadened to include wellbeing alongside performance (Green, Jarden, & Leach, 2021). According to Passmore and Oades (2014), four major positive psychological theories were applied to explain the underlying impacts of coaching on wellbeing in existing literature. They are *strengths theory* (Proctor, Maltby, & Linley, 2011), *broaden-and-build theory* (Fredrickson, 2009), *self-determination theory* (Spence & Oades, 2011), and *PERMA theory* (Seligman, 2012).

According to strengths theory (Proctor, Maltby, & Linley, 2011), personal strengths – including physical, personal, and psychological strengths – are the most critical areas of personal wellbeing. When people identify and use their strengths, they will perform, feel, and function better (Oades, 2016). Moreover, people focusing on their own strengths have higher abilities to complete various tasks, thereby building better self-confidence and image (Ding & Liu, 2022). For this reason, scholars have highlighted the essence of strength identification and utilisation in the coaching process for building one's positive psychological wellbeing (Govindji & Linley, 2007; Linley & Harrington, 2006; Linley et al., 2010; Oades, 2016; Passmore & Oades, 2014). For instance, Linley and Harrington (2006) highlighted that the key role of a coach is to provide a suitably conducive atmosphere for clients to naturally display their strengths so that they can detect and identify their strengths. Govindji and Linley (2007) found that strengths knowledge, strengths use, and organismic valuing (i.e., inner voice or value that guides people in the right and satisfying directions) can increase subjective and psychological wellbeing in the coaching process. Similarly, Linley and colleagues (2010) also found that when coaches help clients to identify, assess, and develop their strengths, it will enhance their subjective wellbeing because of the healthy goal attainment in the coaching process. Oades (2016) indicated that coaches develop and use strengths assessment tools to help clients to explore their strengths and the ways to use these identified strengths.

The second theory is the broaden-and-build theory proposed by Fredrickson (2004). According to Fredrickson (2009), the broaden-and-build theory highlights the important function of positive emotions, such as joy, interest, contentment, and love, and their affects on broadening (or narrowing) one's mindset. Fredrickson (2004) further suggested that when one's mindset is broadened by positive feedback, it will facilitate the building of social and psychological resources such as satisfaction and self-confidence for improving one's subjective wellbeing. In the existing coaching literature, some studies have examined the importance of feedback in the coaching process and its disparate affects on clients' emotions and wellbeing such as emotional exhaustion (e.g., Hui & Sue-Chan, 2016, 2023; Hui, Law, & Lau, 2021; Rosa et al., 2021; Wang & Wentling, 2001). For example, Wang and Wentling (2001) found that digital coaching motivates coaches by providing different social and psychological resources such as information, suggestions, willingness to help, relationship, encouragement, etc., in the coaching process, and that this can contribute to successful outcomes. Rosa and colleagues (2021) also showed that digital coaching programmes can help employees to minimise emotional exhaustion and enhance wellbeing at work. In contrast, Hui, Law, and Lau (2021) provided an alternative view and evidence that clients who received digital coaching experienced more emotional exhaustion than those who received face-to-face coaching because digital communication may induce more stress among clients. More work is needed to better understand these effects and how digital environments affect the cognitive and emotional processes of individuals.

The third theory is self-determination theory (SDT) (Deci & Ryan, 1985; Ryan & Deci, 2000), which emphasises the fulfilment of three innate and universal psychological needs – autonomy, relatedness, and competency needs – which associate with intrinsic motivation and wellbeing. Spence and Oades (2011) conducted a review of SDT and its application in coaching practice. They noted that SDT-informed coaching can support clients with developing their core values (i.e., autonomy support) and acknowledging their competence and abilities (i.e., competence support), providing them with care and trust (i.e., relatedness support). In combination, these aspects can make a positive contribution to wellbeing and underline the value of SDT as a theory to coaching practice.

The final theory is PERMA theory (Seligman, 2012) which proposed five major components of psychological wellbeing: positive emotions (P), engagement (E), (positive) relationships (R), meaning (M), and accomplishment (A). Kern and colleagues (2015) found that each factor is associated differently with psychological outcomes. For example, positive emotion is generally associated with outcomes including life satisfaction, hope, gratitude, physical vitality, and physical activity, while relationships relate to life satisfaction, hope, gratitude, and spirituality (Kern et al., 2015). Among five elements, Huppert and So (2013) suggest that positive emotion is a core part of wellbeing.

In coaching literature, previous studies have examined the relationship between digital coaching and the elements of wellbeing (Filsinger, 2014; Ghods & Boyce, 2013; Green, Jarden, & Leach, 2021; Hui et al., 2017; Poepsel, 2011; Sparrow, 2016). However, the majority of the studies undertaken prior to 2020 focused on phone or email coaching, as opposed to what is now labelled 'digital coaching' (Diller & Passmore, 2023), which involves synchronous audio and visual communication channels.

Poepsel (2011) highlighted the role of goal accomplishment in the positive relationship between e-coaching programmes and subjective wellbeing perceived by coaches. Similarly, Sparrow (2016) also found that e-coaching can enhance employees' subject wellbeing by prompting more emotional self-reflection and positive self-talk. In contrast, some studies have demonstrated the darker sides of e-coaching (Ghods & Boyce, 2013; Hui et al., 2017; Irving, 2021). Ghods and Boyce (2013) and Filsinger (2014) indicated the difficulties in building trust and relationship during the digital coaching process which may affect clients' emotion and wellbeing (Irving, 2021). Hui and colleagues (2017) found that clients who received more digital coaching experienced more emotional exhaustion since the coaching via digital communication lacks social presence and emotional support.

The overall confusion and overlap in language, with similar terms being used for different interventions, such as phone coaching and e-coaching, combined with fast-paced change in technology, has often led to confusion and misunderstandings about which technologies create which effects. Some work has been undertaken in an attempt to clarify terminology and definitions, but past papers have left a legacy of confusion in this space.

The practice of digital-enabled coaching

As we have noted, 'digital-enabled coaching' covers a wide range of coaching practices which share common aspects: a two-way, ICT-mediated communication process which consists of the sender (i.e., coach), receiver (i.e., client), message (i.e., coaching content), and communication channel (i.e., ICTs).

Selection of the medium

Selecting the appropriate ICT medium is one of the keys to successful outcomes (Ghods, Barney, & Kirschner, 2019; Kanatouri, 2020). An ICT medium can be used to facilitate the coaching conversation or to provide resources to aid the coaching process, such as hyperlinks, tests, pictures, and files. Due to the technological advancement of ICT in recent years, more advanced and powerful ICT such as mobile instant messaging applications and video conferencing have become increasingly popular in daily business communication.

ICT media can be classified into two major types: synchronous medium and asynchronous medium. The synchronous medium includes telephone, text-based chat (e.g., SMS and instant messaging applications such as WhatsApp, Line, WeChat, Facebook Messenger), web conferencing (e.g., Skype, Zoom, Microsoft Team, Google Meet), and virtual reality (VR) communication (e.g., Spatial, MeetinVR, Glue, ENGAGE), while the synchronous medium involves email, threaded discussion, voice message, podcast (e.g., Apple Podcast, Google Podcast) and live video streaming (e.g., YouTube, Facebook Live).

To examine the potential impacts of different ICT on digital-enabled coaching effectiveness previous studies (e.g., Boyce & Clutterbuck, 2010; Geissler et al., 2014; Hui, Kong, & Wong, 2024; Kong, Hui, & Tang, 2023; Poepsel, 2011; Wong, Hui, & Kong, 2023) have compared the strengths and weaknesses of different types of ICT based on criteria including: (1) feedback immediacy (i.e., ability to provide instant feedback); (2) amount of information transfer; (3) support transfer of multiple cues; (4) emotions sharing (i.e., ability to show feelings or emotions); (5) message tailoring (i.e., ability to tailor the message to address a specific person); and (6) support of coach–client collaboration. Table 18.2 shows the media abilities of ten different types of ICTs in three categories (i.e., low, medium, and high).

One of the major benefits of ICT is that it enables lower cost and more convenient coaching (Passmore, 2021). As technology has developed, digital coaching platforms have emerged. These aim to provide easy access for global enterprise–sized organisations, making coaching more accessible and available at lower cost. These platform providers have enhanced their coaching offers with the provision of learning content (e.g., assessments and e-library), reflection practice, and organisational data dashboards supporting human resources (HR) business partners with the information to track and report on coaching activity and impact (Rouahi, Boucetta, & Boussaa, 2022; Solis, 2022). It provides an online environment that promotes effective coaching and offers support for coaching programmes with features like personalised dashboard, client management, communication tools, and science-based exercises/tools and assessments.

Coaching behaviour in digital-enabled environments

The second key to success is the coaching behaviour of coaches. To maximise the effectiveness of digital coaching, coaches should use appropriate behaviours to help clients by demonstrating empathy, building trust, and enhancing understanding (Heslin, VandeWalle, & Latham, 2006; Hui, Sue-Chan, & Wood, 2013, 2019). Building on the model of coaching behaviour proposed by Heslin, VandeWalle, & Latham (2006), Hui, Sue-Chan, & Wood (2013, 2019) differentiated two styles of coaching: guidance coaching and facilitation coaching. Each has different impacts on performance of clients,. 'Guidance coaching' entails the coach, as a role model, delivering clear expectations and feedback about how to improve. Guidance approach may not be considered to be 'coaching', for example as defined by the International Coaching Federation (ICF), but in terms of wellbeing and health coaching, the delivery of psycho-social information can be helpful

Table 18.2 Media abilities of different ICTs

	Low	Medium	High
Feedback immediacy	• Email • Threaded discussion • Podcast	• Text-based chat • Voice message • Social media • Live video streaming	• Telephone • Web conferencing • VR communication
Amount of information transfer	• Email • Text-based chat • Voice message • Social media	• Threaded discussion • Telephone • Web conferencing • VR communication	• Podcast • Live video streaming
Support of multiple cues	• Email • Telephone • Threaded discussion • Voice message • Podcast • Social media • Live video streaming • Text-based chat	• Web conferencing	• VR communication
Share emotions	• Email • Threaded discussion • Podcast • Text-based chat • Social media	• Telephone • Voice message • Live video streaming • VR communication	• Web conferencing
Message tailoring	• Threaded discussions • Live video streaming • Podcast • Social media	• Email • Telephone • Voice message • Text-based chat	• Web conferencing • VR communication
Support of collaboration	• Email • Podcast • Voice message • Live video streaming	• Threaded discussion • Text-based chat • Social media • Telephone	• Web conferencing • VR communication

Source: Adapted from Boyce and Clutterbuck (2010) and subsequently revised

in enabling clients to reflect on past health choices and make decisions about future choices to achieve their goals. In comparison, 'facilitation coaching' is more akin to the ICF definition. It involves the coach helping an individual to explore and evaluate the issue and discovering their own solutions (Hui & Sue-Chan, 2018) for themselves.

Regarding the two coaching styles, Hui and Sue-Chan (2018) suggested that guidance and facilitation coaching are differentially associated with job-related anxiety because they vary in the degree to which they are likely to enhance subordinates' feelings of control and/or provide other coping resources. From the perspective of conservation of resources theory (Hobfoll & Shirom, 2000; Niessen & Jimmieson, 2016), recipients of 'guidance coaching', which emphasises behavioural modelling and observational learning (Hui, Sue-Chan, & Wood, 2019), will be deprived of knowledge needed to cope with

Table 18.3 Specific e-coaching behaviour of guidance and facilitation coaching

Coaching style	Digital coaching behaviour
Guidance coaching	• Request the subordinate to report ways of completing a task. • Make suggestions to the subordinate regarding ways of handling a task. • Provide examples or references to the subordinate. • By use of picture(s), emoji icon(s), or any other graphical form(s), instruct the subordinate the job content. • By use of picture(s), emoji icon(s), or any other graphical form(s), explain the job content to the subordinate. • By use of picture(s), emoji icon(s), or any other graphical form(s), illustrate the work procedures to the subordinate.
Facilitation coaching	• Ask a reflective question when the subordinate asked a question. • Ask the subordinate to express his/her view of an incident. • Facilitate the subordinate to identify areas of improvement. • Express encouragement to the subordinate by use of picture(s), emoji icon(s), or any other graphical form(s). • Appreciate the subordinate by picture(s), emoji icon(s), or any other graphical form(s). • Illustrate a(n) action/behaviour by use of picture(s), emoji icon(s), or any other graphical form(s). • Respond to the subordinate by use of picture(s), emoji icon(s), or any other graphical form(s). • Express feelings regarding the subordinate or an incident by use of picture(s), emoji icon(s), or any other graphical form(s).

changing job demands or lifestyle changes. In comparison, 'facilitation coaching' was seen as promoting self-exploration (Hui et al., 2019).

Based on Hui, Sue-Chan, & Wood's (2013, 2019) model of two coaching styles, Hui, Wu, and Luo (2022) explored coaches' digital coaching behaviours by analysing the digital coaching conversation records of 25 pairs of managers using coaching and their subordinates using instant messaging applications. Following Walther's (1996) hyperpersonal communication theory, they identified and classified both verbal cues (e.g., suggestions, questions, comments, hyperlinks) and non-verbal cues (e.g., emoji, pictures) delivered by the coaches via the digital communication. Table 18.3 includes a list of digital coaching behaviours identified by Hui, Wu, and Luo (2022).

Client attitudes toward different forms of ICF

In the existing literature, numerous studies showed that clients' personal characteristics – such as age, gender, expertise, role, and coaching motivation – significantly affect the trust, engagement, and outcomes from ICT-mediated activities (Bucur, 2018; Empaynado-Porto, 2020; Geissler et al., 2014; Sylvestre et al., 2022; Wiredu et al., 2021). For instance, Geissler and colleagues (2014) suggested that a client's attitude towards ICT is important in determining the success of digital-enabled coaching.

The technology acceptance model (TAM; Davis, 1989), which is a widely accepted theoretical model to predict ICT adoption, proposed that client's intention to use ICT is determined by two primary factors – perceived usefulness and perceived ease of use (Davis, 1989; Davis, Bagozzi, & Warshaw, 1989). Perceived usefulness is defined as the degree to which a person believes that ICT would enhance their learning effectiveness, while ease of use is described as the degree to which a person believes that using the ICT would be free of effort. Specifically, when a client perceives that ICT-mediated coaching can enhance their performance (i.e., perceived usefulness), he/she will be motivated to engage in the digital coaching process. On the other hand, when the ICT applied in digital coaching is perceived as easy to interact with (i.e., perceived ease of use), the clients' intention in receiving digital coaching will be greater.

To improve perceived usefulness, coaches need to promote the additional advantages of using ICT-mediated coaching over face-to-face coaching, as well as explain how it benefits the efficiency and effectiveness of their work. For example, a coach may explain how digital coaching saves costs (e.g., time and travel costs) and supports more efficient work (Passmore, Qi, & Tewald, 2021).

Coaches can also emphasise how digital-enabled coaching provides more positive impacts on their psychological and physical wellbeing such as providing a connection when working remotely or at home, reducing exposure to personal contact for employees who prefer to meet in digital environments and providing the flexibility for short notice access to coaching.

On the other hand, to enhance client's perceived ease of use, training should be provided to increase clients' knowledge of tools and functionality, as well as reassurance on data protection and confidentiality. This is the same for coaches, where face-to-face coach training has been the norm, whereas digital coaching has become the dominant mode of delivery since 2020, but few coaching programmes make explicit reference to digital coaching skills or cover these aspects within the programme.

Coaching content for online wellness coaching

The final factor for successful digital-enabled coaching for wellbeing is the application of a suitable coaching approach. While there is a wide diversity of coaching approaches from which health and wellbeing coaches can draw (Passmore, 2021), there is growing evidence that some models are more effective than others (Wang et al., 2021) and this choice is mediated by both the presenting problem and the individual. By making use of an integrated approach, the health and wellbeing coach can enhance their prospects of helping clients achieve their goals.

The following four coaching frameworks are particularly worthy of reference.

1. Cognitive behavioural coaching

    The cognitive behavioural approach has strong evidence (see Willson, 2022), and by enabling clients to identify and challenge unhelpful thoughts and their associated emotions, it has been proven to be highly effective in addressing a range of health-based issues from anxiety to stress and depression. From its background as Cognitive Behavioural Therapy (CBT), it is now widely used in coaching as one of the three most popular coaching approaches. Like the other approaches described in this section, it is particularly well suited to health and wellbeing coaching, given its origins and is equally well suited to digital environments.

2. Acceptance and commitment coaching

    ACC, a variation of Acceptance and Commitment Therapy (ACT), has grown in popularity alongside ACT, and like CBT, has a strong evidence base (see Leach, 2022). Unlike CBT, which focuses on disputation of unhelpful thoughts, ACC focus on enabling individuals to separate these thoughts from themselves and to become more accepting of these thoughts and of themselves.

3. Motivational interview

    As with most of the frameworks for use in health and wellbeing coaching, MI has its origins in the health sector as a therapeutic approach (Miller & Rollnick, 2012). Originally developed to address addictive behaviours, such as with drugs and alcohol, it has developed into a wider behavioural change approach which can be employed with a range of both workplace and non-clinical conditions (Finlay, 2022). The approach is centred around the idea of encouraging clients to identify their core values and contrast these with their current behaviour, thereby building intrinsic motivation towards change, while acknowledging that change is not a simple or smooth pathway and often involves slips and regressions.

4. Meta-cognitive coaching

    Like other third-wave cognitive behavioural approaches, meta-cognitive coaching builds on CBT but recognises that humans – unlike many other mammals – have the ability to both reflect on their thoughts (think about our thinking) and engage in conversations about those thoughts about their thinking. As with other approaches referenced here, the approach has a strong evidence base (Passmore, 2022) and is particularly effective in supporting clients to explore and address depression and low mood.

Conclusion

As health and wellbeing coaching grows in popularity as a sub-clinical intervention provided by coaches, alongside the growth of digital coaching services, we see digital health and wellbeing coaching being employed by health professionals and commercial digital providers to both address health challenges and enhance wellbeing.

However, to optimise its value, both coaches and clients need to be effective in using the technology to be able to exploit its flexibility, accessibility, and cost benefits while managing the issues which can erode trust or reduce the power which coaching can have as a tool to facilitate and support behavioural transformation.

Reflective questions

1. What theoretical perspective do you usually take when conducting digital-enabled coaching?
2. How should coaches operating in digital environments be trained to optimise their use of these environments?
3. What information should be provided to clients to help them make best use of digital coaching?

References

Anthony, A. B., Gimbert, B., & Fultz, D. M. (2013). The effect of e-coaching attendance on alternatively certified teachers' sense of self-efficacy. *Journal of Technology and Teacher Education, 21*(3), 277–299.

Athanasopoulou, A., & Dopson, S. (2018). A systematic review of executive coaching outcomes: Is it the journey or the destination that matters the most? *The Leadership Quarterly, 29*(1), 70–88.

Barrero, J. M., Bloom, N., Davis, S. J., Meyer, B., & Mihaylov, E. (2022). The shift to remote work lessens wage-growth pressures. *Becker Friedman Institute for Economics Working Paper* (No. 2022–80). https://ssrn.com/abstract=4142773

Boyce, L. A., & Clutterbuck, D. (2010). E-coaching: Accept it, it's here, and it's evolving! In G. Hernez-Broome & L. A. Boyce (eds.), *Advancing executive coaching: Setting the course for successful leadership coaching* (pp. 285–315). San Francisco, CA: Jossey-Bass.

Bucur, M. (2018). *Enhancing organizational performance through e-coaching sessions: Quantitative approach.* Proceedings of the 14th International Scientific Conference, Bucharest, Romania. https://doi.org/10.12753/2066-026X-18-051

CNBC (2020). A new normal: Resilience of a digital economy. *CNBC.* https://www.cnbc.com/advertorial/a-new-normal-resilience-of-a-digital-economy/

Cox, E., & Dannahy, P. (2005). The value of openness in e-relationships: Using nonviolent communication to guide online coaching and mentoring. *International Journal of Evidence Based Coaching and Mentoring, 3*(2), 39–51.

Culnan, M. J., & Markus, M. L. (1987). Information technologies. In F. M. Jablin, L. L. Putnam, K. H. Roberts, & L. W. Porter (eds), *Handbook of organizational communication: An interdisciplinary perspective* (pp. 420–443). Newbury Park, CA: Sage.

Daft, R. L., & Lengel, R. H. (1986). Organizational information requirements, media richness and structural design. *Management Science, 32,* 554–571.

Davis, F. D. (1989). Perceived usefulness, perceived ease of use, and user acceptance of information technology. *MIS Quarterly, 13*(3), 319–340.

Davis, F. D., Bagozzi, R. P., & Warshaw, P. R. (1989). User acceptance of computer technology: A comparison of two theoretical models. *Management Science, 35*(8), 982–1003.

Deci, E. L., & Ryan, R. M. (1985). The general causality orientations scale: Self-determination in personality. *Journal of Research in Personality, 19*(2), 109–134.

Diller, S. J., & Passmore, J. (2023). Defining digital coaching: A qualitative inductive approach. *Frontiers in Psychology, 14.* https://doi.org/10.3389/fpsyg.2023.1148243

Ding, H., & Liu, J. (2022). Paying close attention to strengths mindset: The relationship of employee strengths mindset with job performance. *Current Psychology,* 1–12. https://doi.org/10.1007/s12144-022-03400-8

Draca, M., Duchini, E., Rathelot, R., Turrell, A., & Vattuone, G. (2022). Revolution in progress? The rise of remote work in the UK. *Warwick Economics Research Papers* (No. 1408). https://warwick.ac.uk/fac/soc/economics/research/workingpapers/2022/twerp_1408_-_draca.pdf

Empaynado-Porto, A. E. (2020). Adopting e-learning technologies in higher educational institutions: The role of organizational culture, technology acceptance and attitude. *Review of Social Sciences, 5*(1), 1–11.

Fahy, P. J. (2003). Indicators of support in online interaction. *International Review of Research in Open and Distributed Learning, 4*(1), 1–16.

Filsinger, C. (2014). The virtual line manager as coach: Coaching direct reports remotely and across cultures. *International Journal of Evidence Based Coaching and Mentoring, 12*(2), 188–202.

Finlay, K. (2022) Motivational interviewing coaching: Theory, research and practice. In J. Passmore & S. Leach (eds.), *Third wave cognitive behavioural coaching: Contextual, behavioural and neuroscience approaches for evidenced based coaches* (pp. 255–282). Shoreham-on-Sea: Pavilion.

Fredrickson, B. L. (2004). The broaden – and – build theory of positive emotions. *Philosophical Transactions of the Royal Society of London: Series B: Biological Sciences, 359,* 1367–1377.

Fredrickson, B. L. (2009). *Positivity: Groundbreaking research to release your inner optimist and thrive.* New York: Random House.

Fujitsu (2020). *Fujitsu embars towards 'new normal', redefining working styles for its Japan offices, Fujitsu*. https://www.fujitsu.com/global/about/resources/news/press-releases/2020/0706-01.html

Geissler, H., Hasenbein, M., Kanatouri, S., & Wegener, R. (2014). E-coaching: Conceptual and empirical findings of a virtual coaching programme. *International Journal of Evidence Based Coaching and Mentoring, 12*(2), 165–187.

Ghods, N., Barney, M., & Kirschner, J. (2019). Professional coaching: The impact of virtual coaching on practice and research. In R. N. Landers (ed.), *The Cambridge handbook of technology and employee behavior* (pp. 315–346). Cambridge, UK: Cambridge University Press.

Ghods, N., & Boyce, C. (2013). Virtual coaching and mentoring. In J. Passmore, D. Peterson, & T. Freire (eds.), *The Wiley-Blackwell handbook of the psychology of coaching and mentoring* (pp. 502–523). Chichester: Wiley.

Glass, G. (2022, April 6). 3 ways to coach a hybrid workforce. *Entrepreneur*. https://www.entrepreneur.com/article/420887

Govindji, R., & Linley, P. A. (2007). Strengths use, self-concordance and well-being: Implications for strengths coaching and coaching psychologists. *International Coaching Psychology Review, 2*(2), 143–153.

Green, S., Jarden, A., & Leach, C. (2021). Coaching for workplace wellbeing. In W. A. Smith, I., Boniwell, & S. Green, (eds.) *Positive psychology coaching in the workplace* (pp. 199–219). Switzerland: Springer.

Grover, S., & Furnham, A. (2016). Coaching as a developmental intervention in organisations: A systematic review of its effectiveness and the mechanisms underlying it. *PloS One, 11*(7), e0159137.

Hagemann, V., & Klug, K. (2022). Human resource management in a digital environment. *Diginomics Working Paper, 8*, 1–32. https://doi.org/10.26092/elib/1406

Hancock, J. T. (2004). Verbal irony use in face-to-face and computer-mediated conversations. *Journal of Language and Social Psychology, 23*(4), 447–463.

Heslin, P. A., VandeWalle, D., & Latham, G. P. (2006). Keen to help? Managers' implicit person theories and their subsequent employee coaching. *Personnel Psychology, 59*, 871–902.

Hobfoll, S. E., & Shirom, A. (2000). Conservation of resources theory: Applications to tress and management in workplace. In R. T. Golembiewski (ed.), *Handbook of organizational behavior* (2nd revised ed., pp. 57–81). New York: Dekker.

Hui, R. T. Y., Kong, A., & Wong, L. (2024, June 25–28). *Teaming up with AI: Exploring the impact of anthropomorphic features on AI perception, and the roles of openness to experience and team-member exchange with ai teammate*. [Conference presentation]. European Academy of Management Annual Conference 2024, Bath, UK.

Hui, R. T. Y., Law, K. K., & Lau, S C. P. (2021). Online or offline? Coaching media as mediator of the relationship between coaching style and employee work-related outcomes. *Australian Journal of Management, 46*(2), 326–345.

Hui, T. Y. R., Liao, Y. E., Wu, C. W., & Lee, Y. P. (2017, December 5–8). *The mediating role of idiosyncratic deals on the relationships between coaching and organizational citizenship behavior*. [Conference presentation]. 31st Annual Australian and New Zealand Academy of Management Conference, Melbourne, Australia.

Hui, R. T. Y., & Sue-Chan, C. (2016, August 8). *The influence of three aspects of adaptation on the relationships between coaching and work outcomes*. [Paper presentation]. 76th Annual Meeting of the Academy of Management, Anaheim, United States. https://doi.org/10.5465/ambpp.2016.12889abstract

Hui, R. T. Y., & Sue-Chan, C. (2018). Variations in coaching style and their impact on subordinates' work outcomes. *Journal of Organizational Behavior, 39*(5), 663–679. https://doi.org/10.1002/job.2263

Hui, R. T. Y., & Sue-Chan, C. (2023). The mediating role of self-regulatory emotions in the relationship between peer coaching and student learning in higher education. *Studies of Higher Education*. https://doi.org/10.1080/03075079.2023.2298816

Hui, R. T. Y., Sue-Chan, C., & Wood, R. E. (2013). The contrasting effects of coaching style on task performance: The mediating roles of subjective task complexity and self-set goal. *Human Resource Development Quarterly, 24*(4), 429–458.

Hui, R. T. Y., Sue-Chan, C., & Wood, R. E. (2019). Performing versus adapting: How instructor's coaching style matters in Hong Kong. *International Journal of Human Resource Management.* https://doi.org/10.1080/09585192.2019.1569547

Hui, R. T. Y., Wu, D. C. W., & Luo, J. (2022, December 5–7). *E-coaching and work role performance.* [Paper presentation]. 35th Annual Australian and New Zealand Academy of Management Conference, Gold Coast, Australia.

Hui, R. T. Y., Wu, D. C. W., & Luo, J. (2024, March 19–20). *Coaching in hybrid workplace: An examination of face-to-face and online coaching to enhance self-efficacy and knowledge creation.* [Paper presentation]. 12th International Conference on Information and Education Technology, Yamaguchi, Japan.

Huppert, F. A., & So, T. T. C. (2013). Flourishing across Europe: Application of a new conceptual framework for defining well-being. *Social Indicators Research, 110,* 837–861. https://doi.org/10.1007/s11205-011-9966-7

Iqbal, H. (2020). E-mentoring: An effective platform for distance learning. *E-Mentor, 2* (84), 54–61.

Irving, J. (2021). How have workplace coaches experienced coaching during the Covid-19 pandemic? *International Journal of Evidence Based Coaching & Mentoring, 15,* 37–54. https://doi.org/10.24384/6JAB-TV65

Jones, R. J., Woods, S. A., & Guillaume, Y. R. (2016). The effectiveness of workplace coaching: A meta-analysis of learning and performance outcomes from coaching. *Journal of Occupational and Organizational Psychology, 89*(2), 249–277.

Kanatouri, S. (2020). *The digital coach.* London, UK: Routledge.

Kern, M. L., Waters, L. E., Adler, A., & White, M. A. (2015). A multidimensional approach to measuring well-being in students: Application of the PERMA framework. *The Journal of Positive Psychology, 10*(3), 262–271.

Kock, N. (2004). The psychobiological model: Towards a new theory of computer-mediated communication based on Darwinian evolution. *Organization Science, 15,* 327–348.

Kong, A., Hui, R. T. Y., & Tang, J. K. T. (2023). If you believe, you will receive: VR interview training for pre-employment. In T. Jung, M. C. tom Dieck, & S. M. C. Loureiro (eds.), *Extended reality and metaverse* (pp. 106–111). Cham, Switzerland: Springer.

Leach, S. (2022). Acceptance and commitment coaching: Theory, research and practice. In J. Passmore & S. Leach (eds.), *Third wave cognitive behavioural coaching: Contextual, behavioural and neuroscience approaches for evidenced based coaches* (pp. 137–158). Shoreham-on-Sea: Pavilion.

Lee, V., & Wagner, H. (2002). The effect of social presence on the facial and verbal expression of emotion and the interrelationships among emotion components. *Journal of Nonverbal Behavior, 26*(1), 3–25.

Lewandowski, J., Rosenberg, B. D., Parks, M. J., & Siegel, J. T. (2011). The effect of informal social support: Face-to-face versus computer-mediated communication. *Computers in Human Behavior, 27*(5), 1806–1814.

Linley, P. A., & Harrington, S. (2006). Strengths coaching: A potential-guided approach to coaching psychology. *International Coaching Psychology Review, 1,* 37–46.

Linley, P. A., Nielsen, K. M., Wood, A. M., Gillett, R., & Biswas-Diener, R. (2010). Using signature strengths in pursuit of goals: Effects on goal progress, need satisfaction, and well-being, and implications for coaching psychologists. *International Coaching Psychology Review, 5*(1), 6–15.

Miller, W., & Rollnick, S. (2012). *Motivational interviewing.* New York: Guildford Press.

Mortensen, M. (2015, April 20). When you have to coach remotely. *Harvard Business Review.* https://hbr.org/2015/04/when-you-have-to-coach-remotely

Niessen, C., & Jimmieson, N. L. (2016). Threat of resource loss: The role of self-regulation in adaptive task performance. *Journal of Applied Psychology, 101*(3), 450–462. https://doi.org/10.1037/apl0000049

Oades, L. G. (2016). Coaching for wellbeing at work. In C. Van Nieuwerburgh (ed.), *Coaching in professional contexts* (pp. 199–211), London UK: SAGE Publication.

Passmore, J. (2021). *The coaches handbook.* Abingdon: Routledge.

Passmore, J. (2022) Meta-cognitive coaching: Theory, research and practice. In J. Passmore & S. Leach (eds.), *Third wave cognitive behavioural coaching: Contextual, behavioural and neuroscience approaches for evidenced based coaches* (pp. 195–210). Shoreham-on-Sea: Pavilion.

Passmore, J., & Oades, L. G. (2014). Positive psychology coaching: A model for coaching practice. *The Coaching Psychologist*, 10(2), 68–70.

Passmore, J., Qi, L., & Tewald, S. (2021). Future trends in coaching: Results from a global coach survey 2021. *Coaching Psychologist*, 17(2), 41–51.

Passmore, J., & Tee, D. (2023). The future is now. *Coaching Today*, 47(July), 8–13.

Passmore, J., & Woodward, W. (2023). Coaching education: Wake up to the new digital and AI coaching revolution! *International Coaching Psychology Review*, 18(1), 58–72.

Poepsel, M. (2011). *The impact of an online evidence-based coaching program on goal striving, subjective well-being, and level of hope*. Doctoral dissertation, Capella University.

Prasad, D. K., Mangipudi, D. M. R., Vaidya, D. R., & Muralidhar, B. (2020). Organizational climate, opportunities, challenges and psychological wellbeing of the remote working employees during COVID-19 pandemic: A general linear model approach with reference to information technology industry in hyderabad. *International Journal of Advanced Research in Engineering and Technology*, 11(4), 372–389.

Proctor, C., Maltby, J., & Linley, P. A. (2011). Strengths use as a predictor of well-being and health-related quality of life. *Journal of Happiness Studies*, 12(1), 153–169.

Ramayah, T., Ahmad, N. H., & Hong, T. S. (2012). An assessment of e-training effectiveness in multinational companies in Malaysia. *Journal of Educational Technology & Society*, 15(2), 125–137.

Ribbers, A., & Waringa, A. (2015). *E-coaching: Theory and practice for a new online approach to coaching*. Amsterdam: Routledge.

Rosa, W. E., Karanja, V., Kpoeh, J. D., McMahon, C., & Booth, J. (2021). A virtual coaching workshop for a nurse-led community-based palliative care team in Liberia, West Africa, to promote staff well-being during COVID-19. *Nursing Education Perspectives*, 42(6), E194–E196.

Rossett, A., & Marino, G. (2005). If coaching is good, then e-coaching is. *Training and Development*, 59(11), 46–49.

Rouahi, N., Boucetta, N., & Boussaa, S. (2022). Exploratory study of an e-mentoring professional coaching model of novice midwives in Morocco. *The Pan African Medical Journal*, 41(253), 1–12.

Ryan, R. M., & Deci, E. L. (2000). Self-determination theory and the facilitation of intrinsic motivation, social development, and well-being. *American Psychologist*, 55(1), 68–78.

Santucci, M. (2021). Toward an integrated theory of computer-mediated social interaction. *Team Performance Management: An International Journal*, 27(5/6), 353–376.

Seligman, M. E. O. (2012). *Flourish: A visionary new understanding of happiness and well-being*. London, UK: Free Press.

Shockley, K. M., Allen, T. D., Dodd, H., & Waiwood, A. M. (2021). Remote worker communication during COVID-19: The role of quantity, quality, and supervisor expectation-setting. *Journal of Applied Psychology*, 106(10), 1466–1482.

Short, J., Williams, E., & Christie, B. (1976). *The social psychology of telecommunications*. London: Wiley.

Solis, J. (2022, December 9). *5 best online coaching platforms of 2023, teachfloor*. https://www.teachfloor.com/blog/5-best-online-coaching-platforms

Sparrow, J. (2016). *The impact of e-coaching question framing upon emotions in self-reflection, self-efficacy and subjective wellbeing*. Proceedings of Well-Being 2016: The Third International Conference Exploring the Multi-Dimensions of Well-being (pp. 162–167). Birmingham, UK: Birmingham City University.

Spence, G. B., & Oades, L. G. (2011). Coaching with self-determination theory in mind: Using theory to advance evidence-based coaching practice. *International Journal of Evidence Based Coaching and Mentoring*, 9(2), 37–55.

Straus, E., Uhlig, L., Kühnel, J., & Korunka, C. (2022). Remote workers' well-being, perceived productivity, and engagement: Which resources should HRM improve during COVID-19? A longitudinal diary study. *The International Journal of Human Resource Management*, 1–31. https://doi.org/10.1080/09585192.2022.2075235

Sumner, E. M., & Ramirez, A. (2017). Social information processing theory and hyperpersonal perspective. *The International Encyclopedia of Media Effects, 117*, 1–11.

Sylvestre, M., Musengimana, R., Providence, S., Karungi, C., & Gaspard, G. (2022). A smart learner to smart employee: Moodle as a smart e-learning platform to strengthen the smartness of university students in a developing country. *Kibogora Polytechnic Scientific Journal, 2*(1), 1–20.

Theeboom, T., Beersma, B., & van Vianen, A. E. (2014). Does coaching work? A meta-analysis on the effects of coaching on individual level outcomes in an organizational context. *The Journal of Positive Psychology, 9*(1), 1–18.

Walther, J. B. (1992). Interpersonal effects in computer-mediated interaction: A relational perspective. *Communication Research, 19*, 52–89. https://doi.org/10.1177/009365092019001003

Walther, J. B. (1996). Computer-mediated communication: Impersonal, interpersonal, and hyperpersonal interaction. *Communication Research, 23*, 3–43.

Walther, J. B. (2011). Theories of computer-mediated communication and interpersonal relations. In M. L. Knapp & J. A. Daly (eds.), *The handbook of interpersonal communication* (pp. 443–479). Thousand Oaks, US: SAGE Publication.

Wang, L., & Wentling, T. L. (2001, March). *The relationship between distance coaching and the transfer of training*. Proceedings from the Academy of Human Resource Development Conference, Tulsa, Oklahoma.

Wang, Q., Lai, Y-L., Xu, X., & McDowall, A. (2021). The effectiveness of workplace coaching: A meta-analysis of contemporary psychologically informed coaching approaches. *Journal of Work Applied Management, 14*(1), 77–101. https://doi.org/10.1108/JWAM-04-2021-0030

Willson, R. (2022). Cognitive behavioural coaching: Theory, research and practice. In J. Passmore & S. Leach (eds.), *Third wave cognitive behavioural coaching: Contextual, behavioural and neuroscience approaches for evidenced based coaches* (pp. 31–52). Shoreham-on-Sea: Pavilion.

Wiredu, J., Bo, Y., Labaran, U. I., Georgine, F., & Vicinte, N. K. C. (2021). The effect of the adoption of ict on the monetary performance of rural banks in Ghana: A case study of chosen rural banks in eastern region. *International Journal of Recent Research in Commerce Economics and Management, 8*(1), 230–237.

Wong, E. Y. C., Hui, R. T. Y., & Kong, H. (2023). Perceived usefulness of, engagement with, and effectiveness of virtual reality environments in learning industrial operations: The moderating role of openness to experience. *Virtual Reality, 27*, 2149–2165.

Wright, K. B. (2002). Social support within an on-line cancer community: An assessment of emotional support, perceptions of advantages and disadvantages, and motives for using the community from a communication perspective. *Journal of Applied Communication Research, 30*(3), 195–209.

Wright, K. B., & Bell, S. B. (2003). Health-related support groups on the internet: Linking empirical findings to social support and computer-mediated communication theory. *Journal of Health Psychology, 8*, 39–54.

Chapter 19

Developing workplace cultures for wellbeing

Róisín O'Donovan and Mary Collins

Introduction

Developing a positive workplace culture is critical to attract, engage and retain key talent in organisations. Gallup's most recent leadership trends study shows that global engagement levels are around 21%, meaning that only about 1 in 5 employees are emotionally connected to their organisations (Wigert & Pendell, 2023). This highlights the need to focus on developing a positive workplace culture that can support employees to engage fully in their work, in order for both the organisation and the people within it to flourish.

One of the earliest definitions of engagement came from Kahn (1990), who defined employee engagement as "the harnessing of organization members' selves to their work roles; in engagement, people employ and express themselves physically, cognitively, and emotionally during role performances" (p. 694). In this early research, Kahn (1990) also highlighted the role played by psychological safety in making people feel safe to engage in their work. Coaching has a key role to play in fostering a positive workplace culture that has high psychological safety and supportive leadership, in order to improve engagement and performance levels in the workplace.

This chapter will explore the role of coaching in creating a positive workplace through the lens of Positive Organisational Scholarship (POS), psychological safety and leadership. The chapter will conclude with a focus on practical application of strategies to create a culture of wellbeing through coaching.

Theory and research

Coaching and a positive workplace

Coaching can help people achieve a higher level of wellbeing and performance in work. It is a growth promoting relationship that calls on autonomous motivation in order to facilitate a change process (Moore et al., 2016). In contrast to traditional authoritative models of managers giving individuals solutions to follow, coaching helps people develop their own unique solutions for handling challenges (Rock & Schwartz, 2006). By implementing coaching and coaching skills, organisations can improve performance and empower the people working there, ensure they feel valued and – as a result – improve retention (Tompkins, 2018).

DOI: 10.4324/9781003319016-21

Positive Organisational Scholarship

POS offers an alternative to traditional deficit oriented models used in organisations. The POS approach aims to understand and learn from the positive practices, attributes, behaviours and outcomes of extraordinary organisations and their members (Cameron et al., 2003; Cameron & Spreitzer, 2011; Luthans et al., 2006). Within POS, 'positive' represents the focus placed on achieving the best of human potential, 'organisational' refers to a focus on organisational contexts and 'scholarship' highlights the empirically rigorous and theoretically based scientific approach taken within POS (Cameron & Spreitzer, 2012). POS is focused on what is going right, and how we can create positive workplaces where people are thriving, flourishing and resilient (Cameron & Spreitzer, 2012). A central component of POS is to understand how we can create organisations in which people flourish and can build their skills, and in which they feel a sense of purpose, fulfilment and meaning at work (Cameron et al., 2003; Cameron & Spreitzer, 2012).

Flourishing at work

Workplace flourishing is a multidimensional construct that occurs when people feel good (emotional wellbeing), function well (psychological wellbeing) and fit in (social wellbeing) in an organisational setting (Rothmann et al., 2019). When people are flourishing at work, they are self-motivated, happy and continuously learning (Bono & Yoon, 2012; Hart et al., 2015). There are hedonic and eudemonic aspects of flourishing. Hedonic flourishing relates to a positive mindset and the experience of pleasure (Peterson et al., 2005). The eudemonic aspect of flourishing can occur while facing challenges and includes authenticity, meaning and growth (Huta & Waterman, 2014). Recognising one's purpose is a fundamental part of human flourishing (Wiedemann, 2019) and contributes to peoples self-confidence, satisfaction at work and belief in the positive contribution of their work (Hirschi & Herrmann, 2012).

It is important to be aware of the line between a positive workplace and toxic positivity in the workplace. Toxic positivity in the workplace occurs when people's dissent and appraisal of alternatives are suppressed and groupthink is present (Goodman, 2022). This creates a pressure to maintain a façade of positivity and the illusion of there being no conflict or tension. Doing this ultimately makes employees less happy, stifles creativity and hinders workplace performance. To avoid toxic positivity, a positive workplace should be psychologically safe. Psychological safety does not imply a team without any conflict or problems (Edmondson, 2003). In fact, psychological safety is needed in order for productive conflict to occur (Hoenderdos, 2013). When a workplace is psychologically safe, everyone working there believes it is safe to speak up and raise a concern or new idea, even if others disagree. This fosters authenticity, learning and improved performance at work (Bradley et al., 2012; Edmondson & Lei, 2014; Hoenderdos, 2013).

Psychological safety and workplace wellbeing

When psychological safety is present, there is a shared belief that people are safe to take interpersonal risks, such as speaking up, raising concerns and engaging in voice behaviours (Edmondson, 1999). Psychological safety is a complex and dynamic construct that is associated with teamwork, communication, and engagement at work. It plays a key role in creating a dynamic workplace culture where everyone can effectively communicate, collaborate and learn. As a result, it has become increasingly relevant to thriving in a post-pandemic workplace that requires creativity, innovation and experimentation in order to adapt to new ways of working, such as hybrid models (Edmondson & Bransby, 2023). The most recent review of psychological safety literature has concluded that psychological safety research has come of age during the past decade. It is no longer a novel construct in need of theoretical and empirical justification, but has become a mainstream construct in the organizational behaviour literature (Edmondson & Bransby, 2023).

As a complex and dynamic phenomenon, psychological safety affects everyday workplace interactions and experiences. Psychological safety improves team performance, communication, trust and decision-making (Edmondson & Lei, 2014; Newman et al., 2017; Singer & Edmondson, 2012). It creates an environment where failure is not feared but is seen as a learning opportunity by flattening hierarchies and reducing professional boundaries within and across teams (De Hoogh et al., 2015; Edmondson, 1999; Malhotra et al., 2017). Psychological safety plays an important role within a coaching context because it facilitates the behaviour change processes by framing lapses or relapses as normal and as opportunities to grow and learn (Moore et al., 2016). While lack of psychological safety is associated with silence (Brinsfield, 2013; Detert & Edmondson, 2011; Kish-Gephart et al., 2009), speaking up and voice behaviours – such as asking questions and sharing novel ideas – are facilitated by psychological safety (Bienefeld & Grote, 2014; Edmondson & Lei, 2014; Leroy et al., 2012; Nembhard & Edmondson, 2011; Pearsall & Ellis, 2011). When there is psychological safety, people can engage in learning behaviours, including knowledge transfer, knowledge sharing, speaking up and creativity. The presence of psychological safety frees cognitive and emotional resources to allow people to engage in learning, innovation and creative behaviours (Edmondson & Bransby, 2023; Iqbal et al., 2020). Coaching in the workplace can both facilitate and be facilitated by the presence of psychological safety.

Having psychological safety fulfils our basic need for safety and belonging, allowing us to engage in learning behaviour that can ultimately lead to high self-esteem and self-actualisation. Early research on psychological safety focused on the individual level and explored the vital role it plays in making people feel secure, capable of change and engaged in their work (Kahn, 1990; Schein & Bennis, 1965; Schein, 1993). This focus is still present in current research, which centres on how psychological safety improves people's experience at work. This research explores psychological safety in relation to positive psychology constructs, including relationships, emotion, identity, engagement, trust, thriving, job satisfaction, respect and workplace safety. This area of research is directly relevant to coaching and to wellbeing at work. Individuals' experiences of psychological safety are complex and nuanced. They are influenced by leadership, interpersonal relationships and individual characteristics (O'Donovan et al., 2021). When individuals feel psychologically safe, they can be open and honest in their communication, and they can be their authentic selves at work. This ultimately supports people's job engagement and satisfaction, helping them to cope with stress at work (Edmondson & Bransby, 2023).

The role of the leader in fostering psychological safety has played a central role in the psychological safety literature. Many leadership constructs have been found to encourage psychological safety: leader inclusiveness, transformational leadership, leader-member exchange, ethical leadership, servant leadership and change-oriented leaders (Aranzamendez et al., 2015; Frazier et al., 2017; Hassan & Jiang, 2021; Hirak et al., 2012; Miao et al., 2019; Nembhard & Edmondson, 2011; Newman et al., 2017; Tu et al., 2019). Leaders' attitudes and behaviours such as inviting participation, listening and resolving conflict are associated with team psychological safety (Castro et al., 2018; O'Donovan et al., 2021; Remtulla et al., 2021). High power distance, which is when people perceive power to be unequally distributed, is negatively associated with psychological safety at the individual and group levels (Appelbaum et al., 2016; Hu et al., 2018). As a result, leaders must work to reduce the power distance between themselves and other team members. Past research has indicated that inclusive leadership can reduce power distance and encourages team psychological safety (Hirak et al., 2012; Nembhard & Edmondson, 2011). When team members trust their leader, they feel comfortable engaging in interpersonal risk taking because they know that their leaders will not unfairly punish them if an unfavourable outcome occurs (Walumbwa & Schaubroeck, 2009).

Leadership and a wellbeing culture

It is clear that leadership has a key role to play in developing a culture of wellbeing in organisations. Over 40 years of research has shown that transformational leadership positively predicts outcomes for enhancing a positive workplace culture (Bass & Bass, 2009). Transformational leadership can be defined as a process that changes and transforms individuals (Northouse, 2021). It is particularly relevant to create a culture of wellbeing, as it is focused on the ability to get people to want to change, to improve and to be led. Transformational leaders demonstrate inspirational motivation, charisma, intellectual stimulation and a personal approach when communicating with the team (Bass & Avolio, 1994). There are four key factors to transformational leadership, also known as the 'four I's': idealised influence, inspirational motivation, intellectual stimulation and individual consideration. Each factor will be discussed in the context of how leaders can create a culture of wellbeing, as follows.

Idealised influence describes leaders who are exemplary role models for their teams. People with idealised influence can be trusted and respected to make good decisions for the organisation. In the context of wellbeing, these leaders are positive role models in terms of their own health and wellbeing.

Inspirational motivation describes leaders who motivate the team to commit to the vision of the organisation. They encourage team spirit to reach performance goals and can also encourage positive wellbeing behaviours in the team to support the organisational vision around wellbeing.

Intellectual stimulation describes leaders who encourage innovation and creativity through challenging the normal beliefs or views of a group. These leaders promote critical thinking and problem-solving to enhance the organisation's culture of wellbeing.

Individual consideration describes leaders who act as coaches and mentors to their team members, as appropriate. This personalised approach is very connected to SelfDetermination Theory (SDT), defined as a person's ability to reach his/her highest level of motivation, engagement, performance, persistence and creativity.

(Deci & Ryan, 1985)

Self-Determination Theory and leadership

SDT (Deci & Ryan, 1985) is built on the belief that there are three primary psychological needs to be meet in order for people to flourish in the workplace, as follows.

Autonomy: the need to feel autonomous. Leaders need to create an environment in which team members can be in control of their own work and do not feel like they are being 'micro-managed'. West and Dawson (2012) emphasise the need for managers in healthcare roles to give their staff autonomy, as well as providing support and recognition.

Relatedness: the need to feel connected to others. This is particularly important in the context of developing and sustaining a positive organisation culture. Leaders must create a sense of connectedness to the organisation's vision, mission and values. Also, in the emerging world of hybrid working, leaders must be intentional about how best to connect people when they are together in person and be creative around opportunities to connect in an online capacity, e.g., building in networking time before and after online meetings.

Competence: the need to know how well you are doing. Strong leaders have regular coaching conversations with their team members and provide constructive feedback and recognition. Training and development is prioritised and valued in positive workplace cultures.

By working in accordance with autonomy, relatedness and competence, leaders can embody coaching skills in order to elicit autonomous motivation in their teams, encourage them to engage in chance processes and help them to achieve a higher level of wellbeing and performance at work.

The PERMA model is a theoretical framework developed by Seligman (2011) and includes five elements of wellbeing: positive emotion (P), engagement (E), relationships (R), meaning (M) and accomplishment (A). Subsequently, a sixth element, Health (H), was added to the model to include the importance of health for wellbeing (Butler & Kern, 2016; Friedman & Kern, 2014; McQuaid & Kern, 2018). The PERMA-H model can be used to guide workplace policies and practices to support wellbeing. Drawing on coaching skills and techniques can build capacity for change in people and help them to identify what makes them flourish (Moore et al., 2016). Coaching techniques such as appreciative inquiry (Cooperrider & Whitney, 1999) and creating more opportunities for joy and fun in daily workplace routines can create more positive emotions at work. These positive emotions can broaden perspective on situations, allowing people to generate alternative understandings and solutions and build their intellectual, social and physical resources for better engagement and learning at work (Fredrickson, 2013). Creating time to build and maintain relationships in the workplace in another important part of supporting positive workplace culture and wellbeing (Kern et al., 2014; Seligman, 2011).

Coaching in practice

Coaching and coaching leadership skills can help to cultivate psychological safety in the workplace. In this section, we outline a number of practical steps which leaders can take to building psychological safety.

Create safe spaces

Research has highlighted the importance of having private spaces where team members can raise an issue that they find too difficult to raise with the whole team (O'Donovan & McAuliffe, 2020). One-to-one coaching sessions can provide this safe space at work. Building on a coaching contract that has confidentiality at its core, coaching sessions can be an opportunity to brainstorm approaches and set goals for bringing up difficult issues at work and to cultivate behaviours that foster psychological safety.

Foster shared mental models

Group coaching can facilitate the development of shared mental models within teams. Shared mental models refer to team members' overlapping mental representation of knowledge (Van den Bossche et al., 2011). In order for psychological safety to be present, teams should develop a shared understanding for what issues are important to raise at work. Research has found that when team members feel less psychologically safe, they are uncertain about whether it is appropriate to raise complex, personal and/or sensitive issues at work. It is also important that teams develop a shared understanding of their own roles and responsibilities on the team, and those of others. Feeling valued at work fosters psychological safety (O'Donovan & McAuliffe, 2020). Openly sharing the strengths and contributions made by each team member can ensure that members value one another and feel valued themselves. By identifying, exploring and amplifying the best aspects of a person or situation, appreciative inquiry (Cooperrider & Whitney, 1999) offers an opportunity for teams to explore what they do well and how each team member contributes to the overall functioning and performance of the team. This approach is also in line with POS, which seeks to study, understand and enhance what is going well within exceptional organisations.

Play

Taking part in serious play can enhance participants sense of psychological safety by fostering positive emotion, reducing negative bias and creating conditions for flow (Wheeler et al., 2020). In a study using Lego Serious Play (Lego, 2019), participants built their own 3D LEGO® model in response to the facilitator's questions. The models built by participants represented their ideas or experience and served as a basis for group discussion, knowledge sharing, problem-solving and decision-making (Wheeler et al., 2020). This intervention used a coaching style of facilitation to encourage participants' self-discovery and sense-making. Improvisation training has also been found to foster psychological safety by increasing feelings of equality and encouraging team members to be present and listen to one another (Nordean, 2020). Improvisation exercises provide a platform for teams to practise interaction and interpersonal skills that cultivate psychological safety. Improvisation training is structured by four main tenets: co-creation, acceptance and heighten ('Yes and'), celebration of failure, and listening (Leonard & Yorton, 2015).

Inclusive behaviour

Inclusive behaviour involves team members using words and deeds that invite and appreciate contributions from others. Coaches can help all team members to engage in inclusive behaviours. Coaches can model this behaviour in their own coaching by asking open questions and responding with affirming reflections. They can also work with team members to set goals around using more inclusive behaviour, help to build motivation around doing so and identify opportunities for being inclusive in day-to-day working interactions. To improve wellbeing in the workplace, diversity, equity and inclusion (DEI) needs to be a top priority for organisations. Engaging in and promoting inclusive leadership is important in order to build and maintain a positive workplace. Bourke et al. (2020) found that inclusive leaders share the following six signature traits, these can be used by leaders in order to cultivate an open, inclusive and equitable workplace.

1. *Visible commitment:* Demonstrate an authentic commitment to diversity, challenge the status quo, hold others accountable and make diversity and inclusion a personal priority.
2. *Humility:* Be modest about capabilities, admit mistakes and create the space for others to contribute. Not ego-driven; focused on the 'greater good' rather than their own needs.
3. *Awareness of bias:* Show awareness of personal blind spots, as well as flaws in the system, and work hard to ensure fairness across all processes and interactions.
4. *Curiosity about others:* Drawing on key coaching skills to demonstrate an open mindset and deep curiosity about others, listen without judgement and seek with empathy to understand those around them.
5. *Cultural intelligence:* Be attentive to others' cultures and adapt as required.
6. *Effective collaboration:* Empower others, pay attention to diversity of thinking and psychological safety, and focus on team cohesion.

Psychological safety is a multi-level construct (Edmondson & Lei, 2014; Newman et al., 2017), and therefore, a multi-level approach is required to improve it. While team leaders play an important role in creating and supporting psychological safety (Leroy et al., 2012; O'Donovan & McAuliffe, 2020), other team members also play an important role in creating and maintaining psychological safety (O'Donovan & McAuliffe, 2020). Leaders alone cannot improve psychological safety, and there is a need for effort and involvement from all team members to create and maintain a safe environment (O'Donovan & McAuliffe, 2020). Coaches should work with all team members to ensure that inclusive behaviours are being used throughout the workplace to elicit opinions, encourage voices and enhance psychological safety – particularly among individuals who are more likely to experience low psychological safety (O'Donovan & McAuliffe, 2020).

Conclusion

This chapter has outlined the important role that coaching and leadership coaching skills can play in building a positive workplace culture where both the organisation and the people who work within it can flourish. Drawing on concepts such as Positive Organisational Scholarship, flourishing and psychological safety can inform the focus of coaching in the workplace and ensure that people are supported in cultivating a sense of safety, autonomy and positivity at work. Both leaders and other team members can draw on coaching skills to cultivate more positive emotions at work, improve relationships, create safe spaces and ensure that everyone feels included and valued at work.

Reflective questions

1. How can coaching contribute to a culture of workplace wellbeing in your context?
2. What support is needed to embed a culture of coaching?
3. What leadership coaching skills can foster psychological safety in your workplace?

References

Appelbaum, N. P., Dow, A., Mazmanian, P. E., Jundt, D. K., & Appelbaum, E. N. (2016). The effects of power, leadership and psychological safety on resident event reporting. Medical education, 50(3), 343–350.

Aranzamendez, G., James, D., & Toms, R. (2015). Finding antecedents of psychological safety: A step toward quality improvement. Nursing forum, 50(3), 171–178. https://doi.org/10.1111/nuf.12085

Bass, B. M., & Avolio, B. J. (1994). Improving organizational effectiveness through transformational leadership: Sage.

Bass, B. M., & Bass, R. (2009). The Bass handbook of leadership: Theory, research, and managerial applications: Simon and Schuster.

Bienefeld, N., & Grote, G. (2014). Speaking up in ad hoc multiteam systems: Individual-level effects of psychological safety, status, and leadership within and across teams. European journal of work and organizational psychology, 23(6), 930–945.

Bono, J. E., & Yoon, D. J. (2012). Positive supervisory relationships. In L. M. Shore, J. A.-M. Coyle-Shapiro, & L. E. Tetrick (Eds.), The employee–organization relationship: Applications for the 21st century (pp. 43–66): Routledge.

Bourke, J., Titus, A., & Espedido, A. (2020). The key to inclusive leadership. Harvard business review, 6.

Bradley, B. H., Postlethwaite, B. E., Klotz, A. C., Hamdani, M. R., & Brown, K. G. (2012). Reaping the benefits of task conflict in teams: The critical role of team psychological safety climate. Journal of applied psychology, 97(1), 151.

Brinsfield, C. T. (2013). Employee silence motives: Investigation of dimensionality and development of measures. Journal of organizational behavior, 34(5), 671–697.

Butler, J., & Kern, M. L. (2016). The PERMA-Profiler: A brief multidimensional measure of flourishing. International journal of wellbeing, 6(3).

Cameron, K. S., Dutton, J., & Quinn, R. (2003). Positive organisational scholarship: Barrett-Kohler.

Cameron, K. S., & Spreitzer, G. M. (2011). Introduction: What is positive about positive organizational scholarship? In K. S. Cameron, & G. M. Spreitzer (Eds.), The Oxford handbook of positive organizational scholarship (pp. 1–14): Oxford University Press.

Cameron, K. S., & Spreitzer, G. M. (2012). The Oxford handbook of positive organizational scholarship: OUP USA.

Castro, D. R., Anseel, F., Kluger, A. N., Lloyd, K. J., & Turjeman-Levi, Y. (2018). Mere listening effect on creativity and the mediating role of psychological safety. Psychology of aesthetics, creativity, and the arts, 12(4), 489.

Cooperrider, D. L., & Whitney, D. K. (1999). Appreciative inquiry: Berrett Koehler Communications San Francisco.

Deci, E. L., & Ryan, R. M. (1985). The general causality orientations scale: Self-determination in personality. Journal of research in personality, 19(2), 109–134.

De Hoogh, A. H., Greer, L. L., & Den Hartog, D. N. (2015). Diabolical dictators or capable commanders? An investigation of the differential effects of autocratic leadership on team performance. The leadership quarterly, 26(5), 687–701.

Detert, J. R., & Edmondson, A. C. (2011). Implicit voice theories: Taken-for-granted rules of self-censorship at work. Academy of management journal, 54(3), 461–488.

Edmondson, A. (1999). Psychological safety and learning behavior in work teams. Administrative science quarterly, 44(2), 350–383.

Edmondson, A. C. (2003). Speaking up in the operating room: How team leaders promote learning in interdisciplinary action teams. Journal of management studies, 40(6), 1419–1452.

Edmondson, A. C., & Bransby, D. P. (2023). Psychological safety comes of age: Observed themes in an established literature. Annual review of organizational psychology and organizational behavior, 10, 55–78.

Edmondson, A. C., & Lei, Z. (2014). Psychological safety: The history, renaissance, and future of an interpersonal construct. Annual review of organizational psychology and organizational behavior, 1(1), 23–43. https://doi.org/10.1146/annurev-orgpsych-031413-091305

Frazier, M. L., Fainshmidt, S., Klinger, R. L., Pezeshkan, A., & Vracheva, V. (2017). Psychological safety: A meta-analytic review and extension. Personnel psychology, 70(1), 113–165.

Fredrickson, B. L. (2013). Positive emotions broaden and build. In Advances in experimental social psychology (Vol. 47, pp. 1–53): Elsevier.

Friedman, H. S., & Kern, M. L. (2014). Personality, well-being, and health. Annual review of psychology, 65, 719–742.

Goodman, W. (2022). Toxic Positivity: Keeping it real in a world obsessed with being happy: Penguin.

Hart, P. M., Cotton, P., & Scollay, C. E. (2015). Flourishing at work: Improving wellbeing and engagement. In Flourishing in Life, Work and Careers (pp. 281–312): Edward Elgar Publishing.

Hassan, S., & Jiang, Z. (2021). Facilitating learning to improve performance of law enforcement workgroups: The role of inclusive leadership behavior. International public management journal, 24(1), 106–130.

Hirak, R., Peng, A. C., Carmeli, A., & Schaubroeck, J. M. (2012). Linking leader inclusiveness to work unit performance: The importance of psychological safety and learning from failures. The leadership quarterly, 23(1), 107–117.

Hirschi, A., & Herrmann, A. (2012). Vocational identity achievement as a mediator of presence of calling and life satisfaction. Journal of career assessment, 20(3), 309–321.

Hoenderdos, J. W. (2013). Towards an observational measure for team psychological safety: University of Twente.

Hu, J., Erdogan, B., Jiang, K., Bauer, T. N., & Liu, S. (2018). Leader humility and team creativity: The role of team information sharing, psychological safety, and power distance. Journal of applied psychology, 103(3), 313.

Huta, V., & Waterman, A. S. (2014). Eudaimonia and its distinction from hedonia: Developing a classification and terminology for understanding conceptual and operational definitions. Journal of happiness studies, 15, 1425–1456.

Iqbal, A., Latif, K. F., & Ahmad, M. S. (2020). Servant leadership and employee innovative behaviour: Exploring psychological pathways. Leadership & organization development journal, 41(6), 813–827.

Kahn, W. A. (1990). Psychological conditions of personal engagement and disengagement at work. Academy of management journal, 33(4), 692–724.

Kern, M. L., Waters, L., Adler, A., & White, M. (2014). Assessing employee wellbeing in schools using a multifaceted approach: Associations with physical health, life satisfaction, and professional thriving: Oxford University Press.

Kish-Gephart, J. J., Detert, J. R., Treviño, L. K., & Edmondson, A. C. (2009). Silenced by fear: The nature, sources, and consequences of fear at work. Research in organizational behavior, 29, 163–193.

Lego. (2019). Lego serious Play®. https://www.lego.com/en-gb/seriousplay

Leonard, K., & Yorton, T. (2015). Yes, and: Lessons from the second city: Blackstone Audio.

Leroy, H., Dierynck, B., Anseel, F., Simons, T., Halbesleben, J. R., McCaughey, D., Savage, G. T., & Sels, L. (2012). Behavioral integrity for safety, priority of safety, psychological safety, and patient safety: A team-level study. Journal of applied psychology, 97(6), 1273.

Luthans, F., Avey, J. B., Avolio, B. J., Norman, S. M., & Combs, G. M. (2006). Psychological capital development: Toward a micro-intervention. Journal of organizational behavior: The international journal of industrial, occupational and organizational psychology and behavior, 27(3), 387–393.

Malhotra, M. K., Ahire, S., & Shang, G. (2017). Mitigating the impact of functional dominance in cross-functional process improvement teams. Decision sciences, 48(1), 39–70.

McQuaid, M., & Kern, P. (2018). Your wellbeing blueprint: Feeling good and doing well at work: Michelle McQuaid.

Miao, Q., Eva, N., Newman, A., & Cooper, B. (2019). CEO entrepreneurial leadership and performance outcomes of top management teams in entrepreneurial ventures: The mediating effects of
psychological safety. Journal of small business management, 57(3), 1119–1135.

Moore, M., Jackson, E., & Moran, B. (2016). Coaching psychology manual: Williams & Wilkins.

Nembhard, I. M., & Edmondson, A. C. (2011). Psychological safety: A foundation for speaking
up, collaboration, and experimentation in organizations: Oxford University Press.

Newman, A., Donohue, R., & Eva, N. (2017). Psychological safety: A systematic review of the
literature. Human resource management review, 27(3), 521–535.

Nordean, M. M. (2020). Assessing the impacts of work-related applications of improvisation training on psychological safety in teams: Pepperdine University.

Northouse, P. G. (2021). Leadership: Theory and practice: Sage publications.

O'Donovan, R., De Brún, A., & McAuliffe, E. (2021). Healthcare professionals experience of psychological safety, voice, and silence. Frontiers in psychology, 12. doi:10.3389/fpsyg.2021.626689

O'Donovan, R., & McAuliffe, E. (2020). Exploring psychological safety in healthcare teams to
inform the development of interventions: Combining observational, survey and interview data.
BMC health services research, 20(1), 1–16.

Pearsall, M. J., & Ellis, A. P. (2011). Thick as thieves: The effects of ethical orientation and psychological safety on unethical team behavior. Journal of applied psychology, 96(2), 401.

Peterson, C., Park, N., & Seligman, M. E. (2005). Orientations to happiness and life satisfaction:
The full life versus the empty life. Journal of happiness studies, 6, 25–41.

Remtulla, R., Hagana, A., Houbby, N., Ruparell, K., Aojula, N., Menon, A., Fischer, M., Straus,
S. E., Ivers, N. M., & Meyer, E. (2021). Exploring the barriers and facilitators of psychological
safety in primary care teams: A qualitative study. BMC health services research, 21(1), 1–12.
https://doi.org/10.1186/s12913-021-06973-3

Rock, D., & Schwartz, J. (2006). A brain-based approach to coaching. International journal of
coaching in organizations, 4(2), 32–43.

Rothmann, S., Redelinghuys, K., & Botha, E. (2019). Workplace flourishing: Measurement, antecedents and outcomes. SA journal of industrial psychology, 45(1), 1–11.

Schein, E. H. (1993). On dialogue, culture, and organizational learning. Organizational dynamics,
22(2), 40–52.

Schein, E. H., & Bennis, W. G. (1965). Personal and organizational change through group methods: The laboratory approach: JohnWiley and Sons. Inc. Search in.

Seligman, M. (2011). Flourish: Simon Schuster.

Singer, S., & Edmondson, A. (2012). Confronting the tension between learning and performance.
The society for organizational learning journal, 11(4), 34–43.

Tompkins, W. (2018). Coaching in the workplace. Journal of practical consulting, 6(1), 115–122.

Tu, Y., Lu, X., Choi, J. N., & Guo, W. (2019). Ethical leadership and team-level creativity: Mediation of psychological safety climate and moderation of supervisor support for creativity. Journal
of business ethics, 159, 551–565.

Van den Bossche, P., Gijselaers, W., Segers, M., Woltjer, G., & Kirschner, P. (2011). Team learning:
Building shared mental models. Instructional science, 39, 283–301.

Walumbwa, F. O., & Schaubroeck, J. (2009). Leader personality traits and employee voice behavior: Mediating roles of ethical leadership and work group psychological safety. Journal of applied
psychology, 94(5), 1275.

West, M., & Dawson, J. (2012). Employee engagement and NHS performance: King's Fund
London.

Wheeler, S., Passmore, J., & Gold, R. (2020). All to play for: LEGO® SERIOUS PLAY® and its
impact on team cohesion, collaboration and psychological safety in organisational settings using
a coaching approach. Journal of work-applied management, 12(2), 141–157.

Wiedemann, C. S. (2019). Purpose-driven: Employee engagement from a human flourishing perspective: Clemson University,

Wigert, B., & Pendell, R. (2023). 6 trends leaders need to navigate this year: Gallup. https://www.
gallup.com/workplace/468173/workplace-findings-leaders-need-navigate-year.aspx

Chapter 20

Measuring wellbeing in coaching

Aaron Jarden, Annalise Roache, and Rebecca Jarden

Introduction

The assessment of a person's wellbeing is an important link in the coaching–performance connection, which helps a coach gain understanding of the person's wellbeing, and it allows insight into likely wellbeing and coaching approaches. Coaches, practitioners, and leaders are not using research-based practices or theoretically grounded approaches if they progress working with clients without gaining such assessment information to inform their decision-making, which highlights what is influencing wellbeing, and for whom. This is why wellbeing assessments are so important for coaching approaches that target or incorporate wellbeing interventions.

This chapter outlines the fundamentals of assessment, as well as three principles of good assessments. We then summarise wellbeing assessments in a coaching context: what they are and why they are important, and we provide some examples of good assessment tools that coaches could use. Following this, we explain how various stakeholders can use wellbeing assessment data in decision-making. Finally, we suggest a list of questions decision-makers and coaches will find useful in contemplating and choosing assessment approaches and tools. We expect this chapter will aid in promoting proper and relevant wellbeing assessment practice by practitioners and coaches, which will lead to making wellbeing interventions more effective and sustainable.

What is assessment?

The word 'assessment' is often used with three similar terms; testing, measurement, and evaluation. As such, all these terms need some clarification. To start with 'testing': A test is defined as "an instrument or technique that measures someone's knowledge of something to determine what [they] know or [have] learned" (Penn State University, 2019, First section, para 1), and the process of testing as "the act or practice of giving tests to measure someone's knowledge or ability" (Cambridge English Dictionary, 2019a). For example, you might administer a strengths test to an employee. The next term, 'measurement', is when "a 'test' is given, and a 'score' is obtained" (Shum, O'Gorman, Creed, & Myors, 2017, p. 17). For example, the employee's result (the score) of the strengths test (e.g., their score on the strength of leadership) would indicate a measurement has taken place. The term 'evaluation' is "the process of judging or calculating the quality, importance, amount, or value of something" (Cambridge English Dictionary, 2019b), but is also the "appraisal of something, particularly to determine its worth, value, or desirability"

DOI: 10.4324/9781003319016-22

(APA, 2022), such as when using knowledge of the employee's strengths determines their position for a specialised working group. Finally, the term 'assessment' indicates "the act of judging or deciding the amount, value, quality, or importance of something, or the judgment or decision that is made" (Cambridge English Dictionary, 2019c). Assessment incorporates the broad range of tools and methods that coaches and practitioners utilise to test, measure, evaluate, and document the learning progress, states, skill acquisition, or educational requirements of coachees. For example, the coachees' strengths test maybe utilised to ascertain their leadership ability.

As determined by these definitions, and with the commonality between definitions, it may be appropriate to wonder "What's the difference between testing, measurement, evaluation, and assessment"? Instead of distinguishing these terms lexicologically, we take a more pragmatic perspective. Our view (also outlined in Jarden, Jarden, Chyuan Chin, & Kern, 2021) is that a *test* provides a *measurement* of an aspect, or aspects, which can then be *evaluated* against some criteria or knowledge base. This process encompasses the process of *assessment* more generally. In other words, 'assessment' is the more extensive or overarching process incorporating tests, measures, and evaluations. So, an assessment uses a test, which measures something and collects data, and then an evaluation is made of the data.

What does a good assessment look like?

With insight into 'what' assessment encapsulates, there exist certain principles that enable good assessments. We believe in a coaching context that three principles are especially valuable for good assessments: (1) assessments follow good assessment processes; (2) assessments use measures which are psychometrically sound; and (3) assessments adhere to ethical considerations. We now explain and expand on each of these three aspects in more detail.

First, proper assessment processes should be used for all assessments (see Price, 2016). Planning of the assessment is where the assessment process starts (e.g., determining assessment goals and the methods to obtain such goals). Once planning is completed, the commencement of data collection occurs, which may acquire qualitative and quantitative data via methods such as surveys, behavioural measures, observations, experience sampling, or existing records, to name only a few. Once the data is obtained, it is then managed. The raw data is coded and processed, in line with the goals of the assessment; statistical analyses are conducted; and judgements are made about the results of the analyses. Finally, communication of the results happens, usually via a range of methods (e.g., written reports, verbal reporting, infographics, conference presentations, academic papers, and transmission of results to participants and stakeholders of the assessments). These four main overarching processes (planning, data collection, data processing, and communication) indicate proper assessment processes and should be followed.

Second, all assessments ought to be psychometrically sound. All measures and assessment batteries (a battery is a collection of measures) should be empirically validated and rigorously tested, particularly considering their reliability and validity. Reliability entails that consistently accurate results are obtained from the assessment. Making sure that the assessment truly measures what it should measure, and what it purports to measure, relates to its validity. As such, good assessments ought to be both reliable and valid. (See chapters 4–5 of Shum, O'Gorman, Creed, & Myors, 2017; or Cook & Beckman, 2006; or Coolican, 2014, for detailed consideration of validity and reliability.)

Third, appropriate ethical approaches should be followed for all assessments (Jarden, Rashid, Roache, & Lomas, 2021). Taking an approach which is ethical could include various aspects, for instance: considering issues of confidentiality and privacy, gaining proper consent, using appropriate tests for relevant contexts and ages, inspecting and obtaining copyright for tests, safe data storage, collecting data in line with aims and plans, and thinking about the risks and perils related to the outcomes of testing such as feedback around sensitive topics (for examples, see Jarden, Jarden, Chyuan Chin, & Kern, 2021). These various ethical aspects are taken into account by good assessments as they strive to promote the good (beneficence) and avoid harm (non-maleficence).

So, in summary, good assessments in a coaching context follow good assessment processes, use psychometrically sound measures, and fully consider and adhere to ethical considerations. We now turn to assessing wellbeing more specifically.

Assessing wellbeing

Having covered principles of good assessment and what assessments refer to, we now outline wellbeing assessments within coaching contexts. We take a wellbeing assessment to be an assessment that targets wellbeing as largely conceived and defined. As such, it relies on the definition of 'wellbeing' being utilised in each context, and on the particular wellbeing model the description of wellbeing is associated with. In the following subsections, we consider models and definitions of wellbeing used within coaching, and then point to both process and context aspects. We also emphasise the importance of systems considerations as wellbeing assessments generally happen within systems of one sort or another.

Defining wellbeing

In most cases, a definition of wellbeing is based at the level of the individual; for example: "the notion of how well a person's life is going for that person. A person's wellbeing is what is 'good for' them" (Crisp, 2021, The Concept section, para 1), or "wellbeing can be understood as how people feel and how they function both on a personal and social level, and how they evaluate their lives as a whole" (Michaelson, Mahony, & Schifferes, 2012, p. 6).

We take the view that wellbeing incorporates equal qualities of what is not going well in life (e.g., feelings of stress, loneliness, low mood), as well as what is going well in life (e.g., being engaged in life, feeling happy, having meaning). Such a point of view is in keeping with positive psychology's initial notion and intent (Seligman & Csikszentmihalyi, 2000). Consequently, both what is not going well and what is going well for an individual ought to be captured in a wellbeing assessment. In addition, wellbeing is multifaceted (Hone, Jarden, Schofield, & Duncan, 2014) including elements such as behaviours (e.g., meditating, sleeping), cognitions (e.g., judgements of life satisfaction, trouble concentrating), and emotions (e.g., sadness, happiness), as well as physiology (e.g., somatic symptoms, heart rate variability). Moreover, moving past wellbeing's complexity, there are many other issues that could be debated or considered, such as unidimensional versus bidimensional conceptions, hedonic (more pleasure-based) versus eudaimonic (more meaning- and growth-based) notions, subjective versus objective viewpoints, experienced versus evaluative philosophies, and expert versus lay definitions (see OECD, 2013 or Diener, 2009 for discussion of these aspects).

With various issues (as previously noted) related to the definition of wellbeing, there is currently no academic definition of wellbeing that is agreed upon, which is also not surprising. The only aspect which seems to be agreed upon is that wellbeing is multi-faceted and complex (Hone, Jarden, Schofield, & Duncan, 2014). Moreover, 'wellbeing' is frequently used synonymously with terms like 'wellness', 'happiness', 'mental health', 'health', 'quality of life', 'flourishing', and 'thriving', as well as 'mental illness' amongst others (Hone, Jarden, & Schofield, 2014). The combination of these issues provides challenges, with the lack of a clear and agreed-upon definition of 'wellbeing' then leading to challenges with choosing wellbeing models, which then feed into a coach's programme design. Following this, choices about assessment tools are usually made which align with models chosen, so there is (or should be) constructive alignment here – all starting from the definition and conception of wellbeing, to a model, to an intervention strategy, to assessment tools to evaluate. Creating opportunities for interested parties (e.g., coachees, employees) to engage in co-design processes early and throughout the assessment process, from conceptions and definitions, to models, to interventions and measures, is thus invaluable in obtaining the needed constructive alignment moving from definition to model to intervention design to measurement.

Models of wellbeing

For a coach, there are many models of wellbeing available, with a review being past our scope here. However, to illuminate, we outline three wellbeing models which from our experience have frequently been incorporated in coaching in various contexts, and we also note one model which has good potential to be used more in coaching contexts.

First, over the past decade, Martin Seligman's PERMA model (2011) has become popular in conjunction with the rise of positive psychology. In the PERMA model, wellbeing develops from fostering five elements: positive emotion, engagement, relationships, meaning, and accomplishment. Others also modify the model to incorporate relevant aspects for their specific context, for example, by including 'H' for health (i.e., PERMA-H) or 'O' for optimism (i.e., PERMA-O). Also common is to overlay or align the concept of character strengths with all aspects of the model (see Norrish, 2015). Alternatively, some may take a more comprehensive approach with many more elements added. For example, there is PERMA+, whereby the "+" refers to the four elements of optimism, nutrition, sleep, and physical activity used by the Wellbeing and Resilience Centre in South Australia (Iasiello, Bartholomaeus, Jarden, & Kelly, 2017).

Second, the Five Ways to Wellbeing (Aked & Thompson, 2011) was developed by the New Economics Foundation (NEF) in the UK, which has expanded internationally; especially in Western countries, and for more than a decade. Here the NEF was commissioned by the UK government to assist in developing a set of evidence-based actions to improve personal wellbeing. From the starting point of an extensive review of the complete wellbeing literature (i.e., the Foresight Mental Capital and Wellbeing Project, 2008), and by focusing on accessible language, NEF identified five ways to enable and support wellbeing: "Connect", "Be Active", "Take Notice", "Keep Learning", and "Give".

Third, Green and Palmer's RAW model (Green & Palmer, 2018) incorporates the elements of resilience, achievement, and wellbeing. Whilst this model is not technically a wellbeing model, it is a model with a strong emphasis on wellbeing, and developed specially for a coaching context. In this model, flourishing (defined as having high levels of wellbeing), is described as a combination of resilience, achievement, and wellbeing.

Finally, based on Rusk and Waters' (2014) Five Domains of Positive Functioning, we also point to the 'SEARCH' framework (strengths, emotional management, attention and awareness, relationships, coping, and habits and goals: Waters, 2018; Waters & Loton, 2019). In SEARCH, psychosocial functioning is defined as "the moment-by-moment psychological and social processes, states and events that contribute to well-being" (Rusk and Waters, 2014, p. 141). Different than most models and frameworks which are academically developed (i.e., theoretically derived), SEARCH is data-derived and data-driven. Being developed from an evidence base is a particular strength of this framework and is why we highlight it here as having a potential for greater use in coaching.

These frameworks are samples from the many frameworks and models available across the wellbeing sciences. Some coaches use such models to guide practice and measurement of wellbeing; other coaches have refined their own frameworks or variations from such models to fit the context of the people, sectors, or organisations they are working with. Notably, the alignment between the definition of wellbeing chosen and with the model embraced is essential, regardless of the model selected. It is this alignment from the definition to model that allows for assessments to be chosen and refined to fit the definition of wellbeing and the model being utilised.

Looking past models and definitions of wellbeing, attention ought to focus on the process of assessment (i.e., the how), the content that is being assessed (i.e., the what), and the systems involved (i.e., the who). As such, we now consider these three aspects in greater detail.

The content of assessment

Once we have drawn from definitions and models to inform the orientation of the assessment, the next step is to decide what the assessment should comprise. There are options here, first whether to use an existing measurement instrument or to develop a new measurement instrument for the purpose at hand. Currently, there is no claim to a single "gold standard" measure of wellbeing – unsurprisingly, given the heterogeneity of the definitions and multiple worldviews of the instrument developers and target users. However, sound psychometric advice is available when deliberating the content for an assessment, particularly for adults. For example, valuable guidance for a range of essential subjective wellbeing measurement elements, such as the construction of questions, format of response options, contextual and cultural considerations, and survey execution – to name just a few – is offered by the Organisation for Economic Co-operation and Development (OECD) 'Guidelines on Measuring Subjective Wellbeing' (2013). Diener's 'Assessing Well-being' (2009) also offers many such considerations and suggestions.

In considering content, we also suggest considering the four factors that can result in response errors in self-report measures. These include: (1) a *failure in memory*, which might result in inaccurate information being recalled and rated; (2) *motivational considerations*, be they a lack of interest in the process or a desire to be viewed positively;

(3) a *failure to communicate clearly*, such as the survey questions may be misleading or unclear and result in misunderstanding; and finally (4) a *lack of knowledge* that the respondent may not feel as if they know the answer but will respond anyway (Bradburn, Sudman, & Wansink, 2004). Table 20.1 outlines some considerations for survey design and content that can be helpful for coaches and practitioners.

Further to these considerations, the OECD 'Guidelines' (OECD, 2013) recommend the following aspects be considered when assessing wellbeing (Table 20.2).

In addition to those summarised in Table 20.2, 23 areas of positive psychological assessment are reported by Owens, Magyar-Moe, and Lopez (2015), including gratitude, emotions, mindfulness, strengths, and optimism; and 58 specific measures of constructs in these areas, such as the Flourishing Scale (Diener et al., 2009) and Mindfulness Attention Awareness Scale (Brown & Ryan, 2003). Comparing and contrasting recommended measures by experts and those frequently reported in wellbeing promotion and workplace wellbeing research, Jarden and Jarden (2016) highlight nine commonly used measures in the workplace, outlined in Table 20.3.

As we have mentioned, the model or theory of wellbeing which the individual, group, or organisation has adopted, or which best fits with their values and worldview, will inform the content of the assessment. In other words, the measure or measures used in the assessment needs to be aligned with the elements of the adopted model. In addition, a measurement should also include variables of intervention interest and target. For example, if a coachee wants to use their strengths more, then the use of a measure which captures strengths use (such as the Strengths Use and Knowledge Scale: Govindji & Linley, 2007) may be appropriate in conjunction with the variables related to the wellbeing model or definition.

Table 20.1 Considerations for survey design

Considerations	Implementation and design considerations
Question construction	• Is the concept being questioned something that can be recalled from memory? • Is the wording simple and effective? • Is the survey tone neutral so as to not prime or bias respondents? • Does the introductory text indicate that a particular type of answer is preferred? • Could the question be considered invasive or inappropriate? • Is the question likely to fall into a social norm trap, whereby an answer could be considered 'good' or 'bad'?
Response formats	• Can the response options be easily recalled? • Is it easy to distinguish between the response ratings/categories? • Is the format sensitive to tracking changes over time?
Cultural and contextual considerations	• Is the survey translatable to different languages and contexts? • Do respondents' linguistic differences influence how questions may be interpreted? • Are there cultural considerations that must be considered in understanding how participants will respond to specific questions?
Order effects	• Is the order of questions likely to influence the answers given?
Survey context	• Is the timing that the survey is given likely to influence the respondent's motivation or memory recall (i.e., time of day, year, seasonal effects, or before or after a significant event)?

Table 20.2 Organisation for Economic Co-operation and Development (OECD) recommendations

Wellbeing aspect	Description	Example
Life evaluation	Comprises life evaluation judgements on how respondents evaluate their lives and can be framed in the past or future	The 'self-anchoring striving scale', also known as the Cantril Ladder (Bjørnskov, 2010) *"Please imagine a ladder with steps numbered from 0 at the bottom to 10 at the top. Suppose we say that the top of the ladder represents the best possible life for you and the bottom of the ladder represents the worst possible life for you".*
Affect	The reporting of affective states attempts to capture how a person has been feeling over a period of time (i.e., days, weeks, months)	Scale of Positive and Negative Experience (SPANE) (Diener et al., 2009) *"Please think about what you have been doing and experiencing during the past four weeks. Then report how much you experienced each of the following feelings . . .".*
Eudaimonic wellbeing	Reporting on concepts related to psychological functioning such as meaning, purpose, sense of agency and belonging, and locus of control	Flourishing Index (Huppert & So, 2013) *"Most days I feel a sense of accomplishment from what I do".* *"When things go wrong in my life it generally takes me a long time to get back to normal".* *"In general, I feel very positive about myself".*
Domain wellbeing	Reporting on specific life domains or aspects of life (e.g., health status, material stability, housing security, social connectedness), which can be helpful in distinguishing subjective wellbeing results	Personal Wellbeing Index (International Wellbeing Group, 2006) *"How satisfied are you with your standard of living?"* *"How satisfied are your with your health?"* *"How satisfied are you with your future security?"*

A wellbeing assessment that contains valid and reliable measures will be undermined if these measures are inconsistent with the individual's, group's, or organisation's understanding of wellbeing or the drivers of wellbeing or the focus of interest. For example, a team is working on their wellbeing, calling on the Five Ways to Wellbeing (Aked & Thompson, 2011), focusing on "Connect" by strengthening relationships within the team. The team is about to engage in a programme to build high-quality connections (Dutton & Heaphy, 2003) to develop interprofessional relationships. The assessment ought to include a measure of relationships to ensure alignment with this model of wellbeing and to understand whether the programme is working towards achieving its outcomes. Other elements of the Five Ways to Wellbeing, such as "Keep Learning", "Be Active", and "Take Notice", could also be included in the measurement. Measuring these elements over time (longitudinally), on several occasions both before and after the programme commences, provides

Table 20.3 Commonly used workplace wellbeing measures

Measure	Measure authors	Constructs measured	Number of items
Satisfaction with Life Scale (SWLS)	(Diener, Emmons, Larsen, & Griffin, 1985)	Life Satisfaction	5
Scales of Psychological Well-being (SPW)	(Ryff & Singer, 1998)	Wellbeing: • Autonomy • Environmental mastery • Personal growth • Positive relations with others • Purpose in life • Self-acceptance	42
Positive Affect and Negative Affect Schedule (PANAS)	(Watson, Clark, & Tellegan, 1988)	Positive affect Negative affect	20
Quality of Life Inventory (QoLI)	(Frisch, 2004)	Life satisfaction Life domains	32
Steen Happiness Index (SHI)	(Seligman, Steen, Park, & Peterson, 2005).	Happiness	20
Subjective Happiness Scale (SHS)	(Lyubomirsky & Lepper, 1999)	Happiness	4
Life Orientation Test-Revised (LOT-R);	(Scheier, Carver, & Bridges, 1994)	Optimism	10
Flourishing Scale (FS)	(Diener et al., 2009)	Flourishing	8
Mindfulness Attention Awareness Scale (MAAS)	(Brown & Ryan, 2003)	Mindfulness	15

Note: The measures can be located via the reference list at the end of this chapter

an opportunity to determine not just changes in wellbeing over time, but also a greater depth of understanding of potential broader – and sometimes unexpected – impacts of the programme. As an example, the assessment may not initially find any change in perceptions of interprofessional relationships ("Connect") which may come much later, but may identify the team learning a new skill together tapped into "Keep Learning", the team activity tapped into "Be Active", and by exploring what brings joy at work tapped into "Take Notice". Furthermore, the assessment may identify more introverted people of a particular age or gender who responded differently to a particular programme. Balancing assessment length, breadth, and depth for sufficient evidence to inform data-driven decision-making is an essential – and context-dependent – consideration (Green, Jarden, & Leach, 2021; OECD, 2013; Rolstad, Adler, & Ryden, 2011).

The process of assessment

Having determined the assessment's relational definition of wellbeing, model, and content, we now shift to the assessment process. Assessments can be conducted via a range of modalities such as self-report measures (paper-based or online), observation, or interview (to name a few), and may be designed to be executed at a single point in time (e.g., cross-sectional survey) before or after an intervention or coaching session, or across multiple points over time. Each of these modalities and designs is influenced by what one wants to be measured, the context, and the project's scope, and all come with strengths and limitations. Different groups can be compared from one time period to another, or one context to another, such as self-reported perceptions of relationships and intention to leave in one particular department or geographical location compared to another. This provides a snapshot and may inform future potential areas for targeted wellbeing interventions or coaching conversations. With this type of snapshot, it is quicker (than alternatives) and less resource intensive; there is no need to link responses from one time point to another, and responses can be anonymous, which might increase comfort in reporting sensitive information. There is also no chance of not completing subsequent assessments, which may reduce the integrity of the findings. However, there is a range of limitations with a cross-sectional snapshot related to variance between people, times, contexts, limited comparability, and a range of other contributing confounding factors (see Shaughnessy, Zechmeister, & Zechmeister, 2014). The contrasting strengths of longitudinal studies, with multiple assessment points, enable measurement of wellbeing change over time, alongside determining predictors, enablers, and barriers. However, they also have considerable limitations such as participant burden and desirability responding (OECD, 2013). We recommend, at a minimum, assessments designed to measure data over several time points, and where there is an intervention, multiple time points before and after intervention. Where possible, integrating wellbeing measures into existing or routine local or global assessments may support engagement and meet the needs of the various stakeholders, such as a local engagement survey or coaching intake survey, which may be extended to include wellbeing measures.

The systems being assessed

With an understanding of assessment content and process, an important consideration is 'who' needs to be assessed. A systems-informed approach is key to sustainability, particularly in dynamic and interconnected systems such as groups and organisations. A systems-informed approach extends boundaries and, in the system, may include perspectives of coaches, clients, individual professionals, interprofessional teams, organisations, funders, sponsors, and/or regulators (to name a few). There is worth in contemplating assessment across various perspectives from the viewpoint of a system (Kern et al., 2019). Within a system, perspectives may include individuals (such as a coachee, an employee, a manager: 'me'), groups (team on a shift, the interprofessional team across an organisation: 'we') and organisations (a family unit, all people within an organisation or across multiple organisations: 'us'), as illustrated in Figure 20.1 (Jarden & Jarden, 2016, p. 427, used with permission). Within this system, some unique viewpoints and co-dependencies contribute a depth of contextualised understanding.

Wellbeing interventions for the individual (me) might include a person engaging in an intervention they can do by themselves, such as engaging in a mindfulness programme (Niemiec, 2013), the effects of which might be assessed using a measure such as the Mindful Attention Awareness Scale (Brown & Ryan, 2003), or the employee may be identifying and learning to apply their strengths. These effects might be assessed using

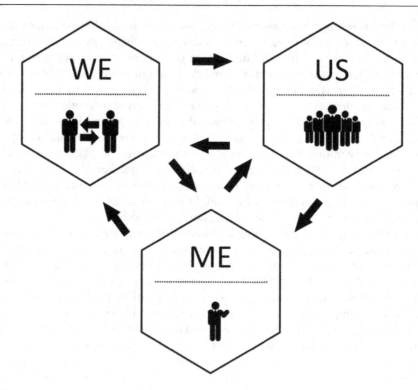

Figure 20.1 Me, We, and Us model

a measure such as the Strength Use and Knowledge Scale (Govindji & Linley, 2007). Wellbeing interventions for the group or relational level (we) might include coaching or a person working on their wellbeing directly with another person from their group, such as job crafting (Wrzesniewski, 2014) in a workplace context, the effects of which might be assessed with the Job Crafting Questionnaire (Slemp & Vella-Brodrick, 2013). Wellbeing interventions for the larger group (e.g., family unit) or organisational (us) context might include an Appreciative Inquiry (AI) summit (Cooperrider & Whitney, 2005), the effects of which might be assessed with a global wellbeing measure anchored to the organisation's definition and model of wellbeing such as the Flourishing Scale (Diener et al., 2009). Interventions might target all 'me', 'we', and 'us' domains, such as building relationships through developing high-quality connections (Dutton & Heaphy, 2003). Here, an individual might be working on 'active constructive responding', the team may be actively connecting through a weekly shared afternoon tea and hobby-photo board, and the organisation may host local forums to determine shared organisational values, as some examples. All three interventions need different approaches to assessment. For the individual, this may be the High-Quality Relationships measure (Carmeli & Gittell, 2009); for the team, it may be the Workplace Wellbeing Index (Page, 2005); and for the organisation, it may include individuals being asked to consider the workplace more universally (e.g., "Does your organisation invest in wellbeing?"). One important consideration from a systems approach is that the whole is considered more than the sum of the parts (Allison, Waters, & Kern, 2020; Kern et al., 2019); whether to start with 'me', 'we', or 'us' – or indeed, all three simultaneously – continues to be one more challenge in the developing science of wellbeing. One of the strengths of the 'me', 'we', and 'us' model remains the accessible language of the model across disciplines and professions. Continuing to develop wellbeing literacy (Oades et al., 2021) across cultures and contexts allows future researchers to develop measures, scales, or tools to holistically account for 'me', 'we', 'us', and their intersections.

Wellbeing assessment tools

Wellbeing assessment tools are widely available, although their cost, quality, reliability, validity, and useability vary greatly. We have suggested that good assessment tools are valid (that is, they measure what they purport to measure) and reliable (that is, they consistently measure the same things each time they are used). Understanding if an assessment measure is valid or reliable requires an evaluation of its psychometric properties; we recommend seeking expert consultation. Information about the psychometric properties of measures, ideally via independent peer-reviewed sources, should preferably be available alongside the measures. Just a few examples of validated measures relevant for various coaching contexts include the Flourishing Scale (Diener et al., 2009), the Temporal Satisfaction with Life Scale (Guitard, Jarden, Jarden, & Lajoie, 2022), and the Scales of Psychological Well-being (Ryff & Keyes, 1995).

Useful assessment questions

With a large number of wellbeing assessment tools accessible, the process of deciding the right wellbeing assessment battery for a coachee or group of individuals can be formidable. As previously mentioned, there is usually no one right approach or measure, as what is best and valuable depends on the specific context of the coachee or group, including the aims of the assessment, the overarching model of wellbeing, the time and resources available, and the interested stakeholders. As such, the following questions can help in making decisions regarding particular tools and approaches. Begin by asking the following questions.

1. What model of wellbeing does the assessment tool purport to measure? Is this in line with the definition and model you are using for your specific current purposes?
2. Has the measure been psychometrically appraised, and ideally independently published in peer-reviewed literature?

If you find a favourable answer to these two questions, only then ask the following.

3. Who has access to the raw data, who owns the data, and how can the data be used by both yourself and anyone else who may have access to it? Here it is important to consider both your intentions with using the data, and any intentions others may also have and benefit from its use.

Our advice is that if you are unclear on the answers to any of these matters, then it may be unsafe to use the particular measure or measures in question. However, if you are satisfied with answers at this point, the following list provides additional questions which may also be helpful in choosing measures and approaches.

1. When the measure was developed, were standard test development procedures followed?
2. If it is an online test, regarding data safety and storage, is the test provider complying with all regulations and industry standards? Does the provider of the measure assert that it is conforming with all privacy requirements?
3. Who is involved in administering the measure? What processes are involved, and are they transparent (e.g., scoring, algorithms)?
4. Can you capture qualitative data with the measure or tool?
5. What cultures and age ranges are appropriate for the measure? Is it available in different languages?
6. What length is the measurement? Is it too long, or an appropriate length for your purposes?
7. Is it clear how the measure aligns with the aims of your assessment?
8. Does the measure provide any immediate value to users or respondents? In other words, is there additional value in the measure beyond the data?

These are challenging questions, for which there are usually no clear answers. Instead, it may be best to take into consideration the benefit the measure has on meeting your purpose and needs for the assessment at hand. These questions help shine a light on the measures of psychometric suitability, flexibility, data safety and use, user experience, fit for purpose, and model of wellbeing alignment.

However, given all of this, we also think it is important to consider the role of assessment in your mission, for example by asking the following questions.

1. How amenable is the person or are the people to wellbeing and coaching?
2. Does the person or do the people have a sense of propriety and energy for wellbeing and coaching?

One suggestion is to include such questions at the first assessment point, as respondents' answers can shape further assessment choices. For example, if priority, energy, and receptivity are minimal, this might call for a brief and less frequent assessment approach; or if there is an extensive history of wellbeing, perhaps using the same measures that have been previously used may prove beneficial.

Conclusion

We suggest that wellbeing assessments play a crucial role in designing coaching interventions proposals, and then in cultivating and sustaining wellbeing. In this chapter, we have reviewed some of the fundamentals of assessment and outlined what wellbeing assessments look like in coaching: why assessments are important, what assessments are, and good assessment practices. We have also highlighted a systems lens – the 'me', 'we', us' framework – showing the advantages of assessment data for making decisions, and presented a list of questions which coaches and practitioners may find useful in considering assessments. We are optimistic that good wellbeing information can be gained via practices that are research-based and theoretically sound, and then that information can be used in coaching processes.

Reflective questions

1. What alternative ways are there to measure wellbeing?
2. In a health and wellbeing coaching assignment, is measuring and tracking client's progress essential?
3. What ethical aspects need to be considered in managing personal data from assessments of this kind, particularly for clients in the European Union?

References

Aked, J., & Thompson, S. (2011). *Five ways to wellbeing: New applications, new ways of thinking.* London: New Economics Foundation.

Allison, L. M., Waters, L., & Kern, M. L. (2020). Flourishing classrooms: Applying a systems-informed approach to positive education. *Contemporary School Psychology.* https://doi.org/10.1007/s40688-019-00267-8

American Psychological Association [APA]. (2022). *APA dictionary.* https://dictionary.apa.org/evaluation

Bjørnskov, C. (2010). How comparable are the Gallup World Poll life satisfaction data? *Journal of Happiness Studies, 11,* pp. 41–60.

Bradburn, N., Sudman, S., & Wansink, B. (2004). *Asking questions: The definitive guide to questionnaire design–From market research, political polls, and social and health questionnaires.* San Francisco: Jossey-Bass.

Brown, K. W., & Ryan, R. M. (2003). The benefits of being present: Mindfulness and its role in psychological well-being. *Journal of Personality and Social Psychology, 84,* 822–848. https://doi.org/10.1037/0022-3514.84.4.822

Cambridge English Dictionary. (2019a). *Assessment.* Retrieved 10th November 2022 from: https://dictionary.cambridge.org/dictionary/english/assessment

Cambridge English Dictionary. (2019b). *Evaluation.* Retrieved 10th November 2022 from: https://dictionary.cambridge.org/dictionary/english/evaluation

Cambridge English Dictionary. (2019c). *Testing.* Retrieved 10th November 2022 from: https://dictionary.cambridge.org/dictionary/english/testing

Carmeli, A., & Gittell, J. H. (2009). High-quality relationships, psychological safety, and learning from failures in work organizations. *Journal of Organizational Behavior, 30*(6), 709–729.

Cook, D. A., & Beckman, T. J. (2006). Current concepts in validity and reliability for psychometric instruments: Theory and application. *The American Journal of Medicine, 119,* 166.e7–166.e16. https://doi.org/10.1016/j.amjmed.2005.10.036

Coolican, H. (2014). *Research methods and statistics in psychology* (6th ed.). London: Psychology Press.

Cooperrider, D., & Whitney, D. (2005). *Appreciative inquiry: A positive revolution in change.* San Francisco: Berrett-Koehler Publishers.

Crisp, R. (2022). Well-being. In E. N. Zalta (Ed.), *The Stanford encyclopedia of philosophy* (Winter 2021 Edition). https://plato.stanford.edu/archives/win2021/entries/well-being/

Diener, E. (2009). *Assessing well-being: The collected works of Ed diener.* Social Indicators Research Series (p. 39). https://doi.org/10.1007/978-90-481-2354-45

Diener, E., Emmons, R. A., Larsen, R. J., & Griffin, S. (1985). The satisfaction with life scale. *Journal of Personality Assessment, 49,* 71–75.

Diener, E., Wirtz, D., Biswas-Diener, R., Tov, W., Kim-Prieto, C., Choi, D. W., & Oishi, S. (2009). New measures of well-being. In *Assessing well-being* (pp. 247–266). Dordrecht: Springer.

Dutton, J., & Heaphy, E. (2003). The power of high quality connections. In K. Cameron, J. Dutton, & R. Quinn (Eds.), *Positive organizational scholarship: Foundations of a new discipline* (pp. 263–278). San Francisco: Berrett – Koehler.

Foresight Mental Capital and Wellbeing Project. (2008). *Final Project report – Executive summary*. London: The Government Office for Science.

Frisch, M. B. (2004). Use of the QoLI or quality of life inventory in quality of life therapy and assessment. In M. R. Maruish (Ed.), *The use of psychological testing for treatment planning and outcome assessment* (vol. 3, pp. 749–798), instruments for adults. Manwah, NJ: Erlbaum.

Govindji, R., & Linley, P. A. (2007). Strengths use, self-concordance and well-being: Implications for strengths coaching and coaching psychologists. *International Coaching Psychology Review*, 2(2), 143–153.

Green, S., Jarden, A., & Leach, C. (2021). Coaching for workplace wellbeing. In W. A. Smith, I. Boniwell, & S. Green (Eds.), *Positive psychology coaching in the workplace*. Cham: Springer. https://doi.org/10.1007/978-3-030-79952-6_11

Green, S., & Palmer, S. (Eds.). (2018). *Positive psychology coaching in practice* (1st ed.). Abingdon, UK: Routledge. https://doi.org/10.4324/9781315716169

Guitard, J., Jarden, A., Jarden, R., & Lajoie, D. (2022). An evaluation of the psychometric properties of the temporal satisfaction with life scale. *Frontiers in Psychology*, 1–10. https://doi.org/10.3389/fpsyg.2022.795478

Hone, L., Jarden, A., & Schofield, G. (2014). Psychometric properties of the flourishing scale in a New Zealand sample. *Social Indicators Research*, 119(2), pp. 1031–1042.

Hone, L., Jarden, A., Schofield, G. M., & Duncan, S. (2014). Measuring flourishing: The impact of operational definitions on the prevalence of high levels of wellbeing. *International Journal of Wellbeing*, 4(1), 62–90. https://doi.org/10.5502/ijw.v4i1.1

Huppert, F. A., & So, T. T. C. (2013). Flourishing across Europe: Application of a new conceptual framework for defining well-being. *Social Indicators Research*, 110(3), 837–1246. http://www.jstor.org/stable/24719080

Iasiello, M., Bartholomaeus, J., Jarden, A., & Kelly, G. (2017). Measuring PERMA+ in South Australia, the state of wellbeing: A comparison with national and international norms. *Journal of Positive Psychology & Wellbeing*, online first.

International Wellbeing Group. (2006). *Personal Wellbeing Index* (4th ed.). Melbourne: Australian Centre on Quality of Life, Deakin University. www.deakin.edu.au/research/acqol/instruments/wellbeing_index.htm

Jarden, A., & Jarden, R. (2016). Positive psychological assessment for the workplace. In L. Oades, M. Steger, A. Della-Fave, & J. Passmore (Eds.), *The Wiley Blackwell Handbook of the psychology of positivity and strengths-based approaches at work* (pp. 415–437). Wiley. https://doi.org/10.1002/9781118977620.ch22

Jarden, A., Jarden, R., Chyuan Chin, T., & Kern, M. (2021). Assessing wellbeing in school communities. In M. Kern & M. L. Wehmeyer (Eds.), *Palgrave handbook on positive education* (pp. 297–324). Cham: Palgrave Macmillan.

Jarden, A., Rashid, T., Roache, A., & Lomas, T. (2021). Ethical guidelines for positive psychology practice (version 2.0: English). *International Journal of Wellbeing*, 11(3), 1–38. https://doi.org/10.5502/ijw.v11i3.1819

Kern, M. L., Williams, P., Spong, C., Colla, R., Sharma, K., Downie, A., Taylor, J. A., Sharp, S., Siokou, C., & Oades, L. G. (2019). Systems informed positive psychology. *The Journal of Positive Psychology*, 1–11. https://doi.org/10.1080/17439760.2019.1639799

Lyubomirsky, S., & Lepper, H. (1999). A measure of subjective happiness: Preliminary reliability and construct validation. *Social Indicators Research*, 46, 137–155.

Michaelson, J., Mahony, S., & Schifferes, J. (2012). *Measuring well-being: A guide for practitioners*. London: New Economics Foundation.

Niemiec, R. (2013). *Mindfulness and character strengths: A practical guide to flourishing*. Gottingen, Germany: Hogrefe Publishing.

Norrish, J. (2015). *Positive education: The Geelong grammar school journey*. Oxford: Oxford University Press.

Oades, L. G., Jarden, A., Hou, H., Ozturk, C., Williams, P. F., Slemp, G. R., & Huang, L. (2021). Wellbeing literacy: A capability model for wellbeing science and practice. *International Journal of Environment Research Public Health*, 18(719), 11–12. https://doi.org/10.3390/ijerph18020719

Organisation for Economic Co-operation and Development [OECD]. (2013). *OECD guidelines on measuring subjective well-being*. OECD Publishing. http://dx.doi.org/10.1787/9789264191655-en

Owens, R. L., Magyar-Moe, J. L., & Lopez, S. J. (2015). Finding balance via positive psychological assessment: Recommendations for practice. *The Counseling Psychologist, 43*(5), 634–670.

Page, K. (2005). *Subjective wellbeing in the workplace.* Unpublished honours thesis, Deakin University, Melbourne, Australia.

Penn State University. (2019). *Differences between testing, assessment, and evaluation.* http://tutorials.istudy.psu.edu/testing/testing2.html

Price, L. R. (2016). *Psychometric methods: Theory into practice.* New York, NY: Guilford Publications.

Rolstad, S., Adler, J., & Ryden, A. (2011). Response burden and questionnaire length: Is shorter better? A review and meta-analysis. *Value in Health, 14*, 1101–1108. https://doi.org/10.1016/j.jval.2011.06.003

Rusk, R., & Waters, L. (2014). A psycho-social system approach to well-being: Empirically deriving the five domains of positive functioning. *Journal of Positive Psychology, 10*(2), 141–152. https://doi.org/10.1080/17439760.2014.920409

Ryff, C. D., & Keyes, C. L. M. (1995). The structure of psychological well-being revisited. *Journal of Personality and Social Psychology, 69*, 719–727.

Ryff, C. D., & Singer, B. (1998). The contours of positive human health. *Psychological Inquiry, 9*, 1–28.

Scheier, M. F., Carver, C. S., & Bridges, M. W. (1994). Distinguishing optimism from neuroticism (and trait anxiety, self-mastery, and self-esteem): A re-evaluation of the life orientation test. *Journal of Personality and Social Psychology, 67*, 1063–1078.

Seligman, M. E. P. (2011). *Flourish.* New York, NY: Free Press.

Seligman, M. E. P., & Csikszentmihalyi, M. (2000). Positive psychology: An introduction. *American Psychologist, 55*, 5–14.

Seligman, M. E. P., Steen, T., Park, N., & Peterson, C. (2005). Positive psychology progress: Empirical validation of interventions. *American Psychologist, 60*, 410–421.

Shaughnessy, J. J., Zechmeister, E. B., & Zechmeister, J. S. (2014). *Research methods in psychology* (10th ed.). New York: McGraw-Hill.

Shum, D., O'Gorman, J., Creed, P., & Myors, B. (2017). *Psychological testing and assessment* (3rd ed.). Melbourne: Oxford University Press.

Slemp, G., & Vella-Brodrick, D. (2013). The job crafting questionnaire: A new scale to measure the extent to which employees engage in job crafting. *International Journal of Wellbeing.* https://doi.org/10.5502/ijw.v3i2.1

Waters, L. (2018). Visible wellbeing: A critical resource for leadership and learning in schools. *Horizon, 8*, 4–10.

Waters, L., & Loton, D. (2019). Search: A meta-framework and review of the field of positive education. *International Journal of Applied Positive Psychology, 4*(1–2), 1–46.

Watson, D., Clark, L. A., & Tellegan, A. (1988). Development and validation of brief measures of positive and negative affect: The PANAS scales. *Journal of Personality and Social Psychology, 54*(6), 1063–1070.

Wrzesniewski, A. (2014). Engage in job crafting. In J. Dutton & G. Spreitzer (Eds.), *How to be a positive leader: Insights from leading thinkers on positive organisations* (pp. 65–76). San Francisco: Berrett-Koehler Publishers.

Chapter 21

Managing wellbeing programmes

Ian Day

Introduction

The investment in health and wellbeing programmes is a growing priority for organisations across the globe. The Chartered Institute of Personnel and Development (CIPD) in the UK noted that "employee wellbeing continues to rise up the corporate agenda, with 70% of leaders having this on their agenda" (CIPD 2022, p. 6). Although this was down from 75% in the 2021 survey (CIPD 2021), 55% of respondents expected their health and wellbeing budget to stay the same in the next 12 months, and 39% expect the budget to increase slightly or significantly. In the United States, the Surgeon General highlighted a clear link between workplace culture and physical and mental health (The Washington Post 2022). Also, as reported by Forbes (2021) in a 2021 survey of 200 U.S.-based human resources (HR) professionals, Future Workplace, noted that employee wellbeing and mental health were key priorities for HR professionals. Against this backdrop of the rising awareness of importance, this chapter will explore the nature and scope of, and detail the business case for, investing in wellbeing programmes. The implementation of a wellbeing programme will be considered as an organisational development change initiative, in which the vital role of the line manager will be explored. The type of interventions organisations can make will be discussed, along with the role of coaching and the evaluation to determine long-term impact. The 'golden thread' which runs through this chapter and the approach taken is that of humanistic psychology, taking the person as a whole, assuming that they have agency and wish to fulfil their potential through personal growth (Moss 2015).

The scope of wellbeing

For the purpose of this chapter, wellbeing programmes are within the context of corporate organisations. Context is important, as managing wellbeing programmes within organisations provides its own challenges because organisations are complex systems of decision-making and implementation, with multiple stakeholders, ostensibly working towards a common goal (Griseri 2013). Wellbeing research tends to focus on larger organisations, rather than SMEs (small and medium enterprises) (Kowalski & Loretto 2017), possibly as larger organisations have more sophisticated HR functions and may have specific HR managers to lead initiatives (Brown et al. 2009). Given this, when discussing wellbeing within organisations, we may assume that what is written in this chapter can be extrapolated to all organisations of any size, but we do not have research

DOI: 10.4324/9781003319016-23

evidence to support this assumption, so generalisability is cautioned. Also, when discussing a wellbeing 'programme', this is more than a transient single activity; a programme is an enduring sequence of integrated interventions, Haynes summarises this by saying, "only cohesively do we optimise value and understand the real impact each element plays" (2013, p. 25). As wellbeing programmes require change which affects the whole organisation, the implementation will be considered as an organisational development intervention (Cacioppe & Edwards 2005).

Before an organisation can implement a wellbeing programme, the definition of wellbeing and the scope of the programme needs to be agreed with stakeholders. It is here that we encounter the first barrier to implementation, as there is no universally agreed definition of 'wellbeing' (Crawshaw 2008). However, what is agreed is that wellbeing is broader than health alone (Crawshaw 2008; Dooris, Farrier & Foggett 2018). Some have argued that wellbeing is not one single thing, but that it is a composite of concepts (Daniels et al. 2019). Crawshaw (2008), however, asks: "If wellbeing is such a broad church how can interventions be designed which are complex and subtle enough to manage this complexity?" (p. 260). This multidimensionality is reiterated by the OECD (2015) and contributes to the confusion and complexity of program design.

When designing a wellbeing programme, what is inside and outside the scope of the programme? For example, each of the following topics could be an element of a wellbeing programme.

- Physical wellbeing.
- Psychological wellbeing and mental health.
- Substance misuse.
- Smoking cessation.
- Healthy eating.
- Relaxation and stress management.
- Sleep management.
- Work/life balance.
- Neurodiversity wellbeing.
- Spiritual wellbeing.
- Financial wellbeing.
- Promotion of flourishing behaviour.
- Or simply the absence of disease or infirmity.
  (Dooris, Farrier & Foggett 2018; Zheng et al. 2015; Daniels et al. 2022).

The discussion of what is wellbeing, its definition, and so therefore what is 'in' or 'out' of scope of a wellbeing programme, is likely to be an ongoing discussion. However, if we pause to compare the nature of wellbeing with a more established and accepted psychological model, we may be able to get a different perspective and a greater understanding. Let us take the humanistic model which Abraham Maslow proposed as the hierarchy of needs and the theory of human motivation (Maslow 1969). Starting at the most basic level, the hierarchy of needs is as follows.

1. Physiological needs: the basic needs of life, food, water, air, reproduction, sleep, shelter, warmth, etc.

2. Safety needs: security, stability, freedom from fear and anxiety, and the presence of law and structure.
3. Belonging and love needs: relationships with friends and others, and belonging within groups and society.
4. Esteem needs: a stable and high evaluation of self, including self-respect.
5. Self-actualisation: doing what each person "is fitted for" (Maslow 1969, p. 46) for selffulfilment and achievement of purpose.

A person can only progress from level 1 to level 5 once the need within the previous level has been satisfied. The wellbeing topics displayed in the preceding list of what could be included in a wellbeing programme relate to – and can be mapped onto – Maslow's five hierarchical needs, and indeed the expanded hierarchy which includes the sixth level of self-transcendence (Maslow 1969). Wellbeing begins at the physiological level, and develops through the levels of need for safety, belonging, esteem and self-actualisation. Wellbeing could be considered to be about the needs of human motivation, in that humans are motivated to satisfy their wellbeing needs. However, what topics are contained within each level of the wellbeing hierarchy of needs, are individual and context-specific. This individualistic and context-specific nature may explain why the definition of wellbeing creates such confusion and debate.

The business case for wellbeing programmes

There is good evidence to link employee wellbeing and organisational performance. Such evidence provides the underpinning for a strong business case for wellbeing in organisations. A multitude of reports over the past decade or more have demonstrated the links between health, wellbeing and performance.

The CIPD's 2022 survey noted that 32.5 million working days are lost each year as a result of health absence. Reported health factors include stress, anxiety and depression, and contribute to over half of the absence reports. Dewa and McDaid (2011) found a link between mental wellbeing and workplace performance, reporting that "Between 30% and 60% of the societal cost of depression is related to losses associated with decreased work productivity.

This individual study was supported by a meta-analysis of 485 studies, in which Faragher, Cass and Cooper (2013) concluded from a comprehensive review of the data, The largest combined statistical correlations found were between job satisfaction and measures of mental health; smaller relationships were detected for measures of physical health." Despite this strong statistical association, the authors cautioned about assuming a causal link, however they, "confirmed that dissatisfaction at work can be hazardous to an employee's mental health and wellbeing" (p. 269).

Zheng and colleagues (2015) found that work/life balance was associated with health and wellbeing. They noted that work life balance "positively contributes to a better employee health and wellbeing" (p. 371). Workplace wellbeing is not only concerned with the reduction of days lost because of employee illness, but also with the positive impact of enhanced wellbeing. In a longitudinal study, Sutton and colleagues found that implementing an employee wellbeing programme could increase employee engagement (Sutton et al. 2016). Employee engagement, in turn, is "intrinsically linked to . . . operational performance or strategic productivity. An engaged workforce can improve profitability and productivity" (Turner 2020, p. 57). This was supported by a CIPD report (2021) which noted that "individuals with higher levels of psychological wellbeing behave differently in ways that would be expected to lead to higher levels of engagement" (p. 334) and employee engagement is more important than the actual health concern when determining if staff take occasional days off sick.

Ryan and colleagues (2021) reviewed 23 studies finding that "Just over 50% of studies reported evidence of either a strong or moderate effect across a physical and psychological outcome providing a positive indication that workplace wellbeing programmes can be effective in promoting physical and psychological wellbeing" (p. 1136). Kowalski and Loretto (2017) highlighted that people are a source of competitive advantage, and wellbeing has "importance of workplace well-being issues both for individual health and for organisational outcomes too" (p. 2230).

Wellbeing programmes

If we accept the evidence already presented in this chapter supporting the business case for managing wellbeing within organisations, reducing the negative effects and promoting the positive enhancements, and agree that wellbeing is within the scope of organisational development, we can consider how a wellbeing programme can be implemented and managed as a change process. This first step of this change is for an organisation to consider why it wants to initiate a wellbeing programme, what change does the organisation want to achieve, what difference does the organisation want to see, and so what is the destination as a result of the wellbeing programme?

Based on the 'broad church' of the wellbeing agenda, as mentioned earlier, for an organisation to manage a wellbeing programme, it must first define wellbeing within its own context: the goal, the scope, the boundaries, and the desired outcome of a wellbeing programme, all of which will be unique to the context within which each organisation operates. The nature of the goal needs conscious consideration (David, Clutterbuck & Megginson 2013) to decide if goals are SMART (specific, measurable, achievable, relevant and time-bound) or courageous (Blakey & Day 2012), or of a different nature. Goal setting begins by examining existing organisational data, for example sickness absence levels, the reasons for absence, staff turnover rates, exit interviews as employees resign from an organisation, staff opinion surveys, feedback from employee and union representatives, customer feedback, production data, quality information, etc. This data may be readily available through normal organisational processes; for example, the HR department is likely to collect sickness absence data, employee opinion surveys may be an annual event, the customer service team will have feedback information, and the production department will hold historic production levels and quality details – so, all that is required is the central collection and evaluation of this existing information. However, some data may be hidden and less readily available, requiring additional organisational activity. For example, the reasons behind and/or meaning of the data trends can be explored through a multi-layer, multi-departmental, employee focus group. The subtleties of the statistical trends can be understood, and insight gained into knowledge that is hidden out of view for most of the time. What is clear is that each organisation will identify their own context-specific wellbeing goals.

Following the notion that the implementation of a wellbeing programme is an organisational change process, we can consider how the large number of organisational change

Table 21.1 Kotter's eight steps of change

1. Establishing a sense of urgency.
2. Forming a powerful guiding coalition.
3. Creating a vision.
4. Communicating the vision.
5. Empowering others to act on the vision.
6. Planning for a creating short-term wins.
7. Consolidating improvements and producing still more change.
8. Institutionalising new approaches.

models (Sveningsson & Sörgärde 2020) can help with the implementation and management. Kotter (2007) identified an eight-step organisational change model, taking into account both the mechanistic and emotional elements of change.

The model offers a possible frame for the implementation and management of a wellbeing programme.

1. Establishing a sense of urgency

    Establishing a sense of urgency is about understanding the 'burning platform' for change. This is by exploring the reality of the situation, the potential threats to the future performance of the organisation, and potential opportunities. Kotter writes:

    > Compared with other steps in the change process, phase one can sound easy. It is not. Well over 50% of the companies I have watched fail in this first phase. What are the reasons for that failure? Sometimes executives underestimate how hard it can be to drive people out of their comfort zones.
    >
    > (Kotter 2007, p. 97)

    For this, we can look at the business case for establishing a wellbeing programme, by collecting and examining data, as detailed in this chapter, so the case for change is clearly identified within the context of the specific organisation.

2. Forming a powerful guiding coalition

    A key step for successful change is to establish a guiding coalition of key stakeholders with the organisational influence and the sense of urgency to make change happen. This coalition needs to begin at the most senior levels of an organisation (Carrington 2014) and include employees, customers, subject experts, and staff representatives. This coalition should also include members who are not part of the senior management team, who operate outside of the normal organisational hierarchy, and as Heifetz and Laurie said, give the work back to the people and protect the voices of leadership from below (1997). The size of the coalition will grow over time as the project moves into implementation. Beyond Kotter's generic change model, this collaborative approach to the development of wellbeing programmes has been recognised by other researchers (Odes 2020; Silcox 2016), adding the weight of validity to this step. The breadth of stakeholders within the guiding coalition will also ensure that a wellbeing programme is not confined to become an HR initiative, but is organisation-wide, in which everyone has 'skin in the game'.

3. Creating a vision

A compelling picture of the future will capture the hearts and minds. The wellbeing change process goes beyond financial numbers and organisational data which are typically found in a five-year business plan. A wellbeing vision helps to create, motivate and clarify the direction of organisational travel.

4. Communicating the vision

This communication is much more than a single 'town hall' meeting or a single email announcement. This is compelling ongoing communication of the wellbeing vision and progress. This is core, crucial to ensure that hearts and minds are engaged, and that commitment is reinforced at every level of the organisation.

5. Empowering others to act on the vision and removing obstacles

Implementation of the wellbeing vision can be incentivised and rewarded, so people are emboldened to adopt new behaviours. Obstacles – which may be in the form of organisational history, culture, policies or structure – can be identified and removed with the help of the powerful guiding coalition.

6. Planning for a creating short-term wins

Short-term wins are created to maintain renewal momentum through visible wellbeing successes, during the yearly planning system, annual objective setting, and rewards and recognition such as promotion and/or financial.

7. Consolidating improvements and producing still more change

Success leads to more success, through increased credibility. The compelling wellbeing vision is reviewed and refreshed, so that momentum is maintained.

8. Institutionalising new approaches

The wellbeing change is anchored deeply into the culture and organisational systems, and it is integrated beyond a single wellbeing policy, so positive behaviour is recognised and rewarded over a long term.

In a review of employee assistance programmes (EAPs), Yen-chen, Ching-wen and Junbang (2019) identified that 'plan-making' represented the greatest variance in the evaluation of wellbeing. Within this, Kotter's notion of the guiding coalition was supported, as two of the seven 'plan-making' items were that specific committees were set up to implement the EAP plan and that the senior management team strongly support the EAP plan.

The role of the manager

A key element in creating a successful outcome is the role of the line managers (CIPD 2022, p. 31). Without wide-scale support from line managers, programs will fail. Daniels and colleagues (2019) noted: "Line managers are considered a foundation for attempts to protect and enhance health and wellbeing in the workplace as well as a fulcrum for implementing reasonable adjustments to facilitate return to work" (p. 8). The UK's Health and Safety Executive recognises the centrality of the line manager, as the 'face' of the organisation and the duty of care they hold to employees (The Health and Safety Executive, n.d.) These management standards identify six areas crucial to support psychological wellbeing, one of which is relationships, which considers the organisational culture such as the promotion of positive working relationships and dealing with unacceptable behaviour. Line managers play a key role in developing and maintaining effective positive relationships in the workplace.

The CIPD (n.d.) emphasises the importance of line manager training. They recommended that employers:

> Train line managers and supervisors to manage people well. Line managers are key to employee wellbeing and should ensure people's workloads and deadlines are manageable .... They [line managers] should have the confidence to have sensitive conversations with people and offer support and flexibility if a team member needs adjustments to help manage their health and work.

This is a very interesting statement, given the juxtaposition that only 38% of HR respondents in the CIPD's 'Health and Wellbeing' report of 2022 agree that line managers are confident to hold sensitive wellbeing conversations, and an even lower 28% of HR respondents agree that line managers are competent to spot early warning signs, with the CIPD stating: "Management style remains among the most common causes of stress at work" (p. 7). Another workplace cultural issue over which managers have influence is sickness presenteeism. Skagen and Collins (2016, p. 1) define this as "as going to work despite illness" and after examining 12 longitudinal studies, presenteeism was found to impact future health and influence sickness absence (Skagen & Collins 2016). This finding was also supported by the CIPD 2022 'Health and Wellbeing at Work Survey Report'. These findings relate to the line manager's influence on wellbeing and presenteeism, and suggest that management training still has a long way to go for managers to fulfil their wellbeing role. As Daniels and colleagues (2019) state, "Training managers has a multiplier effect as each line manager is responsible for a number of workers" (p. 8). To support and focus the mind on the important role of line managers, there is the need for an integrated organisational approach. Reward and recognition systems can be used to reinforce positive management behaviours, the crucial managerial role in enhancing employee wellbeing and during the implementation of a wellbeing programme. As the saying goes, "What gets measured gets done, what gets measured and fed back gets done well, what gets rewarded gets repeated" (Jones & Bearley 2010, p. 155).

Committed line managers, along with wellbeing being integrated into the organisational culture, helps ensure the sustained impact of the wellbeing programme. If we assume the normative nature of culture, then culture can be broken down into individual behaviour and so behaviour of each line manager builds cumulatively to a critical mass. As Cotton and Hart (2003) pointed out: "Organisational climate is the strongest determinant of individual distress .... Thus, it is more important to develop a supportive organisational climate that helps employees to manage their work more effectively" (p. 125).

Practice

Coaching as an intervention

The positive impact of coaching has been researched and reported many times, so here focus will be specifically on wellbeing coaching. Linked to the previous section on the role of line managers, Odes (2020) said, "Coaching for wellbeing at work should also include working with managers and leaders on how they foster the positive relationships of their employees" (p. 204). Dyrbye and colleagues (2019) write that they "suggest that organizationally sponsored professional coaching for physicians can reduce emotional exhaustion, improve overall quality of life, and build resilience" (p. 1412). The medical context of Dyrbye's article may be very narrow, but Zhao and Liu (2020) found that "managerial coaching increased subordinates' workplace well-being by triggering their motivations for autonomy, competence, and personal growth" (p. 305).

Perceived wellbeing is unique to every person. Although organisational programmes can support employee wellbeing, there is a risk that the approach may be top-down and generic (Odes 2020). Coaching has a role to play in overcoming the potentially generic nature of an organisation-wide programme, recognising that employee wellbeing is individual (Gabriel, Moran & Gregory 2014). Odes (2020) emphasises the pre-eminence of coaching in wellbeing enhancement, by saying that "coaching for wellbeing is broader than health coaching by including issues of relationships, belonging and meaning, which would not typically feature within traditional health coaching" (p. 202). The person-centred humanistic nature of coaching is ideally placed to enhance wellbeing and is uniquely placed to address self-determination theory and intrinsic motivation (Deci & Ryan 1985) on an individual level, ensuring longer-lasting results. Focusing on the humanistic approach, Gabriel, Moran and Gregory (2014) said that through coaching, the coach is

> truly treating the client as a whole person rather than an individual who experiences the workplace in isolation from all other parts of his/her life . . . . Coaching practices . . . can ultimately be more tailored to the social context that occurs between a coach and client, potentially leading to higher levels of performance by targeting client needs and driving development.
>
> (p. 68)

Antiss & Passmore (2017) built on a positive psychology foundation noted that wellbeing coaching is "to stimulate and encourage self-awareness, personal responsibility, and behavioural change thought likely to lead to improved wellbeing outcomes over time" (p. 238). This positive psychological orientation is echoed by other authors, such as Govindji & Linley (2007), focusing on strengths to enhance wellbeing, and Boyatzis, Smith and Beveridge (2012), who highlight the importance of "invoking the Ideal Self to initiate and guide the change process" (p. 155).

Coaching has been seen to support organisational culture change initiatives and employee wellbeing (Stout-Rostron 2011; Gormley & van Nieuwerburgh 2014). Also, coaching is well placed to support the development of new behavioural habits on an individual level and reinforce and sustain change in wellbeing behaviour.

Coaching is only one example of a wellbeing intervention, but the message here is that wellbeing programmes also need to be flexible and tailored to the individual, rather than generic. Other wellbeing interventions relate to the early period of industrial psychology, giving people control over their work in terms of decision-making (Ganster & Fusilier 1989). The COVID19 pandemic forced the requirement for remote work from home. As lockdown eased in many parts of the world in late 2021, organisations – instead of returning to work as normal – have instead shifted to hybrid working models, giving people greater control of when, where and how they work, and this personal control has a positive impact on wellbeing (Litchfield et al. 2016). The impact is that organisations can no longer use command and control models, but instead must switch to trust and output-based approaches. Individual control can be further developed in organisations so that employees are agents of their own work.

Evaluation

Once a goal is established for a wellbeing programme, it is important to track progress towards and evaluate achievement. Evaluation answers the "So what?" questions: "So what was the impact of the development intervention?"; "So what was the return of the financial, psychological and time investment?"; or "Has the development intervention made a difference, and if so, was this worthwhile? How can we refine this next time to get even better results?" Kirkpatrick set out the well-known training framework (Kirkpatrick 1979; Reio et al. 2017), identifying four levels for evaluating training: (1) relation; (2) learning; (3) behaviour; and (4) results. With each level, there is an increased duration of time required to establish the impact. The reaction and learning of programme participants are immediate, but behavioural change and individual or organisational results take longer to be observed. As a result, the reliance on workshop 'happy sheets' can only evaluate level 1 of reactions and level 2 of learning. A more considered, patient and long-term evaluation can assess the holistic impact of training and development. Evaluation of wellbeing programmes needs to link back to the organisational data discussed earlier, used to identify the original programme goal. This will ensure that the evaluation is results-based, rather than activity-based. For example, delivering ten employee wellbeing workshops is not a measure of success; it is a measure of busyness. However, an example of a good measure of the result of a wellbeing programme is a comparison of sickness absence levels, employee satisfaction, productivity levels and customer feedback at two points in time – one before and one after implementation of the wellbeing programme. The evaluated difference between T1 and T2, assuming all other things are equal, can be put down to the wellbeing programme. As Passmore and Tee (2021) said, "Unless you are receiving feedback – ideally specific, real-time, objective feedback – it will be hard for you to evaluate the extent to which your goal is being realised" (p. 356).

In additional to the Kirkpatrick evaluation model and specifically relating the evaluation of coaching, Ely and colleagues (2010) proposed a "collection of multi-source data, consideration of multi-level effects, and formative evaluations of the client, coach, client–coach relationship, and coaching process" (p. 596).

Conclusion

There is still more to be done in relation to the management of wellbeing programmes. CIPD (2022) found that 51% of organisations take a strategic approach to employee wellbeing. This is encouraging, but what about the remaining 49%? We would be shocked if only 51% of organisations had a strategic business plan, or a financial strategy, so why is wellbeing different? There is a need for organisations to take a holistic joined-up approach to wellbeing. A wellbeing programme may be in isolation and detached, for example, from organisational remuneration policies which ensure that employees receive a living wage, which aids financial wellbeing. This is just one example to demonstrate the connectedness of the wellbeing agenda, and the need for an integrated approach, which is a cohesive organisational development initiative, with the various company policies linked to wellbeing. Also, wellbeing programmes should recognise the need to tailor wellbeing programmes to the needs of individual employees (Sutton and colleagues (2016). Implementation of wellbeing programmes must recognise the systematic connectedness of organisations on individual, team and organisational levels. Taking a systemic approach will link organisational practises such as management development, reward and recognition, performance appraisal and bonus allocation, engaging with the wider stakeholder community to involve employees and managers in designing interventions evaluated against objectives, with the different elements of wellbeing combined into a whole, with a full understanding of how the organisational system interacts with employees. Over time, as wellbeing continues to rise on the organisational agenda, we may see a new senior post, that of the CWO, the Chief Wellbeing Officer. Alongside the Chief Operating Officer (COO), Chief Financial Officer (CFO), and the Chief Technology Officer (CTO), this would demonstrate the strategic intent of the organisation.

Reflective questions

1. What is the scope/definition of wellbeing within your organization?
2. What change do you want to see because of your wellbeing programme?
3. How will you know that your wellbeing programme has been successful?
4. If you were to complete Kotter's eight steps for change for a wellbeing initiative in your organization, what would it look like?

References

Anstiss, T., & Passmore, J. (2017) Wellbeing Coaching. In: C. Cooper & M. Leiter (eds.) *The Routledge Companion to Wellbeing at Work* (1st ed.). London: Routledge. https://doi.org/10.4324/9781315665979

Blakey, J., & Day, I. (2012) *Challenging Coaching: Going Beyond Traditional Coaching to Face the FACTS*. London: Nicholas Brealey Publishing.

Boyatzis, R. E., Smith, M. L., & Beveridge, A. J. (2012) Coaching with Compassion: Inspiring Health, Well-Being, and Development in Organizations. *Journal of Applied Behavioral Science*, 49(2), pp. 153–178. https://doi.org/10.1177/0021886312462236

Brown, M., Metz, I., Cregan, C., & Kulik, C. T. (2009) Irreconcilable Differences? Strategic Human Resource Management and Employee Well-being. *Asia Pacific Journal of Human Resources*, 47, pp. 270–294. https://doi.org/10.1177/1038411109106859

Cacioppe, R., & Edwards, M. (2005) Seeking the Holy Grail of Organisational Development: A Synthesis of Integral Theory, Spiral Dynamics, Corporate Transformation and Action Inquiry. *Leadership & Organization Development Journal*, 26(2), pp. 86–105.

Carrington, J. (2014) Take the Lead in Wellbeing. *Occupational Health*, 66(8), pp. 24–25.

Chartered Institute of Personnel and Development [CIPD] (2021) *Health and Wellbeing at Work Survey Report 2021*. CIPD: London.

Chartered Institute of Personnel and Development [CIPD] (2022) *Employee Health and Wellbeing*. Retrieved on 25th September 2024 from www.cipd.org/globalassets/media/comms/news/ahealth-wellbeing-work-report-2022_tcm18-108440.pdf

Chartered Institute of Personnel and Development [CIPD] (n.d.) *Employee Health and Wellbeing*. Retrieved on 25th September 2024 from www.cipd.org/uk/views-and-insights/cipd-viewpoint/employee-health-wellbeing/

Cotton, P., & Hart, P. M. (2003) Occupational Wellbeing and Performance: A Review of Organisational Health Research. *Australian Psychologist*, 38(2), pp. 118 127. https://doi.org/10.1080/00050060310001707117

Crawshaw, P. (2008) Whither Wellbeing for Public Health? *Critical Public Health*, 18(3), pp. 259–261. https://doi.org/10.1080/09581590802351757

Daniels, K., Delany, K., Napier, J., Hogg, M., & Rushworth, M. (2019) *The Value of Occupational Health to Workplace Wellbeing*. December 2019 the Society of Occupational Medicine. https://www.som.org.uk/sites/som.org.uk/files/The%20Value%20of%20Occupational%20Health%20to%20Workplace%20Wellbeing%20WEB_0.pdf

Daniels, K., Tregaskis, O., Nayani, R., & Watson. D. (2022) *Achieving Sustainable Workplace Wellbeing, Aligning Perspectives on Health, Safety and Well-Being*. Boston, MA: Springer.

David, S., Clutterbuck, D., & Megginson, D. (2013) *Beyond Goals: Effective Strategies for Coaching and Mentoring*. London: Gower.

Deci, E. L., & Ryan, R. M. (1985) *Conceptualizations of Intrinsic Motivation and Self-Determination*. In: Intrinsic Motivation and Self-Determination in Human Behavior. Perspectives in Social Psychology. Boston, MA: Springer.

Dewa, C. S., & McDaid, D. (2011) Investing in the Mental Health of the Labor Force: Epidemiological and Economic Impact of Mental Health Disabilities in the Workplace. In: I. Schultz & E. Rogers (eds) *Work Accommodation and Retention in Mental Health*. Boston, MA: Springer.

Dooris, M., Farrier, A., & Froggett, L. (2018) Wellbeing: The Challenge of 'Operationalising' An Holistic Concept Within a Reductionist Public Health Programme. *Perspectives in Public Health*, 138(2), pp. 93–99. https://doi.org/10.1177/1757913917711204

Dyrbye, L. N., Shanafelt, T. D., Gill, P. R., Satele, D. V., & West, C. P. (2019) Effect of a Professional Coaching Interventionon the Well-being and Distress of Physicians: A Pilot Randomized Clinical Trial. *Internal Medicine*, 179(10), pp. 1406–1414. https://doi.org/10.1001/jamainternmed.2019.2425

Ely, E., Boyce, L. A., Nelson, J. K., Zaccaro, S. J., Hernez-Broome, G., & Whyman, W. (2010) Evaluating Leadership Coaching: A review and Integrated Framework. *The Leadership Quarterly*, 21(4), pp. 282–599.

Faragher, E. B., Cass, M., & Cooper, C. L. (2013) The Relationship between Job Satisfaction and Health: A Meta-Analysis. In: C. L. Cooper (ed) *From Stress to Wellbeing Volume 1*. London: Palgrave Macmillan. https://doi.org/10.1057/9781137310651_12

Forbes (2021) *The Future of Work Is Employee Well-Being*. Retrieved on 25th September 2024 from www.forbes.com/sites/jeannemeister/2021/08/04/the-future-of-work-is-worker-well-being/#

Gabriel, A. S., Moran, C. M., & Gregory, J. B. (2014) How Can Humanistic Coaching Affect Employee Well-being and Performance? An Application of Self-Determination Theory. *Coaching: An International Journal of Theory, Research and Practice*, 7(1), pp. 56–73. https://doi.org/10.1080/17521882.2014.889184

Ganster, D. C., & Fusilier, M. R. (1989) Control in the Workplace. *International Review of Industrial and Organizational Psychology*, 4, pp. 235–280.

Gormley, H., & van Nieuwerburgh, C. (2014). Developing coaching cultures: A review of the literature. *Coaching: An International Journal of Theory, Research and Practice*, 7(2), 90–101. https://doi.org/10.1080/17521882.2014.915863

Govindji, R., & Linley, P. A. (2007) Strengths Use, Self-Concordance and Well-being: Implications for Strengths Coaching and Coaching Psychologists. *International Coaching Psychology Review*, 2(2), please add page numbers.

Griseri, P. (2013) *An Introduction to the Philosophy of Management*. Thousand Oaks, CA: Sage Publications Ltd.

Haynes, S. (2013) A Healthy Objective. *Occupational Health: September*, 65, 9.

The Health and Safety Executive (n.d.) Retrieved on 25th September 2024 from www.hse.gov.uk/STRESS/mcit.htm

Heifetz, R. A., & Laurie, D. L. (1997) The Work of Leadership: Leaders Do Not Need to Know All the Answers: They do Need to Ask the Right Questions. *Harvard Business Review*, 124–134.

Jones, J. E., & Bearley, W. L. (2010) *360-Degree Feedback: Strategies, Tactics, and Techniques for Developing Leaders*. Boston, MA: HRD Press.

Kirkpatrick, D. L. (1979) Techniques for Evaluating Training Programs. *Training & Development Journal*, 33(6), pp. 78–92.

Kotter, J. P. (2007) Leading Change – Why Transformation Efforts Fail. *Harvard Business Review*. https://hbr.org/1995/05/leading-change-why-transformation-efforts-fail-2

Kowalski, T. H. P., & Loretto, W. (2017) Well-being and HRM in the Changing Workplace. *The International Journal of Human Resource Management*, 28(16), pp. 2229–2255. https://doi.org/10.1080/09585192.2017.1345205

Litchfield, P., Cooper, C., Hancock, C., & Watt, P. (2016) Work and Wellbeing in the 21st Century. *International Journal of Environmental Research and Public Health*, 13(11), 1065. https://doi.org/10.3390/ijerph13111065

Maslow, A. H. (1969) Various Meanings of Transcendence. *Journal of Transpersonal Psychology*, 1(1), pp. 56–66.

Moss, D. (2015) The Roots and Genealogy of Humanistic Psychology. In: K. J. Schneider, J. F. Pierson, & J. F. Bugental (eds) *The Handbook of Humanistic Psychology: Theory, Research, and Practice* (pp. 3–18). Thousand Oaks, CA: SAGE Publications, Inc. https://dx.doi.org/10.4135/9781483387864.n1

Odes, L. (2020) Coaching for Wellbeing at Work. In: C. van Nieuwerburgh (ed) *Coaching in Professional Contexts*, London: SAGE Publications, Inc.

Organisation for Economic Co-operation and Development [OECD] (2015). *How's life? 2015: Measuring well-being*. Paris: OECD Publishing. https://doi.org/10.1787/how_life-2015-en

Passmore, J., & Tee, D. (2021) Feedback and Evaluation in Coaching. In: J. Passmore (ed) *The Coaches' Handbook, the Complete Practitioner Guide for Professional Coaches*. London: Routledge.

Reio, T. G., Jr., Rocco, T. S., Smith, D. H., & Chang, E. (2017) A Critique of Kirkpatrick's Evaluation Model. *New Horizons in Adult Education & Human Resource Development*, 29(2), pp. 35–53.

Ryan, J. C., Williams, C., Wiggins, C. B., Flitton, A. J., McIntosh, J. T., Carmen, M. J., & Cox, D. N. (2021) Exploring the Active Ingredients of Workplace Physical and Psychological Wellbeing Programs: A Systematic Review. *Translational Behavioral Medicine*, 11(5), pp. 1127–1141.

Silcox, S. (2016) Encouraging Employee Participation in Wellbeing Activities. *Occupational Health & Wellbeing*, 68(5), pp. 16–17.

Skagen, K., & Collins, A. M. (2016) The Consequences of Sickness Presenteeism on Health and Wellbeing Over Time: A Systematic Review. *Social Science & Medicine*, 161, p. 169.

Stout-Rostron, S. (2011) How is Coaching Impacting Systematic and Cultural Change within Organisations. *International Journal of Coaching in Organisations*, 32(8), p. 4.

Sutton, A., Evans, M., Davies, C., & Lawson, C. (2016) The Development and Longitudinal Evaluation of a Wellbeing Programme: An Organisational Case Study. *International Journal of Wellbeing*, 6(1), pp. 180–195.

Sveningsson, S., & Sörgärde, N. (2020) *Managing Change in Organizations: How, What and Why?* London: Sage.

Turner, P. (2020) *Employee Engagement in Contemporary Organizations: Maintaining Productivity and Sustained Competeiviness*. Switzerland, Palgrave MacMillan.

The Washington Post. (22 October 2022). https://www.washingtonpost.com/wellness/2022/10/22/toxic-workplaces-stress-surgeon-general/

Yen-chen, H., Ching-wen, W., & Jun-bang, L. (2019) Evaluating the Performance of Employee Assistance Programmes (EAP): A Checklist Developed from a Large Sample of Public Agencies. *Asia Pacific Journal of Management*, 37, pp. 935–955.

Zhao, H., & Liu, W. (2020) Managerial Coaching and Subordinates' Workplace Well-Being: A Moderated Mediation Study. *Human Resource Management Journal*, 30, pp. 293–311. https://www.hse.gov.uk/stress/standards/index.htm

Zheng, C., Molineux, J., Mirsherkary, S., & Scaparo, S. (2015) Developing Individual and Organisational Work Life Balance Strategies to Improve Employee Health and Wellbeing. *Employee Relations* 37(3).

Chapter 22

Coaching for self-care

Tim Anstiss

Introduction

Self-care has been defined as 'the actions that individuals take for themselves, on behalf of and with others, in order to develop, protect, maintain and improve their health, well-being or wellness' (www.selfcareforum.org/). Arguably, a lack of self-care is one of the major drivers of unsustainable pressure on healthcare systems around the world (Riegel et al., 2017; Cravo et al., 2022; Aghajanloo et al., 2021; Paudel et al., 2022), and several initiatives are underway to help healthcare and other organisations get better at enhancing self-care. Research into the topic of self-care and the related topic of self-management has shown a dramatic increase in volume over the last 20 years based on citations in the PubMed database.

This chapter is written for the following four main audiences.

- Health and care professionals seeking to increase self-care behaviours in their patients and clients as part of the wide range of other things they do.
- Professionals with jobs mainly focussing on encouraging people to engage in more or better self-care, including health coaches, wellbeing advisers/coaches, social prescribing link workers, coaching psychologists and therapists.
- Coaches who talk with the clients about a range of things, including health, wellbeing and self-care.
- People with lived experience of poor health who act as peer coaches or peer support workers.

After exploring several models and theories related to the topic of self-care and some of the evidence base for interventions to increase self-care, I outline a process-based approach to self-care coaching to help guide and empower people towards looking after themselves better.

Models and frameworks

The care continuum model

It can be helpful to view care as a continuum, with healthcare at one end and self-care at the other. An example of pure healthcare with no self-care might be when specialists are caring for a patient in a coma in intensive care. An example of pure self-care might be a

DOI: 10.4324/9781003319016-24

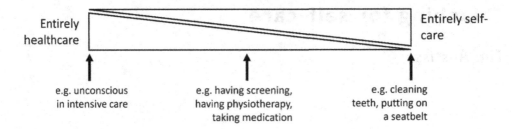

Entirely healthcare

Entirely self-care

e.g. unconscious in intensive care

e.g. having screening, having physiotherapy, taking medication

e.g. cleaning teeth, putting on a seatbelt

Figure 22.1 The care continuum

person cleaning their teeth before they go to bed, or putting on a seatbelt when they get in a car (Figure 22.1).

In between are the many actions a person can take which involve various degrees of healthcare system support or involvement – such as having a screening, engaging in rehabilitation, taking medication, etc.

Self-care and self-management

The terms self-care and self-management are sometimes used interchangeably, but it might be helpful perhaps to see self-care as the larger set of things a person does to look after their health and wellbeing, and self-management as a subset of those things for people with one of more health problems, whereby they have the additional takes of monitoring symptoms, managing symptoms and trying to reduce disease progression and the development of complications (Figure 22.2).

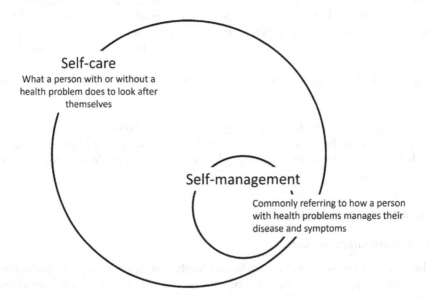

Self-care
What a person with or without a health problem does to look after themselves

Self-management
Commonly referring to how a person with health problems manages their disease and symptoms

Figure 22.2 The relationship between self-care and self-management

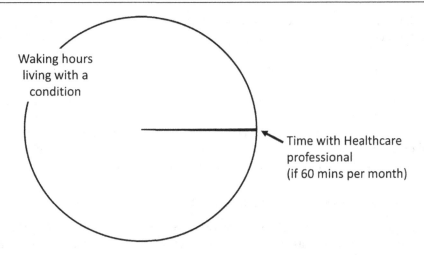

Figure 22.3 Time spent on self-care compared to time spent interacting with healthcare

Time spent self-managing

If a person with one of more long-term conditions sleeps on average seven hours a night, then they will experience 6,205 waking hours living with their condition. If they spend an average of 60 minutes each month interacting with a healthcare professional, then the following graph can be produced (Figure 22.3). This nicely illustrates how important it is for healthcare systems, health professionals and others to get better at guiding, supporting and coaching people towards more and better self-care.

The Information–Motivation–Behaviour Skills (IMBS) model

The IMBS model is a social psychological model for understanding and promoting health-related behaviour (Fisher et al., 2003). Originally developed to help explain psychological determinants of human immunodeficiency virus (HIV) risk and preventive behaviour, it suggests that health behaviour change is dependent upon the individual having the necessary information, motivation and skills. Adapted for broad field of self-care behaviours it would look like Figure 22.4.

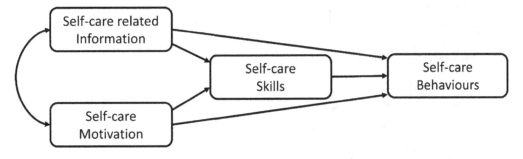

Figure 22.4 IMBS model for self-care

The model suggests that when coaching a person towards more or better self-care, the coach should:

- Check and ensure the person has the information they need to engage in more and better self-care, should they choose to do so.
- Talk with a person to discover and strengthen their reasons for engaging in more or better self-care.
- Check and ensure the person has the skills to engage in more and better self-care, should they choose to do so, e.g., self-monitoring, stress management, exercise, healthy eating, sleep preparation, medication taking, etc.

The Capacity–Opportunity–Motivational model (COMB)

An attempt to synthesise and integrate other health behaviour models, the COM-B model explains behaviour as resulting from a system of interacting factors (Michie et al., 2011b). The model suggests that for a particular behaviour to occur, a person must have sufficient motivation, together with capacity and opportunity to perform the behaviour.

Adapted for self-care behaviours, the model would look like Figure 22.5.

The COM-B model suggests that when coaching a person towards more or better self-care, the coach should:

- Talk with a person to discover and strengthen their reasons for engaging in more or better self-care.
- Help to develop a person's capacity or capability for self-care, their psychological and physical capacity to engage in the behaviour.
- Explore with a person when and where they might engage in more or better self-care, and any changes they may need to make to their physical and/or social environment to make the behaviour possible.

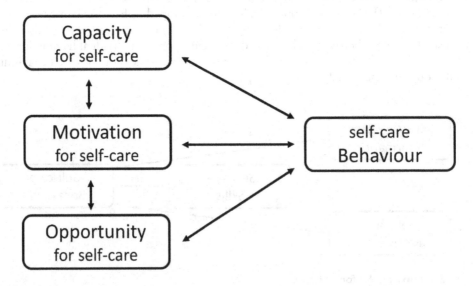

Figure 22.5 The COM-B model for self-care

The Stages of Change element of the TransTheoretical Model (TTM) of behaviour change

Another integrated health behaviour change model, the Stages of Change model (Figure 22.6), is one of several stage-based models which suggest that a person progresses through recognisable stages on their journey towards sustained behaviour change, which may involve backwards steps (Prochaska et al., 1992).

Whilst the evidence for stages matched interventions is mixed, a coach may choose to focus on different tasks according to the stage of change they sense the person may be in regarding a particular self-care behaviour.

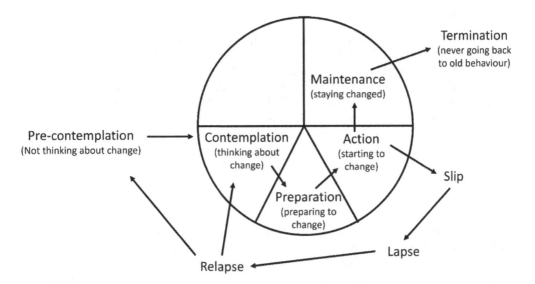

Figure 22.6 The Stages of Change model

Table 22.1 Matching coaching task to Stage of Change

Stages of Change	Description	Possible coach task
Pre-contemplation	Not thinking about engaging in more/better self-care	Raise the topic of self-care in a non-threatening, non-judgemental manner
Contemplation	Thinking about change but ambivalent, undecided	Help the person explore their ambivalence about change and build their readiness to and confidence about changing
Preparation	The person has decided to change, and is getting ready to change, but has not yet started	Work collaboratively with the person to draw out a personalised self-care plan to maximise their chances of success
Action	Taking action on the health behaviour change	Support the person in their efforts to change and stay changed
Maintenance	Keeping going with the behaviour, perhaps with less effort required than during the action phase	Support the person in their efforts to change and stay changed

Research

Self-care can involve a wide range of different behaviours, such as becoming more active, eating a healthier diet, drinking less alcohol, stopping smoking, getting better sleep, becoming more assertive, leaving an abusive relationship, using sunscreen, wearing a seatbelt, cultivating self-acceptance and self-compassion, and taking medication as prescribed. This makes it difficult to summarise the vast amounts of research into what works in helping people make one or more of these behaviour changes. So rather than focus on specific behaviours, this section will review the evidence for different approaches for helping people self-care.

Health coaching

The UK NHS defines health coaching as: 'Helping people gain and use the knowledge, skills and confidence to become active participants in their care so that they can reach their self-identified health and wellbeing goals' (NHS England, u.d.).

Health Education England (HEE, 2014) conducted a rapid review and identified 275 studies about health coaching, along with 67 studies looking at training health professionals to support behaviour change. The authors concluded that there was evidence that health coaching can support people to adopt more healthy lifestyles, including physical activity, healthy eating and reduced smoking, with mixed evidence about the impact of health coaching on physiological variables such as cholesterol, blood pressure and blood sugar levels.

Hill and colleagues (2015) performed a systematic review of health coaching interventions to determine effectiveness for specific outcomes, as well as optimal approaches and techniques. Their analysis showed that 94% of studies reported a positive intervention effect on at least one outcome variable and they concluded that health coaching shows promise as a technique for eliciting positive behaviour change. They attempted to cross-tabulate specific behaviour change techniques with specific outcomes to identify optimal approaches and the more effective techniques. Of a possible 40 behaviour change techniques (BCTs) described in the CALO-RE classification system (Michie et al., 2011a), 25 different BCTs were used in the 16 studies reviewed. The mean number of BCTs described per study was 6.8 (range of 2–15 BCTs). Three issues prevented them drawing firm conclusions about the relative effectiveness of different techniques: the diversity of intervention approaches, the lack of detail in reported studies and the diversity of outcomes.

The Health Services Research and Development Service of the Department of Veterans Affairs (Gierisch et al., 2017) conducted a systematic review to determine the effects of self-identified coaching interventions among adults with chronic medical conditions on clinical, behavioural and self-efficacy outcomes; 41 trials met eligibility criteria. Compared to non-intervention controls, the review found health coaching to have a statistically significant effect on haemoglobin A1C (HBA1c), physical activity levels, body mass index (BMI), dietary fat intake and self-efficacy – but with weaker or no effect when compared to active controls given something other than health coaching. One of the main weaknesses of this review is that it would have excluded hundreds of studies not self-identifying as health coaching – e.g., studies of motivational interviewing (MI) and other behaviour change interventions.

Dejonghe and colleagues (2017) undertook a systematic review to determine the long-term effectiveness of health coaching intervention in rehabilitation and disease prevention;

14 studies met the inclusion criteria, seven each for rehabilitation and prevention. Three studies in each setting showed statistically significant long-term effectiveness for the main outcome. Similar to Hill and colleagues (2015), the wide variation in methods, the poor description of methods and the heterogeneity of outcome measures prevented them drawing any firm conclusions about the most effective or optimal health coaching techniques.

Long and colleagues (2019) systematically reviewed the evidence for health coaching as an intervention to improve health-related quality of life and reduce hospital admissions in people with chronic obstructive pulmonary disease (COPD). Meta-analysis which included ten RCTs showed that health coaching has a significant positive effect on health-related quality of life (HRQoL) and led to a significant reduction in COPD-related hospital admissions. Three of four studies reported significant improvements to self-care behaviours such as medication adherence and exercise compliance.

Singh and colleagues (2019) synthesised the available empirical evidence regarding pharmacy health coaching; ten papers met the eligibility criteria. The most commonly occurring outcome of health coaching was an improvement in a health outcome of a target population. An improvement in medication management/adherence and the relationship between health professionals was also evident, along with an improved attitude towards drug therapy.

An and Song (2020) undertook a systematic review and meta-analysis of the effects of health coaching on physical activities, dietary behaviours, health responsibility, stress management and smoking behaviours among populations with cardiovascular risk factors. The meta-analysis included 15 randomised trials. MI and education sessions were common coaching interventions, with telephone calls or face-to-face contacts as the main contact methods. They found that health coaching for health behaviours showed small but significant effect sizes on physical activity levels, dietary behaviours, health responsibility and stress management.

Motivational interviewing and behavioural counselling

MI specifically has been the subject of over 1,900 clinical trials and over 100 systematic reviews and meta-analyses, covering a broad range of health topics. These generally show that MI can help people to become more active, eat better, lose weight, keep weight off, reduce their blood pressure, reduce their risk of diabetes, take their medication as prescribed, become less anxious, become less depressed, change their drinking patterns and stop smoking. (Miller et al., 2003; Brodie & Inoue, 2005; Macdonald et al., 2012; Spencer & Wheeler, 2016; Ekong & Kavookjian, 2016; Burgess et al., 2017; Al-Ganmi et al., 2016; Armstrong et al., 2011; Hardcastle, 2013)

After reviewing interventions to promote physical activity and dietary lifestyle changes for cardiovascular risk factor modification in adults, the American Heart Association (Artinian et al., 2010) found the strongest level of evidence for the following behaviour change strategies and techniques: interventions to target dietary and physical activity behaviours with specific, proximal goals; providing feedback on progress toward goals; providing strategies for self-monitoring; establishing a plan for frequency and duration of follow-up contacts (e.g., in-person, oral, written, electronic) in accordance with individual needs; assessing and reinforcing progress toward goal achievement; using MI; and using any combination of two of the previously discussed strategies (e.g., goal setting, feedback, self-monitoring, follow-up, MI, self-efficacy) in an intervention.

Olsen and Nesbitt (2010) performed an integrative review of health coaching studies to try to identify elements of effectiveness and key programme features. Significant favourable changes in one or more of the behaviours of nutrition, physical activity, weight management or medication adherence were identified in six of the 15 studies (40%). Common features of effective programmes were use of MI, goal setting and collaboration with healthcare providers.

Morton et al. (2015) conducted a systematic review to examine the evidence base for MI interventions in primary care settings with non-clinical populations to achieve behaviour change for physical activity, dietary behaviours and/or alcohol intake, whilst also exploring the specific behaviour change elements included in MI interventions. Of the 33 papers meeting inclusion criteria, approximately 50% (n=18) demonstrated positive effects on health behaviour change.

McKenzie and colleagues (2015) conducted a systematic review of MI in healthcare to explore its potential in addressing lifestyle factors relevant to multimorbidity. They identified 12 meta-analyses exploring lifestyle factors relevant to multimorbidity, and concluded that MI is as effective as other treatments for each of these lifestyle factors and that it can be delivered by a range of different practitioners.

The US Preventive Services Task Force (USPSTF, 2017) reviewed the evidence on relevant primary care counselling interventions to promote a healthy diet and physical activity. They found adequate evidence that behavioural counselling interventions provide at least a small benefit for reduction of cardiovascular disease (CVD) risk in adults without obesity who do not have the common risk factors for CVD (hypertension, dyslipidaemia, abnormal blood glucose levels or diabetes). They found behavioural counselling interventions to improve healthful behaviours, including beneficial effects on fruit and vegetable consumption, total daily caloric intake, salt intake and physical activity levels, as well as improvements in systolic and diastolic blood pressure levels, low-density lipoprotein cholesterol (LDL-C) levels, BMI and waist circumference that persisted over 6–12 months.

Patnode and colleagues (2017) conducted a systematic review exploring the effects of behavioural counselling for healthful diets and physical activity in the primary prevention of CVD in adults without known CVD risk factors. They concluded that diet and physical activity behavioural interventions resulted in consistent modest benefits across a variety of important intermediate health outcomes, including blood pressure, low-density lipoprotein and total cholesterol levels, as well as adiposity, with evidence of a dose-response effect with higher intensity interventions resulting in greater improvements. Small to moderate improvements were also seen in dietary and physical activity behaviours. They felt that the improvements seen in intermediate and behavioural health outcomes could translate into long-term reduction in CVD-related events, with minimal to no harms, if such changes were maintained over time.

Barrett et al. (2018) performed a systematic review and meta-analysis to investigate whether integrated MI and cognitive behaviour therapy (CBT) leads to changes in lifestyle mediators of overweight and obesity in community-dwelling adults. Ten randomised controlled trials involving 1949 participants were included. Results revealed moderate-quality evidence that integrated MI and cognitive behaviour therapy had a significant effect in increasing physical activity levels in community-dwelling adults, and that the combined intervention resulted in a small, non-significant effect in body composition changes. They stated that the available evidence demonstrates the feasibility of integrating MI with CBT, and that this combined intervention has the potential to improve health-related outcomes.

Soderlund (2018) conducted a review into the effectiveness of MI for physical activity self-management for adults diagnosed with type 2 diabetes mellitus; nine studies met review criteria, and four included MI interventions associated with significant physical activity outcomes.

Melnyk and colleagues (2020) performed a systematic review of randomised controlled trials testing interventions designed to improve the mental health, wellbeing, physical health and lifestyle behaviours of physicians and nurses; 29 studies (N = 2708 participants) met the inclusion criteria. Results indicated that mindfulness and CBT-based interventions were effective in reducing stress, anxiety and depression; that brief interventions incorporating deep breathing and gratitude might also be beneficial; and that visual triggers, pedometers and health coaching with texting increased physical activity.

Fordham and colleagues (2021) conducted an overview of systematic reviews and panoramic meta-analysis in the area of cognitive-behavioural therapy approaches. A total of 494 reviews were mapped, representing 68% of the categories (27 of 40) of the International Classification of Diseases, Eleventh Revision, Mortality and Morbidity Statistics (WHO, 2024). A modest effect was found in favour of CBT for health-related quality of life, anxiety and pain outcomes. The analysis found that CBT consistently improved quality of life across all the conditions where it has been tested, with evidence that it can help children, adolescents and adults, of either sex, who are living in Europe, North America and Australasia.

Wellbeing interventions

Coaching a person towards improved self-care involves coaching them not just towards more and better care for their physical health, but also their psychological health and wellbeing –so to be a good self-care coach, one will need to know what works in helping people protect and improve their mental health.

In a recent systematic review and meta-analysis of interventions to improve psychological wellbeing (van Agteren et al. 2021), the authors looked at over 23,000 citations and assessed almost 2,000 full-text articles. They identified 419 studies that met the inclusion criteria, with 393 studies providing sufficient information for the final quantitative analysis. A total of 53,288 participants were involved in the studies: 41,491 from the general population, 5,712 from populations with a mental illness, and 6,085 from populations with a physical illness.

They found evidence of varying levels of strength that the following approaches can be helpful in improving a person's psychological wellbeing: cognitive therapy or CBT-based interventions, mindfulness and third wave approaches such as acceptance-based and commitment therapy–based, single and multi-component positive psychology interventions, compassion-focussed interventions and reminiscence-based interventions.

Practice

Self-care is: 'The actions that individuals take for themselves, on behalf of and with others, in order to develop, protect, maintain and improve their health, wellbeing or wellness' (What is self-care and why is it good for people and the NHS? – Self Care Forum https://www.selfcareforum.org/about-us/what-do-we-mean-by-self-care-and-why-is-good-for-people/#:~:text=The%20Self%20Care%20Forum%E2%80%99s%20definition%20of%20self-care%20is%3A,maintain%20and%20improve%20their%20health%2C%20wellbeing%20or%20wellness).

Given this definition, coaching for self-care will involve talking with people with or without health problems to help them develop, protect, maintain and improve their health and wellbeing. This obviously makes coaching for self-care very much in the same camp as health coaching, wellbeing coaching and wellness coaching.

The focus of coaching for self-care

Different organisations break down self-care into different components. For instance, the World Health Organization (WHO, 2022) describes self-care as involving the following.

- Making healthy lifestyle choices.
- Avoiding unhealthy lifestyle habits.
- Making responsible use of prescription and non-prescription medicines.
- Self-recognition of symptoms – assessing and addressing symptoms, in partnership with a healthcare professional when necessary.
- Self-monitoring – checking for signs of deterioration or improvement.
- Self-management – managing symptoms of disease, either alone, in partnership with healthcare professionals or alongside other people with the same health condition.

Meanwhile, the International Self-Care Foundation (ISF Global, n.d.) describes the following seven pillars of self-care.

- Knowledge and health literacy.
- Mental wellbeing.
- Physical activity.
- Healthy eating.
- Risk avoidance.
- Good hygiene.
- Rational use of products and services.

The British Society of Lifestyle Medicine (n.d.) suggests conversations with patients about self-care might best be organised around the following topics.

- Healthy eating.
- Mental wellbeing.
- Healthy relationships.
- Physical activity.
- Minimising use of harmful substances.
- Sleep.

To complicate things further (or make the approach more holistic still, depending on your mindset!), coaching a person towards better self-care might even focus on particular body parts, such as the following.

- Skin care: including washing, sun protection, moisturising, applying plaster to wounds, managing skin infections or ulcers, etc.

- Joint care: including taping ankles before a sporting event, resting an injured joint, taking supplements, maintaining good range of motion and strength levels, etc.
- Back care: maintaining strength, paying attention to seating, ensuring good hamstring length, correct lifting technique, using lifting aids, sleeping on a good quality mattress, etc.
- Foot care: using correctly fitting footwear, preventing fungal infections, checking for problems (especially with diabetes), maintaining arch strength, using orthoses, etc.
- Gut care: eating healthily, avoiding dangerous food items, washing some food first, maintaining good gut biome, using probiotics, etc.
- Brain care: wearing cycle helmet, wearing seatbelt, avoiding driving whilst drunk, minimising head contact in sports, avoiding fights, eating healthily, taking exercise, some mindfulness practices, reducing alcohol intake, reducing risk of stroke, etc.
- Heart care: healthy eating, physical activity, screening, medication taking, stress management, blood pressure control, etc.

Another way of categorising self-care coaching might be by condition, with the behaviours to be explored varying from condition to condition, such as the following.

- Self-care in diabetes can include self-monitoring, following a healthy diet, physical activity, medication taking, stopping smoking, foot care, attending screening, etc.
- Self-care for someone with cancer might involve following a healthy or prescribed diet, physical activity, managing fatigue, stoma care, wound care, medication taking, mindfulness, cultivating self-compassion, etc.
- Self-care for someone with lung disease might involve medication taking, self-monitoring, early help seeking in the case of exacerbation, avoiding pollution, breathing exercises, smoking cessation, etc.
- Self-care for someone experiencing depression might involve physical activity, getting back into previously enjoyed activities, eating healthily, cultivating self-compassion, seeking help, taking medication, reducing alcohol intake, spending more time in contact with nature, getting more and better sleep, etc.

Towards a process-based approach

How might a busy practitioner best integrate and apply the various issues explored in this chapter – the different coaching approaches (e.g., health, cognitive-behavioural, MI, positive psychology, compassion focused, acceptance and commitment based, etc.), the different behaviour change models (e.g., Stages of Change, COM-B, IMBS, etc.) and different areas of possible focus?

One solution is to adopt a person centred and process-based coaching approach.

Informed by models such as GROW (goals, reality, options and way forward) (Whitmore et al., 2013) and the four processes (or tasks) of MI (engage, focus, evoke and plan) (Miller & Rollnick, 2013), I would like to suggest a six-stage integrated health and wellbeing coaching framework to support good practice and reduce the chances of a practitioner getting lost in conversations with people around better self-care (Figure 22.7).

Let us look at each step.

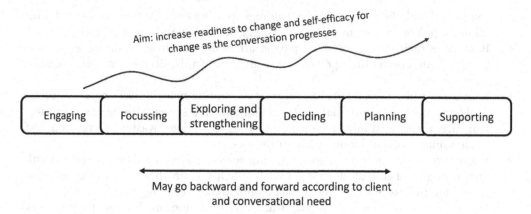

Figure 22.7 A six-step process-based approach to self-care coaching

Engaging

This step or process aims to get a person talking and keep them talking in an open and non-defensive way, using open questions, empathic listening, making affirmations, using summaries, using good non-verbal listening skills, emphasising autonomy, being non-judgemental, ensuring goal congruence and strengthening the sense of alliance, partnership and collaboration.

Focussing

This step or process is about deciding what is to be talked about, such as self-care in general, or more specific behaviours like eating better, taking medications as prescribed or ways to better manage stress. The focus might be determined by the context in which the person is being seen (e.g., a weight management service) or the issue which the person wants to talk about (e.g., back pain), or it might be a topic or issue you want to surface and engage. If the latter, one way to raise the topic might be to ask permission, e.g., 'Would it be OK if we spent a couple of minutes talking about ways to experience less stress over time? I won't be telling you what to do by the way. You'll be the best judge of that'. Another way is to ask an open question: 'What do you know about burnout?' or 'What do you know about the importance of sleep for good health?'

Evoking and strengthening

Things which can be explored in conversations about self-care include how self-care behaviours currently show up (or do not) in a person's life, issues or concerns the person has, their values (what really matter to them) and how these values shape (or do not shape) their behaviour; their hopes for the future; their knowledge about what might help them protect, improve and recover their health and wellbeing into the future; how their medication works; etc. It can also be helpful to explore their ambivalence or mixed feelings about change, and their ideas about how to change if they decided to change.

Things which might be strengthened during a conversation about self-care include knowledge, motivation, self-efficacy, hope, clarity, optimism, self-acceptance, self-compassion, behavioural skills and those all-important relational factors such as alliance, empathy, warmth and goal congruence.

But before a person makes one of more self-directed behaviour changes to look after themselves better, they will need to have good reasons for changing, as well as have a reasonable level of confidence (or self-efficacy) that their attempts at behaviour change will be successful. So it can be helpful to explore and then seek to strengthen first their 'why' for change (their reasons) and then their how.

Box 22.1 Examples of questions to help surface, explore, understand and strengthen a person's reasons for engaging in more and better self-care

- What kinds of things are you already doing to look after your physical health?
- What kinds of things are you already doing to look after your mental health and wellbeing?
- Why do you do these things? What are your main reasons for doing them?
- How important is it for you to look after yourself better, into the future?
- Why? What are your 2–3 best reasons?
- If you did start to make some changes to improve your diet, what do you hope you will notice?
- Looking forward 3–4 years and imagining you continue drinking at your current levels, what do you think might happen?
- What are your thoughts about having a free health check to help you get some sense of your risk of heart disease?
- Let's say you did decide to become more active, and in 10 weeks you were living a more active lifestyle. What would be different? How do you imagine you might be feeling?
- Can I share with you some things other people do to experience better psychological health and wellbeing over time?
- What do you make of some of those ideas?
- You mentioned your family is important to you. What would it be like for them if you had to stop working due to a heart problem or stroke? (Obviously, one would not ask this early in the conversation, only once rapport and trust has been established.)

Box 22.2   Examples of questions to help explore and strengthen a person's confidence or self-efficacy for engaging in more and better self-care

- What kinds of things are you already doing to look after your physical health?
- If you decided to make some changes, where would you start?
- What is the easiest thing you could do to look after yourself better?
- On a scale of 0–10, how confident are you that if you decided to stop smoking, you could stop and stay stopped for, say eight weeks, where 0 is not at all confident and 10 is extremely confident?
- You said 5. Why 5? Why not 1 or 2? What makes you somewhat confident you can do this if you set your mind to it?
- What else?
- What might help increase your confidence to a 6 or 7? What would be helpful to you?
- What else?
- Can you give me an example of when you have made some changes in a different area of life? What helped you be successful?
- What advice might you give to someone else who was thinking of making changes to become less stressed over time?
- Can I share with you a couple of things other people do to help them succeed in this area?
- What do you make of those ideas?
- Who can help you to be successful?
- What help might you want from them?
- What might get in the way of your plan?
- How could you find a way round that?
- Some people find it helpful to have another chat in the future, just to see how things are going. Is that something you might find helpful?
- When do you think it might be helpful for us to catch up?

Deciding

The coaching conversation up to this point has been about helping a person think about why they might want to change and how they might go about it, both of which can help to strengthen their readiness of motivation to change (especially if the coach has noticed and strengthened client change talk and help moderate client sustain talk). But they may not have come to a decision about *actually* changing. To help them decide whether or not to change, it can be helpful to offer them a summary of some of the things they said, and end the summary with the question 'Is that about right?' and if so, ask them what we call the key question: 'So, what are you going to do?' or 'So, what's next for you? Where do you go from here?'. And then let them talk. Do not ask the closed question 'Do you think you will change?' or jump in with advice such as 'Why don't you start with . . . ?'. This will only interfere with the autonomous and self-determined decision-making process you have been working up to, and may even damage the alliance and rapport. Let them talk themselves into changing.

Planning

Where you go next in the conversation depends on what the person decides to do. If they choose not to change, perhaps thank them and let them know you would be happy to chat further if they change their mind. If they cannot decide, perhaps offer to explore things some more with them or let them know that is normal and natural and that maybe they have some more thinking to do. If they do decide to change, and if you have already asked some of the questions listed earlier in this chapter, then it is time to help them generate and strengthen a personalised self-care plan. You can do this by asking some more open questions around when they might get started, how often, where they will make these change, with what kind of help and support, etc. It is at this stage when you might also want to explore goal setting, but do not rush into this and be sensitive to any signs of push-back or resistance, especially if using SMART (specific, measurable, achievable, relevant and time-bound) goal setting as this can be challenging for some people and is not essential to the change process. You might also wish to do some relapse prevention work by asking the person 'What might get in the way of your plan?' or 'How would you find a way around that?' or 'What would you do if that started to happen?' – and then help them develop some implementation intentions such as 'If such and such happened, then I will do X and Y'. This can also be a good time to share with them some helpful tips about habit formation – e.g., focus on simple or small behaviours to start with, link them to a predictable cue or prompt, and reinforce the behaviour after it happens. Finally, having the person write down their personalised self-care plan can also be helpful.

Supporting

Starting a behaviour change for better self-care can be hard, but keeping up new self-care behaviours for several months is harder still. Even if you have helped the person develop a high-quality self-care plan (for instance, including proven BCTs such as self-monitoring, skills development, using social support, goal setting, using prompts and reminders, relapse prevention and signposting), relapse back to an early stage of change is common. Offering and providing ongoing support can therefore be helpful (if your context allows), and this can of course be delivering in a blended or hybrid format involving e-mail, messaging or a support group format.

Some helpful coaching tools and strategies

In addition to these six processes, it can be helpful to use specific coaching strategies and tools.

Asking about what is already happening

A solution-focussed approach to coaching often includes an exploration of what is already happening in the area of the desired solution or outcome, so in the case of coaching someone towards more or better self-care, it might be helpful to ask the person an open question such as:

> I'm wondering: What are some of the things you are already doing to look after your health and wellbeing, including your mental health and wellbeing?

Once this has been explored, then the conversation might move on to what else they might do in order to better look after themselves.

Use ask-share-ask

Sometimes, you may wish to bring up the topic of self-care and do this in a way which reduces the chances of a person becoming defensive, or even talk about a particular self-care option such as becoming more active, eating better, getting better sleep, etc. A way of doing this is the ask-share ask strategy which has the added benefit of helping you discover what the person already knows about a topic. It might sound something like the following.

> May I ask: What do you know about the importance of self-care? [or 'different ways to look after your health', or 'the benefits of strength training', or 'some of the benefits of mindfulness', or 'the key elements of a healthy diet' or 'how this medication works', etc.]

> Let them talk. Listen. And then if you need to, ask: 'Can I share with you a couple more things?'. Only share 2–3 points. Then ask: 'What do I make of what I've just said?'.
> You can use this strategy to raise the topic and get an understanding of what the person already knows or believes, in order to avoid falling into the trap of telling someone things they already know or overwhelming them with too much information. It can also help the person feel listened to and respected.

Decisional balance technique

Many people will be uncertain about whether to engage in more or better self-care. A nice coaching tool for helping a person come to a decision is the decisional balance exercise which helps the person think about the advantages and disadvantages of changing, as well as the advantages and disadvantages about staying the same. For instance, you might ask the following.

> Would it be OK to spend a couple of minutes talking about the pros and cons of looking after yourself better [or 'eating better' or 'stopping smoking' or 'leaving work on time', etc.]?
> What might be some of the good things about [behaviour]? And what else?
> Now, what might be the less good things about [behaviour]? And what else?
> What might be some of the good things about staying as you are? Anything else?
> And what might be some of your concerns about staying as you are? And do you have any other concerns?

At the end of this technique, it can be helpful to offer the person a summary of the things you heard the person say, and then ask them the following key question.

So, what do you think you will do?

Even if they decide not to change, you will have helped them think through the issues for themselves – and you may have even helped to bring forward any decision to look after themselves better.

Importance and confidence scaling questions, with option sharing

Scaling questions ask people to rate something on a scale from 0–10, and then use the number as the basis for some open questions to get the person talking and exploring. In conversations about self-care, you might ask the person how important it is for them to look after themselves better, and then how confident they are they would be able to do this if they chose to, such as in the following example.

> I'm wondering: How important is it for you to look after your health and wellbeing a bit better into the future? Perhaps you could let me know what you are on a scale of 0–10, where 0 would be where better care is not at all important to you and 10 is when it is very important.
>   [They say 5]
>   Why 5, and why not a lower number? What are some of your reasons for looking after yourself better? And are there another reasons? [at the end of this strategy, you will have a better understanding of their reasons, or their motivation, for engaging in more or better self-care. Then perhaps make a transition to exploring and building confidence or self-efficacy for self-care]
>   Thanks for that. And how confident are you that, if you did decide to look after yourself better, you would be able to get started and keep up a programme of self-care for, say, the next 5–6 weeks? Again, on a scale of 0–10, where 0 is not at all confident and 10 is very confident.
>   [they say 4]
>   You said 4. Why 4? You could have said 1 or 2. Why do you think you could look after yourself better if you put your mind to it? Are there any other reasons why you think you could make this change? And what would have to happen for your confidence to be, say, a 5 or a 6? What would help you to become more confident about looking after yourself better into the future?

Once you have heard some of their reasons for why they could look after themselves better, and ideas for becoming more confident, you could if you wanted to offer to share some more ideas. You might then transition into the ask-share-ask strategy to help you respectfully share some additional self-care options. For instance, you might ask the following question.

> Can I share with you some things other people find helpful?' [Then perhaps share with them a sheet like the one in Figure 22.8]
>   What do you make of these options?

Some self-care options

- ❏ Become more active
- ❏ Eat better
- ❏ Spend more time in nature
- ❏ Cultivate positive emotions
- ❏ Sort out finances
- ❏ Strengthen friendships
- ❏ Improve work-life balance
- ❏ Forgive myself or others
- ❏ Get back into a hobby – or develop one!
- ❏ Have therapy or coaching

- ❏ Learn to say no
- ❏ Get better sleep
- ❏ Reduce alcohol
- ❏ Stop smoking
- ❏ Have a massage
- ❏ Become less self-critical
- ❏ Learn to meditate
- ❏ Have screening
- ❏ Take my meds
- ❏ Spend less time with some people
- ❏ Savour pleasure

Figure 22.8 Sheet work sharing possible self-care options

At the end of this three-tool coaching sequence, you may wish to offer the person a summary of what you have heard, and then ask them the following key questions.

So, where do you go from here? What do you think you will do?

Exploring two possible futures

If you sense that the person may not be taking self-care as seriously as they might or should (with awareness that this is a value judgement on your part), you might consider offering them the two possible futures exercise. It might sound a little like this:

Might we talk a little bit about two possible futures? Let's imagine for a moment that you decide that now is the right time for you to look after yourself better, and we met up in say 1–2 years' time and you've developed some self-care habits . . . . What would things be like for you? What do you think would have changed? And now let's imagine that you don't make any changes and you stay as you are . . . again, and we met up in 1–2 year time. What would things be like for you? And what concerns you the most about that?

Conclusion

Coaching another person towards improved self-care and better health and wellbeing is arguably one of the most important services a coach or healthcare professional can provide. There is strong evidence that person-centred conversation-based interventions can make a difference, and there is a range of evidence-based approaches to choose from – including those based on health coaching, cognitive-behavioural therapy, motivational interviewing and positive psychology. A process-based approach may be helpful in providing structure and momentum to any session.

Healthcare systems around the world are under immense pressure from ageing populations and the rise of long-term conditions – including co-morbidities. Coaching people towards more and better self-care is an important response to this challenge.

Reflective questions

1. What are your 2–3 main reasons for engaging in more or better self-care yourself?
2. If you decided to engage in more or better self-care, how would you go about it?
3. What kind of things might get in the way of you looking after yourself better?

References

Aghajanloo A, Negarandeh R, Janani L, Tanha K, Hoseini-Esfidarjani SS. (2021). Self-care status in patients with heart failure: Systematic review and meta-analysis. Nurs Open. Sep;8(5):2235–2248.

Al-Ganmi AH, Perry L, Gholizadeh L, Alotaibi AM. (2016) Cardiovascular medication adherence among patients with cardiac disease: A systematic review. J Adv Nurs. Dec;72(12):3001–3014.

An S, Song R. (2020). Effects of health coaching on behavioral modification among adults with cardiovascular risk factors: Systematic review and meta-analysis. Patient Educ Couns. Oct;103(10):2029–2038.

Armstrong MJ, Mottershead TA, Ronksley PE, Sigal RJ, Campbell TS, Hemmelgarn BR. (2011). Motivational interviewing to improve weight loss in overweight and/or obese patients: A systematic review and meta-analysis of randomized controlled trials. Obes Rev. Sep;12(9):709–723.

Artinian NT, Fletcher GF, Mozaffarian D, Kris-Etherton P, Van Horn L, Lichtenstein AH, Kumanyika S, Kraus WE, Fleg JL, Redeker NS, Meininger JC, Banks J, Stuart-Shor EM, Fletcher BJ, Miller TD, Hughes S, Braun LT, Kopin LA, Berra K, Hayman LL, Ewing LJ, Ades PA, Durstine JL, Houston-Miller N, Burke LE. (2010). American Heart Association prevention committee of the council on cardiovascular nursing. Interventions to promote physical activity and dietary lifestyle changes for cardiovascular risk factor reduction in adults: A scientific statement from the American Heart Association. Circulation. Jul 27;122(4):406–441.

Barrett S, Begg S, O'Halloran P, Kingsley M. (2018). Integrated motivational interviewing and cognitive behaviour therapy for lifestyle mediators of overweight and obesity in community-dwelling adults: A systematic review and meta-analyses. BMC Public Health. Oct 5;18(1):1160.

Brodie, DA, Inoue, A. (2005). Motivational interviewing to promote physical activity for people with chronic heart failure. Journal of Advanced Nursing, 50(5), 518–527.

BSLM (n.d.). Transforming Healthcare Through Lifestyle Medicine. Retrieved on 2nd May 2023 from https://bslm.org.uk/

Burgess E, Hassmén P, Welvaert M, Pumpa KL. (2017). Behavioural treatment strategies improve adherence to lifestyle intervention programmes in adults with obesity: A systematic review and meta-analysis. Clin Obes. 7 Apr;7(2):105–114.

Cravo A, Attar D, Freeman D, Holmes S, Ip L, Singh SJ. (2022). The importance of self-management in the context of personalized care in COPD. Int J Chron Obstruct Pulmon Dis. Jan 22;17:231–243.

Dejonghe LAL, Becker J, Froboese I, Schaller A. (2017) Long-term effectiveness of health coaching in rehabilitation and prevention: A systematic review. Patient Educ Couns. Sep;100(9):1643–1653.

Ekong G, Kavookjian J. (2016). Motivational interviewing and outcomes in adults with type 2 diabetes: A systematic review. Patient Educ Couns. Jun;99(6):944–952.

Fordham B, Sugavanam T, Edwards K, Stallard P, Howard R, das Nair R, Copsey B, Lee H, Howick J, Hemming K, Lamb SE. (2021). The evidence for cognitive behavioural therapy in any condition, population or context: A meta-review of systematic reviews and panoramic meta-analysis. Psychol Med. Jan;51(1):21–29.

Fisher W, Fisher J, Harman J. (2003). The information–motivation– behavioral skills model: A general social psychological approach to understanding and promoting health behavior. In J Suls & KA Wallston (Eds.), Social Psychological Foundations of Health and Illness. Oxford: Blackwell Publishing Ltd.

Gierisch JM, Hughes JM, Edelman D, Bosworth HB, Oddone EZ, Taylor SS, Kosinski AS, McDuffie JR, Swinkels CM, Razouki Z, Masilamani V. (2017). The Effectiveness of Health Coaching [Internet]. Washington (DC): Department of Veterans Affairs (US).

Hardcastle SJ, Taylor AH, Bailey MP, Harley RA, Hagger MS. (2013). Effectiveness of a motivational interviewing intervention on weight loss, physical activity and cardiovascular disease risk factors: A randomised controlled trial with a 12-month post-intervention follow-up. Int J Behav Nutr Phys Act. Mar 28;1.

HEE (2014). Does health coaching work? A rapid review of empirical evidence. Health Education East of England.

Hill B, Richardson B, Skouteris H. (2015). Do we know how to design effective health coaching interventions: A systematic review of the state of the literature. Am J Health Promot. May–Jun;29(5).

ISF Global (n.d.). The seven pillars of self-care. Retrieved on 2nd May 2023 from ISF Global website https://isfglobal.org/

Long H, Howells K, Peters S, Blakemore A. (2019). Does health coaching improve health-related quality of life and reduce hospital admissions in people with chronic obstructive pulmonary disease? A systematic review and meta-analysis. Br J Health Psychol. Sep;24(3):515–546.

Macdonald P, Hibbs R, Corfield F, Treasure J. (2012). The use of motivational interviewing in eating disorders: A systematic review. Psychiatry Res. Nov 30;200(1):1–11.

McKenzie KJ, Pierce D, Gunn JM. (2015). A systematic review of motivational interviewing in healthcare: The potential of motivational interviewing to address the lifestyle factors relevant to multimorbidity. J Comorb. Dec 28;5:162–174.

Melnyk BM, Kelly SA, Stephens J, Dhakal K, McGovern C, Tucker S, Hoying J, McRae K, Ault S, Spurlock E, Bird SB. (2020). Interventions to improve mental health, well-being, physical health, and lifestyle behaviors in physicians and nurses: A systematic review. Am J Health Promot. Nov;34(8):929–941.

Michie S, Ashford S, Sniehotta FF, Dombrowski SU, Bishop A, French DP. (2011a). A refined taxonomy of behaviour change techniques to help people change their physical activity and healthy eating behaviours: The CALO-RE taxonomy. Psychol Health. Nov;26(11):1479–1498.

Michie S, van Stralen MM, West R. (2011b). The behaviour change wheel: A new method for characterising and designing behaviour change interventions. Implement Sci. Apr 23;6:42.

Miller WR., Rollnick S. (2013). Motivational Interviewing: Helping People Change (3rd edition). New York, NY: Guilford Press.

Miller WR., Wilbourne PL, & Hettema JE. (2003). What works? A summary of alcohol treatment outcome research. In RK Hester & WR Miller (Eds.), Handbook of Alcoholism Treatment Approaches: Effective Alternatives (3rd ed., pp. 13–63). Boston, MA: Allyn & Bacon.

Morton K, Beauchamp M, Prothero A, Joyce L, Saunders L, Spencer-Bowdage S, Dancy B, & Pedlar C. (2015). The effectiveness of motivational interviewing for health behaviour change in primary care settings: A systematic review. Health Psychol Rev.9(2):205–223.

NHS England (u.d). Definition of health coaching. Retrieved on 5th May 2023 from https://www.england.nhs.uk/publication/universal-personalised-care-implementing-the-comprehensive-model/

Olsen JM, & Nesbitt BJ. (2010) Health coaching to improve healthy lifestyle behaviors: An integrative review. Am J Health Promot. Sep–Oct;25(1).

Patnode CD, Evans CV, Senger CA, Redmond N, & Lin JS. (2017). Behavioral Counseling to Promote a Healthful Diet and Physical Activity for Cardiovascular Disease Prevention in Adults Without Known Cardiovascular Disease Risk Factors: Updated Systematic Review for the U.S. Preventive Services Task Force [Internet]. Rockville (MD): Agency for Healthcare Research and Quality (US); Jul. Report No.: 15–05222-EF-1.

Paudel G, Vandelanotte C, Dahal PK, Biswas T, Yadav UN, Sugishita T, & Rawal L. (2022). Self-care behaviours among people with type 2 diabetes mellitus in South Asia: A systematic review and meta-analysis. J Glob Health. Aug 3;12.

Prochaska JO, DiClemente CC, Norcross JC. (1992) In search of how people change. Applications to addictive behaviors. Am Psychol. Sep;47(9):1102–1114.

Riegel B, Moser DK, Buck HG, Dickson VV, Dunbar SB, Lee CS, Lennie TA, Lindenfeld J, Mitchell JE, Treat-Jacobson DJ, & Webber DE (2017). American Heart Association council on cardiovascular and stroke nursing; council on peripheral vascular disease; and council on quality of care and outcomes research. Self-care for the prevention and management of cardiovascular disease and stroke: A scientific statement for healthcare professionals from the American Heart Association. J Am Heart Assoc. Aug 31;6(9).

Self Care Forum (ud.). Definition of self care. Retrieved on 5 January 2023 from https://www.self-careforum.org/about-us/what-do-we-mean-by-self-care-and-why-is-good-for-people/

Self Care Forum (ud2). Seven pillars. Retrieved on 5 January 2023 from: https://isfglobal.org/practise-self-care/the-seven-pillars-of-self-care/

Singh HK, Kennedy GA, & Stupans I. (2019). A systematic review of pharmacy health coaching and an evaluation of patient outcomes. Res Social Adm Pharm. 2019 Mar;15(3):244–251.

Soderlund PD.(2018). Effectiveness of motivational interviewing for improving physical activity self-management for adults with type 2 diabetes: A review. Chronic Illn. Mar;14(1):54–68.

Spencer JC, Wheeler SB. (2016). A systematic review of motivational interviewing interventions in cancer patients and survivors. Patient Educ Couns. Jul;99(7):1099–1105.

US Preventive Services Task Force [USPSTF]. (2017). Behavioral counseling to promote a healthful diet and physical activity for cardiovascular disease prevention in adults without cardiovascular risk factors: US preventive services task force recommendation statement. JAMA.;318(2):167–174.

van Agteren J, Iasiello M, Lo L, Bartholomaeus J, Kopsaftis Z, Carey M, Kyrios M. (2021). A systematic review and meta-analysis of psychological interventions to improve mental wellbeing. Nat Hum Behav. May;5(5):631–652.

Whitmore J, Kauffman C, & David, SA. (2013). GROW grows up: From winning the game to pursuing transpersonal goals. In SA David, C David & M David (Eds.), Beyond Goals: Effective Strategies for Coaching and Mentoring. Farnham, Surrey: Gower Publishing Limited. pp. 245–260.

World Health Organization (WHO) (2022). WHO guideline on self-care interventions for health and well-being (2022 revision). Retrieved from WHO website www.who.int/publications/i/item/9789240052192

World Health Organization (WHO) (2024). International Classification of Diseases, 11th Revision (ICD-11) for Mortality and Morbidity Statistics. Geneva: World Health Organization. Retrieved from https://icd.who.int/browse11/l-m/en1.

Chapter 23

Coaching the narcissistic leader

Oriane J. B. Kets de Vries and Caroline Rook

Introduction

The leadership approach most frequently found at top management levels is the narcissist (Chatterjee & Hambrick, 2007): "70% of executives believe they are in the top 25% of their profession in terms of performance" (Kets de Vries et al., 2007, p. 1). People who have narcissistic personality disorder (NPD) tend to act with grandiosity and self-importance, with a fixation on unlimited success and control (*DSM-V-TR*; APA, 2022). Driven by grandiose fantasies about themselves, pathological narcissists feel entitled and pursue power at all costs. They often show no genuine interest in others and do not take responsibility for their own mistakes (Kets de Vries, 2014). But where do we draw the line between healthy self-esteem and an inflated sense of self – or indeed, a narcissistic personality disorder?

In this chapter, we address how to coach a narcissistic client. Specifically, we address the questions: How we can determine whether a client has narcissistic tendencies? Is it possible to help a narcissist (and make positive changes to their behaviour)? How does a leadership coach undertake such a task? What are the challenges of working with such clients? What is the potential positive impact of coaching narcissistic leaders?

Theory and research

Healthy narcissism is an essential part of normal development in children and a survival technique that fuels individuals with the energy and desire for life (Kets de Vries, 2014). As Kets de Vries (2012, p. 176) states: "We all need a modicum of narcissism to function properly." Meta-analytic results of empirical leadership studies show that at the dyadic level of analysis, a positive relationship exists between leader narcissism and leader emergence (Braun, 2017). Leaders perceive themselves and are perceived by others as leaders if they have a certain level of narcissism. The relationship between leader narcissism and leader effectiveness can best be described through a curvilinear function, i.e., there is an optimal midrange of narcissism (Grijalva & Harms, 2013), which enables leaders to be effective. It is high levels of narcissism that are dangerous.

Elizabeth Holmes, the ex-chief executive of Theranos, is one example of where these traits may have contributed to her and her company's demise. At 30 years old, Holmes was a self-made billionaire, with a business valuation of £6.5 billion, and her business was set to revolutionise disease diagnostics with ground-breaking technology that would diagnose diseases such as cancer through blood samples. The apparent success of the

DOI: 10.4324/9781003319016-25

business had drawn allies including U.S. Treasury Secretary George Schultz and media tycoon Rupert Murdoch. In Spring 2022, however, Theranos collapsed and Holmes faced criminal charges for defrauding investors and wire fraud. Looking back at the company culture, Holmes was known for her unforgiving drive for performance, her conviction that she would become a billionaire, her assurance about her own brilliance and for firing anyone who would not agree with her viewpoint. Given these traits, one could say that the founder of Theranos has strong narcissistic tendencies, and these traits may have been significant in both her rise and fall.

To examine narcissism in greater detail, in this section we outline signs and symptoms of NPD and examine the research on narcissism and leader effectiveness in further depth.

According to the *Diagnostic and Statistical Manual of Mental Disorders* (*DSM-IV-TR*), a personality disorder is an enduring and inflexible "pattern of inner experience and behaviour" (American Psychiatric Association, 2000, p. 685) that is sufficiently rigid and ingrained to bring a person into repetitive conflict with his or her environment. The *DSM-IV-TR* states that these dysfunctional patterns "deviate from the expectations of the individual's culture" (APA, 2000, p. 689) and are the cause of significant emotional distress and difficulties in relationships and occupational performance.

The *DSM-5-TR* (APA, 2022) suggests that the diagnosis of NPD can be made when five (or more) out of nine criteria are manifested. These criteria include signals such as exaggerated self-importance, little empathy, ongoing fantasies of infinite power, immense need to be admired and exploiting others. (For a complete and detailed overview of the NPD signal behaviours, please see the *DSM-5-TR* manual; APA, 2022).

NPD affects less than 1% of the general population (APA, 2022). It is considered to affect men more frequently than women. Whereas our introductory example is that of a woman, 75% of the individuals diagnosed with NPD are men (APA, 2022). Furthermore, narcissism manifests differently in men and women (Green, MacLean & Charles, 2022; Hoertel et al., 2018). Whereas the underlying mechanisms are likely the same for men and women, the expression differs (Green, MacLean & Charles, 2022; Hoertel et al., 2018) Narcissistic women might show more vulnerable narcissism features of shame, hyper-sensitivity and low self-esteem (Green, MacLean & Charles, 2022). Narcissistic men – in comparison to narcissistic women – might show more lack of empathy and envy (Hoertel et al., 2018). However, Hoertel and colleagues (2018) found that there was no gender difference in being interpersonally exploitative, having a sense of entitlement, having a grandiose sense of self-importance, and having fantasies of power.

It is generally agreed that narcissism occurs across a spectrum of severity. Almost everyone has some narcissistic traits, which makes it important to understand the difference between a personality trait and a disorder. For example, the psychiatrist Mark Unterberg mentions:

Of all the psychiatric problems that face organizations today, one of the most insidious can be the otherwise high-functioning person with a severe personality problem. These individuals create multilevel difficulties that defy easy detection and definition due to than the obvious depressive or alcoholic, and their personalities cause repeated but subtle disruption in the workforce and the decision-making processes.

(Unterberg, 2003, p. 1)

Like most people, narcissists have patterns of behaviour that can positively or negatively affect their work and the people around them. Otto Fenichel and Helen Tartakoff, two psychoanalysts from the early twentieth century, both stressed the narcissistic personality's drive for success and achievement (Millon, 1996). Fenichel referred to narcissists as the "Don Juans" of achievement, while Tartakoff proclaimed them to have a "Nobel Prize syndrome" (Millon, 1996, p. 396). Narcissists tend to strive towards an ideal self-image and find ways to endorse positive delusions about themselves. In this way, narcissism is linked to ambition and dreams of success, whether success is represented by power, fame, wealth or achievement.

Narcissistic leaders tend to display a high level of self-confidence and are more inclined to self-promote by overstating their talents and achievements. This self-assurance can be perceived as conceit or alternatively associated with competence and can contribute to their advancement at work. Their need for recognition may prompt them to seek positions that provide them with a measure of influence over others.

Narcissistic ambitions tend to foster competitive aspirations and a gruelling work ethic. Narcissists will go to great lengths, work extremely hard, overextend themselves and make personal sacrifices to attain their goals. They will often work to become experts in their fields. All this effort is ultimately driven by a need for affirmation and attention. The charisma that they exude draws followers and may be used to boost their self-esteem and the advancement of their personal goals.

This tendency for narcissists to adopt positions of power may lead us to the assumption that top executives are more narcissistic than the general population. In 2005, psychologists Belinda Board and Katarina Fritzon interviewed and gave personality tests to senior British executives to assess for personality disorders. Their findings suggested that narcissistic traits were as prevalent in the top levels of business as in psychiatric patients, which according to the *DSM-IV* can be as high as 16% (Board & Fritzon, 2005).

As a scholar of politics once said: "It is probably not an exaggeration to state that if individuals with significant narcissistic characteristics were stripped from the ranks of public figures, the ranks would be perilously thinned" (Post, 1993, p. 99). Since narcissistic behaviour exists along a continuum of severity, a high level of narcissism can be interpersonally isolating and may hamper a person's ability to perform in the workplace, therefore reducing their chances for promotion to higher levels of management.

Narcissistic leaders are often visionary. According to Maccoby: "They are gifted and creative strategists who see the big picture and find meaning in the risky challenge of changing the world and leaving behind a legacy" (Maccoby, 2004, p. 94). They can be spontaneous, they are able to make rapid decisions, and they can be great catalysts for change. Their ability to 'think outside the box' or feel unconstrained by the rules and regulations can be innovative but also risky. Narcissistic leadership is often called for in times of great change or in the case of dynamic and competitive industries in which innovation is key. The ability to confidently communicate a vision of the future that inspires and motivates a group of followers, and decision-making confidence, can be real assets in turbulent situations. Their lack of empathy may help narcissistic leaders to make the kinds of difficult decisions that affect other people's lives, like layoffs due to restructuring or because of the enactment of a merger or an acquisition. Conversely, in less turbulent times, risk-taking and quick decision-making may threaten stability.

Narcissists will often believe that they are 'special' (in talent or status) and will be inclined to compare themselves to famous or elite individuals. In fact, they have disdain for those they consider to be less accomplished or otherwise 'unworthy'. Narcissists tend to be more successful in positions that do not require the building of trusting relationships. Their sense of superiority to – and lack of empathy for – others makes it difficult for them to work in a team. "The self-enhancer's manipulation, intimidation, and entitlement tendencies can cause resentment and lead to breakdowns in cooperation" (Morf & Rhodewalt, 1993 as cited in Robins & Paulhus, 2001, p. 210). To them, rules are for others, not for them. They are special.

As bosses, narcissists demand perfection and tend to overwork their staff. They undervalue the work of others, they do not easily praise subordinates and they often take credit for their accomplishments. As quoted by Millon in the *DSM-IV*, Lorna Benjamin writes that the narcissist "will expect great dedication, overwork, and heroic performance from the people associated with him or her without giving any thought to the impact of this pattern on their lives" (1996, p. 402). The charm that they exude in public may not be the same persona that they show privately to their staff. They often have a rather autocratic style of management and have difficulty retaining talented employees. In situations of underperformance, they may deny personal responsibility and blame others for mistakes. They become defensive when criticised and can attack those who question their decisions. The *DSM-IV* also states, "performance may be disrupted due to intolerance of criticism or defeat" (APA, 2000, p. 716), which makes them less able to benefit from the advice of others and are said to surround themselves with 'yes men' who simply compound their stunted view of reality.

Narcissists are prone to 'splitting' as a defence mechanism and view the world in black or white (as good or bad). This bifurcated view can lead them to be very distrustful of others. In their inability to empathise with the feelings and the needs of others, and their difficulty forming interpersonal relationships, they are in danger of becoming emotionally isolated. This may be the source of mood swings, irrational behaviours and volatile decision-making. Narcissistic injuries due to career setbacks and ageing make them prone to bouts of depression or bouts of rage. Their inability to accept feedback poses a challenge to their self-enhancement. Their difficulty forming relationships may make it hard for them to mentor others. The former, combined with their fear of ageing, may stop them from grooming a successor. Their autocratic style may lead organisations to be overly dependent on them, and to be more vulnerable as a result.

In their ambition to achieve greatness, such leaders may be disposed to exploit the organisation (consciously or unconsciously), either by over-extending the company's resources or abilities, or by making excessively risky decisions. "[T]heir leadership is driven by their own personal needs for power and admiration, rather than by an empathetic concern for the constituents they lead" (Rosenthal, n.d., p. 42). Their decisions and performance can be tainted by their bifurcated view of the world, their consuming need for praise, their desire to maintain an image of greatness and their tendency to inhibit the contributions of others. Since narcissistic behaviour at the top serves as an example, it can set the cultural tone for the rest of the organisation which can lead to further problems. In turn, it has been suggested, the cultural environment of an organisation or nation can foster or inhibit the selection of narcissistic leadership.

At the same time, "[T]here can be quite a fine line between narcissists who perform badly in the workplace because of their traits, and those who achieve outrageous success because of them" (Crompton, 2007, p. 159). From a study of 111 CEOs between 1992 and 2004, Arijit Chatterjee and Donald Hambrick (2007) concluded that "narcissistic

CEOs, who tend to pursue dynamic and grandiose strategies, also tend to generate more extreme performance – more big wins and big losses – than their less narcissistic counterparts" (p. 33).

Narcissistic leaders are said to have rapid rise-and-fall trajectories. They are more likely to succeed when their personal goals align with those of the organisation. The reason for their downfall often resides in the personal attributes that have led to their success. Their willingness to change their behaviour is diminished as they progress towards their goals and their weaknesses can, in this way, be amplified by their success. According to Maccoby:

> As he becomes increasingly self-assured, the narcissist becomes more spontaneous. He feels free of constraints. Ideas flow. He thinks he's invincible. This energy and confidence further inspire his followers. But the very adulation that the narcissist demands can have a corrosive effect. As he expands, he listens even less to words of caution and advice. After all, he has been right before, when others had their doubts. Rather than try to persuade those who disagree with him, he feels justified in ignoring them – creating further isolation. The result is sometimes flagrant risk-taking that can lead to catastrophe.
>
> (Maccoby, 2004, p. 96)

Practice

Given the multi-facetted emotional and behavioural world of narcissistic leaders, we now provide concrete advice on how to approach a coaching assignment with a narcissistic client. The 11 aspects in this section are based on our theoretical research, executive coaching experience and a qualitative empirical study conducted by the first author (Kets de Vries, 2013).

Assessment

Information from various sources is needed before making a client evaluation on whether strong narcissistic tendencies are present. Cumulative information about certain behavioural patterns help to get a more complete understanding of the person. The initial interview process (during a chemistry session) allows a coach to dig a little deeper by asking more personal questions to assess the client and clarify his or her objectives. 360-degree feedback instruments can be helpful to call narcissistic traits to attention by observing how the individual reacts to positive and negative feedback. One-to-one interviews with teammates, colleagues, family and friends can be another rich source of information. As a guide, responses to questions like the ones in Table 23.1 should help highlight narcissistic tendencies.

Determining whether a coach is dealing with NPD (and whether a referral to a health professional is needed) is complicated by the fact that many organisations have somewhat narcissistic corporate cultures whereby self-confidence, self-promotion, a driving work ethic, high standards and perfectionism are traits that contribute to an employee's success. As a result, a coach may find that his or her client has adopted a narcissistic façade that, when tested, does not translate into genuine personality traits.

Table 23.1 Assessment questions: narcissistic tendencies

- Is the individual self-confident and prone to talking about him/herself and his or her achievements?
- Is the individual self-focused to the point of excluding others?
- Are the individual willing to make risky decisions with seeming ease?
- Does the individual tend to take the credit for work and blame others for poor performance?
- Does the individual work well in a team?
- Does the individual have difficulty seeing anyone else's point of view but their own?
- How does the individual react to criticism (is the person rigid in his or her views)?
- Does the individual build constructive and trustful relationships?

Creating commitment

After the challenge of diagnosis, getting an individual with strong narcissistic tendencies to commit to coaching can be another obstacle. Narcissistic people rarely seek help of their own accord. Typically, they only ask for help when faced with a major life crisis or when their grandiose perceptions of themselves are shaken or shattered in some way. For a narcissist, accepting the help from a coach is tantamount to admitting weakness; for someone who focuses their energy on concealing personal imperfections, this is a major challenge. Acknowledging vulnerability and accepting dependency on another person is an ability few narcissists have learned, since asking for help is a complete contradiction of the defences they have established over time.

Generally, a narcissistic individual will only seek help if they experience enough pain (whether psychic or physical) – for example, through job loss, failure in an important task or interpersonal issues, either at work or in their private life – that it becomes a road-block to achieving their goals, or if they have been forced to do so by someone else, such as their partner or supervisor. They must reach a point at which changing established patterns of behaviour is less painful than the current situation.

Furthermore, what can foster or hinder the choice of a coach for help may depend on how coaching is viewed within the organisation. The resistance of narcissistic individuals may be less acute if coaching is considered a desirable benefit or a professional perk, rather than a remedial activity – the last resort before getting fired.

In addition, the status, seniority and reputation of the coach are also a key factor. Narcissistic people will choose to associate themselves with people who they deem worthy of respect. It may be possible to play on the status of the coach to entice the individual into a coaching relationship.

Once a coaching initiative with a narcissistic individual has begun, motivating the person to continue the process can be difficult. Narcissistic individuals tend to shy away from negative feedback and their vulnerable self-esteem may cause them to stop the coaching as soon as they are faced with criticism. Clients may choose to end the coaching as soon as they have altered their behaviour enough to no longer feel any pain. However, incremental changes can create a positive feedback loop from colleagues, friends and family, which may help to motivate the individual to continue engaging in the coaching process.

Realistic ambitions for change

Generally, the prognosis for coaching narcissistic individuals depends on the severity of narcissistic traits and the client's motivation to change – be it psychological pain (i.e., separation, divorce, estrangement in the family), negative physical symptoms, ageing, a desire to improve performance or a way to avoid a threat to status, position or influence. It is important to have realistic expectations. Most narcissistic behaviours and defence mechanisms are very well ingrained and resistant to change. The amount of time that needs to be invested, and the level of trust that needs to be established with the client, is likely to determine the extent to which change is possible. Change takes time, and the coach should remain patient about first establishing a solid relationship with the client.

The scope of coaching can vary depending on the length of time, the depth of the client's objectives, and the severity of the problem. For example, West and Milan (2001) outline three types of coaching in their book, *The Reflecting Glass*: These are skills coaching (finite and concrete goals), performance coaching (focus on overall performance) and development coaching (non-directive and longer-term engagements). The design of the engagement needs to vary according to the client. According to them, small changes can make a difference, even if they do not delve into the chronic underlying problems.

Establishing the rules of the game

It is important to establish clear rules and boundaries at the outset of a coaching engagement. Narcissistic clients will initially tend to try and take control of the coaching process, and that it is important for the coach to subtly remain in control of the situation.

One executive coach that we have worked with described his method for establishing a strong position starting from the initial interviews with a client (Kets de Vries, 2013, p. 46):

> I go through three interviews before taking an assignment. I challenge the individual: "I do not quite understand why you want to be coached?". This type of question destabilises them, because you imply that you are interviewing them, and that the decision to work together is taken from both sides. It also forces the client to really think about their objectives. In the third interview, I get into to the deeper issues, and then I am ready to decide whether to work with the client.

Creating transitional space

Creating a working alliance with the client that is based on trust is key as trust is a means by which the individual can begin to show his or her vulnerability and accept another person's perspective. The client should be given the room to access, acknowledge and share their true feelings in the safe environment of the coaching context. Before a client can empathise with others, he or she needs to begin empathising with himself or herself. The process of accepting vulnerability and expressing feelings in an authentic way can help the client become more in tune with him/herself and with others. Once a narcissistic client is ready to admit to his or her weakness, the coach can help them rebuild feelings of self-esteem and develop strategies to deal with the issues involved. In this process, it is important to develop strategies for the client to manage emotions under stress and practice these strategies within the coaching setting.

Transferential observations

The concept of transference and countertransference is invaluable to understand seemingly irrational behaviour. The coach should help the narcissistic client examine their behaviour and the beliefs that motivate their behaviour, and seek the source of these deep-seated beliefs often within the person's family. The narcissistic inability to construct an accurate view of himself/herself may have its roots in parental overindulgence, excessive praise unbalanced by reliable feedback, unpredictable or unreliable parenting, a lack of appropriate mirroring or emotional abuse. Elucidation of the psychological underpinnings of behaviour may help the client better understand how their belief system is different from those around them, and how it affects himself/herself and others.

Clients can be surprised when a coach draws the personal past into discussions about the professional present. The coach would do well to explain the theory of transference and show how repeating patterns established in early childhood may not be beneficial in the present. Self-awareness represents the freedom to disengage from potentially destructive patterns. Searching for clues in the past to explain behaviour in the present is work which ventures into the domain of therapy. The coach can engage in this type of detective work if he or she remains conscious of the boundaries of professional coaching.

Generating interpersonal awareness

Education and feedback about the negative effects of their narcissistic behaviour on others and how emotional distancing can affect their career is key to helping the client address difficult interpersonal relationships. The coach can then help to devise strategies for managing destructive narcissistic traits. A deeper interpersonal awareness will hopefully reduce the client's tendency to see the world in black and white, soften their suspicious nature, and help them take constructive feedback onboard and learn.

Following are some techniques for exploring and improving the client's interpersonal relationships.

- Establish bridges between past relationships and the present relationships at work. Try to highlight the parallels between past and present to single out and discuss transferential behaviours. This may help the individual gain insight into the reasons for their behaviour at work and the reactions of others.
- There is always the option of bringing a person (colleague, spouse, parent) into the room symbolically.
- Dissect and explain feedback from others. Work on the client's ability to be more empathetic towards others.
- Create an honest yet supportive interchange with the client that hopefully gives them an alternative example of interpersonal behaviour.

Resistance judo

There is much debate between those who believe that empathy is the cornerstone of working with narcissistic clients and those who favour confrontation. Generally, to create a working relationship and to provide relevant insights, it is important to try to understand the mental model of the client and the way that they see the world, realising the power of resistance judo- not tackling conflicted issues head-on but reframing them (Kets de Vries, 2010). A client who is defensive or who is pushed to protect himself or herself will not easily progress. Feedback should be presented constructively. It is important to protect the client's feelings of self-respect through praise and recognition without reinforcing their grandiose misconceptions of themselves. Business language, such as words like 'process' and 'strategy', might help the client feel more comfortable. Humour can also be a way to deflect conflict, create a more relaxed atmosphere, and to subtly 'push back' without seeming critical towards the client.

Defensive behaviour can result from a narcissistic client feeling threatened in some way during the coaching process. Thus, timing is important. If the client is too emotional, he or she will not be disposed to receiving feedback about their behaviour. When defence mechanisms are triggered, an empathetic approach may help to diffuse the client's anxiety. A timely interpretation of the client's defences will help elucidate their behaviour through tangible examples that have occurred in the coaching session. This type of real-time, insight-oriented approach can increase a client's awareness of how their defences reduce their possibilities for more meaningful attachments with others.

What follows is a short list of the defensive behaviours that we have seen in coaching work with narcissistic clients.

- Not facilitating the coaching process.
- Re-defining the coaching contract, taking control over the process.
- Undermining the purpose of the coaching or the coach.
- Using the coach as a sparring partner.
- Dominating meetings (speaking first and often, or a need to have the final say).
- Lack of disclosure.
- Hiding the truth and/or lying about the facts.
- Re-writing history, distorting and restructuring past events, making the story fit their view of the world to avoid narcissistic injury.
- Complying without engaging, adopting a posture of aloofness or pseudo-compliance.
- Responding defensively to criticism, either by attacking or subtly undermining.
- Blaming behaviour.
- Rationalising poor performance.

Reality testing

For the narcissistic executive, reality testing is important as their view of the world may be particularly influenced by their need for attention. A coach intending to work with a narcissistic executive should find a way to establish his or her own view of the client's professional situation and relationships. It is important for a coach to test the validity of the client's statements and his or her view of reality.

Understanding the broader context of a client's work situation will help the coach to gauge the true source of problems and areas for development. It will also allow the coach to challenge the client with an alternative view of reality and undeniable facts. It can also be a means by which the coach involves others in the development process, builds relationship bridges and encourages others to help the client improve his or her performance.

There are several information-gathering approaches, in addition to the ones outlined in the 'Assessment' subsection (interviews and 360-degree questionnaires), to gain insight and other perspectives on the potential issues that a client faces in relation to their work.

- Compare the work evaluations with those of a more personal nature. Conversations with people close to the client – such as a spouse, a family member or a friend – may help to get a more rounded picture of an individual.
- Shadow the client in the workplace for a short period of time. Shadowing the client during his/her various interactions at work may be eye-opening with regards to the behaviour of the client and those around him or her. Shadowing can provide real-life situations for the coach to replay with the client to help the individual modify behaviour in a practical way.
- During the process of coaching, cross check actual vs. stated change by discussing with members of the client's team.

Group coaching

Group coaching can be a powerful setting for narcissistic individuals to receive a variety of peer feedback. As in one-to-one coaching, the narcissistic client may become defensive when given negative feedback. Group coaching, however, is a less controlled environment and the coach runs the risk that other members of the group may not be adept at positively re-framing their comments.

Narcissistic clients can be intimidated by group coaching and may be more willing to open up in a one-on-one setting, or they may be too focused on getting the group to feed their narcissistic need for admiration. Certainly, in a group coaching engagement, a narcissistic client can be demanding of attention, ego-centred in discussions or condescending in their advice to others, or they can withdraw altogether. It is important that the coach does not allow the narcissist to take up too much space in the process.

Adjusting goalposts

Once the process of generating self and interpersonal awareness has begun, help the client explore their future goals. It may be useful to discuss their motivations and drive for success and achievement at work. Clarifying these motivations may help the client consciously decide what sacrifices they are willing to make to attain their goals rather than over-extending themselves and others unwittingly.

The coach may also choose to encourage the client to explore other facets of their personality that they rarely access due to an unrelenting work ethic and desire for success. The discovery of different kinds of talents and goals may help to improve the client's work/life balance and self-esteem.

Conclusion

Narcissists continue to play an important role within organisations. Their grandiose visions, high standards and work ethic can have real positive effects on the companies in which they work. Organisations must learn to mitigate the negative aspects of narcissistic leaders and avoid the dramatic downfalls to which they are prone. Companies should identify narcissists, manage their professional development and ascertain the alignment of their goals with those of the business. Through coaching, organisations may help such executives become more receptive to feedback and manage weaknesses before they become a problem. As Gladeana McMahon (n.d.) noted:

> If you monitor an individual, you can head the problems off and find ways of keeping the benefits of that person's talents. At worst you can plan an exit strategy before things go wrong. Narcissism, like everything else, has a place but a place (that is) best controlled.

Coaching narcissistic clients and leaders requires creating client commitment, setting realistic coaching goals, establishing the ground rules, fostering transitional space, paying attention to transferential behaviour, generating interpersonal awareness, dealing with defensive behaviour, fostering reality testing and adjusting client goalposts as the intervention process proceeds. Before coaching a narcissistic executive, preliminary considerations should include an assessment of the coach's personal sensitivity to narcissistic behaviour, consideration of the coaching contract and the management of boundaries. Assessing a client for narcissistic personality characteristics requires the gathering of initial interview information and distinguishing the client's characteristics from the ones pertaining to their organisation's corporate culture. Leadership coaching in organisations can help narcissistic executives obtain insight about dysfunctional behaviour patterns and help them to take preventive action before problems accumulate beyond repair.

Reflective questions

1. How could you evaluate your client's personality profile in the chemistry session?
2. How do you decide when to work with a narcissistic client or when there is a need to refer the client to a psychological or medical professional?
3. How should you manage a narcissistic client's commitment to the coaching process?

References

American Psychiatric Association (2022). *Diagnostic and statistical manual of mentaldisorders* (5th Ed.), Text Revision edition (DSM-5-TR). Washington, DC: American Psychiatric Association Publishing.

American Psychiatric Association (2000). *Diagnostic and Statistical Manual of Mentaldisorders: DSM-IV-TR*. Washington, DC: American Psychiatric Association.

Board, B. J., & Fritzon, K. (2005). Disordered personalities at work. *Psychology, Crime & Law,* 11(1), 17–32. doi: 10.1080/10683160310001634304

Braun, S. (2017). Leader narcissism and outcomes in organizations: A review at multiple levels of analysis and implications for future research. *Frontiers in Psychology*. doi: 0.3389/fpsyg.2017.00773

Chatterjee, A., & Hambrick, D. C. (2007). It's all about me: Narcissistic chief executive officers and their effects on company strategy and performance. *Administrative Science Quarterly,* 52(3), 351–386. doi: 10.2189%2Fasqu.52.3.351

Crompton, S. (2007). *All about me: Loving a narcissist.* London: Harper Collins.

Green, A., MacLean, R., & Charles, K. (2022). *Female Narcissism: Assessment, Aetiology, and Behavioural Manifestations. Psychological Reports.* 125(6), 2833–2864. doi: 10.1177/00332941211027322

Grijalva, E., & Harms, P. D. (2013). Narcissism: An integrative synthesis and dominance complementarity model. *Academy of Management Perspectives,* 28(2), 108–127.

Hoertel, N., Peyre, H., Lavaud, P., Blanco, C., Guerin-Langlois, C., René, M., Schuster, J. P., Lemogne, C., Delorme, R., & Limosin, F. (2018). Examining sex differences in DSM-IV-TR narcissistic personality disorder symptom expression using Item Response Theory (IRT). *Psychiatry Research,* 260, 500–507. doi: 10.1016/j.psychres.2017.12.031

Kets de Vries, M. F. R. (2010). Are you feeling mad, bad, sad, or glad? In *The coaching kaleidoscope.* London: INSEAD Business Press, Palgrave Macmillan. https://doi.org/10.1057/9780230281790_3

Kets de Vries, M. F. R. (2012). Star performers: Paradoxes wrapped up in enigmas. *Organizational Dynamics,* 41, 173–182. doi: 10.1016/j.orgdyn.2012.03.010

Kets de Vries, M. F. R. (2014). Coaching the toxic leader. *Harvard Business Review,* 92(4):100–109. Retrieved on 5th January from: https://hbr.org/2014/04/coaching-the-toxic-leader

Kets de Vries, M. F. R., Vrignaud, P., Florent-Treacy, E., & Korotov, K. (2007). *Insead Global Leadership Centre – 360-Degree Feedback Instruments: An Overview.* INSEAD Business School Research Paper No. 2007/01/EFE. doi: 10.2139/ssrn.1031137

Kets de Vries, O. (2013). *Coaching the narcissistic executive. Implications and Limitations.* Master Thesis. Fontainebleau, INSEAD.

Maccoby, M. (2004, January). The incredible pros, the inevitable cons. *Harvard Business Review,* 82(1), 92–101. Retrieved on 3th October 2024 from: https://hbr.org/2004/01/narcissistic-leaders-the-incredible-pros-the-inevitable-cons

McMahon, G. (n.d.). *Dealing with Narcissism.* Retrieved on 5th Jan 2023 from: http://www.associationforcoaching.com/pages/publications/papers-and-articles/papers-and-handy-guides/dealing-narcissism

Millon, T. (1996). *Disorders of personality: DSM-IV and beyond* (2nd ed.). New York: John Wiley & Sons.

Morf, C. C. Q., & Rhodewalt, F. (1993). Narcissism and self-evaluation maintenance: Explorations in object relations. *Personality and Social Psychology Bulletin,* 19, 668–676. doi: 10.1177/1745691619873350

Post, J. M. (1993). Current concepts of the narcissistic personality: Implications for political psychology. *Political Psychology,* 14, 99–121. doi: 10.2307/3791395

Robins, R. W., & Paulhus, D. L. (2001). The character of self-enhancers: Implications for organizations. In B. W. Roberts & R. Hogan (Eds.), *Personality psychology in the workplace* (pp. 193–219). American Psychological Association. https://doi.org/10.1037/10434-008

Rosenthal, S. A. (n.d.). *Narcissism and Leadership: A Review and Research Agenda.* Retrieved on 5th Jan 2023 from: http://dspace.mit.edu/bitstream/handle/1721.1/55948/CPL_WP_06_04_Rosenthal.pdf?sequence=1

Unterberg, M. (2003). Personality disorders in the workplace. *Business and Health Archive.* Retrieved on 5th January 2023 from: http://www.injurynet.com.au/documents/Article%20-%20Personality%20Disorders%20in%20the%20Workplace%20Series%20-%20M.%20Unterberg%20-%20Business%20%20Health%20-%20June-Oct%202003.pdf

West, L., & Milan, M. (2001). *The Reflecting Glass.* Basingstoke: Palgrave Macmillan.

Chapter 24

Coaching hubristic leaders

Vita Akstinaite and Eugene Sadler-Smith

Introduction

Hubris has been identified as a significant derailment factor for leaders and managers which can result in detrimental outcomes not only for individuals and organizations but sometimes even entire economies and societies (Sadler-Smith, 2018). Examples of hubristic excesses that have led to unanticipated outcomes in geopolitics include the U.S.-led 2003 invasion of Iraq, Russia's invasion of Ukraine in 2022, the 2008 financial crash and the 2022 bankruptcy of the blood testing company Theranos and the jailing of its CEO, Elizabeth Holmes. What is clear is that hubris is not new. The ancient Greeks knew about it and warned against it in their stories and myths (Icarus, Phaeton, Atlantis, etc.), and they often paired hubris with divine retribution in the form of nemesis. Hubris is frequently characterised as intoxication with power and success. Bertrand Russell, the Nobel Prize–winning philosopher, reputedly described hubris as "the greatest danger of our times".

In this chapter, we explore the possibilities for coaching hubristic clients for prevention (i.e., to stop hubristic excesses arising in the first place) and intervention (i.e., to take remedial actions if hubris has established itself). The chapter is organised into three parts as follows: hubris and the dark and destructive sides of leadership, coaching and the 'dark side', and coaching a hubristic client. We conclude with some reflections on the challenges of coaching hubrists. Our aim is to raise awareness of hubris in the coaching context and explore some ideas for ways in which the coaching profession can influence hubristic clients, principally senior leaders and managers, in positive and productive ways.

Hubris and the dark and destructive sides of leadership

Hubris is a form of destructive leadership (Sadler-Smith, 2018). Destructive leadership is the systematic and repeated behaviour by a leader, supervisor or manager that violates, intentionally or unintentionally, "the legitimate interests of the organisation by undermining and/or sabotaging the organisations, goals, tasks, resources and effectiveness and/or the motivation, well-being or job satisfaction of employees" (Einarsen et al., 2007, p. 408). Destructive leadership is a relatively new and emergent field of leadership studies (Dinh et al., 2014) and is of growing interest to researchers (Tierney & Tepper, 2007). It manifests in a variety of forms, ranging from workplace bullying to tyranny (for a review, see: Craig & Kaiser, 2012; Einarsen, 2007; Schyns & Schilling, 2007). Destructive leadership has detrimental effects on various individual and organizational outcomes,

DOI: 10.4324/9781003319016-26

including productivity, financial performance and employees' psychological distress, wellbeing and morale (Krasikova et al., 2013). Hubristic leadership can be viewed as a sub-field of destructive leadership (Sadler-Smith, 2018).

Three further theoretical points are relevant: (1) an excess of leader strengths, such as confidence, may be an underlying cause of destructive leader behaviours (Shipman & Mumford, 2011) based on non-linear (i.e., inverted U-shaped) associations with performance (Judge et al., 2009), which has been referred to as the 'strengths-into-weaknesses' paradox of hubristic leadership (Sadler-Smith, 2018); (2) there is no requirement of intentionality to cause harm for leadership to be destructive – since leaders make choices about what goals to pursue and how to achieve them, they may choose to engage in reckless behaviours and pursue goals that can ultimately, but unintentionally, harm the wellbeing of the organisation or followers (Einarsen et al., 2007; Krasikova, 2013); and (3) concomitantly, harmful but unintended consequences may be implicit in, invited by, or emergent from leaders' actions (Einarsen, 2007; Krasikova et al., 2013; MacKay & Chia, 2013; Padilla et al., 2007). In other words, destructive leader behaviours can create conditions that lead to unintended negative consequences (Sadler-Smith, 2019).

Hubristic leaders systematically and repeatedly take decisions that are over-confident, over-ambitious and contemptuous of the advice and criticism of others; in significantly over-estimating the chances of success and seriously under-estimating what can go wrong, they often invite destructive outcomes (Sadler-Smith, 2018). Hubris aligns with Padilla and colleagues' (2007) definition of destructive leadership as follows.

1. Hubristic leadership is not exclusively destructive. Some of the attributes of hubris (confidence, pride, determination, ambition, etc.) are core requirements for successful leadership.
2. Hubristic leadership involves dominance and coercion of followers and manipulation of circumstances, which may be covert, to attain the leader's goals and ambitions rather than through the processes of influencing and persuading to secure the commitment and loyalty of followers, and organisational success. The interests and ambitions of the hubrist and the organisation may not necessarily be isomorphic; for example, former UK Prime Minister Boris Johnson is described as pursuing his personal agenda and aggrandisement at the expense of that of the country he was elected to lead.
3. Hubristic leadership focuses on leaders' needs through the use of power for self-serving decisions rather than a selfless orientation towards the needs of the wider social group (see the example of Johnson in the preceding list item).
4. The process of hubristic leadership brings about outcomes, albeit unintentionally, that are detrimental both to the individual and the wider context of which s/he is part; again, Johnson's actions have been viewed as detrimental not only to his political party but also to the country as a whole.
5. Destructive organizational outcomes associated with hubris are not exclusive products of individual leaders; rather, they are brought about by the intertwining of hubristic leadership, susceptible followers and conducive contexts. In the case of Johnson, his ascendence to power can be seen as part of the rise of right wing populism in the socio-political context and the support of followers keen to deliver the UK's exit from the European Union (see 'toxic triangle' described in the following section).

The issues of intentionality and outcomes in hubristic leadership (see item 4 in the preceding list) warrant elaboration. Hubristic leaders do not set out to bring about destructive outcomes. For example, Richard Fuld in his hubristic leadership of Lehman Brothers did not seek to contribute significantly to the global financial crisis of 2007–2008; other examples of hubristic recklessness in engineering, finance and management include British Petroleum's Deepwater Horizon oil spill (Ladd, 2012), Long-Term Capital Management's bankruptcy (Lowenstein, 2002) and NASA's Challenger and Columbia tragedies (Mason, 2004). Disaster was not courted intentionally in any of these examples. Johnson did not seek deliberately to bring about the destructive outcomes associated with his behaviours and policies, but negative outcomes accrued nonetheless.

The general point is that hubristic leaders behave ex ante in ways that were not intended to cause harm, but their actions nonetheless prepare the way for and result in detrimental outcomes ex post (see Einarsen et al., 2007, p. 209). As far as volition is concerned, a destructive leadership process arises when a hubristic leader chooses to pursue a goal which "can be" detrimental to the wellbeing of the organisation or followers (Krasikova et al., 2013, p. 1310). In such circumstances, hubristic leadership is volitional and potentially destructive only insofar as goals and actions are chosen from among other ultimately more constructive alternatives against authoritative countervailing opinion. The main practical point for senior leaders and their coaches is that hubrists create conditions from which unintended negative consequences (e.g., financial or reputational damage, employee dissatisfaction or turnover, bankruptcy, litigation) are more likely to arise (Sadler-Smith, 2018).

From the perspective of the coach, it is important to note that there is no requirement that the leader "be consciously aware" (Krasikova et al., 2013, p. 1314) of any intent to, or incipient, harm. This is something to which a coach might be well-placed to draw attention to and highlight the structural relationships and potential consequences of dysfunctional leader behaviours. In this regard, coaches are well-positioned to help leaders think more systematically about the effects of their actions. For example, as far as the 'nasty surprises' that might await leaders as a consequence of their recklessness are concerned, MacKay and Chia (2013) have shown in a study of the automotive industry that volitional actions interacting with environmental circumstances in unexpected and surprising ways can produce unintended consequences that can be decisive in bringing about negative outcomes.

Hubristic leadership entails 'destructive decision-making' (see Craig & Kaiser, 2012) in which ill-advised choices are overtaken by processes that result in negative unintended consequences. The fact that hubristic leaders systematically and repeatedly engage in such behaviours against contrary advice would lead to the expectation that unintended native consequences are more likely to accrue in a hubristic leadership process. In relation to coaching, part of the preventative role of a coach might be to explore the range of possible consequences associated with a hubristic leader's over-confident and over-ambitious behaviours and objectives, and to help leaders in systems thinking (Ackoff, 1994). In sum: hubristic leadership has consequences that are not accidental, but this is not because there is some provable causal link between reckless actions, contempt for criticism and destructive outcomes; rather, there are emergent effects and unintended consequences that a hubristic leadership process invites. Interventions through processes such as coaching may be one way in which to obviate the unintended negative consequences of hubristic leadership.

Coaching and the 'dark side'

Coaching is a developmental technique in which an experienced person (coach) helps a client to achieve a specific goal by providing targeted training and guidance (Nelson & Hogan, 2009). This process usually takes place across several sessions over a period of time, and often employs various techniques to facilitate the client's development (Carvalho et al., 2022). The essence of coaching is to build self-awareness (for example, discovering the perils of one's ego or the potential effects of reckless and over-confident decision-making) which enables a required change (for example, breaking a dysfunctional habit or developing a desirable habit by consciously adhering to requisite checks and balances or moderating one's excesses). Coaching is used across multiple occupations and seniority levels, and for a wide variety of purposes; one of the areas for its use is coaching for the so-called the dark side of personality and the darker and more destructive sides of leadership.

Although the uniqueness of a person comes from their specific set of personality traits, not all personality traits are positive. Some traits are called 'dark side' traits due to their destructive nature. For instance, such often dysfunctional traits include Machiavellianism (Christie & Geis, 1970), narcissism (Raskin & Terry, 1988), psychopathy (Hare, 1985) and hubris (Sadler-Smith et al., 2017). The commonality between such 'dark side' traits is their potentially malicious qualities – such as certain emotional dysfunctions, aggressiveness, self-promotion, deceitfulness and others (Paulhus & Williams, 2002) – and their destructive outcomes. Examples include abusive supervision and bullying at the individual level and other, more wide-ranging outcomes at the organizational level, such as intention to quit, turnover, litigation, etc. Tourish (2013) argues that the conventional view of leaders as heroic, charismatic and transformational may ultimately encourage narcissism, megalomania and poor decision-making as a consequence of hubris and that this can be at great expense to the organizations that they are there to serve and the employees that they have been chosen to lead.

On the other hand, one could also say that any trait has a 'dark' and a 'bright' side and that no trait is universally adaptive or maladaptive, given that different traits are required in various life scenarios and which might make a specific trait adaptive or maladaptive, depending on the circumstances. This relates to the notion of excess and the paradox of a strength turning into a weakness. For instance, attributes such as self-efficacy, ambition and self-confidence can be positively linked to healthy self-esteem and entrepreneurial pursuits. However, if overused, these attributes could lead to reaching the 'tipping point' of hubris, leading to self-absorption, inability to accept mistakes or feedback, and an overall unapproachable character (Akstinaite & Sadler-Smith, 2021). In such circumstances, a leadership strength when practised to excess becomes a weakness (Sadler-Smith, 2018).

At the same time, 'dark side' personality traits could also be associated with and potentially lead to positive outcomes. Apple co-founder Steve Jobs, who is often considered to be hubristic, is a case in point. High egoism and self-confidence often associated with hubris could potentially allow individuals to deal with stressful and uncertain work situations and emergencies or lead them to perform well in high-risk environments (e.g., business venturing, trading, etc.) where such qualities might be necessary drivers for performance. Ambition and drive are attributes which can lead human beings to achieve extraordinary things. For example, Jobs was often criticised for his hubristic tendencies, but the question arises of whether he would, according to a well-known quote of his, have made the "dent in the universe" that he did without his exceptional levels of ambition and drive. Bordoni (2019) characterised this tendency as an innate drive for human beings to seek to 'go beyond their limits' and asked whether redemption for humanity might actually lie in our hubristic tendencies because they give us the scope to find new and innovative paths to progress.

Despite the complexity of leader personality traits and their multifaceted nature, it is important to note that if unchecked and unmonitored, 'dark side' personality characteristics can derail not only an individual's career but can damage those around them and bring about negative consequences for their organisations. Hence, coaching can be helpful in such instances to enhance the leader's self-awareness of the 'dark side' aspects of their personality, the potentially detrimental consequences to the individual and those around them, and finally, identify strategies for intervention and remediation. Moreover, coaching can also be used to draw attention to the interactions between the leader, the context and followers (the so-called 'toxic triangle'; Padilla et al., 2007) and as a means to gain leverage over difficult issues and put in place preventative measures, e.g., putting in checks and balances. The dysfunctional behaviours associated with hubris such as over-confidence, over-ambition, pride and contempt tend to rise when a leader occupies a position of significant power and be amplified when the leader has had a run of successes in a conducive context with the support of complicit followers, thus creating a toxic triangle (Owen & Davidson, 2008; Padilla et al., 2007).

Coaching for the 'dark side' personality traits can be challenging. For instance, the coaching profession has recognised the difficulties in coaching individuals who display narcissistic tendencies. Mansi (2009) identified one of the problems as the paradox that while often attracted to coaching, narcissists can present difficulties in that they do not see much area for improvement and hence will be resistant to coaching, particularly towards those aspects which challenge the person's self-view. The same may be true of hubrists. However, given that hubris tends to emerge in individuals in a specific social or leadership context (i.e., it is more state-like compared to narcissism, which is more trait-like), one positive is that coaching can be applied in advance to make sure that the ego remains in check, even when the power and influence of the individual are growing.

Coaching at the 'dark side'

Although there is – to the best of our knowledge – no research so far which focuses explicitly on coaching hubris (and hence, there is need for more work in this area), there is some literature on coaching the 'dark side' of leadership more generally. It seems that coaching of the 'dark sides' of personality – such as narcissism, Machiavellianism, or psychopathy – has become more prevalent over the last decade, in conjunction with growing awareness and interest in the 'dark side' of personality and especially toxic, destructive leadership (Burke, 2017).

Interest in hubris as a facet of the 'dark side' of leadership both in politics and business has gathered momentum over the past decade. A milestone contribution was the work by David Owen (former politician and neurologist and member of the UK House of Lords) and psychiatry professor Jonathan Davidson of Duke University in the United States. Owen and Davidson (2009) described hubris as an acquired personality change (rather than a personality disorder per se) which manifests as a pattern of behaviour and a collection of symptoms which comprise Hubris Syndrome. The syndrome's 14 symptoms (some of which overlap with *DSM-IV* personality disorders) are listed in Table 24.1.

Table 24.1 Symptoms of Hubris Syndrome (HS)

1. A narcissistic propensity to see their world primarily as an arena in which to exercise power and seek glory.
2. A predisposition to take actions which seem likely to cast the individual in a good light – i.e., in order to enhance image.
3. A disproportionate concern with image and presentation.
4. A messianic manner of talking about current activities and a tendency to exaltation.
5. An identification with the nation or organisation to the extent that the individual regards his/her outlook and interests as identical.*
6. A tendency to speak in the third person or use the royal "we".*
7. Excessive confidence in the individual's own judgement and contempt for the advice or criticism of others.
8. Exaggerated self-belief, bordering on a sense of omnipotence, in what they personally can achieve.
9. A belief that rather than being accountable to the mundane court of colleagues or public opinion, the court to which they answer is history or God.
10. An unshakeable belief that they will be vindicated in that court.*
11. Loss of contact with reality, often associated with progressive isolation.
12. Restlessness, recklessness and impulsiveness.*
13. A tendency to allow their 'broad vision' about the moral rectitude of a proposed course to obviate the need to consider practicality, cost or outcomes.*
14. Hubristic incompetence, whereby things go wrong because too much self-confidence has led the leader not to worry about the 'nuts and bolts' of policy.

Notes: Symptoms 1, 2, 3, 4, 7, 8 and 9 correspond to features of Narcissistic Personality Disorder (NPD); Symptoms 11 and 14 correspond to features of Anti-Social Personality Disorder (APD) and Histrionic Personality Disorder (HPD), respectively. These 14 symptoms could be used to diagnose the extent to which a potential client's behaviours correspond to the symptoms of the syndrome. Owen and Davidson (2009) suggested that in making the diagnosis of Hubris Syndrome, three or more of the 14 defining symptoms should be present – of which at least one must be amongst the five components identified as unique and each indicated by an asterisk (*), i.e., Symptoms 5, 6 10, 12 and 13.

Unlike many other personality disorders which often appear by early adulthood, Hubris Syndrome develops only after significant power has been held for a period of time, and can therefore manifest at any age (Owen and Davidson, 2009), hence its acquired nature and characterisation as a state-like phenomenon. As physicians, Owen and Davidson (2009) recommend that a proper diagnosis should involve an encounter between the client and the diagnostician which draws on information from their interview, as well as collateral information; moreover, any attempt to identify Hubris Syndrome "at a distance must be treated with caution" (p. 1405).

Besides this stated symptomology, no psychometric assessment tools have yet been created for assessing hubris or Hubris Syndrome; however, there are some psychometric tools that can be potentially used in recognition of hubristic traits, e.g., core self-evaluation (CSE; see Hiller and Hambrick, 2005). One of the most prominent figures in the psychometric assessment of the 'dark side' traits is Robert Hogan, who indeed popularised the concept of 'the dark side' of personality (see: Furnham, 2017). Hogan (2009) and suggested that it is possible to measure not only the bright, adaptive, but also the 'dark side', maladaptive, traits which in turn allows to explain and predict leader derailment. This is extremely important, given that research shows that that higher the person is on the leadership ladder, the more 'dark side' traits (i.e., narcissism) can be identified (Diller et al., 2021).

Some authors recommend that coaches should use scientifically validated tools (i.e., such as the Hogan Development Survey [HDS]) for assessing the bright and the 'dark side' of the client. Using such tools would allow a clear determination of the strengths and the weaknesses (and hence, potential derailers) of the client, and in doing so, would help to set the basis for a coaching conversation. The use of the HDS allows the identification of specific attributes (e.g., being over-confident or over-optimistic) that could be used in the coaching process. The main argument for using objective assessments such as the HDS is that the previously mentioned themes would be identified straight away as opposed to emerging late in the coaching process – and by doing so, becoming maladaptive anchor points for the client (Passmore, 2012). In this regard, assessments, annual performance reviews and other feedback processes can create openings for interventions and opportunities for coaching (Otazo, 2018). For example, 360-degree feedback can provoke a realisation of the effects of one's actions on self and others, and could be a good time to get a coach involved to help the leader in understanding the nature of the feedback, especially where this is associated with behaviours that are likely to been seen as negative (e.g., over-confidence, hubristic pride, recklessness) rather than coming from the leader's boss or direct reports. In the case of the CEO, an external coach may be one of the most viable options for delivering negative feedback (Hall et al., 1999).

As noted previously, hubris is a relatively new and under-researched phenomenon in management and leadership, but nevertheless recently scholars have begun to discuss hubris in relation to coaching more often. For example, de Haan (2016) noted that coaches have a 'crucial role to play in working with leaders to provide solutions for dealing with different shadows' (p. 511), hubris being one such shadow. Kim and colleagues (2018) noted that firms should consider "executive coaching in a timely manner when the corporate governing body detects a hubristic tendency among management" and that "licensed psychologists with expertise in psychological dynamics and assessment" may be the "ideal [but not the only] candidates" (p. 553). Similarly, Furnham (2018) suggested that coaching or mentoring could be used as a preventative tool against the derailment towards hubris. More recently still, Sundermeier and colleagues (2020) offered a similar proposition, stating that coaches and consultants can serve as valuable educators about the bright and dark manifestations of hubris. Building on the need for coaching recommendations targeted specifically at hubristic clients, we propose in the next section a three-step approach for coaching hubris.

Coaching a hubristic client

We propose a process for coaching hubristic clients using the following three-step approach: (1) Step 1, assessing and measuring hubristic behaviours; (2) Step 2, understanding the roots and identifying thought patterns; and (3) Step 3, taking action using coaching interventions.

Step 1: assessing and measuring hubristic behaviours

Personality often predicts the effectiveness of an individual (Salgado & Bastida, 2017). Hence, understanding the client's personality can be a good starting point for the coaching process. Stewart and colleagues (2008) found that coaching effectiveness is high when an executive is high on emotional stability, conscientiousness, and openness to experience. Therefore, one of the first steps in the coaching practice for hubristic clients should be the full exploration of the dark and the bright side of personality traits to identify the risk-prone areas for coaching, for example by using a 'dark side' personality assessment (Hogan, 2009) or a 360-degree evaluation. Personality ratings provided by such assessment tools might be a good starting point for a discussion between the coach and the client.

Hubris is a manifestation of excesses of otherwise desirable leader attributes, such as too much confidence becomes over-confidence, etc. As already noted, this has been referred to as the strengths-into-weaknesses paradox of hubris (Sadler-Smith, 2018). For example, when healthy levels of the components of CSE (Judge & Bono, 2001) – i.e., self-esteem (for example, "I am worthy"), self-efficacy (for example, "I succeed at tasks"), locus of control (for example, "Events are within my control") and emotional stability (for example, "I am free from anxiety") – are taken to excess, they become hubristic weaknesses (Hiller & Hambrick, 2005). Healthy self-esteem becomes hyper–self-esteem (for example, "I am the most worthy"), healthy self-efficacy becomes hyper–self-efficacy (for example, "I succeed at every task") and healthy levels of locus of control become hyper–locus of control (for example, "Everything is within my control"). Hiller and Hambrick (2005) argue that established measures of CSE could be used as a composite proxy measure for hubris; moreover, because it is a proxy, it is likely to be less threatening than a direct measure of hubris, which has inherently negative connotations.

Another option for obtaining an independent assessment of the client's hubris and which can be used at a distance is examining their language. This can offer insights into cognitive, emotional and social processes via the leader's lexical choices (see Pennebaker, 2011). A growing body of research has recently explored links between language (as manifested in lexical choices and assessed via word-count approaches) and hubris (Akstinaite et al., 2022; 2020). For example, the high number of self-references (i.e., "I", "my"), vocabulary pertaining to rewards and power (i.e., "money", "powerful"), verbs (i.e., "will do", "achieve") and negations (i.e., "never", "no") have been identified as the linguistic markers of hubris (Akstinaite et al., 2020). The use of the personal pronoun "I" is more nuanced than appears at first sight. Language researchers suggest that power is indicated by the ratio of the use of the first-person personal pronoun "I" to the third person pronoun "we" (Pennebaker, 2011). Greater use of "we" is thought to indicate the presumption of power over others, thus assuming collectivism and control that may not actually exist. Hence, somewhat counter intuitively, a higher "I":"we" ratio may indicate less of a presumption of power, while a lower "I":"we" ratio may be more indicative. This is consistent with Hubris Syndrome's Symptom 6, the use of the royal "we" in conversation. Hence, analysing the client's language might be another way of assessing the individual's hubris and allowing for the coaching conversations between the coach and the client to start. Although there are currently no instruments that allow for measuring leaders' hubris from samples of their linguistic utterances, work by Akstinaite (2020; 2022) has provided some recommendations for how to identify the linguistic markers of hubris using proprietary software (e.g., Linguistic Inquiry and Word Count [LIWC]; Pennebaker, 2011) and machine learning approaches (Akstinaite et al., 2022).

Step 2: understanding the roots and identifying the leader's thought patterns

'Dark side' personality traits tend to develop over time. For instance, narcissism often develops in childhood, while hubris develops over time when an individual is placed in a position of power, followed by a track record of success. These trait-like vs. state-like distinctions can help understanding potential causes of narcissism (intoxication with self) and hubris (intoxication with power), respectively. Hence, it is important to understand the root cause of individual leaders' hubris from a perspective which takes into account the relationship between leader behaviours (e.g., recklessness and pride), conducive context (e.g., position of power, praise from media, a track record of success, organisational culture and an unstable external environment) and susceptible followers (e.g., opportunists, acolytes, etc.). This toxic triangle of hubristic leadership (Padilla et al., 2007; Sadler-Smith, 2018) is a useful framework for the analysis of a leader behaviours, the context in which they are operating and their relationship with followers and may be a useful but as yet under-used tool for coaches to frame a conversation by highlighted the roles played, for example by instability in the business environment, perceived threat and hubris as a stress response, the role of organisational culture, the presence or lack of checks and balances, the existence of susceptible followers such as conformers with unmet needs, low core-self-evaluations and low maturity or colluders with personal ambitions, similar worldview to the leader, etc. Padilla and colleagues (2007) fargue that the use of the toxic triangle as a means to identify undesirable leader behaviours, conductive contexts and supportive follower behaviours could help to "stave off" the destructive consequences of the interactions between these three domains (p. 189). We concur with this view, and propose it as a potentially useful analytical framework that coaches could use in working with hubristic leaders. Once the coach has explored what may have triggered and sustains the leader's hubris (including contextual or followership factors, as well as leader behaviours themselves), then it is possible to start considering various interventions to address these underlying causes and contextual factors that may lead to unintended negative consequences.

An important part of this step is exploring the mental model (a cognitive structure, existing as frameworks or schemas) of the individual in order to understand any specific thought patterns or assumptions that a client might have about the self and others and their environment. Given that having shared mental models allow people to anticipate the actions and needs of each other, this, in turn, can have a positive impact on the effectiveness of a team (Weick & Roberts, 1993). Therefore, creating a shared mental model between the coach and the client might be helpful to increase the understanding of each other and potentially positively influence the client's behaviour (Druskat & Pescosolido, 2002).

Another important issue when coaching hubristic clients is establishing trust (see Schiemann et al., 2019). Given that coaching for hubris involves working with high achievers and involves constantly treading a thin line between direct questions and challenges to the client's ego and gently allowing it to the surface, showcasing the expertise and the knowledge of the coach is vital for the hubristic client to respond positively to coaching (Jones & Spooner, 2006). Coaching is a conversational process in which the client has to be prepared to engage; reflecting on feedback, confronting their assumptions and working to develop new behaviours and ways of being. Moreover, given that one of the criteria for hubris is contempt for the advice of others and the rejection of the opinions of other people (Sadler-Smith, 2018), conversations between the coach and the client by itself may be insufficient to overcome the client's hubris and might even cause some potentially aggressive emotional reactions and responses from the client; 360-degree assessments and approaches such as Motivational Interviewing can be helpful in working with senior leaders (Passmore, 2007). Hence, the coach must address these issues carefully, by first broadening the self-awareness of the client and only then working on pinpointing and analysing specific hubristic behaviours using some of the frameworks previously discussed: the Hogan approach, CSE, toxic triangle, linguistic analysis, etc.

Step 3: taking action using coaching interventions

Specific techniques can be used to help the client to address his/her hubristic traits and their behavioural expressions. One of the ways to address hubris is shifting the coaching focus from the person to the issue at hand, e.g., how an over-ambitious project went wrong rather than the over-ambitious behaviour of an individual leader. Individuals tend to react with heightened sensitivity when they assume that someone is identifying the flaws in their personality. Therefore, the starting point of the coaching intervention might be addressing the problem or an issue that brought the person to coaching in the first place (e.g., the results of an employee survey reporting low employee morale and high intention to quit, a project that went wrong) rather than focusing on the hubris of the leader directly (e.g., that the manager believes that she/he knows everything best and takes decisions without any consultations).

Intervention 1: coaching conversations

Some of the questions to ask when coaching a hubristic client that encourages self-reflection and is a coaching conversation starter could include the following examples (see Table 24.2).

Table 24.2 Ten questions for reflecting on with potentially hubristic leaders

1. Elon Musk is recognised by many people as one of the greatest business innovators but also is regarded by some people as a toxic leader. Is it OK to (ab)use power in the pursuit of achievement?
2. Is the leader's ego their friend or foe?
3. What irritates you the most about other people? Why?
4. What common shortcomings or mistake(s) usually prevent people from progressing in their careers?
5. How would you like your behaviour to be when you are angry/in a conflict situation?
6. What skills do your colleagues overestimate and underestimate in you?
7. What skills do you overestimate and underestimate in yourself?
8. What skills or strengths do you overexercise and underexercise?
9. What might be the consequences of doing so (for Questions 6–8)?
10. If you could improve one skill, what would that be?

There are many questions that a coach can ask, depending on the specific situation; however, the phrasing is important when posing those questions. For instance, a discussion on whether "an ego is our friend or foe" is likely to be more constructive compared to direct questioning of one's ego. Over time, questions can become more direct when a relationship of trust has been developed, but at the very start, it is helpful to keep the questioning broader in order not to trigger the client's psychological defence mechanisms.

Intervention 2: "outside-in" approach

An "outside-in" approach is a behavioural coaching technique whereby the focus of the coaching is on addressing the behavioural expressions of the issue at hand (Watts & Blazek, 2022). For instance, if an issue is that a client is reported by a colleague as having excessive pride and confidence that negatively affects the team, then the coach could work with a client to create an action plan to address these specific behavioural expressions. For example, actions to address hubristic behaviours could include not cutting people off in conversations, stopping criticisms, showing gratitude for the work of others, being open to new ideas, etc. A benefit of such a technique is that it could work as an immediate remedy to some negative hubristic behaviours. However, its limitation is that it focuses on the outcomes of hubris rather than addressing the antecedent factors that may underlie hubris directly, such as over-estimating the components of one's CSE to the extent that they become hyper-CSE (i.e., self-efficacy, self-esteem, locus of control and emotional stability, see: Hiller and Hambrick, 2005). For such a coaching conversation to be successful, it is likely that both outcomes and antecedents of hubris will need to be addressed.

Intervention 3: "inside-out" approach

This coaching technique focuses on the strengths of the client when addressing the issue. In other words, it attempts to change the underlying mindset (Watts & Blazek, 2022). For instance, if we have the cornerstone issue of hubris – contempt for the advice of, and hence inability to listen to, others – then using the "outside-in" approach, the coach should focus the coaching efforts on providing some recognition for the client's ego (this is the 'inside' which may be driving excessive behaviours, such as too much confidence in the first place) and focusing on this as an aspect of client strengths. For example, the coaching efforts could be targeted at helping the client to develop open-mindedness through the ability to ask great questions of others before pushing their opinion first. Hence, a coach could focus on improving the client's behaviour/tendency to ask questions – in other words, converting the client's weakness of providing strong opinion into a strength that could more strategically benefit their workplace, and by doing so, to minimise the behavioural expressions of hubris.

Summary and conclusion

Coaching for the 'dark side' personality traits can be challenging. For instance, the coaching profession has recognised the challenges in coaching individuals who display narcissistic tendencies. As discussed in this chapter, Mansi (2009) identified one of the problems as the paradox that while often attracted to coaching, narcissists can present difficulties in that they do not see much area for improvement and hence will be resistant to coaching, particularly towards those aspects which challenge the person's self-view. The same may be true of hubrists. However, given that hubris is seen as an acquired personality change, rather than a personality disorder, coaching may be a useful tool for mitigating or reducing one's hubristic tendencies. Dealing with hubristic leader behaviours (which is only one part of the toxic triangle) is unlikely to fix the problem. Coaching to counteract the hubris hazard needs to focus on leadership as well as leaders, which takes into account the leadership which needs to be shown by other stakeholders in mitigating hubris, such as the role played by board members and non-executive directors in exercising checks and balances. We agree with Kets de Vries (2016), who argues the case for the evaluation and the education of board members about the risks associated with hubris, as well as offering coaching and counselling to executives showing signs of hubris. In terms of the practicalities, hubris is a complex and paradoxical phenomenon. A certain amount of hubris may be necessary and productive if leaders are to push the boundaries of what is possible (Bordoni, 2019), but it may not take much to transform a confident, ambitious and authentically proud leader or manager into an over-confident, over-ambitious and hubristically proud one (Kets de Vries & Rook, 2018). We must avoid the switch from productive (bright side) hubris (Zeitoun et al., 2019) to 'dark side' destructive hubris (Picone et al., 2021). The investor Warren Buffett commented that the best results come from a carefully calibrated balance of hubris and humility (Miller, 2016). In this respect, senior leaders have to tread a fine line between deficiency and excess of leader behaviours (Sadler-Smith, 2018). Coaching is uniquely placed to provide leaders who may find themselves walking the tightrope of excess or deficiency with the necessary feedback and support to keep them grounded in reality and help to check potentially dysfunctional behaviours, and as such, has much to contribute to the mitigation of the hazard of hubristic leadership.

Reflective questions

1. Leaders such as Steve Jobs and Elon Musk are noted as great business leaders but some people also argue that they are hubristic. Is it ever ok to be hubristic even if it brings remarkable success? Do remarkably successful people need to be hubristic? In your experience is hubris a leader's friend or foe?
2. What are your main leadership strengths? Have you ever taken these strengths to excess? If you have, were the consequences always positive or have your strengths ever morphed into weaknesses? If they have what could you do in the future to prevent this from happening again?
3. What are the darker sides of your leadership style or your personality? Are these darker sides likely to manifest (or have they ever manifested) when you have occupied a position of power? What were the consequences? What steps could you take to rein-in this darker side?
4. Who are your role model good leaders? Why are they so good? Who are your role model bad leaders? Why are they so bad? Is there one ethical principle that for you is a red line that you could never step over? If so what is it? Why is it important to you?
5. What steps can you take to avoid hubris taking hold of your own leader behaviours or the behaviours of others in your organisation?

References

Ackoff, R. L. (1994). Systems thinking and thinking systems. *System Dynamics Review*, 10(2–3), 175–188.

Akstinaite, V., Garrard, P., & Sadler-Smith, E. (2022). Identifying linguistic markers of CEO hubris: A machine learning approach. *British Journal of Management*, 33(3), 1163–1178.

Akstinaite, V., & Sadler-Smith, E. (2021). Entrepreneurial hubris. In *World Encyclopaedia of Entrepreneurship* (pp. 139–144). Cheltenham, UK: Edward Elgar Publishing.

Akstinaite, V., Robinson, G., & Sadler-Smith, E. (2020). Linguistic markers of CEO hubris. *Journal of Business Ethics*, 167(4), 687–705.

Bordoni, C. (2019). *Hubris and Progress: A Future Born of Presumption*. Abingdon: Routledge.

Burke, R. J. (2017). Toxic leaders: Exploring the dark side. *Effective Executive*, 20(1), 10–14.

Carvalho, C., Carvalho, F. K., & Carvalho, S. (2022). Managerial coaching: Where are we now and where should we go in the future? *Development and Learning in Organizations: An International Journal*, 36(1), 4–7.

Christie, R., & Geis, F. L. (1970). Chapter I-Why Machiavelli. *Studies in Machiavellianism*, 1–9.

Craig, S. B., & Kaiser, R. B. (2012). Destructive leadership. In Rumsey, M. G. (ed.), *The Oxford Handbook of Leadership* (pp. 439–453). Oxford, UK: Oxford University Press.

de Haan, E. (2016). The leadership shadow: How to recognise and avoid derailment, hubris and overdrive. *Leadership*, 12(4), 504–512.

Diller, S. J., Frey, D., & Jonas, E. (2021). Coach me if you can! Dark triad clients, their effect on coaches, and how coaches deal with them. *Coaching: An International Journal of Theory, Research and Practice*, 14(2), 110–126.

Dinh, J. E., Lord, R. G., Gardner, W. L., Meuser, J. D., Liden, R. C., & Hu, J. (2014). Leadership theory and research in the new millennium: Current theoretical trends and changing perspectives. *The Leadership Quarterly*, 25, 36–62.

Druskat, V. U., & Pescosolido, A. T. (2002). The content of effective teamwork mental models in self-managing teams: Ownership, learning and heedful interrelating. *Human Relations*, 55(3), 283–314.

Einarsen, S., Aasland, M. S., & Skogstad, A. (2007). Destructive leadership behaviour: A definition and conceptual model. *The Leadership Quarterly*, 18(3), 207–216.

Furnham, A. (2017). Measuring the dark side. *Psychometric Testing: Critical Perspectives*, 197–211.

Furnham, A. (2018). Management failure and derailment. In *The Leadership Hubris Epidemic* (pp. 69–92). Cham: Palgrave Macmillan. https://link.springer.com/chapter/10.1007/978-3-319-57255-0_4

Hall, D. T., Otazo, K. L., & Hollenbeck, G. P. (1999). Behind closed doors: What really happens in executive coaching. *Organizational Dynamics*, 27(3), 39–53.

Hare, R. D. (1985). Comparison of procedures for the assessment of psychopathy. *Journal of Consulting and Clinical Psychology*, 53(1), 7–16.

Hiller, N. J., & Hambrick, D. C. (2005). Conceptualizing executive hubris: The role of (hyper-) core self-evaluations in strategic decision-making. *Strategic Management Journal*, 26(4), 297–319.

Hogan, R. (2009). *Hogan Development Survey Manual*. Tulsa, OK: Hogan Assessment Systems.

Jones, G., & Spooner, K. (2006). Coaching high achievers. *Consulting Psychology Journal: Practice and Research*, 58(1), 40–50.

Judge, T. A., & Bono, J. E. (2001). Relationship of core self-evaluations traits – self-esteem, generalized self-efficacy, locus of control, and emotional stability – with job satisfaction and job performance: A meta-analysis. *Journal of Applied Psychology*, 86, 80–92.

Judge, T. A., Piccolo, R. F., & Kosalka, T. (2009). The bright and dark sides of leader traits: A review and theoretical extension of the leader trait paradigm. *The Leadership Quarterly*, 20, 855–875.

Kets de Vries, M. K. (2016). The Hubris Factor in Leadership. In *The Intoxication of Power: Interdisciplinary Insights* (pp. 89–99). London: Palgrave Macmillan UK.

Kets de Vries, M. F., & Rook, C. (2018). *Coaching challenging executives. Mastering Executive Coaching* (2018), Jonathan Passmore and Bryan Underhill,(Eds.) Routledge, INSEAD Working Paper, (2018/01).

Kim, M., Xiong, G., & Kim, K. H. (2018). Where does pride lead? Corporate managerial hubris and strategic emphasis. *Journal of the Academy of Marketing Science*, 46(3), 537–556.

Krasikova, D. V., Green, S. G., & LeBreton, J. M. (2013). Destructive leadership: A theoretical review, integration, and future research agenda. *Journal of Management*, 39(5), 1308–1338.

Ladd, A. E. (2012). Pandora's well: Hubris, deregulation, fossil fuels, and the BP oil disaster in the Gulf. *American Behavioral Scientist*, 56, 104–127.

Lowenstein, R. (2002). *When Genius Failed*. London: Fourth Estate.

MacKay, R. B., & Chia, R. (2013). Choice, chance, and unintended consequences in strategic change: A process understanding of the rise and fall of NorthCo automotive. *Academy of Management Journal*, 56(1), 208–230.

Mansi, A. (2009). Coaching the narcissist: How difficult can it be? Challenges for coaching psychologists. *The Coaching Psychologist*, 5(1), 22–25.

Mason, R. O. (2004). Lessons in organizational ethics from the Columbia Disaster: Can a culture be lethal? *Organizational Dynamics*, 33, 128–142.

Miller, J. (2016). *Warren Buffett's Ground Rules: Words of Wisdom from the Partnership Letters of the World's Greatest Investor*. New York: Harper Business.

Nelson, E., & Hogan, R. (2009). Coaching on the dark side. *International Coaching Psychology Review*, 4(1), 9–21.

Otazo, K. (2018). Preventing and curing hubris in leaders. In Garrard, P. (ed.), *The Leadership Hubris Epidemic* (pp. 193–221). Basingstoke: Palgrave Macmillan.

Owen, D., & Davidson, J. (2009). Hubris syndrome: An acquired personality disorder? A study of US Presidents and UK Prime Ministers over the last 100 years. *Brain*, 132(5), 1396–1406.

Padilla, A., Hogan, R., & Kaiser, R. B. (2007). The toxic triangle: Destructive leaders, susceptible followers, and conducive environments. *The Leadership Quarterly*, 18(3), 176–194.

Passmore, J. (2007). Addressing deficit performance through coaching: Using motivational interviewing for performance improvement in coaching. *International Coaching Psychology Review*, 2(3), 265–279. https://doi.org/10.53841/bpsicpr.2007.2.3.265

Passmore, J. (Ed.). (2012). *Psychometrics in Coaching: Using Psychological and Psychometric Tools for Development*. Kogan Page Publishers. https://books.google.ch/books?hl=en&lr=&id=dXv6yoHlEiEC&oi=fnd&pg=PR5&dq=Psychometrics+in+Coaching:+Using+Psychological+and+Psychometric+Tools+for+Development&ots=Dvi2ABfLl7&sig=O3-tu1T84EcjqcIN14a4vPFBlMs&redir_esc=y#v=onepage&q=Psychometrics%20in%20Coaching%3A%20Using%20Psychological%20and%20Psychometric%20Tools%20for%20Development&f=false

Paulhus, D. L., & Williams, K. M. (2002). The dark triad of personality: Narcissism, machiavellianism, and psychopathy. *Journal of Research in Personality*, 36(6), 556–563.

Pennebaker, J. W. (2011). The secret life of pronouns. *New Scientist*, 211(2828), 42–45. https://sciencedirect.com/science/article/abs/pii/S0262407911621672

Picone, P. M., Pisano, V., & Dagnino, G. B. (2021). The bright and dark sides of CEO hubris: Assessing cultural distance in international business. *European Management Review*, 18(3), 343–362.

Raskin, R., & Terry, H. (1988). A principal-components analysis of the narcissistic personality Inventory and further evidence of its construct validity. *Journal of Personality and Social Psychology*, 54(5), 890.

Sadler-Smith, E. (2018). *Hubristic leadership*. Sage publications.

Sadler-Smith, E. (2019). *Hubristic Leadership*. London: SAGE.

Sadler-Smith, E., Akstinaite, V., Robinson, G., & Wray, T. (2017). Hubristic leadership: A review. *Leadership*, 13(5), 525–548.

Salgado, J. F., & Bastida, M. (2017). Predicting expatriate effectiveness: The role of personality, cross-cultural adjustment, and organizational support. *International Journal of Selection and Assessment*, 25(3), 267–275.

Schiemann, S. J., Mühlberger, C., Schoorman, F. D., & Jonas, E. (2019). Trust me, I am a caring coach: The benefits of establishing trustworthiness during coaching by communicating benevolence. *Journal of Trust Research*, 9(2), 164–184.

Shipman, A. S., & Mumford, M. D. (2011). When confidence is detrimental: Influence of overconfidence on leadership effectiveness. *The Leadership Quarterly*, 22, 649–665.

Schyns, B., & Schilling, J. (2013). How bad are the effects of bad leaders? A meta-analysis of destructive leadership and its outcomes. *The Leadership Quarterly*, 24(1), 138–158.

Stewart, L. J., Palmer, S., Wilkin, H., & Kerrin, M. (2008). The influence of character: Does personality impact coaching success? *International Journal of Evidence Based Coaching & Mentoring*, 6(1), 32–42.

Sundermeier, J., Gersch, M., & Freiling, J. (2020). Hubristic start-up founders–the neglected bright and inevitable dark manifestations of hubristic leadership in new venture creation processes. *Journal of Management Studies*, 57(5), 1037–1067.

Tierney, P., & Tepper, B. J. (2007). Introduction to the leadership quarterly special issue: Destructive leadership. *The Leadership Quarterly*, 18, 171–173.

Tourish, D. (2013). *The Dark Side of Transformational Leadership*. Abingdon: Routledge.

Watts, G., & Blazek, L. (February, 2022). 5 Ego traps and strategies to overcome them. Retrieved from: https://trainingmag.com/five-ego-traps-and-strategies-to-overcome-them/

Weick, K. E., & Roberts, K. H. (1993). Collective mind in organizations: Heedful interrelating on flight decks. *Administrative Science Quarterly*, 357–381.

Zeitoun, H., Nordberg, D., & Homberg, F. (2019). The dark and bright sides of hubris: Conceptual implications for leadership and governance research. *Leadership*, 15(6), 647–672.

Chapter 25

Coaching for a harsh inner critic

Tim Anstiss

Introduction

Self-talk or inner dialogue is perfectly normal and natural. Indeed, it is a large part of what thinking actually is. Some self-talk takes the form of self-criticism, which in turn is a normal part of our self-regulation system. However, not all self-criticism is the same. Some self-criticism can be hostile, attacking, condemning and shaming, and this type of self-criticism is associated with a wide range of poor health, wellbeing and performance outcomes.

Different coaching approaches offer different solutions for clients experiencing harsh and negative self-related thoughts. Cognitive approaches aim to change the content of a client's thoughts, helping them become aware of various cognitive errors or thinking traps whilst guiding them to dispute and debate their negative thoughts and develop more helpful, functional and less self-disturbing beliefs. Mindfulness-based approaches can involve helping clients to notice and change their relationship with their inner experience, rather than seeking to change the mind's content. These approaches are helpful, well described and will not be the focus of this chapter.

Instead, this chapter outlines an evolutionary neuroscience informed approach to helping clients switch from one innate motivational brain state (or social mentality) to another – from a competitive mental state to a caring mental state. In the competitive mental state, one self-part (the inner critic) attacks and seeks to shame, condemn, put down and undermine the client for their shortcomings, mistakes and failings, and this attack can result in the client experiencing and living as their 'criticised' self, which can involve feelings and behaviours associated with defeat, submission, avoidance and shame. In the caring mental state, a different self-part (the caring inner coach) helps the client respond to difficulties and mistakes with compassionate self-correction involving reassurance, warmth, safety and more motivational and approach-type behaviours.

For ease of reference, I will call this approach to switching brain states and motivational systems 'inner coach development'.

Theory

Self-parts and multiplicity of mind

The view that the mind is made up of different parts which interact with each other has a long history and includes Freud's Tripartite model of Ego, Id and Super-ego (Freud, 1923); Jung's archetypes, e.g., persona, shadow, anima/animus, etc. (Jung, 1991), and Schwartz's Internal Family Systems approach, e.g., exiles, managers and firefighters (Schwartz & Sweezy, 2020). The multiplicity of mind theory even underpins the popular

DOI: 10.4324/9781003319016-27

2015 movie *Inside Out* (Docter & Del Carmen, 2015). Each self-part comes with its own motivations and things it pays attention to, and may be associated with different emotional and behavioural reactions. Some of the main self-parts talked about and worked with in compassion focussed approaches (Gilbert & Simos, 2022) are the critical self, the criticised self, the compassionate self and the reassured self.

One aim of the inner coach development approach is to help the client come to view some of their difficulties as arising from an internal conflict between different self-parts, or an overly active self-part, e.g., a vocal, attacking and harsh critical self-part (or inner critic) which triggers a particular motivational, emotional and behavioural response, and then to guide and support them to cultivate and strengthen a different self-part – their caring inner coach – which can help them experience a significantly improved inner world, quality of life and personal development.

Evolutionary neuroscience and social mentality theory

Human brains have evolved over millions of years to help respond adaptively to such challenges as detecting and responding to threats, the gathering of resources necessary for survival and reproduction, and finding safety (Gilbert, 2020). Brains are pre-programmed with multiple algorithms which largely operate outside of our awareness, algorithms of the form 'if x is present, then do y': if danger is present, then escape, hide, freeze or attack. As humans evolved, most threats and opportunities came to arise from within the social domain. As a result, we evolved various 'social mentalities' or innate response patterns which become automatically activated in the context of other people's behaviour and help choreograph our behaviour in turn, e.g., how to best respond to the presence of a dominant, aggressive other; an attractive mate who seems interested in us; or the presence of an injured friend or relative.

As is the case with some compassion-focussed approaches, the main aim of the inner coach development approach is to help the client switch from a competitive social mentality (in which they are responding to a harsh inner critic or bully in an innate and often unhelpful way) to a caring social mentality (in which they are responding to a wise, caring, kind and reassuring self-part, which may need some strengthening).

Control theory

Dynamic systems (including humans) contain error detection processes which detect deviation from a desired state, e.g., low blood sugar, falling body temperature, feelings of threat, feelings of isolation, low status, – which in turn are linked to response processes which attempt to return the system to the desired state, e.g., eat food, get warm, get safe, get connected, climb in status) (Mansell & Marken, 2015). These control systems also apply to our behavioural standards – when we notice a fall in our desired behaviour and life performance, mechanisms are activated to try to return the performance to the desired level. Unfortunately for some people, when their behaviour falls short of a desired standard or performance, a harsh, attacking, undermining self-part (the inner critic) shows up and can actually make things worse. In fact, this self-criticism can kick in even before a performance deficit has been noticed, just when thinking about opportunities where performance may be less good than expected – e.g., public speaking, going to a social event, asking for a promotion, going on a date, competing in sports, sitting an exam.

One aim of the inner coach development approach is to help the client respond differently to any poor performance, mistakes, difficulties and challenges they experience, away from hostile self-criticism to compassionate self-correction.

Hostile Inner Critic

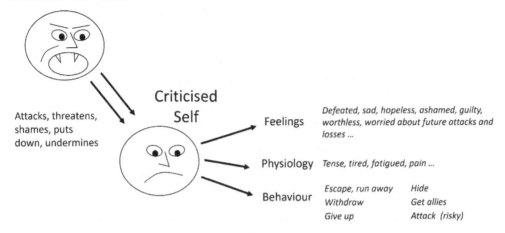

Attacks, threatens, shames, puts down, undermines

Criticised Self

Feelings — Defeated, sad, hopeless, ashamed, guilty, worthless, worried about future attacks and losses ...

Physiology — Tense, tired, fatigued, pain ...

Behaviour — Escape, run away   Hide
Withdraw   Get allies
Give up   Attack (risky)

Figure 25.1 An attacking self-part can trigger an ancient brain algorithm or programme in which the client responds as they might if they were attacked for real by a dominant, aggressive other

Caring Inner Coach

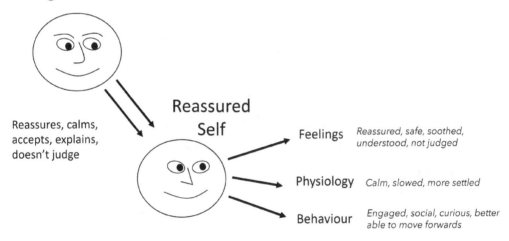

Reassures, calms, accepts, explains, doesn't judge

Reassured Self

Feelings — Reassured, safe, soothed, understood, not judged

Physiology — Calm, slowed, more settled

Behaviour — Engaged, social, curious, better able to move forwards

Figure 25.2 A caring, compassionate, coaching self-part can trigger an ancient brain algorithm or programme in which the client responds as they might if they were comforted, reassured and encouraged for real by a caring, compassionate other

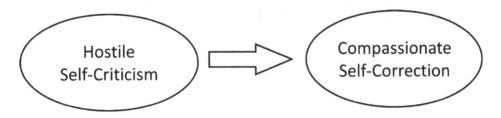

Figure 25.3 Core aim of the caring inner coach development approach

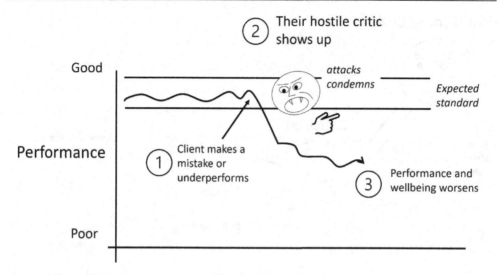

Figure 25.4 The critical self-part is part of our self-regulation system, but its harsh, attacking tone can make wellbeing and performance worse

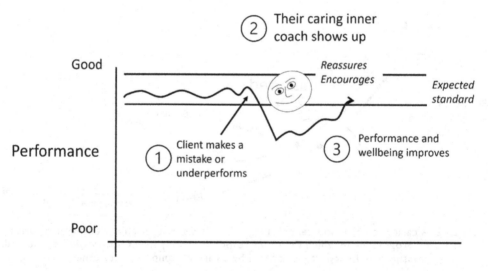

Figure 25.5 The caring inner coach is also part of our self-regulation system, and its warm, reassuring tone can help wellbeing and performance improve

Humanistic (Rogerian) theory

Carl Rogers (1957) suggested that the chances of clients reaching their potential, becoming fully human and self-actualising are increased when the practitioner helps to create and maintain several core or facilitative conditions including empathic understanding, congruence, genuineness, and unconditional positive regard. He stated:

> [T]he individual has within himself or herself vast resources for self-understanding, for altering his or her self-concept, attitudes and self-directed behaviour – and that these resources can be tapped if only a definable climate of facilitative psychological attitudes can be provided.
>
> (Rogers, 1980, p. 115)

So, while you as the actual, external real coach should be paying as attention to creating these facilitative conditions, one aim of the inner coach development approach is to help the client create these facilitative and enabling conditions within and for themselves – helping to dramatically improve their internal relating, to help them strengthen and cultivate an inner, caring self-part which related to them with understanding, warmth, non-judgment, genuineness, and authenticity. This reminds me a little of the saying 'give a man a fish, and he will eat for a day; teach him to fish, and he will never go hungry'. If we can help our clients to strengthen their caring inner coach, then this internal resource may serve them well years into the future.

Attachment theory

Attachment theory assumes that humans possess innate behavioural systems for caregiving, care-seeking and attachment. According to Bowlby (1969/1982), the attachment system helps to protect individuals from danger by ensuring that they stay close to caring and supporting others, and the system includes motivations and abilities for both expressing distress and being responsive to others' signals of care. The theory also proposes that how human beings relate to each other as they grow up and develop is shaped by their early experiences with primary care givers (Ainsworth & Bowlby, 1991). Ideally, primary care givers act as a 'secure base' from which the infant can explore the world, learn and grow, as well as a 'safe haven' to which the distressed infant can return and be comforted and feel safe and protected.

Gilbert (2005) suggests that in the same way that the care-seeking and caregiving mentalities are activated when relating to others (e.g., crying child and comforting mother), they can also be activated when relating to the self. In this way, self-compassion/reassurance is viewed as a form of self-to-self relating in which the innate care-seeking mentality signals distress and need for care, and the innate caregiving mentality responds with compassionate thoughts, emotions and intentions directed inward.

Some of the aims of the inner coach development approach flow from these discussions. One is to help the client become more sensitive to their own suffering, and respond to this with care. Another is to help the client create within themselves more of a secure base which can enable less fearful approach behaviours so that they are more likely to obtain the resources they need to live their best possible life, whilst also helping them create within themselves more of a safe haven to which they can return and be soothed, comforted and reassured when they encounter failure, difficulty and struggle – as they will, being human.

Research

There is a growing body of evidence establishing that harsh, attacking critical self-process can be extremely harmful, and that approaches focusing on helping people cultivate self-compassion can be helpful.

Longe and colleagues (2010) used a novel fMRI (functional magnetic resonance imaging) task to investigate the neuronal correlates of self-criticism and self-reassurance. Participants were presented with statements describing two types of scenarios, with the instruction to either imagine being self-critical or self-reassuring in that situation. Self-criticism was associated with activity in lateral prefrontal cortex (PFC) regions and the dorsal anterior cingulate (dAC), linking self-critical thinking to error processing and resolution and also to behavioural inhibition. Self-reassurance was associated with left temporal pole and insula activation, suggesting that efforts to be self-reassuring engage similar regions to expressing compassion and empathy towards others. They suggested that their findings may have implications for the neural basis of a range of mood disorders that are characterised by a preoccupation with personal mistakes and failures, and a self-critical response to such events.

Thew and colleagues (2017) explored the phenomenology of self-criticism and its relationship with constructs such as rumination and perfectionism in three groups – 26 people with depression, 26 with eating disorders and 26 non-clinical. They found that people in the clinical groups reported more frequent, persistent and less controllable self-criticism compared to controls, present on average 50–60% of the time, and reported a negative impact on mood and a moderately severe impact on daily activities. They indicated a greater desire to change self-criticism whilst judging it more difficult to reduce. Habitual self-criticism was highly correlated with lower self-esteem, lower self-compassion, greater rumination and greater negative perfectionism.

In a review of 48 studies appearing in the literature from 2012–2018, Werner and colleagues (2019) showed that besides depressive symptoms, self-criticism showed positive relations to symptoms of eating disorders, social anxiety disorder, psychosis, personality disorders and interpersonal problems. Harsh forms of self-criticism were more persistent and difficult to change.

Levine and colleagues (2019) examined the influence of personal standards and self-critical perfectionism on depressive and anxiety symptoms in high school students (N = 174). Students were surveyed in autumn and early spring. Path modelling demonstrated that self-critical perfectionism predicted an increase in depressive symptoms over time, whilst personal standards perfectionism was unrelated to changes in mental health. They recommended that future interventions should focus on reducing self-critical cognitive biases in youth.

Zelkowitz and Cole (2019) performed a systematic review and meta-analysis of self-criticism as a transdiagnostic correlate for non-suicidal self-injury (NSSI) and disordered eating (DE), two highly comorbid disorders which may be regarded as belonging to a spectrum of self-harm behaviours. Their aims included testing the hypothesis that self-criticism is a transdiagnostic process for non-suicidal self-injury and disordered eating, learning about the size of any effects, and exploring possible moderators of the relationship between self-criticism and NSSI and DE. Examining over 45 effect sizes across 39 studies, they found moderate to large effects for the relation of self-criticism to both NSSI (r = .38) and DE (r = .40). They described three key points emerging from the research. First, correlations of self-criticism with NSSI and DE were markedly similar – both forms of pathology showed large and significant relations to the self-criticism. Second, none of the tested moderators accounted for significant portions of variation in the strength of the relationships. Third, the relation of self-criticism to DE varied significantly from one form of DE to another. The authors believed that their results highlight the importance of self-criticism in any transdiagnostic conceptualisation of self-harm behaviour, and suggested that clinicians treating patients who engage in NSSI, DE or both behaviours should evaluate and potentially target self-critical cognitions in treatment.

In a systematic review and meta-analysis (49 studies, 3,277 patients) into the relationship between self-criticism and psychotherapy outcome, Löw et al (2019) found an association between pre-treatment self-criticism and psychotherapy outcome at r = –.20, suggesting that higher levels of self-criticism are related to poorer outcome.

O'Neill and colleagues (2021) assessed the relative contribution of self-criticism to suicide probability. Results demonstrated that self-attacking has a direct relationship with suicide probability, alongside such established predictors as entrapment and hopelessness. They concluded that addressing particularly hostile forms of self-criticism may be a promising area in terms of future research and clinical practice.

Kotera and colleagues (2021) evaluated the relationships between mental wellbeing, academic motivation (intrinsic motivation, extrinsic motivation and amotivation), self-compassion (self-reassurance) and self-criticism (self-inadequacy and self-hate) in a convenience sample of 119 psychology students. Correlation, regression and path analyses were conducted. Mental wellbeing was positively associated with intrinsic motivation and self-compassion, and negatively associated with amotivation and self-criticism. They concluded that helping students to cultivate self-compassion may help protect their mental wellbeing.

In a meta-analysis of the association between self-compassion and psychopathology, MacBeth and Gumley (2012) found a large effect size for the relationship between compassion and psychopathology (r = –0.54). The authors stated that compassion is an important explanatory variable in understanding mental health and resilience, and that more work is needed to develop the evidence base for compassion in psychopathology and explore correlates of compassion and psychopathology.

In a study of 419 subjects, Petrocchi et al. (2019) found that at higher levels of self-reassurance, the relationship between self-criticism and depressive symptoms became non-significant, supporting the buffering hypothesis of self-reassurance in a way that self-esteem (which is rooted in a different motivational system) did not. They concluded that their results support the growing evidence that not all positive self-relating processes exert the same protective function against psychopathological consequences of self-criticism and that compassion-focussed interventions are promising avenues to help clients counteract the negative impact of self-criticism on mood.

Zhang and colleagues (2019) explored the role of self-compassion in alleviating the effect of self-criticism on depressive symptoms in 147 urban, low-income African Americans who had recently tried to take their own life. Their cross-sectional investigation showed self-criticism to be positively associated with depressive symptoms and negatively associated with self-compassion, with self-compassion associated with less depressive symptoms. Bootstrapping analysis suggested that self-compassion ameliorates the negative impact of self-criticism on depressive symptoms.

Kim and colleagues (2021) had participants engage in self-criticism and self-reassurance toward written descriptions of negative life events (mistakes, setbacks, failures), and found that neural markers of negative emotion during fMRI are down-regulated under conditions of self-reassurance, relative to self-criticism. They concluded that engagement in self-reassurance can reduce the 'sting' of negative life events, both neural and self-report, which holds important implications for therapy.

Wakelin et al. (2021) conducted a systematic review and meta-analysis of the effectiveness of self-compassion–related interventions for reducing self-criticism. Twenty randomised controlled trials (RCTs) met the inclusion criteria and Nineteen papers (n = 1,350 participants) had sufficient data to be included in the meta-analysis. Meta-analysis indicated that self-compassion–related interventions produce a significant, medium reduction in self-criticism in comparison with control groups (Hedges' g = 0.51, 95% CI [0.33–0.69]), and moderator analysis found greater reductions in self-criticism when interventions were longer and compared with passive controls rather than active. Overall, the review provides promising evidence of the effectiveness of self-compassion-related interventions for reducing self-criticism.

Egan and colleagues (2022) investigated the efficacy of self-compassion as an active ingredient in the treatment and prevention of anxiety and depression in youth, via a systematic review of the literature and qualitative consultation with young people and researchers in self-compassion. Fifty studies met the inclusion criteria. Eight studies evaluated self-compassion interventions among youth aged 14–24, and the remaining studies measured the association between self-compassion and anxiety, and/or depression among this age group. Higher self-compassion was related to lower symptoms of anxiety, r = –0.49 and depression, r = –0.50. They also found evidence for self-compassion interventions in decreasing anxiety and depression in young people. Consultation with young people indicated that they were interested in self-compassion interventions, and self-compassion experts emphasised the importance of decreasing self-criticism as a reason why self-compassion interventions work. The importance of targeting self-criticism is supported by the preferences of young people who said that they would be more likely to engage in a treatment reducing self-criticism than engage in a treatment increasing self-kindness.

Practice

The inner coach development approach is a multi-modal approach to coaching drawing heavily on compassionate mind informed approaches such as Compassion Focussed Therapy (Gilbert, 2014) and Mindful Self-Compassion (Neff & Germer, 2013) and incorporating psychoeducation, functional analysis, Socratic questioning, skills development, relationship factors, visualisation and guided imagery, reframing, exposure, writing exercises, mindfulness, bodywork, chairwork and between-session practice.

The main aim of the approach is to help clients experiencing a hostile, attacking form of self-criticism (coming from a competitive, rank-driven social mentality) shift into a caring, compassionate social mentality by cultivating and experiencing and responding to the presences of a caring inner coach.

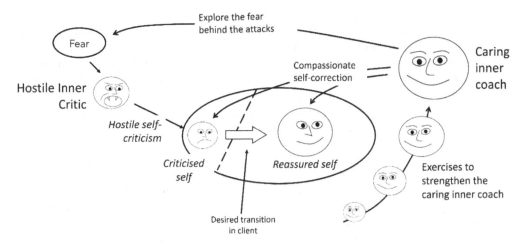

Figure 25.6 How the caring inner coach development approach may help clients spend less time as their criticised self and more time as their reassured self

Inner coach development coaching is a process-based approach in two senses. First, it seeks to activate, stimulate and use certain psychological and physiological processes inside the client – specifically those related to: (1) noticing their own suffering; (2) becoming motivated to act so as to alleviate and prevent their current and future suffering (self-compassion); and (3) developing the skills to do so, including those involving better and more self-care and self-management. Since compassionate mind approaches seek to activate and strengthen neural pathways and processes, they have been likened to physiotherapy for the brain.

The other sense in which the inner coach development approach is process-based is that coaches can follow a process to help them deliver the desired client outcomes. Building on the four-process model of motivational interviewing (Miller & Rollnick, 2013), coaches are invited to explore the following seven step process to help guide them.

Engaging: You want client engagement, and so will be using open-ended questions, empathic listening, affirmations and summaries (Anstiss, 2021), as well as maintaining a spirit of partnership and acceptance.

Focussing: The approach involves a conversation and exercises to do with the inner critic and the strengthening of the inner coach. How this topic comes into focus will vary from client to client. It may be they bring the topic up directly, or talk about something related – e.g., harsh negative self-related thoughts, feelings of shame, internal entrapment or defeat, etc. You might bring the topic into focus by using the ask-share-ask approach – asking them what they have heard about the inner critic, sharing some more things with them about the approach, asking what they make of what you have shares, and then asking them if they would like to, or be willing to, explore the idea or approach further.

Evoking: Drawing out from them their ideas and concerns, experiences, hopes, reasons for strengthening their inner coach, etc. The inner coach development approach is strengths-based in that it assumes the person has many of the resources within them to make good progress – e.g., a compassionate mind, a motivation to care for themselves and others better, to prevent and alleviate suffering, etc. This process can involve further psychological education about the approach, as well as performing a functional analysis of the inner critic and the inner coach, and chairwork (discussed later in this section) involving the different self-parts.

Strengthening: Things you may wish to strengthen during inner coach development may include readiness to engage in the approach, self-efficacy for the approach and hope that the approach can help them experience a better quality of life, as well as the various skills and competencies associated with self-compassion such as being willing to engage with their own suffering and struggles; the ability to tolerate discomfort; entering into a soothing rhythm of breathing; visualising and connecting with a safe space; visualising and feeling the presence of a wise, caring compassion other; and talking to themselves with a warm, gentle tone.

Deciding: Once the client has become aware of the approach, they have to decide whether or not to learn more about it, engage with it during the session, and continue to use the approach into the future.

Planning: If the client decides to engage with the approach, then just as a fitness instructor will (hopefully) co-design a programme to help their client get in better physical shape, you as a coach will work with the client to co-design a plan or programme to help them cultivate, strengthen and experience their inner coach over time.

Supporting: This process involves both what you do with a client inside the session and how you plan to help, guide and support them into the future.

Having briefly looked at seven processes to guide your work with the client, let us now look in a bit more detail at some specific practices and activities.

Psychoeducation

Many clients do not have a good understanding of how their mind works, why they struggle as much as they do, and evidence-informed approaches to improved life performance, reduced suffering and improved wellbeing. Things it may be helpful to educate them about include the following.

- That inner speech is entirely normal and common – that we all experience an inner dialogue.
- That the tone of the inner dialogue matters as much as (or more than) the content of the words spoken.
- The modular basis of the mind and that we are all made up of different self-parts.
- That we can consider our inner world as a little like a committee, with some members of the committee rather loud and hostile (the inner critic).
- That self-criticism is a normal part of self-regulation.
- That a harsh, condemning, attacking, self-hating, undermining inner critic can be extremely harmful to a person's health, wellbeing, quality of life and life chances.
- That it is possible to cultivate and strengthen our caring, compassionate self-part, and that this can help improve our health, wellbeing and quality of life.

- That everyone suffers and can experience a harsh and hurtful inner voice. It is one of the things brains and minds do.
- That they are not alone in suffering the way they do (the common humanity message).

Clients may also benefit from education about the power of visualisation. One way of doing this is to discuss with them that just as the presence of real or imagined food can stimulate salivation when hungry, or the presence of a real or imagined intimate partner can stimulate changes associated with sexual arousal, so too the presence of a real or imagined aggressive bully can stimulate fear, avoidance and submission, and the presence of a real or imagined caring compassionate other can stimulate feelings of being protected, cared for, understood and reassured.

The child and the classroom

The child and the classroom example can help clients understand why they might wish to cultivate their caring inner coach. You might say something like:

> Imagine taking a child you love and care about to a school, and you look into two classrooms, Classroom A and Classroom B. In classroom A, you see the teacher standing over the child, telling them they are stupid, pointing out their mistakes to the rest of the class and telling the child they always knew they were never going to amount to anything, that they are a failure and that they are going to beat them until they improve. Then you look into classroom B and see a teacher down at the level of the child and helping them figure something out, telling them to take their time, that they have got this, that there is no real learning without making some mistakes, that we all make mistakes and that they know they are bright.

Then ask the client: 'What kind of teacher would you like a child you love to have, the teacher in classroom A or B?'. They will typically say B and you can then spend some time exploring why teacher B. After this exploration, ask them: 'And what kind of teacher are you to yourself, when you make mistakes?' and see what they say!

Functional analysis of the inner critic and the inner coach

Some clients find it helpful to get to know their critic a little better, to help objectify it, to separate it out from themselves, and to understand its motivation and impact. A good way of doing this is via a functional analysis.

You can start this activity by asking them if they would be happy to let you meet their self-critical process (or critical self-part or inner critic – you choose the phrase) in order that you may both get a better understanding of how it is actually functioning for them. If they agree, a nice early question might be: 'To help us get started, what would be your greatest fear if you gave it up, or lost your critical self-part?'. You can also ask this playfully, for instance: 'Imagine that is this coaching session today we are going to take away your self-criticism so that you never get angry with yourself or beat yourself up again. What concerns would you have? What might be different?'

Common concerns which often surface include becoming lazy, arrogant or less nice to others, letting their standards drop or around lacking direction or motivation. Explore any concerns a little further. Ask them what might happen if they were to become lazy or complacent or unmotivated. What is their greatest fear about that? Why would that be a problem? The aim is to try to tap into the fear behind the critic. This can sometimes lead to concerns about being rejected, unwanted or undesirable. You then may wish to offer a small summary to check for and demonstrate understanding: 'so your concerns about losing your critic are that you might find yourself less x and y and that might result in a and b; is that right?'.

The next phase of the exploratory process involves guided discovery. You might say something like: 'So we've talked about what the inner critic does for you; shall we meet it? Would that be OK for you?', and reassure the client that if things become too uncomfortable, you can always stop.

Perhaps then say:

> To start with, I would like you to think of something that you are critical of yourself about, or tend to feel angry or upset with yourself about? You do not have to tell me what it is, just spend some time with this in order to stimulate the self-critical process.

Once we have primed the critical self-process, we help the client to mentalise and objectify the self-critical process (or inner critic) by doing the following.

*   Exploring its appearance and physical sense, or form. For instance, you might say:

    > If you could imagine your critic outside of yourself, if you took it out of your head and looked at it, what form might it take? What would it look like? How would it appear to you? What colours or textures would you associate with it?

    (Do not worry if they struggle; reassure them that that is OK.)
*   Exploring what it tends to say, its specific messages and its attacks and putdowns, including its tone of voice. For instance, you might say:

    > So now just sit quietly, listening, and let your critic say what it really thinks about you. Try to hear what this part of you wants to say. No matter how critical, try and find the courage just to hear your own critical thoughts.

*   Exploring the feelings it has towards the client, e.g.:

    > As you're sitting there, listening to your critic, what emotions is it directing at you, what does it actually feel about you and towards you?

*   And then finally, exploring what it would like to do to the client, (its behaviour), e.g.:

    > So, you have heard what your critic thinks about you, and you know what it feels for you. What would it like to do to you or with you?

At the end of this activity, ask the client to step back, let go of their inner critic and reflect on what they are now thinking and feeling – including in the body – and are wanting to do. Perhaps saying:

> OK, so well done, you've been very brave and looked at your critic, taking it out of the cupboard so to speak, and really listened to what it thinks about you, noticing what it feels about you, and what it wants to do to you or with you. Now we've done that,

how does that leave you feeling? What happens in your body? [Leave spaces between these questions to allow for reflection.]

It is not uncommon at this stage for clients to report feeling rather down, defeated, crushed, hopeless, demotivated, etc. This is an important part of the process if it happens, as the client is realising that this critical self-part which they may have felt was motivating and stopping them from messing up may actually be making them feel bad and reducing their energy, confidence and motivation. Some other questions you might ask include: 'Are you surprised at how unpleasant your critic was?'; 'Are you surprised by how put down, depressed, or crushed you feel?'; 'How powerful did you find your critic?'; 'How easy would it be to stand up against?'; 'What do you think it might do if you tried?'. You might also ask the client: 'To what extent do you think your inner critic cares about the distress it causes you?'. These questions can help the client realise that engaging in a fight with their critic might not be the best way forward.

Having done a functional analysis of the inner critic, you might then offer the client the opportunity to get to know another self-part a bit better – that of their caring, compassionate inner coach or self-part.

For this part of the exercise, rather than have the client bring to mind something they are critical about, ask them to think about something they would like their caring self-part or inner coach to help them with. This could be something they felt their critic helps them with, e.g., not to be arrogant or lazy or hurt people, but it also might be more clearly linked to their values and approach goals, things they want more of, their desired future self, etc.

Before starting the functional analysis of their caring inner coach, you may wish to let them know that their critic might decide to chip in! Perhaps say something like:

> One thing to watch out for when we look at the caring inner coach self-part is the intrusion of the critic. Remember that the critic can be a bit of a bully, and just assumes it has got a right to comment and undermine. If you notice inner speech telling you not to pay attention to your caring self-part, or you notice some 'yes but . . . ' comments and complaints, do not stress about them; they are common. Just notice and bring your mind back mindfully to the task.

Before doing a functional analysis of the inner coach, it can be helpful to have the client engage in some compassionate mind exercises such as practising a soothing breathing rhythm, bringing a gentle smile to the face and noticing self-talk in a friendly warm tone. These exercises are well described elsewhere (Gilbert, 2010; Kolts, 2016; Irons & Beaumont, 2017). This kind of preparatory self-calming may be especially important after exploring the client's self-criticism system, which may have activated their bodies' threat systems. You may also wish to prime their caring mental state by having them recall a time when they were very helpful to somebody, and what they felt their motivation was – e.g., caring, reassuring and supportive.

Then perform a similar, structure guided exploration of the caring inner coach, progressively enquiring about and exploring the following.

- Its appearance and physical sense, or form. For instance, you might say:

  > Imagine you could see the caring, inner coach as part of you outside of yourself. What form might it take? What might it look like? What colours and textures

would this part of you have? For some people it might be an animal, or a person, or a mixture – something that cares for you and wants the best for you.

- What it tends to say, its specific messages, its wisdom, including its tone of voice. For instance:

  Now listen carefully to what your caring inner coach (compassionate self-part) wants to say to you. What would you like to hear that would be helpful? What messages would you like to get from it? Try and feel your way into what is helpful and imagine your inner coach having that wisdom for you.

- The feelings the caring inner coach has towards them, e.g.:

  What does your caring inner coaching (wise, compassionate self-part) feel about you? What emotions is it directing at you and have for you?

- What their inner coach would like to do to them, (its behaviour), e.g.:

  What does your inner coach (compassionate self) want to do with you or for you?'

  and perhaps add:

  How would your compassionate mind like to help and support you?'

Once the client has engaged in this guided functional analysis of their inner coach, ask them how they are feeling, what they are noticing. What we are hoping for – and what many clients experience – is feeling encouraged and supported to make progress towards their values, goals and desired future self.

We then might have the client reflect on their different experiences of making contact with and being exposed to their inner critic and then their inner coach. We might offer some psychoeducation around the fact that the inner critic and the inner coach are approaching things from different directions – one comes from a place of hostile self-criticism motivated by a competitive mental state, and one comes from a place of compassionate self-correction motivated by a caring mental state – and that a main aim of this approach to coaching and personal development is to help the client get better at 'switching' from one brain state (competitive) to another (caring).

Cultivating the image of the caring, inner coach

This exercise builds on the functional analysis of the caring inner coach and seeks to further strengthen the client's ability to switch on their caring social mentality. Have the client think about and imagine a caring and compassionate other being, one that cares deeply for them. Ask them to get a feeling for this other being, whether it is old or young, male or female, of a particular ethnicity, or perhaps of a different species than human. Have the client imagine the qualities they want their caring inner coach to have – perhaps it is warm and completely accepting, perhaps it has a deep concern and care for them, perhaps it has experienced some of the same things the client has experienced and had a deep wisdom to share. Ask the client: 'What kind of words and messages would you like to hear from your caring inner coach, what would be helpful to you' and 'how would you like to respond to the presence of your caring inner coach?'. After this guided visualisation, explore with the client what they noticed – and perhaps reassure them that this is something that can take time, like strengthening a muscle which has not been used for some time. Reassure them also that any image does not have to be pixel perfect; what is more important is the felt sense of the presence, and the feelings in the mind and the body that can come from being in contact with the caring inner coach.

Using chairwork to help improve internal relationships between parts

Chairwork can also be used to deepen your client's understanding of their critical and caring self-parts, or their inner critic and their caring inner coach (Bell, 2022; Bell et al., 2021). Explain to your client some people find it helpful to use different chairs to help them 'get into' or experience or learn more about different self-parts and get some insight into more helpful or improved ways of talking with and relating to themselves.

If they are willing, set out three chairs and have the client sit in one chair as themselves. Ask them to describe a particular issue or concern they have, something which frustrates them or which they tend to beat themselves up about. Then ask them to move over to the 'inner critic' chair and have the critic self say things to the chair they were just in, as it they were still sitting in it. You can prompt the critic with such questions as: 'What would you like to say to [client's name]? What else would you like to say? What do you want them to know? What would you like them to do?' (This process is really just 'externalising' what the client's inner critic may already be saying to them inside their heads on a regular basis.)

Then have the client return to the normal self-chair and ask them what they would like to say to their critical self. Some clients may adopt a posture of defeat and submission and tend to agree with and give into the critical self. Empathise with the client: 'That was quite nasty' or 'It must be hard, having to listen to that inner talk. No wonder you're struggling', for instance.

Then invite the client to move to the third chair – the caring inner coach chair – and ask them to prepare themselves with breathing and postural exercises, think about themselves at their most caring and accepting, and adopt their caring inner coach mentality. Then have the caring inner coach address the 'normal' chair they were just in. You can prompt the caring coach with such questions as: 'What would you like to say to [client's name]? What else would you like to say? What do you want them to do? What would you like them to know?', then have the client return to the normal self-chair and ask them what it was like hearing those messages from their caring inner coach. Perhaps ask them how helpful it might be to experience the presence of their caring, wise inner coach more often.

One final activity you may choose to facilitate is to have the client return to the caring inner coach chair and look at the chair which contained the inner critic and think about what is behind the critic's attacks, what it is that the critic most frightened of, what might have been some of the hurts or disappointments that set it going however many years ago. The aim here is to help the caring inner coach to recognise the fears which lie behind the self-critical process, and to help the caring inner coach become more important as an integrating voice inside the client.

Strengthening the caring inner coach through writing

This exercise might best be done as a between-session activity. Have the client write about an aspect of themselves they do not like, something they judge themselves about, put themselves down about, or attack themselves about. Then either have them imagine they have a good friend with the exact same issues, and have them write a caring, supporting, reassuring letter to that friend. Or have them write an imaginary letter to themselves as if it was coming from a very wise, caring and compassionate friend. In either case, once the letter is written, have them read the letter as if it was coming to themselves. Once with the client again, have them reflect on the experience. Explore with them how the message might be tweaked or enhanced, and help them see that this is the kind of message and communication which their wise, inner, caring coach may be seeking to offer them.

Conclusion

Many clients experience problems arising from a harsh, condemning self-critical process or inner critic. Three different ways of helping clients with negative, unhelpful self-directed thoughts are helping them to change the content of their thinking (cognitive-based coaching), helping them change their relationship with their inner experience (mindfulness-based coaching) and the approach outlined in this chapter, caring inner coach development. This involves helping clients shift from hostile self-criticism to caring self-correction, developing their ability to switch from a competitive mental state or social mentality in which they experience a losing, sub-originate, defeated position, to a caring mental state of social mentality in which they come to experience a more reassured, engaged and optimistic position.

The inner coach development approach is a process-based, multi-modal approach heavily informed by compassion-based approaches and associated models including multiple selves, social mentality theory and attachment theory. Helping a client become better able to activate and experience their caring inner coach may help them not just with their presenting issue, but also help them better manage other frustrations, disappointments and setbacks in the future, helping them to become more resilient.

Further, if the inner critic is holding them back from taking important steps forward in their life towards valued goals, then helping them activate their caring inner coach may also help reduce avoidance, develop a more growth-oriented mindset (Dweck, 2006) and be more likely to thrive and flourish over time.

Reflective questions

1. What proportion of your clients might benefit from an improved ability to regulate their emotional state, and as a result of experience less self-criticism and more self-reassurance?
2. How strong is your own inner critic?
3. In what situations, circumstances and contexts does your own inner critic become most vocal?

References

Ainsworth, M. D., & Bowlby, J. (1991). An ethological approach to personality development. *American Psychologist, 46*, 333–341.

Anstiss, T. (2021). Affirmations, reflections and summaries in coaching. In J. Passmore (ed.) *The Coaches Handbook* (pp. 114–124). Abingdon: Routledge.

Bell, T. (2022). Compassion focussed therapy chairwork. In P. Gilbert & G. Simos. (Eds.), *Compassion Focused Therapy: Clinical Practice and Applications* (pp. 445–458). Abingdon: Routledge.

Bell, T., Montague, J., Elander, J., & Gilbert, P. (2021). Multiple emotions, multiple selves: Compassion focused therapy chairwork. *The Cognitive Behaviour Therapist.* 14.

Bowlby (1969/1982). *Attachment and Loss: Vol 1. Attachment* (2nd ed.). New York: Basic Books.

Docter, P., & Del Carmen, R. (2015). *Inside Out.* Walt Disney Studios Motion Pictures.

Dweck, C. S. (2006). *Mindset: The New Psychology of Success.* New York, NY: Random House.

Egan, S. J., Rees, C. S., Delalande, J., Greene, D., Fitzallen, G., Brown, S., Webb, M., & Finlay-Jones, A. (2022). A review of self-compassion as an active ingredient in the prevention and treatment of anxiety and depression in young people. *Administrative Policy Mental Health.* 49(3), 385–403.

Freud, S. (1923). The ego and the Id. In J. Strachey et al. (Trans.), *The Standard Edition of the Complete Psychological Works of Sigmund Freud*, Volume XIX. London: Hogarth Press.

Gilbert, P. (2005). Compassion and cruelty: A biopsychosocial approach. In P. Gilbert (Ed.), *Compassion Conceptualisations, Research and Use in Psychotherapy*, (pp. 9–74). London, UK: Brunner-Routledge.

Gilbert, P. (2010). *Compassion Focused Therapy: Distinctive Features.* Abingdon: Routledge.

Gilbert, P. (2014). The origins and nature of compassion focused therapy. *British Journal of Clinical Psychology.* 53(1), 6–41.

Gilbert, P. (2020). Compassion: From its evolution to a psychotherapy. *Frontiers in Psychology.* 11. Article 586161.

Gilbert, P., & Simos, G. (Eds.). (2022). *Compassion Focused Therapy: Clinical Practice and Applications* (1st ed.). Abingdon: Routledge.

Irons, C., & Beaumont, E. (2017). *The Compassionate Mind Workbook. A Step-by-Step Guide to Developing Your Compassionate Self.* Robinson (London: Little Brown).

Jung, C. G. (1991). *The Archetypes and the Collective Unconscious* (R. F. C. Hull, Trans., 2nd ed.). New York, NY: Routledge.

Kim, J. J., Doty, J. R., Cunnington, R., & Kirby, J. N. (2021). Does self-reassurance reduce neural and self-report reactivity to negative life events? *Frontiers of Psychology.* Sep 28, 12.

Kolts, R. L. (2016). *CFT Made Simple: A Clinician's Guide to Practicing Compassion-Focused Therapy.* Oakland, CA: New Harbinger.

Kotera, Y., Dosedlova, J., Andrzejewski, D., Kaluzeviciute, G., & Sakai, M. (2021). From stress to psychopathology: Relationship with self-reassurance and self-criticism in czech university students. *International Journal of Mental Health and Addiction.* 20(4), 2321–2332. https://doi.org/10.1007/s11469-021-00516-z

Levine, S. L., Green-Demers, I., Werner, K. M., & Milyavskaya, M. (2019). Perfectionism in adolescents: Self-critical perfectionism as a predictor of depressive symptoms across the school year. *Journal of Social and Clinical Psychology,* 38(1), 70–86.

Longe, O., Maratos, F. A., Gilbert, P., Evans, G., Volker, F., Rockliff, H., & Rippon, G. (2010). Having a word with yourself: Neural correlates of self-criticism and self-reassurance. *Neuroimage.* Jan 15; 49(2), 1849–1856.

Löw, A. C., Schauenburg, H., & Dinger, U. (2019). Self-criticism and psychotherapy outcome: A systematic review and meta-analysis. *Clinical Psychology Review.* 75, 101808.

MacBeth, A., & Gumley, A. (2012). Exploring compassion: A meta-analysis of the association between self-compassion and psychopathology. *Clinical Psychology Review.* Aug; 32(6), 545–552.

Mansell, W., & Marken, R. (2015). The origins and future of control theory in psychology. *Review of General Psychology.* 19, 425–430. https://doi.org/10.1037/gpr0000057.

Miller, W. R., & Rollnick, S. (2013). *Motivational Interviewing: Helping People Change* (3rd ed.). New York, NY: Guildford Press.

Neff, K. D., & Germer, C. K. (2013). A pilot study and randomized controlled trial of the mindful self-compassion program. *Journal of Clinical Psychology.* 69, 28–44.

O'Neill, C., Pratt, D., Kilshaw, M., Ward, K., Kelly, J., & Haddock, G. (2021). The relationship between self-criticism and suicide probability. *Clinical Psychology & Psychotherapy.* 28(6), 1445–1456.

Petrocchi, N., Dentale, F., & Gilbert, P. (2019). Self-reassurance, not self-esteem, serves as a buffer between self-criticism and depressive symptoms. *Psychology and Psychotherapy: Theory, Research and Practice.* 92(3), 394–406.

Rogers, C. R. (1957). The necessary and sufficient conditions of therapeutic personality change. *Journal of Consulting Psychology.* 21, 95–103.

Rogers, C. R. (1980). *A Way of Being.* Boston: Houghton Mifflin.

Schwartz, R. C., & Sweezy, M. (2020). *Internal Family Systems Therapy* (2nd ed.). New York: The Guilford Press.

Thew, G. R., Gregory, J. D., Roberts, K., & Rimes, K. A. (2017). The phenomenology of self-critical thinking in people with depression, eating disorders, and in healthy individuals. *Psychology and Psychotherapy: Theory, Research and Practice.* 90(4), 751–769.

Wakelin, K., Perman, G., & Simonds, L. (2021). Effectiveness of self-compassion related interventions for reducing self-criticism: A systematic review and meta-analysis. *Clinical Psychology & Psychotherapy.* 29. https://doi.org/10.1002/cpp.2586.

Werner, A. M., Tibubos, A. N., Rohrmann, S., & Reiss, N. (2019). The clinical trait self-criticism and its relation to psychopathology: A systematic review – update. *Journal of Affective Disorders.* 246, 530–547.

Zelkowitz, R. L., & Cole, D. A. (2019). Self-criticism as a transdiagnostic process in non-suicidal self-injury and disordered eating: Systematic review and meta-analysis. *Suicide & Life Threat Behaviour.* Feb; 49(1), 310–327.

Zhang, H., Watson-Singleton, N. N., Pollard, S. E., Pittman, D. M., Lamis, D. A., Fischer, N. L., Patterson, B., & Kaslow, N. J. (2019). Self-criticism and depressive symptoms: Mediating role of self-compassion. *Omega: Journal of Death and Dying.* 80(2), 202–222.

Chapter 26

Artificial intelligence coaching for wellbeing

Bergsveinn Olafsson, Danny Martin and Augusto Gonzalez-Bonorino

Introduction

Creating a world where everyone has access to wellness services when they need them seems difficult to do. According to the American Psychological Association (2022), 71% of people never receive adequate mental health services and 46% of practitioners cannot meet service demands. Furthermore, 44 million Americans reported feelings of suffering or languishing pre-pandemic (Our World in Data, n.d.). Multiple meta-analytic reviews of nearly 650,000 participants across 4000 randomized control trials have concluded that these service gaps are driven in part by the reactive nature of traditional pharmacological treatments and psychotherapeutic approaches to mental wellness and that the field is in need of a paradigm shift in the towards more proactive approaches (Leichsenring et al., 2022). Such approaches, like those embodied in several classes of coaching, are limited because individuals generally require consistent exposure to high-cost interventions to gain any substantive benefits (Bolier et al., 2013). The integration of coaching and artificial intelligence (AI) represents one path toward circumventing these challenges and making such a paradigm shift possible.

In this chapter, we will briefly overview the science of coaching and wellbeing before giving a more comprehensive review of the AI landscape as it pertains to capabilities that can be usefully applied in coaching settings. In doing so, we will discuss pathways to effectively integrate AI into coaching practice, open questions and challenges surrounding such integration, and best practices regarding the design, implementation, and deployment of AI systems in coaching contexts. In doing so, we will highlight several case studies surrounding real-life AI systems currently being used in coaching contexts, including the particularly exciting case of Novem, an AI coaching application that utilises evidence-backed frameworks to help people set and achieve goals related to enhancing their overall wellbeing.

Coaching

Coaching describes a collaborative relationship between a coach and client to facilitate the client's personal development (Grant & Stober, 2006). Meta-analyses indicate that coaching increases coping, skill development, self-efficacy, problem-solving, wellbeing, and self-regulated goal-attainment capacities (Cannon-Bowers et al., 2023). There are many different outcomes that coaching can be applied to optimise in clients, each eliciting a specialised set of approaches and methodologies. Regardless of these nuances in

DOI: 10.4324/9781003319016-28

coaching practice, the core philosophy of coaching is goal attainment, or the process of helping clients set and achieve some specific goal (Grant, 2012). This first step in this process involves helping clients develop a sense of awareness around how their thoughts, emotions, and behaviours affect their lives. The next step involves moving beyond awareness to creating a sense of responsibility for one's life outcomes, as well as the role that one's thoughts, emotions, and behaviours play in affecting these outcomes. By developing responsibility, clients will be more likely to monitor their thoughts, emotions, and behaviours outside of the coaching session and actively work towards changing these in a manner that will lead to desired changes in one's life (Nieuwerburgh, 2014).

Between awareness and responsibility is a goal. A goal describes the specific type of change to either our thoughts, behaviours, or emotions that we want to implement in order to see some desired change in our lives. Without a goal in place, it is difficult to move beyond awareness because there is nothing specific for a client to take responsibility for. So much of what coaches do involves helping clients set attainable goals that will also lead to meaningful changes in their lives. The rich literature on goal theory generally contends that goals should also be challenging, alongside noting the importance of commitment, feedback, and moderate complexity (Locke & Latham, 1990). However, vague goals have also been shown to enhance behaviour change as long as they are accompanied by concrete plans and sub-goals (Schippers & Ziegler, 2019).

While goal-setting may seem a daunting task, given the proper framework, goal-setting does not have to be a complex task (Saddawi-Konefka et al., 2017). Examples of such frameworks include SMART, which contends that goals should be specific, measurable, achievable, relevant, and time-bound; and WOOP, which stands for wish, outcome, obstacles, and plans. WOOP utilises mental contrasting with implementation intentions (MCII) to set high-quality goals (Saddawi-Konefka et al., 2017). Mental contrasting involves assessing one's motivation behind a specific goal (wish) by outlining what the world will look like when that goal is achieved (outcome), and contrasting this alternate world with the barriers stopping one from making it a reality (obstacles). Implementation intentions involve developing specific responses that one will implement in response to these barriers (plans). WOOP has been shown to substantially enhance rates of goal attainment relative to other popular goal-setting frameworks (Adriaanse et al., 2010; Oettingen et al., 2015; Saddawi-Konefka et al., 2017).

We build on insights from goal theory and the WOOP framework to offer an alternate goal-setting framework called SCMT-MOP. SCMT stands for specific, challenging, measurable, and timely – all elements of effective goals, according to both the SMART framework and goal theory in general. MOP stands for motivation, obstacles, and plans. This framework directly builds on WOOP, replacing outcome with motivation to allow for greater generality in assessing one's reasons for wanting to achieve a specific goal and wish with SCMT to outline characteristics of an effective goal from which to build out subsequent elements of WOOP. As we outline moving forward, the effectiveness of AI coaching systems is largely contingent upon the level of detail built into the structure of their task. As such, by offering a more granular process of goal-setting, the SCMT-MOP framework should be more effective when implemented by AI coaching systems than less granular frameworks like SMART and WOOP.

Wellbeing coaching

Coaching is an applied arm of positive psychology (Grant & Atad, 2022), the scientific study of positive states, traits, and institutions (Seligman & Csikszentmihalyi, 2000). One of the primary foci of positive psychology is the study of wellbeing. Wellbeing is a fundamental coaching outcome because all coaching outcomes – in one way or another – involve enhancing the client's wellbeing. Wellbeing coaching is a specialised branch of coaching whose focus is aimed at helping clients craft and attain goals that are explicitly related to identifiable components of wellbeing. Effective wellbeing coaching thus requires wellbeing frameworks that outline these components.

Within the context of positive psychology and coaching, wellbeing frameworks have often been conceptualised in terms of hedonia and eudaimonia (Huta & Waterman, 2014). Hedonia is captured by the construct of subjective wellbeing (SWB), which describes the quality of one's life and the momentary presence of positive emotion and absence of negative emotion. Eudaimonia is more closely captured by the construct of psychological wellbeing (PWB), which describes living a virtuous life characterised by a devotion to personal growth and a higher purpose, regardless of positive emotionality in the present moment. Where SWB is about feeling good, PWB is about doing good.

There are several competing frameworks of wellbeing within positive psychology, each with its own benefits and drawbacks. One framework that has seen great success in coaching contexts is the PERMA4 framework (Donaldson et al., 2022). PERMA4 is an extension of the PERMA model of wellbeing, which was built out of Seligman's (2002) theory of authentic happiness. PERMA4 posits nine components of wellbeing whose presence constitutes the experience of both SWB and PWB. These components are positive emotions, engagement, relationships, meaning, accomplishment, physical health, mindset, economic security, and environment.

Positive emotions describe enjoyable affective states like the experience of love, joy, and gratitude. Engagement is all about being fully absorbed and immersed in the daily activities of life. Positive relationships are characterised by support, warmth, and love. Meaning is about contributing to something beyond the self, making sense of yourself and the world, and perceiving that life is worth living. Accomplishment describes experiencing a sense of competence and mastery within a domain of interest and achieving important life goals (Seligman, 2011). Physical health goes beyond the absence of illness, describing a balance of both high psychological and physiological functioning. Mindset consists of having high levels of Psycap (hope, efficacy, resilience, and optimism) and a growth mindset. Environment is being in a psychologically and physically safe environment and having access to things such as natural light and fresh air. Economic security describes the effect of one's financial assets on their wellbeing (Donaldson & Donaldson, 2020; Donaldson et al., 2022).

Artificial intelligence

Despite private-sector initiatives historically leading the charge in AI research and development, academic interest in this space has skyrocketed during the last ten years. This trend, fuelled by the increasing popularity of open-source initiatives, will likely drive both innovation and uncertainty regarding the future of AI. Despite this uncertainty, we hope to elucidate the wonderful things we can do with this technology today, while pointing out the limitations we should strive to surpass in the near future.

Demystifying artificial intelligence

AI's journey from a nascent theoretical concept to a practical tool mirrors the evolution of human knowledge, both within individuals and across the history of our species. Initially, AI followed a symbolic approach based on the idea of representing knowledge in a structured way using symbols and rules. Powered by networks, which represent entities (e.g., "the chair") and relationships (e.g., "I *SIT ON* the chair"), these models eliminate the risk of generating false information by providing responses grounded in the networks of validated knowledge. The drawback is that these models are both computationally expensive and rigid in the information they can generate. However, the advent of Big Data and machine learning – a subset of AI that enables computers to learn from data and make predictions or decisions without being explicitly programmed – marked a paradigm shift that allowed computers to both accurately and efficiently generate knowledge based on statistical patterns contained in enormous repositories of information. This paradigm shift in computational knowledge generation marked the beginning of the AI revolution. AI is a field of computer science that focuses on creating systems capable of performing tasks that usually require human intelligence. These tasks include problem-solving, pattern recognition, and decision-making. AI systems can process vast amounts of data, learn from this data, and make predictions or decisions based on it. This ability is particularly useful in identifying health behaviours and suggesting personalised interventions for behaviour change.

AI can be broadly categorised into two types: artificial general intelligence (AGI) and Narrow AI. AGI refers to a type of AI that possesses the ability to understand, learn, and apply knowledge across a wide range of tasks at a level comparable to that of a human being. Achieving AGI is a complex task due to several limitations. For instance, current AI systems lack common sense reasoning, a fundamental aspect of human intelligence, and require massive amounts of energy to run.

On the other hand, Narrow AI – which is the focus of most current AI research – is designed to perform specific tasks, such as voice recognition or image analysis. These systems can process and analyse large datasets, recognise patterns, and make decisions or predictions. However, it's important to note that the "intelligence" of these systems is vastly different from human intelligence. They excel in tasks that involve processing large amounts of data and making predictions based on patterns, but they do not possess the broad range of cognitive abilities that humans do. Therefore, while AI has made significant strides in many fields, it is crucial to understand its limitations and the differences between human intelligence and machine "intelligence".

In recent years, the progress in AI, especially in areas like natural language processing (NLP), has been remarkable. Innovations such as the transformer model, introduced in the groundbreaking paper "Attention Is All You Need" (Vaswani et al., 2017), laid the foundation for modern large language models (LLMs) such as BERT (Bidirectional Encoder Representations from Transformers; Devlin et al., 2018) and the Generative Pre-trained Transformers (GPTs) family (Radford et al., 2018) These models can be applied in various coaching domains to provide personalised and interactive feedback, guidance, and support.

Prompt engineering – the systematic design and optimisation of input instructions to guide the responses of LLMs conditional on specific contexts – involves curating the context provided to the model to generate responses that are factual, useful, and aligned with one's beliefs (Chen et al., 2023). Prompt engineering plays a crucial role in leveraging LLMs for coaching. For instance, providing LLMs with repositories of empirically based knowledge and instructions on how to use them, detailed descriptions of the persona the model should mimic, specifying the model's desired output, and outlining what the model should avoid can all guide the model's responses. Identification of such techniques in the context of coaching applications – whereby AI models need to adhere to ethical guidelines, maintain a positive and empathetic tone, and provide advice that is both accurate and insightful, is an active field of research (Terblanche, 2020).

Crafting effective prompts requires a deep understanding of both the coaching process and the workings of LLMs. Best practice guidelines suggest starting with a broad prompt and iteratively refining it based on either subjective feedback or testing the model's responses against some predefined standard of a "good response". It's also important to manage expectations during this process: while LLMs can generate impressively human-like text, they don't possess human-like understanding or common-sense reasoning (Albrecht et al., 2022; Valmeekam et al., 2022); therefore, their responses should always be reviewed and interpreted within the context of their desired purpose. Despite these challenges, the potential of LLMs in coaching is immense, offering scalable, personalised, and affordable coaching solutions (Terblanche et al., 2022b). In general, the application of LLMs in the workplace has the potential to automate routine tasks such as intake form processing or building client profiles from multiple data points, thereby freeing up time for coaches to focus on more rewarding tasks.

AI in the landscape of coaching and wellbeing

The integration of AI into healthcare and psychology has seen a significant uptick in recent years. LLMs in particular have gained interest among coaching communities since the launch of tools like GPT-3, BERT, and ChatGPT, with several scholars noting the potential of LLMs to revolutionise coaching as a field (Graßmann & Schermuly, 2021; Terblanche et al., 2022b; Passmore & Tee, 2023a, 2023b). Powered by these models, modern AI chatbots are beginning to demonstrate the potential to operate as useful coaching modalities of themselves. Such systems boast several benefits, including increased consistency and objectivity, affordability, personalisation, accessibility, and a capacity to be deployed at a greater scale than human coaches.

Several recent studies have examined AI chatbots in the context of psychology and healthcare. AI chatbots specialised in administering cognitive behavioural therapy (CBT) have been shown to effectively reduce anxiety and depression compared to controls receiving no treatment (Fulmer et al., 2018). In healthcare, (Greer et al., 2019) found that young adults with cancer diagnoses who interacted with AI chatbots developed to deliver positive psychology–based coping skills for four weeks exhibited lower levels of anxiety. A systematic review also found that AI chatbots effectively reduced general psychological distress among users (Gaffney et al., 2019). Furthermore, Naor and colleagues (2022) demonstrated that AI-powered Acceptance Commitment Therapy tools were effective at improving wellbeing.

Recently, more studies have explored the efficacy of AI-driven methodologies for well-being coaching. Personal narratives, the stories we tell ourselves about ourselves, help us make sense of our lives and are important contributors to wellbeing (McAdams & McLean, 2013). Blyler and Seligman (2023) prompted ChatGPT to construct personal narratives from a collection of participants' stream-of-consciousness–style thoughts collected over the course of 48 hours; 25 of 26 participants reported that the narrative crafted by ChatGPT was highly or completely accurate, and 19 of 26 reported that they learned something new about themselves by reading it, indicating that ChatGPT could help enhance the self-discovery process for clients.

In a 2022 study on the effectiveness of AI-based coaching interventions relative to traditional human coaches, Terblanche developed an AI chatbot called Vici specialised in goal attainment, which he subsequently employed in an experiment to test rates of successful goal attainment among participants who engaged in either no coaching intervention, intervention delivered via human professionals, or intervention delivered via Vici (Terblanche et al., 2022b). Terblanche found that, over a nine-month period, participants in the AI and human coaching groups exhibited similar rates of goal attainment, which were both significantly higher than in controls. The results of this study indicate that AI chatbots can provide continuous, longstanding support to help individuals continually set, work towards, and achieve goals across extended periods of time. In a follow-up study, Terblanche et al. (2022a) found that Vici's impact did not extend to coaching outcomes outside of goal attainment, such as PWB and resilience, indicating that the effects of AI coaches may be constrained by their specialised functions.

Open questions in AI coaching

Although studies on AI coaching on goal attainment have demonstrated promising results, the field of coaching needs to answer several important questions regarding the role of AI systems in coaching praxis and the efficacy of AI coaching with respect to several outcomes of interest to coaching researchers and practitioners alike. First, the field needs to establish best practices with respect to assessing the efficacy of such systems, as well as a hierarchy of evidence that can be used to judge the quality of evidence coming out of any given study with regard to assessing the efficacy of AI coaching systems. Randomised controlled trials (RCTs) comparing longitudinal outcomes among groups randomly assigned to interventions involving AI coaching, human coaching, hybrid coaching approaches, and controls may serve as a baseline for such standards. Such studies should implement strict experimental procedures to control for confounds like the frequency of interaction between participants and their coaching modality, which has been shown to affect AI coaching outcomes (Terblanche et al., 2022b). Furthermore, such studies may also require the development of specialised AI coaching systems aimed at enhancing specific outcomes to be tested under the RCT paradigm, as there exists little evidence to suggest that AI coaches can effectively impact multiple types of outcomes (Terblanche et al., 2022a). For example, AI tools which specialise in goal attainment, like Vici, may not help enhance overall wellbeing unless they are further specialised to help individuals set and attain goals that are strictly aimed at enhancing outcomes that have been empirically demonstrated to enhance wellbeing.

Some scholars contend that AI coaching has developed to the point of being able to replace novice coaching practitioners, who rely heavily on strict models and frameworks, but not more experienced coaches, who rely more on experience and intuition, sometimes referred to as a meta-wisdom (Megginson & Clutterbuck, 2010). Preliminary evidence from testing AI has highlighted the current gaps (as of 2023) with the ability of AI to engage in competent coaching conversations, even to the level of a novice coach (Passmore & Tee, 2023b). However, AI is likely to continue to improve.

An important question regarding the potential for AI systems to serve as replacements to – rather than amplifiers of – human coaching pertains to the efficacy of working alliances between AI coaching systems and human users (Graßmann et al., 2020). Working alliances encompass the extent to which the coach (whether human or AI) and the client can establish rapport, trust, connection, and mutually agreed goals. Graßmann & Schermuly (2021) contend that AI coaches should be effective in forming working alliances with users, building on studies demonstrating that users develop bonds with AI chatbots in therapeutic contexts, and that these bonds become stronger over time (Bickmore et al., 2005; Bickmore et al., 2010;). Furthermore, people who engage with an AI chatbot report human-like empathy emanating from AI therapists (Jiang et al., 2022). Moreover, in therapeutic settings, AI chatbots have been shown to serve as an effective mechanism to circumvent issues with client self-disclosure (Gratch et al., 2014), as people often describe reduced feelings of social judgement when interacting with AI therapists. Although these are promising findings, the question if AI chatbots are effective in establishing working alliances with users remains open, and will need to be explored in much greater depth by coaching researchers and practitioners alike.

Furthermore, there exists some preliminary evidence that AI coaching systems do not need to establish human-like working alliances with users to produce similar outcomes to human coaches. In a 2022 study, Terblanche and Kidd noted that trust – a key component of working alliance formation – might not be as important for AI coaches as for human coaches in terms of predicting engagement with the coaching process. Terblanche & Kidd (2022) instead found that performance expectations, social influence, and attitudes toward technology were far more influential on behavioural intentions to engage with AI coaching systems. Despite these findings, whether working alliance formation is predictive of engagement with and outcomes of AI coaching in the presence of positive attitudes toward technology has yet to be rigorously tested, and thus represents an open question for the field.

These findings also relate to the more high-level question of whether people want AI coaches to be more like humans or technological tools. While it is seemingly rational to think that AI coaches should mimic human-like attributes, the uncanny valley effect is a well-researched phenomenon whereby people report negative impressions of robotic objects with overly human-like qualities, and experts have argued that it should be actively avoided when designing AI coaching systems (Sasaki et al., 2017; Terblanche, 2020). Indeed, studies have shown that individuals develop fewer negative impressions of conversational targets when engaging with text-based chatbots than with photorealistic human-like avatars (Ciechanowski et al., 2019). Contrasting with these findings, studies have also shown that social presence is enhanced when a chatbot has human-like features such as having a name, using formal language, and speaking in the first person (Araujo, 2018). These findings indicate that the question of how human-like AI coaching systems should be is very much an open one.

Rapid advancements in AI technology across several domains have led many experts to view AI systems as serious threats to displace knowledge workers in general, and there have been active calls from within the coaching community for greater regulation surrounding the application of these tools (Passmore & Tee, 2023a). Even if experienced coaches are indeed more effective than AI coaching systems, given the rapid pace of development surrounding AI coaching systems, as well as the comparative snail's pace of regulatory bodies, it remains to be seen just how long the field can ignore these seemingly inevitable trends. It may instead behove coaches to seek out avenues towards integration of these tools into their own praxis sooner rather than later (Passmore & Tee, 2023a). If effectively integrated into our practice as coaches, LLMs can help increase the supply of coaching services available to fill the mental health gap that has persisted since COVID19. To manifest a reality whereby coaches and AI work symbiotically to better serve the needs of diverse clientele, researchers and practitioners alike must work to better systems will serve as symbiotes to – rather than usurpers of – the practice of coaching.

Finally, in an age during which data is gold, how do we ensure the confidentiality, privacy, and security of clients and their personal information? This issue remains underexplored in the area of AI coaching and represents an important opportunity for collaboration between coaching researchers, practitioners, and a host of specialists from disparate fields like machine learning, AI, IT, and cyber-security. Such collaborative efforts will be necessary in the coming years to develop tools, standards, and techniques that can be employed towards minimising the risk of data leakage, prompt injections, and other security issues related to the usage of LLMs (and AI in general) throughout various coaching contexts.

Designing AI wellbeing coach

One recent development in AI that will be especially important for coaching is the proliferation of software that allows users to develop specialised LLM systems, or agents, that can be deployed to carry out specific tasks, such as coaching users towards specific, narrow outcomes. One such software is Evoach, a platform that allows users to build several customised coaching agents aimed at optimising specified coaching outcomes for themselves or clients (Mai & Rutschmann, 2023). This technology has started a race to develop best practices for designing AI coaches.

One promising set of best practices for developing AI coaching chatbots is captured by Nicky Terblanche's Designing AI Coach (DAIC) Framework (Terblanche, 2020). The DAIC is broken into two components, chatbot design best practices and elements of effective human coaching. Chatbot design best practices include incorporating a level of human likeness appropriate for the purpose of a given chatbot, setting and managing expectations regarding a chatbot's purpose and capabilities, transparency regarding the potential for a chatbot to change its behaviour in response to data from previous interactions, and ensuring that the chatbot is explicitly designed to acknowledge its mistakes as they are highlighted by users and remind users that it is actively undergoing a process of self-improvement. In an effort to support this last feature, chatbots should continually ask for user feedback throughout the interaction process. Finally, it is important for chatbots to actively disclose to users that they themselves are not humans and do not have human capacities such as conscious awareness, empathy, or emotion.

Elements of effective human coaching include aspects of the coach–client relationship like trust, empathy, transparency, predictability, reliability, ability, benevolence, and integrity. As such, chatbots should be designed to mimic and embody these elements when interacting with users. Effective human coaching also requires ethical conduct, and consideration of such issues as privacy and data protection, client autonomy, liability and division of responsibilities between coach and client, and identification of how bias may influence one's coaching practice.

Effective human coaching is also narrow in scope, with human coaches generally focusing on one coaching outcome at a time. Human coaches can choose from a number of potential outcomes to optimise for when trying to help clients, including one-shot goal attainment, overall wellbeing, or creating lasting behavioural change of some specific form. Effective human coaching thus generally requires defining a specific coaching outcome to work towards optimising. Effective human coaching also relies on the use of evidence-backed theoretical models that have been empirically validated across all contexts in which they are being employed. The purpose of these models is to specify what elements of human coaching efficacy are most important to emphasise when attempting to optimise for a specific coaching outcome. For example, if one's goal as a coach is to help a client achieve one specific goal which they have laid out for themselves, then elements of empathy may not be as important for the human coach to emphasise compared to a situation whereby the human coach is attempting to optimise the client's overall wellbeing. Whether or not this is the case must be based on some line of reasoning. Theoretical models supply these lines of reasoning, with their effectiveness hanging on the degree of empirical support available for their claims.

Moving beyond Terblanche's framework for a moment, scholars have noted that to be able to develop an AI coach that can provide evidence-based and personalised insights, one needs large amounts of data from coaching conversations (Passmore & Tee, 2023a). However, this requires access to that sensitive data, which practitioners may not have access to or permission to use. It is thus important that developers of AI coaching systems design such systems to meet some minimal threshold of efficacy, even in the absence of any data from real-life coaching conversations or from prior interactions with users.

The utilisation of specific coaching outcomes in conjunction with theoretical models, as laid out by Terblanche, provides one avenue to meet this threshold. For example, by using wellbeing frameworks, AI coaching systems can help people evaluate their wellbeing against evidence-based standards before enacting elements of the coach–client relationship that will best help people build their wellbeing over time, even if the system has little data on the client to inform its output. The application of wellbeing frameworks like PERMA4, SWB, and PWB allows us to constrain AI systems to optimise outcomes that have been empirically demonstrated to make meaningful contributions to people's overall wellbeing. For instance, one challenge with AI coaching is how to prompt LLMs to help individuals identify their problems (Graßmann & Schermuly, 2021). Without having appropriate contexts, goals, and constraints, LLMs are subject to generating inaccurate or counterproductive assessments of what an individual's problems are and what they should do to address them. By incorporating wellbeing frameworks into the prompts provided to LLMs, AI coaches can help individuals understand and evaluate where they stand with respect to specific components of wellbeing. This in turn helps individuals identify for themselves the problems that are currently detracting from their overall wellbeing.

The same can be said of designing AI systems to mimic strengths-based coaching. AI systems need to be given similar constraints, contexts, and goals to help people become aware of and better utilise character strengths or positive character traits that energise them and reflect their best selves, which has been empirically demonstrated to enhance over-all wellbeing (Peterson & Park, 2006). By leveraging empirically supported theories and frameworks, both human and AI-based coaches can better help individuals identify where they stand on relevant contributors to wellbeing and where they might want to improve.

By using frameworks of behavioural change, AI coaching systems can more effec-tively support users in developing lasting habits that can support them in achieving other coaching outcomes like wellbeing or self-awareness. Theoretical models on behaviour change suggest that factors such as self-monitoring, psychological distancing, social norms, and commitment all support behavioural change processes (Duckworth et al., 2018). AI coaching systems should thus leverage such models to inform themselves how to effectively utilise tools like digital nudging to serve as accountability partners. For instance, when people are in the process of working towards some goal, AI systems could rely on theories of behaviour change to inform how often they should notify users about their goal, how often to ask users for progress updates, how often to provide encourage-ment to users, how often to ask user s whether they need to revise as a goal, and so on, all while leveraging elements of the coach–client relationship that will be most effective for the particular type of "nudge" being given to a user.

Novem, founded in 2023, offers AI coaching that highlights these design principles by integrating specific coaching outcomes with theoretical models and frameworks of behavioral change to enhance user wellbeing (Olafsson et al., 2024). Novem helps users assess their wellbeing, identify improvement pathways, set actionable goals around them, and develop action plans for a smooth transition to the real world. Digital nudging systems support this transition, encouraging sustained action toward goal attainment. Grounded in user profile data and frameworks like PERMA4 and SCMT-MOP, Novem optimizes for empirically validated outcomes that meaningfully contribute to wellbeing within users' unique social contexts.

Conclusion

The role of artificial intelligence (AI) in coaching is not just a fleeting trend, but a trans-formative movement reshaping the landscape of personal development. Advancements in AI, particularly with respect to large language models (LLMs) and their application in tools like Cai (EZRA), AIMY (CoachHub) Vici, eVoach, and Novem have already begun to open up new possibilities for enhancing wellbeing and personal growth. Furthermore, recent AI development trends seem to promise more change and disruption. Only by developing a deep understanding of how AI coaching systems work and what outcomes they can generate will coaching as a field be able to exploit this technology to the benefit of clients and coaches alike. We thus call for greater transparency from developers of AI coaching systems, more scientific research on the structure, use, and impact of these systems from academic communities; and more exploratory integration of these systems by coaches into their personal practice.

Reflective questions

1. What is your definition of an AI coach?
2. In your coaching practice, how could AI enhance your coaching practice?
3. What safeguards are needed to protect clients when using an AI coach?

References

Adriaanse, M. A., Oettingen, G., Gollwitzer, P. M., Hennes, E. P., De Ridder, D. T. D., & De Wit, J. B. F. (2010). When planning is not enough: Fighting unhealthy snacking habits by Mental Contrasting with Implementation Intentions (MCII). *European Journal of Social Psychology*, 40(7), 1277–1293. https://doi.org/10.1002/ejsp.730

Albrecht, J., Kitanidis, E., & Fetterman, A. J. (2022). *Despite "super-human" performance, current LLMs are unsuited for decisions about ethics and safety.* https://doi.org/10.48550/ARXIV.2212.06295

American Psychological Association. (2022, November). *Psychologists struggle to meet demand amid mental health crisis: 2022 COVID-19 practitioner impact survey.* American Psychological Association. www.apa.org/pubs/reports/practitioner/2022-covid-psychologist-workload.pdf

Araujo, T. (2018). Living up to the chatbot hype: The influence of anthropomorphic design cues and communicative agency framing on conversational agent and company perceptions. *Computers in Human Behavior*, 85, 183–189. https://doi.org/10.1016/j.chb.2018.03.051

Bickmore, T., Gruber, A., & Picard, R. (2005). Establishing the computer–patient working alliance in automated health behavior change interventions. *Patient Education and Counseling*, 59(1), 21–30. https://doi.org/10.1016/j.pec.2004.09.008

Bickmore, T., Schulman, D., & Yin, L. (2010). Maintaining engagement in long-term interventions with relational agents. *Applied Artificial Intelligence*, 24(6), 648–666. https://doi.org/10.1080/08839514.2010.492259

Blyler, A. P., & Seligman, M. E. P. (2023). Personal narrative and stream of consciousness: An AI approach. *The Journal of Positive Psychology*, 1–7. https://doi.org/10.1080/17439760.2023.2257666

Bolier, L., Haverman, M., Westerhof, G. J., Riper, H., Smit, F., & Bohlmeijer, E. (2013). Positive psychology interventions: A meta-analysis of randomized controlled studies. *BMC Public Health*, 13(1), 1–20.

Cannon-Bowers, J. A., Bowers, C. A., Carlson, C. E., Doherty, S. L., Evans, J., & Hall, J. (2023). Workplace coaching: A meta-analysis and recommendations for advancing the science of coaching. *Frontiers in Psychology*, 14, 1204166. https://doi.org/10.3389/fpsyg.2023.1204166

Chen, B., Zhang, Z., Langrené, N., & Zhu, S. (2023). *Unleashing the potential of prompt engineering in large language models: A comprehensive review.* https://doi.org/10.48550/ARXIV.2310.14735

Ciechanowski, L., Przegalinska, A., Magnuski, M., & Gloor, P. (2019). In the shades of the uncanny valley: An experimental study of human–chatbot interaction. *Future Generation Computer Systems*, 92, 539–548. https://doi.org/10.1016/j.future.2018.01.055

Devlin, J., Chang, M.-W., Lee, K., & Toutanova, K. (2018). *BERT: Pre-training of deep bidirectional transformers for language understanding.* https://doi.org/10.48550/ARXIV.1810.04805

Donaldson, S. I., & Donaldson, S. I. (2020). The positive functioning at work scale: Psychometric assessment, validation, and measurement invariance. *Journal of Well-Being Assessment*, 4(2), 181–215. https://doi.org/10.1007/s41543-020-00033-1

Donaldson, S. I., Van Zyl, L. E., & Donaldson, S. I. (2022). PERMA+4: A framework for work-related wellbeing, performance and positive organizational psychology 2.0. *Frontiers in Psychology*, 12, 817244. https://doi.org/10.3389/fpsyg.2021.817244

Duckworth, A. L., Milkman, K. L., & Laibson, D. (2018). Beyond willpower: Strategies for reducing failures of self-control. *Psychological Science in the Public Interest*, 19(3), 102–129. https://doi.org/10.1177/1529100618821893

Fulmer, R., Joerin, A., Gentile, B., Lakerink, L., & Rauws, M. (2018). Using psychological artificial ontelligence (Tess) to relieve symptoms of depression and anxiety: Randomized controlled trial. *JMIR Mental Health*, 5(4), e64. https://doi.org/10.2196/mental.9782

Gaffney, H., Mansell, W., & Tai, S. (2019). Conversational agents in the rreatment of mental health problems: Mixed-method systematic review. *JMIR Mental Health*, 6(10), e14166. https://doi.org/10.2196/14166

Grant, A. M. (2012). An integrated model of goal-focused coaching: An evidence-based framework for teaching and practice. *International Coaching Psychology Review*, 7(2), 146–165.

Grant, A. M., & Atad, O. I. (2022). Coaching psychology interventions vs. positive psychology interventions: The measurable benefits of a coaching relationship. *The Journal of Positive Psychology*, 17(4), 532–544. https://doi.org/10.1080/17439760.2021.1871944

Grant, A., & Stober, D. (2006). Introduction. In D. Stober & A. Grant (Eds.), *Evidence based coaching: Putting best practices to work for your clients* (pp. 114). Wiley & Sons.

Graßmann, C., & Schermuly, C. C. (2021). Coaching with artificial intelligence: Concepts and capabilities. *Human Resource Development Review*, 20(1), 106–126. https://doi.org/10.1177/1534484320982891

Graßmann, C., Schölmerich, F., & Schermuly, C. C. (2020). The relationship between working alliance and client outcomes in coaching: A meta-analysis. *Human Relations*, 73(1), 35–58. https://doi.org/10.1177/0018726718819725

Gratch, J., Lucas, G. M., King, A. A., & Morency, L. P. (2014, May). It's only a computer: The impact of human-agent interaction in clinical interviews. In *Proceedings of the 2014 International Conference on Autonomous Agents and Multi-Agent Systems* (pp. 85–92).

Greer, S., Ramo, D., Chang, Y.-J., Fu, M., Moskowitz, J., & Haritatos, J. (2019). Use of the chatbot "Vivibot" to deliver positive psychology skills and promote well-being among young people after cancer treatment: Randomized controlled feasibility trial. *JMIR MHealth and UHealth*, 7(10), e15018. https://doi.org/10.2196/15018

Huta, V., & Waterman, A. S. (2014). Eudaimonia and its distinction from hedonia: Developing a classification and terminology for understanding conceptual and operational definitions. *Journal of Happiness Studies*, 15(6), 1425–1456. https://doi.org/10.1007/s10902-013-9485-0

Jiang, Q., Zhang, Y., & Pian, W. (2022). Chatbot as an emergency exist: Mediated empathy for resilience via human-AI interaction during the COVID-19 pandemic. *Information Processing & Management*, 59(6), 103074. https://doi.org/10.1016/j.ipm.2022.103074

Leichsenring, F., Steinert, C., Rabung, S., & Ioannidis, J. P. (2022). The efficacy of psychotherapies and pharmacotherapies for mental disorders in adults: An umbrella review and meta-analytic evaluation of recent meta-analyses. *World Psychiatry*, 21(1), 133–145.

Locke, E. A., & Latham, G. P. (1990). *A theory of goal setting & task performance*. Prentice Hall.

Mai, V., & Rutschmann, R. (2023). Best practices in chatbot coaching: Einblicke in Forschung und Entwicklung des StudiCoachBots der TH Köln und in die Coaching Chatbot Plattform evoach. *Organisationsberatung, Supervision, Coaching*, 30(1), 111–125. https://doi.org/10.1007/s11613-022-00802-2

McAdams, D. P., & McLean, K. C. (2013). Narrative identity. *Current Directions in Psychological Science*, 22(3), 233–238. https://doi.org/10.1177/0963721413475622

Megginson, D., & Clutterbuck, D. (2010). *Further techniques for coaching and mentoring*. Routledge.

Naor, N., Frenkel, A., & Winsberg, M. (2022). Improving well-being with a mobile artificial intelligence–powered acceptance commitment therapy Tool: Pragmatic retrospective study. *JMIR Formative Research*, 6(7), e36018. https://doi.org/10.2196/36018

Nieuwerburgh, C. van. (2014). *An introduction to coaching skills: A practical guide*. SAGE.

Oettingen, G., Kappes, H. B., Guttenberg, K. B., & Gollwitzer, P. M. (2015). Self-regulation of time management: Mental contrasting with implementation intentions. *European Journal of Social Psychology*, 45(2), 218–229. https://doi.org/10.1002/ejsp.2090

Olafsson, B., Martin, D., & Gonzalez-Bonorino, A. (2024, January). PERMA+4 in action: Advancing well-being through AI-facilitated coaching. *Paper presented at the Western Positive Psychology Association's 8th Annual Conference*, Albuquerque, NM.

Our World in Data. (n.d.). *Happiness and life satisfaction*. Retrieved on 26 November 2023 from https://ourworldindata.org/grapher/happiness-cantril-ladder

Passmore, J., & Tee, D. (2023a). Can chatbots like GPT-4 replace human coaches: Issues and dilemmas for the coaching profession, coaching clients and for organisations. *The Coaching Psychologist*, 19(1), 47–54. https://doi.org/10.53841/bpstcp.2023.19.1.47

Passmore, J., & Tee, D. (2023b). The library of babel: Assessing the powers of artificial intelligence in coaching conversations and knowledge synthesis. *Journal of Work Applied Management*. https://doi.org/10.1108/JWAM-06-2023-0057

Peterson, C., & Park, N. (2006). Character strengths in organizations. *Journal of Organizational Behavior*, 27(8), 1149–1154. https://doi.org/10.1002/job.398

Radford, A., Narasimhan, K., Salimans, T., & Sutskever, I. (2018). *Improving language understanding by generative pre-training*. OpenAI. https://www.mikecaptain.com/resources/pdf/GPT-1.pdf

Saddawi-Konefka, D., Baker, K., Guarino, A., Burns, S. M., Oettingen, G., Gollwitzer, P. M., & Charnin, J. E. (2017). Changing resident physician studying behaviors: A randomized, comparative effectiveness trial of goal setting versus use of WOOP. *Journal of Graduate Medical Education*, 9(4), 451–457. https://doi.org/10.4300/JGME-D-16-00703.1

Sasaki, K., Ihaya, K., & Yamada, Y. (2017). Avoidance of novelty contributes to the uncanny valley. *Frontiers in Psychology*, 8, 1792. https://doi.org/10.3389/fpsyg.2017.01792

Schippers, M. C., & Ziegler, N. (2019). Life crafting as a way to find purpose and meaning in life. *Frontiers in Psychology*, 10, 2778. https://doi.org/10.3389/fpsyg.2019.02778

Seligman, M. E. P. (2002). *Authentic happiness: Using the new positive psychology to realize your potential for lasting fulfillment*. Free Press.

Seligman, M. E. P. (2011). *Flourish: A visionary new understanding of happiness and well-being*. Free Press.

Seligman, M. E. P., & Csikszentmihalyi, M. (2000). Positive psychology: An introduction. *American Psychologist*, 55(1), 5–14. https://doi.org/10.1037/0003-066X.55.1.5

Terblanche, N. (2020). *A design framework to create artificial intelligence coaches*. https://doi.org/10.24384/B7GS-3H05

Terblanche, N., & Kidd, M. (2022). Adoption factors and moderating effects of age and gender that influence the intention to use a non-directive reflective coaching chatbot. *SAGE Open*, 12(2), 215824402210961. https://doi.org/10.1177/21582440221096136

Terblanche, N., Molyn, J., De Haan, E., & Nilsson, V. O. (2022a). Comparing artificial intelligence and human coaching goal attainment efficacy. *PLoS One*, 17(6), e0270255.

Terblanche, N., Molyn, J., De Haan, E., & Nilsson, V. O. (2022b). *Coaching at scale: Investigating the efficacy of artificial intelligence coaching*. https://doi.org/10.24384/5CGF-AB69

Valmeekam, K., Olmo, A., Sreedharan, S., & Kambhampati, S. (2022). *Large language models still can't plan (A Bbnchmark for LLMs on planning and reasoning about change)*. https://doi.org/10.48550/ARXIV.2206.10498

Vaswani, A., Shazeer, N., Parmar, N., Uszkoreit, J., Jones, L., Gomez, A. N., Kaiser, L., & Polosukhin, I. (2017). *Attention is all you need*. https://doi.org/10.48550/ARXIV.1706.03762

Health and wellbeing coaching tools

Chapter 27

Using coaching tools

Jonathan Passmore

This section of the book focuses on health and wellbeing tools. The implication of a separate section like this in a handbook could be that tools are themselves separate devices to be used separately or in isolation, dropped into a conversation like a parachute to magically transform a client or their perception of their 'problem'. This is not the case. While we have created a tools section, we did so because several authors included tools with their chapters. Rather than have three or four longer chapters with tools, and some without, we thought we would gather the tools together in a separate section, and also add five or six widely used health and wellbeing tools.

It is our view that coaching tools should not be used as one-offs, devoid of the model approach and mindset from which they originated. Instead, tools should be embedded with the model or approach from which they were drawn, used with skills and only when appropriate to the client and the issue under discussion.

Further, tools and the approaches they are drawn from, only have value, when they themselves are embedded within the container of a relationship. Carl Rogers, a person-centred therapist, writing in the 1950s, highlighted the importance of the relationship through his "necessary and sufficient conditions" (Rogers, 1957, p. 103). One aspect of these conditions is the role of relationship between the coach (therapist), who is congruent, and a client who brings for discussion an aspect of themselves which is incongruence in the form of an issue, a problem, or a topic to be explored. Of course, this congruence/incongruence relationship means that it is not a normal conversation between two friends which moves back and forth between their respective interests or concerns. In coaching, all of the focus is towards the interest or concern of the client.

It is also worth noting that while the coach may act as congruent in the coaching conversation, we all have aspects of incongruence – issues of our selves which we are wrestling with to bring our behaviours into line with our values or realign our values or beliefs with new values or beliefs we believe we should adopt.

Such relationships emerge between the coach and their clients when the coach is able to draw on advanced interpersonal skills, such as active listening and insightful open questions, but also use effective summarising, reflecting, and affirming as tools to demonstrate their listening and understanding, and thus show empathy and compassion towards their client. These skills help the client to navigate their way through the conversation and emerge with new insights, plans, and personal learning. It is these skills (tools) that are the basic ingredients of all effective coaching. Only once these have been mastered should the coach turn to the tool in this section, while keeping in mind the frameworks or approaches from which they are drawn.

DOI: 10.4324/9781003319016-30

The tools are drawn from a variety of approaches. Most common amongst them are cognitive behavioural coaching, acceptance, commitment coaching, compassion-based coaching, and motivational interviewing. As evidence-based approaches, these should sit at the heart of the health and wellbeing coach's work.

Before moving to the tools, we also wanted to share a few words of caution about the use of tools in general.

One of the biggest dangers of learning to apply a new tool or framework is what's know as Maslow's Hammer. This is a common challenge for us all. We may be highly skilled in using a particular tool, but the question is: Is it the right tool for this client, for this issue, or at this moment in the conversation? Our view is that by creating a wide-ranging collection of approaches and tools within these approaches, we can better serve our clients.

A second danger is a belief that tools can always get us out of a situation. When we stop listening and think about the laundry or the latest episode of a TV show, then suddenly realise we should have been present, the temptation may be to throw in a tool. Instead, we would argue that returning to listening and reflecting back is almost always more powerful than a tool. Tools are an amazing resource, but only when combined with the core coaching skills we referred to previously.

A third danger of tools is how the coach may set up or introduce a tool. Some coaches might be tempted to suggest to clients that the tool will create a transformational moment. While new insights might emerge from their use, we would advocate lowering client expectations. One way to do this is by using the word 'experiment': "Would you be happy to try an experiment?" We have found that many clients sometimes find this helpful. This allows the client to try it, and find out the tool – for them – does not lead to the magic outcome suggested, or to try it and decide they don't like it. Because it is an 'experiment', the language implies that no one knows what will happen, so all outcomes are acceptable. If it 'works', great; if not, great! There is learning and insight to be gained from both outcomes.

The fourth danger is experimenting with a new tool on a paying client. We would advocate that coaches practise in supervision or with peers before they try out a tool with a new client. In this way, the coach can get used to the language they wish to use to introduce the tool – the 'script'. It also allows the coach to get a sense of how the tool lands and how to explore the insights from the tool with the client. Practice makes perfect.

The final danger is one we have witnessed a lot. We might describe this the 'party piece'; some coaches even say, "When I get to this stage I always use the ABC tool". This use of a signature tool in our view means coaching has become all about the coach and not about the client and breaks the No. 1 rule of coaching: Coaching is all about the client and never about the coach. By having a wide range of model approaches, frameworks available coaches can avoid this problem and instead adapt and flex to meet their client where they are instead of forcing the client to watch the coach's 'magic show'.

Reference

Rogers, C. R. (1957). The necessary and sufficient conditions of therapeutic personality change. *Journal of Consulting Psychology, 21*(2), 95–103. https://doi.org/10.1037/h0045357

Chapter 28

Sky and weather

Jonathan Passmore

Description

Sky and weather is a tool drawn from the work of Buddhist writer Pema Chodron (1997). Like many of the tools from Third Wave cognitive behavioural approaches, it has aspects of mindfulness (present moment awareness with a non-judgemental mind), compassion and acceptance weaved together.

As Russ Harris (2009) notes, this one fits nicely within a Acceptance and Commitment Coaching approach, and it is one of my most favourite tools, only because I use it so frequently myself when I need to remind myself that these difficult moments are just 'weather'.

The tool aims to help the client to differentiate between a short term, unpleasant event (weather) and themselves and the other positive aspects in their life (the sky). The sky is so much bigger and constant (or at least only slowly changing), while the weather changes from hour to hour, day to day and season to season. Some days it rains, or there is thunder, but behind it, the sky remains constant. Bad weather passes.

When it works best

The tool works well within an Acceptance and Commitment Therapy (ACT) framework, whereby the client may be struggling to manage unhelpful, negative or irrational thoughts; specifically when clients are catastrophising, or generalising – when one bad event is being used to define them and or their life: "I have lost my job and I will never get another job again. I am a failure"

ACT encourages clients to recognise that these thoughts are not truths – that they are part of who they are now, but the thoughts do not define them, they are not part of all of their life and these thoughts (events) will pass. The client has the choice to ignore the thoughts and to refocus their thinking towards more positive or other aspects of their life.

Step by step

1. The client may express their unhelpful thought: "This has been a dreadful week. There is so much to do at work. I can't get through it."
2. Describe the metaphor, sky and weather: "While the weather may change, the sky remains constant. We may see the weather in the sky, but they are different. Today,

DOI: 10.4324/9781003319016-31

it's raining. Tomorrow, it may be windy. By the weekend, it could be sunny. In what ways is your thinking similar to this situation?"

3. Help the client to explore how our mood and emotions may change, but these emotions do not define who we are. They are the weather. Help the client to find their own umbrella for the rainy days, a coat for cold days and sun cream for sunny days, while recognising that neither the sun nor the rain defines who they are.

References

Chodron, P. (1997) *When Things Fall Apart: Heart Advice for Difficult Times*. Boulder, CO: Shambhala.
Harris, R. (2009) *ACT Made Simple*. Oakland, CA: New Harbinger Publications, Inc.

Chapter 29

The GENIAL Roadmap to Wellbeing tool

Zoe Fisher, Lowri Wilkie, Alexandra Hamill, and Andrew H. Kemp

Description

The 'GENIAL Roadmap to Wellbeing' (Figure 29.1) is a self-reflection tool designed to support clients to: (1) reflect on the key domains of wellbeing as they relate to their own life; and (2) set targeted goals based on these reflections to help them build their wellbeing.

When does it work best?

The roadmap is an outline of the key factors which contribute to health and wellbeing based on the GENIAL theoretical framework (Fisher et al., 2019; Kemp et al., 2017; Kemp & Fisher, 2022; Mead et al., 2021). The roadmap assumes that if an individual can improve one or more domains of the roadmap, they increase the likelihood of improving their sense of wellbeing. The roadmap works best when respondents create space and time to truthfully reflect on each domain, identifying current strengths and weaknesses. Respondents are more likely to positively change their wellbeing-related behaviours if they take time to set concrete goals using the 'Goal setting' section on page 2 (Figure 29.2).

Step by step

1. The client should carefully read through each domain of the roadmap.
2. The client should use the questions to prompt them to reflect on how each component of the roadmap is currently going for them in their life (the past two weeks).
3. Clients should mark one number on each arm to indicate which components are going well for them right now (6), versus which components might need some attention (1).
4. After they have completed each arm of the roadmap, they can turn to page 2 to start goal setting. The roadmap should be used to guide goals and daily habits set, based on recognised areas for improvement. For example, if they scored 'connection to nature' as low on the roadmap, they might set the goal of going for a daily 30-minute walk in nature.
5. Clients should use the goal setting prompts to help them clarify a plan and get clear on their goal.

DOI: 10.4324/9781003319016-32

The GENIAL Roadmap to Wellbeing

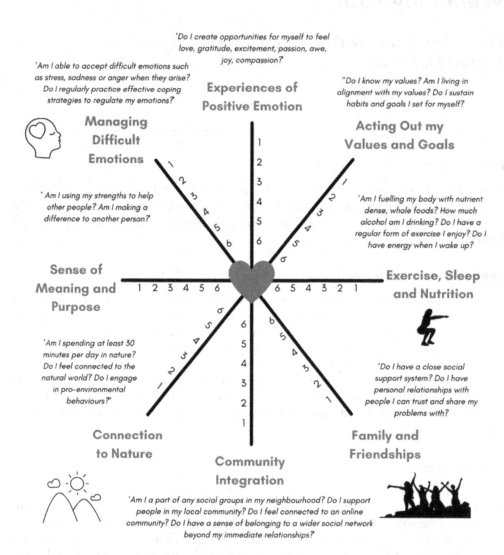

'Do I create opportunities for myself to feel love, gratitude, excitement, passion, awe, joy, compassion?'

'Am I able to accept difficult emotions such as stress, sadness or anger when they arise? Do I regularly practice effective coping strategies to regulate my emotions?'

Experiences of Positive Emotion

"Do I know my values? Am I living in alignment with my values? Do I sustain habits and goals I set for myself?"

Managing Difficult Emotions

Acting Out my Values and Goals

' Am I using my strengths to help other people? Am I making a difference to another person?'

'Am I fuelling my body with nutrient dense, whole foods? How much alcohol am I drinking? Do I have a regular form of exercise I enjoy? Do I have energy when I wake up?

Sense of Meaning and Purpose

Exercise, Sleep and Nutrition

'Am I spending at least 30 minutes per day in nature? Do I feel connected to the natural world? Do I engage in pro-environmental behaviours?'

'Do I have a close social support system? Do I have personal relationships with people I can trust and share my problems with?

Connection to Nature

Family and Friendships

Community Integration

'Am I a part of any social groups in my neighbourhood? Do I support people in my local community? Do I feel connected to an online community? Do I have a sense of belonging to a wider social network beyond my immediate relationships?

Figure 29.1 GENIAL Roadmap, page 1

The GENIAL Roadmap to Wellbeing

Goal Setting

Which domain would I like to try and improve?

....

Prompts to help you get clear on your plan:

- *What is one small daily habit I need to develop?*
- *When and where will I perform this ?*
- *What changes can I make to my environment to make it easy to perform this behaviour?*
- *How can my close social network support me?*
- *Can I join a community of people with similar goals to mine?*
- *What are the benefits of this new behaviour?*
- *How will I reward myself for sticking to the behaviour?*
- *How will I track my progress?*

....

....

....

....

....

....

Figure 29.2 GENIAL Roadmap, page 2

References

Fisher, Z., Wilkie, L., Gibbs, K., Pridmore, J., Tree, J., & Kemp, A. (2019). Rethinking wellbeing: Toward a more ethical science of wellbeing that considers current and future generations. Authorea Preprints.

Kemp, A. H., Arias, J. A., & Fisher, Z. (2017). Social ties, health and wellbeing: A literature review and model. Neuroscience and Social Science, 397–427.

Kemp, A. H., & Fisher, Z. (2022). Wellbeing, whole health and societal transformation: Theoretical insights and practical applications. Global Advances in Health and Medicine, 11, 21649561211073076. https://doi.org/10.1177/21649561211073077

Mead, J., Fisher, Z., & Kemp, A. H. (2021). Moving beyond disciplinary silos towards a transdisciplinary model of wellbeing: An invited review. Frontiers in Psychology, 12.

Chapter 30

Rituals for wellbeing

Badri Bajaj

Description

Diwali is a Hindu festival. It is celebrated in India and across the world. When Lord Rama, Goddess Sita, and Luxman returned to Ayodhya (their kingdom) after completing their exile of 14 years in jungles, the people of Ayodhya lighted earthen lamps filled with ghee (clarified butter) to celebrate the return of lord Rama and Goddess Sita. Since then, this day has been celebrated by lighting earthen lamps, candles, decorative lights, etc. Later, the trend of giving sweets to loved ones also started. Around Diwali, people clean their houses, paint, decorate them, and give sweets and gifts to each other. People also remove some old stuff and buy some new stuff as well. People worship Lord Ganesha and Goddess Luxmi on this auspicious day, and they visit temples as well. Many people do most of the Diwali-related rituals/things every year.

When does it work best?

The tool works best when a client is tired of the status quo of low wellbeing levels, and the client is willing to do some overhauling exercises to enhance wellbeing levels.

Step by step

1. Explain the Diwali festival to the client.
2. Invite the client to recognize the old stuff and consider removing it. Old stuff may be in terms of thoughts, habits, environment/people patterns, or any other relevant thing.
3. Like on Diwali, when people clean almost every spot of their houses, the coach may invite the client to consider looking into each area of their life with a focal lens. Invite the client to explore any factors which are affecting their wellbeing negatively.
4. Like on Diwali, people paint their houses. The coach may invite the client to explore what old positive things they would like to fill in their lives. The client may also be encouraged to explore what new positive things they would like to fill in their lives.
5. As people worship the god and goddess on Diwali, client may be encouraged to nurture more their key values which affect their wellbeing.
6. People share Diwali greetings, sweets, and gifts with their loved ones and other known people; the client may be invited to explore what they can plan to support others in enhancing their wellbeing. The feeling of supporting others may increase

DOI: 10.4324/9781003319016-33

the social wellbeing dimension of the client and may also enhance the positive relationships with others dimension of psychological wellbeing for the clients.

7. As people celebrate Diwali every year, the client may be encouraged to explore planning annual self-reflection using the Diwali celebration analogy.

8. The client may be encouraged to make an overall plan using insights from the preceding steps.

Chapter 31

Meaningful autonomy

Wendy-Ann Smith

Description

Meaningful autonomy (MA) is grounded in the science and theory of self-determination theory, a motivation theory purporting that humans are well motivated when they have their basic needs of connection, mastery and autonomy fulfilled.

When does it work best?

MA is best used when a client lacks motivation to take action on a project or other desired outcome. MA is an invaluable process to use in the coaching session to support a client's thriving, through building awareness of the meaning of autonomy for the client to support independent decision-making.

Step by step

1. The coach invites the client to identify their goal or area where they have been stuck.
2. Draw the Meaningful Autonomy Model as shown in Figure 31.1.

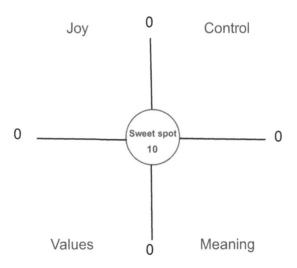

Figure 31.1 Meaningful Autonomy Model

Note: 0 = none at all to 10 = maximum

DOI: 10.4324/9781003319016-34

3. Coach explains the model to the client.
4. The coach guides the client to rate their goal or point where they are stuck on each quadrant of the model.
5. Coach invites the client to explore with the client the reasons they scored as they did, so that both coach and coachee increase the awareness of the area in need of work, and perhaps enable more insight and learning, offering new mindset or new possible courses of action – and perhaps score adjustment.
6. Invite the client to choose an area to work on, working through each quadrant to:

    a. Understand either the goal, the task or set new goals and tasks.
    b. Explore how they can reframe, rework or refine in order to:

        i.   Be more closely aligned with their values.
        ii. Make sense of its importance.
        iii. Increase joy.
        iv. Increase sense of control.

7. Work with the client to refine the goal, goal tasks or area of life they are experiencing a block/stuck, with the aim to increase their score nearer to 10.
8. Repeat for each goal, area of perceived stuckness/block and/or goal tasks.

Chapter 32

Relational mindfulness

Emma Donaldson-Feilder

Description

Relational mindfulness (RM) is about paying attention on purpose, non-judgmentally (or dispassionately) in the present moment, whilst speaking, listening or otherwise interacting with others. It is about awareness of self, others and the relationship.

As with individual mindfulness, RM can be cultivated through formal 'practice'. Formal RM practice would generally be relational meditation: meditating on a contemplation topic in dialogue with another person, bringing full attention and receptivity right into the moment of speaking and listening. The approach to RM that I offer provides guidelines for this form of meditation and is based on insight dialogue (Kramer, 2007). The aim is to generate insight and greater capacity to bring awareness, receptivity and wisdom into daily interactions (Donaldson-Feilder, 2020a, 2020b, 2020c, 2021; Donaldson-Feilder & Comalie, 2021).

When does it work best?

As individuals and for coaching clients, RM is powerful in helping us deal with challenging situations in relationships. It helps us be more resilient in relationships by allowing us to be fully present, receptive rather than reactive, bringing a wider perspective and making wiser choices about what to say and do. It also supports 'vertical' development, helping us become more aware of our habitual patterns in relationships, challenge our assumptions and broaden our mind-set. As coaches, RM helps us develop our capacity to be fully present with our clients, aware of what we embody, more empathetic and compassionate, and enabling insight for clients.

Step by step

The following are guidelines, rather than steps. While they offer a progression, they are non-linear and holographic, with each guideline pointing to the other five.

- *Pause* is about being fully present moment by moment, being aware, noticing what is happening and stepping back from doing, saying or thinking to bring attention to immediate experience.
- *Relax/allow* invites a calming of the body, heart and mind, and acceptance of whatever sensations, emotions and thoughts are present. It is about being with our

DOI: 10.4324/9781003319016-35

experience, even if it is unpleasant, releasing the habit of resisting, avoiding or judging it, and instead bringing a friendly awareness.

- *Open* is an expansion of awareness beyond internal sensations, thoughts and emotions to take in the external world, other people and the environment. This spacious awareness allows us to be aware of ourselves, others and the relationship.
- *Attune to emergence* brings flexibility to be with the constant change and complexity of the world, supporting us to be fully present with the ebb and flow of experience, letting go of preconceptions, planning and trying to control what happens next.
- *Listen deeply* is a stable, receptive awareness that provides kindness, empathy and sensitivity, while being fully present to the person who is speaking – to their words, body language, tone, energy and context.
- *Speak the truth* involves mindful discernment of the subjective truth of experience and sharing what is useful. At a gross level, this is about not lying, and instead telling things as we actually see them; at a more subtle level, it is about expressing what is true in the moment and discerning what is valuable, kind and timely to be spoken.

References

Donaldson-Feilder, E. J. (2020a). Part 1. Relational mindfulness: Why the enthusiasm and what is it? March/April 2020, Vol 15, Issue 2 https://www.coaching-at-work.com/2020/02/29/mindfulness-a-magical-shift/

Donaldson-Feilder, E. J. (2020b). Part 2. What does relational mindfulness mean for coaches, mentors and coaching supervisors? May/June 2020, Vol 15, Issue 3 https://www.coaching-at-work.com/2020/05/05/relational-mindfulness-part-2-an-anchored-connection/

Donaldson-Feilder, E. J. (2020c). Part 3. What does relational mindfulness mean for leadership development? July/Aug 2020 Vol 15, Issue 4 https://www.coaching-at-work.com/2020/06/29/developing-leadership/

Donaldson-Feilder, E. J. (2021). Relational mindfulness. *Coaching Perspectives*. July 2021, Issue 30.

Donaldson-Feilder, E. J. and Comalie, L. (2021). In the moment (Case study article). *Coaching at Work*. May/June 2021, Vol 16, Issue 3.

Kramer, G. (2007). *Insight Dialogue: The interpersonal path to freedom*. Boston: Shambhala.

Chapter 33

Passengers on a bus

Jonathan Passmore

Description

I am a fan of metaphors and regularly use these in my coaching practice for both leadership and wellbeing work. Metaphors are an efficient and effective tool to communicate complex ideas. The 'passengers on the bus' metaphor is an excellent example. The tool is drawn from Acceptance and Commitment Therapy (ACT). It can help clients reflect on how internal thoughts can drive our external behaviour. This metaphor can be used to address irrational and unhelpful thinking and to demonstrate that life is full of possibilities, and that we are not victims but rather have many choices available to us.

When does it work best

The tool is drawn from ACT framework, and works well when clients have irrational thoughts – particularly invasive irritation thoughts – which disputation approaches have failed to address. These thoughts jump into the head of the clients and they can often find it hard to quieten these thoughts, and instead find themselves hijacked by them, as these thoughts run away with themselves and grow and lead to escalating negative thinking, which we might term 'catastrophisation'.

Step by step

The following steps can be used to guide your client through the process:

1. We might start by inviting them to imagine themselves as the driver of a great big double-decker bus. But remind them that this is a metaphor! The bus symbolises our mind. Our thoughts are represented by passengers on the bus, while we are the driver. On the journey, some passengers sit quietly, while others make critical and distracting comments: for example "Fatty you will never get fit", or "You cant sleep, can you? Why not get up and have a drink and watch some TV?" or "You are rubbish, always have been, always will be, you will never get a job".
2. The driver can choose how they react to these passengers. They can choose to listen and accept these comments. Or the driver can choose to ignore them. Likewise, we can choose how we react to our negative and critical thoughts. We can allow these thoughts to drive our behaviour, or like the bus driver, we can just accept them as

DOI: 10.4324/9781003319016-36

comments but acknowledge that we are the driver, that we are in charge of the bus, and that we can choose what we do next.

3. Some clients even like to 'name' some of these passengers (these inner critical voices) 'Mr Nasty' and 'Mrs Whinge', or names which suit them. For some clients, this can help to reduce their power.

4. As we move forward with the client, we can help them to notice more of these comments as being separate from them and to become more choosy about what they want to achieve and to see these critical comments as passing and unhelpful distractions.

Chapter 34

Wellbeing Vision Development tool

Simon Matthews and Margaret Moore

Description

The Wellbeing Vision Development tool (Moore et al., 2016) helps a client or patient create a robust foundation for sustainable behavioral change that improves wellbeing. It supports a client in expanding awareness of their values, strengths, future dreams, and desired outcomes, and is implemented primarily using an appreciative (strengths-based) lens (Cooperrider & Whitney, 2005).

When does it work best?

The tool is best introduced at the outset of a client coaching program around wellbeing behavioral change. It is often preceded by the review of a self-assessment of personal health and wellbeing habits. Vision-setting best precedes any behavioral or SMART (specific, measurable, achievable, relevant and time-bound) goal setting, providing the compass direction and a change foundation on which the wellbeing-promoting goals can be identified and implemented. It is a deep collaboration between the coach and client/patient.

Step by step

1. Introduction of wellbeing vision

    The coach first describes the nature, value, and importance of creating a vision as a compelling statement of a desired future and/or best or ideal self.

2. Cultivate resources

    a. In order to cultivate energy and resources, the coach starts by inquiring about strengths and current successes in areas where a client subjectively feels efficacious, based on a self-assessment if available.
    b. The coach and client collaboratively identify strengths, successes, and sources of satisfaction and efficacy for the client.

3. Thriving

    The client identifies examples of their thriving and the elements that enable their thriving: When do they feel most alive? What conditions enable the thriving experience? (Sheldon, 2009).

DOI: 10.4324/9781003319016-37

4. Internal motivation

    a. The client explores what matters to them most now – what they wish for most for themselves.
    b. Ask: What are the main benefits of improved wellbeing that ignite your motivation to move forward? (Miller & Rollnick, 2012).

5. Priorities

    Then the client prioritizes: "What areas of your wellbeing would you most like to improve now? What areas would you like to start with?"

6. Visualization

    The coach guides the client in imagining or visualizing, and describe in detail, a mental picture of their desired future self. Ask: "What would you be doing? What would you be experiencing? How would you be feeling?" (Miller & Frisch, 2009).

7. Cultivate positive resources

    a. The client explores positive experiences or successes in related areas, even if they only represents a small part of what they currently wish for. Exploring and unpacking a positive story can be invigorating.
    b. The client identifies the strengths which will most help them realize their vision. Ask: "Without being modest, what do you value most about you? What strengths do you have to draw upon? What past lessons in life can you apply here?"

8. Improve confidence

    a. The client identifies key obstacles and challenges which may impede or slow progress, and if resolved, would boost confidence in a meaningful way. Ask: "What concerns you the most?" The coach responds with empathy.
    b. The client selects one challenge for immediate exploration, and then explores past or potential strategies, structures, and resources (especially people) which or who would help them navigate this challenge and improve their confidence.

9. Summarize

    The coach and client reflect and summarize the discussion.

10. Commit

    The client is asked to commit their vision description and statement to paper.

References

Cooperrider, D., & Whitney, D. (2005). *Appreciative inquiry: A positive revolution in change.* San Francisco: Berrett-Koehler.

Miller, C. A., & Frisch, M. B. (2009). *Creating your best life: The ultimate life list guide.* New York, NY: Sterling Publishing Company, Inc.

Miller, W. R., & Rollnick, S. (2012). *Motivational interviewing: Helping people change.* New York, NY: Guilford Press.

Moore, M., Jackson, E., & Tschannen-Moran, B. (2016). Wellcoaches corporation. *Coaching Psychology Manual.* Second ed. Philadelphia, PA: Wolters Kluwer.

Sheldon, K. (2009). Providing the scientific backbone for positive psychology: A multi-level conception of human thriving. *Psihologijske Teme, 18*(2), 267–284.

Name of tool

Quick Intervention for Change (QIC).

Description

The QIC is a straightforward tool for physicians and others, designed to initiate and support sustainable health behavior change. It is predicated on the primacy of the therapeutic alliance (Hubble et al., 1999) and principles of Appreciative Inquiry (Cooperrider et al., 2005), solution-oriented thinking (Ratner et al., 2012; Roberts & Jackson, 2013; Soltero et al., 2017), and motivational interviewing (Rollnick & William, 2013). It is an application of the Fogg Model of Change (Fogg, 2009).

When does it work best?

The QIC was designed for use by busy and time-pressured physicians and other medical and health practitioners. It can be executed in as little as five minutes. Its purpose is to "jump start" useful health related behavioral change rather than manage complex comorbid lifestyle disease.

Step by step

The QIC administration process requires no specific training. With a little practice, the tool can be applied in just a few minutes. It is a conversational tool which involves straightforward inquiries and brief reflections only, before asking the patient for a commitment to the change they're describing

1. Inquire of the patient: "What's the area of your health and wellness/wellbeing you'd most like to see some immediate change in?"
2. Listen for an "area" rather than a specific "problem." For example, if a patient responds, "I need to lose some weight", reflect and reframe this as "You want to be effectively managing your weight".
3. Inquire of the patient: "What makes this area of your health important to you?" Listen for a need or value to be named, for example, "I want to be in good condition to play with my grandchildren". If the need is framed as an avoidance such as "I don't want my diabetes to get worse", ask "what *would* you like here?"
4. Inquire of the patient: "What's already working well for you in this area, even if in a small way?" Reflect what you hear the patient say.
5. Inquire: "If 10 represents having reached your goal in this area of your health, where are you on a 0–10 scale right now?"
6. Whatever rating given by the patient, take care not to challenge or dispute it. Instead, follow up by asking: "What's the main reason for that number?" Reflect what you hear the patient say.
7. Ask the patient to describe: "How would a 1-point change look different?" The small increment is important here – it encourages the framing of a manageable next step. Do a "sense check" with the response. If the patient's one-point change seems very large, reply with "That's bold. It sounds like more of a 5- or 6-point change on the scale. What would just a 1-point change look like?"

8. After the patient describes the change, ask: "How confident are you on a scale of 0–10 to begin working towards this 1-point change?"
9. If the patient rates their confidence to make the change at < 7–10, inquire: "What would it take to increase your confidence just 1 point?"
10. Reflect that modification to the patient.
11. Now conclude by requesting that the patient either begin the 1-point step change, or the "increased confidence" change.
12. Be clear with the patient that you will review this with them at the next consultation. If the next consultation is intended to be more than two weeks later, consider scheduling a consultation to review their progress.
13. This process can be repeated as often as desired with any type of behavioral lifestyle change.

References

Cooperrider DL., Sorenson P, Yeager T, Whitney D. (eds.). *Appreciative Inquiry: Foundations in Positive Organization Development*. Stipes; 2005.

Fogg BJ. (2009, April). A behavior model for persuasive design. In *Proceedings of the 4th international Conference on Persuasive Technology* (pp. 1–7).

Hubble M, Duncan B, Miller S. *The Heart and Soul of Change – What Works in Therapy*. APA; 1999.

Ratner H, George E, Iveson C. *Solution Focussed Brief Therapy: 100 Key Points and Techniques*. Routledge; 2012.

Roberts I, Jackson R. Beyond disease burden: Towards solution-oriented population health. *Lancet Lond Engl*. 2013;381(9884):2219–2221. doi:10.1016/S0140-6736(13)60602-9

Rollnick S, William, M. *Motivational Interviewing – Helping People Change*. 3rd ed. Guilford Press; 2013.

Soltero EG, Konopken YP, Olson ML, et al. Preventing diabetes in obese Latino youth with prediabetes: A study protocol for a randomized controlled trial. *BMC Public Health*. 2017;17(1):261. doi:10.1186/s12889-017-4174-2

Chapter 35

The 'Snakes and Ladders' tool

Zoe Fisher, Lowri Wilkie, Alexandra Hamill, and
Andrew H. Kemp

Description

The 'Snakes and Ladders Tool for Wellbeing' (Figure 35.1, Figure 35.2, Figure 35.3) draws on concepts from acceptance and commitment therapy and positive psychotherapy to illustrate barriers to meaningful and valued action and ways to overcome those barriers. The 'snakes' represent the difficult internal experiences and unhelpful actions that move people away from their values, while the 'wooden ladders' represent the antidote

Figure 35.1 'Snakes and Ladders' tool

DOI: 10.4324/9781003319016-38

Figure 35.2 Photograph of the giant 'Snakes and Ladders' tool used in the final session of our positive psychotherapy group to help consolidate what has been taught

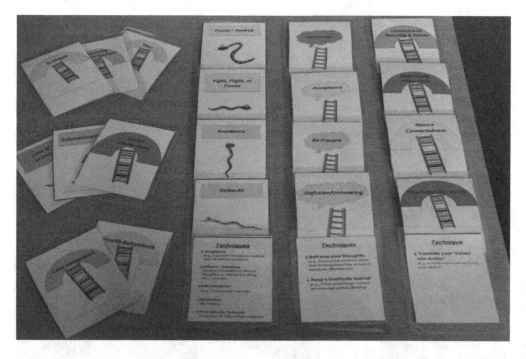

Figure 35.3 A photograph of the 'snake', wooden ladder' and 'rainbow ladder' cards which are used in conjunction with the 'Snakes and Ladders' board (Figures 35.1 and 35.2)

Table 35.1 Examples of snakes and (wooden) ladders

Types of snakes	Wooden ladders: antidotes to snakes
Avoidance of difficult emotions and experiences	Acceptance Be present (mindfulness)
Fusion (in other words, getting 'hooked' by thoughts)	Defusion Be present (mindfulness)
Exhaustion, lack of will power or headspace	Be present (mindfulness) Acceptance Clarifying values and strengths Goal setting
Uncomfortable bodily sensations (e.g., fight, flight or freeze response)	Acceptance
Setbacks	Acceptance Be present (mindfulness)
Feeling lost or lacking in direction	Clarifying values and strengths Goal setting
Feeling disconnected from your sense of self (in other words, loss of or change in identity)	Be present (Mindfulness) Clarifying values and strengths Goal setting
Feeling overwhelmed by difficult emotions	Acceptance Be present (Mindfulness)

to the 'snake bites' – actions that move people towards their values (Table 35.1). The 'rainbow ladders' represent evidence-based strategies to promote wellbeing, even in the absence of snakes (Table 35.2).

When does it work best?

The 'Snakes and Ladders' board is used as a gamified exercise of moving toward or away from personal values and goals. The tool helps people to build awareness of potential snakes that could derail their efforts and the ladders to 'climb' to move in a valued direction.

Step by step

1. Setup and play: Players roll a giant inflatable die to move their marker along a giant replica of the 'Snakes and Ladders' board (see Figure 35.2). The objective of the game is to be first to reach the square at the top of the board.
2. Slide down the snakes: When landing on a snake, the player slides down the snake and then locates that snake in their pack of cards (see Figure 35.3). Each snake represents a different barrier such as avoidance or difficult emotions (Table 35.1), and the player reflects on examples of where they have encountered that snake in real life. On the back of the card is a list of techniques/actions that could be used in response to that snake next time it is encountered.
3. Climb up the ladders: When landing on a 'wooden' or 'rainbow' ladder, the player moves up the ladder, and depending on whether they landed on a wooden ladder or rainbow ladder, they are asked to select either a rainbow or wooden ladder card from the pack. They are then asked to reflect on the technique presented on that card. Those techniques that are less familiar are practiced more in the session.

Table 35.2 Examples of 'rainbow' ladders and their descriptions

Ladder type	Description
Character strengths	Use one of your signature strengths in a new way each day (e.g., remind yourself of your top five signature strengths described in the VIA Survey you completed)
	Positive self-statements (e.g., list five positive statements or phrases about yourself)
Practice optimism	Reframe your thoughts (e.g., focus on the solutions rather than thinking about how an issue is negatively affecting you)
	Keep a Gratitude Journal (e.g., 'Three good things' exercise to encourage positive thinking)
Practice gratitude	Wake up with gratitude
	Use gratitude affirmations (e.g., "I constantly remind myself to enjoy all the good I have in my life")
	Keep a daily gratitude journal (Spend five minutes a day writing down something you are grateful for, e.g., 'three good things' exercise)
Flow	Pick up an activity that you see yourself enjoying; not too easy or too challenging
	(e.g., This varies for each person – composing music, dancing, reading, writing or gardening; this activity will lead you to further activities that help you to become engaged in and attain a 'flow state')
Build positive emotions and savour positive emotions	Savouring experiences (intentionally focusing your attention on appreciating positive events, from the past and present, e.g., 'mindful eating')
	Reflecting on acts of kindness (e.g., record your acts of kindness toward others over seven days)
	'Three good things' exercise (write down three events and reflect upon the reasons why they happened – practice this daily)
Building health behaviours	Diet (aim to consume whole foods, e.g., fruit, vegetables, protein, and whole grains every day)
	Sleep (aim for an average of eight hours of sleep per night)
	Smoking cessation
	Physical action (aim to exercise for around 30 minutes per day)
Cold immersion	Ice baths (15°C or colder – build up stamina to withstand the cold over time)
	Brisk cold daily showers (Take warm to cold showers: Even 30 seconds of cold water towards the end can yield significant health benefits)
	Outdoor swim (sea swimming, lakes and rivers)
Nature Connectedness	Time spent in nature (120 minutes of time spent in nature per week can yield significant health benefits)
	'Three good things in nature' (focusing on specifics, such as the beauty within nature)
Social connectedness	Reflecting on acts of kindness (e.g., record your acts of kindness toward others over seven days)
	Expressing gratitude (three good things exercise)
	Make time for new connections
Community integration	Volunteering opportunities in the community (contact local volunteer bureau)
	Brain injury and stroke charities (contact local charities)
	Get involved in local social groups of shared interests (e.g., contact your local area coordinator to connect to others within your community)
Connection with meaning and values	Identify your values (e.g., using a values clarification exercise)
	Identify what is meaningful in your life (e.g., focus your time and energy into areas of meaning in your life)
Positive behaviour change	Translate your 'values into action' (e.g., to what extent are you living your values?)
	Goal setting (SMART [specific, measurable, achievable, relevant and time-bound] goals)

4. Homework: Players may be given a board and set of cards to take home with them. Participants are encouraged to play with their families to share what they have learnt. This tool gives individuals room to consolidate learning and the tool can be adapted to reflect different techniques and approaches. Also, when participants notice encountering a 'snake' in real life and feel overwhelmed, they are encouraged to find that snake in the pack and look at the back of the card for suggestions of things they might to do to help manage the situation.

Chapter 36

Wellbeing through savouring

Badri Bajaj and Jonathan Passmore

Description

Savouring is termed as thoughts or actions aimed at appreciating or amplifying positive experiences. According to work by Bryant and Veroff (2007), savouring is about attending to, appreciating, and enhancing the positive experiences in peoples' lives. They argue that everyone has the capacity to savour, but that in the rush to move into the next thing in life, too few of us allow ourselves this experience. They suggested there are broadly the following three types of savouring.

1. Savouring the past, or *reminiscence*. For example, remembering funny/enjoyable moments from positive experiences.
2. Savouring the present or being in the *moment*. For instance, enjoying a new meal by drawing your attention to the flavours and smells.
3. Savouring the future, or *anticipation*. For example, visualise the trip you have planned with your friends for the next month.

When does it work best?

The tool works well when a client is looking forward to easy-to-implement ways to enhance their wellbeing, for example, when facing depression or negative thinking. It may best be used alongside other tools as a suite of interventions offering clients a series of experiments as homework to try out over the period between sessions.

Step by step

1. Coach explains savouring and its types to the client.
2. Coach invites the client to recall positive experiences and enjoyable moments from those positive experiences.
3. The coach may encourage the client to be aware and reflect on a positive experience and also be grateful for that experience.
4. Invite the client to explore things/events which, if they pay more attention to them, may deepen their positive experiences.
5. The coach may encourage the client to be aware of positive emotions while being immersed and engaged in a particular experience.

DOI: 10.4324/9781003319016-39

6. The client may explore planned future positive events and visualise some of those positive events.
7. The client may be encouraged to gather insights from the preceding steps.
8. The coach may invite the client to plan actions/activities based on the three types of savouring described in this chapter.

References

Bryant, F. & Veroff, J. (2007) *Savouring: A new model of positive experience* Erlbaum Associates.

Index

Holmes, E. 300, 312
homeostasis 166
hope: The Good Life and 42; stress, coaching for 94
Hübl, T. 142
hubris: defined 316; and leadership 312–314
hubris syndrome (HS) 316, **317**
hubristic behaviours 318–319
hubristic clients 312–323; assessing and measuring hubristic behaviours 318–319; coaching and dark side of traits 315–318; coaching conversations 321–322; dark side personality traits 320–321; hubris and leadership 312–314; inside-out approach 322; outside-in approach 322
humanistic (Rogerian) theory 331
humanity of coaches 78
humility 78, 208, 247, 323
Huppert, F. A. 230
hyperpersonal communication theory 228, 233

Iasenza, S. 161
ICT-mediated communication 230–231
idealised influence 244
idea of parts, trauma 145
ill health *see* bereavement and ill health
illness as normality narrative 77–78
improvements and change 271
inclusive behaviour 246–247
individual consideration 244
individual domain **21**
individual-level coach 206–209
infants, vulnerable to trauma 141–142
information transfer 231, **232**
informed consent, neurodiversity 193
inner coach 337–342; development approach 328, 329, 330, 331, 334, 335, *335*; self-regulation system *330*
inner critic 327–342; attachment theory 331–332; caring and 340–341; chairwork in improving internal relationships 341; child and the classroom 337; control theory 328–330, *329–330*; evolutionary neuroscience 328; functional analysis of 337–340; humanistic (Rogerian) theory 331; inner coach 337–342; multiplicity of mind 327–328; practice 334–342; psychoeducation 336–337; research 332–334; self-parts 327–328; social mentality theory 328; theory 327–332
innovative moments 77
inside-out approach 322
inspirational motivation 244
institutionalising new approaches 271
integrative model, stress coaching for 91–93

intellectual stimulation 244
intention, importance in meaning and purpose 78–80
intentionality, related to wellbeing **14**
internal family systems (IFS) 140
internal relationships, chairwork in improving 341
International Coaching Federation (ICF) 231; client attitudes toward different forms of 233–234; Core Competency model 211
International Labour Office (ILO) 175
International Self-Care Foundation 288
interpersonal communication 102
interpersonal relationships 152, 243, 303, 307
interpersonal skills 102, 246, 361
intersectional sexuality 161, 162
interventions 62–63, 125, 260; based on meaning and purpose 74–75; coaching 321–322; self-management 129; self-select positive psychological 25; wellbeing 287
Ivey, S. L. 206
Ivezaj, V. 62

Jacka, F. 58
Jackson, M. 43
James, J. 216
Jobs, S. 315
Johnson, M. 164, 165, 166
joint care 289
Jones, C. 208
Jun-bang, L. 271
Jung, C. 177
Juster, F. 38–39

Kahlo, F. 43
Kahn, R. L. 175–177
Kahn, W. A. 241
Kaplan, S. **28**
Karpman, S. 146, 218
Kashdan, T. B. 41
Katzmarzyk, P. T. 205
Kaufman, S. B. 209
Kelly, G. 13
Kendall, G. 83
Kennedy 60
Kern, M. L. 230
Kessler, D. 217
Keyes, C. L. M. 12, 39, 45, 47–48, 150, 152
Kidd, M. 351
Kim, E. S. 76
Kim, J. J. 334
Kim, K. H. 318
Kirkpatrick, D. L. 274
Kleist, D. M. 77
Knobe, J. 15

Printed in the United States
by Baker & Taylor Publisher Services